LESSON PLANS FOR

DYNAMIC PHYSICAL EDUCATION FOR ELEMENTARY SCHOOL CHILDREN

ELEVENTH EDITION

Robert P. Pangrazi

Arizona State University
Tempe, Arizona

Victor P. Dauer

Washington State University
Pullman, Washington

Allyn and Bacon
Boston   London   Toronto   Sydney   Tokyo   Singapore

Contents

Page numbers for individual Lesson Plans appear on pages 1–2, 125–127, and 253–254

Using Lesson Plans for Dynamic Physical Education, 11th Edition

Lesson Plans for Dynamic Physical Education, are designed for use with the text *Dynamic Physical Education for Elementary School Children, 11th Edition. (DPE).* The activities presented in the plans are covered in detail in the text. The lesson plans provide a guide for presenting movement experiences in a sequential and well-ordered manner. The series of plans should be regarded as an aid in curriculum planning. The lessons can serve as a framework for modifying and developing a curriculum which is shaped to meet the needs of individual teachers. Teachers still need to plan lessons and reshape yearly curriculums based on local needs.

Many teachers take activities from the lesson plans and write them on 4" by 6" note cards. Writing the activities on cards helps teachers mentally organize the lesson and results in a more effective presentation. All lesson presentations should be mentally rehearsed to prevent excessive use of written notes. Lesson plan notes relieve the burden of trying to remember the proper sequence of activities and the worry of forgetting key points of instruction.

Using the Lesson Plans

Three sets of lesson plans are included to cover three developmental levels. Yearly plans for each of the three developmental levels are listed at the start of each set of lessons. The following is a brief description of the curriculum by developmental level:

Developmental Level I. For the majority of children, activities placed in developmental level I are appropriate for *kindergarten through 2nd-grade* children. Learner characteristics in developmental level I make it necessary to create an enjoyable and instructional learning environment. By stressing joy and rewards through physical activity, positive behaviors are developed that last a lifetime. The majority of activities for younger children are individual in nature and center on learning movement concepts through theme development. Children learn about movement principles and educational movement themes are used to teach body identification and body management skills.

Developmental Level II. Developmental level II activities are usually appropriate for the majority of *3rd- and 4th-grade* children. However, it is common to find youngsters who are performing at level I or level III. In developmental level II activities, refinement of fundamental skills occurs and the ability to perform specialized skills begins to surface. Visual-tactile coordination is enhanced by using a variety of manipulative skills. Children should be allowed the opportunity to explore, experiment, and create activities without fear. While not stressing conformity, children need to absorb the how and also the why of activity patterns. Cooperation with peers is important as more emphasis is placed on group and team play. Initial instruction in sport skills begins in developmental level II and a number of lead-up activities are utilized so youngsters can apply newly learned skills in a small group setting.

Developmental Level III. Developmental level III activities are characterized by a shift toward specialized skills and sport activities. The majority of activities at this level can be used with *5th- and 6th-grade* students. Football, basketball, softball, track and field, volleyball, and hockey are added to the sport offerings. Students continue learning and improving sport skills while participating in cooperative sport lead-up games. Less emphasis is placed on movement concept activities and a larger percentage of instructional time is devoted to manipulative activity. Adequate time is set aside for the rhythmic program and for the program area involving apparatus, stunts, and tumbling. At this level, increased emphasis is placed on physical fitness and developmental activities. Organized and structured fitness routines are offered so that students can begin to make decisions about personal approaches to maintaining fitness levels.

Format of the Lesson Plans

Each lesson plan is divided into four instructional parts as described in Chapter 5 of *DPE*. Each plan offers an outline of activities for approximately one week. When necessary, teachers should refer to *DPE* for in-depth instruction. Briefly, the four instructional parts of the lesson plan and major purposes of each are as follows:

1. **Introductory Activity:** Introductory activities change weekly and are used to physiologically prepare children for activity when entering the gymnasium or activity area. Activities used in this section demand little instruction and allow time for practicing class management skills. Descriptions of introductory activities can be found in *DPE*, Chapter 12.

2. **Fitness Development Activity:** Fitness activities take 7 to 8 minutes of a 30 minute lesson. The length of fitness modules varies depending on the developmental level of youngsters. Younger children need frequent change while older children can benefit by staying with a fitness routine for two to four weeks. The activities should be personalized, progressive in nature, and exercise all parts of the body. Allied to the workout should be brief discussions about the values of fitness for a healthy lifestyle. A comprehensive discussion of fitness principles, activities, and routines is found in *DPE*, Chapter 13.

3. **Lesson Focus Activities**: The purpose of the lesson focus is to help children attain major program objectives such as the development of eye-hand coordination, body management competency, and fundamental and specialized skills (e.g., folk dancing, shooting a basket, and catching an object). The lesson focus uses 15–20 minutes of the daily lesson depending on the length of the teaching period. Lesson focus activities are organized into units and vary in length depending on the developmental level of children. Lesson focus activities are changed weekly except when continuity of instruction demands longer units. Enough activities are placed in each lesson focus section to accommodate three to four teaching periods.

   The content in each lesson is organized in a developmental sequence, with the first activity being the easiest and the last activity the most difficult. Usually, instruction starts with the first activity and proceeds forward regardless of developmental level. The implications are twofold: This progression ensures that each unit begins with success, since all children are capable of performing the beginning activities. It also assures that a proper sequence of activities will be followed during instruction. Obviously, developmentally mature children will progress further along the continuum of activities than less capable children.

4. **Game Activity**: This part of the lesson plan takes place at the closing of the lesson, utilizing the last 5–7 minutes of the period. Games are often used as a culminating activity for practicing skills emphasized in the lesson focus. In other lessons, games are unrelated to the lesson focus and are presented for the purpose of completing the lesson with a fun and enjoyable activity. The game should leave children with positive feelings so they look forward with anticipation to the next lesson. If the lesson has been physically demanding, a less active game can be played and vice versa. In some cases, a low key, relaxing activity might be chosen so that children can unwind before returning to the classroom.

Contents of the Lesson Plans

The contents of the lesson plans is placed into three columns:

1. **Movement Content—Experience**: This column lists movement sequences that will be taught in the lesson. The content in this column offers progression and sequence for activities that will be presented during the week. Movement progressions should allow opportunity for creativity and exploration. Note that throughout the lesson plans, time is offered to allow youngsters a chance to explore the range of movement possibilities.

2. **Organization and Teaching Hints**: This section provides points for efficient organization of the class and important learning cues. Emphasis in this column is on teaching for quality of movement rather than quantity. Page numbers in this section refer to the *DPE* text which should be used for in-depth discussions and teaching techniques.

3. **Expected Student Objectives and Outcomes**: Objectives that students are expected to reach are listed in this area. The objectives are written in three learning domains; psychomotor, cognitive, and affective. The objectives are not listed as concise behavioral objectives, but do offer direction for student learning. In particular, the affective learning objectives offer direction for discussions which can enhance positive attitudes toward fitness and skill learning.

A Note of Appreciation

Acknowledgments and appreciation go to Debbie Pangrazi and Connie Orlowicz of the Mesa (Arizona) School District for their field testing and numerous contributions. Both teachers field-tested and improved the quality of the lesson plans. Donald Hicks, Supervisor of Physical Education for the Fort Worth (Texas) Country Day School contributed heavily to this edition. The professionalism of these three teachers is unparalleled. A warm note of thanks goes to Nicki Rippee, professor at University of Nevada, Reno and Carole Casten, professor at CSU - Dominguez Hills for their contributions to this edition.

Self-Evaluation Guide

The following points can be used for evaluating the daily lesson.

1. Did you prepare ahead of time? Few lessons can be properly taught without prior mental preparation.
2. Did you understand the "whys" behind your lesson? Did they lead you in the direction you wanted the class to go?
3. Was the equipment necessary for your lesson arranged before class? If so, it will allow more time to chat with students.
4. Did you constantly change positions in relationship to the class while you were teaching? This allows you to be close to all students so that you can attempt to acknowledge each of them on a daily basis.
5. Did you carefully observe for the child who was having trouble performing the activities? He or she needs help but doesn't want a big fuss made in order to receive aid.
6. Did you tell the class what your goals for the lesson are? Students must be told what the purpose of the activity is so that they believe it is relevant and useful.
7. Were you excited and enthusiastic about the lesson? If not, the student probably didn't enjoy the lesson. Remember that enthusiasm begets enthusiasm.
8. Did you praise children for the improvement or effort they made during the lesson? Finding something positive to tell children when you know they are putting forth an effort will make them try harder next time.
9. Did you give sufficient attention to the development of student independence and creativity? You must allow time for students to create.
10. Did you give students a sense of responsibility? Using student leaders and allowing the class an opportunity to make decisions about choice of activity is a start.
11. Were enough activities in the lesson plan? Did you cover enough in the lesson or too much?
12. Did you teach for quality of movement or just quantity of movement? Usually, activities must be performed more than once if they are going to be learned.
13. Did you ask for student evaluation of the lesson? This doesn't have to be done every lesson; however, students should be able to provide feedback about the presentation.
14. What activities used in this lesson were effective or ineffective? Why?
15. What overt signs of misbehavior, if any, were present? Who were the students directly involved? To what causes, either the teaching or the personalities, can this misbehavior be attributed?
16. Was the major objective of the lesson reached? Did the students grasp the idea or ideas presented? If not, why not?

Finally, put down any other comments that will make the lesson more effective in the future. Constant updating and evaluation of the lesson plans will make them more useful and in line with your style of teaching.

LESSON PLANS FOR THE SCHOOL YEAR
Developmental Level I

1

DYNAMIC PHYSICAL EDUCATION LESSON PLAN
Orientation and Class Management Games
Level I

Orientation Lesson Plan

The first week of school should be used to teach students the system you are going to use throughout the year. The following are reminders you might find useful in establishing your expectations and routines.

1. Establish rules and expectations. Discuss your expectations with the class to assure students understand reasons for your guidelines. Explain what the consequences are when rules are not followed. Show where time-out boxes are located and how they will be used.
2. Explain to the class the method you will use to learn names. It might be helpful to ask classroom teachers to have students put their name on a piece of masking tape (name tag). Tell students that you will ask them their name on a regular basis until it is learned.
3. Develop entry and exit behaviors for students coming and leaving physical education classes. Students should know how to enter the instructional area and to leave equipment alone until told to use it. If squads are used for instruction, place students into squads and practice moving into formation on signal.
4. Decide how excuses for non-participation will be handled. If possible, set up a routine where the school nurse determines which students are excused for health reasons.
5. Safety is important. Children should receive safety rules to be followed on apparatus and playground equipment. Safety procedures to be followed in physical education classes should be discussed.
6. Illustrate how you will stop and start the class. In general, a whistle (or similar loud signal) and a raised hand is effective for stopping the class. A voice command should be used to start the class. Telling the class when before what (*DPE*, Chapter 6) will assure they do not begin before instructions are finished.
7. Discuss the issue, distribution, and care of equipment. Make students responsible for acquiring a piece of equipment and returning it at the end of the lesson. Place equipment around the perimeter of the teaching area to reduce the chance of students fighting over a piece of equipment.
8. Explain to the class that the format of the daily lesson will include an introductory activity, fitness development, lesson focus, and finish with a game activity.
9. Practice various teaching formations such as open-squad formation and closed-squad formation. Practice moving into a circle while moving (fall-in). Transitions between formations should be done while moving, i.e., jogging from scatter formation into a circular formation.
10. Refer to Chapters 5, 6, and 7 in *DPE* for detailed information about planning, developing an effective learning environment, and class management strategies.

INTRODUCTORY ACTIVITY (2 — 3 MINUTES)

Move and Freeze on Signal
  Have students move throughout the area using a variety of locomotor movements. On signal (whistle), they quickly freeze. Try to reduce the response latency by reinforcing students who stop quickly on signal. The primary objective should be to teach students the importance of moving under control (without bumping others or falling down) and quickly freezing, ready to listen to upcoming instructions.

FITNESS DEVELOPMENT ACTIVITIES (7 — 8 MINUTES)

Teacher Leader Movement Challenges
  The goal should be to move students through a number of movement challenges. Emphasis should be placed on starting the fitness activities at a level where all students can feel successful.

***Alternate locomotor movements with strength and flexibility challenges. Repeat the
challenges as necessary.***

Locomotor Movement: Walk for 30 seconds.

Flexibility and Trunk Development Challenges
1. Bend in different directions.
2. Stretch slowly and return quickly.
3. Combine bending and stretching movements.
4. Sway back and forth.
5. Twist one body part; add body parts.
6. Make your body move in a large circle.

Locomotor Movement: Skip for 30 seconds.

Shoulder Girdle Challenges
In a push-up position, do the following challenges:
1. Lift one foot; the other foot.
2. Wave at a friend; wave with the other arm.
3. Scratch your back with one hand; use the other hand.
4. Walk your feet to your hands.
5. Turn over and face the ceiling; shake a leg; crab walk.

Locomotor Movement: Jog for 30 seconds.

Abdominal Development
From a supine position:
1. Lift your head and look at your toes.
2. Lift your knees to your chest.
3. Wave your legs at a friend.
From a sitting position;
1. Slowly lay down with hands on tummy.
2. Lift legs and touch toes.

Locomotor Movement: Run and leap for 30 seconds.

LESSON FOCUS (15 — 20 MINUTES)

Since much time during the first week is used for orientation procedures and management, no lesson focus activity is scheduled.

GAME (5 — 7 MINUTES)

Play one or two management games to teach students how to move into partner and small group formation. The following games can be used to teach students such management goals in an enjoyable and efficient manner.

Back to Back — *DPE, p. 556*
Supplies: None
Skills: Fundamental locomotor movements
Students move under control throughout the area using a variety of locomotor movements. On signal, each child stands back to back (or toe to toe) with another child. If one child ends up without a partner, the teacher takes this student as a partner. Youngsters who do not find a partner nearby run to a designated spot in the center of the area. This helps assure that students do not run around looking for a partner or feel left out. Students who move to the center spot quickly find a partner and move out of the area (to avoid crowding around the center spot). Emphasis should be placed finding a partner near them, not searching for a friend, and taking a different partner each time.

Whistle Mixer — *DPE, p. 580*

Supplies: None

Skills: All basic locomotor movements

Children are scattered throughout the area. To begin, they move in any direction they wish. The teacher whistles a number of times in succession and raises the same number of fingers above their head to signal the group size. Children then form small groups with the number in each group equal to the number of whistles. For example, if there are four short whistles, children form circles of four—no more, no less. The goal is to find the correct number of students as quickly as possible. As soon as a group has the desired number, they sit down to signal that other may not join the group. Children who cannot find a group nearby should be encouraged to move to the center of the area and raise their hands to facilitate finding others without a group.

DYNAMIC PHYSICAL EDUCATION LESSON PLAN
Manipulative Skills Using Beanbags
Level I

Supplies and Equipment Needed:
One beanbag per child   Music
One parachute   Tape player

MOVEMENT EXPERIENCE—CONTENT	ORGANIZATION AND TEACHING HINTS	EXPECTED STUDENT OBJECTIVES AND OUTCOMES

INTRODUCTORY ACTIVITY (2 – 3 MINUTES)

| **Move and Assume Pose** | *DPE* p. 253 | |
| Have children move using a variety of locomotor movements. Freeze on signal and assume a pose. The following position are suggested:
1. Balance on different body parts
2. Stretch
3. Curl
4. Bridge
5. Push-up position
6. V-Sit position
7. Seat Circle
8. Stork Stand | Scatter formation. Emphasize proper method of stopping quickly.

Discourage falling and lack of body control.

Encourage creativity in various poses

Try continuous movement without freeze command. Different poses and locomotor movements can be named. | PM.—The student will be able to perform the basic poses on command.

Cog.—The student will be able to recognize the basic command names and nonlocomotor movement.

PM.—The student will be able to stop quickly with good balance.

Aff.—Physical activity is an excellent means of releasing tension. Students will begin to appreciate the importance of exercise to enhance wellness. |

FITNESS DEVELOPMENT ACTIVITIES (7 – 8 MINUTES)

| **Parachute Fitness** | *DPE* p. 285 | |
| Tape alternating segments of silence and music to signal duration of exercise. Music segments indicate aerobic activity with the parachute while intervals of silence announce using the chute to enhance flexibility and strength development.
1. Jog while holding the chute in the left hand - 20 seconds.
2. Shake the chute.
3. Slide while holding the chute with both hands - 20 seconds.
4. Sit and perform curl-ups - 30 seconds.
5. Skip for 20 seconds.
6. Freeze, face the center, and stretch the chute tightly. Hold for 8–12 seconds. Repeat five to six times.
7. Run in place while holding the chute taut at different levels.
8. Sit with legs under the chute. Do a seat walk toward the center. Return to the perimeter. Repeat four to six times.
9. Move into push-up position holding the chute with one hand. Shake the chute.
10. Place the chute on the ground. Jog away from the chute and return on signal. Repeat for 30 seconds.
11. Shake the chute and jump in place. | Evenly space youngsters around the chute.

Use different grips to add variation to the activities.

Develop group morale by encouraging students to move together.

Use music to motivate youngsters.

To cool down, allow youngsters a minute to perform parachute stunts like the Dome or Mushroom. | Cog.—The student will be able to explain verbally why correct form is important when performing fitness activities.

PM.—The student will be able to perform all activities at the teacher established level.

Aff.—One of the reasons for fitness activities now is to establish patterns for later life. Establish the need for fitness throughout life through example and brief comments. |

MOVEMENT EXPERIENCE— CONTENT	ORGANIZATION AND TEACHING HINTS	EXPECTED STUDENT OBJECTIVES AND OUTCOMES

12. Lie on back with feet under the chute. Shake the chute with the feet.
13. Hop to the center of the chute and return. Repeat for 20 seconds.
14. Sit with feet under the chute. Stretch by touching the toes with the chute. Relax with other stretches while sitting.

LESSON FOCUS (15 – 20 MINUTES)

Beanbag Activities

Give students two or three activities to practice so you have time to move and help youngsters. Alternate activities from each of the categories so students receive a variety of skills to practice.
In Place, Tossing to Self
1. Toss and catch with both hands - right hand, left hand
2. Toss and catch with the back of hands. This will encourage children to catch with "soft hands."
3. Toss the beanbag to increasingly high level, emphasizing a straight overhead toss. To encourage straight tossing, have the child sit down.

In Place, Adding Stunts
1. Toss overhead and perform the following stunts and catch the bag.
   a. ¼ and ½ turns, right and left
   b. Full turn
   c. Touch floor
   d. Clap hands
   e. Clap hands around different parts of body, behind back, under legs.
   f. Heel click
   g. Sit down, get up
   h. Look between legs

Toss, Move, and Catch
1. Toss overhead, move to another spot, and catch.
2. Toss, do a locomotor movement, and catch.
3. Move from side to side.
4. Toss overhead behind self, move, and catch.

Balance the Beanbag
1. Balance on the following body parts
   a. Head
   b. Back of hand
   c. Shoulder
   d. Knee
   e. Foot

DPE pp. 409 – 413

Scatter formation.

Stress soft catch.

Keep eyes on the bag.

Try all challenges in sitting, back, or side positions.

Try all the toss and catch activities with the feet and combinations of feet, hands, and body parts.

Emphasize keeping eyes on object while performing stunts.

Give them two or three activities to attempt so that you have time to move around and help children in need.

Catching is more important than the stunt.

Make sure that students are making good throws and catching the bag.

Use a change-of-pace activity. For example, place the beanbags on the floor and hop over five blue beanbags. Use different challenges.

Encourage the class to look where they are moving. This will force them to take their eyes off the object, recover, focus, and catch the bag, which is a more advanced skill.

Look for new and exciting ways of balancing the bags. Allow students to show their ideas to the rest of the class.

See who can balance her bag the longest on various body parts while moving.

PM.—The student will enhance his development of visual concentration on a moving object.

PM.—The student will be able to demonstrate "giving" with body to create a soft home for beanbag.

Cog.—The student will be able to recite the necessary ingredients for successful catching.

Cog.—The student will be able to verbalize the importance of visually tracking moving projectiles.

Cog.—The student will be able to explain why catching is more difficult when the person is moving.

PM.—The student will be able to propel the body and balance an object simultaneously.

Aff.—Visual–tactile coordination demands a great deal of practice and repetition if the student is going to improve. Discuss the importance of tenacity and persistence in achieving a goal.

MOVEMENT EXPERIENCE— CONTENT	ORGANIZATION AND TEACHING HINTS	EXPECTED STUDENT OBJECTIVES AND OUTCOMES

    f. Elbow
    g. Exploratory activity
  2. Balance and move as follows:
    a. Walk
    b. Run
    c. Skip
    d. Gallop
    e. Sit down
    f. Lie down
    g. Turn around
    h. Combinations of the above
    i. Exploratory activity

Organization and teaching hints: If time allows, go back and polish some of the activities performed earlier in the week.

Challenge Activities
1. Hold the beanbag between knees and play tag with a partner or small group.
2. Place the beanbag on tummy and shake it off.
3. Place the beanbag on back and Mule Kick it off.
4. Push the beanbag across the floor with different body parts.
5. Toss the beanbag up and touch specified body parts.
6. Put beanbags on floor. Rotate various body parts on a beanbag.
7. Beanbag Balance Tag - balance a beanbag on selected body parts. Announce a color to identify those who are it.

GAME (5 – 7 MINUTES)

Midnight — *DPE,* p. 564
  Supplies: None
  Skills: Running, dodging

    A safety line is established about 40 ft from a den in which one player, the fox, is standing. The others stand behind the safety line and move forward slowly, asking, "Please, Mr. Fox, what time is it?" The fox answers in various fashions, such as "Bedtime," "Pretty late," "Three-thirty." The fox continues to draw the players toward him. At some point, he answers the question by saying "Midnight," and then chases the others back to the safety line. Any player who is caught joins the fox in the den and helps to catch others. No player in the den may leave, however, until the fox calls out "Midnight."

    Variation: <u>Lame Wolf</u>. The wolf is lame and advances in a series of three running steps and a hop. Other children taunt, "Lame Wolf, can't catch me!" or "Lame Wolf, tame wolf, can't catch me!" The wolf may give chase at any time. Children who are caught join the wolf and must also move as if lame.

Leap the Brook — *DPE,* p. 563
  Supplies: None
  Skills: Leaping, jumping, hopping, turning

    A brook is marked off on the floor for a distance of about 30 ft. For the first 10 ft, it is 3 ft wide; for the next 10 ft, it is 4 ft wide; for the last 10 ft, it is 5 ft wide. Children form a single file and jump over the narrowest part of the brook. They should be encouraged to do this several times, using different styles of jumping and leaping. After they have satisfactorily negotiated the narrow part, they move to the next width, and so on.

    Teaching suggestion: The teacher should stress landing lightly on the balls of the feet in a bent-knee position. Good form should be stressed throughout the game. The selection of the distances is arbitrary, and the distances can be changed if they seem unsuitable for any particular group of children.

    Variation: Children can use different means of crossing the brook--leaping, jumping, hopping. They also can vary the kinds of turns to be made--right or left; or quarter, half, three quarter, or full. They should use different body shapes, different arm positions, and so on.

DYNAMIC PHYSICAL EDUCATION LESSON PLAN
Fundamental Skills Using Individual Mats
Level I

Supplies and Equipment Needed:
  Record player and records
  Individual mats—one for each child

MOVEMENT EXPERIENCE—CONTENT	ORGANIZATION AND TEACHING HINTS	EXPECTED STUDENT OBJECTIVES AND OUTCOMES

INTRODUCTORY ACTIVITY (2 – 3 MINUTES)

Locomotor Movements and Freeze

Perform the locomotor movements below; freeze quickly on signal with a wide base of support. A suggestion is to tape alternating segments of silence and music to signal duration of the locomotor movements. Segments of silence to indicate the "freeze" position can be decreased in duration until the desired response latency is reached.
  1. Walk
  2. Run
  3. Jump
  4. Hop
  5. Skip
  6. Gallop
  7. Leap
  8. Slide

DPE p. 253

Scatter formation.

Have the class try different methods of stopping such as stiff body, flat feet, etc., and have them choose best method.

Explain terms as needed.

PM.—The student will be able to stop the body quickly after moving, using the basic locomotor movements.

Cog.—The student will be able to explain what is necessary to stop quickly.

FITNESS DEVELOPMENT ACTIVITIES (7 – 8 MINUTES)

Fitness Challenges

Alternate locomotor movements with strength and flexibility challenges. Repeat the challenges as necessary.
Locomotor Movement: Walk for 30 seconds.

Flexibility and Trunk Development Challenges
  1. Bend in different directions.
  2. Stretch slowly and return quickly.
  3. Combine bending and stretching movements.
  4. Sway back and forth.
  5. Twist one body part; add body parts.
  6. Make your body move in a large circle.
Locomotor Movement: Skip for 30 seconds.

Shoulder Girdle Challenges
In a push-up position, do the following challenges:
  1. Lift one foot; the other foot.
  2. Wave at a friend; wave with the other arm.
  3. Scratch your back with one hand; use the other hand.

DPE pp. 281 – 283

Scatter formation.

Individual mats can be used as a "home" to keep youngsters spaced properly.

Repeat the various trunk challenges as necessary.

Young children will perform best when locomotor movements are alternated with stationary challenges that allow them to recover aerobically.

Add Animal Walks to replace some of the locomotor movements and to create interest.

Use different qualities of movement such as giant skips, tiny and quick gallops, or slow giant steps to motivate youngsters.

As children become more fit, repeat the entire sequence.

PM.—The student will be able to perform all activities at teacher established level.

PM.—The student will demonstrate the ability to make maximum movements as directed.

Aff.—With regular exercise the heart muscle is strengthened. Encourage student understanding and appreciation of this fact through discussion.

9

MOVEMENT EXPERIENCE—CONTENT	ORGANIZATION AND TEACHING HINTS	EXPECTED STUDENT OBJECTIVES AND OUTCOMES

4. Walk your feet to your hands.
5. Turn over and face the ceiling; shake a leg; crab walk.
Locomotor Movement: Jog for 30 seconds.

Abdominal Development
From a supine position:
   1. Lift your head and look at your toes.
   2. Lift your knees to your chest.
   3. Wave your legs at a friend.
From a sitting position;
   1. Slowly lay down with hands on tummy.
   2. Lift legs and touch toes.
Locomotor Movement: Run and leap for 30 seconds.

LESSON FOCUS (15 – 20 MINUTES)

Individual Mats	*DPE* pp. 475 – 477	
Give students two or three activities to practice so you have time to move and help youngsters. Alternate activities from each of the categories so students receive a variety of skills to practice.		
Command Movements		
1. Stretch	Each child gets a mat and sits (cross-legged) on it.	PM.—The student will be able to move the body into various shapes and positions quickly and efficiently.
a. Different directions.		
b. Different parts of body.	Emphasize a full stretch.	
2. Curl		Cog.—The student will know the shapes and be able to identify the positions by name.
3. Balance	Try to secure variety. Use levels.	
a. Balance on different body parts.	Tightly on different parts.	
b. Balance on different number of parts.	Hold for a few seconds.	PM.—The student will be able to develop versatility and variation in movement.
c. Go from one balance to another.	Go 5, 4, 3, 2, 1 parts.	
4. Bridge	Try to work some nice arches.	Cog.—The student will be able to describe the proper care and use of mats.
a. Bridge across the short width, long width.		
b. Different parts or number of parts.	Try activities on tummy and back.	
c. Bridge to a full arch.		
5. Reach	Pupil demonstration.	
a. Keep toes on mat, reach as far as possible.	Full stretch out.	
b. Keep hand on mat, reach as far as possible.		
c. Keep hand on mat, reach as far as possible with a foot.		
6. Rock	Pupil demonstration.	
a. On different parts		
7. Roll	Forward, backward, sideways, log.	
a. Different types of rolls.		
b. Roll up in the mat.	Work each movement separately and then combine them.	
8. Twist		
a. Full twist, held.	Get pupil input.	
b. Moving twists		
c. Twist and untwist.		

MOVEMENT EXPERIENCE— CONTENT	ORGANIZATION AND TEACHING HINTS	EXPECTED STUDENT OBJECTIVES AND OUTCOMES
9. Use other Terms a. Straight, curved, narrow, wide, prone melt, shake, fall, collapse. 10. Combination Movements	Develop this well. Four or five changes.	PM.—The student will be able to change from one pattern to another smoothly.

On and off the Mats
  1. Different locomotor movements-hop, jump, leap.
  2. Weight on the hands. Crouch jumps, forward and backward.
  3. Animal imitations, i.e., Rabbit, Frog, etc.
	Use levels. Add turns, shapes, patterns.
	
	Secure suggestions.
		Cog.—The student will be able to differentiate and describe the following movements: hopping, jumping, and leaping.
		
		PM.—The student will be able to perform the hop, jump, and leap.

Over the Mat
  1. Locomotor movements: Add turns, secure height.
  2. Weight on the hands.
  3. Combinations: Over one way and back another way.
  4. How many mats can you jump over in 10 seconds? Change the movements over the mat.
  5. Hop over fine blue mats. Change the movement, number, and color of the mats.
	Body shapes.
	
	Stress soft landing—relaxed.
	
	Stress levels.
	
	Allow choice.	

Movements around the Mats
  1. Different locomotor movements.
  2. Animal Walks, i.e., Dog, Bear, Cat, Rabbit.
  3. Keep hands on the mat.
  4. Keep feet on the mat.
	Use both clockwise and counterclockwise directions.
	
	Allow exploration.
	
	Build up variation here.
		Aff.—Discuss the importance of watching out for others while moving. This could initiate a good discussion about concern for the welfare of other people.

Mats as a Base
  1. Use different magic numbers.
    a. A number of movements out and back.
    b. Different number combinations.
    c. Animal imitations.
	Stress general space.
	
	Use magic numbers.	

Challenge Activities
  1. Try some individual and partner stunts with the mats as a base.
    a. Coffee Grinder
    b. Chinese Get-up
    c. Wring the Dishrag
  2. Jump from mat to mat without touching the floor. Can you move across the area? Skip from mat to mat.
  3. Play "Ring around the Mat." Skip around the mat and all fall down.
  4. Move between five mats and cartwheel over two mats. Use different movements and tumbling activities.
  5. Put your mat together with a partner and make different shapes, numbers, and letters. Do the same thing in small groups.
  6. Magic Carpet Ride - one person pulls a partner sitting on the mat.
	Encourage students to build new challenges and sequences of movement.
	
	Turn the mat over and drive it like a car. (Push the mat with hands on the mat.)	

MOVEMENT EXPERIENCE— CONTENT	ORGANIZATION AND TEACHING HINTS	EXPECTED STUDENT OBJECTIVES AND OUTCOMES

GAME (5 – 7 MINUTES)

Sneak Attack — *DPE,* p. 567

Supplies: None

Skills: Marching, running

Two parallel lines are drawn about 60 ft apart. Children are divided into two teams. One team takes a position on one of the lines, with their backs to the area. These are the chasers. The other team is on the other line, facing the area. This is the sneak team. The sneak team moves forward on signal, moving toward the chasers. When they get reasonably close, a whistle or some other signal is given, and the sneak team turns and runs back to their line, chased by the other team. Anyone caught before reaching the line changes to the chase team. The game is repeated, with the roles exchanged.

Mat Games — *DPE,* p. 477

Supplies: Individual Mats

Skills: Running, jumping

Each child is seated on a mat. On signal, each rises and jumps over as many different mats as possible. On the next signal, each child takes a seat on the nearest mat. The last child to be seated can pay a penalty. The game can also be played by eliminating one or two mats so that one or two children are left without a home base. The teacher can stand on a mat or turn over mats to put them out of the game. To control roughness, the rule should be that the first child to touch a mat gets to sit on it.

A variation of this game is to have each child touch at least ten mats and then sit cross-legged on his own mat, or a child can be required to alternate touching a mat and jumping over the next mat until a total of ten is reached. "See how many mats you can cartwheel or jump over in 10 seconds." Change the challenge and try again.

DYNAMIC PHYSICAL EDUCATION LESSON PLAN
Kicking, Trapping, Bowling, and Rolling Skills
Level I

Supplies and Equipment Needed:
  One partially deflated playground or foam training ball for each child
  Cones for marking areas for lead-up activities
  One hoop for each child
  Bowling pins or Indian clubs

MOVEMENT EXPERIENCE— CONTENT	ORGANIZATION AND TEACHING HINTS	EXPECTED STUDENT OBJECTIVES AND OUTCOMES

INTRODUCTORY ACTIVITY (2 – 3 MINUTES)

Hoops—Free Activity

Issue a hoop for each child. Give them 2 to 3 minutes of free activity. If necessary, suggest some of the following challenges:
  1. Run or hop with hoop, stop and jump the hoop.
  2. Run and roll the hoop like a tire.
  3. Spin the hoop and see how many time you can run around it.
  4. Roll the hoop and go through it.
  5. Combine two hoop activities with two locomotor movements.

DPE p. 256

Scatter formation.

Encourage variety of response by asking individuals to show their activity.

Students should combine some locomotor movement with their hoop activities.

Cog.—Introductory activity is performed in order to warm up the body for more strenuous activity.

PM.—The student will develop an introductory activity that combines two hoop activities with a locomotor movement.

FITNESS DEVELOPMENT ACTIVITIES (7 – 8 MINUTES)

Walk, Trot, and Sprint

Move to the following signals:
  1. One drumbeat - walk.
  2. Two drumbeats - trot.
  3. Three drumbeats - sprint.
  4. Whistle - freeze and perform exercises.

Perform various strength and flexibility exercises between bouts of walk, trot, and sprint. Examples are:
  1. Bend and Twist
  2. Sitting Stretch
  3. Push-up variations
  4. Abdominal Challenges
  5. Body Twist
  6. Standing Hip Bend

DPE pp. 285 – 286

Use a tom-tom or tambourine.

Scatter formation.

Emphasize quality of movement and rapid changes

Alternate bouts of movement with strength and flexibility exercises.

Cog.—The student will be able to explain why it is necessary to increase the activity work load in order to provide additional stress on the body and increase fitness levels.

Aff.—Physically fit people are rewarded by society. Teachers, parents, and peers respond much more favorably to those fit and attractive. Discuss the social importance of fitness.

LESSON FOCUS (15 – 20 MINUTES)

Kicking, Trapping, Rolling, and Bowling Skills

Give students two or three activities to practice so you have time to move and help youngsters. Alternate activities from each of the categories so students receive a variety of skills to practice.

DPE pp. 663 – 665

Begin with informal kicking and trapping to get the feel of the ball.

Partner work or triangle formation.

One ball for three children.

Keep head down. Eyes on ball. Follow through.

PM.—The student will be able to pass, kick, and trap the ball successfully at the end of the week.

Cog.—The student will be able to explain why in kicking, accuracy is much preferred over raw power and lack of control.

13

MOVEMENT EXPERIENCE— CONTENT	ORGANIZATION AND TEACHING HINTS	EXPECTED STUDENT OBJECTIVES AND OUTCOMES
Kicking and Ball Control Skills 1. Inside of Foot Kick Approach at 45° angle; inside of foot meets ball. Place non-kicking foot alongside ball. 2. Outside of Foot Kick Short distance kick; keep toe down. 3. Long (instep) Pass Contact the ball with the shoelaces. Not as accurate, but used for distance. 4. Sole of Foot Control Use sole of foot to stop ball; make sure weight is placed on the non-receiving foot. 5. Inside of Foot Control Use inside of foot and learn to "give" with leg so ball doesn't ricochet off foot.	If short supply of gray foam balls, partially deflate 8-1/2-inch playground balls. They will move more slowly and be easier for youngsters to handle. Make sure students don't handle the balls with their hands. They must retrieve and move the balls with feet only. Practice the kicking skills against a wall. Emphasis should be on velocity of the kick rather than accuracy if a correct pattern is to be developed.	Aff.—Even in basic lead-up games, teamwork is necessary for success and enjoyment by all.
Lead-Up Activities Note: It is possible to teach soccer-related activities at the primary level. However, emphasis must be placed on the individual. Give each child a ball when possible and work in as small groups as possible. Drills have little value as do complicated team games. It might be necessary to play an unrelated game in the middle of the lesson when interest wanes. Emphasize correct movement patterns—it is important that youngsters develop proper motor patterns so they will not have to be changed at a later date. Skill level will vary widely, but if children learn to handle an object with their feet, they will be much more advanced than most American students.	Teach skills from a stationary position; as students improve, introduce movement. Practice individual dribbling skills. Students move throughout the area and dodge other students. Foam training balls are excellent for teaching lead-up activities to prevent fear of being hurt.	Aff.—It is acceptable to make mistakes when learning a skill. Even professional athletes make many performance mistakes.
1. Circle Kickball - *DPE*, p. 674. For youngster children, put them in a circle and kick the ball back and forth. Use small circles. 2. Soccer Touch Ball - *DPE*, p. 674. 3. Dribblerama - *DPE*, p. 675.	Circle formation, two circles necessary. Emphasize kicking the ball below *waist* level. Two circles. Emphasize short, accurate passes. Pass quickly; don't hold the ball.	Aff.—Students will learn to appreciate individual differences and show concern for the welfare of others. Take time to discuss this important attitude.
Bowling and Rolling Skills 1. Two-handed roll—between the legs, with wide straddle stance. 2. Roll the ball with one hand. Use both left and right hands. 3. Roll the ball and put spin on the ball so it will curve to the left and right.	When bowling with one hand, the other hand should serve as a guide. Use the opposite rule; when bowling with the right hand, step forward with the left foot. Use beachballs or foam balls for very small children.	PM.—The student will be able to explain the opposition rule in his own words. PM.—The student will be able to roll the ball properly utilizing opposition of body parts and body coordination.

MOVEMENT EXPERIENCE— CONTENT	ORGANIZATION AND TEACHING HINTS	EXPECTED STUDENT OBJECTIVES AND OUTCOMES

3. Roll the ball and put spin on the ball so it will curve to the left and right.
4. Roll the ball through human straddle targets:
  a. Start rolling at moderate stances and gradually increase as bowlers become more proficient.
  b. Use left and right hands.
  c. Scoring can be done giving two points for a ball that goes through the target without touching and one point for a ball going through, but touching a leg.
5. Use objects such as milk cartons, clubs, or bowling pins for targets. Various bowling games can be developed using the targets.
6. Stand with your back facing your partner. Bend over, look through your legs and bowl.
7. Play **Bowling One-Step** (*DPE*, p. 578) as a culminating activity.
8. Soccer skills can be practiced by the receiver. For example, the following skills are suggested:
  a. Toe Trap
  b. The Foot Pickup
  c. Bowl with Your Feet
	Encourage students to keep their eyes on the target.
	
	Work in groups of three—one on each end and one in the middle.
	
	Some students should retrieve the ball, others reset the pins, and the rest bowl. Rotate responsibilities often.
	
	Emphasize the importance of accuracy over speed.
	
	The playground balls can be deflated somewhat to make them easier to handle.
		PM.—While using human straddle targets, the student will be able to score 7 points from a distance of 15 feet.
		
		Aff.—The student will demonstrate a desire to help others by performing all the duties necessary such as retrieving the ball and setting up the pins.
		
		Cog.—The student will be able to explain the difference between a "hook" ball and a "backup" ball.

GAME (5 – 7 MINUTES)

Back to Back — *DPE*, p. 556
  Supplies: None
  Skills: Fundamental locomotor movements
  The number of children must be uneven. (If not, the teacher can play.) On signal, each child stands back to back with another child. One child will be without a partner. This child claps the hands for the next signal, and all children change partners, with the extra player from the previous game seeking a partner.
  Variation: Considerably more activity can be achieved by putting in an extra command. After children are in partner formation back to back, the teacher says, "Everybody run [skip, hop, jump, slide]!" Other commands, such as "Walk like an elephant," can also be given. Children move around in the prescribed manner. When the signal is sounded, they immediately find a new partner and stand back to back.

Change Sides — *DPE*, p. 559
  Supplies: None
  Skill: Body management
  Two parallel lines are established 30 ft apart. Half of the children are on each line. On signal, all cross to the other line, face the center, and stand at attention. The first group to do this correctly wins a point. Children must be cautioned to use care when passing through the opposite group. They should be spaced well along each line; this allows room for them to move through each group. The locomotor movements should be varied. The teacher may say, "Ready--walk!" Skipping, hopping, long steps, sliding, and other forms of locomotion can be specified. The position to be assumed at the finish can be varied also.
  Teaching suggestion: Because success depends on getting across first, the teacher should watch for shortcutting of the rules and talk this problem over with the children.
  Variation: The competition can be by squads, with two squads on each line.

Musical Ball Pass — *DPE*, p. 565
  Supplies: Playground ball per group, music
  Skills: Passing and handling
  Players stand in circle formation facing the center. One ball is given to a player and is passed to the circle players when the music starts. When the music stops, the player with the ball (or the last player to touch the ball) goes into the "well" in the center of the circle. The player in the well stays there until another player is caught with the ball.
  Variation: More than one ball may be used, depending on the skill of the class.

DYNAMIC PHYSICAL EDUCATION LESSON PLAN
Educational Movement (Lesson 1)
Level I

Fundamental Skill: Walking
Manipulative Activity: Beachballs
Educational Movement Themes: Identification of body parts, personal space

Supplies and Equipment Needed:
  One inflated beachball for each child (or use balloons)
  Tom-tom or dance drum
  One jump rope for each child
  Lummi sticks
  Stocking paddles
  One beanbag for each child
  Tape player

MOVEMENT EXPERIENCE—CONTENT	ORGANIZATION AND TEACHING HINTS	EXPECTED STUDENT OBJECTIVES AND OUTCOMES

INTRODUCTORY ACTIVITY (2 – 3 MINUTES)

European Running

1. Run and stop.
2. Run, and on signal make a full turn; continue in same direction. Turn the other way.
3. Run, and on signal run in general space. On next signal, re-form the original pattern.
4. Run and bend the upper body forward in four counts. Return to the upright position in four counts.
5. Run and clap the rhythm.

DPE pp. 252 – 253

Scatter around perimeter of area.

Check on stopping techniques.

Turn is made with four running steps. Lift knees.

PM.—The student will be able to develop a smooth, rhythmic run.

PM.—Students will be able to develop the ability to space themselves while running.

Cog.—The student will be able to describe stopping techniques.

FITNESS DEVELOPMENT ACTIVITIES (7 – 8 MINUTES)

Tape alternating segments of silence and music to signal duration of exercise. Music segments indicate aerobic activity while intervals of silence announce flexibility and strength development activities.

Jump Rope Exercises

1. Jump rope - 45 seconds. If not able to jump, practice swinging the rope to the side while jumping
2. Place the rope on the floor and perform locomotor movements around and over the rope. Make different shapes and letters with the rope.
3. Hold the folded rope overhead. Sway from side to side. Twist right and left.
4. Lie on back with rope held with outstretched arms toward ceiling. Bring up one leg at a time and touch the rope with toes. Lift both legs together. Sit up and try to hook the rope over the feet. Release and repeat.

DPE p. 286

Place the ropes around the perimeter of the area so they can quickly pick up and return a jump rope.

If youngsters have difficulty jumping the rope, offer alternate challenges.

An alternative is to substitute long-rope jumping. Since not all children are jumping, it is less demanding and easier for children to perform.

PM.—The student will demonstrate the ability to change from slow to fast and vice versa.

Cog.—The student will know the meaning of the terms "slow" and "fast" times.

MOVEMENT EXPERIENCE— CONTENT	ORGANIZATION AND TEACHING HINTS	EXPECTED STUDENT OBJECTIVES AND OUTCOMES

5. Jump rope - 45 seconds.
6. Fold the rope and perform various isometric exercises.
7. Play "Tail Tag." Fold the rope and use it as a tail. Try to keep others from pulling the tail.
8. Touch toes with the folded rope.
9. Jump rope - 45 seconds.
10. Place rope on the floor and do various Animal Walks along or over the rope.
11. Do Push- variations with the rope folded and help between the hands.
12. Jump rope - 45 seconds.

LESSON FOCUS (15 – 20 MINUTES)

Movement Skills and Concepts (1)

Select a few activities from each of the categories so students receive a variety of skills to practice. When possible, integrate the manipulative skills activities with fundamental skill activities.

Fundamental Skill: Walking

1. Walk in different directions, changing direction on signal (90°).
2. While walking, bring up the knees and slap with the hands on each step.
3. Walk on heels, toes, side of the foot, Charlie Chaplin fashion (toes pointed way out).
4. Gradually lower the body while walking; gradually raise body.
5. Walk with a smooth gliding step.
6. Walk with a wide base on tip-toes; rock from side to side.
7. Clap hands alternately front and back. Clap hands under the thighs (slow walk).
8. Walk slowly. Accelerate. Decelerate.
9. Take long strides. Tiny steps.
10. Change levels on signal.
11. Walk quickly and quietly. Slowly and heavily. Quickly and heavily, etc.
12. Change direction on signal while facing the same way.
13. Walk angrily, then happily; add others.
14. Hold arms in different positions. Try different arm movements as you walk.
15. Walk different patterns: circle, square, rectangle, figure-eight, etc.
16. Walk through heavy mud, on ice of slick floor on a rainy day.
17. Walk like a soldier, a giant, a robot; add other.
18. Duck under trees or railings while walking.

DPE pp. 292 – 294

Select from formations on pp. 81 – 85
Cue by saying:

"Head up—eyes forward. Point toes straight ahead. Nice, easy, relaxed arm swing.

Lift chest, stand tall. Shoulders back and easy. Hold tummy in, chest up."

Drum rhythm can be provided throughout.

Cue: "Reach with the toes."

Explain terms.

Cog.—The student will know the meaning of the term "walking."

PM.—The student will be able to walk smoothly and rhythmically in good postural position.

Cog.—The student will understand and react in conformance to the different directives.

Cog.—The student will be able to create unique responses.

MOVEMENT EXPERIENCE— CONTENT	ORGANIZATION AND TEACHING HINTS	EXPECTED STUDENT OBJECTIVES AND OUTCOMES

19. Point toes out in different directions while walking—in, forward, and out.
20. Walk with high knees, stiff knees, one stiff knee, sore ankle.
21. Walk toward a spot, turn around in four steps. Move in a different direction.
22. Practice changing steps while walking.
23. Walk with a military goose step.
24. Walk a different way.

Skills: Working with Balloons or Beachballs

1. Keep your balloon in the air by rebounding it from the hand, fist, arm, elbow, knee, shoulder, head, and other body parts. Use one finger. Use the feet to keep balloon in the air.
2. Work out combinations of body parts, four different parts in succession.
3. Add contrasting terms:
   a. close—far
   b. in front of—behind
   c. near—far
   d. right—left
   e. high—low
   f. sudden—smooth
4. Use Lummi sticks and/or paddles:
   a. Explore keeping balloon or beachball up in the air.
   b. Hit with different parts of stick or paddle. Work out sequences. Alternate a body part with the stick or a paddle.
   c. Use contrasting terms.
   d. Work with a partner.
   e. Change sticks with paddles.
5. Keep one foot in place, control balloon or beachball.
6. Play "let's pretend" we are volleyball players. Practice overhand, underhand, dig passes. Show serving.
7. Exploratory activity by individuals or partners.

DPE pp. 408 – 409

Scattered formation.

Some movement in general space.

Begin with specific body parts and move to general areas.

Challenge with directives using the terms.

Half with sticks, half with paddles.

PM.—The student will develop the ability to track the descending balloon or beachball and control it.

Cog.—The student will understand the meaning of contrasting terms as used.

Cog.—An object rebounds according to the amount of force applied to it. The student will be able to explain this concept in his own words.

Could use hoops, individual mats, carpet squares, etc.

Explain volleyball terms.

Movement Concept: Identifying Body Parts

1. Children can be standing or seated. Touch the part of parts with both hands without looking at it. Children should repeat out loud the designated part touched by saying, "I am touching _____."
   a. Touch your shoulders
   b. Touch your ankles
   c. Touch your head
   d. Touch your toes
   e. Touch your ears
   f. Touch your knees

DPE pp. 331 – 332

Scatter formation or circle.

This is a thinking–doing activity.

Give commands briskly.

Children hold until the following command is given.

Order can be varied.

PM.—The student will be able to demonstrate the ability to touch the designated parts with assurance.

Cog.—The student will know the names of the various body parts.

MOVEMENT EXPERIENCE— CONTENT	ORGANIZATION AND TEACHING HINTS	EXPECTED STUDENT OBJECTIVES AND OUTCOMES

g. Touch your eyes

h. Touch your hips

i. Touch your cheeks

j. Touch your forehead

k. Touch your thighs

l. Touch your elbows

2. Fun Activity
   Teacher touches the incorrect part of the body as commands are given.

3. As a part is named, form a pose so that this part is the highest position of your body; the lowest.

Add other body parts, such as face, eyebrows, nose, jaw, chin, neck, chest, back, stomach, arms, forearms, wrists, thumbs, waist, feet, arches, heels.

4. Move about general space in any manner you wish. When I call out a body part, stop and put both hands on the part.

Check for accuracy.

Name muscles such as biceps, abdominals, quadriceps, etc.

5. Toss your beanbag in personal space. When I call out the name of a body part, sit down and put the beanbag on or against the part.

Issue beanbags.

6. Select some kind of a way you wish to move in general space. The signal to move will be the name of a body part. Move around the room with one hand on the body part. When another body part is called out, change the type of movement and also hold that body part.

Movement Concept: Exploring Personal Space

DPE pp. 327 – 328

Issue jump ropes.

Cog.—Each child will be able to grasp the concept and define personal space.

1. Each child has a jump rope. Double the rope and grasp it by the handles. In a kneeling position, swing the rope in a full arc along the floor. Use other positions: Sitting cross-legged, or others.

Circle both clockwise and counterclockwise. Ropes do not touch other ropes or children.

Put ropes to one side.

PM.—Each student will be able physically to define her personal space.

2. Keeping one foot in place on a spot, make a full arc with the other foot. Keep both one foot and one hand touching the spot, arc again with other foot.

Also identifies personal space.

Stretch fully, all directions.

Cog.—Students should find that a wide base is best.

3. Keeping your feet in place, sway and reach out as far as you can without losing balance or moving feet. Try with feet together and feet apart. Which is better for balance? Sit down and repeat movements. Do you need more or less space?

Provide choice.

Look for unilateral, bilateral, and cross-lateral movements.

Cog.—Students should find that less space is needed when seated.

Aff.—The children will have the urge to explore and create.

4. Here are some of the kinds of movements you can do in personal space:

   a. Make yourself as wide as possible. Change to narrow. Experiment with narrow, small—large, high—low, etc. Try from other positions—kneeling, sitting balancing of seat, standing on one foot, lying on stomach, and other.

MOVEMENT EXPERIENCE—CONTENT	ORGANIZATION AND TEACHING HINTS	EXPECTED STUDENT OBJECTIVES AND OUTCOMES
b. In supine position, move arms and legs in different combinations out and back.		
c. Select one part of the body to keep in place. Make big circles with the rest of the body. Select other parts.		
d. Explore different positions where one foot is higher than any other body part.		
e. Pump yourself up like a balloon. Get bigger and bigger until I say, "Pop!"		
f. Let's pretend you are a snowman melting to the ground under a hot sun.	May need to speed up the melting a bit.	
g. With your feet in place, twist as far as you can one way and then the other (arms out to sides). Show me how a top spins.		

GAME (5 – 7 MINUTES)

Jack Frost and Jane Thaw — *DPE,* p. 563
   Supplies: A white streamer for Jack Frost, a streamer of another color for Jane Thaw
   Skills: Running, dodging, holding position
   Children are scattered and move to avoid being frozen (tagged) by Jack Frost, who carries a white streamer in one hand. Frozen children must remain immobile until touched (thawed) by Jane Thaw, identified by a streamer of a different color. Freezing occurs instantly, but thawing is a more gradual process. Two Jack Frosts can help keep the action moving.

Marching Ponies — *DPE,* p. 563
   Supplies: None
   Skills: Marching, running
   One child, the ringmaster, crouches in the center of a circle of ponies formed by the other children. Two goal lines on opposite sides of the circle are established as safe areas. The ponies march around the circle in step, counting as they do so. At a predetermined number (whispered to the ringmaster by the teacher), the ringmaster jumps up and attempts to tag the others before they can reach the safety lines. Anyone tagged joins the ringmaster in the center and helps catch the other children the next time. The game should be reorganized after six to eight children have been caught. Those left in the circle are declared the winners.
   Variation: Other characterizations, such as lumbering elephants, jumping kangaroos, and the like, can be tried. A child who suggests a unique movement could be allowed to be the ringmaster.

Tag Games — *DPE,* p. 568
   Supplies: None
   Skills: Fundamental locomotor movements, dodging
   Tag is played in many ways. Children are scattered about the area. One child is it and chases the others, trying to tag one of them. When a tag is made, she says, "You're it." The new it chases other children.
   Variations:
   1. Object Tag. Touching a specified type of object (e.g., wood, iron) or the floor or an object of a specified color makes the runner safe.
   2. Mimic Tag. Children can be safe by mimicking a particular action or pose.
   3. Locomotor Tag. The child who is it specifies how the others should move—skipping, hopping, jumping. The tagger must use the same kind of movement.
   4. Frozen Tag. Two children are it. The rest are scattered over the area. When caught, they are "frozen" and must keep both feet in place. Any free player can tag a frozen player and thus release her. The goal of the tagger is to freeze all players. Frozen players can be required to hop in place until released.

DYNAMIC PHYSICAL EDUCATION LESSON PLAN
Rhythmic Movement (Lesson 1)
Level I

Supplies and Equipment Needed:
Magic number cards
Record player and records
Parachute
Tom-tom
Balls
Cones
Wands
Hoops
Mats

Dances Taught:
Ach Ja
Let Your Feet Go Tap, Tap, Tap
Did You Ever See a Lassie
Carrousel
Movin' Madness
Jolly Is the Miller

MOVEMENT EXPERIENCE— CONTENT	ORGANIZATION AND TEACHING HINTS	EXPECTED STUDENT OBJECTIVES AND OUTCOMES

INTRODUCTORY ACTIVITY (2 – 3 MINUTES)

Magic Number Challenges

Students put together a series of movements based on the magic numbers given. For example, hold a card with three numbers on it (10, 8, 14). The students must then perform any three movements the specified number of times, respectively.

DPE pp. 254

Encourage variety of response.

Scatter formation.

Encourage students to use all the available space.

If difficulty occurs, use only two numbers in the sequence.

PM.—The student will be able to change movements quickly and correctly count the desired number of repetitions.

FITNESS DEVELOPMENT ACTIVITIES (7 – 8 MINUTES)

Mini-Challenge Course

Arrange four courses with a group at each course. Students perform the challenges from start to finish and jog back to repeat the course. On signal, groups move to a new course.
Course 1. Do crouch jumps, pulls or scooter movements down a bench; through two hoops; and skip to a cone.
Course 2. Weave in and out of four wands held upright by cones; Crab Walk, hang from a climbing rope for 5 seconds; and gallop to a cone.
Course 3. Do a tumbling activity length of mat; agility run through hoops; Frog Jump; and slide to a cone.
Course 4. Move over and under six obstacles; Log Roll length of mat; while jumping, circle around three cones; and run to a cone.

DPE pp. 284 – 285

Set up four parallel (side-by-side) courses in one-half of the area. Rotate groups to each course after a specified time.

An alternative is to organize the courses into a single circuit around the perimeter of the area.

Movement should be continuous.

Since young children fatigue and recover quickly, stop the class after 30–45 seconds and perform fitness movement challenges.

Cog.—The students will be able to name each of the movements they select.

Cog.—The student will recognize and perform all verbally designated tasks.

PM.—The student will be able to perform the new fitness routine by the end of the week,

Aff.—In most sports, performance falls off when muscular fatigue sets in. Muscular endurance is an important factor in delaying fatigue. Discuss the value of fitness for better athletic performance.

MOVEMENT EXPERIENCE— CONTENT	ORGANIZATION AND TEACHING HINTS	EXPECTED STUDENT OBJECTIVES AND OUTCOMES

LESSON FOCUS (15 – 20 MINUTES)

Rhythmic Movement (1)

Alternate activities from each of the categories so students receive a variety of skills to practice.
Marching

Try the following sequence:
1. Clap hands while standing in place to the beat of a tom-tom or record.
2. March in place; always start with the left foot.
3. March to the music in scatter formation, adding some of the following challenges;
   a. Be a big or small as you can.
   b. Count the rhythm.
   c. Change direction on signal.
   d. March backwards.
   e. March loudly or quietly.
   f. Make up a rhythmic poem like "Sound Off."
4. Try some simple patterns such as the following:
   a. Single-line formation.
   b. Double-line formation (with a partner).
   c. Two lines meet and go up the center.
   d. Two lines meet and split on signal.
   e. Make up your own formation.

DPE pp. 355 – 406

Scatter formation.

Use any piece of music that has a steady rhythm.

Try to keep head up and stay in good posture.

By adding different challenges to the marching, it will force the student to concentrate and remain motivated.

When marching in line, try to maintain even spacing between people.

This activity can be an excellent lead-up for the Grand March.

Wave at the "people" while marching. Pretend you are in a parade.

Try teaching commands such as "mark time," "about face," "forward march," and "halt." Be a drum major.

Pretend to play an instrument in a marching band.

PM.—The student will be able to march in time to the rhythmic beat.

Aff.—Discuss the difficulty of learning to perform two or more skills at the same time: for example, a marching band or ice skating to music.

Cog.—Temperature affects physical performance. Discuss how heat will decrease performance in endurance activities and the need for replenishing body fluids.

Parachute Rhythmic Routine

A sample routine follows:
Beats
1–8   Eight walking steps to the left. Hold chute in both hands.
9–16   Eight backward steps to the right.
17–20 Raise parachute above head (up-2-3-4).
21–24 Lower chute to floor (Down-2-3-4).
25–32 Shake the chute (Up and Down).
33–36 Raise the chute overhead.
37–44 Lower chute quickly to floor and form a dome. Hold the dome for eight beats.

DPE pp. 477 – 482

Before trying this routine to music, it might be wise to practice with the beat of a tom-tom.

A good idea for practice might be to first try the routine without the chute.

Offer youngsters an opportunity to develop simple routines and parachute movements.

Cog.—Parachute activities require teamwork. Students must work together to perform the tasks.

PM.—The student will be able to perform the parachute activities to the rhythm of the music.

MOVEMENT EXPERIENCE— CONTENT	ORGANIZATION AND TEACHING HINTS	EXPECTED STUDENT OBJECTIVES AND OUTCOMES

Dances

1. Movin' Madness (*DPE*, p. 368)

2. Did You Ever See a Lassie? (*DPE*, p. 368)

3. Let Your Feet Go Tap, Tap, Tap (*DPE*, p. 370)

4. Ach Ja (*DPE*, p. 371)

5. Carrousel (*DPE*, pp. 375)

6. Jolly Is the Miller (*DPE*, p. 376)

When teaching a dance, use the following steps:
1. Tell about the dance and listen to the music.
2. Clap the beat and learn the verse.
3. Practice the dance steps without the music and with verbal cues.
4. Practice the dance with the music.

Make dances easy for students to learn by using some of the following ideas:
1. Teach the dances without partners.
2. Allow youngsters to move in any direction—avoid the left–right orientation.
3. Use scattered formation instead of circles—it helps avoid embarrassment.
4. Emphasize strong movements such as clapping and stomping to encourage involvement.
5. Tape the music at a slower speed when first learning the dance.

Rhythms should be taught like other sport skills. Avoid expecting perfection when teaching rhythms. Teach a variety of dances rather than one or two in depth. Youngsters will enjoy rhythms if they know it is acceptable to make mistakes without being ridiculed.

Cog.—The student will be able to sing the verses of the singing games.

Aff.—Rhythmic activities are a learned skill. Performers need to practice them many times before they are mastered. Discuss the need for understanding individual differences in rates of learning.

GAMES (5 – 7 MINUTES)

Squirrel in the Trees — *DPE*, p. 567
Supplies: None
Skills: Fundamental locomotor movements
A number of trees are formed by two players facing each other and holding hands or putting hands on each other's shoulders. A squirrel is in the center of each tree, and one or two extra squirrels are outside. A signal to change is given. All squirrels move out of their tree to another tree, and the extra players try to find a free tree. Only one squirrel is allowed in a tree.
Teaching suggestion: As a system of rotation, when each squirrel moves into a tree, he can change places with one of the players forming the tree. The rotation is important, because it ensures that all children eventually are active.

Stop Ball — *DPE*, p. 568
Supplies: A ball
Skills: Tossing, catching
One child, with hands over the eyes, stands in the center of a circle of children. A ball is tossed clockwise or counterclockwise from child to child around the circle. Failing to catch the ball or making a bad toss incurs a penalty. That child must take one long step back and stay out of the game for one turn.
At a time of her own selection, the center player calls, "Stop." The player caught with the ball steps back and stays out for one turn. The center player should be allowed three or four turns and then be changed.

DYNAMIC PHYSICAL EDUCATION LESSON PLAN
Long-Rope Jumping Skills
Level I

Supplies and Equipment Needed:
  One long-jump rope (16 ft.) for each group of 4–6 children
  Individual jump ropes
  Tom-tom
  Cones
  Circuit training signs
  Balls
  Hula hoops
  Beanbags

MOVEMENT EXPERIENCE— CONTENT	ORGANIZATION AND TEACHING HINTS	EXPECTED STUDENT OBJECTIVES AND OUTCOMES

INTRODUCTORY ACTIVITY (2 – 3 MINUTES)

Crossing the River

A river is designated by two lines about 40 feet apart. Each time the youngsters cross the river the must perform a different movement. For example:
  1. Run, walk, hop, skip, leap.
  2. Animal Walks such as bear, crab, and puppy dog.
  3. Partner run, back to back, side by side.

DPE p. 254

Delineate two lines 40 feet apart with cones.

Divide class with one-half on each side of the river.

Perform movements for 1 minute, rest, and stretch. Perform movements again.

PM.—The student will be able to perform the various movement activities for one minute.

Cog.—The student will understand and be able to explain the need for introductory activities.

FITNESS DEVELOPMENT ACTIVITIES (7 – 8 MINUTES)

Circuit Training

Tape alternating segments of silence and music to signal duration of exercise. Music segments (begin at 30 seconds) indicate activity at each station while intervals of silence (10 seconds) announce it is time to stop and move forward to the next station.
  1. Tortoise and Hare
  2. Curl-up variations
  3. Hula Hooping on arms
  4. Jumping boxes—step on and off continuously
  5. Agility run—run back and forth between two designated lines
  6. Bench Pulls—pull body along bench
  7. Crab Walk
  8. Bend and Twist

DPE pp. 300 – 303

Increase the amount of time at each station to 25 seconds and decrease the amount of rest between stations.

The students must be able to perform the exercises well to assure the effectiveness of circuit training.

Have youngsters point to the next station before rotating to avoid confusion.

Perform aerobic activities at the end of the circuit.

PM.—The student will be able to perform all exercises on the circuit.

Cog.—The student will be able to explain how the circuit exercises all areas of the body: arm–shoulder girdle, trunk, and legs.

Aff.—Most fitness gains are made when the body is exercised past the point of initial fatigue. Thus, briefly discuss the value of pushing one's self past the first signs of tiring.

LESSON FOCUS (15 – 20 MINUTES)

Long-Rope Jumping Skills

  1. Jump a stationary rope, gradually raise the rope.
  2. Ocean Waves—Shake the rope with an up-and-down motion. Students try to jump a "low spot."

DPE pp. 446 – 451

Groups of three to four children.

These are introductory activities that should aid nonjumpers.

PM.—The student will be able to jump the rope a minimum of eight times consecutively without a miss.

Cog.—In terms of physical exercise, 10 minutes of rope jumping is equal to 30 minutes of jogging. The student will be able to explain this fact in his own words.

24

MOVEMENT EXPERIENCE—CONTENT	ORGANIZATION AND TEACHING HINTS	EXPECTED STUDENT OBJECTIVES AND OUTCOMES

3. Snake in the grass—Wiggle the rope back and forth on the grass. Jump without touching the rope.
4. Pendulum swing—Move the rope back and forth like a pendulum. Jump the rope as it approaches the jumper.
5. Practice turning the rope with a partner. The skill of turning *must* precede jumping skills. Standard 16 ft. long ropes are difficult for young children to turn. Substitute 8 to 12 ft ropes depending on the maturity of the youngsters.
6. Practice turning the rope to rhythm. Music with a strong beat or a steady tom-tom beat is useful for developing rhythmic turning. Turning the rope to a steady rhythm *must* precede jumping skills.
7. Stand in the center of the turners and jump the rope as it is turned once. Add more jumps.
8. Run through a turning rope.
9. Run in, jump once, and run out.
10. Front door—turn the rope toward the jumper.
11. Try the following variations:
    a. Run in front door and out back door.
    b. Run in back door and out front door.
    c. Run in back door and out back door.
    d. Run in front or back door, jump a specified number of times, and out.
    e. Run in front or back door, jump, and do a quarter, half, and full turn in the air.
    f. Touch the ground while jumping.
    g. Turn around while jumping.
12. Hot Pepper — *gradually* increase the speed of the rope.
13. High Water — *gradually* raise the height of the rope while it is turned.

Concentrate on *not* touching the rope (body awareness).

Primary-grade children must be taught *how* to start and maintain proper turning of the long rope. Work hard on this step.

Tying one end of a rope to a hook on the wall or a chair will make it easier for children to turn long ropes.

Use 9- 12-foot ropes for teaching primary grade rope turning. The shorter ropes are easier for young children to turn.

Cross-age tutoring is excellent. Have older students teach kindergarten children to turn.

Two children turn and the others jump. Make sure that all children get a chance to both turn and jump.

Back door is much more difficult. Approach the rope at a 45° angle.

Make sure the turners maintain a constant rhythm with the rope. Children who have trouble should face one of the turners and key their jumps to both the visual and audio cues (hand movement and sound of the rope hitting the floor).

It might be helpful to review beanbag activity as a change-of-pace activity.

Try to eliminate excessive body movement while jumping, i.e., jumping too high.

Use Hot Pepper verse, p. 402.

Cog.—Rope jumping burns a large number of calories as compared to other activities. The youngster will understand that exercise helps prevent obesity.

Aff.—Rope jumping is neither a masculine nor feminine activity. It is performed by boxers, football players, and dancers for fitness development. Discuss its value for both sexes.

PM.—The student will be able to turn the rope front and back door, hot pepper, and high water.

GAME (5 – 7 MINUTES)

Ball Passing — *DPE*, p. 558
  Supplies: Five or six different kinds of balls for each circle
  Skill: Object handling
  The class is divided into two or more circles, with no more than 15 children in any one circle. Each circle consists of two or more squads, but squad members need not stand together.
  The teacher starts a ball around the circle; it is passed from player to player in the same direction. The teacher introduces more balls until five or six are moving around the circle at the same time and in the same direction. If a child drops a ball, he must retrieve it, and a point is scored against his squad. After a period of time, a whistle is blown, and the points against each squad are totaled. The squad with the lowest score wins. Beanbags, large blocks, or softballs can be substituted for balls.

MOVEMENT EXPERIENCE— CONTENT	ORGANIZATION AND TEACHING HINTS	EXPECTED STUDENT OBJECTIVES AND OUTCOMES

Hot Potatoes — *DPE,* p. 562

Supplies: One to three balls or beanbags for each group

Skill: Object handling

Children are seated in small circles (8 to 12 per circle) so that objects can be passed from one to another around the circle. Balls or beanbags or both are passed around the circle. The teacher or a selected student looks away from the class and randomly shouts, "stop!" The point of the game is to avoid getting stuck with an object. If this happens, the player(s) with an object must get up and move to the next circle. The teacher should begin the game with one object and gradually add objects if the class is capable.

Variation: The passing direction can be reversed on signal.

Aviator — *DPE,* p. 556

Supplies: None

Skills: Running, locomotor movements, stopping

Players are parked (in push-up position) at one end of the playing area. The air traffic controller (ATC) is in front of the players and calls out, "Aviators aviators, take off!" Youngsters take off and move like airplanes to the opposite side of the area. The first person to move to the other side and land the plane (get into push-up position facing the ATC) is declared the new ATC.

If the ATC yells out some type of stormy weather, all planes must return to the starting line and resume the parked position. Examples of stormy weather commands are lightning, thunder, hurricane, and tornado. Each ATC is allowed to give stormy weather warnings once.

DYNAMIC PHYSICAL EDUCATION LESSON PLAN
Manipulative Skills Using Playground Balls
Level I

Supplies and Equipment Needed:
One 8-1/2" playground ball for each student
Tom-tom

MOVEMENT EXPERIENCE— CONTENT	ORGANIZATION AND TEACHING HINTS	EXPECTED STUDENT OBJECTIVES AND OUTCOMES

INTRODUCTORY ACTIVITY (2 – 3 MINUTES)

Combination Movements

1. Hop, turn around, and shake.
2. Jump, make a shape in the air, balance.
3. Skip, collapse, and roll.
4. Curl, roll, jump with a half turn.
5. Whirl, skip, sink slowly.
6. Hop, collapse, creep.
7. Kneel, sway, jump to feet.
8. Lift, grin, and roll.

DPE p. 254

Scatter formation.

Use the tambourine to signal movement changes.

Challenge students to develop their own sequences.

Repeat the challenges so youngsters can create different movements using the same words.

PM.—The student will be able to perform the various combinations and demonstrate an understanding of the movements' terms.

Cog.—The student will be able to recognize various movements by name.

FITNESS DEVELOPMENT ACTIVITIES (7 – 8 MINUTES)

Fitness Challenges

Alternate locomotor movements with strength challenges. Repeat the challenges as necessary.
Locomotor Movement: Walk for 30 seconds.

Flexibility and Trunk Development Challenges
1. Bend in different directions.
2. Stretch slowly and return quickly.
3. Combine bending and stretching movements.
4. Sway back and forth.
5. Twist one body part; add body parts.
6. Make your body move in a large circle.
7. In a sitting position, wave your legs at a friend; make circles with your legs.
Locomotor Movement: Skip for 30 seconds.

Shoulder Girdle Challenges
In a push-up position, do the following challenges:
1. Lift one foot; the other foot.
2. Wave at a friend; wave with the other arm.
3. Scratch your back with one hand; use the other hand.
4. Walk your feet to your hands.
5. Turn over and face the ceiling; shake a leg; Crab Walk.
Locomotor Movement: Jog for 30 seconds.

DPE pp. 281 – 283

Scatter formation.

Individual mats can be used as a "home" to keep youngsters spaced properly.

Repeat the various trunk challenges as necessary.

Young children will perform best when locomotor movements are alternated with stationary challenges that allow them to recover aerobically.

Add Animal Walks to replace some of the locomotor movements and to create interest.

Use different qualities of movement such as giant skips, tiny and quick gallops, or slow giant steps to motivate youngsters.

As children become more fit, repeat the entire sequence.

Cog.—The student will be able to recognize the names of the activities and be able to demonstrate each one.

PM.—The student will be able to perform the challenges at an increased dosage level.

MOVEMENT EXPERIENCE— CONTENT	ORGANIZATION AND TEACHING HINTS	EXPECTED STUDENT OBJECTIVES AND OUTCOMES

Abdominal Development
From a supine position:
1. Lift your head and look at your toes.
2. Lift your knees to your chest.
3. Wave your legs at a friend. From a sitting position:
1. Slowly lay down with hands on tummy.
2. Lift legs and touch toes.
Locomotor Movement: Run and leap for 30 seconds.

LESSON FOCUS (15 – 20 MINUTES)

Manipulative Skills Using Playground Balls

Give students two or three activities to practice so you have time to move and help youngsters. Alternate activities from each of the categories so students receive a variety of activities for practice.
Individual Activities
1. Bounce and Catch
   a. Two hands, one hand.
   b. Bounce at different levels.
   c. Bounce between legs.
   d. Close eyes and bounce.
   e. Dribble ball in a stationary and/or moving position.
   f. Dribble and follow the commands, such as move forward, backward, in a circle, or sideways, while walking, galloping, trotting, etc.
   g. Exploratory activity.
2. Toss and Catch
   a. Toss and catch, vary height.
   b. Add various challenges while tossing (i.e., touch floor, clap hands, turn, sit down, lie down).
   c. Toss and let bounce. Also add some challenges as above.
   d. Toss up and catch behind back—toss from behind back and catch in front of body.
   e. Create moving challenges (i.e., toss, run five steps and catch, toss and back up five hops and catch.)
   f. Exploratory activity.
3. Foot Skills
   a. Lift the ball up with both feet and catch. Both front and rear of body catch.
   b. From a sitting position with the ball between feet, toss it up, and catch with hands.
   c. Keep the ball in the air with feet and different body parts.

DPE pp. 413 – 417

One 8-1/2" playground ball per child.

Warm up with controlled rolling while sitting. Also practice rolling from standing position.

Emphasize keeping the eyes on the ball and catching with the fingertips.

Make sure children "give" when they catch the ball and make a soft home.

Encourage children to start with a low toss in the air and gradually increase the height of the throw as skill increases.

The purpose of the many variations is to force children to keep their eyes on the moving object while performing another activity with their bodies.

Practice tossing the ball straight up and accurately.

See how many catches can be made in a row.

Strive for quality, good throws, and a high percentage of catches.

PM.—The students will be able to keep their eyes on the ball during all challenges and activities.

PM.—The student will be able to make a good toss to enable a good catch.

Cog.—The student will be able to interpret orally the many uses of the basic ball skills introduced in this lesson.

Aff.—Develop the attitude that mere accomplishment of a skill is not a goal of people who excel. Rather, a person must be able to master the skill many times and with consistency to be a champion.

Cog.—The student will be able to identify the sport in which the various passes are used.

PM.—The student will be able to pass (all variations) and catch the ball without dropping it, three times in succession.

MOVEMENT EXPERIENCE—CONTENT	ORGANIZATION AND TEACHING HINTS	EXPECTED STUDENT OBJECTIVES AND OUTCOMES

Partner Activities: Rolling, Bouncing, and Throwing
 	
1. Roll ball back and forth.
   a. Two-handed, right and left.
   b. Targets, straddle, pins, etc.
2. Bouncing and throwing.
   a. Begin with bouncing skills.
   b. Different tosses first.
   c. Different throws. Two-handed right and left.
3. Basketball Activities
   a. Bounce pass to partner.
   b. Dribble in a variety of ways.
   c. Dribble and pass to a partner.
4. Throwing from different positions.
   a. Kneeling, sitting.
5. Use follow activity; one partner leads and the other follows.
6. Allow for exploration and creativity.
	Partner organization.
	
	Distances should be short, then increased.
	
	Keep body low.
	
	Use one-step.
	
	Use underhand first. One bounce to partner.
	
	Keep distances short. Show technique. Use a line or bench.
	
	If possible, have students throw against a wall and catch on the rebound.
	
	Take three turns, then change.
		PM.—The students will be able to demonstrate the ability to control the balls so their partners can handle them successfully.
		
		Aff.—For people to improve throwing and catching skills, they must have the cooperation of a partner. Discuss the importance of helping others improve their skills and how that relates to self-development.
		
		Cog.—Students will understand it is easier to catch larger objects, i.e., the difference between a small sponge ball and a beachball.

GAME (5 – 7 MINUTES)

Teacher Ball — *DPE,* p. 569

Supplies: A grey foam ball or rubber playground ball

Skills: Throwing, catching

One child is the teacher or leader and stands about 10 ft in front of three other students, who are lined up facing him. The object of the game is to move up to the teacher's spot by avoiding making bad throws or missing catches. The teacher throws to each child in turn, beginning with the child on the left, who must catch and return the ball. Any child making a throwing or catching error goes to the end of the line, on the teacher's right. Those in the line move up, filling the vacated space.

If the teacher makes a mistake, he must go to the end of the line and the child at the head of the line becomes the new teacher. The teacher scores a point by remaining in position for three rounds (three throws to each child). After scoring a point, the teacher takes a position at the end of the line and another child becomes the teacher.

Teaching suggestion: This game should be used only after children have a minimal competency in throwing and catching skills. It can be a part of the skill-teaching program.

Variation: The teacher can suggest specific methods of throwing and catching, such as "Catch with the right hand only" or "Catch with one hand and don't let the ball touch your body."

The Scarecrow and the Crows — *DPE,* p. 567

Supplies: None

Skills: Dodging, running

Children form a large circle representing the garden, which one child, designated the scarecrow, guards. From six to eight crows scatter on the outside of the circle, and the scarecrow assumes a characteristic pose inside the circle. The circle children raise their joined hands and let the crows run through, into the garden, where they pretend to eat. The scarecrow tries to tag the crows. The circle children help the crows by raising their joined hands and allowing them to leave the circle, but they try to hinder the scarecrow. If the scarecrow runs out of the circle, all the crows immediately run into the garden and start to nibble at the vegetables, while thes circle children hinder the scarecrow's reentry.

When the scarecrow has caught one or two crows, a new group of children is selected. If, after a reasonable period of time, the scarecrow has failed to catch any crows, a change should be made.

DYNAMIC PHYSICAL EDUCATION LESSON PLAN
Educational Movement Using Rope Patterns
Level I

Supplies and Equipment Needed:
  Tambourine
  Music for rope jumping
  One jump rope for each child
  One beanbag for each child
  Tape player

MOVEMENT EXPERIENCE—CONTENT	ORGANIZATION AND TEACHING HINTS	EXPECTED STUDENT OBJECTIVES AND OUTCOMES

INTRODUCTORY ACTIVITY (2 – 3 MINUTES)

Bend, Stretch, and Shake

1. Bend various body parts individually and then bend various combinations of body parts.
2. Stretch the body in various levels. Encourage stretching from various positions such as standing, sitting, and prone position.
3. Practice shaking individual body parts when the tambourine is shaken. Progress to shaking the entire body.
4. Bend body parts while doing different locomotor movements. Bend limbs while shaking.

DPE p. 259

Use a tambourine to signal changes.

Encourage smooth bending movements through the full range of joint movement.

Stretch beyond usual limits.

As children learn variations of the movements, increase the speed of change from one movement to the other.

Encourage creative and new responses.

Cog.—The student will recognize the meaning of the word "level" in relation to her body in space.

Cog.—Stretching beyond normal limits is necessary to maintain flexibility and range of motion at the joints.

PM.—The student will be able to perform at least five variations of stretch, bend, and shake.

FITNESS DEVELOPMENT ACTIVITIES (7 – 8 MINUTES)

Fitness Games and Challenges

Tape alternating segments of silence and music to signal duration of exercise. Music segments indicate fitness game activity while intervals of silence announce flexibility and strength development activities.
1. Stoop Tag - 45 seconds.
2. Freeze; perform stretching activities.
3. Back-to-Back Tag - 45 seconds.
4. Freeze; perform Abdominal Challenges using Curl-up variations.
5. Balance Tag - 45 seconds.
6. Freeze; perform Arm-Shoulder Girdle Challenges using Push-up variations.
7. Elbow Swing Tag - 45 seconds.
8. Freeze; perform Trunk Development challenges.
9. Color Tag - 45 seconds.

DPE p. 284

Maximize movement by using simple fitness games that require little explanation.

Many Fitness Challenges are found in *DPE*, pp. 281 – 283.

Remember that the goal of fitness games is to stimulate movement rather than teach children to follow rules.

Assign many youngsters to be it to increase the amount of movement.

Cog.—The body starts to perspire in an attempt to maintain a constant temperature. The student will verbalize this in his own words.

PM.—The student will be able to perform all challenges of the fitness activities.

Aff.—Regulation of body temperature is essential for comfort and safety. Discuss the many ways we attempt to regulate this temperature: more or fewer clothes, perspiring, swimming, and heating.

MOVEMENT EXPERIENCE—CONTENT	ORGANIZATION AND TEACHING HINTS	EXPECTED STUDENT OBJECTIVES AND OUTCOMES

LESSON FOCUS (15 – 20 MINUTES)

Movement Skills and Concepts Using Rope Patterns

Alternate rope pattern activities with rope jumping activities. This offers students time for recovery after rope jumping.

A. Rope Patterns

Lay rope lengthwise on floor.
1. Walk as on a balance beam.
   a. Forward
   b. Backward
   c. Sideways
2. Jump/hop down length and back.
   a. Vary time—slow, fast, accelerate, decelerate, even, uneven
   b. Vary levels and force—light, heavy, high to low.
3. Other locomotor movements.
   a. Crisscross
   b. Jumps with one-half turn
   c. Allow student choice
4. Imitate animals.
5. Crouch jumps.
   a. Various combinations; forward, backward, sideways.
   b. Allow exploration.
6. Put rope in shapes, letters, numbers.
   a. Move in and out of figures.
   b. Add movements, keeping the body inside figure.
7. Partner work.
   a. Make figure with two ropes. Move in and out of figure.
   b. Using one rope, do follow activity. Take turns.

B. Rope Jumping

This lesson should introduce youngsters to rope jumping. It should not be too instructional, but should be used for the purpose of giving them a positive introduction to rope jumping. Instruction will come in a later lesson.
1. Hold rope. Jump in time.
2. Perform the slow-time and fast-time rhythm with the rope held in one hand and turned (propellers).
3. Jump the rope and practice slow to fast time.
4. Introduce a few basic steps.
   a. Two-step basic
   b. Alternating basic
   c. Backwards
   d. One foot

DPE pp. 444 – 446

Throughout the lesson use much student choice.

Use right and left. When hopping, change feet on reversing, or repeat with the other foot the next time.

Could add—leading with different parts of the body.

Use demonstration.

Use demonstration and have class guess.

Place some of the body weight on hands.

Alternate the rope pattern activities with rope jumping activities. This will give students a needed rest from jumping.

Allow enough time for exploration. Have achievement demonstration.

DPE pp. 451 – 458

Use a record that possesses a rhythm that is steady, unchanging, and easy to hear.

Turn up the tape player so the music is loud and easy to hear.

It may be necessary to take a short break and work with something like beanbags or play an inactive game, as children tire easily in this activity.

PM.—The student will be able to develop versatility in movement.

Cog.—The student will be able to develop the ability to solve problem situations.

Aff.—The student will develop an understanding of movements principles and terms.

PM.—The student will be able to create three movements and teach them to a partner.

PM.—The student will be able to jump rope.

Cog.—The student will be able to recognize the basic underlying beat and clap his hands to the rhythm after listening to a variety of records.

Aff.—The student will learn the value of overlearning a skill. Here is a chance to discuss the overlearning principle and explain that it is hard to listen for the rhythm if you haven't overlearned the skill of rope jumping. If you *have* overlearned rope jumping, you can easily listen to the music *without* thinking about rope jumping.

MOVEMENT EXPERIENCE— CONTENT	ORGANIZATION AND TEACHING HINTS	EXPECTED STUDENT OBJECTIVES AND OUTCOMES

GAME (5 – 7 MINUTES)

Tag Games — *DPE,* p. 568
Supplies: None
Skills: Fundamental locomotor movements, dodging
Tag is played in many ways. Children are scattered about the area. One child is it and chases the others, trying to tag one of them. When a tag is made, she says, "You're it." The new it chases other children.
Variations:
1. Object Tag. Touching a specified type of object (e.g., wood, iron) or the floor or an object of a specified color makes the runner safe.
2. Mimic Tag. Children can be safe by mimicking a particular action or pose.
3. Locomotor Tag. The child who is it specifies how the others should move—skipping, hopping, jumping. The tagger must use the same kind of movement.
4. Frozen Tag. Two children are it. The rest are scattered over the area. When caught, they are "frozen" and must keep both feet in place. Any free player can tag a frozen player and thus release her. The goal of the tagger is to freeze all players. Frozen players can be required to hop in place until released.

Charlie Over the Water — *DPE,* p. 560
Supplies: A volleyball or playground ball
Skills: Skipping, running, stopping, bowling (rolling)
The children are in circle formation with hands joined. One child, Charlie (or Sally, if a girl), is in the center of the circle, holding a ball. The children skip around the circle to the following chant.
Charlie over the water,
Charlie over the sea,
Charlie caught a bluebird,
But he can't catch me!
On the word me, Charlie tosses the ball in the air and children drop hands and scatter. When Charlie catches it, he shouts "Stop!" All of the children stop immediately and must not move their feet. Charlie rolls the ball in an attempt to hit one of the children. If he hits a child, that child becomes the new Charlie. If he misses, he must remain Charlie, and the game is repeated. If he misses twice, however, he picks another child for the center.

Flowers and Wind — *DPE,* p. 561
Supplies: None
Skill: Running
Two parallel lines long enough to accommodate the children are drawn about 30 ft apart. Children are divided into two groups. One is the wind and the other the flowers. Each of the teams takes a position on one of the lines and faces the other team. The flowers secretly select the name of a common flower. When ready, they walk over to the other line and stand about 3 ft away from the wind. The players on the wind team begin to call out flower names—trying to guess the flower chosen. When the flower has been guessed, the flowers run to their goal line, chased by the players of the other team. Any player caught must join the other side. The roles are reversed and the game is repeated. If one side has trouble guessing, a clue can be given to the color or size of the flower or the first letter of its name.

DYNAMIC PHYSICAL EDUCATION LESSON PLAN
Educational Movement (Lesson 2)
Level I

Fundamental Skill: Jumping
Manipulative Activity: Yarn balls
Educational Movement Themes: Moving in general space, use of force (effort)

Supplies and Equipment Needed:
  One yarn ball for each child
  Tom-tom or drum
  Parachute
  Tape player

MOVEMENT EXPERIENCE—CONTENT	ORGANIZATION AND TEACHING HINTS	EXPECTED STUDENT OBJECTIVES AND OUTCOMES

INTRODUCTORY ACTIVITY (2 – 3 MINUTES)

Marking

"Mark" by touching partner. After touch, reverse and the other partner attempts to mark.

Variations:
1. Use the eight basic locomotor movements.
2. Use positions such as Crab Walk, Puppy Dog Walk, etc.
3. Allow a point to be scored only when they touch a specified body part, i.e., knee, elbow, left hand.
4. Use a whistle signal to change partners' roles. (If chasing partner, reverse and attempt to move *away* from the other.)

DPE p. 257

Encourage students to "watch where they are going" so they won't run into each other.

Partners should be somewhat equal in ability.

Change partners once or twice.

PM.—Be able to move with agility and quickness, which would allow students to catch as well as evade their partners.

Cog.—The student will be able to verbalize a simple reason for warm-up prior to strenuous activity.

FITNESS DEVELOPMENT ACTIVITIES (7 – 8 MINUTES)

Parachute Fitness

Tape alternating segments of silence and music to signal duration of exercise. Music segments indicate aerobic activity with the parachute while intervals of silence announce using the chute to enhance flexibility and strength development.
1. Jog while holding the chute in the left hand - 20 seconds.
2. Shake the chute.
3. Slide while holding the chute with both hands - 20 seconds.
4. Sit and perform curl-ups - 30 seconds.
5. Skip for 20 seconds.
6. Freeze, face the center, and stretch the chute tightly. Hold for 8–12 seconds. Repeat five to six times.
7. Run in place while holding the chute taut at different levels.

DPE p. 285

Evenly space youngsters around the chute.

Use different grips to add variation to the activities.

Develop group morale by encouraging students to move together.

To cool down, allow youngsters a minute to perform parachute stunts like the Dome or Mushroom.

PM.—The student will be able to perform all the movement challenges.

MOVEMENT EXPERIENCE—CONTENT	ORGANIZATION AND TEACHING HINTS	EXPECTED STUDENT OBJECTIVES AND OUTCOMES

8. Sit with legs under the chute. Do a seat walk toward the center. Return to the perimeter. Repeat four to six times.
9. Move into push-up position holding the chute with one hand. Shake the chute.
10. Place the chute on the ground. Jog away from the chute and return on signal. Repeat for 30 seconds.
11. Shake the chute and jump in place.
12. Lie on back with feet under the chute. Shake the chute with the feet.
13. Hop to the center of the chute and return. Repeat for 20 seconds.
14. Sit with feet under the chute. Stretch by touching the toes with the chute. Relax with other stretches while sitting.

LESSON FOCUS (15 – 20 MINUTES)

Movement Skills and Concepts (2)

Select a few activities from each of the categories so students receive a variety of skills to practice. When possible, integrate the manipulative skill activities with fundamental skill activities.

Fundamental Skill—Jumping

1. Jump upward, trying for height.
2. Alternate low and high jumps.
3. Jump in various floor patterns—triangle, circle, square, letters, figure-eight, diamond shape.
4. Over a spot, jump forward, backwards, sideways, criss-cross.
5. Jump with the body stiff, like a pogo stick. Explore with arms in different positions.
6. Practice jump turns—quarter, half, three-quarter, full. Add heel clicks with turns.
7. Increase and decrease the speed of jumping. The height of jumping.
8. Land with the feet apart sideways and together again. Try it forward and backward (stride).
9. Jump and land as quietly as possible.
10. Jump and criss-cross the feet sideways.
11. See how far you can jump in two, three, or four consecutive jumps.
12. Pretend you are a bouncing ball.
13. Clap hands or slap thighs when in the air.
14. Jump so the hands contact the floor.
15. Select a line. Proceed down it by jumping back and forth over the line. Add turns.

DPE pp. 337 – 338

Scatter formation.

Cue by saying:
"Swing your arms forward as fast as possible."
"Bend your knees."
"Land lightly, bend knees"
"On your toes"
"Jump up and touch the ceiling."

Change activities rapidly.

Concentrate on good landings with the body in good control.

PM.—The student will be able to make a good jump and landing.

Cog.—The student will be able to verbally explain the important stress points that should be followed while jumping.

Cog.—The student will be able to name four sport or recreational activities where the jump is used.

Cog.—The student will understand that strength in relation to body size is an important factor in learning motor skills.

MOVEMENT EXPERIENCE—CONTENT	ORGANIZATION AND TEACHING HINTS	EXPECTED STUDENT OBJECTIVES AND OUTCOMES
Manipulative Activity: Yarn Balls	*DPE* pp. 413 – 417	
Individual Activity	Scatter formation.	Aff.—The student will appreciate that to become skilled, one must practice.
1. Toss and catch to self.	Keep eyes on ball, stress "give."	
a. Increase height gradually.		PM.—The student will be able to improve in the ability to track and catch objects.
b. Side to side.		
c. Front to back.		PM.—Students will throw yarn balls using the principle of opposition.
d. Toss underneath the legs, around the body, etc.		
e. Toss and clap the hands. Clap around the body. Underneath the legs.		
f. Toss and make turns—quarter and half.		
g. Toss, perform the following, catch: Heel click Touch both elbows, knees, shoulders, and heels.		
h. Use contrasting tosses: High and low Near and far Front and back		
2. Bat the ball upward as in volleyball, catch. Bat the ball, run forward and catch.		
3. Toss forward, run and catch. Toss sideways and catch. Toss overhead, turn around, run and catch.	Watch out for others. Use these with caution. Be sure of readiness.	
4. Bonk Ball—throw at anyone and say "Bonk" before throwing. Stress opposition of feet and throwing arm. Specify area to be hit.		
Partner Activity	Keep distances close. Will take some force.	
1. Roll the ball back and forth.		
2. Toss the ball back and forth, various ways.		
3. Throw the ball back and forth.		
4. Exploratory activity—batting, kicking, etc.	Seek ideas.	
Movement Concept: Moving in General Space	*DPE* p. 327	
1. Run lightly in the area, changing direction as you wish without bumping or touching anyone. How many were able to do this? Try running zigzag fashion.	Can use yarn balls for spots. Stress light running under control.	PM.—Children move in general space without interfering with others.
2. Run again in general space. On signal, change direction abruptly. Try again, only this time change both direction and the type of locomotor movement you are doing.		Aff.—Each child will respect the rights of others in general space.
3. Run lightly and pretend you are dodging another runner. Run directly at another runner and dodge him or her.		Cog.—Each student will grasp the difference between personal and general space.
4. Use a yarn ball to mark your personal space (spot); run in general space until the signal is given; return to your yarn ball and sit down.	Change the type of locomotor activity.	

MOVEMENT EXPERIENCE—CONTENT	ORGANIZATION AND TEACHING HINTS	EXPECTED STUDENT OBJECTIVES AND OUTCOMES
5. We are going to do orienteering. Point to a spot on a wall, walk directly to the spot in a straight line. You may have to wait for other so as not to bump them. Pick another spot on a different wall and repeat. Return to home base on signal.	Explain orienteering briefly.	
6. What happens when general space is decreased? Walk in general space. Now as space is decreased, walk again. Once more we are decreasing the space.	Decrease space by half and then by another half. (One quarter left.)	
7. Run around your yarn ball until I Say, "Bang." Then explode in a straight direction until the stop signal is sounded. Return.		
8. From your spot, take three (four or five) jumps (hops, skips, gallops, slides) in one direction, turn around and do the same back to home base. Try with long steps away and tiny steps back.	Remind again about not bumping or interfering with others. Expand this with different number challenges and different movements.	
9. Using movement combinations (run-jump-roll, skip-spin-collapse), move out from your spot and back. Set up a combination of three movements of your own.		
10. Blow yourself up and pretend you are a soap bubble. Float around in general space. If you touch someone or if I touch you, the bubble bursts and you collapse. Return to your spot and begin again. This time you may say "pop" and break the bubble when you wish.		
11. I am going to challenge you on right and left movements. First, let's walk in general space. When I say "right" (or "left") you change direction abruptly. Now we'll try some other movements.		PM.—Each child should be able to move right and left without mistakes.
12. This time run rapidly toward another child. Stop and bow. Now stop and shake hands.		
13. From your home spot, run to a selected spot on a wall and return home. Pick spots on two different walls and return home. Pick spots on two different walls and return.		

Movement Concept: Use of Force

	DPE pp. 330 – 331	
1. Show us how you do some forceful movements, such as chopping batting, hitting with a sledge, punching the punchbag. Try karate chops and kicks, kicking a soccerball, etc.	Scatter formation. Practice these movements. Use brief discussion of factors. Yell "timber" when chopping. Run the bases after batting.	PM.—The student will be able to develop the ability to create more forceful movement. Cog.—The student will understand that torque is the tendency of force to produce rotation around an axis.
2. Show us a light movement you can make with the arm. Repeat the same movement more forcefully.		Cog.—The student will be able to understand and apply the terms defining light and forceful movement.

MOVEMENT EXPERIENCE—CONTENT	ORGANIZATION AND TEACHING HINTS	EXPECTED STUDENT OBJECTIVES AND OUTCOMES

3. Make some movements that are light and sustained, heavy and sudden, heavy and sustained, light and sudden.
4. Make one part of the body move lightly, while another moves heavily.

GAME (5 – 7 MINUTES)

Firefighter — *DPE,* p. 561
  Supplies: None
  Skill: Running
  A fire chief runs around the outside of a circle of children and taps a number of them on the back, saying "Firefighter" each time. After making the round of the circle, the chief goes to the center. When she says "Fire," the firefighters run counterclockwise around the circle and back to place. The one who returns first and is able to stand in place motionless is declared the winner and the new chief.
  The chief can use other words to fool children, but they run only on the word <u>Fire</u>. This merely provides some fun, since there is no penalty for a false start. The circle children can sound the siren as the firefighters run.

Animal Tag — *DPE,* p. 556
  Supplies: None
  Skills: Imagery, running, dodging
  Two parallel lines are drawn about 40 ft apart. Children are divided into two groups, each of which takes a position on one of the lines. Children in one group get together with their leader and decide what animal they wish to imitate. Having selected the animal, they move over to within 5 ft or so of the other line. There they imitate the animal, and the other group tries to guess the animal correctly. If the guess is correct, they chase the first group back to its line, trying to tag as many as possible. Those caught must go over to the other team. The second group then selects an animal, and the roles are reversed. If the guessing team cannot guess the animal, however, the performing team gets another try. To avoid confusion, children must raise their hands to take turns at naming the animal. Otherwise, many false chases will occur. If children have trouble guessing, the leader of the performing team can give the initial of the animal.

Sneak Attack — *DPE,* p. 567
  Supplies: None
  Skills: Marching, running
  Two parallel lines are drawn about 60 ft apart. Children are divided into two teams. One team takes a position on one of the lines, with their backs to the area. These are the chasers. The other team is on the other line, facing the area. This is the sneak team. The sneak team moves forward on signal, moving toward the chasers. When they get reasonably close, a whistle or some other signal is given, and the sneak team turns and runs back to their line, chased by the other team. Anyone caught before reaching the line changes to the chase team. The game is repeated, with the roles exchanged.

DYNAMIC PHYSICAL EDUCATION LESSON PLAN
Individual Rope Jumping Skills
Level I

Supplies and Equipment Needed:
  Jump rope for each child
  Appropriate music
  Beanbag or hoop for each child
  Tom-tom
  Four cones
  Tape player

MOVEMENT EXPERIENCE— CONTENT	ORGANIZATION AND TEACHING HINTS	EXPECTED STUDENT OBJECTIVES AND OUTCOMES

INTRODUCTORY ACTIVITY (2 – 3 MINUTES)

Individual Movement with Manipulation

Each child is given a beanbag and moves around the area using various basic locomotor movements. Students toss and catch their beanbag while moving. On signal, they drop the beanbags and jump, hop, or leap over as many bags as possible.

DPE p. 256

Scatter formation.

Hoops can be used instead of beanbags.

Specify the number or color of beanbags they must move, leap over, or around.

Add many challenges while moving to both the locomotor movements and manipulative activities.

PM.—The student will be able to toss and catch an object while moving.

Cog.—The student will be able to recite the fact that it is easier to toss and catch an object while standing stationary than while moving.

FITNESS DEVELOPMENT ACTIVITIES (7 – 8 MINUTES)

Four-Corners Movement

Outline a large rectangle with four cones. Place signs with pictures on both sides of the cones. Youngsters move around the outside of the rectangle and change movements as they pass a corner sign. The following movement activities are suggested:
  1. Jogging
  2. Skipping/Jumping/Hopping
  3. Sliding/Galloping
  4. Various animal movements
  5. Sport imitation movements
  6. Bench pulls
  7. Bench crouch jumps
Stop the class after 30–45 seconds of movement and perform fitness challenges. Tape alternating segments of silence and music to signal duration of exercise. Music segments indicate aerobic activity while intervals of silence announce flexibility and strength development activities.

DPE p. 287

If signs are not placed at the corners, teachers can specify movements for students to perform.

Increase the demand of the routine by increasing the size of the rectangle.

Faster-moving students can pass on the outside (away from the center) of the rectangle. Also, change directions periodically.

Assure that abdominal and shoulder girdle strength development activities are included.

Cog.—It is interesting to measure the breathing rate at rest and during and after exercise. The student will be able to explain why breathing rate varies.

Aff.—Many experts feel people are overweight due to lack of activity rather than eating too much. Discuss why this might be true.

LESSON FOCUS (15 – 20 MINUTES)

Individual Rope Jumping Skills

The following are lead-up activities for beginning jumpers:
  1. Clap hands to a tom-tom beat.

DPE pp. 451 – 458

Children get tired when learning to jump. It might be wise to split the lesson focus and use a less active activity such as hoops.

PM.—The student will be able to jump the rope at least ten times in succession.

Cog.—The student will be able to recognize the difference between slow and fast time.

MOVEMENT EXPERIENCE— CONTENT	ORGANIZATION AND TEACHING HINTS	EXPECTED STUDENT OBJECTIVES AND OUTCOMES

2. Jump in place to a beat without rope. Jump back and forth over rope on floor.
3. Hold both ends of the jump rope in one hand and turn it so a steady rhythm can be made through a consistent turn. Just before the rope hits the ground, the student should practice jumping.
4. Count the rhythm out loud to cue students when to jump.
5. Start jumping the rope one turn at a time—gradually increase the number of turns.
6. Try jogging and jumping rope. The even rhythm of running often makes it easier for some youngsters to jump the rope.

Introduce the two basic jumps:
1. Slow time.
2. Fast time

Introduce some of the basic step variations:
1. Alternate foot basic step
2. Swing step forward
3. Swing step sideways
4. Backward

Add music to the two basic jumps so students can practice following a basic underlying beat.

After introducing the basic skills, play music that has a strong beat. (Turn it up so it is easy for children to hear.)

Some students will find it helpful to jump with the teacher or another good jumper turning the rope.

Give the children plenty of room so they don't hit someone with their ropes.

For slow time: Slow rope, slow feet with a rebound.

For fast time: Fast rope, fast feet. Jump the rope every turn.

To offer rest intervals, try making numbers, letters, name, and shapes with the jump rope. Cowboy turns (hold by handle and spin the rope), circling the rope under the legs, and tail tag are good rest activities.

Allow students to progress at their own rate. It is good to show the better jumpers some of the more difficult variations and allow them to practice by themselves.

Aff.—Often, boys think rope jumping is a "sissy" activity. Emphasize the fact that many athletes use it for achieving a high level of fitness. You might also mention that 10 minutes of rope jumping is equal to 30 minutes of jogging.

GAME (5 – 7 MINUTES)

Tommy Tucker's Land — *DPE,* p. 569
    Supplies: About ten beanbags for each game
    Skills: Dodging, running
    One child, Tommy Tucker (or Tammi Tucker, if a girl), stands in the center of a 15-ft square, within which the beanbags are scattered. Tommy is guarding his land and the treasure. The other children chant,
I'm on Tommy Tucker's land,
Picking up gold and silver.
Children attempt to pick up as much of the treasure as they can while avoiding being tagged by Tommy. Any child who is tagged must return the treasure and retire from the game. The game is over when only one child is left or when all of the beanbags have been successfully filched. The teacher may wish to call a halt to the game earlier if a stalemate is reached. In this case, the child with the most treasure becomes the new Tommy.
    Variation: This game can be played with a restraining line instead of a square, but there must be boundaries that limit movement.

Change Sides — *DPE,* p. 559
    Supplies: None
    Skill: Body management
    Two parallel lines are established 30 ft apart. Half of the children are on each line. On signal, all cross to the other line, face the center, and stand at attention. The first group to do this correctly wins a point. Children must be cautioned to use care when passing through the opposite group. They should be spaced well along each line; this allows room for them to move through each group. The locomotor movements should be varied. The teacher may say, "Ready—walk!" Skipping, hopping, long steps, sliding, and other forms of locomotion can be specified. The position to be assumed at the finish can be varied also.
    Teaching suggestion: Because success depends on getting across first, the teacher should watch for shortcutting of the rules and talk this problem over with the children.
    Variation: The competition can be by squads, with two squads on each line.

DYNAMIC PHYSICAL EDUCATION LESSON PLAN
Educational Movement (Lesson 3)
Level I

Fundamental Skill: Running
Educational Movement Themes: Over and under, moving in different ways
Manipulative Activity: Paddles and balls

Supplies and Equipment Needed:
  Playground balls (rubber)
  Paddles and balls—one set for each child
  Jump ropes
  Circuit training signs
  Climbing ropes
  Tape player
  Hula hoops
  2 Benches
  4 Jumping Boxes

MOVEMENT EXPERIENCE—CONTENT	ORGANIZATION AND TEACHING HINTS	EXPECTED STUDENT OBJECTIVES AND OUTCOMES

INTRODUCTORY ACTIVITY (2 – 3 MINUTES)

Movement Varieties

Move using a basic locomotor movement. Then add variety to the movement by asking students to respond to the following factors:
  1. Level—low, high, in between.
  2. Direction—straight, zigzag, circular, curved, forward, backward, upward, downward.
  3. Size—large, tiny, medium movements.
  4. Patterns—forming squares, diamonds, triangles, circles, figure-eights.
  5. Speed—slow, fast, accelerate.

DPE p. 253

Scatter formation.

Emphasize and reinforce creativity.

Change the various factors often and take time to explain the concepts the words describe, if children cannot interpret them.

Cog.—The student will be able to interpret the concepts the words describe by moving the body in a corresponding manner.

PM.—The student will be able to move the body with ease throughout the range of movement varieties.

FITNESS DEVELOPMENT ACTIVITIES (7 – 8 MINUTES)

Circuit Training

Tape alternating segments of silence and music to signal duration of exercise. Music segments (begin at 30 seconds) indicate activity at each station while intervals of silence (10 seconds) announce it is time to stop and move forward to the next station.
  1. Tortoise and Hare
  2. Curl-up variations
  3. Hula Hooping on arms
  4. Jumping boxes—step on and off continuously
  5. Agility run—run back and forth between two designated lines
  6. Bench Pulls—pull body along bench
  7. Crab Walk
  8. Bend and Twist

DPE pp. 300 – 303

Divide class into equal groups at each station.

Have one piece of equipment for each child in the group.

Other activities to try are rope jumping, agility run, swinging on climbing ropes, and arm circles.

PM.—The student will be able to perform each activity in the circuit.

Cog.—The student will be able to identify what part(s) of the body each activity exercises.

MOVEMENT EXPERIENCE— CONTENT	ORGANIZATION AND TEACHING HINTS	EXPECTED STUDENT OBJECTIVES AND OUTCOMES

LESSON FOCUS (15 – 20 MINUTES)

Movement Skills and Concepts (3)

Select a few activities from each of the categories so students receive a variety of skills to practice. When possible, integrate the manipulative skill activities with fundamental skill activities.

Fundamental Skill: Running

1. Run lightly around the area; stop on signal.
2. Run lightly and change directions on signal.
3. Run, turn around with running steps on signal and continue in a new direction.
4. Pick a spot away from you. Run to it and return without bumping anyone.
5. Run low, gradually increase the height. Reverse.
6. Run patterns. Run inside and around objects.
7. Run with high knee action. Add a knee slap with the hand as you run.
8. Run with different steps—tiny, long, light, heavy, criss-cross, wide and others.
9. Run with arms in different positions—circling, overhead, stiff at sides and others (choice).
10. Free running. Concentrate on good knee lift.
11. Run at different speeds.
12. Touch the ground at times with either hand as you run.
13. Run backwards, sideways.
14. Run with exaggerated arm movements and/or high bounce.
15. Practice running, crossing from one line to another.
    a. Cross your feet as you run.
    b. Touch the ground with one and both hands as you run.
    c. Run forward, looking backward over your right shoulder.
    d. Same, but look over the left shoulder.
    e. Change direction every few steps.
    f. Run to the center, stop completely, then continue.
    g. Make two stops going across— first with the right side forward and then with the left side forward as you stop.
    h. Run forward and stop. Come back three steps and stop. Continue in forward direction.
    i. Do a two-count stop on the way.

DPE pp. 336 – 337

Teaching cues:
 "Run on the balls of the feet."
 "Head up, look ahead."
 "Lift knees."
 "Relax upper body."
 "Breathe naturally."
Scatter formation.

Stress courtesy.

Patterns can be outlined with objects.

Pretend you are a football player (running for a touchdown) or a track star.

Stress body lean for faster running.

Caution to look to avoid possible collisions.

Use appropriate formation for crossing over.

Must be a "one, two" count, slapping the feet.

PM.—The students will improve their running form—lightness, and rhythmic pattern.

Cog.—The student will be able to express the mechanics of good running form.

Aff.—The student will show concern for others when moving through general space.

Cog.—Students will be able to express that gravity is always working and always acts in a vertical direction.

Cog.—Students will learn to share space and take turns.

Aff.—The student will work for control rather than just moving across.

Cog.—Students will understand that a fast walk is more difficult than an easy jog. The body is more efficient during the easy jog.

MOVEMENT EXPERIENCE—CONTENT	ORGANIZATION AND TEACHING HINTS	EXPECTED STUDENT OBJECTIVES AND OUTCOMES
j. Run sideways across, leading with one side. Next time lead with the other. k. Run forward halfway and then backward the rest. l. Run backward halfway and then forward the rest. m. Make a full turn in the center and continue. Do this right and left. n. Provide for student choice.		
Manipulative Activity—Paddles and Balls Individual Activity 1. Place the ball on the paddle face. Roll it around the face. 2. Hit the ball into the air with the paddle. Retrieve and repeat. 3. Bounce the ball into the air, using the paddle, specify number. 4. Bounce the ball into the air, decreasing the height of the bounce until it rests on the face of the paddle. 5. Bounce the ball on the floor. 6. Alternate bouncing upward and to the floor. 7. Dribble the ball and move while dribbling. 8. Choice activity.	*DPE* pp. 423 – 425 Scatter formation. Try for control rather than distance. Track ball. Stay with the basics until some progress is made. Can have show-and-tell demonstration.	PM.—The student will develop the ability to contact the ball solidly and also control it. PM.—The student will develop better hand-eye coordination, leading to increased automatic play. Aff.—The student will gain an appreciation that skill in paddle activities comes only from proper practice. Cog.—The student will be able to explain the best place on the racket to contact the ball. PM.—The students will improve their object tracking skills.
Partner Activity 1. One partner tosses the the other hits it back. 2. Try batting it back and forth. If using a tennis ball, let it bounce between hits. 3. Place ball on floor and roll it back and forth.	Stress easy, controlled tossing (feeding). Need sufficient room.	PM.—The student will be able to make controlled returns to the partner tossing the ball. PM.—The student will be able to bat the ball back and forth four times without a miss.
Movement Concept: Over and Under 1. One partner is an obstacle and the other goes over, under, and around the "obstacle." Reverse positions. 2. Copying action. One partner takes a position and the other goes over and under the first. Reverse positions, but try to copy the same sequence. 3. Progressive sequencing. The first child does a movement (over, under, or around). The second child repeats the movement and adds another. The first child repeats the first two movements and adds a third. The second child repeats and adds a forth.	*DPE* p. 331 Partner activity. Look for unique ideas. This is about the limit for changes.	PM.—The student will demonstrate the ability to interpret the themes in a variety of responses. Aff.—Working cooperatively with a partner is necessary.

MOVEMENT EXPERIENCE—CONTENT	ORGANIZATION AND TEACHING HINTS	EXPECTED STUDENT OBJECTIVES AND OUTCOMES
Movement Concept: Moving in Different Ways 1. Show me different ways to move when your body is in the air part of the time; when your body is always in contact with the floor. 2. Show me different ways you can progress along the floor without using your hands or feet. Can you "walk" using your seat? 3. What are the different ways you can roll and move? 4. What ways can you move sideways? How can you move on all fours? 5. Move across the floor halfway with one movement and the other half with a decidedly different movement. 6. Explore the different ways you ca move when leading with selected parts of the body.	*DPE* p. 329 Select from formations pp. 89 – 93 Stress not colliding with others. Get pupil demonstration.	Cog.—The student will demonstrate the ability to understand the directions and make broad interpretations.

GAME (5 – 7 MINUTES)

Rollee Pollee — *DPE,* p. 567
  Supplies: Many 8-in. foam balls
  Skills: Ball rolling, dodging
  Half of the children form a circle; the other half are in the center. Balls are given to the circle players. The circle players roll the balls at the feet and shoes of the center players, trying to hit them. The center players move around to avoid the balls. A center player who is hit leaves the center and joins the circle.
  After a period of time or when all of the children have been hit, the teams trade places. If a specified time limit is used, the team having the fewer players hit wins, or the team that puts out all of the opponents in the shorter time wins.
  Teaching suggestion: The instructor can have the children practice rolling a ball first. Balls that stop in the center are dead and must be taken back to the circle before being put into play again. The preferable procedure is to have the player who recovers a ball roll it to a teammate rather than return to place

Mix and Match — *DPE,* p. 564
  Supplies: None
  Skills: Fundamental locomotor movements
  A line is established through the middle of the area. Half of the children are on one side and half are on the other. There must be an odd person, the teacher or another child. The teacher gives a signal for children to move as directed on their side of the line. They can be told to run, hop, skip, or whatever. At another signal, children run to the dividing line, and each reaches across to join hands with a child from the opposite group. The goal is to not be left out. Children may reach over but may not cross the line. The person left out is moved to the opposite side so that players left out come from alternating sides of the area.
  Variation: The game also can be done with music or a drumbeat, with the players rushing to the centerline to find partners when the rhythm stops.

DYNAMIC PHYSICAL EDUCATION LESSON PLAN
Fundamental Skills Using Benches
Level I

Supplies and Equipment Needed:
  Six balance-beam benches
  Six tumbling mats
  One jump rope for each child
  Beanbags or fleece balls
  Foam balls, 8-1/2"
  Music
  Tape player
  Plastic jugs

MOVEMENT EXPERIENCE—CONTENT	ORGANIZATION AND TEACHING HINTS	EXPECTED STUDENT OBJECTIVES AND OUTCOMES

INTRODUCTORY ACTIVITY (2 – 3 MINUTES)

New Leader Warm-Up

Groups move around the area, following the leader. On signal, the last person moves to the head of the squad and become the leader. Various types of locomotor movements and/or exercises should be used.

When learning this activity, it is sometimes helpful to work in pairs or triads.

DPE p. 258

Squad formation.

Encourage students not to stand around. Keep moving unless an exercise or similar activity is being performed.

Assign each squad a specific area if desired. Each area could include a piece of equipment to aid in the activity (beanbag, fleece ball, etc.)

Cog.—Warm-up is necessary to get the blood to the periphery of the body. Always warm up before strenuous exercise.

Aff.—Students will all be capable of leading as well as following. Discuss the necessity of both in our society.

FITNESS DEVELOPMENT ACTIVITIES (7 – 8 MINUTES)

Jump Rope Exercises

Tape alternating segments of silence and music to signal duration of exercise. Music segments indicate aerobic activity while intervals of silence announce flexibility and strength development activities.
  1. Jump rope - 45 seconds. If not able to jump, practice swinging the rope to the side while jumping
  2. Place the rope on the floor and perform locomotor movements around and over the rope. Make different shapes and letters with the rope.
  3. Hold the folded rope overhead. Sway from side to side. Twist right and left.
  4. Lie on back with rope held with outstretched arms toward ceiling. Bring up one leg at a time and touch the rope with toes. Lift both legs together. Sit up and try to hook the rope over the feet. Release and repeat.
  5. Jump rope - 45 seconds.
  6. Fold the rope and perform various isometric exercises.

DPE p. 286

Place the ropes around the perimeter of the area so they can quickly pickup and return a jump rope.

If youngsters have difficulty jumping the rope, offer alternate challenges.

An alternative is to substitute long-rope jumping. Since not all children are jumping, it is less demanding and easier for children to perform.

Cog.—Rope jumping demands a great deal from all parts of the body. For the conditioning effect to take place, the pulse rate should be elevated above 150 beats per minute for 5 minutes. It might be interesting to use a stop watch and have students check their own pulse rate.

MOVEMENT EXPERIENCE—CONTENT	**ORGANIZATION AND TEACHING HINTS**	**EXPECTED STUDENT OBJECTIVES AND OUTCOMES**

7. Play "Tail Tag." Fold the rope and use it as a tail. Try to keep others from pulling the tail.
8. Touch toes with the folded rope.
9. Jump rope - 45 seconds.
10. Place rope on the floor and do various Animal Walks along or over the rope.
11. Do Push- variations with the rope folded and help between the hands.
12. Jump rope - 45 seconds.

LESSON FOCUS (15 – 20 MINUTES)

Fundamental Skills Using Benches

Give students two or three activities to practice so you have time to move and help youngsters. Alternate activities from each of the categories so students receive a variety of skills to practice.

1. Animal walks on the bench:
   a. Seal walk
   b. Cat walk
   c. Lame dog walk
   d. Rabbit jump
   e. Choice activity
2. Locomotor movements:
   a. Skip on the bench.
   b. Gallop on the bench.
   c. Step on and off the bench.
   d. Jump on and off the bench.
   e. Hop on and off the bench.
   f. Choice activity
3. Pulls—Pull body along the bench in various positions.
   a. Prone position—head first, feet first.
   b. Supine position—head first, feet first.
   c. Side position—head first, feet first.
4. Pushes—same as above activity except push with the arms in all positions.
5. Movements alongside the benches—proceed alongside the bench in the following positions. (Keep the limbs on the floor as far away as possible from the bench to achieve maximum effort.)
   a. Prone position—hands on bench.
   b. Supine position—hands on bench.
   c. Turn over—proceed along bench changing from prone to supine positions with hands on bench.
   d. All of the above positions performed with the feet on the bench.

DPE pp. 425 – 427

Six benches—one group behind each bench. Place a mat at end of bench for dismounts.

Use a dismount at the end of each activity. See item 7 for suggestions.

Have the next person in line begin when the person in front of him is halfway across the bench.

Have the youngsters perform a return activity on the way back to their lines.

Differentiate between pulling and pushing movements.

Set up lists of return activities at the end of the gym. After doing the bench activity, students jog to the list and perform a listed activity.

PM.—The student will be able to perform all the animal walks across the bench.

PM.—The student will be able to perform the locomotor movements across the bench.

Cog.—The student will be able to identify which bench activities develop arm and shoulder girdle strength.

Cog.—Quality of movement is necessary on the benches to insure adequate results, and speed is not a goal.

Cog.—Students will understand that force for jumping is increased when extensor muscles of the lower limbs are stretched quickly.

Aff.—Satisfaction results from attaining realistic goals. Discuss the importance of viewing your ability correctly so meaningful goals can be set.

MOVEMENT EXPERIENCE—CONTENT	ORGANIZATION AND TEACHING HINTS	EXPECTED STUDENT OBJECTIVES AND OUTCOMES

6. Scooter movements—sit on bench and proceed along bench without using hand.
   a. Regular scooter—feet leading.
   b. Reverse scooter—legs trailing.
   c. Seat walk—walk on the buttocks.
7. Jump dismounts:
   a. Single jump—forward or backward.
   b. Jump with turns—$\frac{1}{2}$ or $\frac{3}{4}$ or full.
   c. Jackknife (Pike).
   d. Jackknife split (straddle).
   e. Jump and follow with a log or forward roll.

Put hands on head while scooting.

The dismounts should be integrated into all the bench activities.

Encourage variety.

GAME (5 – 7 MINUTES)

Hill Dill — *DPE*, p. 562
   Supplies: None
   Skills: Running, dodging
   Two parallel lines are established 50 ft apart. One player is chosen to be it and stands in the center between the lines. The other children stand on one of the parallel lines. The center player calls,
Hill Dill! Come over the hill,
Or else I'll catch you standing still!
Children run across the open space to the other line, while the one in the center tries to tag them. Anyone caught helps the tagger in the center. The first child caught is it for the next game. Once children cross over to the other line, they must await the next call.

Bottle Kick Ball — *DPE*, p. 559
   Supplies: Plastic gallon jugs (bleach or milk containers) and 8-in. foam balls
   Skills: Kicking, trapping
   Players form a large circle around 10 to 12 plastic gallon jugs (bowling pins) standing in the middle of the circle. Students kick the balls and try to knock over the bottles.
   Variation: Use as many foam balls as necessary to keep all children active. If the group is large, make more than one circle of players.

DYNAMIC PHYSICAL EDUCATION LESSON PLAN
Throwing Skills (Lesson 1)
Level I

Supplies and Equipment Needed:
  Beanbags or fleece balls
  Yarn balls
  Rag balls or tennis balls
  Hoops
  Mats for targets
  Tape player
  Music

MOVEMENT EXPERIENCE— CONTENT	ORGANIZATION AND TEACHING HINTS	EXPECTED STUDENT OBJECTIVES AND OUTCOMES

INTRODUCTORY ACTIVITY (2 – 3 MINUTES)

Group Over and Under

One-half of the class is scattered and is in a curled position. The other half of the class leap or jump over the down children. On signal, reverse the groups quickly. In place of a curl, the down children can bridge and the others go under. The down children can also alternate between curl and bridge, as well as move around the area while in bridge position.

DPE p. 257

Scatter formation.

Encourage the students to go over or under a specified number of classmates.

Vary the down challenges, i.e., bridge using two body parts, curl face down or on your side.

Do various locomotor movements when moving from student to student.

PM.—The student will be able to perform the activities of bridge, curl, leap, jump, and hop at a teacher-acceptable level.

FITNESS DEVELOPMENT ACTIVITIES (7 – 8 MINUTES)

Astronaut Drills

Tape alternating segments of silence and music to signal duration of exercise. Music segments indicate aerobic activity while intervals of silence announce flexibility and strength development activities.
  1. Walk.
  2. Walk on tiptoes while reaching for the sky.
  3. Walk with giant strides.
  4. Freeze; perform various stretches.
  5. Do a Puppy Dog Walk.
  6. Jump like a pogo stick.
  7. Freeze; perform Push-up variations.
  8. Walk and swing arms like a helicopter.
  9. Trot lightly and silently.
 10. Slide like and athlete.
 11. Freeze; perform Curl-up variations.
 12. Crab Walk.
 13. Skip
 14. Freeze; perform trunk development challenges.
 15. Walk and cool down.

DPE p. 304

Use circle or scatter formation with ample space between youngsters.

Children should be in constant movement except when stopped to do strength and flexibility activities.

Emphasize quality movement.

Change direction often.

When they are moving on all fours, youngsters should be encouraged to place much of their weight on the hands in order to develop arm–shoulder girdle strength.

Aff.—Very little resting time occurs in Astronaut Drills. When one exercises for a long period of time, without rest, muscular and cardiovascular endurance is developed.

MOVEMENT EXPERIENCE—CONTENT	ORGANIZATION AND TEACHING HINTS	EXPECTED STUDENT OBJECTIVES AND OUTCOMES

LESSON FOCUS (15 – 20 MINUTES)

Throwing Skills (1)
Mimetics

1. "Pretend you:
   a. have to throw a rock across a big river!"
   b. want to throw a ball over a very tall building!"
   c. are a javelin thrower and you want to make the longest throw ever!"
   d. are a baseball pitcher and you are throwing a fast ball!"

Individual Activities

1. Throw beanbag or fleece ball against the wall. Concentrate on the following points:
   a. Feet together
   b. Contralateral foot forward
   c. Start with non-throwing side to the wall
2. Throw from one side of the gym and try to hit the other wall.

Mimetics

1. The teacher should cue students and model a good throw.
   a. Teacher should use terms such as "turn your non-throwing side to the target," "wind-up," "step toward the target," "follow through."
   b. Teacher can also use this time to observe and coach.
   c. *Encourage* the children to throw *hard.*
   d. Modeling of good throws by the teacher should be a major objective for this exercise.

Individual Activities

1. Throwing yarn balls
   a. Throw against wall:
      Throw from a standing position 20 feet from the wall.
      Throw five balls, retrieve, and repeat.
2. Throwing rag balls or tennis balls
   a. Teach the proper grip.
   b. Throw against mats on the wall. Throw from 20–25 feet depending on skill level. Student should be able to hit the wall. Student should pick up any ball rolling behind the throwing line and throw again. Step and retrieve balls when necessary.

DPE pp. 349 – 351

Mimetics are to be done before every lesson for 1–2 minutes.

Scattered formation teacher modeling.

Cue if necessary:
1. "Take a big wind-up!"
2. "Turn your side to the target." etc.

At least one beanbag per child.

Students should be 4–5 ft. from the wall.

Encourage children to throw hard.

Redirect children with key points:
1. Start with your throwing hand behind your head.
2. Raise elbow to shoulder level.
3. Turn your side to the wall.
4. Take a big step and throw hard.
Have the entire class throw at once if possible, retrieve, and run to wall. Repeat.

These should be done for 1–2 minutes.

The teacher should encourage and praise good *form.*

The teacher should talk about what the components of a good throw are and how to produce force.

The cue of "turn, step, throw" may be useful.

The children should be generating maximum force.

Redirect with appropriate cues:
1. "Throw hard!"
2. "Take a big step, then throw!"
3. "Really get your throwing arm behind your head to start the throw!"

May need to set up a diagonal throwing line so that all skill levels are challenged to throw hard.

PM.—Students will begin to turn their nonthrowing shoulder to the target.

PM.—Students will begin to take a step toward the target with the contralateral foot.

Cog.—The student will begin to understand the importance of body rotation to produce force.

Cog.—The student will understand the importance of opposition of limbs.

PM.—The student will perform the throw by stepping with the contralateral foot.

Cog.—The student will understand the importance of the shoulder turn and step in producing a forceful throw.

Cog.—Students will know what a mature throw looks like.

Cog.—Students will know the components of a mature throw.

Cog.—Students should begin to realize what parts of the throw result in the greatest force production.

Aff.—Students will begin to value throwing hard.

PM.—The student should begin every throw from a side-facing position.

PM.—The student should take a big step with the contralateral foot.

MOVEMENT EXPERIENCE—CONTENT	ORGANIZATION AND TEACHING HINTS	EXPECTED STUDENT OBJECTIVES AND OUTCOMES
c. Throw at hoops leaning against the mats. Throw from a distance so that children can hit the wall, but only with a forceful throw.	The hoops can be used as targets, but the emphasis should still be throwing hard. Teacher comments should emphasize good form rather than hitting the target.	Aff.—The student should value good form more than hitting a target. Discuss the importance of throwing with good form.

GAME (5 – 7 MINUTES)

Aviator — *DPE,* p. 556

Supplies: None

Skills: Running, locomotor movements, stopping

Players are parked (in push-up position) at one end of the playing area. The air traffic controller (ATC) is in front of the players and calls out, "Aviators aviators, take off!" Youngsters take off and move like airplanes to the opposite side of the area. The first person to move to the other side and land the plane (get into push-up position facing the ATC) is declared the new ATC.

If the ATC yells out some type of stormy weather, all planes must return to the starting line and resume the parked position. Examples of stormy weather commands are lightning, thunder, hurricane, and tornado. Each ATC is allowed to give stormy weather warnings once.

Sneak Attack — *DPE,* p. 567

Supplies: None

Skills: Marching, running

Two parallel lines are drawn about 60 ft apart. Children are divided into two teams. One team takes a position on one of the lines, with their backs to the area. These are the chasers. The other team is on the other line, facing the area. This is the sneak team. The sneak team moves forward on signal, moving toward the chasers. When they get reasonably close, a whistle or some other signal is given, and the sneak team turns and runs back to their line, chased by the other team. Anyone caught before reaching the line changes to the chase team. The game is repeated, with the roles exchanged.

DYNAMIC PHYSICAL EDUCATION LESSON PLAN
Tumbling, Stunts, and Animal Movements (Lesson 1)
Level 1

Supplies and Equipment Needed:
  Tumbling mats
  Balls
  Tape player
  Music

MOVEMENT EXPERIENCE—CONTENT	ORGANIZATION AND TEACHING HINTS	EXPECTED STUDENT OBJECTIVES AND OUTCOMES

INTRODUCTORY ACTIVITY (2 – 3 MINUTES)

Countdown

Students and teacher begin a countdown (10, 9, 8, 7, etc.) and gradually crouch with each count. On the words "blast off," they explode and move in different directions.

Vary with challenges such as:
  1. Different locomotor movements.
  2. Various animal walks.
  3. Change intervals of counting—slow, fast.
  4. Point to a student who says, "Blast Off!"

DPE p. 254

Scatter formation.

Other positions can be used. Students can be challenged to "copy" the teacher's position (curl, stretch, etc.).

Have students run to markers around the area rather than running to the walls.

Try a group countdown where everyone holds hands and moves as a unit.

PM.—The student will be able to move in a controlled fashion during the countdown.

PM.—The student will be able to stop and start rapidly under control.

FITNESS DEVELOPMENT ACTIVITY (7 – 8 MINUTES)

Animal Movements and Fitness Challenges

Tape alternating segments of silence and music to signal duration of exercise. Music segments indicate animal movements while intervals of silence announce flexibility and strength development activities.
  1. Puppy Dog Walk—30 seconds.
  2. Freeze; perform stretching activities.
  3. Measuring Worm Walk—30 seconds
  4. Freeze; perform abdominal challenges.
  5. Seal Crawl —30 seconds.
  6. Frog Jump—30 seconds.
  7. Freeze; perform push-up position challenges.
  8. Elephant Walk —30 seconds.
  9. Bear Walk—30 seconds.
  10. Freeze; perform abdominal challenges.
  11. Crab Walk—30 seconds.
  12. Lame Dog Walk
A variation is to place animal movement signs throughout the area and instruct students to move from sign to sign performing the appropriate animal movement each time they reach a new sign.

DPE pp. 283 – 284

Emphasize placing the weight on the hands for shoulder girdle development.

Quality of movement should be emphasized rather than speed.

Vary the length of the intervals to match the fitness level of youngsters.

Cog.—The student will be able to perform the fitness activities at the beginning level.

Cog.—The student will be able to react to the different word cues.

Aff.—The student will take pride in being able to perform strenuous physical activity.

Aff.—Smoking shortens the average life span by seven years. Students will understand that choosing *not* to smoke enhances wellness.

MOVEMENT EXPERIENCE—CONTENT	ORGANIZATION AND TEACHING HINTS	EXPECTED STUDENT OBJECTIVES AND OUTCOMES

LESSON FOCUS (15 – 20 MINUTES)

Tumbling, Stunts, and Animal Movements (1)

Five groups of activities in this lesson ensure that youngsters receive a variety of experiences. Pick a few activities from each group and teach them alternately. For example, teach one or two animal movements, then a tumbling and inverted balance, followed by a balance stunt, etc. Give equal time to each group of activities

1. Animal Movements
   a. Alligator Crawl
   b. Kangaroo Jump
   c. Puppy Dog Run
   d. Cat Walk
   e. Monkey Run
2. Tumbling and Inverted Balances
   a. Rolling Log
   b. Side Roll
   c. Forward Roll
   d. Back Roller
3. Balance Stunts
   a. One-Leg Balance
   b. Double-Knee Balance
   c. Head Touch
   d. Head Balance
   e. One-Leg Balance Stunts
4. Individual Stunts
   a. Directional Walk
   b. Line Walking
   c. Fluttering Leaf
   d. Elevator
   e. Cross-Legged Stand
   f. Walking in Place
   g. Jump Turns
5. Partner and Group Stunts
   a. Bouncing Ball
   b. Seesaw

DPE pp. 491 – 507

Scatter as many tumbling mats as possible throughout the area in order to avoid waiting lines.

Do not perform many repetitions of tumbling and inverted balances. For most children, limiting the number of forward or backward roll repetitions to four or five will prevent fatigue and injury.

Don't force students to perform tumbling and inverted balances. If they are fearful, gradual encouragement will accomplish more in the long run than intimidation and force.

Demonstrate the activities so students are aware of how they should be performed.

A major concern for safety is the neck and back region. Overweight children are at greater risk and might be allowed to avoid tumbling and inverted balances.

PM.—The student will be able to perform a forward and backward roll.

PM.—The student will be able to balance her body in the balance stunts and manage it easily in the individual stunts.

Cog.—The student will be able to recite the stress points necessary to know in performing the forward and backward roll.

Cog.—The student will be able to identify the activities by name.

PM.—The student will be able to perform the animal movements for a distance of at least 25 feet.

Aff.—Approximately two to three quarts of water are needed for the body to function properly. Students should drink one quart (or four to eight glasses) of water daily and more when exercising strenuously.

GAME (5 – 7 MINUTES)

Circle Straddle Ball — *DPE*, p. 560
   Supplies: Two or more 8-in. foam balls
   Skills: Ball rolling, catching
   Children are in circle formation, facing in. Each stands in a wide straddle stance with the side of the foot against the neighbor's. The hands are on the knees. Two balls are used. The object of the game is to roll one of the balls between the legs of another player before he can get his hands down to stop the ball. Each time a ball goes between the legs of an individual, a point is scored. The players having the fewest points scored against them are the winners. Keep the circles small so students have more opportunities to handle the ball.
   Teaching suggestion: The teacher should be sure that children catch and roll the ball, rather than batting it. Children must keep their hands on their knees until a ball is rolled at them. After some practice, the following variation can be played.
   Variation: One child is in the center with a ball and is it. The other children are in the same formation as before. One ball is used. The center player tries to roll the ball through the legs of any child. She should mask her intent, using feints and changes of direction. Any child allowing the ball to go through his legs becomes it.

MOVEMENT EXPERIENCE— CONTENT	ORGANIZATION AND TEACHING HINTS	EXPECTED STUDENT OBJECTIVES AND OUTCOMES

Statues — *DPE,* p. 568

Supplies: None

Skills: Body management, applying force, balance

Children are scattered in pairs around the area. One partner is the swinger and the other the statue. The teacher voices a directive, such as "Pretty," "Funny," "Happy," "Angry," or "Ugly." The swinger takes the statue by one or both hands, swings it around in a small circle two or three times (the teacher should specify), and releases it. The statue then takes a pose in keeping with the directive, and the swinger sits down on the floor.

The teacher or a committee of children can determine which children are the best statues. The statue must hold the position without moving or be disqualified. After the winners are announced, the partners reverse positions. Children should be cautioned that the purpose of the swinging is to position the statues and that it must be controlled.

Variation: In the original game, the swinging is done until the directive is called. The swinger then immediately releases the statue, who takes the pose as called. This gives little time for the statue to react. Better and more creative statues are possible if the directive is given earlier.

Soap Bubbles — *DPE,* p. 567

Supplies: Cones to delineate space, music

Skills: Body management

Each player is a soap bubble floating throughout the area. The teacher calls out the locomotor movement youngsters use to move in the area. The entire area is used to start the game. As the game progresses, the size of the area is decreased by moving the cones. Bubbles freeze on signal. Music can be used to stimulate movement.

The object of the game is not to touch or collide with another bubble. When this occurs, both bubbles burst and sink to the floor and make themselves as small as possible. The space is made smaller until those who have not been touched are declared the winners. Those players who are broken bubbles may move to the unrestricted area and move. This is an

DYNAMIC PHYSICAL EDUCATION LESSON PLAN
Manipulative Ball Skills—Basketball Related
Level I

Supplies and Equipment Needed:
One 8 1/2" playground or foam rubber ball for each student
Hoops
Wastepaper basket or box

MOVEMENT EXPERIENCE— CONTENT	ORGANIZATION AND TEACHING HINTS	EXPECTED STUDENT OBJECTIVES AND OUTCOMES

INTRODUCTORY ACTIVITY (2 – 3 MINUTES)

Free Activity with Playground (Rubber) Balls

Explore as many activities as possible combining locomotor movements with ball skills.

DPE p. 256

Scatter formation. Individual or partner as per choice.

Use efficient way to distribute and collect balls such as placing them at five or six locations in the area.

PM.—The student will be able to combine three ball skills and two locomotor movements into a routine.

FITNESS DEVELOPMENT ACTIVITIES (7 – 8 MINUTES)

Fitness Games and Challenges

Tape alternating segments of silence and music to signal duration of exercise. Music segments indicate fitness game activity while intervals of silence announce flexibility and strength development activities.
1. Stoop Tag - 45 seconds.
2. Freeze; perform stretching activities.
3. Back-to-Back Tag - 45 seconds.
4. Freeze; perform Abdominal Challenges using Curl-up variations.
5. Balance Tag - 45 seconds.
6. Freeze; perform Arm-Shoulder Girdle Challenges using Push-up variations.
7. Elbow Swing Tag - 45 seconds.
8. Freeze; perform Trunk Development Challenges.
9. Color Tag - 45 seconds.

DPE pp. 281 – 284

Maximize movement by using simple fitness games that require little explanation.

Remember that the goal of fitness games is to stimulate movement rather than teach children to follow rules.

Assign many youngsters to be it to increase the amount of movement.

PM.—The student will be able to perform the various fitness activities.

Aff.—A balanced diet low in saturated fat, cholesterol, and sugar will help reduce the incidence of heart attacks. Discuss the role of diet in maintaining wellness.

Cog.—Stretching allows the body to move with more efficiency. The student will be able to explain why stretching activities are desirable.

Aff.—In order to develop a higher level of physical fitness, it is necessary to exercise to the point of discomfort at times. Discuss the importance of pushing to higher achievement and the need for overloading.

LESSON FOCUS (15 – 20 MINUTES)

Manipulative Ball Skills—Basketball Related

1. Warm-up with informal passing back and forth between partners.
2. Push (chest) pass—two handed. Emphasize one or two of the following points at a time depending on the skill level of students:
   a. Ball at chest level, face partner.
   b. Fingers spread above center of ball.
   c. Step toward partner and extend arms.
   d. Throw to chest level.

DPE pp. 615 – 620

Organize by partners.

Explain that this is one of the basic passes and must be mastered.

Get the "push" first, then later stress the finger action.

Lower the baskets to encourage development of a "shooting touch." This contrasts with throwing the ball at a basket that is too high.

PM.—The student will be able to adequately perform the following skills:
1. Push and one-handed pass.
2. Dribbling—right and left hands in a stationary position.
3. Shooting—one-handed shot at a target on the floor.
4. Catching—high and low passes.

MOVEMENT EXPERIENCE— CONTENT	ORGANIZATION AND TEACHING HINTS	EXPECTED STUDENT OBJECTIVES AND OUTCOMES

e. Catch with finger tips.
f. Thumbs together for high pass.
g. Little fingers together for low pass.
h. Hands relaxed, provide a little "give."
i. Practice on the fly.
j. Add the bounce pass—same technique.
k. Avoid forward spin.
3. One-Handed Pass
  a. Side toward catcher.
  b. Ball back with both hands to side of head or above shoulder. Fingers spread, directly behind the ball.
  c. Release the forward hand and throw with a wrist snap.
  d. Practice both right and left.
4. Birdie in the Cage
  a. Form circles of 7–8 children.
  b. Pass ball among the circle for practice. Be sure everyone handles the ball.
  c. Select "Birdie," put in center until he touches the ball, or there is a loose ball leaving the circle.
5. Dribbling (each has a ball)
  a. Explain technique: wrist action, finger control, eyes ahead.
  b. Dribble in different directions. Use right and left in turn.
  c. Use whistle dribble. Stop on whistle.
6. One-Handed Shot
  a. Raise ball up to eye level, sight, and shoot to a partner (demonstrate).
  b. Shoot from close position around the basket with partners alternating.
7. Add a short dribble and a shot.
	Bounce the ball just beyond the half-way mark.
	
	Avoid the "hip pocket" windup.
	
	Foam rubber balls bounce in a fashion similar to a basketball and do not create fear of the object.
	
	Let the children call the fault.
	
	Watch for collisions. Loose balls—stop the ball or just return it.
	
	Move through the area and encourage students to look for you. This causes them to take their eyes off the ball from time to time.
	
	Each person takes two shots per turn.
	
	Shoot at wastepaper baskets, boxes, etc. Regulation baskets are much too high and prevent students from developing a proper shooting touch.
	
	Shoot at a hula hoop held by a partner. Dribble and shoot into inverted boxes.
		Aff.—People who live a long time tend to be satisfied. Discuss the importance of self-acceptance. Encourage self-evaluation, rather than comparison to others, as a way of reducing stress and encouraging wellness.
		
		Aff.—Basketball-related skills demand a great deal of fine motor coordination. Discuss the necessity of much repetition and practice over a long period of time before good results appear.
		
		Cog.—Accuracy is relative. All shooters miss more shots than they make.

GAME (5 – 7 MINUTES)

Blindfolded Duck — *DPE*, p. 558
   Supplies: A wand, broomstick, cane, or yardstick
   Skills: Fundamental locomotor movements
   One child, designated the duck (Daisy if a girl, Donald if a boy), stands blindfolded in the center of a circle and holds a wand or similar article. She taps on the floor and tells children to hop (or perform some other locomotor movement). Children in the circle act accordingly, all moving in the same direction. Daisy then taps the wand twice on the floor, which signals all children to stop. Daisy moves forward with her wand, still blindfolded, to find a child in the circle. She asks, "Who are you?" The child responds, "Quack, quack." Daisy tries to identify this person. If the guess is correct, the identified child becomes the new duck. If the guess is wrong, Daisy must take another turn. After two unsuccessful turns, another child is chosen to be the duck.

MOVEMENT EXPERIENCE— CONTENT	ORGANIZATION AND TEACHING HINTS	EXPECTED STUDENT OBJECTIVES AND OUTCOMES

Cat and Mice — *DPE,* p. 559

Supplies: None

Skills: Running, dodging

Children form a large circle. One child is the cat and four others are the mice. The cat and mice cannot leave the circle. On signal, the cat chases the mice inside the circle. As they are caught, the mice join the circle. The last mouse caught becomes the cat for the next round.

Teaching suggestions: The teacher should start at one point in the circle and go around the circle selecting mice so that each child gets a chance to be in the center.

Sometimes, one child has difficulty catching the last mouse or any of the mice. If this is the case, children forming the circle can take a step toward the center, thus constricting the running area. The teacher should cut off any prolonged chase sequence.

Freeze — *DPE,* p. 562

Supplies: Music or tom-tom

Skills: Locomotor movements to rhythm

Children are scattered about the room. When the music starts, they move throughout the area, guided by the music. They walk, run, jump, or use other locomotor movements, depending on the selected music or beat. When the music is stopped, they freeze and do not move. Any child caught moving after the cessation of the rhythm pays a penalty. A tom-tom or a piano is a fine accompaniment for this game, because the rhythmic beat can be varied easily and the rhythm can be stopped at any time.

This is an excellent game for practicing management skills. The game reinforces freezing on a stop signal.

Variations:

1. Specify the level at which children must freeze.

2. Have children fall to the ground or balance or go into a different position, such as the Push-Up, Crab, Lame Dog, or some other defined position.

DYNAMIC PHYSICAL EDUCATION LESSON PLAN
Educational Movement (Lesson 4)
Level I

Fundamental Skills: Sliding and galloping
Educational Movement Themes: Movement combinations, activities with tires
Manipulative Activity: Yarn balls

Supplies and Equipment Needed:
  Hoop—one for each child
  Beanbags—one for each child
  Yarn balls—one for each child
  Tires—16–20 (hoops may be substituted)
  Balls
  Parachute
  Tape player
  Music

MOVEMENT EXPERIENCE—CONTENT	ORGANIZATION AND TEACHING HINTS	EXPECTED STUDENT OBJECTIVES AND OUTCOMES

INTRODUCTORY ACTIVITY (2 – 3 MINUTES)

Body Part Identification

Enough beanbags for every child are scattered on the floor. Students are instructed to move over and around the beanbags. When a body part is called, students place that body part on the nearest beanbag.

Variations:
  1. Use different movements.
  2. Use different equipment such as hoops or jump ropes.
  3. Call combinations of body parts.

DPE p. 258

Scatter formation.

Put names of body parts on flash cards.

To encourage fast thinking (after students have learned body parts), scatter one or two fewer beanbags than there are students in the class.

Cog.—The student will be able to identify body parts by name.

PM.—The student will be able to place the proper body parts on the beanbag.

FITNESS DEVELOPMENT ACTIVITY (7 – 8 MINUTES)

Parachute Fitness

Tape alternating segments of silence and music to signal duration of exercise. Music segments indicate aerobic activity with the parachute while intervals of silence announce using the chute to enhance flexibility and strength development.
  1. Jog while holding the chute in the left hand - 20 seconds.
  2. Shake the chute.
  3. Slide while holding the chute with both hands - 20 seconds.
  4. Sit and perform curl-ups - 30 seconds.
  5. Skip for 20 seconds.
  6. Freeze, face the center, and stretch the chute tightly. Hold for 8–12 seconds. Repeat five to six times.
  7. Run in place while holding the chute taut at different levels.

DPE p. 285

Evenly space youngsters around the chute.

Use different grips to add variation to the activities.

Develop group morale by encouraging students to move together.

To cool down, allow youngsters a minute to perform parachute stunts like the Dome or Mushroom.

PM.—The student will be able to perform the grass drill continuously for 60–90 seconds.

Aff.—Grass drills are an old football drill. Discuss the value of this activity in developing endurance and quickness.

MOVEMENT EXPERIENCE—CONTENT	ORGANIZATION AND TEACHING HINTS	EXPECTED STUDENT OBJECTIVES AND OUTCOMES

8. Sit with legs under the chute. Do a seat walk toward the center. Return to the perimeter. Repeat four to six times.
9. Move into push-up position holding the chute with one hand. Shake the chute.
10. Place the chute on the ground. Jog away from the chute and return on signal. Repeat for 30 seconds.
11. Shake the chute and jump in place.
12. Lie on back with feet under the chute. Shake the chute with the feet.
13. Hop to the center of the chute and return. Repeat for 20 seconds.
14. Sit with feet under the chute. Stretch by touching the toes with the chute. Relax with other stretches while sitting.

LESSON FOCUS (15 – 20 MINUTES)

Movement Skills and Concepts (4)

Select a few activities from each of the categories so students receive a variety of skills to practice. When possible, integrate the manipulative skill activities with fundamental skill activities.

Fundamental Skill: Sliding

1. Slide in one direction, stop and slide in another.
2. Begin with short slides in crease slide length. Reverse.
3. Do a number of slides (3, 4, 5, 6), do a half turn, continue in the same direction, but leading with the other leg.
4. Slide with a 4–4 pattern.
5. Slide in a figure-eight pattern.
6. Change levels while sliding; touch the floor occasionally while sliding.
7. Slide lightly and noiselessly.
8. Pretend to be a defensive basketball player, sliding.
9. Slide with a partner.
10. Exploratory activity.

DPE pp. 339–340

Scatter formation.

Cue by saying:
"Move sideways."
"Smooth, light movement."
"Don't bounce."
"Slide your feet."

Use a drum to guide the movements.

Basic movement music for sliding is excellent here.

PM.—The student will develop the ability to slide in both directions and make changes at will.

Cog.—The student will be able to explain the difference between sliding techniques and those of galloping.

Aff.—The student will exhibit an appreciation of the fact that sliding has future use in many sport and leisure time activities.

Fundamental Skill: Galloping

1. Form a circle. Slide in one direction (clockwise or counterclockwise). Gradually turn the body to face the line of direction; this is galloping.
2. Practice galloping freely in general space. Gallop backwards.
3. Gallop in a figure-eight and other patterns.
4. Change gallops (leading foot) on 8, 4 and 2 gallops.

DPE pp. 340–341

Cue by saying:
"Lead with one foot."
"Lead with the other foot."

Use music here. This leads to the polka.

PM.—The student will be able to gallop in various directions.

PM.—The student will demonstrate the ability to gallop backward.

PM.—The student will be able to change the leading foot at will while galloping.

MOVEMENT EXPERIENCE—CONTENT	ORGANIZATION AND TEACHING HINTS	EXPECTED STUDENT OBJECTIVES AND OUTCOMES
5. Gallop with a partner.		
6. Play Ponies in the Stable, (*DPE*, p. 253)	Use as a fun activity.	

Manipulative Skills: Yarn Ball Activities

This is to be free practice and exploration. Children can work as individuals or as partners. Students should work on needed skills and also come up with activities of their own origin.

DPE pp. 413–417

Scatter formation.

Encourage children to work on skills that need practice.

See Educational Movement Lesson 2 for ideas.

PM.—The student will improve skills that need work.

Aff.—Students will be stimulated to work on improving skills.

Movement Concept: Movement Combinations

1. Run, leap, roll.
2. Shake (all over), gallop, freeze.
3. Hop, collapse, explode.
4. Whirl, skip, sink (melt) slowly.
5. Creep, pounce, curl.
6. Begin low, lift, grin, roll.
7. Kneel, sway, jump to feet.
8. Shrink, expand, slide.
9. On all fours, run, roll, jump.
10. Do a Jumping Jack (two or three times), slide, jump turn.
11. Hop forward, collapse, creep forward.
12. Jump forward (several jumps), shake yourself, whirl.
13. Rock back and forth on the heels, jump high, sit down quickly.
14. Sink slowly from a high position, roll, do a jump turn.
15. Click heels right and left, jump half turn, run backwards.
16. Twist, skip, sit down, smile.
17. Turn around three times, clap hands behind the back, run, balance on one foot when you stop.
18. Do fast, tiny steps in place; fall forward to the hands; move forward on all fours.
19. Take a deep breath, expel the air, saying, "Ah-h-h", jump forward, spin, sink.
20. Spin on your seat, roll sideways, stand, take five jumps ahead.
21. Allow exploratory activity to put together three or four movements of your choice.
22. From item 21, select one or more unique patterns, have the student verbalize and demonstrate, have all follow the pattern.

Scatter formation. Use of general space.

Allow individual response within framework of challenge.

Repeat two or three times.

Caution to avoid collisions.

Ask for student demonstration when a unique or well-done response appears.

PM.—The student will be able to combine the movements together as described.

Cog.—Proper diet is necessary if students are to retain optimum wellness. Generally, one serving from each of the following basic food groups is desirable:
1. Leafy green and yellow vegetables.
2. Citrus fruits, tomatoes, and salad greens.
3. Potatoes and other vegetables and fruits.
4. Milk and milk products.
5. Meat, poultry, fish, eggs, dried beans and peas, and nuts.
6. Bread and cereals.
7. Butter and margarine.

Allow sufficient time. Encourage smooth linking of patterns.

Cog.—On the basis of the pattern experiences, the student will be able to put together smooth patterns of his own choosing.

Manipulative Skills: Hoop Activities

Each group uses four or five hoops and places them in a line on the floor.
1. Walk, hop, and jump through or on the sides of the hoops.
2. Leap over the hoops from the side.
3. Run around the hoops.

MOVEMENT EXPERIENCE— CONTENT	ORGANIZATION AND TEACHING HINTS	EXPECTED STUDENT OBJECTIVES AND OUTCOMES

4. Jump astride the hoop and inside it alternately.
5. Jump through each center without touching the hoop.
6. Use different animal walks— Bunny Jump, Frog Jump, Crab Walk.
7. Jump down the line of hoops.
8. Using one hoop, take a push-up position. Keeping the hands on the hoop, circle with the feet. Then put the feet on the hoop and circle with the hands.
9. Jog through with high knees.
10. Heel clicks in the center of each hoop.
11. Roll a hoop at a partner, who jumps over it as it approaches.
12. Stand the hoops upright (two or three hoops) and jump in and out of the hoops.

GAME (5 – 7 MINUTES)

Corner Spry — *DPE,* p. 561
  Supplies: Blindfold
  Skills: Light, silent walking
  One person is blindfolded and stands in the center of the square. The other players are scattered in the corner areas. On signal they travel as quietly as possible from corner area to corner area. When the blindfolded person is ready (less than 20 seconds), he calls out "Corner Spry!" All players finish their trips to the corner nearest them. The blindfolded person then picks (by pointing) the corner he thinks has the most players. A new player is then selected to be blindfolded.
  Variation: The corners can be numbered 1, 2, 3, 4. The leader then calls out the corner number. The leader can also start class movement by naming the locomotor movement to be used.

Hot Potatoes — *DPE,* p. 562
  Supplies: One to three balls or beanbags for each group
  Skill: Object handling
  Children are seated in small circles (8 to 12 per circle) so that objects can be passed from one to another around the circle. Balls or beanbags or both are passed around the circle. The teacher or a selected student looks away from the class and randomly shouts, "stop!" The point of the game is to avoid getting stuck with an object. If this happens, the player(s) with an object must get up and move to the next circle. The teacher should begin the game with one object and gradually add objects if the class is capable.
  Variation: The passing direction can be reversed on signal.

Popcorn — *DPE,* p. 565
  Supplies: None
  Skills: Curling, stretching, jumping
  The teacher should give a short preliminary explanation of how popcorn pops in response to the heat applied. Half of the children are designated as popcorn; they crouch down in the center of the circle formed by the rest of the children. The circle children, also crouching, represent the heat. One of them is designated the leader, and his actions serve as a guide to the other children. The circle children gradually rise to a standing position, extend their arms overhead, and shake them vigorously to indicate the intensifying heat. In the meantime, the popcorn in the center starts to pop. This should begin at a slow pace and increase in speed and height as the heat is applied. In the final stages, children are popping up rapidly. After a time, the groups change places and the action is repeated.

DYNAMIC PHYSICAL EDUCATION LESSON PLAN
Recreational Activities
Level I

Supplies and Equipment Needed:
  One beanbag or hoop for each child
  Recreational activities equipment
  Tape player
  Music

MOVEMENT EXPERIENCE—CONTENT	ORGANIZATION AND TEACHING HINTS	EXPECTED STUDENT OBJECTIVES AND OUTCOMES

INTRODUCTORY ACTIVITY (2 – 3 MINUTES)

Ponies in the Stable

A beanbag or hoop is used to mark each child's stable. On signal, youngsters gallop around the area and "stables." On a second signal, students return to the nearest stable.

Variations.

1. Use different locomotor movement.
2. Take different positions in the stable such as seated, balanced, collapsed.

DPE p. 253

Place one fewer stable on the floor than children to add challenge.

Have students move in different directions such as northbound, etc.

Place different colors of beanbags (or hoops) on floor. Stipulate that the students must go over (or through) five green bags (or hoops) before returning to their stables.

Cog.—The student will understand that galloping is an uneven rhythmic movement.

PM.—The students will be able to gallop smoothly to and from their stables.

Cog.—Students will understand that it is necessary to warm up the body before doing activities.

FITNESS DEVELOPMENT ACTIVITIES (7 – 8 MINUTES)

Astronaut Drills

Tape alternating segments of silence and music to signal duration of exercise. Music segments indicate aerobic activity while intervals of silence announce flexibility and strength development activities.
  1. Walk
  2. Walk on tiptoes while reaching for the sky.
  3. Walk with giant strides.
  4. Freeze; perform various stretches.
  5. Do a Puppy dog Walk.
  6. Jump like a pogo stick.
  7. Freeze; perform Push-up variations.
  8. Walk and swing arms like a helicopter.
  9. Trot lightly and silently.
  10. Slide like and athlete.
  11. Freeze; perform Curl-up variations.
  12. Crab Walk.
  13. Skip.
  14. Freeze; perform trunk development challenges.
  15. Walk and cool down.

DPE p. 304

Use circle or scatter formation with ample space between youngsters.

Children should be in constant movement except when stopped to do strength and flexibility activities.

Change direction often.

When they are moving on all fours, youngsters should be encouraged to place much of their weight on the hands in order to develop arm–shoulder girdle strength.

PM.—The student will be able to perform all the activies without stopping.

Cog.—Exercise routines, to be effective, must be done regularly. The student will be able to explain the necessity of exercising at least every other day.

MOVEMENT EXPERIENCE—CONTENT	ORGANIZATION AND TEACHING HINTS	EXPECTED STUDENT OBJECTIVES AND OUTCOMES

LESSON FOCUS (15 – 20 MINUTES)

Recreational Activities

The purpose of this unit is to teach children activities that they can use for recreation outside of school or during recess. Suggested activities are:

1. Shuffleboard
2. Two Square
3. Hopscotch
4. Beanbag Horseshoes
5. Jacks
6. Marbles
7. Sidewalk tennis
8. Quoits
9. Rubber Horseshoes
10. Four Square
11. Formulating original, creative games

Emphasis should be placed on teaching the rules of the activities so children can enjoy them on their own time.

It might be useful to set up the activities at four or five different stations and then rotate the students from one station to the next. Three or four activities should be available at each station.

If you know a traditional game played by children in your area for many years, now is a good time to teach it.

Play some background music while children are participating.

PM.—The student will be able to play at least four of the given activities.

Cog.—The student will be able to recite the rules for playing four or more of the activities.

Aff.—The recreational unit demands that students be self-directed. Emphasis should be placed on working with others cooperatively. Discuss the need for learning to self-direct oneself as an adult in recreational activities.

Aff.—Recreational activities are excellent activities for reducing stress. Constant anxiety and stress increases heart rate, blood pressure, and blood cholesterol. Discuss the importance of playing for the "joy and fun of it."

GAME (5 – 7 MINUTES)

Recreational Activities

A game is unnecessary for this lesson. Continue the recreational activities specified in the lesson focus.

DYNAMIC PHYSICAL EDUCATION LESSON PLAN
Educational Movement (Lesson 5)
Level I

Fundamental Skill: Skipping
Education Movement Themes: Taking the weight on the hands, leading with different body parts, making bridges
Manipulative Activity: Scoops and balls

Supplies and Equipment Needed:
  Four traffic cones
  Scoops and balls—one for each child

MOVEMENT EXPERIENCE—CONTENT	ORGANIZATION AND TEACHING HINTS	EXPECTED STUDENT OBJECTIVES AND OUTCOMES

INTRODUCTORY ACTIVITY (2 – 3 MINUTES)

Following Activity

One partner leads and performs various kinds of movements. The other partner must move in a similar fashion. This can also be used with squads or small groups, allowing the captain to lead.

DPE p. 257

If the movements seem to be limited, suggest a few ideas for challenges for the students to try.

PM.—The student will be able to lead as well as follow in this activity.

Cog.—The student will be able to create three movement patterns for her partner to follow.

FITNESS DEVELOPMENT ACTIVITIES (7 – 8 MINUTES)

Four-Corners Movement

Outline a large rectangle with four cones. Place signs with pictures on both sides of the cones. Youngsters move around the outside of the rectangle and change movements as they pass a corner sign. The following movement activities are suggested:
  1. Jogging
  2. Skipping/Jumping/Hopping
  3. Sliding/Galloping
  4. Various animal movements
  5. Sport imitation movements
  6. Bench pulls
  7. Bench crouch jumps
Stop the class after 30–45 seconds of movement and perform fitness challenges. Tape alternating segments of silence and music to signal duration of exercise. Music segments indicate aerobic activity while intervals of silence announce flexibility and strength development activities.

DPE p. 287

If signs are not placed at the corners, teachers can specify movements for students to perform.

Increase the demand of the routine by increasing the size of the rectangle.

Faster-moving students can pass on the outside (away from the center) of the rectangle.

Assure that abdominal and shoulder girdle strength development activities are included.

Aff.—Very little resting time occurs in Four-Corners Movement. When one exercises for a long period of time, without rest, muscular and cardiovascular endurance is developed. Discuss the importance of this type of conditioning.

MOVEMENT EXPERIENCE—CONTENT	ORGANIZATION AND TEACHING HINTS	EXPECTED STUDENT OBJECTIVES AND OUTCOMES

LESSON FOCUS (15 – 20 MINUTES)

Movement Skills and Concepts (5)

Select a few activities from each of the categories so students receive a variety of skills to practice. When possible, integrate the manipulative skill activities with fundamental skill activities

Fundamental Skill: Skipping

1. Skip in general space.
2. Vary the skip with exaggerated arm action and lifted knees; side-to-side motion; skip lightly; skip heavily.
3. Skip backward.
4. Clap as you skip.
5. Skip twice on the same side (double skip). Alternate double skips (two on each side).
6. Form a circle. Skip clockwise and counterclockwise.
7. Form by partners or by threes. Skip in general space.

DPE pp. 341 – 342

Scatter formation

Use drum beat to stimulate.

Cue by saying:
"Skip high."
"Swing your arms."
"Skip smoothly."
"On your toes."
"Be happy."

Use the alternative step–hop method for those having trouble.

PM.—The student will be able to skip in a straight line action.

Cog.—It is a misconception that physical activity is self-defeating because it increases appetite. Decreasing activity does not reduce appetite. Thus, under-exercising rather than overeating is the more important cause of obesity.

PM.—The student will be able to skip with a partner.

Manipulative Skills: Scoop And Ball Activities

Individual Activities

1. Place the ball on the floor, scoop it up with the scoop.
2. Toss the ball upward and catch it with the scoop. Change scoop to the other hand and repeat.
3. Explore various ways of tossing the ball with the hand and catching in the scoop.
4. Throw the ball against a wall and catch with the scoop.
5. Throw the ball against the wall with the scoop and catch with the scoop.
6. Toss either with the hand or with the scoop and do a stunt before catching. Use heel click, quarter turn, touch scoop to floor.
7. Exploratory opportunity.

DPE pp. 421 – 422

Scatter with enough personal space.

Yarn balls or whiffle balls can be used. Beanbags are a possibility. Eyes on the ball. Some "give" with the scoop.

Plastic scoops can be made from 1-gallon jugs. See *DPE*, p. 714 for instructions.

Omit if no wall space.

PM.—The student will develop the ability to catch the ball in the scoop.

PM.—The student will be able to propel the ball with a toss from the scoop.

Cog.—Scoops increase the length of the lever used for throwing. This allows objects to be thrown harder and farther.

Partner Activities

1. Roll the ball and pick up with the scoop.
2. Throw the ball back and forth, catching in the scoop.
3. Toss the ball on first bounce and catch in the scoop.
4. Play One-Step (*DPE*, p. 578)
5. Repeat as much of a-d as possible, tossing with the scoop.
6. Matching activities—repeat throw of the partner.
7. Explore from other positions—sitting, kneeling, back to back, prone position.

One ball for partners.

Keep distances relative.

Seek variety. Specify different levels. Limit the distance.

PM.—The student will be able to play catch with a partner using only the scoop to both throw and catch.

MOVEMENT EXPERIENCE— CONTENT	ORGANIZATION AND TEACHING HINTS	EXPECTED STUDENT OBJECTIVES AND OUTCOMES
Movement Concept: Taking the Weight on the Hands 1. Begin in all-fours position, practice taking the weight on the hands by kicking up the feet in a one-two fashion. 2. From standing position with the arms overhead, bring the hands to the floor and take the weight on the hands. 3. Take the weight successively on the hands by moving from the side as a preliminary to the cart-wheel. 4. Have a partner hold your knees in a wheelbarrow position. Life the legs as high as possible. May need to shift hands underneath.	*DPE* p. 326 Scatter formation. Try crouch jumps and the mule kick. Keep elbows straight. Fingers spread, pointed forward. Some may be able to do a cartwheel.	PM.—The student will be able to take the weight momentarily on the hands. PM.—The student will be able to devise a task where the body weight is placed on the hands.
Movement Concept: Leading with Different Body Parts Children move across the space as indicated: 1. Move across with one arm leading. 2. Now a different movement with the other arm leading. 3. Repeat 1 with one foot leading. 4. Repeat 2 with other fool leading. 5. Move so one arm and one foot are leading. 6. Show us a movement where the shoulder leads. 7. How about a movement where one side leads? 8. Show a movement along the floor where the foot is leading. 9. Can you move so your head leads the movement? 10. What other kinds of leading parts can you show?	*DPE* p. 332 Use movement formations, pp. 89 – 93. Allow variation and choice. Other factors should be used—light and heavy, soft and loud, tiny and large, slow and fast.	PM.—The student will be able to move in accordance with the selected body part(s) leading.
Movement Concept: Making Bridges 1. Make a bridge using five, four, three, and two parts of the body. 2. Select the number of body parts you wish to use and see how many different bridges you can make from this base. 3. Select three different bridges and go from one to the next smoothly in sequence (sustained flow). 4. Work with a partner and make different kinds of bridges. 5. Have your partner go under your bridge.	*DPE* p. 324 Scatter formation. Could use achievement demonstration here.	PM.—The student will be able to show a variety of bridges. Aff.—The student will demonstrate cooperation with a partner in making bridges.

MOVEMENT EXPERIENCE— CONTENT	ORGANIZATION AND TEACHING HINTS	EXPECTED STUDENT OBJECTIVES AND OUTCOMES

GAME (5 – 7 MINUTES)

Hill Dill — *DPE,* p. 562

Supplies: None

Skills: Running, dodging

Two parallel lines are established 50 ft apart. One player is chosen to be it and stands in the center between the lines. The other children stand on one of the parallel lines. The center player calls,

Hill Dill! Come over the hill,

Or else I'll catch you standing still!

Children run across the open space to the other line, while the one in the center tries to tag them. Anyone caught helps the tagger in the center. The first child caught is it for the next game. Once children cross over to the other line, they must await the next call.

Mousetrap — *DPE,* p. 564

Supplies: None

Skills: Skipping, running, dodging

Half of the children form a circle with hands joined and face the center. This is the trap. The other children are on the outside of the circle. These are the mice. Three signals are given for the game. These can be word cues or other signals. On the first signal, the mice skip around, outside the circle, playing happily. On the second signal, the trap is opened. (The circle players raise their joined hands to form arches.) The mice run in and out of the trap. On the third signal, the trap snaps shut. (The arms come down.) All mice caught inside join the circle.

The game is repeated until all or most of the mice are caught. The players then exchange places, and the game begins anew. A child should not run in and out of the trap through adjacent openings.

Variation: This game is excellent with a parachute. The chute drops down and traps the mice.

DYNAMIC PHYSICAL EDUCATION LESSON PLAN
Stunts and Tumbling Skills (Lesson 2)
Level I

Supplies and Equipment Needed:
  Cones
  Tumbling mats
  Equipment for Mini-Challenge Course

MOVEMENT EXPERIENCE—CONTENT	ORGANIZATION AND TEACHING HINTS	EXPECTED STUDENT OBJECTIVES AND OUTCOMES

INTRODUCTORY ACTIVITY (2 – 3 MINUTES)

Popcorn

Students pair up with one person on the floor in push-up position and the other standing ready to move. On signal, the standing students move over and under the persons on the floor. The person on the floor changes from a raised to a lowered push-up position each time the partner goes over or under her. On signal, reverse positions.

DPE p. 258

Partner formation.

Encourage students to move as quickly as possible.

Challenge them to see how many times they can go over and under each other, or to be the quickest pair to go over, under, and around each other a specified number of times.

For a more difficult activity, the children on the floor can move around the area on all fours.

PM.—The student will be able to move quickly over, under, and around her partner.

Aff.—Warm-up activities only work when an individual motivates himself to move quickly and with quality. Discuss the need for self-motivation.

FITNESS DEVELOPMENT ACTIVITIES (7 – 8 MINUTES)

Mini-Challenge Course

Arrange four courses with a group at each course. Students perform the challenges from start to finish and jog back to repeat the course. On signal, groups move to a new course.
Course 1. Do crouch jumps, pulls or scooter movements down a bench; through two hoops and skip to a cone.
Course 2. Weave in and out of four wands held upright by cones; Crab Walk; hang from a climbing rope for 5 seconds; and gallop to a cone.
Course 3. Do a tumbling activity length of mat; agility run through hoops; Frog Jump; and slide to a cone.
Course 4. Move over and under six obstacles; Log Roll length of mat; while jumping, circle around three cones; and run to a cone.

DPE pp. 284 – 285

Set up four parellel (side-by-side) courses in one-half of the area. Rotate groups to each course after a specified time.

An alternative is to organize the courses into a single circuit around the perimeter of the area.

Movement should be continuous.

Since young children fatigue and recover quickly, stop the class after 30-45 seconds and perform fitness movement challenges.

PM.—The student will be able to perform the various movements offered in the Mini-Challenge Course.

Aff.—Contrary to popular belief, girls can become stronger through exercise and weight training without fear of developing huge, unattractive muscles. Discuss this fact with the class.

It might be helpful to bring pictures of various women athletes as examples of fitness.

MOVEMENT EXPERIENCE—CONTENT	ORGANIZATION AND TEACHING HINTS	EXPECTED STUDENT OBJECTIVES AND OUTCOMES

LESSON FOCUS (15 – 20 MINUTES)

Tumbling, Stunts, and Animal Movements (2)

Five groups of activities in this lesson ensure that youngsters receive a variety of experiences. Pick a few activities from each group and teach them alternately. For example, teach one or two animal movements, then a tumbling and inverted balance, followed by a balance stunt, etc. Give equal time to each group of activities

1. Animal Movements
   a. Bear Walk
   b. Gorilla Walk
   c. Rabbit Jump
   d. Elephant Walk
2. Tumbling and Inverted Balances
   a. Forward Roll-Straddle
   b. Backward Curl
   c. Backward Roll-Handclasp Position
   d. Climb-Up
3. Balance Stunts
   a. Kimbo Stand
   b. Knee-Lift Stand
   c. Stork Stand
   d. Balance Touch
   e. Single-Leg Balance
4. Individual Stunts
   a. Rubber Band
   b. Pumping Up the Balloon
   c. Rising Sun
   d. Heel Click
   e. Lowering the Boom
   f. Turn-Over
   g. Thread the Needle
5. Partner and Group Stunts
   a. Wring the Dishrag
   b. Partner Toe Toucher

DPE pp. 491 – 507

Scatter as many tumbling mats as possible throughout the area in order to avoid waiting lines.

Do not perform many repetitions of tumbling and inverted balances. For most children, limiting the number of forward or backward roll repetitions to four or five will prevent fatigue and injury.

Don't force students to perform tumbling and inverted balances. If they are fearful, gradual encouragement will accomplish more in the long run than intimidation and force.

Avoid lines to increase activity and avoid the embarrassment of performing in front of others.

A major concern for safety is the neck and back region. Overweight children are at greater risk and might be allowed to avoid tumbling and inverted balances.

Cog.—Momentum needs to be developed and applied when performing rolls. The student will be able to name three ways of developing momentum, i.e., tucking, starting from a higher point, preliminary raising of the arms.

Cog.—The center of weight must be positioned over the center of support in balance stunts. The student will be able to describe and demonstrate this in his own fashion.

PM.—The student will be able to perform at least two of the activities in each of the groups.

Aff.—Tumbling and stunts are activities in which there is a wide range of student ability which is evident to others. Discuss the sensitivity of the situation and the need to understand the shortcomings of others.

GAME (5 – 7 MINUTES)

Where's My Partner? — *DPE,* p. 569
   Supplies: None
   Skills: Fundamental locomotor movements
   Children are in a double circle by couples, with partners facing. The inside circle has one more player than the outside. When the signal is given, the circles skip (or walk, run, hop, or gallop) to the right. This means that they are skipping in opposite directions. On the command "Halt," the circles face each other to find partners. The player left without a partner is in the mush pot (the center area of the circle). When play starts again, this child enters either circle. The circles should be reversed after a time.
   Variation: The game can also be played with music or a drumbeat. When the music stops, the players seek partners.

Change Sides — *DPE,* p. 559
   Supplies: None
   Skill: Body management
   Two parallel lines are established 30 ft apart. Half of the children are on each line. On signal, all cross to the other line, face the center, and stand at attention. The first group to do this correctly wins a point. Children must be cautioned to use care when passing through the opposite group. They should be spaced well along each line; this allows room for them to move through each group. The locomotor movements should be varied. The teacher may say, "Ready—walk!" Skipping, hopping, long steps, sliding, and other forms of locomotion can be specified. The position to be assumed at the finish can be varied also.
   Teaching suggestion: Because success depends on getting across first, the teacher should watch for shortcutting of the rules and talk this problem over with the children.
   Variation: The competition can be by squads, with two squads on each line.

DYNAMIC PHYSICAL EDUCATION LESSON PLAN
Educational Movement (Lesson 6)
Level I

Fundamental Skill: Hopping
Educational Movement Themes: Body shapes, letters with the body
Manipulative Activity: Hoops

Supplies and Equipment Needed:
  Hoops, one for each child
  Balls

MOVEMENT EXPERIENCE— CONTENT	ORGANIZATION AND TEACHING HINTS	EXPECTED STUDENT OBJECTIVES AND OUTCOMES

INTRODUCTORY ACTIVITY (2 – 3 MINUTES)

Tag Games

Use some of the following tag games to offer children immediate activity.
  1. Skunk
  2. Stork
  3. Stoop
  4. Turtle
  5. Nose-and-Toe

DPE p. 568

Scatter formation.

Allow many players to be it.

PM.—The student will be able to dodge and evade the person(s) who is it.

FITNESS DEVELOPMENT ACTIVITIES (7 – 8 MINUTES)

Fitness Challenges

Alternate locomotor movements with strength challenges. Repeat the challenges as necessary.
Locomotor Movement: Walk for 30 seconds.

Flexibility and Trunk Development Challenges
  1. Bend in different directions.
  2. Stretch slowly and return quickly.
  3. Combine bending and stretching movements.
  4. Sway back and forth.
  5. Twist one body part; add body parts.
  6. Make your body move in a large circle.
  7. In a sitting position, wave your legs at a friend; make circles with your legs.
  Locomotor Movement: Skip for 30 seconds.

Shoulder Girdle Challenges
In a push-up position, do the following challenges:
  1. Lift one foot; the other foot.
  2. Wave at a friend; wave with the other arm.
  3. Scratch your back with one hand; use the other hand.
  4. Scratch your back with one hand; use the other hand.
  5. Walk your feet to your hands.

DPE pp. 281 – 283

Scatter formation.

Individual mats can be used as a "home" to keep youngsters spaced properly.

Repeat the various trunk challenges as necessary.

Young children will perform best when locomotor movements are alternated with stationary challenges, which allow them to recover aerobically.

Add Animal Walks to replace some of the locomotor movements and to create interest.

Use different qualities of movement such as giant skips, tiny and quick gallops, slow giant steps, to motivate youngsters.

As children become more fit, repeat the entire sequence.

PM.—The student will be able to move around the rectangle using different movements.

Cog.—The student will understand and be able to express verbally the fact that strenuous activity for months will tend to decrease resting heart rate.

MOVEMENT EXPERIENCE— CONTENT	ORGANIZATION AND TEACHING HINTS	EXPECTED STUDENT OBJECTIVES AND OUTCOMES

6. Turn over and face the ceiling; shake a leg; Crab Walk.
Locomotor Movement: Jog for 30 seconds.

Abdominal Development
From a supine position:
1. Lift your head and look at your toes.
2. Lift your knees to your chest.
3. Wave your legs at a friend. From a sitting position:
   1. Slowly lay down with hands on tummy.
   2. Lift legs and touch toes.
Locomotor Movement: Run and leap for 45 seconds.

LESSON FOCUS (15 – 20 MINUTES)

Movement Skills and Concepts (6)

Select a few activities from each of the categories so students receive a variety of skills to practice. When possible, integrate the manipulative skill activities with fundamental skill activities.

Fundamental Skill: Hopping

DPE pp. 338 – 339

1. Hopping
   a. Hop in place lightly, changing the feet at will.
   b. Hop numbered sequences, right and left: 1-1, 2-2, 3-3, 4-4, 5-5, 1-2, 2-1, 2-3, 3-2 (hop in place).
   c. Hop, increasing height, reverse.
   d. From your spot, take two, three, or four hops out, turn around and hop back on other foot. How much space can you cover?
   e. Hop on one foot, do a heel and toe pattern with the other. Can you change feet each time doing this?
   f. Pick two spots away from you. Hop in place, then move to one spot. Hop in place, then to the other. Return to spot.
   g. Hop forward, backward, sideways.
   h. Hop different patterns—square, triangle, circle, figure-eight, diamond, etc.
   i. Explore different positions in which you can hold the foot while hopping.
   j. Hold the free foot in different positions while hopping.
   k. Hop with the body in different leaning positions—forward, sideways, backward.
   l. Hop lightly, heavily.

Cue by saying: "Hop or jump with good upward arm motion." "Stay on your toes." "Use your arms for balance." "Reach for the sky." "Land lightly."

In hopping, be sure to change feet regularly. Hop 10 to 20 seconds in each sequence.

Stress form more than distance.

Encourage variety. Allow some choice here.

Try for variety.

PM.—The student will be able to hop using correct body form and a proper landing.

Cog.—The student will be able to identify the major stress points involved in hopping.

Cog.—The student will be able to name four sports where a hopping movement is used.

PM.—The student will be able to perform a satisfactory hop while performing all the variations.

Aff.—Alcohol allows people to fail and still feel good. This may be why it is habit forming. Discuss the importance of understanding that failure is an important part of learning and must be accepted.

Cog.—The ultimate range of motion at a joint is the distance between absolute flexion and extension. Exercises should involve the full range of motion to maintain flexibility.

MOVEMENT EXPERIENCE—CONTENT	ORGANIZATION AND TEACHING HINTS	EXPECTED STUDENT OBJECTIVES AND OUTCOMES
m. While hopping, touch the floor with either or both hands. n. Hop back and forth over a board or line, moving down the line. o. Trace out letters or numbers. Write your name hopping. p. Do quarter or half turns while hopping.		
Manipulative Skills: Floor Targets and Hula Hooping	*DPE* pp. 431 – 433	PM.—The student will be able to do the movements without touching the hoops.
1. Use six to eight hoops to form floor targets for each squad. Walk, run, hop or jump through the hoops. One the way back, do a movement on all fours (return activity).	Hoops should be placed with dispatch.	
2. Have each squad demonstrate the above movements.	Others watch.	
3. Design a different target with the hoops and repeat #1. 4. Hula hoop around the waist.	Remove extras.	PM.—The student will be able to do simple hula hooping around the waist.
5. Hula hoop around the hands and arms, the neck, or legs (on back position). 6. Exploratory activity.		
Movement Concept: Body Shapes	*DPE* p. 323	
Possibilities include: Long or short; wide or narrow; straight or twisted; stretched or curled; large or small; symmetrical or asymmetrical.	Scatter formation. Each in personal space.	PM.—The student will demonstrate the ability to assume the different named shapes.
1. Show me a _____ (use terms above) shape. 2. When I say "change," go from a ____ shape to a _____ shape (vary these).	Go briskly through this. As unique shapes appear, let the child demonstrate.	Cog.—The student will be able to distinguish between the different kinds of shapes.
3. Explore symmetrical and asymmetrical. Take one of the above and make it symmetrical. Then change the same to an asymmetrical shape. 4. Explore other kinds of shapes. 5. Contrasting shapes. Do one kind of shape and its contrast. Or name a shape with its contrast or opposite.	Explain the terms, expecially the prefix.	Aff.—One of the most important things to achieve in life is a good feeling about one's self. Physical fitness is an important contributing factor to positive feelings. Discuss how physical and mental health are interrelated and necessary to develop total wellness.
Movement Concept: Letters with the Body		
1. Make letters standing. 2. Make letters lying on the floor. 3. Divide class into two sets of groups: one group makes a letter and the other names it. Give only one guess. Change groups.	Can be done individually, but is a fine partner activity. Scatter formation.	Aff.—The student will exhibit a willingness to cooperate with a partner. PM.—The student will be able to form the letters as named.
4. Make simple words of two letters or three letters, using one child per letter. 5. Form numbers of two digits.	Demonstrate unique or excellent letters.	Cog.—The student will be able to mentally visualize how the body is forming the letters.

MOVEMENT EXPERIENCE— CONTENT	ORGANIZATION AND TEACHING HINTS	EXPECTED STUDENT OBJECTIVES AND OUTCOMES

GAME (5 – 7 MINUTES)

Rollee Pollee — *DPE,* p. 566

Supplies: Many 8-in. foam balls

Skills: Ball rolling, dodging

Half of the children form a circle; the other half are in the center. Balls are given to the circle players. The circle players roll the balls at the feet and shoes of the center players, trying to hit them. The center players move around to avoid the balls. A center player who is hit leaves the center and joins the circle.

After a period of time or when all of the children have been hit, the teams trade places. If a specified time limit is used, the team having the fewer players hit wins, or the team that puts out all of the opponents in the shorter time wins.

Teaching suggestion: The instructor can have the children practice rolling a ball first. Balls that stop in the center are dead and must be taken back to the circle before being put into play again. The preferable procedure is to have the player who recovers a ball roll it to a teammate rather than return to place

Stop Ball — *DPE,* p. 568

Supplies: A ball

Skills: Tossing, catching

One child, with hands over the eyes, stands in the center of a circle of children. A ball is tossed clockwise or counterclockwise from child to child around the circle. Failing to catch the ball or making a bad toss incurs a penalty. That child must take one long step back and stay out of the game for one turn.

At a time of her own selection, the center player calls, "Stop." The player caught with the ball steps back and stays out for one turn. The center player should be allowed three or four turns and then be changed.

DYNAMIC PHYSICAL EDUCATION LESSON PLAN
Fundamental Skills Using Magic Ropes
Level I

Supplies and Equipment Needed:
  Six to ten magic ropes per class
  Balance-beam benches or jumping boxes (optional)
  Tape player
  Music

MOVEMENT EXPERIENCE—CONTENT	ORGANIZATION AND TEACHING HINTS	EXPECTED STUDENT OBJECTIVES AND OUTCOMES

INTRODUCTORY ACTIVITY (2 – 3 MINUTES)

Run, Stop, and Pivot

Have the children run, and on signal, stop and pivot. Begin teaching a 90° pivot and move gradually to a 180° pivot. Relate the use of the pivot to various sport activities, such as basketball.

DPE p. 254

Concentrate on teaching quick reaction and shifting weight to the pivot foot.

Students should be able to bend their knees (to lower the center of gravity) for stability.

Cog.—The student will be able to explain the use of the pivot as a common movement in many sports. For example, football and basketball.

PM.—The student will be able to do a 180° pivot with the body in good control.

FITNESS DEVELOPMENT ACTIVITIES (7 – 8 MINUTES)

Astronaut Drills

Tape alternating segments of silence and music to signal duration of exercise. Music segments indicate aerobic activity while intervals of silence announce flexibility and strength development activities.
  1. Walk.
  2. Walk on tiptoes while reaching for the sky.
  3. Walk with giant strides.
  4. Freeze; perform various stretches.
  5. Do a Puppy dog Walk.
  6. Jump like a pogo stick.
  7. Freeze; perform Push-up variations.
  8. Walk and swing arms like a helicopter.
  9. Trot lightly and silently.
  10. Slide like an athlete.
  11. Freeze; perform Curl-up variations.
  12. Crab Walk.
  13. Skip.
  14. Freeze; perform trunk development challenges.
  15. Walk and cool down.

DPE p. 304

Use circle or scatter formation with ample space between youngsters.

Children should be in constant movement except when stopped to do strength and flexibility activities.

Change direction often.

When moving on all fours, encourage youngsters to place much of their weight on the hands in order to develop arm–shoulder girdle strength.

Cog.—Astronaut Drills were a common way of developing fitness in the armed services.

PM.—All students should be able to perform the Astronaut Drills.

Aff.—There is no easy way to fitness. It demands self-discipline. Discuss the importance of possessing a positive attitude toward activity in later life.

LESSON FOCUS (15 – 20 MINUTES)

Fundamental Skills Using Magic Ropes
Single-Rope Activities

  1. Jump back and forth, feet uncrossed.
  2. Jump back and forth, feet crossed.

DPE pp. 474 – 475

Divide the class into small groups of five or six members.

Start activities with the rope at a 6" height and progressively raise it to increase the challenge.

PM.—The students will be able to hop back and forth from one end of the rope to the other without touching the rope at a height of 10".

MOVEMENT EXPERIENCE— CONTENT	ORGANIZATION AND TEACHING HINTS	EXPECTED STUDENT OBJECTIVES AND OUTCOMES

3. Jump back and forth, feet crossed and uncrossed alternately.
4. Hop back and forth over rope using right and left feet in turn.
5. Jump the rope and perform various body turns while jumping.
6. Change body shapes and sizes while jumping.
7. Crawl or slide under the rope.
8. Alternate going over and under the rope.
9. Perform crouch jumps back and forth the length of the rope
10. Exploratory activity.

Emphasize the point that students are *not* supposed to touch the rope. The objective is body management and learning to control the body in space.

Try the activities while holding hands with a partner.

Tie one end of the magic rope to a jumping box or balance-beam bench. This reduces the number of rope holders needed.

Cog.—The student will understand and be able to recite why magic ropes are used in the program—to develop body management skills.

Aff.—Carbon monoxide in tobacco smoke reduces the physical endurance of the smoker. Discuss the detrimental effects of this habit.

Double Rope Activities

1. Ropes parallel to each other:
   a. Jump in one side, out other.
   b. Hop in one side, out other.
   c. Crouch jump in and out.
   d. Perform various animal walks in and out.
   e. Exploratory activity
2. Ropes crossed at right angles to each other.
   a. Perform various movements from one to the other.
   b. Jump into one area, crawl out the other.

Rotate the rope holders.

Students should approach the rope from one end and perform their activities to the other end of the rope.

The child next in turn should begin a movement when the performing child is near the end of the rope.

Try holding one end near the floor and the other end 2–3' high. Children then progress from the low end to the high and more difficult end.

Aff.—Discuss the need for all students to be willing to share rope-holding responsibilities.

Cog.—Readiness for learning a motor skill is necessary for optimal learning. Readiness is individual in nature and occurs at different times.

GAME (5 – 7 MINUTES)

One, Two, Button My Shoe — *DPE,* p. 565
Supplies: None
Skill: Running
Two parallel lines are drawn about 50 ft apart. One child is the leader and stands to one side. The rest of the children are behind one of the lines. The leader says "Ready." The following dialogue takes place between the leader and the children.
Children: One, two.
Leader: Button my shoe.
Children: Three, four.
Leader: Close the door.
Children: Five, six.
Leader: Pick up sticks.
Children: Seven, eight.
Leader: Run, or you'll be late!
As children carry on the conversation with the leader, they toe the line, ready to run. When the leader says the word late, children run to the other line and return. The first child across the original line is the winner and becomes the new leader. The leader can give the last response ("Run, or you'll be late!") in any timing she wishes—pausing or dragging out the words. No child is to leave before the word late is uttered.

Twins (Triplets) — *DPE,* p. 569
Supplies: None
Skills: Body management
Formation: Scattered with partner
Youngsters find a space in the area. Each youngster has a partner (twin). The teacher gives commands such as "Take three hops and two leaps" or "Walk backward four steps and three skips." When the pairs are separated, the teacher says, "Find your twin!" Players find their twin and stand frozen back to back. The goal is to not be the last pair to find each other and assume the frozen position.
Students need to move away from each other during the movements. One alternative is to find a new twin each time. Another variation is to separate twins in opposite ends of the playing area.
Variation: The game becomes more challenging when played in groups of three (triplets). When using this variation, new partners should be selected each time.

MOVEMENT EXPERIENCE— CONTENT	ORGANIZATION AND TEACHING HINTS	EXPECTED STUDENT OBJECTIVES AND OUTCOMES

Firefighter — *DPE,* p. 561

Supplies: None

Skill: Running

A fire chief runs around the outside of a circle of children and taps a number of them on the back, saying "Firefighter" each time. After making the round of the circle, the chief goes to the center. When she says "Fire," the firefighters run counterclockwise around the circle and back to place. The one who returns first and is able to stand in place motionless is declared the winner and the new chief.

The chief can use other words to fool children, but they run only on the word Fire. This merely provides some fun, since there is no penalty for a false start. The circle children can sound the siren as the firefighters run.

DYNAMIC PHYSICAL EDUCATION LESSON PLAN
Fundamental Skills Using Balance Beams
Level I

Supplies and Equipment Needed:
Six tumbling mats
Six balance-beam benches
24 beanbags
12 wands
Equipment for Mini-Challenge Course
Cones

MOVEMENT EXPERIENCE—CONTENT	ORGANIZATION AND TEACHING HINTS	EXPECTED STUDENT OBJECTIVES AND OUTCOMES

INTRODUCTORY ACTIVITY (2 – 3 MINUTES)

European Running with Variations

Review variations previously used.
1. Clap hands on various beats.
2. On signal, make a complete turn using four running steps.
3. On signal, scatter and run in general space. On next signal, resume circular running.
4. Stamp feet, say "hey!" and do a hop on stipulated beats.

DPE pp. 252 – 253

Try different formations using different leaders.

Have the students move in individual directions and, on signal, have them move into a specified formation.

Work on quality of movement. Students should be able to move to the beat of the tom-tom and maintain proper spacing.

PM.—The student will be able to run to the beat of the tom-tom.

PM.—The student will be able to move into the following formations—circle, triangle, and rectangle—from scatter formation.

FITNESS DEVELOPMENT ACTIVITIES (7 – 8 MINUTES)

Mini-Challenge Course

Arrange four courses with a group at each course. Students perform the challenges from start to finish and jog back to repeat the course. On signal, groups move to a new course.
Course 1. Do crouch jumps, pull, or scooter movements down a bench; through two hoops; and skip to a cone.
Course 2. Weave in and out of four wands held upright by cones; Crab Walk; hang from a climbing rope for 5 seconds; and gallop to a cone.
Course 3. Do a tumbling activity the length of mat; agility run through hoops; Frog Jump; and slide to a cone.
Course 4. Move over and under six obstacles; Log roll length of mat; while jumping, circle around three cones; and run to a cone.

DPE pp. 284 – 285

Set up four parallel (side-by-side) courses in one-half of the area. Rotate groups to each course after a specified time.

An alternative is to organize the courses into a single circuit around the perimeter of the area.

Movement should be continuous.

Since young children fatigue and recover quickly, stop the class after 30–45 seconds and perform fitness movement challenges.

PM.—The student will be able to perform all the activities by the end of the week.

Cog.—The student will be able to name the immediate changes in body functions that occur when one exercises, i.e., increased heart rate, breathing rate.

MOVEMENT EXPERIENCE— CONTENT	ORGANIZATION AND TEACHING HINTS	EXPECTED STUDENT OBJECTIVES AND OUTCOMES

LESSON FOCUS (15 – 20 MINUTES)

Fundamental Skills Using Balance Beams

1. Practice walking on floor lines to establish qualities of controlled movement and not looking at feet.
2. Walk length of beam and dismount correctly.
    a. Walk forward.
    b. Walk backward.
    c. Walk sideways—lead with both left and right sides of body.
    d. Try other steps—follow steps, heel and toe, on toes, etc.
    e. Allow for exploratory activity.
3. Walk different directions and vary arm and body positions.
    a. Hands on hips.
    b. Hand on head.
    c. Arms folded across chest.
    d. Lean to one side or the other.
    e. Body bent forward or backward.
    f. Hands on knees or feet.
    g. Student choice.
4. Balance objects such as beanbags or wands while walking across beam. (Use exploratory approach.)
5. Pause momentarily in good balance and dismount with a small controlled jump.
6. Allow a few minutes for students' exploration of ideas.

DPE pp. 467 – 469

Use at least six beams with equal number of students behind each beam.

Use a mat at the finishing end of the beam for students to perform their dismounts.

Assign a return activity for students so they are busy off as well as on the beam.

Place return activity signs on cones. Students perform one of activities after dismounting from the beam. Return activities should be done for the length of area to assure students don't stand in line.

Stress quality of the movement across the beam as well as during the dismount.

If a child falls, have her step back on the beam and continue. This will assure her of the same amount of practice as the gifted child.

Place a target on the wall in front of the beams for students to focus their eyes.

Make sure student performs a dismount. Pause first.

Encourage a variety of dismounts such as:
    a. Jumps
    b. Quarter and half turns
    c. Pike and Straddle Jumps

Encourage a broad variety of activities.

PM.—The student will be able to balance self while walking across beam. A desirable goal would be for the child to walk across the beam without falling.

Cog.—Balance is a learned activity. The student will be able to state that practice and concentration are necessary for improvement.

Cog.—Changing arm and leg positions or direction of movement creates a new task for the body and it must compensate to maintain balance. The student will be able to explain this in her own words.

Aff.—Awareness of the status and prestige given to a skilled performer. Discuss the payoff when one is skilled such as friends, money, prizes, etc.

Cog.—Muscle size is determined by gender (testosterone in male) and exercise. The student will understand the physical differences between males and females in terms of musculature.

GAME (5 – 7 MINUTES)

Back to Back — *DPE,* p. 556
Supplies: None
Skills: Fundamental locomotor movements
   The number of children must be uneven. (If not, the teacher can play.) On signal, each child stands back to back with another child. One child will be without a partner. This child claps the hands for the next signal, and all children change partners, with the extra player from the previous game seeking a partner.
   Variation: Considerably more activity can be achieved by putting in an extra command. After children are in partner formation back to back, the teacher says, "Everybody run [skip, hop, jump, slide]!" Other commands, such as "Walk like an elephant," can also be given. Children move around in the prescribed manner. When the signal is sounded, they immediately find a new partner and stand back to back.

MOVEMENT EXPERIENCE— CONTENT	ORGANIZATION AND TEACHING HINTS	EXPECTED STUDENT OBJECTIVES AND OUTCOMES

Mousetrap — *DPE,* p. 564

Supplies: None

Skills: Skipping, running, dodging

Half of the children form a circle with hands joined and face the center. This is the trap. The other children are on the outside of the circle. These are the mice. Three signals are given for the game. These can be word cues or other signals. On the first signal, the mice skip around, outside the circle, playing happily. On the second signal, the trap is opened. (The circle players raise their joined hands to form arches.) The mice run in and out of the trap. On the third signal, the trap snaps shut. (The arms come down.) All mice caught inside join the circle.

The game is repeated until all or most of the mice are caught. The players then exchange places, and the game begins anew. A child should not run in and out of the trap through adjacent openings.

Variation: This game is excellent with a parachute. The chute drops down and traps the mice.

Aviator — *DPE,* p. 556

Supplies: None

Skills: Running, locomotor movements, stopping

Players are parked (in push-up position) at one end of the playing area. The air traffic controller (ATC) is in front of the players and calls out, "Aviators aviators, take off!" Youngsters take off and move like airplanes to the opposite side of the area. The first person to move to the other side and land the plane (get into push-up position facing the ATC) is declared the new ATC.

If the ATC yells out some type of stormy weather, all planes must return to the starting line and resume the parked position. Examples of stormy weather commands are lightning, thunder, hurricane, and tornado. Each ATC is allowed to give stormy weather warnings once.

DYNAMIC PHYSICAL EDUCATION LESSON PLAN
Manipulative Skills Using Hoops
Level I

Supplies and Equipment Needed:
  One hoop per child
  Tom-tom
  Bottle bat and balls

MOVEMENT EXPERIENCE— CONTENT	ORGANIZATION AND TEACHING HINTS	EXPECTED STUDENT OBJECTIVES AND OUTCOMES

INTRODUCTORY ACTIVITY (2 – 3 MINUTES)

Marking

To teach marking, start by teaching partner tag. One partner moves whiles while the other partner attempts to tag him. Once tagged, the partners change roles and the other attempts to tag. Progress to marking which requires one of the partners to move in a desired fashion while the other attempts to stay near him. On signal, both partners freeze and cannot move their feet. The following partner tries to reach and touch (mark) the partner. If a mark is made, that partner receives a point. Resume the chase with the roles reversed.

DPE p. 257

Partners in general space.

Can use various locomotor movements.

Challenges can be made by marking certain body parts.

PM.—The student will be able to demonstrate the ability to mark his partner, to stay with him so when the whistle sounds he is within one yard of his partner.

FITNESS DEVELOPMENT ACTIVITIES (7 – 8 MINUTES)

Walk, Trot, and Sprint

Move to the following signals:
  1. One drumbeat - walk.
  2. Two drumbeats - trot.
  3. Three drumbeats - sprint.
  4. Whistle - freeze and perform exercises.
Perform various strength and flexibility exercises between bouts of walk, trot, and sprint. Examples are:
  1. Bend and Twist
  2. Sitting Stretch
  3. Push-up variations
  4. Abdominal Challenges
  5. Body Twist
  6. Achilles Tendon Stretch

DPE pp. 285 – 286

Use a tom-tom or tambourine.

Scatter formation.

Emphasize quality of movement and rapid changes.

Check heart rate after bouts of sprinting.

Alternate bouts of movement with strength and flexibility exercises.

PM.—The student will be able to perform the activity at an increased pace.

Cog.—One method often used to measure fitness is to count the pulse rate after exercise within 2 or 3 minutes. It might be interesting to measure pulse rate at various intervals after exercise. The more fit one is, the faster pulse rate returns to normal.

Cog.—A well-balanced diet provides fuel for physical activity. Discuss the basics of a good diet and the need for such.

LESSON FOCUS (15 – 20 MINUTES)

Manipulative Skills Using Hoops

  1. Hula-hoop using various body parts such as waist, neck, knees, arms and fingers.
     a. While hula-hooping on the arms, try to change the hoop from one arm to the other.

DPE pp. 431 – 433

Scatter formation.

Hula hooping demands that body part is moved back and forth, *not* in a circle.

PM.—The student will be able to hula–hoop on at least one part of their body.

PM.—The student will be able to place a reverse spin on the hoop, causing it to return to them.

MOVEMENT EXPERIENCE— CONTENT	ORGANIZATION AND TEACHING HINTS	EXPECTED STUDENT OBJECTIVES AND OUTCOMES

b. Change hoop from one partner to another while hula-hooping around the waist.
  c. Try leg skippers—hula-hoop with one leg and jump the hoop with the other leg.
  d. Hula-hoop around waist while on knees. While hooping, try to stand up and go back to knees.
  e. Exploratory activity.
	Have the class drop their hoops when you desire their attention.
	
	When jumping through hoops, encourage children to hold them loosely to prevent falls.
		Aff.—Many students will not immediately be able to hula-hoop or apply the reverse spin. Discuss the value of continued practice versus the alternative of quitting and never learning the skill.

2. Place the hoops on the floor to create various patterns. Have the children perform various fundamental locomotor movements and animal walks in, out of and between the hoops. Create different challenges by having students go in and out of various color hoops and specify a certain number of hoops they must enter.	Use the hoops as a home area for children. This will keep them in a designated area.	Cog.—Spin reduces the amount of force available for forward projection. Discuss the effect reverse spin of the hoop has on forward movement of the hoop.
3. Jump rope with the hoop—forward and backward. Begin with a back-and-forth pendulum swing. Try sideways jumping.		Cog.—Fiber is an important part of a healthy diet. Vegetables and fruit play significant roles in the health of the digestive tract.
4. Thread the needle. Balance the hoop on head and try to step through the hoop. Do it forward, backward and sideways.		Cog.—Muscular strength is an important defense against joint injury. Discuss how professional athletes lift weights in an attempt to lessen potential injury.
5. Roll hoop and run alongside it. Run ahead of it. Cross in front of it. Go through the hoop.		
6. Spin the hoop like a top. How many times can you make it spin? How many times can you run around the spinning hoop before it falls?		
7. Balance the hoop and then go through it before it falls.		
8. For a change-of-pace activity, put hoops on floor. Perform various locomotor movements around many hoops. On signal, curl up inside a hoop. For challenge, have fewer hoops than students.		
9. Roll hoop with a reverse spin to make it return to the thrower.	The reverse spin must be taught and practiced. Many students find it to be a difficult skill.	
10. Reverse spin, catch on arm, and hula-hoop it. Try catching on foot.		
11. Partner Activities—roll hoops back and forth. Play catch with the hoops.	When throwing and catching two hoops, each partner should throw one and then progress to both hoops being thrown at the same time by one partner.	
12. Roll with a reverse spin and see how many times partner can go through with it.		
13. Exploratory activity.		

MOVEMENT EXPERIENCE— CONTENT	ORGANIZATION AND TEACHING HINTS	EXPECTED STUDENT OBJECTIVES AND OUTCOMES

GAME (5 – 7 MINUTES)

Animal Tag — *DPE,* p. 556
    Supplies: None
    Skills: Imagery, running, dodging
    Two parallel lines are drawn about 40 ft apart. Children are divided into two groups, each of which takes a position on one of the lines. Children in one group get together with their leader and decide what animal they wish to imitate. Having selected the animal, they move over to within 5 ft or so of the other line. There they imitate the animal, and the other group tries to guess the animal correctly. If the guess is correct, they chase the first group back to its line, trying to tag as many as possible. Those caught must go over to the other team. The second group then selects an animal, and the roles are reversed. If the guessing team cannot guess the animal, however, the performing team gets another try. To avoid confusion, children must raise their hands to take turns at naming the animal. Otherwise, many false chases will occur. If children have trouble guessing, the leader of the performing team can give the initial of the animal.

Bottle Bat Ball — *DPE,* p. 558
    Supplies: A plastic bottle bat, whiffle ball, batting tee (optional), home plate, base marker
    Skills: Batting, retrieving balls
    Formation: Scattered
    A home plate is needed, and a batting tee can be used. Foul lines should be marked wide enough so as not to be restrictive. The batter gets three pitches (or swings) to hit a fair ball, or she is out. The pitches are easy (as in slow-pitch softball), so that the batter has a good chance to hit the ball. The batter hits the ball and runs around the base marker and back to home. If the ball is returned to the pitcher's mound before the batter reaches home, she is out. (A marker should designate the pitcher's mound.) Otherwise, the batter has a home run and bats again. One fielder other than the pitcher is needed, but another can be used. The running distance to first base is critical. It can remain fixed or can be made progressively (one step) longer, until it reaches such a point that the fielders are heavily favored.
    Teaching suggestion: The game should make use of a plastic bottle bat and fun (whiffle) ball. A rotation system should be established when an out is made.
    Variation: A batting tee can be used.

DYNAMIC PHYSICAL EDUCATION LESSON PLAN
Educational Movement (Lesson 7)
Level I

Fundamental Skill: Leaping
Educational Movement Themes: Levels and speed, partner; jump ropes as floor targets, partner; supporting the weight wholly or in part; acceleration and deceleration

Supplies and Equipment Needed:
  Jump ropes—one for each child
  Benches and other obstacles to leap over
  Tom-tom

MOVEMENT EXPERIENCE—CONTENT	ORGANIZATION AND TEACHING HINTS	EXPECTED STUDENT OBJECTIVES AND OUTCOMES

INTRODUCTORY ACTIVITY (2 – 3 MINUTES)

Locomotor movement Variations

Using the basic locomotor movements (walking, running, skipping, hopping, etc.), try the following variations:
  1. Changes in speed
  2. Weight bearing on different parts of foot (toes, heels, sides of feet)
  3. Change directions
  4. Making different patterns (triangles, squares, etc.)
  5. Putting together sequences of various locomotor movements.

DPE p. 253

Try to encourage children to move with quality.

The tom-tom can be used to offer different qualities to the movement.

Cog.—The student will be able to verbalize the importance of locomotor movements and their variations in sports activities.

PM.—The student will be able to originate his sequence of locomotor movements and variations.

FITNESS DEVELOPMENT ACTIVITIES (7 – 8 MINUTES)

Animal Movements and Fitness Challenges

Tape alternating segments of silence and music to signal duration of exercise. Music segments indicate animal movements while intervals of silence announce flexibility and strength development activities.
  1. Puppy Dog Walk—30 seconds.
  2. Freeze; perform stretching activities.
  3. Measuring Worm Walk—30 seconds
  4. Freeze; perform abdominal development challenges.
  5. Seal Crawl —30 seconds.
  6. Frog Jump—30 seconds.
  7. Freeze; perform push-up position challenges.
  8. Elephant Walk —30 seconds.
  9. Bear Walk—30 seconds.
  10. Freeze; perform abdominal challenges.
  11. Crab Walk—30 seconds.
  12. Lame Dog Walk
A variation is to place animal movement signs throughout the area and instruct students to move from sign to sign performing the appropriate animal movement each time they reach a new sign.

DPE pp. 281 – 284

Emphasize placing the weight on the hands for shoulder girdle development.

Quality of movement should be emphasized rather than speed.

Vary the length of the intervals to match the fitness level of youngsters

Cog.—It is interesting to measure the breathing rate at rest and during and after exercise. The student will be able to explain why breathing rate varies.

Aff.—Many experts feel people are overweight due to lack of activity rather than eating too much. Discuss why this might be true.

Cog.—Flexor muscles decrease the angle of a joint. Extensors return the movement from flexion. Identify flexors and extensors among students.

MOVEMENT EXPERIENCE—CONTENT	ORGANIZATION AND TEACHING HINTS	EXPECTED STUDENT OBJECTIVES AND OUTCOMES

LESSON FOCUS (15 – 20 MINUTES)

Movement Skills and Concepts (7)

Select a few activities from each of the categories so students receive a variety of skills to practice. When possible, integrate the manipulative skill activities with fundamental skill activities.

Fundamental Skill: Leaping

1. Run in different directions and practice your leaping. Alternate the leading foot.
2. As you run, try a leap for good height; for distance; for both.
3. Explore the different arm positions you can use in leaping. Which is best? Try sailing through the air like an airplane.
4. Leap with a quarter or half turn.
5. If there are benches or other obstacles present, leap over these. Put several in succession for consecutive leaps.
6. Put one-half the children down scattered in curled position, face to the floor. The others leap over as many as possible.
7. Practice making two or three leaps in succession.
8. Practice Leap the Brook.

DPE p. 341

Scatter formation.

Stress "soft" landing.

Alternate leading foot.

Cues:
  "Up and over."
  "Push off and reach."
  "Use your arms to help."

Change groups.

Use a mat for landing.

PM.—The student will be able to secure good height in leaping.

PM.—The student will be able to land lightly.

Cog.—The student will be able to explain how force is applied to result in an effective leap.

Cog.—The number and size of muscles used for a movement will determine the amount of force generated. Identify the size and number of muscles used when leaping.

Movement Concept: Levels and Speed

Each set of partners has a line on the floor. Each partner goes down the line and explores the following:
1. Show me a slow, low level movement down and back.
2. What other ways can you go down and back at a slow, low level?
3. Change to a high level, fast movement.
4. What other ways can you do a high level, fast movement?
5. Combine a low, fast movement down with a high, slow movement back.
6. Explore other ways to move at different levels and speeds.

DPE p. 329

By partners.

Each takes a turn.

Encourage student-developed ideas and responses.

Students should be given a chance to share their ideas with each other.

PM.—The student will demonstrate the ability to react to the level and speed as challenged.

Cog.—The student will be able to explain the concepts of levels and speed.

Aff.—Emotional health is impossible unless individuals can acknowledge and express their feelings. Discuss the importance of accepting our own and others' feelings in a gentle and empathetic fashion.

Movement Concept: Partner Activity and Jump Rope Floor Targets

Begin with the rope laid in a straight line along the floor and perform movements down the rope:
1. Jumping, hopping, cross-steps, scissors steps, heel clicks, etc.
2. Add quarter and half-turns, levels.

DPE pp. 444 – 446

Partners scattered around the space.

Go down the rope one way only.

Develop this well.

Each takes a turn.

Challenge for variety.

Low, in-between, high levels.

PM.—The student will be able to move down the rope with a variety of movements.

MOVEMENT EXPERIENCE—CONTENT	ORGANIZATION AND TEACHING HINTS	EXPECTED STUDENT OBJECTIVES AND OUTCOMES

3. Take the weight partially on the hands; crouch jumps, bunny jump, cartwheel, etc.
4. Form a selected shape with the rope. Repeat 1, 2, 3. Form the same shape with your body.
5. Matching activity. One partner performs and the other matches the movement.
6. Partner activity. Join hands in some way; hop, jump, or use other movements down the rope or figure. Wheelbarrow or use partner-support activities and move down the rope.

Movement Concept: Supporting the Weight Wholly or in Part (Partners)

1. Support with partner's feet on floor; with one foot on the floor.
2. Support with partner's hands on the floor.
3. Support with partner completely off the floor.
4. Support and turn the partner in a full circle.

DPE p. 321

Scatter formation with partners. This should be flexible, with emphasis on variety of response.

Use half-and-half achievement, demonstration. One-half the class watches the other half.

PM.—The student will be able to create a variety of responses.

Cog.—Aerobic endurance is important for long-term, low-intensity activities. Discuss how aerobic endurance can be improved.

Movement Concept: Acceleration and Deceleration

1. Begin a movement and accelerate.
2. Begin with a fast movement and decelerate.
3. Accelerate to a fast speed and decelerate the same movement.
4. Accelerate with one movement to fast speed, shift to another movement, and decelerate.
5. Can you accelerate one movement of the body while decelerating another at the same time?

Suggested movements for practicing acceleration and deceleration: Stepping in place, running in place, circling body parts, arm thrust movements, jumping, hopping, changing stride, arm and leg movement while lying on back, pretending to be a locomotive engine of a railroad train.

DPE pp. 329 – 330

Scatter formation.

Explain prefixes.

Get other suggestions from the children.

PM.—The student will demonstrate the ability to interpret acceleration and deceleration in selected movements.

Cog.—The student will be able to verbally explain the terms "acceleration" and "deceleration."

Cog.—Strength is an important factor for learning motor skills. Exercises designed to develop strength are not effective in developing endurance. Discuss the need for separate conditioning activities that will develop fitness in endurance and strength activities.

GAME (5 – 7 MINUTES)

Mix and Match — *DPE,* p. 564
  Supplies: None
  Skills: Fundamental locomotor movements
  A line is established through the middle of the area. Half of the children are on one side and half are on the other. There must be an odd person, the teacher or another child. The teacher gives a signal for children to move as directed on their side of the line. They can be told to run, hop, skip, or whatever. At another signal, children run to the dividing line, and each reaches across to join hands with a child from the opposite group. The goal is to not be left out. Children may reach over but may not cross the line. The person left out is moved to the opposite side so that players left out come from alternating sides of the area.
  Variation: The game also can be done with music or a drumbeat, with the players rushing to the centerline to find partners when the rhythm stops.

MOVEMENT EXPERIENCE— CONTENT	ORGANIZATION AND TEACHING HINTS	EXPECTED STUDENT OBJECTIVES AND OUTCOMES

Colors — *DPE,* p. 561

    Supplies: Colored paper (construction paper) cut in circles, squares, or triangles for markers

    Skills: Color or other perceptual concepts, running

    Five or six different-colored markers should be used, with a number of children having the same color. Children are standing or seated in a circle with a marker in front of each child. The teacher calls out a color, and everyone having that color runs counterclockwise around the circle and back to place. The first one seated upright and motionless is declared the winner. Different kinds of locomotor movement can be specified, such as skipping, galloping, walking, and so on. After a period of play, the children leave the markers on the floor and move one place to the left.

    Variation: Shapes (e.g., circles, triangles, squares, rectangles, stars, and diamonds) can be used instead of colors, as can numbers or other articles or categories, such as animals, birds, or fish. This game has value in teaching identification and recognition.

DYNAMIC PHYSICAL EDUCATION LESSON PLAN
Stunts and Tumbling Skills (Lesson 3)
Level I

Supplies and Equipment Needed:
Tumbling mats
Cones
Balls

MOVEMENT EXPERIENCE—CONTENT	ORGANIZATION AND TEACHING HINTS	EXPECTED STUDENT OBJECTIVES AND OUTCOMES

INTRODUCTORY ACTIVITY (2 – 3 MINUTES)

Move, Perform Task on Signal

Do a locomotor movement; on signal, stop and perform a task such as an exercise or stunt.
  1. Seat Circles
  2. Balances—foot, seat, and knee
  3. Crab Kicks
  4. Heel Clicks
  5. Coffee Grinder
  6. Wring the Dishrag
  7. Partner Hopping

DPE p. 254

Many individual stunts such as the heel click, heel slap, or jump turn can be performed. These add challenge and excitement to the activity.

Vary the locomotor movements by adding quality words, i.e., slow–fast, high–low.

PM.—The student will be able to perform the basic locomotor movement variations as well as the designated stunts or exercises.

Aff.—The body should be gradually warmed up, rather than moving into demanding activity immediately. Discuss with the class a need to self-pace and gradually work toward maximum output. Incorporate this principle into your teaching by demanding more as the introductory and fitness work progress.

FITNESS DEVELOPMENT ACTIVITIES (7 – 8 MINUTES)

Four-Corners Movement

Outline a large rectangle with four cones. Place signs with pictures on both sides of the cones. Youngsters move around the outside of the rectangle and change movements as they pass a corner sign. The following movement activities are suggested:
  1. Jogging
  2. Skipping/Jumping/Hopping
  3. Sliding/Galloping
  4. Various animal movements
  5. Sport imitation movements
  6. Bench pulls
  7. Bench crouch jumps
Stop the class after 30–45 seconds of movement and perform fitness challenges. Tape alternating segments of silence and music to signal duration of exercise. Music segments indicate aerobic activity while intervals of silence announce flexibility and strength development activities.

DPE p. 287

If signs are not placed at the corners, teachers can specify movements for students to perform.

Increase the demand of the routine by increasing the size of the rectangle.

Faster-moving students can pass on the outside (away from the center) of the rectangle.

Assure that abdominal and shoulder girdle strength development activities are included.

PM.—The student will be able to perform the activities on all sides of the rectangle.

Cog.—The students will be able to explain in their own words how exercise, if demanding enough, will cause the training effect to occur in a short period of time.

MOVEMENT EXPERIENCE—CONTENT	ORGANIZATION AND TEACHING HINTS	EXPECTED STUDENT OBJECTIVES AND OUTCOMES

LESSON FOCUS (15 – 20 MINUTES)

Tumbling, Stunts, and Animal Movements (3)

Five groups of activities in this lesson ensure that youngsters receive a variety of experiences. Pick a few activities from each group and teach them alternately. For example, teach one or two animal movements, then a tumbling and inverted balance, followed by a balance stunt, etc. Give equal time to each group of activities

1. Animal Movement
   a. Siamese Twin Walk
   b. Tightrope Walk
   c. Lame Dog Walk
   d. Crab Walk
2. Tumbling and Inverted Balances
   a. Forward and Backward Roll review
   b. Three Point Tip-up
   c. Mountain Climber
   d. Switcheroo
3. Balance Stunts
   a. Forward Balance
   b. Backward Balance
   c. Side Balance
   d. Hand and Knee Balance
   e. Single-Knee Balance
4. Individual Stunts
   a. Heel Slap
   b. Pogo Stick
   c. Top
   d. Turk Stand
   e. Crazy Walk
   f. Seat Circle
5. Partner and Group Stunts
   a. Double Top
   b. Rollee Pollee

DPE pp. 491 – 507

Scatter as many tumbling mats as possible throughout the area in order to avoid waiting lines.

Present students with two or three activities and allow them to choose one they feel able to perform.

Review activities from previous lessons and allow less gifted students to practice less difficult challenges.

Don't force students to perform tumbling and inverted balances. If they are fearful, gradual encouragement will accomplish more in the long run than intimidation and force.

Demonstrate the activities so students are aware of how they should be performed.

A major concern for safety is the neck and back region. Overweight children are at greater risk and might be allowed to avoid tumbling and inverted balances.

PM.—The student will be able to perform a forward and backward roll with at least two variations.

PM.—The student will be able to perform at least two activities from each of the categories.

Cog.—The student will be able to describe positioning of the hands and knees in partner support activities.

Cog.—The student will be able to name at least three safety principles that are important in tumbling and inverted balance activities.

Aff.—Tumbling is an excellent activity for overcoming personal fear of harm from the activities. Discuss how many athletes must conquer fears and take risks in order to succeed.

Cog.—Regular aerobic exercise lowers blood pressure. Discuss the importance of regular exercise and blood pressure monitoring.

Cog.—Regular exercise keeps the bones from demineralizing. When bones demineralize, they become brittle and less resistant to breakage.

GAME (5 – 7 MINUTES)

Charlie Over the Water — *DPE,* p. 560
   Supplies: A volleyball or playground ball
   Skills: Skipping, running, stopping, bowling (rolling)
   The children are in circle formation with hands joined. One child, Charlie (or Sally, if a girl), is in the center of the circle, holding a ball. The children skip around the circle to the following chant.
Charlie over the water,
Charlie over the sea,
Charlie caught a bluebird,
But he can't catch me!
   On the word me, Charlie tosses the ball in the air and children drop hands and scatter. When Charlie catches it, he shouts "Stop!" All of the children stop immediately and must not move their feet. Charlie rolls the ball in an attempt to hit one of the children. If he hits a child, that child becomes the new Charlie. If he misses, he must remain Charlie, and the game is repeated. If he misses twice, however, he picks another child for the center.

MOVEMENT EXPERIENCE— CONTENT	ORGANIZATION AND TEACHING HINTS	EXPECTED STUDENT OBJECTIVES AND OUTCOMES

Circle Straddle Ball — *DPE,* p. 560

    Supplies: Two or more 8-in. foam balls

    Skills: Ball rolling, catching

    Children are in circle formation, facing in. Each stands in a wide straddle stance with the side of the foot against the neighbor's. The hands are on the knees. Two balls are used. The object of the game is to roll one of the balls between the legs of another player before he can get his hands down to stop the ball. Each time a ball goes between the legs of an individual, a point is scored. The players having the fewest points scored against them are the winners. Keep the circles small so students have more opportunities to handle the ball.

    Teaching suggestion: The teacher should be sure that children catch and roll the ball, rather than batting it. Children must keep their hands on their knees until a ball is rolled at them. After some practice, the following variation can be played.

    Variation: One child is in the center with a ball and is it. The other children are in the same formation as before. One ball is used. The center player tries to roll the ball through the legs of any child. She should mask her intent, using feints and changes of direction. Any child allowing the ball to go through his legs becomes it.

Flowers and Wind — *DPE,* p. 561

    Supplies: None

    Skill: Running

    Two parallel lines long enough to accommodate the children are drawn about 30 ft apart. Children are divided into two groups. One is the wind and the other the flowers. Each of the teams takes a position on one of the lines and faces the other team. The flowers secretly select the name of a common flower. When ready, they walk over to the other line and stand about 3 ft away from the wind. The players on the wind team begin to call out flower names—trying to guess the flower chosen. When the flower has been guessed, the flowers run to their goal line, chased by the players of the other team. Any player caught must join the other side. The roles are reversed and the game is repeated. If one side has trouble guessing, a clue can be given to the color or size of the flower or the first letter of its name.

DYNAMIC PHYSICAL EDUCATION LESSON PLAN
Rhythmic Movement (Lesson 2)
Level I

Supplies and Equipment Needed:
  Tom-tom and beater
  Tape player and selected music
  Cones
  Equipment for Mini-Challenge Course

Dances Taught:
  How D'Ye Do, My Partner
  Jump Jim Jo
  Children's Polka
  Chimes of Dunkirk
  Turn the Glasses Over
  Shortnin' Bread
  Bombay Bounce
  Jingle Bells, Var. 1

MOVEMENT EXPERIENCE— CONTENT	ORGANIZATION AND TEACHING HINTS	EXPECTED STUDENT OBJECTIVES AND OUTCOMES

INTRODUCTORY ACTIVITY (2 – 3 MINUTES)

Drill Sergeant

Designate a student in each squad to be a drill sergeant. The sergeant then gives commands to the squad such as:
  1. Walk, jump twice, and roll
  2. Lean, jump twice, and freeze (pose)
  3. Shake, leap, and roll
  4. Seal Walk, forward roll, and jump
The sergeant can call the squad to group to attention, give them directions, and command them to move.

DPE p. 258

Teacher may want to act out the drill sergeant role with the entire class first, then appoint student leaders.

Squad formation.

Commands can be written on note cards to prompt the leaders.

Allow students to act out the role of soldiers.

A "military drumbeat" on the tom–tom may be used with this activity.

PM.—The student will be able to change quickly from one movement to the next.

Cog.—When a person exercises, breathing becomes deeper and more frequent. Discuss the reason why— working muscles need more oxygen.

FITNESS DEVELOPMENT ACTIVITIES (7 – 8 MINUTES)

Mini-Challenge Course

Arrange four courses with a group at each course. Students perform the challenges from start to finish and job back to repeat the course. On signal, groups move to a new course.
Course 1. Crouch jumps, pulls or scooter movements down a bench; through two hoops; and skip to a cone.
Course 2. Weave in and out of four wands held upright by cones; Crab Walk; hang from climbing rope for 5 seconds; and gallop to a cone.
Course 3. Do a tumbling activity length of mat; agility run through hoops; Frog Jump; and slide to a cone.
Course 4. Move over and under six obstacles; Log Roll length of mat; while jumping, circle around three cones; and run to a cone.

DPE pp. 284 – 285

Set up four parallel (side-by-side) courses in one-half of the area. Rotate groups to each course after a specified time.

Set up four parallel (side-by-side) courses in one-half of the area. Rotate groups to each course after a specified time.

An alternative is to organize the courses into a single circuit around the perimeter of the area.

Movement should be continuous.

Since young children fatigue and recover quickly, stop the class after 30– 45 seconds and perform fitness movement challenges.

Cog.—When a person exercises regularly, additional capillaries form in the muscle tissue so that the muscle cells are better supplied with blood. The student will be able to describe this occurrence in her own words.

Aff.—Lack of exercise is one of the key factors in heart disease. Symptoms of heart disease are often found in young people, and thus fitness activities may help retard this health problem. Discuss heart disease and the role of exercise.

MOVEMENT EXPERIENCE—CONTENT	ORGANIZATION AND TEACHING HINTS	EXPECTED STUDENT OBJECTIVES AND OUTCOMES

LESSON FOCUS (15 – 20 MINUTES)

Rhythmic Movement (2)

Practice the following locomotor and nonlocomotor movements to the beat of a tom-tom or tambourine.

Locomotor Movements

1. Walk, run, skip, hop, jump, gallop, slide, draw steps, leap.
2. Gallop in different directions.
   a. Change on 8, 4, 2.
3. Jump patterns. Hopping practice.
   a. Back and forth over a spot (board, line or jump rope).
   b. Circle or other form.
   c. Use numbers and letters.
   d. Exploratory opportunity.
4. Crab Kick and Walk
   a. Alternate kicking.
   b. Together kicking.
   c. Walk to slow beat.
5. Sprinter (Treadmill)
   a. Change feet. Try together.
6. Combinations
   a. Walk and run (4 and 8)
   b. Walk-walk-hop-hop-hop.
   c. Run 4 and jump 3.
   d. Draw steps 2 and walk 4.
   e. Slide 4 and skip 4.
   f. Gallop 4 and jump 3.
   g. Others (exploratory).

Nonlocomotor Movements

1. Elevator, piston machine (use arms).
2. Clock, rubber band, balloon.
3. Exploratory opportunity.

Dances

1. Hokey Pokey (*DPE*, p. 369)
2. How D'Ye Do, My Partner? (*DPE*, p. 370)
3. Chimes of Dunkirk (Var. 1) (*DPE*, p. 372)
4. Shortnin' Bread (*DPE*, p. 372)
5. Children's Polka (*DPE*, p. 372)
6. Jump Jim Jo (*DPE*, p. 373)
7. Bombay Bounce (*DPE*, p. 375)
8. Turn the Glasses Over (*DPE*, p. 377)
9. Jungle Bells (Var. 1) (*DPE*, p. 378)

DPE pp. 356 – 361

Selected movement formations.

Change hopping foot in center (can use loud beat).

Signal with loud beat.

Use right and left in hopping.

Can use rope for different patterns on the floor.

Add turns.

Stimulate different tempos, qualities, and intensities of movement by varying the beat.

This is a somewhat creative lesson and you should allow yourself and students a great amount of freedom of movement and exploration.

A heavy drum beat can be used to signal changes.

Let children develop others.

Discuss these objects and their movements and have children mimic them in their own way.

When teaching a dance, use the following steps:
1. Tell about the dance and listen to the music.
2. Clap the beat and learn the verse.
3. Practice the dance steps without the music and with verbal cues.
4. Practice the dance with the music.

Make dances easy for students to learn by using some of the following ideas:
1. Teach the dances without partners.
2. Allow youngsters to move in any direction—avoid the left–right orientation.
3. Use scattered formation instead of circles—it helps avoid embarrassment.

PM.—The student will be able to move rhythmically (keep time).

Cog.—The student will be able to recognize the various tom-tom rhythms, i.e., slow, fast, gallop, skip, walk.

Cog.—To minimize muscle soreness, static stretching exercises should be performed. Significant soreness occurs when exercise work load is increased too rapidly. Discuss the importance of progression when developing higher levels of fitness.

PM.—The student will be able to move using combinations of basic locomotor movements.

Cog.—Rhythm and timing are important elements in motor skill performance. Discuss the need for learning rhythmic activities through correct practice and repetition.

Cog.—The student will be able to sing the verses of the singing games.

Aff.—Rhythmic activities are a learned skill. Performers need to practice them many times before they are mastered. Discuss the need for understanding individual differences in rates of learning.

MOVEMENT EXPERIENCE— CONTENT	ORGANIZATION AND TEACHING HINTS	EXPECTED STUDENT OBJECTIVES AND OUTCOMES

4. Emphasize strong movements such as clapping and stomping to encourage involvement.
5. Tape the music at a slower speed when first learning the dance.

Rhythms should be taught like other sport skills. Avoid expecting perfection when teaching rhythms. Teach a variety of dances rather than one or two in depth. Youngsters will enjoy rhythms if they know it is acceptable to make mistakes without being ridiculed.

GAME (5 – 7 MINUTES)

Skunk Tag — *DPE,* p. 568
   Supplies: None
   Skills: Fundamental locomotor movements, dodging
   Children are scattered about the area. One child is it and chases the others, trying to tag one of them. When a tag is made, she says, "You're it." The new it chases other children. Children are safe when they move into the skunk position which is assumed by kneeling and reaching one arm under a knee and holding their nose. The skunk position can only be held for five seconds; students are then eligible to be tagged.

Aviator — *DPE,* p. 556
   Supplies: None
   Skills: Running, locomotor movements, stopping
   Players are parked (in push-up position) at one end of the playing area. The air traffic controller (ATC) is in front of the players and calls out, "Aviators aviators, take off!" Youngsters take off and move like airplanes to the opposite side of the area. The first person to move to the other side and land the plane (get into push-up position facing the ATC) is declared the new ATC.
   If the ATC yells out some type of stormy weather, all planes must return to the starting line and resume the parked position. Examples of stormy weather commands are lightning, thunder, hurricane, and tornado. Each ATC is allowed to give stormy weather warnings once.

Right Angle — *DPE,* p. 566
   Supplies: Music
   Skills: Rhythmic movement, body management
   A tom-tom can be used to provide the rhythm for this activity. Some of the basic rhythm records also have suitable music. Children change direction at right angles on each heavy beat or change of music. The object of the game is to make the right-angle change on signal and not to bump into other players.

DYNAMIC PHYSICAL EDUCATION LESSON PLAN
Fundamental Skills Using Jumping Boxes
Level I

Supplies and Equipment Needed:
  Jumping boxes
  Tumbling mats
  Cones and lists of return activities
  Secret movement cards
  Tom-tom
  Balls
  Beanbag
  Hula hoop
  Wand

MOVEMENT EXPERIENCE— CONTENT	ORGANIZATION AND TEACHING HINTS	EXPECTED STUDENT OBJECTIVES AND OUTCOMES

INTRODUCTORY ACTIVITY (2 – 3 MINUTES)

Secret Movement

Many different movements and/or combinations of movements are written on large flash cards. Without looking, the teacher or a student selects a card and directs the class to "show me" the secret movement. Youngsters select a movement and perform it until signaled to stop. The card is then revealed to the class to see which youngsters, by chance, guessed the secret movement.

DPE p. 254

Scatter formation.

Use demanding movements (locomotor movements, animal walks, stunts, exercises, sports imitation activities) so youngsters will move and warm up quickly.

Challenge the students to see who can correctly guess the most movements.

PM.—The student will be able to perform the movement combinations and create three new patterns.

Cog.—The student will be able to distinguish between a nonlocomotor movement and a locomotor movement.

FITNESS DEVELOPMENT ACTIVITIES (7 – 8 MINUTES)

Fitness Games and Challenges

Tape alternating segments of silence and music to signal duration of exercise. Music segments indicate fitness game activity while intervals of silence announce flexibility and strength development activities.
  1. Stoop Tag - 45 seconds.
  2. Freeze; perform stretching activities.
  3. Back-to-Back Tag - 45 seconds.
  4. Freeze; perform Abdominal Challenges using Curl-up variations.
  5. Balance Tag - 45 seconds.
  6. Freeze; perform Arm-Shoulder Girdle Challenges using Push-up variations.
  7. Elbow Swing Tag - 45 seconds.
  8. Freeze; perform Trunk Development challenges.
  9. Color Tag - 45 seconds.

DPE pp. 281 – 284

Maximize movement by using simple fitness games that require little explanation.

Many fitness challenges are found in *DPE* pp. 281 – 283.

Remember that the goal of fitness games is to stimulate movement rather than teach children to follow rules.

Assign many youngsters to be it to increase the amount of movement.

Cog.—When a person exercises, the muscular action aids in returning the venous blood to the heart. The student will be able to explain why this occurs. (One-way valves and pressure of muscular contraction.)

MOVEMENT EXPERIENCE— CONTENT	ORGANIZATION AND TEACHING HINTS	EXPECTED STUDENT OBJECTIVES AND OUTCOMES

LESSON FOCUS (15 – 20 MINUTES)

Fundamental Skills Using Jumping Boxes

Activities fall into three basic categories: approaching the box, mounting the box, and dismounting the box. A wide range of activities can be developed by combining these variables and making many different routines.

Approaches to the Boxes

1. Basic movements such as skip, hop, jump, etc.
2. Various animal walks.
3. Stunts like heel clicks, half turns, and scooter movements can be used to approach the box.

Mounting the Box

1. Step, jump, leap or hop onto the box.
2. Rabbit jump or leap frog onto the box.

Dismounting

1. Jump off with a quarter, half and full turn.
2. Jump off forward, backward and sideways.
3. Jump off with different body shapes, i.e., stretch, curl, jack-knife.
4. Jump off followed by a forward or backward roll.
5. Change the above dismounts by substituting a hop or leap in place of the jump.
6. Hold a hoop in front of the box. Have the rest of the squad jump through the hoop.

Challenge Activities

1. Crouch jump over the boxes.
2. Use a beanbag, toss in air, dismount and catch.
3. Dribble a playground ball while mounting and dismounting boxes.
4. Hula-hoop to the box, mount and dismount without losing control of hoop.
5. Jump over a wand on the dismount.
6. Jump-rope to the box. Mount and dismount maintaining jumping rope.

DPE pp. 472 – 474

Squad formation—one squad per box with tumbling mats used in front of the boxes to cushion landings.

List return activities on signs so that students are busy and doing some activity on their way back to the end of the line.

Emphasize landing softly so that students "meet the ground." Stress lightness, bending the knees, balance, and body controlling. Students should not fall to the ground upon landing.

Encourage students to be creative and think of their own activities.

Use the larger boxes for the upper grades, as well as combinations of both large and small.

Combine the approach, mount, and dismount in a smooth, skillful manner.

To encourage landing with knees bent, ask students to touch the floor with the hands.

Challenge students to think of other activities for their squad.

Tape signs to cones listing return activities to perform on the return to line.

The leader of the squad can raise a hand on returning so the teacher knows when to introduce a new activity.

PM.—The student will be able to dismount from the box with a controlled landing.

PM.—The student will be able to manage her body in the air and perform different stunts in the air.

Aff.—Jumping boxes are used for learning body management skills. Discuss the need for learning to control the body in the air and prepare it for the landing.

Cog.—Students will understand that limbs must be bent and "give" in order to absorb force.

Cog.—The student will be able to describe the proper technique of landing from a jump off the box.

MOVEMENT EXPERIENCE— CONTENT	ORGANIZATION AND TEACHING HINTS	EXPECTED STUDENT OBJECTIVES AND OUTCOMES

GAME (5 – 7 MINUTES)

Squirrel in the Trees — *DPE,* p. 567
  Supplies: None
  Skills: Fundamental locomotor movements
  A number of trees are formed by two players facing each other and holding hands or putting hands on each other's shoulders. A squirrel is in the center of each tree, and one or two extra squirrels are outside. A signal to change is given. All squirrels move out of their tree to another tree, and the extra players try to find a free tree. Only one squirrel is allowed in a tree.
  Teaching suggestion: As a system of rotation, when each squirrel moves into a tree, he can change places with one of the players forming the tree. The rotation is important, because it ensures that all children eventually are active.

Stop Ball — *DPE,* p. 568
  Supplies: A ball
  Skills: Tossing, catching
  One child, with hands over the eyes, stands in the center of a circle of children. A ball is tossed clockwise or counterclockwise from child to child around the circle. Failing to catch the ball or making a bad toss incurs a penalty. That child must take one long step back and stay out of the game for one turn.
  At a time of her own selection, the center player calls, "Stop." The player caught with the ball steps back and stays out for one turn. The center player should be allowed three or four turns and then be changed.

DYNAMIC PHYSICAL EDUCATION LESSON PLAN
Educational Movement (Lesson 8)
Level I

Fundamental Skills: Pushing and pulling
Educational Movement Themes: Balancing the body
Manipulative Activity: Rope jumping
Parallel Sequence Building: Circles in the body—planes of movement
Creative Activity: Sports imitation activities

Supplies and Equipment Needed:
  Objects to push—jumping boxes, cardboard boxes (filled), sacks of balls, etc.
  Beanbags—one for each child
  Partner tug-of-war ropes—one for each two children
  Tape player and tapes for rope jumping to music
  Cones
  Jump rope—one for each student
  Balls
  Tom-tom
  Plastic jugs
  Pictures of athletes (optional)

MOVEMENT EXPERIENCE—CONTENT	ORGANIZATION AND TEACHING HINTS	EXPECTED STUDENT OBJECTIVES AND OUTCOMES

INTRODUCTORY ACTIVITY (2 – 3 MINUTES)

Run and Assume Shape

Place emphasis on making a variety of shapes and balances. Vary the locomotor movements.
  1. Run and move to a prone (one drumbeat) or supine (two drumbeats) position on signal.
  2. Run and move into a balance position.
  3. Run and freeze in various shapes.

DPE p. 253

Scatter formation.

If outside and wet, use only the balances.

Other challenges such as curl, stretch, rock can be used.

PM.—The student will be able to respond to a signal and quickly change movements.

FITNESS DEVELOPMENT ACTIVITIES (7 – 8 MINUTES)

Walk, Trot, and Sprint

Move to the following signals:
  1. One drumbeat - walk.
  2. Two drumbeats - trot.
  3. Three drumbeats - sprint.
  4. Whistle - freeze and perform exercises.
Perform various strength and flexibility exercises between bouts of walk, trot, and sprint. Examples are:
  1. Bend and Twist
  2. Sitting Stretch
  3. Push-up variations
  4. Abdominal Challenges
  5. Body Twist
  6. Standing Hip Bend

DPE pp. 285 – 286

Use a tom-tom or tambourine.

Scatter formation.

Emphasize quality of movement and rapid changes.

Check heart rate after bouts of sprinting.

Alternate bouts of movement with strength and flexibility exercises.

PM.—The student will demonstrate proper form in the following movements:
  1. Walk
  2. Trot
  3. Sprint

Cog.—Walk, trot, and sprint only develops the leg region and cardiovascular endurance. The student will be able to explain this in his own words.

MOVEMENT EXPERIENCE—CONTENT	ORGANIZATION AND TEACHING HINTS	EXPECTED STUDENT OBJECTIVES AND OUTCOMES

LESSON FOCUS (15 – 20 MINUTES)

Movement Skills and Concepts (8)

Select a few activities from each of the categories so students receive a variety of skills to practice. When possible, integrate the manipulative skill activities with fundamental skill activities.

Fundamental Skill: Pushing

1. Push against a wall first in an erect position and then with knees bent and one foot braced behind the other. Which is better
2. Push an imaginary object that is very light. Now try pushing a very heavy object.
3. Try to push a partner who is sitting on the floor. Then try to push your partner sitting on a gym scooter. What changes are made?
4. Can you push an object with your feet without using your arms and hands? Try with the hands braced behind you.
5. Put your back against an object and push with your feet.
6. Explore different ways to push your object.
7. Find a friend to explore different ways to push him or her over a line.
8. Sit down back to back with your partner and see whether you can move him or her.
9. Lie on the floor and push yourself backward, forward, sideways. Which is easiest?
10. Lie on the floor and push yourself forward with one hand and one foot. Which hand-foot combination is best?
11. Put a beanbag on the floor and push it with the elbow, shoulder, nose and other selected body parts.
12. Show how you can push a ball to a friend. Push slowly and steadily.
13. Push something toward the ceiling—a ball or other object.

DPE p. 347

Cues:
   "Widen your feet."
   "Lower your body."
   "Get body in line with push."
   "Push steadily and evenly."

Make the comparison.

What changes occur?

Show differences. Discuss friction.

Partner uses passive resistance.

Partner resists.

Opposition probably works best.

Cog.—The student will learn the most effective pushing techniques.

PM.—The student will learn to execute forceful pushing.

Aff.—Students will work together cooperatively to explore pushing movements.

Cog.—To improve performance, feedback is necessary. Students need to identify and use feedback about the outcome of the performance and feedback about how the skill was performed. In pushing activities, they can easily gauge outcome and the effect that modifications of pushing technique have on the outcome.

Cog.—Static stretching is the best means for increasing flexibility. This means holding the stretch for 15–30 seconds. Help students understand the difference between ballistic and static stretching.

Fundamental Skill: Pulling

1. Reach for an imaginary object near the ceiling and pull the object toward you quickly. Now slowly and smoothly.
2. Use a partner tug-of-war rope and practice pulling at different levels against a partner.
3. With the rope, pull from a kneeling position.
4. With the rope on your feet, pull from a sitting position.

DPE pp. 347 – 348

Cues:
   "Widen base."
   "Lower body."
   "Lean away from object."
   "Take a good grip."

Practice a variety of pulling movements.

Cog.—The student will learn how best to exert force in pulling.

PM.—The student will be able to execute forceful pulling movements.

Cog.—Weak abdominal muscles are a major cause of low back pain. Discuss the importance of exercises to strengthen abdominal muscles and maintain proper posture.

MOVEMENT EXPERIENCE—CONTENT	ORGANIZATION AND TEACHING HINTS	EXPECTED STUDENT OBJECTIVES AND OUTCOMES
5. Clasp your hands together and pull against each hand as hard as you can. Vary the positions of the arms. 6. Hold hands with your partner and try to pull against each other balancing on one foot. 7. Hold hands with partner, drop low, and pull hard against each other. 8. Have partner sit down. Pull partner slowly by the feet. 9. Pretend to pull a heavy object while you are lying on the floor. 10. With partner seated on the floor, pull him or her to his or her feet.	Use one-hand and two-hand grips. Practice pulling but avoid contests. Pull like a water skier.	Cog.—Not practicing at all is better than practicing incorrect motor patterns. Discuss the importance of seeking feedback in developing correct motor patterns.
Manipulative Skills: Rope Jumping Encourage children to work on needed skill areas. Suggest working first without music and then with music.	*DPE* pp. 451 – 458 The progress of the children will determine the approach. See what they can do and then provide necessary coaching.	PM.—The student will improve in rope jumping skills. Aff.—The student will be stimulated to work on areas needing improvement.
Movement Concepts: Circles in the Body and Planes of Movement 1. How many joints of the body can do circular motion (circles)? 2. How many different ways can you make the arms circle, using both arms at once? 3. Lie on your back, lift your legs. Can you make the arms and legs go in circles? Can you make them go in different circles? 4. In a standing position, show arm circles in horizontal, vertical and diagonal planes using one arm at a time. 5. Repeat item 4, using both arms in bilateral movements. 6. Lie on back and lift the legs. Make the feet describe the three planes of movement first singly and then together. 7. Explore different ways where two different body parts illustrate two different planes of movement. 8. Make a large circle with one part of the body and a small one with another. Explore with different planes of movement. 9. With which part of the body can you make the biggest circle? 10. What joints can also twist as well as circle? Explore.	*DPE* pp. 328 – 329 Scatter formation. When a child comes up with a suggestion, have all practice that movement. Show examples and then all practice. Explain terms. Bilateral means that the arms move the same way. Come up with some answers.	PM.—The student will be able to make circles with five different body parts. Cog.—The student will be able to differentiate among the various planes of movement—horizontal, vertical, and diagonal. Cog.—Rotation occurs when force is applied off-center. To make a ball spin, the force must be applied away from the center of gravity.
Movement Concept: Balancing the Body 1. On different parts of the body. 2. On different number of body parts, varying from one through five. Different combinations. 3. Balancing on different levels.	*DPE* pp. 323 – 324 Scatter or circle formation. Hold balance poses for 3–5 seconds.	PM.—The student will be able to form and hold a variety of balance poses.

MOVEMENT EXPERIENCE— CONTENT	ORGANIZATION AND TEACHING HINTS	EXPECTED STUDENT OBJECTIVES AND OUTCOMES

4. Work out a sequence of three or four balance poses. Move from one to the next (sustained flow).
5. Try to balance on both hands.
6. With a partner, form different balances.

Utilize pupil demonstration.

Movement Concept: Sports Imitation Activities

1. Pretend you are a football player—kicking the ball, passing the ball, making a tackle, centering the ball.
2. Pretend you are a basketball player—shooting a basket, dribbling, guarding, jump ball, a free throw shot.
3. Let's pretend you are a track and field star performing at: the shot-put, the javelin throw, or the discus. Move like a hurdler.
4. Pretend you are a baseball player—pitching, catching a fly ball, fielding a grounder and throwing to first, batting, bunting, sliding into a base.

This is a "let's pretend" activity. Scatter in general space.

Allow students to imitate various movements and have others guess what sport it is.

It might be useful to show pictures of various athletes if students have not seen the sport activity previously.

PM.—The student will be able to imitate the movements found in the various sport activities.

Cog.—The student will be able to identify the sport when other students imitate various movements.

GAME (5 – 7 MINUTES)

Change Sides — *DPE,* p. 559
Supplies: None
Skill: Body management
Two parallel lines are established 30 ft apart. Half of the children are on each line. On signal, all cross to the other line, face the center, and stand at attention. The first group to do this correctly wins a point. Children must be cautioned to use care when passing through the opposite group. They should be spaced well along each line; this allows room for them to move through each group. The locomotor movements should be varied. The teacher may say, "Ready—walk!" Skipping, hopping, long steps, sliding, and other forms of locomotion can be specified. The position to be assumed at the finish can be varied also.
Teaching suggestion: Because success depends on getting across first, the teacher should watch for shortcutting of the rules and talk this problem over with the children.
Variation: The competition can be by squads, with two squads on each line.

Bottle Bat Ball — *DPE,* p. 558
Supplies: A plastic bottle bat, whiffle ball, batting tee (optional), home plate, base marker
Skills: Batting, retrieving balls
A home plate is needed, and a batting tee can be used. Foul lines should be marked wide enough so as not to be restrictive.
The batter gets three pitches (or swings) to hit a fair ball, or she is out. The pitches are easy (as in slow-pitch softball), so that the batter has a good chance to hit the ball. The batter hits the ball and runs around the base marker and back to home. If the ball is returned to the pitcher's mound before the batter reaches home, she is out. (A marker should designate the pitcher's mound.) Otherwise, the batter has a home run and bats again. One fielder other than the pitcher is needed, but another can be used. The running distance to first base is critical. It can remain fixed or can be made progressively (one step) longer, until it reaches such a point that the fielders are heavily favored.
Teaching suggestion: The game should make use of a plastic bottle bat and fun (whiffle) ball. A rotation system should be established when an out is made.
Variation: A batting tee can be used.

DYNAMIC PHYSICAL EDUCATION LESSON PLAN
Jogging Skills
Level I

Supplies and Equipment Needed:
  One parachute

MOVEMENT EXPERIENCE— CONTENT	ORGANIZATION AND TEACHING HINTS	EXPECTED STUDENT OBJECTIVES AND OUTCOMES

INTRODUCTORY ACTIVITY (2 – 3 MINUTES)

Simple Games

Use a game that requires little teaching and much gross motor activity. The following might be good selections:
  1. Back to Back, p. 556
  2. Twins, p. 569
  3. Jack Frost & Jane Thaw, p. 563
  4. Change Sides, p. 559
  5. Freeze, p. 562

Tag games require only a light tag, not a push or shove.

Emphasize the importance of admitting when you were tagged and thus the need for sportsmanship.

PM.—The student will be able to evade the tagger through effective use of dodging.

Aff.—All games that are competitive demand cooperation as well. Discuss the value of sportsmanship as well as self-officiating.

FITNESS DEVELOPMENT ACTIVITIES (7 – 8 MINUTES)

Parachute Fitness

Tape alternating segments of silence and music to signal duration of exercise. Music segments indicate aerobic activity with the parachute while intervals of silence announce using the chute to enhance flexibility and strength development.
  1. Jog while holding the chute in the left hand - 20 seconds.
  2. Shake the chute.
  3. Slide while holding the chute with both hands - 20 seconds.
  4. Sit and perform curl-ups - 30 seconds.
  5. Skip for 20 seconds.
  6. Freeze, face the center, and stretch the chute tightly. Hold for 8–12 seconds. Repeat five to six times.
  7. Run in place while holding the chute taut at different levels.
  8. Sit with legs under the chute. Do a seat walk toward the center. Return to the perimeter. Repeat four to six times.
  9. Move into push-up position holding the chute with one hand. Shake the chute.
  10. Place the chute on the ground. Jog away from the chute and return on signal. Repeat for 30 seconds.
  11. Shake the chute and jump in place.
  12. Lie on back with feet under the chute. Shake the chute with the feet.
  13. Hop to the center of the chute and return. Repeat for 20 seconds.

DPE p. 285

Evenly space youngsters around the chute.

Use different grips to add variation to the activities.

Develop group morale by encouraging students to move together.

Use music to motivate youngsters.

To cool down, allow youngsters a minute to perform parachute stunts like the Dome or Mushroom.

Cog.—Muscles grow when exercised regularly. To support the stronger muscles, larger bones are developed.

PM.—The student will be able to perform the parachute exercises using three different grips.

MOVEMENT EXPERIENCE—CONTENT	ORGANIZATION AND TEACHING HINTS	EXPECTED STUDENT OBJECTIVES AND OUTCOMES

14. Sit with feet under the chute. Stretch by touching the toes with the chute. Relax with other stretches while sitting.

LESSON FOCUS (15 – 20 MINUTES)

Walking and Jogging

The walking and jogging lesson should be a relaxed lesson with emphasis on developing activity patterns that can be used outside of the school environment. An educational approach to this lesson can teach students that walking and jogging is done without equipment and offers excellent health benefits. It is an activity that can literally be done for a lifetime. The following are suggestions for implementing this unit of instruction:

1. Youngsters should be allowed to find a friend with whom they want to jog or walk. The result is usually a friend of similar ability level. A way to judge correct pace is to be able to talk with a friend without undue stress. If students are too winded to talk, they are probably running too fast. A selected friend will encourage talking and help assure that the experience is positive and within the student's aerobic capacity. *Pace, not race* is the motto.
2. Jogging and walking should be done in any direction so people are unable to keep track of the distance covered. Doing laps on a track is one of the surest ways to discourage less able youngsters. They always finish last and are open to chiding by the rest of the class.
3. Jogging and walking should be done for a specified time rather than a specified distance. All youngsters should not have to run the same distance. This goes against the philosophy of accompanying individual differences and varying aerobic capacities. Running or walking for a set amount of time will allow the less able child to move without fear of ridicule.

DPE pp. 309 – 310

Teach the children the proper style of running.

Start students at a short distance so they will not become discouraged.

Concentrate on teaching the values of jogging and encouraging students to start their own jogging program.

A good motivating technique is to jog across the state or United States. The distance each student runs could be added together for a class total. This total is then the distance the class has progressed across the country.

Praise students running with pace, not the first few people coming back from their run, if you are working on pace.

Bring in a high school track or cross-country runner to talk about their running.

"Train, don't strain."

"Pace, not race."

PM.—The student will be able to demonstrate proper jogging style.

PM.—The student will be able to jog 220 yards nonstop.

Aff.—Jogging is one of the best activities for developing cardiovascular endurance. Discuss the value of jogging for personal health.

Cog.—The student will be able to list three chronic effects jogging has on the body.

Cog.—Fast walking is less efficient than a slow jog due to internal resistance created by the body. Discuss the importance of jogging rather than walking at a pace that is comfortable. (Be able to talk with a friend while jogging.)

Cog.—Jogging strengthens the back, in relation to the abdominal muscles. Discuss the importance of choosing exercises to strengthen the abdominal muscles and stretch the back muscles.

MOVEMENT EXPERIENCE— CONTENT	ORGANIZATION AND TEACHING HINTS	EXPECTED STUDENT OBJECTIVES AND OUTCOMES

4. Teachers should not be concerned about foot action, since the child selects naturally the means that is most comfortable. Arm movement should be easy and natural, with elbows bent. The head and upper body should be held up and back. The eyes look ahead. The general body position in walking and jogging should be erect but relaxed. Jogging on the toes should be avoided.

5. Jogging and walking should not be a competitive, timed activity. Each youngster should move at a self-determined pace. Racing belongs in the track program. Another reason to avoid speed is that racing keeps youngsters from learning to pace themselves. For developing endurance and gaining health benefits, it is more important to move for a longer time at a slower speed than to run at top speed for a shorter distance.

6. It can be motivating for youngsters if they run with a piece of equipment, i.e., beanbag or jump rope. They can play catch with a beanbag or roll a hoop while walking or jogging.

GAME (5 – 7 MINUTES)

Low Organization Games

When the jogging activity is finished, students may be somewhat fatigued. Play games that do not place high demand on the cardiovascular system.

DYNAMIC PHYSICAL EDUCATION LESSON PLAN
Throwing Skills (Lesson 2)
Level I

Supplies and Equipment Needed:
  Tumbling mats for targets
  Tires, hoops, or jump ropes
  Cones
  Tennis balls, rag balls, fleece balls, beanbags
  Tape player
  Music

MOVEMENT EXPERIENCE—CONTENT	ORGANIZATION AND TEACHING HINTS	EXPECTED STUDENT OBJECTIVES AND OUTCOMES

INTRODUCTORY ACTIVITY (2 – 3 MINUTES)

Hoop Activities

Each child is given a hoop. For a short time, the children may work with the hoops as they wish. On the first signal, drop the hoops and move in and out of as many hoops as possible; on the second signal, pick up a hoop and resume exploration.

DPE p. 256

Scatter formation.

Encourage using the hoops as jump ropes or to hula-hoop.

Use different locomotor movements to move in and out of the hoops.

PM.—The student will be able to change quickly from one movement to the next.

Cog.—When a person exercises, breathing becomes deeper and more frequent. Discuss the reason that working muscles need more oxygen.

FITNESS DEVELOPMENT ACTIVITIES (7 – 8 MINUTES)

Circuit Training

Tape alternating segments of silence and music to signal duration of exercise. Music segments (begin at 30 seconds) indicate activity at each station while intervals of silence (10 seconds) announce it is time to stop and move forward to the next station.
  1. Tortoise and Hare
  2. Curl-up variations
  3. Hula Hooping on arms
  4. Jumping boxes—step on and off continuously
  5. Agility run—run back and forth between two designated lines
  6. Bench Pulls—pull body along bench
  7. Crab Walk
  8. Bend and Twist

DPE pp. 300 – 303

Establish "starting stations" and maintain them throughout the unit.

Use signals such as "start," "stop," and "move up" to ensure quick and effective movement from station to station. An effective method is to use timed music segments recorded on tape. Children exercise when the music plays and move to the next station when it stops.

Cog.—The student will be able to explain why circuit training should work all parts of the body, but no two similar parts in succession.

Cog.—The student will be able to explain how overload is achieved by increasing the length of activity at each station and decreasing the rest between stations.

Cog.—In order that circuit training be effective, *quality* exercise must be performed at each station. The student will be able to verbalize this concept.

LESSON FOCUS (15 – 20 MINUTES)

Throwing Skills (2)
Mimetics

  1. The teacher should cue students and model a good throw.
    a. Teacher should use terms such as "wind-up," "turn your non-throwing side to the target," "step toward the target, follow through."

DPE pp. 349 – 351

These should be done for 1–2 minutes.

The teacher should encourage and praise good *form*.

The teacher should talk about what the components of a good throw are and how to produce force.

Cog.—Students will know what a mature throw looks like.

Cog.—Students will know the components of a mature throw.

Cog.—Students should begin to realize what parts of the throw result in the greatest force production.

MOVEMENT EXPERIENCE—CONTENT	ORGANIZATION AND TEACHING HINTS	EXPECTED STUDENT OBJECTIVES AND OUTCOMES
b. Teacher can also use this time to observe and coach. c. *Encourage* children to throw *hard*. d. Modeling of good throws by the teacher should be a major objective for this exercise.	The cue of "turn, step, throw" may be useful. The children should be generating maximum force.	Aff.—Students will begin to value throwing hard. PM.—The students should begin every throw from a side facing position. PM.—The student should take a big step with the contralateral foot.

Station Format
1. Activities emphasizing form.
  a. Mats 5–6" thick
  The student stands on the edge of the mat and steps to the floor with their contralateral foot as they throw toward the wall. (The other foot remains on the mat.)
  b. Both feet in hoop.
  The student begins in side-facing position to the target, with both feet inside the hoop they then step outside of the hoop with the contralateral foot and throw to the wall.
  c. Cone behind the student.
  The student must touch the cone with the throwing hand on the back-swing, them throw to the wall.
	All students should do these activities a minimum of two days.
	
	All throws are made to the wall and with force.
	
	This activity forces the student to take a long stride toward the target.
	
	If tires or hoops are not available, use jump ropes. The circle should be large enough to encourage the student to take a long stride.
	
	This activity should encourage the student to rotate and take a wind-up before throwing.
	
	The cone should be directly behind the student and about an arm's length distance.
		Aff.—The student should understand that a lot of practice is necessary to master the skill of throwing.
		
		PM.—The student should begin to take a long stride with the throw.
		
		Cog.—The student should understand that a longer stride helps increase force production.

Using large targets to allow forceful throwing:
 	
1. Throw at mats on the wall.
  a. Throw tennis or rag balls hard from 15–20 ft.
  b. Retrieve only if the balls roll behind the throwing line.
2. Mats laid over tables.
  a. If tables are on rollers, see if forceful throws can move the table.
3. Throw at hoops leaning against mats against the wall.
4. Large target throw.
  a. A circle or square 4 ft. in diameter should be placed on the wall.
  b. Students should throw from 20–25 ft.
	Each student should start with five balls.
	
	The teacher should continue to give feedback to the students that will help them improve their form.
	
	The mats should be placed on the table so they hang to the floor.
	
	Put hoops touching one another for easier targets; spread apart for more difficult target.
	
	Another excellent large target is a 4- ft. cage ball.	

GAME (5 – 7 MINUTES)

Animal Tag — *DPE,* p. 556
  Supplies: None
  Skills: Imagery, running, dodging
  Two parallel lines are drawn about 40 ft apart. Children are divided into two groups, each of which takes a position on one of the lines. Children in one group get together with their leader and decide what animal they wish to imitate. Having selected the animal, they move over to within 5 ft or so of the other line. There they imitate the animal, and the other group tries to guess the animal correctly. If the guess is correct, they chase the first group back to its line, trying to tag as many as possible. Those caught must go over to the other team. The second group then selects an animal, and the roles are reversed. If the guessing team cannot guess the animal, however, the performing team gets another try. To avoid confusion, children must raise their hands to take turns at naming the animal. Otherwise, many false chases will occur. If children have trouble guessing, the leader of the performing team can give the initial of the animal.

MOVEMENT EXPERIENCE— CONTENT	ORGANIZATION AND TEACHING HINTS	EXPECTED STUDENT OBJECTIVES AND OUTCOMES

Forest Ranger — *DPE,* p. 562

Supplies: None

Skill: Running

Half of the children form a circle and face the center. These are the trees. The other half of the children are forest rangers and stand behind the trees. An extra child, the forest lookout, is in the center. The forest lookout starts the game by calling, "Fire in the forest. Run, run, run!" Immediately, the forest rangers run around the outside of the circle to the right. After a few moments, the lookout steps in front of one of the trees. This is the signal for each of the rangers to step in front of a tree. One player is left out, and she becomes the new forest lookout. The trees become rangers and the rangers become trees. Each time the game is played, the circle must be moved out somewhat, because the formation narrows when the rangers step in front of the trees.

DYNAMIC PHYSICAL EDUCATION LESSON PLAN
Educational Movement (Lesson 9)
Level I

Fundamental Skill: Bending and Stretching
Educational Movement Themes: Receiving and transferring weight, partner matching movements,
  partner obstacle movements
Manipulative Activity: Parachute

Supplies and Equipment Needed:
  Jumping boxes or benches
  Parachute
  Cones

MOVEMENT EXPERIENCE— CONTENT	ORGANIZATION AND TEACHING HINTS	EXPECTED STUDENT OBJECTIVES AND OUTCOMES

INTRODUCTORY ACTIVITY (2 – 3 MINUTES)

Bridges by Three

Children work in groups of three, with two of the children making bridges and the third moving under them. As soon as the third person has moved under the other two, she moves forward 5 to 7 steps and makes a bridge. Each child in turn moves under the bridges of the other two students.

DPE p. 258

Groups of three.

Different challenges can be tried by specifying different types of bridges or having the moving child perform different movements and tasks.

To increase challenges, increase distance between bridging youngsters.

PM.—The student will be able to make at least five different bridges.

Cog.—The student will identify the isometric exercises (bridging) as well as the isotonic exercises (moving).

FITNESS DEVELOPMENT ACTIVITY (7 – 8 MINUTES)

Four-Corners Movement

Outline a large rectangle with four cones. Place signs with pictures on both sides of the cones. Youngsters move around the outside of the rectangle and change movements as they pass a corner sign. The following movement activities are suggested:
1. Jogging
2. Skipping/Jumping/Hopping
3. Sliding/Galloping
4. Various animal movements
5. Sport imitation movements
6. Bench pulls
7. Bench crouch jumps

Stop the class after 30–45 seconds of movement and perform fitness challenges. Tape alternating segments of silence and music to signal duration of exercise. Music segments indicate aerobic activity while intervals of silence announce flexibility and strength development activities.

DPE p. 287

If signs are not placed at the corners, teachers can specify movements for students to perform.

Increase the demand of the routine by increasing the size of the rectangle.

Faster-moving students can pass on the outside (away from the center) of the rectangle.

Assure that abdominal and shoulder girdle strength development activities are included.

PM.—The student will be able to perform the grass drills and challenge activities.

Cog.—Sweating occurs when the body is overheated due to stress in an attempt to maintain a constant body temperature. The student will be able to explain why the body sweats.

MOVEMENT EXPERIENCE—CONTENT	ORGANIZATION AND TEACHING HINTS	EXPECTED STUDENT OBJECTIVES AND OUTCOMES

Movement Skills and Concepts (9)

Select a few activities from each of the categories so students receive a variety of skills to practice. When possible, integrate the manipulative skill activities with fundamental skill activities.

Fundamental Skill: Bending

1. Can you bend forward and up?
2. Show how far you can bend backward. Can you see behind you on your backward bend?
3. Combine a forward bend with a backward bend.
4. Bend right and left. Try with your hands out to the sides. Overhead.
5. Explore different ways the body can bend in a standing position.
6. Sit down. How does this affect the bending possibilities of the body? Can you bend forward so your chin touches the floor?
7. How many body parts (joints) can you bend below the waist? Above the waist?
8. Who can lie down and bend two, three, four, five, six parts?
9. Pick two similar parts. Bend one while unbending the other.
10. Pick two body parts (joints). Beginning at the same time, bend one quickly and one slowly. Bend one smoothly and one with jerks.
11. Make a familiar shape by bending two body parts.
12. Think of a toy that bends, and you bend the same way.
13. Working with a partner, do matching bending movements. Try having one partner make big bends while the other makes small bends at corresponding joints.
14. Show how you can bend to look funny, happy, sad, slow, and quick.

DPE pp. 342 – 343

Cues:
"Bend as far as possible."
"Bend one part while holding other fixed."

Repeat movements several times.

Learn names of body joints that bend.

In straightening (unbending), straighten completely.

Begin with two parts.

Matching movements can begin with one joint and then add multiple movements.

Seek other terms.

Cog.—The student will learn what bending means and what parts of the body do this.

PM.—The student will be able to bend joints independently of others as specified.

Cog.—There are many ways to evaluate performance and improvement. For example, accuracy, distance, speed, and time are commonly used. Students should begin to learn different ways to measure their performance.

Aff.—Competency in physical skill increases a youngster's desire to participate. Discuss the importance of practicing skills that are difficult to master in order to increase the range of activities one is willing to participate in regularly.

PM.—The student will be able to match single and double bending movements with a partner.

Fundamental Skill: Stretching

1. Stretch as many body parts as you can.
2. Stretch your arms, legs and feet in as many ways as possible.
3. At the same time stretch your feet in one direction and your arms in another.
4. Stretch one body part quickly, slowly, smoothly. Try another. Repeat.
5. Bend a body part and tell me which muscles or muscle groups are being stretched.
6. How many ways can you stretch while sitting on the floor?

DPE pp. 346 – 347

Cues:
"Stretch as far as you can."
"Make it hurt a little."
"Keep it smooth, don't jerk."
"Involve as many parts (joints) as you can."

Much emphasis on exploratory movement.

Look to stimulate wide application to many body parts.

Stress smoothness.

Stress the fun aspect, as this needs spicing up.

PM.—The student will be able to stretch many parts of the body to full range.

Cog.—The student will understand the meaning of the word "stretch" and be able to apply this to her movement vocabulary.

Aff.—The student will apply herself fully to the movement challenges. Discuss the importance of effort and intensity when performing motor tasks. Use the illustration of outstanding athletes practicing with intensity so they will be able to perform well in games.

MOVEMENT EXPERIENCE—CONTENT	ORGANIZATION AND TEACHING HINTS	EXPECTED STUDENT OBJECTIVES AND OUTCOMES
7. Lie on the floor (prone or supine) and stretch two parts at once. Add others up to five.	Repeat movements several times for S-R bonds. Keep this nontechnical.	Cog.—Stretching to increase the range of motion at a joint should be done slowly and under control. Stretches should be held for 15–30 seconds. Encourage smooth sustained movements in stretching activities.
8. From any position you like, see if you can at the same time stretch one part quickly (but smoothly) and one part slowly. Try one part quickly and two parts slowly.		
9. From a kneeling position, set a mark on the floor where you can reach (stretch) without losing balance. Increase the distance.	Use a spot, line, or beanbag.	Aff.—Nonsmokers who are in residence with smokers suffer many of the same effects. For example, a nonsmoker inhales 11 cigarettes when living with a person who smokes a pack a day. Discuss the effects of smoking on wellness.
10. Stretch your one arm while your other curls (bends). Reverse.		
11. Find a partner and show how many different ways you can help each other stretch.		
12. Can you stretch as tall as a giraffe? As wide as an elephant? As long as a snake?	Add other animals. Show that some body parts are more difficult to stretch than others.	
13. Stretch and make a wide bridge. Have a partner go under, around and over the bridge.		
14. Try bending forward slowly and touch your toes.		
15. Can you stretch the muscles in your chest, back, ankles, wrist, and fingers? Is this easy?	Use small–tall, wide–thin, stretched–curled. Make up other verses.	
Manipulative Skill: Parachute Activities	*DPE* pp. 477 – 482	
Use locomotor activities with the parachute as the prior activities (bending and stretching) are non-moving activities.	Make this mostly locomotor movements. The drum beat can direct the movements.	
1. Shake the Rug		
2. Making Waves.		
3. Walk, run, skip, slide, hop, jump CW or CCW as the parachute rotates.		
Movement Concept: Receiving and Transferring Weight	*DPE* pp. 325 – 326	Cog.—The student will learn correct landing techniques.
1. Project yourself high into the air and land. Try to land now with as little noise as possible.	Cues: "Be relaxed." "Keep knees slightly bent on landing." "Provide 'give' on landing." No noise means soft landing.	PM.—The student will be able to control his landing from a jump into the air to a jump from a height of 24 to 30 in.
2. Practice projecting yourself into the air and landing in different fashions.		
3. Experiment with different landings where one or both hands touch the floor at the completion of the landing.	Crouching helps take the landing shock.	Cog.—To absorb force from a jump upon landing, as many joints as possible should be flexed. Discuss the importance of "giving" with the knees, hips, and ankles in order to land softly.
4. Experiment with turns as you land.		
5. Begin your movement through the air with a short run and practice landings.		
6. Jumping boxes and inclined benches can project you higher. Practice some types of landings. Begin low and increase the height.	Use whatever you have—chairs, tables, benches (inclined)—to provide height for jumping and landing. Landing over benches; through hoops.	
7. Swinging and landing from climbing ropes also can be a part.	Weight transfer to be made smoothly.	

MOVEMENT EXPERIENCE— CONTENT	ORGANIZATION AND TEACHING HINTS	EXPECTED STUDENT OBJECTIVES AND OUTCOMES

8. Take a position with the body balanced on two different parts. Transfer the weight to another two parts. Go from three to three.

9. Transfer the weight from a rounded part of the body to the hands and/or the feet. Go back to the rounded part.

10. Jump and land under control. Transfer the weight to another two body parts.

11. Explore different combinations of transferring the weight from various parts to others.

Movement Concept: Partner Obstacle Movements

With one partner acting as an obstacle, the other partner goes over, under and around the partner posing as the obstacle. Explore different ways this can be accomplished.

DPE pp. 321 – 322

Exploratory emphasis.

Show-and-tell demonstration.

GAME (5 – 7 MINUTES)

Marching Ponies — *DPE,* p. 563
  Supplies: None
  Skills: Marching, running
  One child, the ringmaster, crouches in the center of a circle of ponies formed by the other children. Two goal lines on opposite sides of the circle are established as safe areas. The ponies march around the circle in step, counting as they do so. At a predetermined number (whispered to the ringmaster by the teacher), the ringmaster jumps up and attempts to tag the others before they can reach the safety lines. Anyone tagged joins the ringmaster in the center and helps catch the other children the next time. The game should be reorganized after six to eight children have been caught. Those left in the circle are declared the winners.
  Variation: Other characterizations, such as lumbering elephants, jumping kangaroos, and the like, can be tried. A child who suggests a unique movement could be allowed to be the ringmaster.

Cat and Mice — *DPE,* p. 559
  Supplies: None
  Skills: Running, dodging
  Children form a large circle. One child is the cat and four others are the mice. The cat and mice cannot leave the circle. On signal, the cat chases the mice inside the circle. As they are caught, the mice join the circle. The last mouse caught becomes the cat for the next round.
  Teaching suggestions: The teacher should start at one point in the circle and go around the circle selecting mice so that each child gets a chance to be in the center.
  Sometimes, one child has difficulty catching the last mouse or any of the mice. If this is the case, children forming the circle can take a step toward the center, thus constricting the running area. The teacher should cut off any prolonged chase sequence.

DYNAMIC PHYSICAL EDUCATION LESSON PLAN
Fundamental Skills Using Parachute Activity
Level I

Supplies and Equipment Needed:
Six jump ropes
Beanbags or playground balls, one for each child
Parachute
Six to ten beanbags
Two basketballs or cageballs
Tom-tom

MOVEMENT EXPERIENCE—CONTENT	ORGANIZATION AND TEACHING HINTS	EXPECTED STUDENT OBJECTIVES AND OUTCOMES

INTRODUCTORY ACTIVITY (2 – 3 MINUTES)

European Running with Equipment

Review European running and emphasize the following points:
1. Move to the rhythm
2. Lift the knees and trot
3. Maintain proper spacing between each other

After the review, give each child a beanbag or playground ball. Every fourth step, toss the beanbag upward or bounce the ball.

DPE p. 252

Since the parachute will be used in the Lesson Focus, it might be enjoyable to do European Running while holding the chute.

Encourage the students to try different challenges with their beanbag or ball.

PM.—The student will be able to toss the beanbag into the air and catch it while doing European Running.

PM.—The student will be able to create three activities with the beanbag or ball while doing European Running.

FITNESS DEVELOPMENT ACTIVITIES (7 – 8 MINUTES)

Walk, Trot, and Sprint

Move to the following signals:
1. One drumbeat - walk.
2. Two drumbeats - trot.
3. Three drumbeats - sprint.
4. Whistle - freeze and perform exercises.

Perform various strength and flexibility exercises between bouts of walk, trot, and sprint. Examples are:
1. Bend and Twist
2. Sitting Stretch
3. Push-up variations
4. Abdominal challenges
5. Body Twist
6. Standing Hip Bend

DPE pp. 285 – 286

Use a tom-tom or tambourine.

Scatter formation.

Emphasize quality of movement and rapid changes.

Check heart rate after bouts of sprinting.

Altentate bouts of movement with strength and flexibility exercises.

PM.—The student will be able to perform the activity at an increased pace.

Cog.—One measure often used to measure fitness is to count the pulse rate after exercise within 2 or 3 minutes. It might be interesting to measure pulse rate at various intervals after exercise. The more fit one is, the faster pulse rate returns to normal.

Cog.—A well-balanced diet provides fuel for physical activity. Discuss the basics of a good diet and the need for such.

LESSON FOCUS (15 – 20 MINUTES)

Fundamental Skills Using Parachute Activity

1. Circular movements.
   Move utilizing locomotor movements and holding the chute at various levels—walk, run, hop, jump, skip, slide, draw steps.

DPE pp. 477 – 482

Teach the proper terminology so students can identify the various activities.

Perform the activities with different grips.

Cog.—The student will be able to identify the various parachute activities by name.

MOVEMENT EXPERIENCE— CONTENT	ORGANIZATION AND TEACHING HINTS	EXPECTED STUDENT OBJECTIVES AND OUTCOMES

MOVEMENT EXPERIENCE—CONTENT

2. Shaking the Rug and Making Waves.
   Shaking the Rug should involve small, rapid movements, whereas Making Waves is large movements.
3. Making a Dome.
   Parachute should be on the floor and held with both hands. Make a dome by standing up and rapidly lifting the chute overhead.
4. Mushroom.
   Similar to the Dome except three or four steps toward the center are taken by each student.
   a. Mushroom Release—all students release the chute at its peak of inflation.
   b. Mushroom Run—Make a mushroom, students move toward center; a few selected students release grip, and run around the inside of the chute back to place.
5. Activities with Balls and Beanbags.
   a. Ball Circle—Use a basketball or cageball and make it circle around the outside of the chute. Add a second ball.
   b. Popcorn—Place six to ten whiffle balls on the chute and shake them into the air.
   c. Giant Popcorn—Use beachballs instead of whiffle balls.
   d. Poison Snake—Place six to ten jump ropes on the chute. Divide the players in half. Try to shake the ropes so they touch a player on the opposing team.
   e. Cannonball—Use a 24" cageball on the chute. On the command "load," place the chute on the floor. On "fire," life the chute and fire the cageball into the air.
6. Kite Run.
   Half the class holds the chute on one side. They run in any direction together and as fast as possible. The parachute should trail like a kite.
7. Tug-of-War.
   Divide the class into two equal halves. On signal, they pull and try to move each other.
8. Hole in One.
   Use six or eight small balls of two different colors. The objects is to get the other team's balls to fall through the hole in the center.
9. Ocean Walk.
   The class is on their knees, making waves with the chute. Three or four youngsters are selected to walk or jog "in the ocean" without falling.

ORGANIZATION AND TEACHING HINTS

Various patterns can be made by having the class work in small groups around the chute.

Try making a dome while moving in a circle.

Teach the proper technique of standing and lifting the parachute to avoid back strain.

Work for precision so that all students are together in their movement.

Proper care of the chutes should be taught so that they are not ripped.

Many routines to music can be developed and incorporated with the various chute activities. Many singing games can be done utilizing parachute activities, which increases motivation for students.

Teach students to place the chute in "home" position (on the floor) during instruction.

EXPECTED STUDENT OBJECTIVES AND OUTCOMES

Aff.—The parachute requires group cooperation for successful implementation of the activities. Discuss the importance of working together to improve everybody's welfare.

PM.—The student will be able to cooperatively perform the following activities:
1. Making Waves
2. Making a Dome
3. Popcorn
4. Ball Circles

Cog.—Air resistance has an effect on athletic performances. When using the parachute, the effect of air resistance is obvious. Discuss the difference between a slow parachute movement and a fast one. Which is more difficult? Why?

Cog.—Stability is increased by lowering the center of gravity and widening the base of support in the direction of the force. Discuss how youngsters automatically do this in the Tug-of-War activity.

MOVEMENT EXPERIENCE—CONTENT	ORGANIZATION AND TEACHING HINTS	EXPECTED STUDENT OBJECTIVES AND OUTCOMES

GAME (5 – 7 MINUTES)

May I Chase You? — *DPE,* p. 563

Supplies: None

Skills: Running, dodging

The class stands behind a line long enough to accommodate all. The runner stands about 5 ft in front of the line. One child in the line asks, "May I chase you?" The runner replies, "Yes, if you are wearing," naming a color, an article of clothing, or a combination of the two. All who qualify immediately chase the runner until she is tagged. The tagger becomes the new runner. Children can think of other ways to identify those who may run.

Tommy Tucker's Land — *DPE,* p. 569

Supplies: About ten beanbags for each game

Skills: Dodging, running

One child, Tommy Tucker (or Tammi Tucker, if a girl), stands in the center of a 15-ft square, within which the beanbags are scattered. Tommy is guarding his land and the treasure. The other children chant,

I'm on Tommy Tucker's land,

Picking up gold and silver.

Children attempt to pick up as much of the treasure as they can while avoiding being tagged by Tommy. Any child who is tagged must return the treasure and retire from the game. The game is over when only one child is left or when all of the beanbags have been successfully filched. The teacher may wish to call a halt to the game earlier if a stalemate is reached. In this case, the child with the most treasure becomes the new Tommy.

Variation: This game can be played with a restraining line instead of a square, but there must be boundaries that limit movement.

Colors — *DPE,* p. 561

Supplies: Colored paper (construction paper) cut in circles, squares, or triangles for markers

Skills: Color or other perceptual concepts, running

Five or six different-colored markers should be used, with a number of children having the same color. Children are standing or seated in a circle with a marker in front of each child. The teacher calls out a color, and everyone having that color runs counterclockwise around the circle and back to place. The first one seated upright and motionless is declared the winner. Different kinds of locomotor movement can be specified, such as skipping, galloping, walking, and so on. After a period of play, the children leave the markers on the floor and move one place to the left.

Variation: Shapes (e.g., circles, triangles, squares, rectangles, stars, and diamonds) can be used instead of colors, as can numbers or other articles or categories, such as animals, birds, or fish. This game has value in teaching identification and recognition.

DYNAMIC PHYSICAL EDUCATION LESSON PLAN
Rhythmic Movement (Lesson 3)
Level I

Supplies and Equipment Needed:
  One playground ball per student
  Parachute
  Appropriate music for dances
  Tape player

Dances Taught:
  Muffin Man
  Danish Dance of Greeting
  Seven Jumps
  Yankee Doodle
  Eins Zwie Drei
  Bleking
  Pease Porridge Hot
  Nixie Polka
  Chimes of Dunkirk

MOVEMENT EXPERIENCE—CONTENT	ORGANIZATION AND TEACHING HINTS	EXPECTED STUDENT OBJECTIVES AND OUTCOMES

INTRODUCTORY ACTIVITY (2 – 3 MINUTES)

Ball Activities

Children dribble their ball around the area. On signal:
  1. Stop and pivot.
  2. Balance on different body parts.
  3. Handle the ball—around back, over head, under leg, etc.

DPE p. 256

Dribble both as a basketball and soccer player.

Dribble under control—slowly without running into other students.

Encourage variety.

PM.—The student will be able to dribble the ball for 10 seconds without losing control.

Cog.—The student will be able to describe the relationships between the height and speed of the dribble.

FITNESS DEVELOPMENT ACTIVITIES (7 – 8 MINUTES)

Parachute Fitness

Tape alternating segments of silence and music to signal duration of exercise. Music segments indicate aerobic activity with the parachute while intervals of silence announce using the chute to enhance flexibility and strength development.
  1. Jog while holding the chute in the left hand - 20 seconds.
  2. Shake the chute.
  3. Slide while holding the chute with both hands - 20 seconds.
  4. Sit and perform curl-ups - 30 seconds.
  5. Skip for 20 seconds.
  6. Freeze, face the center, and stretch the chute tightly. Hold for 8–12 seconds. Repeat five to six times.
  7. Run in place while holding the chute taut at different levels.
  8. Sit with legs under the chute. Do a seat walk toward the center. Return to the perimeter. Repeat four to six times.
  9. Place the chute on the ground. Jog away from the chute and return on signal. Repeat for 30 seconds.
  10. Shake the chute and jump in place.
  11. Lie on back with feet under the chute. Shake the chute with the feet.

DPE, p. 285

Evenly space youngsters around the chute.

Use different grips to add variation to the activities.

Develop group morale by encouraging students to move together.

To cool down, allow youngsters a minute to perform parachute stunts like the Dome or Mushroom.

Cog.—Muscles grow when exercised regularly. To support the stronger muscles, larger bones are developed.

PM.—The student will be able to perform the parachute exercises using three different grips.

111

MOVEMENT EXPERIENCE— CONTENT	ORGANIZATION AND TEACHING HINTS	EXPECTED STUDENT OBJECTIVES AND OUTCOMES

12. Hop to the center of the chute and return. Repeat for 20 seconds.
13. Sit with feet under the chute. Stretch by touching the toes with the chute. Relax with other stretches while sitting.

LESSON FOCUS (15 – 20 MINUTES)

Rhythmic Movement (3)

1. Muffin Man (*DPE*, pp. 369)
2. Danish Dance of Greeting (*DPE*, p. 370)
3. Seven Jumps (*DPE*, pp. 371)
4. Pease Porridge Hot (*DPE* pp. 373)
5. Yankee Doodle (*DPE*, p. 374)
6. Eins Zwie Drei (*DPE*, pp. 374)
7. Chimes of Dunkirk, Var. 2 (*DPE*, p. 375)
8. Bleking (*DPE*, p. 376)
9. Nixie Polka (*DPE*, p. 377)

When teaching a dance, use the following steps:
1. Tell about the dance and listen to the music.
2. Clap the beat and learn the verse.
3. Practice the dance steps without the music and with verbal cues.
4. Practice the dance with the music.

Make dances easy for students to learn by using some of the following ideas:
1. Teach the dances without partners.
2. Allow youngsters to move in any direction—avoid the left–right orientation.
3. Use scattered formation instead of circles—it helps avoid embarassment.
4. Emphasize strong movements such as clapping and stomping to encourage involvement.
5. Tape the music at a slower speed when first learning the dance.

Rhythms should be taught like other sport skills. Avoid expecting perfection when teaching rhythms. Teach a variety of dances rather than one or two in depth. Youngsters will enjoy rhythms if they know it is acceptable to make mistakes without being ridiculed.

Cog.—The student will be able to sing the verses of the singing games.

Aff.—Rhythmic activities are a learned skill. Performers need to practice them many times before they are mastered. Discuss the need for understanding individual differences in rates of learning.

GAME (5 – 7 MINUTES)

Circle Stoop — *DPE,* p. 560
   Supplies: Music or tom-tom
   Skills: Moving to rhythm
   Children are in a single circle, facing counterclockwise. A march or similar music, or a tom-tom beat, can be used. The children march with good posture until the music stops. As soon as a child no longer hears the music or the tom-tom beat, he stoops and touches both hands to the ground without losing his balance. The last child to touch both hands to the ground and those children who lost balance pay a penalty by going into the mush pot (the center of the circle) and waiting out the next round of the game. The children must march in good posture, and anyone stooping, even partially, before the music stops should be penalized. The duration of the music should be varied, and children should not be able to observe the stopping process if a record player is used.
   Variations:
   1. Using suitable music, have children employ different locomotor movements, such as skipping, hopping, or galloping.
   2. Vary the stooping position. Instead of stooping, use positions such as the Push-Up, Crab, or Lame Dog, or balancing on one foot or touching with one hand and one foot. Such variations add to the interest and fun.

MOVEMENT EXPERIENCE—CONTENT	ORGANIZATION AND TEACHING HINTS	EXPECTED STUDENT OBJECTIVES AND OUTCOMES

Blindfolded Duck — *DPE,* p. 558

Supplies: A wand, broomstick, cane, or yardstick

Skills: Fundamental locomotor movements

One child, designated the duck (Daisy if a girl, Donald if a boy), stands blindfolded in the center of a circle and holds a wand or similar article. She taps on the floor and tells children to hop (or perform some other locomotor movement). Children in the circle act accordingly, all moving in the same direction. Daisy then taps the wand twice on the floor, which signals all children to stop. Daisy moves forward with her wand, still blindfolded, to find a child in the circle. She asks, "Who are you?" The child responds, "Quack, quack." Daisy tries to identify this person. If the guess is correct, the identified child becomes the new duck. If the guess is wrong, Daisy must take another turn. After two unsuccessful turns, another child is chosen to be the duck.

DYNAMIC PHYSICAL EDUCATION LESSON PLAN
Educational Movement (Lesson 10)
Level I

Fundamental Movements: Twisting, turning, and rocking
Educational Movement Themes: Stretching and curling, contrasting movements, tension and relaxation
Manipulative Activities: Teacher's choice

Supplies and Equipment Needed:
  Tambourine, scoops and balls, or beanbags
  Tape player
  Music

MOVEMENT EXPERIENCE—CONTENT	ORGANIZATION AND TEACHING HINTS	EXPECTED STUDENT OBJECTIVES AND OUTCOMES

INTRODUCTORY ACTIVITY (2 – 3 MINUTES)

Creative and Exploratory Opportunities

1. Put out enough equipment for all children to have a piece. Allow them to explore and create activities while moving.
2. Work with a piece of equipment with a partner or small group.

DPE pp. 258 – 259

Use hoops, balls, or beanbags.

Use different locomotor movements.

Rotate on signal.

PM.—The student will be able to manipulate his or her piece of equipment while moving.

Aff.—Partner activity is more enjoyable for youngsters. Discuss the need for gracefully selecting a partner.

FITNESS DEVELOPMENT ACTIVITIES (7 – 8 MINUTES)

Animal Movements and Fitness Challenges

Tape alternating segments of silence and music to signal duration of exercise. Music segments indicate animal movements while intervals of silence announce flexibility and strength development activities.
  1. Puppy Dog Walk—30 seconds.
  2. Freeze; perform stretching activities.
  3. Measuring Worm Walk—30 seconds
  4. Freeze; perform abdominal development challenges.
  5. Seal Crawl—30 seconds.
  6. Frog Jump—30 seconds.
  7. Freeze; perform push-up position challenges.
  8. Elephant Walk—30 seconds.
  9. Bear Walk—30 seconds.
  10. Freeze; perform abdominal challenges.
  11. Crab Walk—30 seconds.
  12. Lame Dog Walk
A variation is to place animal movement signs throughout the area and instruct students to move from sign to sign performing the appropriate animal movement each time they reach a new sign.

DPE pp. 281 – 284

Emphasize placing the weight on the hands for shoulder girdle development.

Quality of movement should be emphasized rather than speed.

Vary the length of the intervals to match the fitness level of youngsters.

Cog.—The student will recognize the animal movements by name.

PM.—The student will be able to perform each of the animal movements over a distance of 25 feet.

MOVEMENT EXPERIENCE—CONTENT	ORGANIZATION AND TEACHING HINTS	EXPECTED STUDENT OBJECTIVES AND OUTCOMES

Movement Skills and Concepts (10)

Select a few activities from each of the categories so students receive a variety of skills to practice. When possible, integrate the manipulative skill activities with fundamental skill activities.

Fundamental Skill: Twisting

1. Glue your feet to the floor. Can you twist your body to the right and to the left? Can you twist slowly, quickly? Can you bend and twist at the same time? How far can you twist your hands back and forth?
2. Twist two parts of the body at the same time. Try three. More?
3. Can you twist one part of the body in one direction and another in a different direction?
4. Is it possible to twist the upper half of your body without twisting the lower part? How about the reverse?
5. Seated on the floor, what parts of the body can you twist?
6. Can you twist one part of the body around another? Why or why not?
7. Balance on one foot and twist your body. Can you bend and twist in this position?
8. Show different shapes that can be made using twisted body parts.
9. Can you twist like a spring?

DPE pp. 345 – 346

Cue by saying:
   "Twist far (fully)."
   "Hold supporting parts firm."
   "Twist the other way."

Seek full exploration.

PM.—The student will be able to isolate different parts of the body for twisting.

Cog.—Students will give meaning to the term to be added to their movement vocabularies.

Fundamental Skill: Turning

1. Turn your body left and right with quarter and half turns. Turn clockwise and counterclockwise.
2. Post compass directions on the walls—north, south, east, and west. Have children face the correct direction on call. Introduce some in-between directions—northwest, southeast, etc.
3. Can you stand on one foot and turn around slowly, quickly, with a series of small hops?
4. Show me how you can cross your legs with a turn and then sit down. Can you get up without moving your feet too much.
5. When you hear the signal, turn completely around one. Next time turn the other way. Now try with two full turns; three.
6. Lie on your tummy and turn yourself around in an arc. Try seated position.
7. Find a friend and see how many different ways one can turn the other.
8. Play follow-the-leader activities with your friend.

DPE p. 345

Cue by saying:
   "Keep your balance."
   "Turn smoothly."
   "Make turns definite— 1/4, 1/2, or full turns."

Turn right and left.

Expand these activities.

PM.—The student will be able to turn right and left on signal.

Cog.—The student will understand the differences between twisting and turning.

MOVEMENT EXPERIENCE—CONTENT	ORGANIZATION AND TEACHING HINTS	EXPECTED STUDENT OBJECTIVES AND OUTCOMES

Fundamental Skill: Rocking
 	
1. How many different ways can your rock? Which part of the body is used to rock the highest?
2. Select a part of the body and show me how you can rock smoothly and slowly. How about quickly and smoothly?
3. Can you rock like a rocking chair?
4. Lie on your back and rock. Point both hands and feet toward the ceiling and rock on the back.
5. Lie on your tummy and rock. Rock as high as you can. Can you hold your ankles and make giant rocks?
6. Can you rock in a standing position? Try forward, sideways and diagonal rocking directions.
7. Select a position where you can rock and twist at the same time.
8. Who can lie on his or her back, with knees up and rock side to side?
9. From a standing position, sway back and forth, right and left. Experiment with different foot positions. Sway slowly and as far as you can without losing your balance.
10. Repeat swaying movements from a kneeling position.
11. Show three different ways you can rock with a partner.
	DPE pp. 343 – 344
	
	Cue by saying:
	  "Rock smoothly."
	  "Rock higher (farther)."
	  "Rock in different directions."
	  "Use your arms (legs) to help you rock."
	
	Emphasize exploration.
	
	Arms and feet can aid the tummy rock.
	
	Swaying maintains a stable base.
		PM.—The student will be able to do rocking movements smoothly and rhythmically on several parts of the body.
		
		Cog.—The student will learn the ways to apply force with arms and legs to increase momentum in rocking.

Manipulative Skill: Teacher's Choice Select one or more manipulative activities that need additional developing with respect to the children's needs and progress. During the week's work, a different activity might be scheduled each individual day.	*DPE* pp. 407 – 441 Use balls, beanbags, jump ropes, scoops and balls, etc.	
Movement Concept: Stretching and Curling 1. While on your feet, show us a stretched position. A curled position. 2. Go very slowly from your stretched position to the curled one you select. Go rapidly. 3. Keeping one foot in place (on a spot), show how far you can stretch in different directions. 4. Show us a straight (regular) curled position. A twisted curled position. A tight curled position. 5. Select three different curled positions. On signal, go from one to the other rapidly. Repeat with stretch positions.	*DPE* p. 326 Emphasize personal space. Scatter formation.	Cog.—The meaning of "curled" and "stretched" will be clarified and reinforced through activity and discussion. PM.—The student will demonstrate the ability to make changes as defined.

MOVEMENT EXPERIENCE—CONTENT	ORGANIZATION AND TEACHING HINTS	EXPECTED STUDENT OBJECTIVES AND OUTCOMES
6. Explore and show the different ways that the body can support itself in curled positions.	Have a show-and-tell demonstration.	

Movement Concept: Contrasting Movements

1. Above—below, beneath, under. Make arm circles above your head. Below. With your partner, you make a bridge above him or her. Beneath (under).
2. Across—around, under. Jump across your partner. Move under your partner.
3. Around clockwise—around counterclockwise. Jump around your partner in a clockwise direction, and skip around your partner counterclockwise.
4. Between—beside. Crawl between your partner's legs. Stand beside your partner.
5. Make different shapes to illustrate:
   a. Big—little, small
   b. Crooked—straight
   c. Curved—flat, straight
   d. Large—small
   e. Round—straight, flat
   f. Short—long, tall
   g. Tiny—beg, large
   h. Wide—narrow, thin
6. Using locomotor movements, illustrate:
   a. Zig-zag—straight
   b. Fast—slow
   c. Forward—backward, back
   d. Graceful—awkward
   e. Heavy—light
   f. Right—left
   g. Sideways—forward, backward
   h. High—low

DPE p. 330

Begin by showing the contrasting movements first. Later, stress the opposite movement. In the latter, the teacher gives the one term and the children move to the opposite term. For example: the teacher says "reach high." The children will reach low.

Emphasize exploration.

Stress: "Do it a different way."

Some of the activities are best illustrated with partners.

With partners, repeat actions, so roles change.

Cog.—The student will understand and be able to employ the majority of these contrasting terms in her movement patterns.

Movement Concept: Tension and Relaxation

1. Make yourself as tense as possible. Now relax.
2. Take a deep breath, hold it tight. Expel the air and relax.
3. Reach as high as you can tensed, slowly relax and droop to the floor.
4. Show how you can tense different parts of the body.
5. Tense one part of the body and relax another. Shift the tenseness to the relaxes part and vice-versa.
6. Press your fingers hard against your tensed abdominal muscles. Take your fists and beat lightly against the tensed position. Relax. Repeat.

DPE p. 331

Scatter formation.

Emphasize exploration.

Illustrate this with the basketball free-throw shooter, who does this to relax.

Cog.—Physical activity is an excellent outlet for stress and tension.

MOVEMENT EXPERIENCE— CONTENT	ORGANIZATION AND TEACHING HINTS	EXPECTED STUDENT OBJECTIVES AND OUTCOMES

7. Run forward, stop suddenly in a tensed position. Relax. Repeat.
8. Run in a tensed position, change direction on signal, and run relaxed.

GAME (5 – 7 MINUTES)

Midnight — *DPE,* p. 564
   Supplies: None
   Skills: Running, dodging
   A safety line is established about 40 ft from a den in which one player, the fox, is standing. The others stand behind the safety line and move forward slowly, asking, "Please, Mr. Fox, what time is it?" The fox answers in various fashions, such as "Bedtime," "Pretty late," "Three-thirty." The fox continues to draw the players toward him. At some point, he answers the question by saying "Midnight," and then chases the others back to the safety line. Any player who is caught joins the fox in the den and helps to catch others. No player in the den may leave, however, until the fox calls out "Midnight."
   Variation: <u>Lame Wolf</u>. The wolf is lame and advances in a series of three running steps and a hop. Other children taunt, "Lame Wolf, can't catch me!" or "Lame Wolf, tame wolf, can't catch me!" The wolf may give chase at any time. Children who are caught join the wolf and must also move as if lame.

Twins (Triplets) — *DPE,* p. 569
   Supplies: None
   Skills: Body management
   Youngsters find a space in the area. Each youngster has a partner (twin). The teacher gives commands such as "Take three hops and two leaps" or "Walk backward four steps and three skips." When the pairs are separated, the teacher says, "Find your twin!" Players find their twin and stand frozen back to back. The goal is to not be the last pair to find each other and assume the frozen position.
   Students need to move away from each other during the movements. One alternative is to find a new twin each time. Another variation is to separate twins in opposite ends of the playing area.
   Variation: The game becomes more challenging when played in groups of three (triplets). When using this variation, new partners should be selected each time.

DYNAMIC PHYSICAL EDUCATION LESSON PLAN
Balance Beam Activities with Manipulative Equipment
Level I

Supplies and Equipment Needed:
  Balance beams
  Mats (placed at ends of beams)
  Playground balls
  Hoops
  Beanbags
  Tape player
  Music

MOVEMENT EXPERIENCE— CONTENT	ORGANIZATION AND TEACHING HINTS	EXPECTED STUDENT OBJECTIVES AND OUTCOMES

INTRODUCTORY ACTIVITY (2 – 3 MINUTES)

Airplanes

Children pretend to be airplanes. They take off, zoom with arms out, swoop, turn, and glide. On signal, they drop to the floor in prone position. To begin again, they must "refuel" their engines by doing a series of Push-ups while making a "vroom, vroom" engine sound.

DPE p. 254

Utilize different locomotor movements.

Repeat the pattern.

Imitate different types of airplanes.

Substitute a rocket or helicopter for an airplane and allow students to create a new pattern.

PM.—The student will be able to effectively imitate an airplane and a rocket.

FITNESS DEVELOPMENT ACTIVITIES (7 – 8 MINUTES)

Astronaut Drills

Tape alternating segments of silence and music to signal duration of exercise. Music segments indicate aerobic activity while intervals of silence announce flexibility and strength development activities.
  1. Walk.
  2. Walk on tiptoes while reaching for the sky.
  3. Walk with giant strides.
  4. Freeze; perform various stretches.
  5. Do a Puppy Dog Walk.
  6. Jump like a pogo stick.
  7. Freeze, perform Push-up variations.
  8. Walk and swing arms like a helicopter.
  9. Trot lightly and silently.
 10. Slide like an athlete.
 11. Freeze; perform Curl-up variations.
 12. Crab Walk.
 13. Skip.
 14. Freeze; perform trunk development challenges.
 15. Walk and cool down.

DPE, p. 304

Use circle or scatter formation with ample space between youngsters.

Children should be in constant movement except when stopped to do strength and flexibility activities.

Change direction often.

When they are moving on all fours, youngsters should be encouraged to place much of their weight on the hands in order to develop arm–shoulder girdle strength.

Cog.—Astronaut Drills were a common way of developing fitness in the armed services.

PM.—All students should be able to perform the Astronaut Drills.

Aff.—There is no easy way to fitness. It demands self-discipline. Discuss the importance of possessing a positive attitude toward activity in later life.

119

MOVEMENT EXPERIENCE—CONTENT	ORGANIZATION AND TEACHING HINTS	EXPECTED STUDENT OBJECTIVES AND OUTCOMES

LESSON FOCUS (15 – 20 MINUTES)

Balance Beam Activities with Manipulative Equipment

Using Beanbags

1. Try some of the following steps forward, backward and sideways:
   a. Walk
   b. Follow steps
   c. Heel and Toe
   d. Side or Draw Step
   e. Tip Toes
   f. Grapevine
2. Try with beanbag on head and different arm positions:
   a. On hips
   b. On knees
   c. Behind Back
   d. Folded across chest
   e. Pointing toward ceiling
3. Move across the beam using animal walks.

DPE pp. 467 – 469

Move deliberately, catching balance after each step. Quality, not speed, is the goal.

Mats should be placed at the end of each beam to cushion the dismount and allow selected rolls and stunts.

Encourage a wide variety of dismounts. Students should pause at the end of the beam before dismounting.

PM.—The student will be able to walk the beam forward and backward while manipulating a piece of equipment.

Cog.—The student will be able to name five activities where balance is the major factor.

Using Hoops

1. Carry a hoop on various body parts while moving across the beam.
2. Step through a hoop while walking beam in various fashions—forward, sideways, backward.
3. Step through a series of hoops held by a partner.
4. Hula-hoop around waist while moving across the beam.
5. Twirl a hoop around different body parts and proceed across the beam.

Both sides of the body should receive equal treatment. If students walk with the left side leading, they should also walk with the right side leading.

If the student steps off the beam, he should step back on at that point and continue to the end of the beam.

Aff.—Balance is affected a great deal by the auditory and visual senses. Experiment by trying various balance activities and eliminating some of the senses.

Using Playground Balls

1. Walk across the beam and dribble the ball on the floor.
2. Walk across the beam and toss and catch the ball.
3. Walk backward on the beam and toss and catch with a friend waiting in line.
4. Walk across the beam and toss the ball back and forth overhead.
5. Walk across the beam with the ball held between the legs.

Place visual targets in front of the beams (on the wall at eye level). Those students with competency can look at the targets instead of the beam.

Allow each student to determine the degree of challenge desired.

Cog.—Walking and moving across balance beams involves dynamic balance. Dynamic balance involves balancing while moving. Static balance involves a minimal amount of movement. Students can learn to combine static and dynamic balance when performing on the beam.

GAME (5 – 7 MINUTES)

Stork Tag — *DPE,* p. 568
Supplies: None
Skills: Fundamental locomotor movements, dodging
Children are scattered about the area. One child is it and chases the others, trying to tag one of them. When a tag is made, she says, "You're it." The new it chases other children. Children are safe when they move into the stork position which is assumed by balancing on one foot with the eyes closed. The sole of the foot must be placed alongside the knee to compete the stork position. The stork position can be held until the lifted foot touches the floor; students are then eligible to be tagged.

MOVEMENT EXPERIENCE— CONTENT	ORGANIZATION AND TEACHING HINTS	EXPECTED STUDENT OBJECTIVES AND OUTCOMES

Flowers and Wind — *DPE,* p. 561

Supplies: None

Skill: Running

Two parallel lines long enough to accommodate the children are drawn about 30 ft apart. Children are divided into two groups. One is the wind and the other the flowers. Each of the teams takes a position on one of the lines and faces the other team. The flowers secretly select the name of a common flower. When ready, they walk over to the other line and stand about 3 ft away from the wind. The players on the wind team begin to call out flower names—trying to guess the flower chosen. When the flower has been guessed, the flowers run to their goal line, chased by the players of the other team. Any player caught must join the other side. The roles are reversed and the game is repeated. If one side has trouble guessing, a clue can be given to the color or size of the flower or the first letter of its name.

DYNAMIC PHYSICAL EDUCATION LESSON PLAN
Fundamental Skills Using Climbing Ropes
Level I

Supplies and Equipment Needed:
Climbing ropes
Mats (placed under ropes)
Bench, box, or stool

MOVEMENT EXPERIENCE—CONTENT	ORGANIZATION AND TEACHING HINTS	EXPECTED STUDENT OBJECTIVES AND OUTCOMES

INTRODUCTORY ACTIVITY (2 – 3 MINUTES)

Substitute from an earlier lesson

FITNESS DEVELOPMENT ACTIVITIES (7 – 8 MINUTES)

Substitute from an earlier lesson

LESSON FOCUS (15 – 20 MINUTES)

Fundamental Skills Using Climbing Ropes

Supported Pull-Ups

1. Knee and pull to feet, return.
2. Sit, pull to feet and back to seat.
3. Stand, keep body straight while lowering body to the floor.

Hangs

1. Sit, pull body off floor except for feet, and hold.
2. Jump up, grasp the rope, and hang and perform the following movements:
   a. One or both knees up
   b. Bicycling movement
   c. Half-lever
   d. Choice of movement
3. Hang upside down with the rope hanging and looking like a "monkey's tail."

Pull-Ups

Repeat all the activities suggested under Hands, except substitute the pull-up for the hang.

Swinging and Jumping

Use a bench, box or stool for a take-off point. The student should reach high and jump to a bent-arm position while swinging.

1. Swing and jump. Add one-half and full turns.
2. Swing and return to perch.
3. Jump for distance or land on a target. (Place a rubber spot or chalk mark on the floor.)

DPE pp. 460 – 464

Place tumbling mats under all the climbing apparatus.

Caution students not to slide quickly down the rope to prevent rope burns.

The pull-up and hang activities are excellent lead-ups for students who are not strong enough to climb the rope.

Students should be encouraged to learn the various techniques of climbing and descending.

If there are only a few climbing ropes, it would be a good teaching technique to have the nonclimbing students work on another unit. Some good units are beanbags, hoops, wands, and playground balls.

Rope climbing is a very intense and demanding activity. A good idea is to break up the lesson focus with a game or relay. This will also offer leg development activities.

If other climbing equipment is available such as a horizontal ladder and/or exercise bar, many activities are offered in *DPE* (see Chapter 19).

P.M.—The student will be able to demonstrate proper techniques in the following activities:
1. Supported pull-ups
2. Hangs
3. Swinging and jumping
4. Climbing and descending with the scissors grip

Cog.—The student will be able to describe the safety rules necessary when climbing ropes.

Aff.—Strength development activities do not significantly increase cardiovascular efficiency. Discuss the need for both strength and endurance activities when developing total fitness.

MOVEMENT EXPERIENCE—CONTENT	ORGANIZATION AND TEACHING HINTS	EXPECTED STUDENT OBJECTIVES AND OUTCOMES

4. Swing and pick up a bowling pin and return to perch.
5. Play Tarzan—take a running start, jump up and swing as far as possible.

Climbing the Rope

1. Scissors grip—Place the rope inside of the knee and outside the foot. Climb halfway up and practice descending using the reverse scissors grip before climbing to the top of the rope.

GAME (5 – 7 MINUTES)

Alternate Lesson

Change Sides — *DPE,* p. 559
  Supplies: None
  Skill: Body management
  Two parallel lines are established 30 ft apart. Half of the children are on each line. On signal, all cross to the other line, face the center, and stand at attention. The first group to do this correctly wins a point. Children must be cautioned to use care when passing through the opposite group. They should be spaced well along each line; this allows room for them to move through each group. The locomotor movements should be varied. The teacher may say, "Ready—walk!" Skipping, hopping, long steps, sliding, and other forms of locomotion can be specified. The position to be assumed at the finish can be varied also.
  Teaching suggestion: Because success depends on getting across first, the teacher should watch for shortcutting of the rules and talk this problem over with the children.
  Variation: The competition can be by squads, with two squads on each line.

Where's My Partner? — *DPE,* p. 569
  Supplies: None
  Skills: Fundamental locomotor movements
  Children are in a double circle by couples, with partners facing. The inside circle has one more player than the outside. When the signal is given, the circles skip (or walk, run, hop, or gallop) to the right. This means that they are skipping in opposite directions. On the command "Halt," the circles face each other to find partners. The player left without a partner is in the mush pot (the center area of the circle). When play starts again, this child enters either circle. The circles should be reversed after a time.
  Variation: The game can also be played with music or a drumbeat. When the music stops, the players seek partners.

LESSON PLANS FOR THE SCHOOL YEAR
Developmental Level II

WEEK	INTRODUCTORY ACTIVITY	FITNESS DEVELOPMENT ACTIVITY	LESSON FOCUS ACTIVITY	GAME ACTIVITY	PAGE
1	Move and Freeze on Signal	Teacher Leader Movement Challenges	Orientation	Class Management Games	128
2	Fundamental Movements and Stopping	Teacher Leader Exercises	Manipulative Skills Using Beanbags	Galloping Lizzie Crows and Cranes	131
3	Move and Assume Pose	Teacher Leader Exercises	Throwing Skills(1)	Whistle Mixer Couple Tag Partner Stoop	134
4	Walk, Trot, and Sprint	Teacher Leader Exercises	Soccer Related Activities(1)	Circle Soccer Soccer Touch Ball Diagonal Soccer Soccer Take-Away	137
5	Partner Over and Under	Teacher Leader Exercises	Soccer Related Activities(2)	Diagonal Soccer Sideline Soccer Dribblerama Bullseye	140
6	Run, Stop, Pivot	Circuit Training	Fundamental Skills Through Playground Games	Playground Games	143
7	European Rhythmic Running	Circuit Training	Long Rope Jumping Skills	Trades Fly Trap	145
8	Magic Number Challenges	Circuit Training	Manipulative Skills Using Playground Balls	Fox Hunt Bounce Ball One Step	148
9	Fastest Tag in the West	Walk, Trot, and Sprint	Throwing Skills(2)	In the Prison Snowball Center Target Throw Target Ball Throw	152
10	Group Tag	Walk, Trot, and Sprint	Walking and Jogging Skills	Recreational Activity	155
11	Locomotor and Manipulative Activity	Exercises to Music	Rhythmic Movement(1)	Whistle March Arches Home Base	158
12	Movement Varieties	Exercises to Music	Hockey Related Activities(1)	Circle Keepaway Star Wars Modified Hockey Circle Straddleball	162
13	New Ladder	Astronaut Drills	Hockey Related Activities(2)	Modified Hockey Lane Hockey	165
14	Group Over and Under	Astronaut Drills	Individual Rope Jumping Skills	Trades Follow Me Beachball Bat Ball	167
15	Low Organization Games	Continuity Drills	Stunts and Tumbling Skills(1)	Whistle Mixer Competitive Circle Contests Alaska Baseball	170

WEEK	INTRODUCTORY ACTIVITY	FITNESS DEVELOPMENT ACTIVITY	LESSON FOCUS ACTIVITY	GAME ACTIVITY	PAGE
16	Following Activity	Continuity Drills	Rhythmic Movement(2)	Fox Hunt Steal the Treasure Addition Tag	173
17	Leapfrog	Aerobic Fitness and Partner Resistance Exercises	Fundamental Skills Using Benches	Cageball Kick-Over Squad Tag	177
18	Bridges by Three	Aerobic Fitness and Partner Resistance Exercises	Basketball Related Activities(1)	Birdie in the Cage Dribble Take-Away Captain Ball Basketball Tag	180
19	Jumping and Hopping	Challenge Course	Basketball Related Activities(2)	Circle Guard and Pass Captain Basketball Around the Key	184
20	Fleece Ball Fun	Challenge Course	Recreational Activities	Recreational Activities	187
21	Ball Activities	Challenge Course	Fundamental Skills Using Balance Beams	Nonda's Car Lot Fly Trap	189
22	Moving to Music	Aerobic Fitness	Stunts and Tumbling Skills(2)	Partner Stoop Crows and Cranes	192
23	European Rhythmic Running with Variations	Aerobic Fitness	Manipulative Skills Using Wands	Home Base Indianapolis 500 Nine Lives	195
24	Tortoise and Hare	Aerobic Fitness	Rhythmic Movement(3)	Jump the Shot Beach-Ball Batball Club Guard	198
25	Bend, Stretch, and Shake	Astronaut Drills	Volleyball-Related Skills	Beach Ball Volleyball Informal Volleyball Shower Service Ball	202
26	Move, Perform Task	Astronaut Drills	Manipulative Skills Using Hoops	Hand Hockey Cageball Kick Over	206
27	Tag Games	Continuity Drills	Manipulative Skills Using Paddle and Balls	Steal the Treasure Addition Tag	209
28	Combination Movement Patterns	Continuity Drills	Stunts and Tumbling Skills(3)	Trades Benchball Batball	212
29	European Rhythmic Running with Equipment	Exercises to Music	Fundamental Skills Using Tug-of-War Ropes	Wolfe's Beanbag Exchange Arches	215
30	Marking	Exercises to Music	Rhythmic Movement with Equipment(4)	Alaska Baseball Trees	218
31	Stretching	Jogging	Track and Field Related Activities(1)	Potato Shuttle Relay Shuttle Relays One on One Contests	222
32	Stretching	Jogging	Track and Field Related Activities(2)	Circular Relays Shuttle Relays One on One Contests	225
33	Creative Routine	Hexagon Hustle	Fundamental Skills Using Parachute Activities	Nonda's Car Lot Box Ball	227

WEEK	INTRODUCTORY ACTIVITY	FITNESS DEVELOPMENT ACTIVITY	LESSON FOCUS ACTIVITY	GAME ACTIVITY	PAGE
34	Four Corner Movement	Hexagon Hustle	Manipulative Skills Using Frisbees	Frisbee Keep-Away Frisbee Golf	230
35	Long Rope Routine	Parachute Exercises	Softball Related Activities(1)	Throw It and Run Two-Pitch Softball Hit and Run	233
36	Squad Leader Movement	Parachute Exercises	Softball Related Activities(2)	Beat Ball Kick Softball In a Pickle	237
Alternate Lesson Plans					
A	Substitute	Substitute	Football Related Activities(1)	Football End Ball Five Passes	240
B	Substitute	Substitute	Football Related Activities(2)	Football Box Ball Fourth Down	242
C	Substitute	Substitute	Softball Related Activities(3)	Beat Ball Kick Softball Two-Pitch Softball	244
D	Substitute	Substitute	Fundamental Skills Using Balance Beams and Manipulative Equipment	Hand Hockey Nine Lives	246
E	Substitute	Substitute	Fundamental Skills Using Climbing Ropes	Nonda's Car Lot Indianapolis 500	248
F	Substitute	Substitute	Fundamental Skills Using Magic Ropes	Busy Bee Box Ball	250

DYNAMIC PHYSICAL EDUCATION LESSON PLAN
Orientation and Class Management Games
Level II

Orientation Lesson Plan

The first week of school should be used to teach students the system you are going to use throughout the year. The following are reminders you might find useful in establishing your expectations and routines.

1. Establish rules and expectations. Discuss your expectations with the class to assure students understand reasons for your guidelines. Explain what the consequences are when rules are not followed. Show where time-out boxes are located and how they will be used.
2. Explain to the class the method you will use to learn names. It might be helpful to ask classroom teachers to have students put their name on a piece of masking tape (name tag). Tell students that you will ask them their name on a regular basis until it is learned.
3. Develop entry and exit behaviors for students coming and leaving physical education classes. Students should know how to enter the instructional area and to leave equipment alone until told to use it. If squads are used for instruction, place students into squads and practice moving into formation on signal.
4. Decide how excuses for non-participation will be handled. If possible, set up a routine where the school nurse determines which students are excused for health reasons.
5. Safety is important. Children should receive safety rules to be followed on apparatus and playground equipment. Safety procedures to be followed in physical education classes should be discussed.
6. Illustrate how you will stop and start the class. In general, a whistle (or similar loud signal) and a raised hand is effective for stopping the class. A voice command should be used to start the class. Telling the class when before what (*DPE,* Chapter 6) will assure they do not begin before instructions are finished.
7. Discuss the issue, distribution, and care of equipment. Make students responsible for acquiring a piece of equipment and returning it at the end of the lesson. Place equipment around the perimeter of the teaching area to reduce the chance of students fighting over a piece of equipment.
8. Explain to the class that the format of the daily lesson will include an introductory activity, fitness development, lesson focus, and finish with a game activity.
9. Practice various teaching formations such as open-squad formation and closed-squad formation. Practice moving into a circle while moving (fall-in). Transitions between formations should be done while moving, i.e., jogging from scatter formation into a circular formation.
10. Refer to Chapters 5, 6, and 7 in *DPE* for detailed information about planning, developing an effective learning environment, and class management strategies.

INTRODUCTORY ACTIVITY (2–3 MINUTES)

Move and Freeze on Signal
   Have students move throughout the area using a variety of locomotor movements. On signal (whistle), they quickly freeze. Try to reduce the response latency by reinforcing students who stop quickly on signal. The primary objective should be to teach students the importance of moving under control (without bumping others or falling down) and quickly freezing, ready to listen to upcoming instructions.

FITNESS DEVELOPMENT ACTIVITIES (7–8 MINUTES)

Teacher Leader Movement Challenges
   The goal should be to move students through a number of movement challenges. Emphasis should be placed on starting the fitness activities at a level where all students can feel successful.

Alternate locomotor movements with strength and flexibility challenges. Repeat the challenges as necessary.

Locomotor Movement: Walk for 30 seconds.

Flexibility and Trunk Development Challenges
1. Bend in different directions.
2. Stretch slowly and return quickly.
3. Combine bending and stretching movements.
4. Sway back and forth.
5. Twist one body part; add body parts.
6. Make your body move in a large circle.

Locomotor Movement: Skip for 30 seconds.

Shoulder Girdle Challenges
In a push-up position, do the following challenges:
1. Lift one foot; the other foot.
2. Wave at a friend; wave with the other arm.
3. Scratch your back with one hand; use the other hand.
4. Walk your feet to your hands.
5. Turn over and face the ceiling; shake a leg; crab walk.

Locomotor Movement: Jog for 30 seconds.

Abdominal Development
From a supine position:
1. Lift your head and look at your toes.
2. Lift your knees to your chest.
3. Wave your legs at a friend.
From a sitting position;
1. Slowly lay down with hands on tummy.
2. Lift legs and touch toes.

Locomotor Movement: Run and leap for 30 seconds.

LESSON FOCUS (15–20 MINUTES)

Since much time during the first week is used for orientation procedures and management, no lesson focus activity is scheduled.

GAME (5–7 MINUTES)

Play one or two management games to teach students how to move into partner and small group formation. The following games can be used to teach students such management goals in an enjoyable and efficient manner.

Back to Back — *DPE, p. 556*
Supplies: None
Skills: Fundamental locomotor movements
Students move under control throughout the area using a variety of locomotor movements. On signal, each child stands back to back (or toe to toe) with another child. If one child ends up without a partner, the teacher takes this student as a partner. Youngsters who do not find a partner nearby run to a designated spot in the center of the area. This helps assure that students do not run around looking for a partner or feel left out. Students who move to the center spot quickly find a partner and move out of the area (to avoid crowding around the center spot). Emphasis should be placed finding a partner near them, not searching for a friend, and taking a different partner each time.

Whistle Mixer — *DPE, p. 580*

Supplies: None

Skills: All basic locomotor movements

Children are scattered throughout the area. To begin, they move in any direction they wish. The teacher whistles a number of times in succession and raises the same number of fingers above their head to signal the group size. Children then form small groups with the number in each group equal to the number of whistles. For example, if there are four short whistles, children form circles of four—no more, no less. The goal is to find the correct number of students as quickly as possible. As soon as a group has the desired number, they sit down to signal that other may not join the group. Children who cannot find a group nearby should be encouraged to move to the center of the area and raise their hands to facilitate finding others without a group.

DYNAMIC PHYSICAL EDUCATION LESSON PLAN
Manipulative Skills Using Beanbags
Level II

Supplies and Equipment Needed:
Two beanbags per child
Tom-tom or tambourine
Jump ropes

MOVEMENT EXPERIENCE—CONTENT	ORGANIZATION AND TEACHING HINTS	EXPECTED STUDENT OBJECTIVES AND OUTCOMES

INTRODUCTORY ACTIVITY (2 – 3 MINUTES)

Fundamental Movements and Stopping

1. Teach the run, walk, hop, jump, leap, slide, gallop and skip with proper stopping.
2. Practice moving and stopping correctly—emphasize basics of proper movement.
3. Tape alternating segments of silence and music to signal duration of the locomotor movements. Segments of silence that indicate the "freeze" position can be decreased in duration until the desired response latency is reached.

DPE p. 253

Scatter formation.

PM.—The student will be able to stop quickly under control.

Cog.—Know the elements involved in stopping quickly.

PM.—The student will be able to execute the various locomotor movements.

FITNESS DEVELOPMENT ACTIVITIES (7 – 8 MINUTES)

Teacher Leader Exercises

Tape alternating segments of silence (10 seconds) to signal a change of exercise and music to signal the duration of exercise (25 seconds).

Arm Circles	25 seconds
Bend and Twist	25 seconds
Treadmill	25 seconds
Abdominal Challenges	25 seconds
Single-Leg Crab Kick	25 seconds
Knee to Chest Curl	25 seconds
Run in Place	25 seconds
Trunk Twister	25 seconds

Conclude the routine with 2 to 4 minutes of jogging, rope jumping or other continuous activity.

DPE pp. 289 – 299

Scatter formation.

Allow students to adjust the work load to their ability and fitness level. This implies that some students will perform more repetitions in the same amount of time.

Emphasize proper form and technique.

Rotate to different parts of the teaching area and help motivate students.

Cog.—Know why it is necessary to increase the number of repetitions (overload principle).

PM.—The student will be able to perform all activities.

LESSON FOCUS (15 – 20 MINUTES)

Beanbag Activities

Give students two or three activities to practice so you have time to move and help youngsters. Alternate activities from each of the categories so students receive a variety of skills to practice.

In place, Tossing to self

1. Toss and catch with both hands - right hand, left hand

DPE pp. 409 – 413

Scatter formation.

Stress soft catch. Keep eyes on the bag.

Students should practice the activities with both the left and right hands.

PM.—The student will develop the necessary visual concentration to follow a moving object.

PM.—The student will be able to "give" with the body to create a soft home for the beanbag.

MOVEMENT EXPERIENCE— CONTENT	ORGANIZATION AND TEACHING HINTS	EXPECTED STUDENT OBJECTIVES AND OUTCOMES
2. Toss and catch with the back of hands. This will encourage children to catch with "soft hands." 3. Toss the beanbag to increasingly high level, *emphasizing* a straight overhead toss. To encourage straight tossing, have the child sit down. 4. Exploratory activity.		Cog.—The student will be able to recite the necessary ingredients for successful catching.

In Place, Adding Stunts
 	
1. Toss overhead and perform the following stunts and catch the bag.
  a. ¼ and ½ turns, right and left
  b. Full turn
  c. Touch floor
  d. Clap hands
  e. Clap hands around different parts of body, behind back, under legs.
  f. Heel click
  g. Student choice
	Emphasize keeping eyes on object while performing stunts.
	
	Catching is more important than the stunt. Make sure that they are making good throws and catching the bag.
		Cog.—The length of the lever determines the amount of force that can be generated when propelling an object. Discuss how the length of the lever is shortened when making accurate tosses.

In place, kicking to self 1. Place beanbag on foot, kick up and catch—right foot, left foot. 2. Try above activity from sitting and lying positions. 3. Kick up and catch behind back. 4. Kick up overhead, make ½ turn and catch. 5. Put beanbag between feet, jump up and catch beanbag. 6. Toss beanbag with one foot and catch with the other foot.		
Locomotor movements (Toss, Move and Catch) 1. Toss overhead, move to another spot and catch. 2. Toss, do a locomotor movement and catch. 3. Move from side to side. 4. Toss overhead behind self, move and catch. 5. Exploratory movements.	Encourage the class to look where they are moving. This will force them to take their eyes off the object, relocate it, and catch it, which is a more advanced skill.	Cog.—The student will be able to state why catching is more difficult when the person is moving.

Balance the beanbag
 	
1. Balance on the following body parts:
  a. Head
  b. Back of hand
  c. Shoulder
  d. Knee
  e. Foot
  f. Elbow
  g. Others (choice)
2. Balance and move as follows:
  a. Walk
  b. Run
  c. Skip
  d. Gallop
	Look for new and exciting ways of balancing the bags. Allow students to show their ideas to the rest of the class.
	
	See who can balance a bag the longest on various body parts while moving.
	
	If time allows, go back and polish some of the activities performed earlier in the week.
		PM.—The student will be able to propel the body and balance an object simultaneously.
		
		Cog.—Proper nutrition is important for ensuring strong physical performance. Studies show that Americans eat too much salt, sugar, and fat. Discuss the types of foods that can be eaten to reduce these areas of excessive intake.

MOVEMENT EXPERIENCE—CONTENT	ORGANIZATION AND TEACHING HINTS	EXPECTED STUDENT OBJECTIVES AND OUTCOMES

    e. Sit down
    f. Lie down
    g. Turn around
    h. Balance beanbag on body part and move on all fours.
    i. Play Beanbag Balance Tag
    j. Other (choice)

Those students balancing red beanbags are it, or those with blue beanbags are it, etc.

Partner activities

1. Toss back and forth using the following throws:
    a. Two-handed throws—overhead, underhand, side and over shoulder.
    b. One-handed throws and catches.
    c. Throw at different levels and targets such as high, low, left, right.
    d. Throw under leg, around body, from behind back, center, as in football, etc.
    e. Sit down and play catch—try different throws and catches.
    f. Toss in various directions to make partner move and catch. Have one partner move around other in a circle while catching and throwing.
    g. Propel more than one beanbag back and forth. Toss both beanbags together, as well as at opposite times.

Start partners close together and gradually increase distance to increase challenge.

Aff.—Most sport activities require teamwork (working with a partner) for success to occur. Discuss with the students the need for working closely with their partner in the beanbag activities.

A motivating idea is to challenge students by asking them to perform an activity a certain number of times in a row without missing.

Also, try to follow activities where one partner throws or catches exactly as the lead thrower does.

PM.—The student will be able to throw and catch at various distances and levels.

PM.—The student will be able to throw and catch the beanbag while moving in circular formation.

GAME (5 – 7 MINUTES)

Galloping Lizzie—*DPE*, p. 576
    Supplies: A beanbag or fleece ball
    Skills: Throwing, dodging, running
    One player is it and has a beanbag or fleece ball. The other players are scattered around the playground. The player with the bag or ball runs after the others and attempts to hit another player below the shoulders with the object. The person hit becomes it, and the game continues. The tagger must throw the bag or ball, not merely touch another person with it.
Variation: A pair of children is it, with one of the players handling the bag or ball. A specific kind of toss can be called for (e.g., overhand, underhand, left-handed).

  Crows and Cranes—*DPE*, p. 574
    Supplies: None
    Skills: Running, dodging
    Two goal lines are drawn about 50 ft apart. Children are divided into two groups—the crows and the cranes. The groups face each other at the center of the area, about 5 ft apart. The leader calls out either "Crows" or "Cranes," using a cr-r-r-r-r sound at the start of either word to mask the result. If "Crows" is the call, the crows chase the cranes to the goal line. If "Cranes" is the call, then the cranes chase. Any child caught goes over to the other side. The team that has the most players when the game ends is the winner.
Variations:
    1. Instead of facing each other, children stand back to back, about a foot apart, in the center.
    2. The game can be played with the two sides designated as red and blue. A piece of plywood painted red on one side and blue on the other can be thrown into the air between the teams, instead of having someone give calls. If red comes up, the red team chases, and vice versa.
    3. Blue, black, and baloney. On the command "Blue" or "Black," the game proceeds as described. On the command "Baloney," no one is to move. The caller should draw out the bl-l-l-l sound before ending with one of the three commands.
    4. Another variation of the game is to have a leader tell a story using as many words beginning with cr- as possible. Words that can be incorporated into a story might be crazy, crunch, crust, crown, crude, crowd, crouch, cross, croak, critter. Each time one of these words is spoken, the beginning of the word is lengthened with a drawn out cr-r-r-r sound. No one may move on any of the words except crows or cranes.

DYNAMIC PHYSICAL EDUCATION LESSON PLAN
Throwing Skills (Lesson 1)
Level II

Supplies and Equipment Needed:
  Beanbags or fleece balls
  Yarn balls
  Rag balls or tennis balls
  Hoops
  Mats for targets
  Jump ropes (optional)

MOVEMENT EXPERIENCE—CONTENT	ORGANIZATION AND TEACHING HINTS	EXPECTED STUDENT OBJECTIVES AND OUTCOMES

INTRODUCTORY ACTIVITY (2 – 3 MINUTES)

Move and Assume Pose

1. Have youngsters move using a variation of a basic movement. Freeze on signal; assume a pose using the following commands.
   a. Balance
   b. Stretch
   c. Curl
   d. Bridge
   e. Push-Up position
   f. Make shape with a partner (double bridge, arch)
   g. Choice

DPE p. 253

Scatter formation.

Emphasize proper method of stopping quickly.

Discourage falling and lack of body control.

Encourage creativity in various poses.

Stretching exercises should be slow and sustained movements.

PM.—The student will be able to perform the basic poses on command.

Cog.—The student will recognize the basic command names and nonlocomotor movements.

PM.—The student will be able to stop quickly with good balance.

FITNESS DEVELOPMENT ACTIVITIES (7 – 8 MINUTES)

Teacher Leader Exercises

Tape alternating segments of silence (10 seconds) to signal a change of exercise and music to signal the duration of exercise (30 seconds).

Arm Circles	30 seconds
Sitting Stretch	30 seconds
Treadmill	30 seconds
Abdominal Challenges	30 seconds
Single-Leg Crab Kick	30 seconds
Knee to Chest Curl	30 seconds
Power Jumper	30 seconds
Trunk Twister	30 seconds

Conclude the routine with 2 to 4 minutes of jogging, rope jumping or other continuous activity.

Increase the duration of exercises by 10 to 20% over the previous week.

DPE pp. 289 – 299

Scatter formation.

Allow students to adjust the work load to their ability and fitness level. This implies that some students will perform more repetitions in the same amount of time.

Emphasize proper form and technique.

Rotate to different parts of the teaching area and help motivate students.

Cog.—The student will be able to explain verbally why correct form is important when performing fitness activities.

Aff.—One of the reasons for fitness activities now is to establish patterns for later life. Establish the need for fitness throughout life through example and brief comments.

LESSON FOCUS (15 – 20 MINUTES)

Throwing Skills
Individual activities

1. Throw beanbag or fleece ball against the wall. Emphasize the following points:
   a. Feet together.

DPE pp. 349 – 351

At least one object per child.

Students should be 4–5 ft from the wall.

Encourage children to throw hard.

Cog.—The student will begin to understand the importance of body rotation to produce force.

MOVEMENT EXPERIENCE— CONTENT	ORGANIZATION AND TEACHING HINTS	EXPECTED STUDENT OBJECTIVES AND OUTCOMES

b. Contra-lateral foot forward.
c. Start with non-throwing side to the wall.
2. Throw from one side of the gym and try to hit the other wall.

Redirect children with key points:
1. Start with your throwing hand behind your head.
2. Turn your side to the wall.
3. Take a big step and throw hard.

Have the entire class throw at once if possible, retrieve, and run to wall. Repeat.

Cog.—The student will understand the importance of opposition of limbs.

PM.—The student will perform the throw by stepping with the contralateral foot.

Cog.—Student will understand the importance of the shoulder turn and step in producing a forceful throw.

Station (Small Group) Instruction

1. Activities emphasizing form
   a. Throwing at tumbling mats. The student stands on the edge of the mat and steps to the floor with his contra-lateral foot as he throws toward the wall. (The other foot remains on the mat.)

   b. Throwing with both feet in a hoop. The student begins in side-facing position to the target, with both feet inside the hoop; she then steps outside the hoop with the contra-lateral foot and throws to the wall.
   c. Touching a cone. The student must touch the cone with the throwing hand on the backswing, then throw to the wall.

Throwing for velocity

1. Throw at mats on the wall
   a. Throw tennis or rag balls hard from 15 to 20 feet
   b. Retrieve only if the balls roll behind the throwing line.
2. Throw at mats laid over tables
3. Throw at hoops leaning against mats against the wall

All students should do these activities a minimum of two days.

All throws are made to the wall and with force.

This activity forces the student to take a long stride toward the target.

If tires or hoops are not available, use jump ropes. The circle should be large enough to encourage the student to take a long stride.

This activity should encourage the student to rotate and take a wind-up before throwing.

The cone should be directly behind the student and about at arm's length–distance.

Organize 2 to 3 students per group depending on available space.

Verbal cues of "throw and retrieve" add clarity to instruction.

Each student should start with five balls.

The teacher should continue to give feedback to the students that will help them improve their form.

The mats should be placed on the table so they hang to the floor.

Put hoops touching one another for easier targets; spread apart for more difficult target.

Another excellent large target is a 4-ft. cage ball.

Aff.—The student should understand that a lot of practice is necessary to master the skill of throwing.

PM.—The student should begin to take a long stride with the throw.

Cog.—The student should understand that a longer stride helps increase force production.

MOVEMENT EXPERIENCE— CONTENT	ORGANIZATION AND TEACHING HINTS	EXPECTED STUDENT OBJECTIVES AND OUTCOMES

GAME (5 – 7 MINUTES)

Whistle Mixer—*DPE*, p. 580
    Supplies: A whistle
    Skills: All basic locomotor movements
    Children are scattered throughout the area. To begin, they walk around in any direction they wish. The teacher blows a whistle a number of times in succession with short, sharp blasts. Children then form small circles with the number in the circles equal to the number of whistle blasts. If there are four blasts, children form circles of four—no more, no less. The goal is not to be left out or caught in a circle with the incorrect number of students. Children should be encouraged to move to the center of the area and raise their hands to facilitate finding others without a group.
    After the circles are formed, the teacher calls "Walk," and the game continues. In walking, children should move in different directions.
    Variation: A fine version of this game is done with the aid of a tom-tom. Different beats indicate different locomotor movements—skipping, galloping, slow walking, normal walking, running. The whistle is still used to set the number for each circle.

Couple Tag—*DPE*, p. 574
    Supplies: None
    Skills: Running, dodging
    Two goal lines are established about 50 ft apart. Children run in pairs, with inside hands joined. All pairs, except one, line up on one of the goal lines. The pair in the center is it. They call "Come," and the children, keeping hands joined, run to the other goal line. The pair in the center, also retaining joined hands, tries to tag any other pair. As soon as a couple is caught, they help the center couple. The game continues until all are caught. The last couple caught is it for the next game.
    Variation: Triplet Tag. The game can be played with sets of threes. Tagging is done with any pair of joined hands. If a triplet breaks joined hands, it is considered caught.

Partner Stoop—*DPE*, p. 578
    Supplies: Music
    Skills: Marching rhythmically
    The game follows the same basic principle of stooping as in Circle Stoop, but it is played with partners. The group forms a double circle, with partners facing counterclockwise, which means that one partner is on the inside and one is on the outside. When the music begins, all march in the line of direction. After a short period of marching, a signal (whistle) is sounded, and the inside circle reverses direction and marches the other way—clockwise. The partners are thus separated. When the music stops, the outer circle stands still, and the partners making up the inner circle walk to rejoin their respective outer circle partners. As soon as a child reaches her partner, they join inside hands and stoop without losing balance. The last couple to stoop and those who have lost balance go to the center of the circle and wait out the next round.
    Insist that players walk when joining their partner. This avoids the problem of stampeding and colliding with others.

DYNAMIC PHYSICAL EDUCATION LESSON PLAN
Soccer-Related Activities (Lesson 1)
Level II

Supplies and Equipment Needed:
  8 1/2" foam rubber balls (8 1/2" playground balls may be substituted)
  Cones for marking areas for lead-up activities
  Tom-tom
  Jump ropes (optional)

MOVEMENT EXPERIENCE— CONTENT	ORGANIZATION AND TEACHING HINTS	EXPECTED STUDENT OBJECTIVES AND OUTCOMES

INTRODUCTORY ACTIVITY (2 – 3 MINUTES)

Walk, Trot and Sprint

Youngsters move throughout the area and change the pace of their movement depending on the number of signals (whistles or tom-tom beats) given. When four signals are given, the class freezes and performs a variety of stretches.
  1. One signal—walk
  2. Two signals—trot
  3. Three signals—run
  4. Whistle—freeze and stretch

DPE pp. 285 – 286

Scatter formation.

Work on quality of movements and quick changes.

Try to "fool" the class by changing signals and catching them "off guard."

May vary this activity by adding a fourth tom-tom beat to signal an exercise.

Cog.—Introductory activity is performed in order to warm up the body for more strenuous activity.

FITNESS DEVELOPMENT ACTIVITIES (7 – 8 MINUTES)

Teacher Leader Exercises

Tape alternating segments of silence (10 seconds) to signal a change of exercise and music to signal the duration of exercise (35 seconds).

Arm Circles	35 seconds
Bend and Twist	35 seconds
Treadmill	35 seconds
Abdominal Challenges	35 seconds
Single-Leg Crab Kick	35 seconds
Knee to Chest Curl	35 seconds
Run in Place	35 seconds
Standing Hip Bend	35 seconds

Conclude the routine with 2 to 4 minutes of jogging, rope jumping or other continuous activity.

Increase the duration of exercises by 10 to 20% over the previous week.

DPE pp. 289 – 299

Scatter formation.

Allow students to adjust the work load to their ability and fitness level. This implies that some students will perform more repetitions in the same amount of time.

Emphasize proper form and technique.

Rotate to different parts of the teaching area and help motivate students.

Cog.—It is necessary to increase the workload to provide additional stress on the body and increase fitness levels.

PM.—The student will be able to perform one to two more repetitions of each exercise than he was capable of two weeks ago.

Aff.—Physically fit people are rewarded by society. Teachers, parents, and peers respond much more favorably to those fit and attractive.

LESSON FOCUS (15 – 20 MINUTES)

Soccer Related Activities (1)
Skills

  1. The long pass:
     Approach at 45° angle, top of instep meets ball. Place non-kicking foot alongside ball.

DPE pp. 663 – 665

Partner or triangle formation, one ball for two or three children.

Keep head down, eyes on ball, follow through.

8 1/2" foam rubber training balls should be used as they remove the fear of being hurt by a kicked soccer ball.

PM.—The student will be able to pass, kick, and trap the ball successfully at the end of the week.

Cog.—The student will be able to state two reasons why, in soccer activities, accuracy is much preferred over raw power and lack of control.

137

MOVEMENT EXPERIENCE— CONTENT	ORGANIZATION AND TEACHING HINTS	EXPECTED STUDENT OBJECTIVES AND OUTCOMES

2. Side of foot pass (short pass): Short distance kick, keep toe down. Use both the inside and out-side of the foot.
3. Sole of the foot control: Use sole of foot to stop ball, make sure weight is placed on the non-re-ceiving foot.
4. Foot control: Use inside of foot, lean to "give" with leg so ball doesn't ricochet off foot.
5. Dribbling: Practice moving the ball with a se-ries on controlled taps. Practice dribbling with the left and the right foot.

If short supply of foam rubber balls, use 8 1/2" playground balls. Partially deflate them and they will move more slowly and offer children more success.

Make sure students handle the ball with their feet, not the hands. They should retrieve and move the balls with feet only.

Aff.—Even in basic lead-up games, teamwork is necessary for success and enjoyment by all.

Cog.—The student will be able to state the basic rules necessary for soccer lead-up games.

Aff.—The student will learn to appreci-ate individual differences and show concern for the welfare of others.

Aff.—Cooperation needs to be learned before students can compete with oth-ers. Discuss how it is impossible to have a competitive game if others choose not to cooperate and follow rules.

Drills

DPE pp. 668 – 674

Each student should practice dribbling and handling the ball individually. Part-ner or triplet work is excellent for prac-ticing kicking, passing and trapping skills.
1. Circle formation: Useful for kicking, trapping and passing.
2. Circle and leader: Useful for emphasizing accuracy and allowing all a chance to lead.

Teach skills from a stationary position; as students improve, introduce move-ment.

Drills should be used after students' in-dividual skills have improved to enable them to participate successfully. Pro-gress from *individual* work to group drills.

The grid system described on pages 669 – 673 is excellent for skill practice and drills.

GAME (5 – 7 MINUTES)

Soccer Lead-Up Games

Circle Kickball—*DPE*, p. 674
Supplies: Two soccer balls or 8-in. foam rubber balls
Skills: Kicking, controlling
Players are in circle formation. Using the side of the foot, players kick the balls back and forth inside the circle. The object is to kick a ball out of the circle beneath the shoulder level of the circle players. A point is scored against each of the players where a ball leaves the circle between them. If, however, a lost ball is clearly the fault of a single player, then the point is scored against that player only. Any player who kicks a ball higher than the shoulders of the circle players has a point scored against him. Players with the fewest points scored against them win. Players must watch carefully since two balls are in action at one time. A player cannot be penalized if she leaves the circle to recover a ball and the second ball goes through her vacated spot.

Soccer Touch Ball—*DPE*, p. 674
Supplies: A soccer ball
Skills: Kicking, controlling
Players are spaced around a circle 10 yd in diameter with two players in the center. The object of the game is to keep the players in the center from touching the ball. The ball is passed back and forth as in soccer. If a center player touches the ball with a foot, the person who kicked the ball goes to the center. If a circle player commits an error (i.e., misses a ball), the person responsible changes places with a center player. A rule that no player may contain or hold the ball longer than 3 seconds tends to keep the game moving.

Diagonal Soccer—*DPE*, p. 674
Supplies: A soccer ball, pinnies (optional)
Skills: Kicking, passing, dribbling, some controlling, defending, blocking shots
Two corners are marked off with cones 5 ft from the corners on both the sides, outlining triangular dead areas. Each team lines up and protects two adjacent sides of the square. The dead area on the opposite corner marks the opposing team's goal lines. To begin competition, three players from each team move into the playing area in their own half of the space. These are the active players. During play, they may roam anywhere in the square. The other players act as line guards.

MOVEMENT EXPERIENCE— CONTENT	ORGANIZATION AND TEACHING HINTS	EXPECTED STUDENT OBJECTIVES AND OUTCOMES

The object of the game is for active players to kick the ball through the opposing team's line (beneath shoulder height) to score. When a score is made, active players rotate to the sidelines and new players take their place. Players on the sidelines may block the ball with their bodies but cannot use their hands. The team against whom the point was scored starts the ball for the next point. Only active players may score. Scoring is much the same as in Circle Kickball in that a point is awarded for the opponents when any of the following occur.

1. A team allows the ball to go through its line below the shoulders.
2. A team touches the ball illegally.
3. A team kicks the ball over the other team above shoulder height.

Variations:

1. If the class is large, a bigger area and more active players can be used.
2. If scoring seems too easy, the line defenders can use their hands to stop the ball.

Soccer Take-Away

Supplies: A soccer ball for each student

Skills: Dribbling and defensive skills

Four or five players are designated as defensive players. Each of the rest of the students have a soccer ball and dribble it around the area. The defensive players try to take away a ball from the offensive players. When a successful steal is made, the player losing control of the ball becomes a defensive player.

DYNAMIC PHYSICAL EDUCATION LESSON PLAN
Soccer-Related Activities (Lesson 2)
Level II

Supplies and Equipment Needed:
One foam rubber or playground ball per two or three children
Cones for marking playing areas
Tape player
Music
Jump ropes (optional)

MOVEMENT EXPERIENCE— CONTENT	ORGANIZATION AND TEACHING HINTS	EXPECTED STUDENT OBJECTIVES AND OUTCOMES

INTRODUCTORY ACTIVITY (2 – 3 MINUTES)

Partner Over and Under

Students pair up with one person on the floor and the other standing ready to move. On signal, the standing students move over, under and/or around the persons on the floor. On signal, reverse positions. Students on the floor can also alternate between positions such as curl, stretch and bridge.

DPE p. 257

Partner formation.

Encourage students to move as quickly as possible.

Challenge them to see how many times they can go over and under each other.

PM.—The student will be able to move quickly over, under, and around his or her partner.

Aff.—Warm-up activities work only when an individual is motivated to move quickly and with intensity.

FITNESS DEVELOPMENT ACTIVITIES (7 – 8 MINUTES)

Teacher Leader Exercises

Tape alternating segments of silence (10 seconds) to signal a change of exercise and music to signal the duration of exercise (40 seconds).

Sitting Stretch	40 seconds
Power Jumper	40 seconds
Jumping Jacks	40 seconds
Abdominal Challenges	40 seconds
Single-Leg Crab Kick	40 seconds
Knee to Chest Curl	40 seconds
Windmill	40 seconds
Trunk twister	40 seconds

Conclude the routine with 2 to 4 minutes of jogging, rope jumping or other continuous activity.

Increase the duration of exercises by 10 to 20% over the previous week.

DPE pp. 289 – 299

Scatter formation.

Allow students to adjust the work load to their ability and fitness level. This implies that some students will perform more repetitions in the same amount of time.

Rotate to different parts of the teaching area and help motivate students.

Cog.—The student will be able to identify the activities by name.

Aff.—Compare performances occurring three weeks ago with present performances. Discuss the attitude that self-improvement is self-rewarding and motivates the learner to continue the effort.

LESSON FOCUS (15 – 20 MINUTES)

The soccer lesson works well in a circuit of instructional stations. Divide the skills into four to six stations and place the necessary equipment and instructions at each.

Soccer-Related Activities (2)
Skills

1. Review long pass and short pass.
2. Outside foot pass: Use the outside of the foot. More of a push than a kick.
3. Dribbling: Move the ball with a series of taps. Start slowly and don't kick the ball too far away from the player.

DPE pp. 663 – 665

One ball per two children or triangle formation; one ball for each group of three children.

8 1/2" foam rubber training balls are best for learning proper form in soccer activities.

Start expecting quality and accuracy in the kicks, passes, and traps.

PM.—The student will be able to kick, dribble, trap, and pass the soccer ball by the end of the week.

Cog.—The student will be able to describe the situations in which the heel and outside foot kicks should be used.

MOVEMENT EXPERIENCE—CONTENT	ORGANIZATION AND TEACHING HINTS	EXPECTED STUDENT OBJECTIVES AND OUTCOMES
4. Passing: Start passing the ball from a stationary position and then progress to moving while passing.	Heel kick and outside foot kick are used for short distances only.	Aff.—When soccer is taught in a co-ed situation, students must appreciate individual differences. Aff.—Good passes can be easily handled by a teammate. Praise passes and teamwork.
Drills 1. Shuttle turnback: Use this drill to practice passing for accuracy. 2. Shuttle dribbling: Use to practice dribbling and short passes. 3. Three-man shuttle dribble drill. A good drill to use to encourage well-controlled dribbling. 4. Passing drill: Use a double shuttle formation. Two players progress down the field. 5. Dribbling Keep-Away: Half of class has a ball for each player. The other half of the class tries to take away a ball and retain control while dribbling. Activity is continuous.	*DPE* pp. 668 – 674 Review the skills taught last lesson and integrate them into this lesson. Proper motor patterns can be learned only when they are reviewed and practiced many times. Keep the lines short in the drill activities. Use a series of cones as objects to dribble around. Use short lines with an emphasis on passing accuracy. Emphasis should be placed on controlled, accurate dribbling. The grid system described on pages 669 – 673 is excellent for skill practice and drills.	Cog.—Flexibility is the range of motion at a joint. Flexibility is important in kicking activities as more force can be generated over a greater range of motion. Discuss the importance of stretching in order to lengthen connective tissue. PM.—The student will practice and use the soccer skills learned previously. Cog.—The student will be able to recite the basic rules of soccer. Cog.—Muscle soreness may occur from the breakdown of connective tissue. Excessive exercise (in relation to the amount of activity a person normally performs) may cause an imbalance in the breakdown–buildup process, and soreness will result. Students should understand the need for progressively increasing work load to minimize soreness.

GAME (5 – 7 MINUTES)

Soccer Lead-Up Games

Diagonal Soccer—*DPE*, p. 674

Supplies: A soccer ball, pinnies (optional)

Skills: Kicking, passing, dribbling, some controlling, defending, blocking shots

Two corners are marked off with cones 5 ft from the corners on both the sides, outlining triangular dead areas. Each team lines up and protects two adjacent sides of the square. The dead area on the opposite corner marks the opposing team's goal lines. To begin competition, three players from each team move into the playing area in their own half of the space. These are the active players. During play, they may roam anywhere in the square. The other players act as line guards.

The object of the game is for active players to kick the ball through the opposing team's line (beneath shoulder height) to score. When a score is made, active players rotate to the sidelines and new players take their place. Players on the sidelines may block the ball with their bodies but cannot use their hands. The team against whom the point was scored starts the ball for the next point. Only active players may score. Scoring is much the same as in Circle Kickball in that a point is awarded for the opponents when any of the following occur.

1. A team allows the ball to go through its line below the shoulders.
2. A team touches the ball illegally.
3. A team kicks the ball over the other team above shoulder height.

Variations:

1. If the class is large, a bigger area and more active players can be used.
2. If scoring seems too easy, the line defenders can use their hands to stop the ball.

MOVEMENT EXPERIENCE— CONTENT	ORGANIZATION AND TEACHING HINTS	EXPECTED STUDENT OBJECTIVES AND OUTCOMES

Soccer Touch Ball—*DPE*, p. 674

Supplies: A soccer ball

Skills: Kicking, controlling

Players are spaced around a circle 10 yd in diameter with two players in the center. The object of the game is to keep the players in the center from touching the ball. The ball is passed back and forth as in soccer. If a center player touches the ball with a foot, the person who kicked the ball goes to the center. If a circle player commits an error (i.e., misses a ball), the person responsible changes places with a center player. A rule that no player may contain or hold the ball longer than 3 seconds tends to keep the game moving.

Dribblerama—*DPE*, p. 675

Supplies: One soccer ball for each player

Skills: Dribbling, protecting the ball

The playing area is a large circle or square, clearly outlined. All players dribble within the area. The game is played on two levels.

Level 1: Each player dribbles throughout the area, controlling the ball so that it does not touch another ball. If a touch occurs, both players go outside the area and dribble counterclockwise around the area. Once youngsters have completed dribbling one lap of the counterclockwise path, they may reenter the game.

Level 2: While dribbling and controlling the ball, each player attempts to kick any other ball out of the area. When a ball is kicked out, the player owning that ball takes it outside and dribbles around the area. Play continues until only two or three players who have not lost control of their ball are left. These are declared the winners. Bring all players back into the game and repeat.

Bull's Eye—*DPE*, p. 675

Supplies: One soccer ball per player

Skills: Dribbling, protecting the ball

The playing area is a large outlined area—circle, square, or rectangle. One player holds a ball in her hands, which serves as the bull's-eye. The other players dribble within the area. The player with the bull's-eye attempts to throw her ball (basketball push shot) at any other ball. The ball that is hit now becomes the new bull's-eye. The old bull's-eye becomes one of the dribblers. A new bull's-eye cannot hit back immediately at the old bull's-eye. A dribbler should protect the ball with her body. If the group is large, have two bull's-eyes. No score is kept and no one is eliminated.

DYNAMIC PHYSICAL EDUCATION LESSON PLAN
Fundamental Skills Through Playground Games
Level II

Supplies and Equipment Needed:
 Jump ropes
 Signs for circuit training stations
 Cones
 Balls
 Hula hoops

MOVEMENT EXPERIENCE—CONTENT	ORGANIZATION AND TEACHING HINTS	EXPECTED STUDENT OBJECTIVES AND OUTCOMES

INTRODUCTORY ACTIVITY (2 – 3 MINUTES)

Run, Stop and Pivot

The class should run, stop on signal and pivot. Vary the activity by having the class pivot on the left or right foot and increase the circumference of the pivot.

Movement should be continuous. Students should continue running after the pivot.

DPE p. 254

Emphasize correct form in stopping and absorbing force.

Make sure students do not cross legs or lose balance while pivoting.

Allow a few moments of free practice.

Cog.—The pivot is used in many sports such as basketball and baseball.

PM.—The student will be able to stop, pivot, and move by the end of the week.

FITNESS DEVELOPMENT ACTIVITIES (7 – 8 MINUTES)

Circuit Training

Tape alternating segments of silence and music to signal duration of exercise. Music segments (begin at 30 seconds) indicate activity at each station while intervals of silence (10 seconds) announce it is time to stop and move forward to the next station.
Rope Jumping
Triceps Push-Ups
Agility Run
Body Circles
Hula Hoop
Knee Touch Curl-Ups
Crab Walk
Tortoise and Hare
Bend and Twist

Conclude circuit training with 2–4 minutes of walking, jogging, rope jumping or other aerobic activity.

DPE pp. 300 – 303

Use signals such as "start," "stop," "move up" to ensure rapid movement to the next station.

Move randomly from station to station to offer help for students who are not using correct technique.

Cog.—Circuit training should work all parts of the body, but no two similar parts in succession.

Cog.—The student will be able to describe how overload is achieved (by increasing the length of activity at each station and decreasing the rest between stations).

Cog.—In order that circuit training be effective, *quality* exercise must be performed at each station.

143

MOVEMENT EXPERIENCE—CONTENT	ORGANIZATION AND TEACHING HINTS	EXPECTED STUDENT OBJECTIVES AND OUTCOMES

LESSON FOCUS AND GAME (15 – 20 MINUTES)

Fundamental Skills Through Playground Games

The objective of this lesson should be to teach youngsters the rules and methods for playing games during their free time. Emphasis should be on self-direction so students do not need supervision.
1. Tetherball, (*DPE,* p. 592)
2. Four Square, (*DPE,* p. 589)
3. Two Square, (*DPE,* P. 592)
4. Volley Tennis, (*DPE,* p. 592)
5. Basketball
   a. Around the Key (*DPE,* p. 629)
   b. Twenty One, (*DPE,* p. 631)
   c. Freeze Out, (*DPE,* p. 632)
6. Hopscotch
7. Jump Rope
8. Soccer (2 on 2)
9. Frisbee Golf, (*DPE,* p. 589)
10. Wall Handball
11. Any recreational games played at your school.

Emphasis should be placed on teaching the rules of the activities so children can enjoy them on their own time.

It might be useful to set up the activities at four or five different stations and then rotate the students from one activity to the next.

If you know a traditional game played by children in your area for many years, now is a good time to teach it.

PM.—The student will be able to play at least four of the given activities.

Cog.—The student will be able to recite the rules for playing four or more of the activities.

Aff.—Recreational activities can be an excellent release for reducing stress. Relaxation demands playing for enjoyment and personal pleasure. Adults spend millions of dollars searching for activities that are relaxing and rewarding.

DYNAMIC PHYSICAL EDUCATION LESSON PLAN
Long-Rope Jumping Skills
Level II

Supplies and Equipment Needed:
  Two long-jump ropes (16 ft.) for a group of four to six children
  Individual jump ropes
  Tom-tom
  Cones
  Circuit training signs
  Balls or beanbags
  Cageball
  Tape player
  Music
  Hula hoops

MOVEMENT EXPERIENCE—CONTENT	ORGANIZATION AND TEACHING HINTS	EXPECTED STUDENT OBJECTIVES AND OUTCOMES

INTRODUCTORY ACTIVITY (2 – 3 MINUTES)

European Rhythmic Running

To introduce a group of children to Rhythmic Running, have them clap to the beat of the drum. Next, as they clap, have them shuffle their feet in place, keeping time. Following this, have them run in place, omitting the clapping. Finally, the class can run in single-file formation, develop the ability to follow a leader, maintain proper spacing and move to the rhythm of the tom-tom.

Variation: have leader move in different shapes and designs. Have class freeze and see if they can identify the shape or formation.

DPE pp. 252 – 253

Single-file formation with a leader.

Start the class by moving feet, in place, to the beat of the tom-tom at a slow pace and gradually speed up. Add clapping hands. Add movement after the above is accomplished. The beat must be fast enough so students move at a fast trot with knees up.

Cog.—The student will describe six sport and recreational activities in which the body moves rhythmically.

PM.—The student will be able to move rhythmically with the beat of the tom-tom by the end of the week.

FITNESS DEVELOPMENT ACTIVITIES (7 – 8 MINUTES)

Circuit Training

Tape alternating segments of silence and music to signal duration of exercise. Music segments (begin at 30 seconds) indicate activity at each station while intervals of silence (10 seconds) announce it is time to stop and move forward to the next station.
Rope Jumping
Triceps Push-Ups
Agility Run
Body circles
Hula Hoop
Knee Touch Curl-Ups
Crab Walk
Tortoise and Hare
Bend and Twist

Conclude circuit training with 2–4 minutes of walking, jogging rope jumping or other aerobic activity.

DPE pp. 300 – 303

Emphasize quality of movement rather than quantity and lack of technique.

PM.—The student will be able to perform all exercises.

Cog.—The student will be able to state which circuit exercises develop the various areas of the body.

Aff.—Most fitness gains are made when the body is exercised past the point of initial fatigue. Thus, briefly discuss the value of pushing one's self past the first signs of tiring.

MOVEMENT EXPERIENCE—CONTENT	ORGANIZATION AND TEACHING HINTS	EXPECTED STUDENT OBJECTIVES AND OUTCOMES

LESSON FOCUS (15 – 20 MINUTES)

Long-Rope Jumping Skills

1. Run through turning rope from front door approach.
2. Run through turning rope from back door approach.
3. Try different approaches, a few jumps and varied exits
   a. Run in front door, out back door.
   b. Run in front door and out front door.
   c. Run in back door and out back door.
   d. Run in back door and out front door.
   e. Run in front or back door, jump and do a quarter, half and full turn in the air.
   f. Add individual rope.
   g. Individual choice or with a partner.
4. Hot Pepper: *Gradually* increase the speed of the rope. Use the verse, (*DPE*, p 448).
5. High Water: *Gradually* raise the height of the rope while it is turned.
6. Have more than one child jump at a time. Students can enter in pairs or any other combination. Have jumpers change positions while jumping.
7. Have jumper attempt to jump while holding beanbag or playground ball between knees.
8. Have one of the turners jump the long rope.
9. Play catch with a partner while jumping the rope.
10. Egg Beater: Two long ropes are turned simultaneously with four turners.
11. Double Dutch: Requires two long ropes turned alternately. Rope near jumper is turned back door and far rope front door.
12. Combination movements: three or four ropes in sequence.

DPE pp. 446 – 451

Groups of 4 or 5 children.

Change turners frequently. Make sure that all children get a chance to both turn and jump.

When jumping front door, the rope is turned toward the jumper, as compared to back door where the rope is turned away from the jumper.

Back door is much more difficult. Approach the rope at a 45° angle.

Turners maintain a constant rhythm with the rope.

Children who have trouble jumping should face one of the turners and key their jumps to both the visual and audio cues (hand movement and sound of the rope hitting the floor).

It might be helpful to review beanbag activities briefly as a change of pace (rest) activity.

Try to eliminate excessive body movement while jumping, i.e., jumping too high, knees too high, or excessive arm movement.

Double Dutch contests for speed and endurance may be motivating.

The jumper must jump twice as fast as each rope is turning to succeed (Double Dutch).

Students can be challenged to perform a different activity as they pass through each rope.

PM.—The student will be able to jump the rope a minimum of 15 times consecutively without a miss.

Cog.—In terms of physical exertion, 10 minutes of rope jumping is equal to 30 minutes of jogging.

Aff.—Rope jumping is neither a male nor a female activity. It is performed by boxers, football players, and dancers for fitness development.

Cog.—The student will learn to react to rope jumping terms: front door, back door, hot pepper, high water, etc.

Cog.—Two misconceptions prevail in regard to weight control. One is that exercise burns a small amount of calories and thus has no impact on weight, and the other is that exercise increases appetite. This ignores the fact that if a mile were run every day, the person would burn 12 lbs. of fat in a year. Activity does not appear to significantly increase appetite.

Cog.—Aerobic endurance is usually measured by speed or distance in a given time frame. Allow students to devise some informal methods of evaluating their aerobic fitness.

MOVEMENT EXPERIENCE— CONTENT	ORGANIZATION AND TEACHING HINTS	EXPECTED STUDENT OBJECTIVES AND OUTCOMES

GAME (5 – 7 MINUTES)

Fly Trap—*DPE*, p. 575
  Supplies: None
  Skills: Fundamental locomotor movements
  Half of the class is scattered around the playing area, sitting on the floor in cross-legged fashion. These children form the trap. The other children are the flies, and they buzz around the seated children. When a whistle is blown, the flies must freeze where they are. If any of the trappers can touch a fly, that fly sits down at that spot and becomes a trapper. The trappers must keep their seats glued to the floor.
  The game continues until all of the flies are caught. Some realism is given to the game if the flies make buzzing sounds and move their arms as wings.
  Teaching suggestion: Some experience with the game enables the teacher to determine how far apart to place the seated children. After all (or most) of the flies have been caught, the groups trade places. The method of locomotion should be changed occasionally also.

Trades—*DPE*, p. 579
  Supplies: None
  Skills: Imagery, running, dodging
  The class is divided into two teams of equal number, each of which has a goal line. One team, the chasers, remains behind its goal line. The other team, the runners, approaches from its goal line, marching to the following dialogue:
  Runners: Here we come.
  Chasers: Where from?
  Runners: New Orleans.
  Chasers: What's your trade?
  Runners: Lemonade.
  Chasers: Show us some.
  Runners move up close to the other team's goal line and proceed to act out an occupation or a specific task that they have chosen previously. The opponents try to guess what the pantomime represents. On a correct guess, the running team must run back to its goal line chased by the others. Any runner tagged must join the chasers. The game is repeated with roles reversed. The team ending with the greater number of players is the winner.
  Teaching suggestion: If a team has trouble guessing the pantomime, the other team should provide hints. Teams also should be encouraged to have a number of activities selected so that little time is consumed in choosing the next activity to be pantomimed.

Fox Hunt—*DPE*, p. 575
  Supplies: None
  Skills: Running, dodging
  Two players form trees by facing each other and holding hands. The third member of the group is a fox and stands between the hands of the trees. Three players are identified as foxes without trees and three players are designated as hounds. The hounds try to tag foxes who are not in trees. The extra foxes may move to a tree and displace the fox who is standing in the tree. In addition, the foxes in trees may leave the safety of their trees at any time. If the hound tags a fox, their roles are reversed immediately, the fox becoming the hound.
  The game should be stopped at regular intervals to allow the players who are trees to change places with the foxes and hounds. Different locomotor movements can be specified to add variety to the game.

DYNAMIC PHYSICAL EDUCATION LESSON PLAN
Manipulative Skills Using Playground Balls
Level II

Supplies and Equipment Needed:
One 8 1/2" playground ball for each student
Tambourine
Eight cones
Magic number cards
Circuit training signs
Balls
Tape player
Music
Jump ropes
Hula hoops and scarves

MOVEMENT EXPERIENCE— CONTENT	ORGANIZATION AND TEACHING HINTS	EXPECTED STUDENT OBJECTIVES AND OUTCOMES

INTRODUCTORY ACTIVITY (2 – 3 MINUTES)

Magic Number Challenges

Students are challenged to put together a combination of movements corresponding to the magic numbers designated (e.g., 10, 8 and 7). Students would have to do three different movements 10, 8 and 7 time, respectively. The number of movements, the repetitions and the types of movements can be changed to offer a wide variety of challenges.

DPE p. 254

Scatter formation.

Movements can be stretching, locomotor, nonlocomotor, and specialized sport skills.

Challenge students to develop new sequences.

PM.—The student will be able to perform the challenges rapidly and with concise changes from one movement to the next.

Cog.—The student will be able to immediately identify the total number of repetitions as well as movements.

FITNESS DEVELOPMENT ACTIVITIES (7 – 8 MINUTES)

Circuit Training

Tape alternating segments of silence and music to signal duration of exercise. Music segments (begin at 30 seconds) indicate activity at each station while intervals of silence (10 seconds) announce it is time to stop and move forward to the next station.
Rope Jumping
Push-Up Challenges
Agility Run
Lower Leg Stretch
Juggling Scarves
Abdominal Challenges
Alternate Leg Extension
Tortoise and Hare
Bear Hug

Conclude circuit training with 2–4 minutes of walking, jogging, rope jumping or other aerobic activity.

DPE pp. 300 – 303

Increase to 35 seconds of exercise followed by 10 seconds of time to move and prepare for the next station.

Hula hoops and juggling scarves placed at a station allow youngsters a chance to rest and are motivating activities.

This is the last week of circuit training. Encourage improvement of performance and technique.

Cog.—Muscles atrophy without exercise and grow stronger with use. The student will be able to describe in his own words the need for exercise.

MOVEMENT EXPERIENCE—CONTENT	ORGANIZATION AND TEACHING HINTS	EXPECTED STUDENT OBJECTIVES AND OUTCOMES

LESSON FOCUS (15 – 20 MINUTES)

Manipulative Skills Using Playground Balls

Give students two or three activities to practice so you have time to move and help youngsters. Alternate activities from each of the categories so students receive a variety of skills to practice.

Individual Activities
Controlled rolling and handling

1. Sit, stand, or on back—roll ball around and handle it between legs, behind back to develop a proper "feel" of the ball.

Bounce and catch

1. Two hands, one hand.
2. Bounce at different levels.
3. Bounce between legs.
4. Close eyes and bounce.
5. Dribble ball in a stationary and/or moving position.
6. Dribble and follow the commands, such as: move forward, backward, in a circle, sideways, while walking, galloping, trotting, etc.
7. Exploratory activity.

Toss and catch

1. Toss and catch, vary height.
2. Add various challenges while tossing (i.e., touch floor, clap hands, turn, make body turns, sit down, lie down).
3. Toss and let bounce. Also add some challenges as above.
4. Toss up and catch behind back—toss from behind back and catch in front of body.
5. Create moving challenges (i.e., toss, run five steps, catch, toss, back up five hops, and catch).
6. Exploratory activity.

Bat the ball (as in volleyball) to self (teach a low-controlled bat).

1. Bat the ball—use palm, back, and side of hand.
2. Bat the ball using different body parts.

Foot skills

1. Pick the ball with both feet and catch. Both front and rear of body catch.
2. From a sitting position, ball between feet, toss ball up and catch with hands.

DPE pp. 413 – 417

Emphasize keeping the eyes on the ball and catching with the fingertips.

One 8 1/2" playground ball is needed for each child.

Make sure children "give" when they catch the ball and make a soft home.

Encourage children to start with a low toss in the air and gradually increase the height of the throw as skill increases.

The purpose of the many variations is to force children to keep their eyes on the moving object while performing other activities with their bodies.

Strive for quality, good throws, and a high percentage of catches.

Watch for proper challenges. Change activities rapidly.

The music "Sweet Georgia Brown" may stimulate special ball-handling skills.

Allow student choice.

PM.—The students will be able to catch the balls on their fingertips.

PM.—The student will be able to keep her eyes on the ball during all challenges and activities.

PM.—The student will be able to make a toss that enables her to make a catch.

Cog.—The student will be able to interpret orally the many uses of the basic ball skills introduced in this lesson.

Aff.—Develop the attitude that mere accomplishment of a skill is not a goal of people who excel. Rather, a person must be able to master the skill many times and with consistency to be a champion.

Cog.—A study in England classified 2.5 million people by occupation (sedentary and nonsedentary). Findings revealed that people engaged in occupations requiring only light physical work had a higher rate of death due to coronary heart disease compared with people engaged in heavy physical work. Discuss the need for exercise to ensure cardiovascular health.

MOVEMENT EXPERIENCE— CONTENT	ORGANIZATION AND TEACHING HINTS	EXPECTED STUDENT OBJECTIVES AND OUTCOMES

3. While sitting, toss ball up with hands and catch with feet.
4. Put ball between feet or knees and play tag games.
5. Keep ball in air by using feet, knees, head. How many times can you bounce it in succession.
6. Exploratory activity.

Partner Activities

Passing skills

1. Two-handed, right and left.
2. Throw to various targets—high, low, right and left.
3. Odd throws—under leg, around body, football center, shot-put, windmill, discus. Off floor.
4. Push-shot types. Straight push, arch.
5. Roll the ball to partner. Flick it in the air with foot and catch.
6. Have one partner dribble and the other attempt to take it away without fouling.
7. Exploratory activity.

Partner formation. Distance about 15 feet.

Chest target first.

Stress passing and catching skills.

Seek variety.

Watch finger position.

Cog.—The student will be able to identify the sport in which various passes are used.

PM.—The student will be able to pass (all variations) and catch the ball without dropping it, three times in a row.

Cog.—"Giving" at the elbow and shoulder joint when catching a ball increases the distance over which the force is absorbed. This lessens rebound and makes catching easier.

Volleyball and handball-type skills

1. Serve. Toss and return. Overhand serve.
2. Bat back and forth like hand tennis. Bat over a line.

Experiment with hand positions.

Stress control.

Aff.—Ask students to keep an activity diary for 24 hours. At the next meeting, the amounts of time involved in activity can be compared. The amount of calories expended can be evaluated.

Use follow activity

One partner tries something and the other follows. Specify number of turns; then reverse.

Seek variety.

Could set up sequences.

GAME (5 – 7 MINUTES)

Bounce Ball—*DPE*, p. 572
   Supplies: Volleyballs or rubber playground balls of about the same size
   Skills: Throwing, ball rolling
   The court is divided into halves (30 by 40 ft each). Children form two teams. Each team occupies one half of the court and is given a number of balls. One or two players from each team should be assigned to retrieve balls behind their own end lines. The object of the game is to bounce or roll the ball over the opponents' end line. A ball thrown across the line on a fly does not count.
   Two scorers are needed, one at each end line. Players can move wherever they wish in their own area but cannot cross the centerline. After the starting signal, the balls are thrown back and forth at will.
   Variation: A row of benches is placed across the center line. Throws must go over the benches and bounce in the other team's area to score.

One Step—*DPE*, p. 578
   Supplies: A ball or beanbag for each pair of children
   Skills: Throwing, catching
   Two children stand facing each other about 3 ft apart. One has a ball or a beanbag. The object of the game is to throw or toss the item in the stipulated manner so that the partner can catch it without moving his feet on or from the ground. When the throw is completed successfully, the thrower takes one step backward and waits for the throw from her partner. Children can try to increase their distance to an established line, or the two children who move the greatest distance apart can be declared the winners. Variables to provide interest and challenge are type of throw, type of catch, and kind of step. Throwing can be underhand, overhand, two-handed, under one leg, around the back, and so on. Catching can be two-handed, left-handed, right-handed, to the side, and so on. The step can be a giant step, a tiny step, a hop, a jump, or a similar movement.

MOVEMENT EXPERIENCE— CONTENT	ORGANIZATION AND TEACHING HINTS	EXPECTED STUDENT OBJECTIVES AND OUTCOMES

When either child misses, moves the feet, or fails to follow directions, the partners move forward and start over. A double line of children facing each other makes a satisfactory formation.

Variation: <u>Bowling One Step.</u> In groups of squad size or smaller, each of the players in turn gets a chance to roll the ball at a bowling pin. A minimal distance (5 to 10 ft) is established, so that most bowlers can hit the pin on the first try. The player takes a step backward each time the pin is knocked down, and keeps rolling until he misses. The winner is the child who has moved the farthest from the pin. Instead of backward steps, stipulated distances (5, 10, 15, and 20 ft) can be used.

DYNAMIC PHYSICAL EDUCATION LESSON PLAN
Throwing Skills (Lesson 2)
Level II

Supplies and Equipment Needed:
  Tumbling mats for targets
  Tires, hoops, or jump ropes
  Cones
  Yarn balls, beanbags, and beach balls
  Scooters
  Tom-tom or tambourine
  Tennis or rug balls
  Blocks or bottles

MOVEMENT EXPERIENCE— CONTENT	ORGANIZATION AND TEACHING HINTS	EXPECTED STUDENT OBJECTIVES AND OUTCOMES

INTRODUCTORY ACTIVITY (2 – 3 MINUTES)

Fastest Tag in the West

All students are it. On signal, they try to tag each other. If they are tagged, they must freeze, but they are eligible to tag other students who pass near them. If two or more players tag each other simultaneously, they are both/all "frozen."

DPE p. 257

Avoid playing the game when only one or two players are left untagged. Start the game over a number of times to assure all students will have the opportunity to be active.

FITNESS DEVELOPMENT ACTIVITIES (7 – 8 MINUTES)

Walk, Trot and Sprint

Move to the following signals:
  1. One drumbeat - walk.
  2. Two drumbeats - trot.
  3. Three drumbeats - sprint.
  4. Whistle - freeze and perform exercises.

Perform various strength and flexibility exercises between bouts of walk, trot and sprint. Examples are:
  1. Bend and Twist
  2. Sitting Stretch
  3. Push-Up Challenges
  4. Abdominal Challenges
  5. Trunk Twister
  6. Body Circles
  7. Crab Walk

Tape alternating segments of silence and music to signal duration of exercise. Music segments indicate aerobic activity (30–45 seconds) while intervals of silence announce flexibility and strength development activities (30 seconds).

DPE pp. 285 – 286

Use a tom-tom.

Scatter formation.

Emphasize quality of movement and rapid changes.

Check heart rate after bouts of sprinting.

Assure that sprinting is done under control to avoid collisions.

Encourage students to change directions sharply, even to the point of pivoting at each turn.

Cog.—Static stretching involves stretching without bouncing. Stretches should be held for 15–30 seconds for maximum benefit.

PM.—The student will demonstrate the ability to put proper stress on muscles in stretching.

MOVEMENT EXPERIENCE— CONTENT	ORGANIZATION AND TEACHING HINTS	EXPECTED STUDENT OBJECTIVES AND OUTCOMES

LESSON FOCUS (15 – 20 MINUTES)

Throwing Skills (2)
Individual Activities

1. Throw yarn balls from a standing position 20 feet from the wall. Throw five balls, retrieve and repeat.
2. Throwing rag balls or tennis balls using the proper grip. Throw against mats on the wall. Throw from a distance of 20 to 25 feet depending on skill level. Student should be able to hit the wall.

Throwing for Velocity

Set up activities using large targets so students will throw forcefully.

a. Throw at mats on the wall. Throw tennis balls hard from 16 to 20 feet. Retrieve only if the balls roll beyond the throwing line.

b. Throw at hoops leaning against mats on the wall.

c. Large target throw. Use a circle or square 4 feet in diameter placed on the wall. Students should throw from 20 to 35 feet.

Throwing at targets

1. Intermediate-level target activities.
   a. Throw through hoops suspended from goals.
   b. Allow a partner to hold the hoop target.
   c. Use large boxes for targets and try to throw inside the box. Try throwing at the side of the box.

   d. Cageball throw. Throwers try to move it into the corner by throwing at it.
   e. Upright hoops set on floor.
   f. Graduated-size target throw. Use a large concentric circle (or square) with 4 feet, 3 feet and 2 feet diameter circles.

DPE pp. 349 – 351

Redirect with appropriate cues:
   1. Throw hard!
   2. Take a big step, then throw!
   3. Really get your throwing arm behind your head to start the throw!
May need to set up a diagonal throwing line so that all skill levels are challenged to throw hard.

Everyone should do the stations a minimum of two days.

Each student should start with five balls.

The teacher should continue to give feedback to the students that will help them improve their form.

Put hoops touching one another for easier targets; spread apart for more difficult target.

The teacher should make a special effort to encourage throwing with force and good form, rather than hitting a target.

Use firm yarn balls.

Washer/dryer or refrigerator boxes.

Two types of targets:
a. Cut the side out of the box so that the opening faces the student. Use beanbags.
b. Paint targets on the side of the box and throw at the target. Use yarn balls or beanbags.

Use small playground balls.

Place the cageball 15 ft. from the wall, in a corner.

Student should be encouraged to hit the target anywhere.

Student should be encouraged to set goals as his skill increases.

Cog.—Students will know what a mature throw looks like.

Cog.—Students will know the components of a mature throw.

Cog.—Students should begin to realize what parts of the throw result in the greatest force production.

Aff.—Students will begin to value throwing hard.

PM.—The students should begin every throw from a side-facing position.

PM.—The student should take a step with the contralateral foot.

Aff.—Students should value throwing with good form more than hitting a target.

Aff.—Students should feel comfortable choosing any task.

MOVEMENT EXPERIENCE— CONTENT	ORGANIZATION AND TEACHING HINTS	EXPECTED STUDENT OBJECTIVES AND OUTCOMES

GAMES (5 – 7 MINUTES)

In the Prison
Supplies: 15–20 throwing balls
Skill: Throwing
Two teams, one assigned to each half of the gym. Balls (15–20) are placed on the center line. On signal, each team throws the balls to the other side of the gym. The object of the game is to get all the balls into the other team's backcourt area (or prison) which extends 10 feet from the wall. The teacher stops play by blowing a whistle, then counting the number of balls in the "prison."

Snowball
Supplies: 36 yarn balls
Skill: Throwing
Two teams, one assigned to each half of the gym. Each student has a yarn ball. Players can be hit three times. Each time they are hit they call out the number (1, 2, 3) of times they have been hit. After the third hit they must go to the side of the area and count to 25 before they can reenter. Teams must stay in their half of the gym.

Center Target Throw
Supplies: 20 - 8" gray foam balls and 20 bowling pins
Skill: Throwing
The area is divided into quadrants. Two teams compete, and each team has its own set of targets (bowling pins) set on a center line.
Half of each team is placed in opposing quadrants with the pins in the middle. Team A, on the left half of the area, has players on both sides of the center line behind restraining lines 15 to 20 feet away from the center target line. Team B is positioned the same way on the right half of the area. Each team tries to knock down all of its bowling pins as quickly as possible.

Target Ball Throw
Supplies: 10 - 18" beachballs and 36 yarn balls
Skill: Throwing
Beachballs are placed on the center line of the gym. There are two teams and each must stay in its half of the gym. Players have yarn balls. The object of the game is to roll the beachballs into the other team's court by hitting them with the yarn balls. The team that has the least number of beachballs on its side when the teacher blows the whistle is the winner.

DYNAMIC PHYSICAL EDUCATION LESSON PLAN
Walking and Jogging Skills
Level II

Supplies and Equipment Needed:
  Recreational and individual equipment as desired
  Tom-tom or tambourine

MOVEMENT EXPERIENCE—CONTENT	ORGANIZATION AND TEACHING HINTS	EXPECTED STUDENT OBJECTIVES AND OUTCOMES

INTRODUCTORY ACTIVITIES (2 – 3 MINUTES)

Group Tag

A number of players are designated to be it. On signal, they try to tag other players. If a player is tagged, that player becomes it and must try to tag another. In other words, each person who is it tags only one player. If players want to be "safe," they must hold hands in a group of three or more students.

DPE p. 568

This should be a continuous-movement tag game. Players who are it should simultaneously tag and verbalize "you're it" to avoid confusion.

FITNESS DEVELOPMENT ACTIVITIES (7 – 8 MINUTES)

Walk, Trot and Sprint

Move to the following signals:
  1. One drumbeat - walk.
  2. Two drumbeats - trot.
  3. Three drumbeats - sprint.
  4. Whistle - freeze and perform exercises.

Perform various strength and flexibility exercises between bouts of walk, trot and sprint. Examples are:
  1. Bend and Twist
  2. Sitting Stretch
  3. Push-Up Challenges
  4. Abdominal Challenges
  5. Trunk Twister
  6. Body Circles
  7. Crab Walk

Tape alternating segments of silence and music to signal duration of exercise. Music segments indicate aerobic activity (30–45 seconds) while intervals of silence announce flexibility and strength development activities (30 seconds).

DPE pp. 285 – 286

Use a tom-tom or tambourine.

Scatter formation.

Emphasize quality of movement and rapid changes.

Check heart rate after bouts of sprinting.

Assure that sprinting is done under control to avoid collisions.

Encourage students to change directions sharply, even to the point of pivoting at each turn.

PM.—The student will demonstrate the ability to put proper stress on muscles in stretching.

Cog.—Flexors decrease the angle of a joint, and extensors cause the return from flexion. Identify different flexor and extensor muscle groups and the joint they affect.

155

MOVEMENT EXPERIENCE—CONTENT	ORGANIZATION AND TEACHING HINTS	EXPECTED STUDENT OBJECTIVES AND OUTCOMES

LESSON FOCUS (15 – 20 MINUTES)

Walking and Jogging Skills

The walking and jogging lesson should be a relaxed lesson with emphasis on developing activity patterns that can be used outside of the school environment. An educational approach to this lesson can teach students that walking and jogging is done without equipment and offers excellent health benefits. It is an activity that can literally be done for a lifetime. The following are suggestions for implementing this unit of instruction:

1. Youngsters should be allowed to find a friend with whom they want to jog or walk. The result is usually a friend of similar ability level. A way to judge correct pace is to be able to talk with a friend without undue stress. If students are too winded to talk, they are probably running too fast. A selected friend will encourage talking and help assure that the experience is positive and within the student's aerobic capacity. *Pace, not race* is the motto.

2. Jogging and walking should be done in any direction so people are unable to keep track of the distance covered. Doing laps on a track is one of the surest ways to discourage less able youngsters. They always finish last and are open to chiding by the rest of the class.

3. Jogging and walking should be done for a specified time rather than a specified distance. All youngsters should not have to run the same distance. This goes against the philosophy of accompanying individual differences and varying aerobic capacities. Running or walking for a set amount of time will allow the less able child to move without fear of ridicule.

4. Teachers should not be concerned about foot action, since the child selects naturally the means that is most comfortable. Arm movement should be easy and natural, with elbows bent. The head and upper body should be held up and back. The eyes look ahead. The general body position in walking and jogging should be erect but relaxed. Jogging on the toes should be avoided.

DPE pp. 309 – 310

Teach children the proper style of running.

Start students at a short distance so they will not become discouraged.

Concentrate on teaching the values of walking and jogging and encourage students to start their own jogging program.

"Train, don't strain."

PM.—The student will be able to demonstrate proper jogging style.

Aff.—Jogging and walking are some of the best activities for developing cardiovascular endurance. Discuss the value of jogging and walking for personal health.

Cog.—The student will be able to list three chronic training effects jogging and walking has on the body.

5. Jogging and walking should not be a competitive, timed activity. Each youngster should move at a self-determined pace. Racing belongs in the track program. Another reason to avoid speed is that racing keeps youngsters from learning to pace themselves. For developing endurance and gaining health benefits, it is more important to move for a longer time at a slower speed than to run at top speed for a shorter distance.

6. It can be motivating for youngsters if they run with a piece of equipment, i.e., beanbag or jump rope. They can play catch with a beanbag or roll a hoop while walking or jogging.

"Pace, not race."

Reinforce students who work on pacing. The praise will encourage students to run with pace rather than running all-out and then fading.

Bring in high school track or cross-country runners to talk about their training.

GAME

Individual or Recreational Activity

Since youngsters will finish at different times, individual equipment can be placed out so those youngsters who have completed the course and are warming down can be actively involved. Another good choice would be a recreational activity, such as Four Square, Beanbag, Horseshoes, and Sidewalk Tennis.

DYNAMIC PHYSICAL EDUCATION LESSON PLAN
Rhythmic Movement (Lesson 1)
Level II

Supplies and Equipment Needed:
- One beanbag for each child
- Exercise-to-music tape
- One jump rope for each child
- One 8 1/2" playground ball per child
- Hoops or yarn balls
- Tape player
- Music for rhythms

Dances Taught:
- The Bird Dance
- La Raspa
- Csebogar
- Teddy Bear Mixer
- Pop Goes the Weasel
- Crested Hen
- Greensleeves
- Grand March

MOVEMENT EXPERIENCE—CONTENT	ORGANIZATION AND TEACHING HINTS	EXPECTED STUDENT OBJECTIVES AND OUTCOMES

INTRODUCTORY ACTIVITIES (2 – 3 MINUTES)

Locomotor and Manipulative Activity

Each child is given a bean bag and moves around the area using various basic locomotor movements. Students toss and catch their beanbags while moving. On signal, they drop the beanbags and jump and/or hop over as many bags as possible.

DPE p. 258

Scatter formation.

Playground balls or yarn balls can be used instead of beanbags.

Specify the number or color of beanbags they must move, leap over, or around.

Add many challenges while moving to both the locomotor movements and the manipulative activities.

PM.—The student will be able to toss and catch an object while moving.

Cog.—The student will recite the fact that it is easier to toss and catch an object while standing stationary than while moving.

FITNESS DEVELOPMENT ACTIVITIES (7 – 8 MINUTES)

Exercises to Music

Side Flex (switch sides)	40 seconds
Trunk Twister	25 seconds
Abdominal Challenges	40 seconds
Slide/Skip	25 seconds
Jumping Jack variations	40 seconds
Triceps Push-Ups	25 seconds
Curl-Up Challenges	40 seconds
Gallop	25 seconds
Push-Up challenges	40 seconds
Aerobic Bouncing and Clapping	25 seconds
Leg Extensions	40 seconds
Walking to cool down	25 seconds

DPE p. 300

Students should know the exercises before trying to do them rhythmically.

The exercise music should be taped prior to the routine. This frees the teacher to move and help students.

Voice instructions can be dubbed onto the tape to tell students when to change to a new exercise.

Cog.—The student will recognize the names of the activities and be able to demonstrate each one.

PM.—The student will be able to perform the exercises to the beat of the music on the tape.

LESSON FOCUS (15 – 20 MINUTES)

Rhythmic Movement (1)

When teaching a dance, use the following steps:
1. Tell about the dance and listen to the music.
2. Clap the beat and learn the verse.
3. Practice the dance steps without the music and with verbal cues.
4. Practice the dance with the music.

Make dances easy for students to learn by using some of the following ideas:
1. Teach the dances without partners.
2. Allow youngsters to move in any direction—avoid the left–right orientation.

158

MOVEMENT EXPERIENCE—CONTENT	ORGANIZATION AND TEACHING HINTS	EXPECTED STUDENT OBJECTIVES AND OUTCOMES
	3. Use scattered formation instead of circles—it helps avoid embarrassment. 4. Emphasize strong movements such as clapping and stomping to encourage involvement. 5. Tape the music at a slower speed when first learning the dance. Rhythms should be taught like other sport skills. Avoid expecting perfection when teaching rhythms. Teach a variety of dances rather than one or two in depth. Youngsters will enjoy rhythms if they know it is acceptable to make mistakes without being ridiculed.	
a. The Bird Dance (also called The Chicken Dance) (*DPE*, p. 378)	Basic dance skills: 1. Skipping or walking 2. Elbow swing or star 3. Grand right and left 4. Click, flap, twist, and clap pattern Scattered or circle formation.	PM.—The student will participate in the dance successfully with others.
b. Csebogar (*DPE*, p. 379)	A Hungarian dance. Basic dance skills: 1. Skipping and sliding 2. Draw step 3. Elbow swing Single circle of partners facing center.	Aff.—The student will gain an appreciation of the Hungarian culture.
c. Pop Goes the Weasel (*DPE*, p. 379)	An American dance. Basic dance skills: 1. Walking, skipping 2. "Popping" under This dance may be done in circles or sets of either three or four. Try the jump rope version of Pop Goes the Weasel. Ball routines may be performed to the song, with students dribbling during the verse and passing the ball during the chorus.	PM.—The student will develop enough skill to perform this dance successfully. Cog.—The student will recognize the name of this dance and be able to demonstrate the major step in the dance.
d. Teddy Bear Mixer (*DPE*, p. 380)	An American dance. Basic dance skill: 1. Walking, with changing directions Double circle of couples facing counterclockwise.	PM.—The student will develop the proper rhythm to do this dance successfully.
e. La Raspa (*DPE*, p. 380)	A Mexican dance. Basic dance skills: 1. Bleking step 2. Elbow turn As a variation, this dance may begin with students scattered individually around the room, finding different partners for the elbow turn. Change partners each time the dance starts over.	Aff.—The student will gain some appreciation of the Mexican culture. PM.—The student will do the bleking step well enough to employ it in this dance and in other dances.

MOVEMENT EXPERIENCE—CONTENT	ORGANIZATION AND TEACHING HINTS	EXPECTED STUDENT OBJECTIVES AND OUTCOMES
f. Grand March (*DPE,* p. 383)	An American dance. Any good marching music may be used. May want to use pinnies on the students on one-half of the gym. Various Grand March formation and terms: 1. "Head" and "foot" of the hall 2. Down the center by fours 3. Form arches 4. Couples arch 5. Over and under 6. Down the center by eights	PM.—The student will be able to go through various formations in the Grand March without difficulty. Cog.—Failing to learn an activity is not necessarily a negative outcome. Focus on the importance of learning to make failure a positive and necessary experience in the total learning process.
g. Greensleeves (*DPE,* p. 384)	An English dance. Basic dance steps: 1. Walking 2. Star formation 3. Over and under (arches) Circle of couples. Couples are numbered one and two. Two couples form a set.	PM.—The student will be able to go through the entire dance without difficulty.
h. Crested Hen (*DPE,* p. 386)	A Danish dance. Basic dance skills: 1. Step-hop 2. Turning under Circles of three, either in one large circle or scattered in the gym. This dance may also be done in a single circle of partners. There are many variations of this dance.	Aff.—The student will gain some appreciation of the Danish culture. Aff.—The student will recognize the importance of cooperation when performing dances.

GAME (5 – 7 MINUTES)

Whistle March—*DPE*, p. 580
  Supplies: Music
  Skill: Moving rhythmically
  A record with a brisk march is needed. Children are scattered around the room, individually walking in various directions and keeping time to the music. A whistle is blown a number of times. At this signal, lines are formed of that precise number of children, no more and no fewer. To form the lines, children stand side by side with locked elbows. As soon as a line of the proper number is formed, it begins to march to the music counterclockwise around the room. Any children left over go to the center of the room and remain there until the next signal. On the next whistle signal (a single blast), the lines break up, and all walk individually around the room in various directions.
  When forming a new line, make a rule that children may not form the same combinations as in the previous line.

Arches—*DPE*, p. 571
  Supplies: Music
  Skills: Moving rhythmically
  The game is similar to London Bridge. An arch is placed in the playing area. (To form an arch, two players stand facing one another with hands joined and arms raised.) When the music starts, the other players move in a circle, passing under the arch. Suddenly, the music stops, and the arch is brought down by dropping the hands. All players caught in an arch immediately pair off to form other arches, keeping in a general circle formation. If a caught player does not have a partner, he waits in the center of the circle until one is available. The last players caught (or left) form arches for the next game.
  The arches should be warned not to bring down their hands and arms too forcefully so that children passing under are not pummeled.
  Variation: Different types of music can be used, and children can move according to the pattern of the music.

MOVEMENT EXPERIENCE— CONTENT	ORGANIZATION AND TEACHING HINTS	EXPECTED STUDENT OBJECTIVES AND OUTCOMES

Home Base—*DPE*, p. 576

Supplies: Cones to delineate the area, four pinnies

Skills: Reaction time, locomotor movements, body management

The area is divided into four quadrants with cones or floor lines. Each quadrant is the home base for one of the squads. The captain of the squad wears a pinnie for easy identification. The teams begin in a straight line sitting on the floor. The teacher calls out a locomotor movement which the players use to move throughout the area. When the teacher calls "Home base," the students return to their quadrant and return to the starting position behind their captain. The first team to return to proper position (sitting in a straight line) is awarded 2 points. Second place receives 1 point.

Teaching suggestion: Avoid calling "Home base" until the students have left the area of their quadrant. A number of different formations can be specified which students must assume upon return to their home base.

DYNAMIC PHYSICAL EDUCATION LESSON PLAN
Hockey-Related Activities (Lesson 1)
Level II

Supplies and Equipment Needed:
  Exercise tape
  One puck or whiffle ball and stick for each student
  Tumbling mats for goals
  Tape player
  Music

MOVEMENT EXPERIENCE— CONTENT	ORGANIZATION AND TEACHING HINTS	EXPECTED STUDENT OBJECTIVES AND OUTCOMES

INTRODUCTORY ACTIVITY (2 – 3 MINUTES)

Movement Varieties

Move using a basic locomotor movement. Then add variety to the movement by asking students to respond to the following factors:
  1. Level—low, high, in-between.
  2. Direction—straight, zigzag, circular, curved, forward, backward, upward, downward.
  3. Size—large, tiny, medium movements.
  4. Patterns—forming squares, diamonds, triangles, circles, figure eights.

DPE p. 254

Scatter formation.

Emphasize and reinforce creativity.

Change the various factors often and take time to explain the concepts the words describe if children cannot interpret them.

Cog.—The student will be able to interpret the concepts the words describe by moving the body in a corresponding manner.

PM.—The student will be able to move the body with ease throughout the range of movement varieties.

FITNESS DEVELOPMENT ACTIVITIES (7 – 8 MINUTES)

Exercises to Music

Side Flex (switch sides)	40 seconds
Trunk Twister	25 seconds
Abdominal Challenges	40 seconds
Slide/Skip	25 seconds
Jumping Jack variations	40 seconds
Triceps Push-Ups	25 seconds
Curl-Up Challenges	40 seconds
Gallop	25 seconds
Push-Up challenges	40 seconds
Aerobic Bouncing and Clapping	25 seconds
Leg Extensions	40 seconds
Walking to cool down	25 seconds

DPE p. 300

Students should know the exercises before trying to do them rhythmically.

Students can lead the exercise to music routine while the instructor monitors student progress.

Voice instructions can be dubbed onto the tape to tell students when to change to a new exercise.

Cog.—The overload principle dictates that to increase strength, one must perform progressively larger work loads. Duration, frequency, and intensity can be modified to progressively overload the system. Students should be able to develop work loads that are meaningful to their fitness levels.

LESSON FOCUS (15 – 20 MINUTES)

Hockey-Related Activities (1)
Skills

  1. Gripping and carrying of stick.
  2. Controlled Dribble: Ball controlled by individual. Keep the ball in front of stick while moving.

DPE pp. 652 – 655

Individual or partner work.

Use a plastic puck or fleeceball indoors and a whiffle ball outdoors.

Keep stick below waist level to ensure accuracy and safety.

Cog.—The student will be able to describe the meaning of the following terms: grip, carry, dribble, field, dodge, tackle, and drive.

PM.—The student will be able to perform each of the skills listed.

162

MOVEMENT EXPERIENCE— CONTENT	ORGANIZATION AND TEACHING HINTS	EXPECTED STUDENT OBJECTIVES AND OUTCOMES
3. Front Field: This is catching the puck or ball with the stick. As the ball approaches, get in line with the ball and extend the flat side of the stick forward to meet it.	The ball is pushed with the flat side of the stick in front of the body.	Aff.—Safety and concern for others is important. Others can be hurt by wild swinging of the stick. Discuss the need for rules in all sports in order to protect the participants.
4. Hit: Short pass which usually occurs from the dribble.	Good fielding requires learning to "give" with the stick.	
5. Dodging: Maintaining control of the ball while evading a tackler. Hold the ball as long as possible until one can determine which direction the tackler is going to move—then pass the puck or ball.	Practice with a partner—field in front of the body.

Do not lift the stick too high and hit through the ball. Strive for accuracy.

Pass the ball to one side of the tackler and move self around the opposite side. | Cog.—The distance over which a muscle contracts determines, in part, the amount of force to be generated. Various backswings and wind-ups are performed to increase the range of motion prior to contraction. Students will understand why preliminary movements are carried out in sports activities. |
6. Driving: Hitting the ball or puck for distance or trying to score a goal.	The stick is raised higher (waist level) and the hands are brought together to give the player a longer level.	
Drills	*DPE* pp. 656 – 657	
1. Dribbling	Scatter formation.	PM.—The student will be able to control the ball while moving.
a. Each student has a stick and ball. On signal, change directions while maintaining control of the ball.	Stress control.	
b. Dribble and dodge imaginary tacklers or dodge around a set of cones. Partners may act as tacklers.	Allow students time to learn hockey skills before placing them in competitive situations. Competition before skills are learned will lower performance.	Cog.—Hockey is a team game and passing is a needed skill. The student will be able to describe what factors make up a good hit.
c. Students in pairs—20 feet apart. One partner dribbles toward the other, goes around him or her, and returns to starting point. The first student then drives the ball to the second, who completes the same sequence.		Aff.—In fine motor control skills, much practice is needed to approach a desirable level. Discuss the need for drills and repeated practice.
2. Driving and Fielding	Partner formation.	
a. Partners drive the ball back and forth to each other both from moving and stationary positions.	Students should also practice their driving and fielding in this drill.	
b. Partners 20 feet apart—players pass the ball back and forth with emphasis on *fielding* and *immediately* hitting the ball back.	Passes should be fielded from all angles and sides of the body.

Call words might be "field," "set feet," and "pass." | |

HOCKEY LEAD-UP GAMES (6 – 7 MINUTES)

Circle Keep-Away—*DPE*, p. 657
Supplies: One stick per person, a puck or ball
Skills: Passing, fielding
Players are spaced evenly around the circle, with one player in the center. The object of the game is to keep the player in the center from touching the puck. The puck is passed back and forth, with emphasis on accurate passing and fielding. If the player in the center touches the puck, the player who last passed the puck takes the place of the center player. A change of players also can be made after a passing or fielding error.

Star Wars Hockey—*DPE*, p. 657
Supplies: One stick per player, four pucks or balls
Skill: Dribbling
Each team forms one side of a square formation. The game is similar to Star Wars (*DPE*, p. 587), with the following exceptions:
1. Four pucks (or balls) are used. When a number is called, each player with that number goes to a puck and dribbles it out of the square through the spot previously occupied, around the square counterclockwise, and back to the original spot. Circles 12 in. in diameter are drawn on the floor to provide a definite place to which the puck must be returned. If the game is played outdoors, hoops can mark the spot to which the puck must be returned.
2. No player is permitted to use anything other than the stick in making the circuit and returning the puck to the inside of the hoop. The penalty for infractions is disqualification.

MOVEMENT EXPERIENCE— CONTENT	ORGANIZATION AND TEACHING HINTS	EXPECTED STUDENT OBJECTIVES AND OUTCOMES

Lane Hockey—*DPE*, p. 657

Supplies: Hockey stick per player, puck, two goals

Skills: All hockey skills

The field is divided into eight lanes. A defensive and an offensive player are placed in each of the eight lanes. A goalkeeper for each team is also positioned in front of the goal area. Players may not leave their lane during play. A shot on goal may not be taken until a minimum of two passes have been completed. This rule encourages looking for teammates and passing to someone in a better position before a shot on goal is taken.

Players should be encouraged to maintain their spacing during play. The purpose of the lanes is to force them to play a zone rather than rushing to the puck. Rules used for regulation hockey (*DPE*, p. 659) enforce situations not described here. A free hit (unguarded) is awarded a team if a foul occurs. Players should be rotated after a goal is scored or at regular time intervals.

Variation: Increase the number of lanes to five or six. This involves a larger number of players. On a large playing area, the lanes may be broken into thirds rather than halves. Increase the number of passes that should be made prior to a shot on goal.

Circle Hockey Straddleball

Supplies: Hockey sticks and pucks or yarnballs

Skills: Passing and fielding

Children are in circle formation, facing in. Each player stands in a wide straddle stance two or three feet apart. The object of the game is to pass one of the pucks between the legs of another. Each time a puck goes between the legs of an individual, a point is scored. The players having the fewest points scored against them are winners. Keep the circles small so students have more opportunities to handle the puck.

DYNAMIC PHYSICAL EDUCATION LESSON PLAN
Hockey-Related Activities (Lesson 2)
Level II

Supplies and Equipment Needed:
  Hockey sticks and pucks
  Tumbling mats for goals
  Cones
  Tape player
  Music

MOVEMENT EXPERIENCE—CONTENT	ORGANIZATION AND TEACHING HINTS	EXPECTED STUDENT OBJECTIVES AND OUTCOMES

INTRODUCTORY ACTIVITY (2 – 3 MINUTES)

New Leader

Squads move around the area, following the squad leader. On signal, the last person can move to the head of the squad and become the leader. Various types of locomotor movements and/or exercises should be used.

DPE p. 258

Squad formation. Encourage students to keep moving unless an exercise or similar activity is being performed.

Assign each squad a specific area if desired. Each area could include a piece of equipment to aid in the activity (beanbag, fleece ball, etc.).

Cog.—The student will be able to give two reasons why warm-up is necessary prior to strenuous exercises.

Aff.—The student will be capable of leading as well as following. Discuss the necessity of both in our society.

FITNESS DEVELOPMENT ACTIVITIES (7 – 8 MINUTES)

Astronaut Drills

Tape alternating segments of silence and music to signal duration of exercise. Music segments indicate aerobic activity while intervals of silence announce flexibility and strength development activities.

Walk while doing	
Arm circles	30 seconds
Crab Alternate-Leg	
Extension	35 seconds
Skip	30 seconds
Body Twist	35 seconds
Slide	30 seconds
Jumping Jack variations	35 seconds
Crab Walk to center	
and back	30 seconds
Abdominal Challenges	35 seconds
Hop to center and back	30 seconds
Push-Up Challenges	35 seconds
Gallop	30 seconds
Bear Hugs	35 seconds
Pogo Stick Jump	30 seconds

Cool down with stretching and walking or jogging for 1–2 minutes.

DPE p. 304

Use circle or scatter formation with ample space between youngsters. If a circle formation is used, establish a "passing lane" to the outside for faster students.

Change directions occasionally to keep students spread out.

Emphasize quality movement over quantity. Allow students to adjust the work load pace. They should be able to move at a pace that is consistent with their fitness level.

Cog.—The student will be able to explain the need to exercise on "all fours" to increase arm and shoulder girdle strength.

PM.—The student will be able to perform the fitness activities at the beginning level.

Aff.—This routine is used by astronauts. They need to be fit, as fitness is extremely useful when unexpected demands are made on the body. Discuss some of these unexpected demands.

LESSON FOCUS (15 – 20 MINUTES)

Hockey-Related Activities (2)
Review skills taught in previous lesson:

1. Controlled dribble
2. Front field

DPE pp. 652 – 655

See previous hockey lesson plan for description and teaching hints.

PM.—The student will be able to perform the basic skills in hockey.

Cog.—The student will be able to recite the proper time to tackle.

MOVEMENT EXPERIENCE— CONTENT	ORGANIZATION AND TEACHING HINTS	EXPECTED STUDENT OBJECTIVES AND OUTCOMES

3. Quick hit
4. Dodging
5. Driving

Introduce:

1. Tackling—tackling is an attempt to intercept the ball from an opponent.
2. Goalkeeping—the goalie should practice moving in front of the ball and bringing the feet together. Turn the stick sideways and stop the puck or ball.

Review the following drills:

1. Dribble around a set of cones.
2. Students dribbling in pairs.
3. Partner driving and fielding drill—stationary and moving.

Introduce:

1. Tackling and dribbling drill—one partner dribbles toward the other player, who attempts to make a tackle.
2. Three-on-three drill—Many goals can be set up, and six students can work in small groups of three offensive and three defensive players.
3. Shooting Drill—Mats are set up as goals (three or four on each end of the floor). Half of class on each half of the floor. Each team attempts to hit pucks into opponents' goals without crossing center line of gym. Use a large number of pucks.

The proper time to tackle is when the ball is *off* the opponent's stick.

Assure students that it is impossible to make a successful tackle every time.

The goalie may kick the puck, stop it with any body part, or allow it to rebound off any body part.

DPE pp. 656 – 657

An 8-ft folding tumbling mat set on end makes an excellent goal.

See previous hockey lesson plan for description of the drills reviewed.

Emphasize the importance of proper timing to facilitate a "clean" tackle. Tripping with the stick is illegal and should be avoided.

In the three-on-three drill, the offensive team should concentrate on passing, dribbling, and dodging, and the defense on tackling and good body position.

Cog.—Wellness demands learning to cope with stressful situations. A study demonstrated that a 15-minute walk reduced tension more effectively than a tranquilizer. Students will understand the importance of exercise for stress reduction.

PM.—The student will be able to demonstrate the proper manner of blocking a shot on goal.

PM.—The student will be able to successfully participate in the three-on-three drill.

Cog.—The student will be able to explain the importance of practicing and developing basic hockey skills before playing a regulation game.

Aff.—Violence in sport is evident, particularly in hockey. Discuss the need for ethics in sport including self-discipline, accepting one's own and others' feelings, and the immorality of physical violence.

HOCKEY LEAD-UP GAMES (5 – 7 MINUTES)

Modified Hockey—*DPE*, p. 658
   Supplies: One stick per person, a puck or ball
   Skills: Dribbling, passing, dodging, tackling, face-off
   The teams may take any position on the field as long as they remain inside the boundaries. The object of the game is to hit the puck through the opponent's goal. No goalies are used. At the start of the game and after each score, play begins with a face-off. Each goal is worth one point.
   Teaching suggestion: The distance between goal lines is flexible but should be on the long side. If making goals is too easy or too difficult, the width of the goals can be adjusted accordingly.

Lane Hockey—*DPE*, p. 657
   Supplies: Hockey stick per player, puck, two goals
   Skills: All hockey skills
   The field is divided into eight lanes. A defensive and an offensive player are placed in each of the eight lanes. A goalkeeper for each team is also positioned in front of the goal area. Players may not leave their lane during play. A shot on goal may not be taken until a minimum of two passes have been completed. This rule encourages looking for teammates and passing to someone in a better position before a shot on goal is taken.
   Players should be encouraged to maintain their spacing during play. The purpose of the lanes is to force them to play a zone rather than rushing to the puck. Rules used for regulation hockey (*DPE*, p. 659) enforce situations not described here. A free hit (unguarded) is awarded a team if a foul occurs. Players should be rotated after a goal is scored or at regular time intervals.
   Variation: Increase the number of lanes to five or six. This involves a larger number of players. On a large playing area, the lanes may be broken into thirds rather than halves. Increase the number of passes that should be made prior to a shot on goal.

DYNAMIC PHYSICAL EDUCATION LESSON PLAN
Individual Rope Jumping Skills
Level II

Supplies and Equipment Needed:
  Jump rope for each student
  Appropriate music
  Tape player
  Balls
  Beach balls
  Tom-tom
  Wands

MOVEMENT EXPERIENCE— CONTENT	ORGANIZATION AND TEACHING HINTS	EXPECTED STUDENT OBJECTIVES AND OUTCOMES

INTRODUCTORY ACTIVITY (2 – 3 MINUTES)

Group Over and Under

One half of the class is scattered. Each is in a curled position. The other half of the class leap or jump over the down children. On signal, reverse the group quickly. In place of a curl, the down children can bridge and the other go under. The down children can also alternate between curl and bridge, as well as move around the area while in a bridged position.

DPE p. 257

Scatter formation.

Encourage the students to go over or under a specified number of classmates.

Vary the down challenges (i.e., bridge using two body parts, curl face down or on your side).

PM.—The student will be able to perform the activities of bridge, curl, leap, jump, and hop at a teacher-acceptable level.

Cog.—Warm-up loosens the muscles, tendons, and ligaments, decreasing the risk of injury. It also increases the flow of blood to the heart muscle.

FITNESS DEVELOPMENT ACTIVITIES (7 – 8 MINUTES)

Astronaut Drills

Tape alternating segments of silence and music to signal duration of exercise. Music segments indicate aerobic activity while intervals of silence announce flexibility and strength development activities.

Walk while doing	
Arm circles	30 seconds
Crab Alternate-Leg	
Extension	35 seconds
Skip	30 seconds
Body Twist	35 seconds
Slide	30 seconds
Jumping Jack variations	35 seconds
Crab Walk to center	
and back	30 seconds
Abdominal Challenges	35 seconds
Hop to center and back	30 seconds
Push-Up Challenges	35 seconds
Gallop	30 seconds
Bear Hugs	35 seconds
Pogo Stick Jump	30 seconds

Cool down with stretching and walking or jogging for 1–2 minutes.

DPE p. 304

Use circle or scatter formation with ample space between youngsters. If a circle formation is used, establish a "passing lane" to the outside for faster students.

Change directions occasionally to keep students spread out.

Emphasize quality movement over quantity. Allow students to adjust the work load pace. They should be able to move at a pace that is consistent with their fitness level.

Aff.—Very little resting time occurs in Astronaut Drills. When one exercises for a long period of time without rest, muscular and cardiovascular endurance is developed.

MOVEMENT EXPERIENCE— CONTENT	ORGANIZATION AND TEACHING HINTS	EXPECTED STUDENT OBJECTIVES AND OUTCOMES

LESSON FOCUS (15 – 20 MINUTES)

Individual Rope Jumping Skills

1. As a lead-up activity for individual rope jumping, it might be useful to try some of the following activities:
   a. Clap hands to a tom-tom beat.
   b. Jump in place to a beat without rope.
   c. Hold both ends of the jump rope in one hand and turn it to the side so a steady rhythm can be made through a consistent turn. Just before the rope hits the ground, the student should practice jumping.
   d. Start jumping the rope one turn at a time—gradually increase the number of turns.
2. Introduce the two basic jumps:
   a. Slow time
   b. Fast time
3. Introduce some of the basic step variations:
   a. Alternate foot basic step
   b. Swing step forward
   c. Swing step sideways
   d. Rocker step
   e. Spread legs, forward and backward
   f. Toe touch, forward and backward
   g. Shuffle step
   h. Cross arms, forward and backward
   i. Double jump
4. Teach how to go from rope turning forward to rope turning backward without stopping the rope.
5. Using an individual rope with one partner holding each end: Each partner turns, partners take turns jumping in while turning.
6. One partner holds and turns rope. Second partner jumps with partner.

DPE pp. 451 – 458

Children get tired easily when learning to jump. It might be wise to split the lesson focus and use a less strenuous activity such as wands or hoops.

After introducing the basic skills, play some music that has a good strong beat. (Turn it up so it is easy for children to hear.)

Give the children plenty of room so they don't hit someone with their rope.

For slow time: Slow rope, slow feet with a rebound.

For fast time: Fast rope, fast feet. Jump the rope every turn.

Allow students to progress at their own rate. It is good to show the better jumpers some of the more difficult variations and allow them to practice by themselves.

All of the variations can be done with the turning in a forward or backward direction.

PM.—Youngsters will be able to jump rope to slow and fast time rhythm for 30 to 60 seconds.

Cog.—High-density lipoproteins (HDL) can slow the deposit of fat on arteries. The ratio of HDL to low-density lipoproteins (LDL) can be enhanced through exercise.

Aff.—Stress can be detrimental to a person's health. Discuss various situations that create stress among students. Discuss ways of coping with the stress.

Cog.—Some doctors estimate that young people eat 150–200 pounds of sugar per year. Sugar offers "empty calories"—calories, but no nutritional value. Eating too much sugar releases insulin to handle the extra sugar and soon depresses the blood sugar level to make you feel sluggish. Discuss the importance of reducing raw sugar intake.

GAME (5 – 7 MINUTES)

Follow Me—*DPE*, p. 575
   Supplies: A marker for each child (squares of cardboard or plywood can be used; individual mats or beanbags work well)
   Skills: All locomotor movements, stopping
   Children are arranged in a rough circle, each standing or sitting with one foot on a marker. An extra player is the guide. He moves around the circle, pointing at different players and asking them to follow. Each player chosen falls in behind the guide. The guide then takes the group on a tour, and the members of the group perform just as the guide does. The guide may hop, skip, do stunts, or execute other movements, and children following must do likewise. At the signal "Home," all run for places with a marker. One child is left without a marker. This child chooses another guide.
   Teaching suggestions: Making the last child the new leader is not a good idea, because this causes some children to lag and try to be last. Another way to overcome the tendency to lag is to make the first one back the guide. The teacher can also use a special marker; the first one to this marker becomes the new leader. A penalty can be imposed on the one who does not find a marker.

MOVEMENT EXPERIENCE—CONTENT	ORGANIZATION AND TEACHING HINTS	EXPECTED STUDENT OBJECTIVES AND OUTCOMES

Trades—*DPE*, p. 579

Supplies: None

Skills: Imagery, running, dodging

The class is divided into two teams of equal number, each of which has a goal line. One team, the chasers, remains behind its goal line. The other team, the runners, approaches from its goal line, marching to the following dialogue:

Runners: Here we come.

Chasers: Where from?

Runners: New Orleans.

Chasers: What's your trade?

Runners: Lemonade.

Chasers: Show us some.

Runners move up close to the other team's goal line and proceed to act out an occupation or a specific task that they have chosen previously. The opponents try to guess what the pantomime represents. On a correct guess, the running team must run back to its goal line chased by the others. Any runner tagged must join the chasers. The game is repeated with roles reversed. The team ending with the greater number of players is the winner.

Teaching suggestion: If a team has trouble guessing the pantomime, the other team should provide hints. Teams also should be encouraged to have a number of activities selected so that little time is consumed in choosing the next activity to be pantomimed.

Beachball Batball—*DPE*, p. 571

Supplies: Four to six beachballs

Skills: Batting, tactile handling

Two games are played across the gymnasium area. The teams are scattered throughout the area without restriction as to where they may move. To begin the game, the balls are placed on the centerline dividing the court area. Four to six beachballs are in play at the same time. A score occurs when the beachball is batted over the end line. Once the ball moves across the end line it is dead. Players concentrate on the remaining balls in play.

If a ball is on the floor, it is picked up and batted into play. At no time may a ball be carried. After all four balls are scored, the game ends. A new game is started after teams switch goals.

DYNAMIC PHYSICAL EDUCATION LESSON PLAN
Stunts and Tumbling Skills (Lesson 1)
Level II

Supplies and Equipment Needed:
  Tumbling mats
  Jump ropes
  Tape player
  Music
  Bowling pins
  Grey foam balls

MOVEMENT EXPERIENCE—CONTENT	ORGANIZATION AND TEACHING HINTS	EXPECTED STUDENT OBJECTIVES AND OUTCOMES

INTRODUCTORY ACTIVITY (2 – 3 MINUTES)

Low Organization Games

Play a game such as:
  1. Addition Tag, (*DPE*, p. 570)
  2. Squad Tag, (*DPE*, p. 579)
  3. Couple Tag, (*DPE*, p. 574)

Students should know the game so that immediate activity occurs.

Make sure the games are active enough so *all* students are warmed up simultaneously.

PM.—The student will be active in the games to ensure physiological warm-up.

FITNESS DEVELOPMENT ACTIVITY (7 – 8 MINUTES)

Continuity Drills

Students alternate jump rope activity with exercises done in two-count fashion. Exercises are done with the teacher saying "Ready;" the class answers "One-two" and performs a repetition of exercise. In activities like Push-Ups and Curl-Ups, students can pick any challenge activity (*DPE*, pp. 281–283) they choose. Teachers or students can lead.

Rope Jumping - Forward	30 seconds
Double Crab Kick	45 seconds
Rope Jumping - Backward	30 seconds
Knee Touch Curl-Up	45 seconds
Jump and Slowly Turn Body	30 seconds
Push-Up Challenges	45 seconds
Rocker Step	30 seconds
Bend and Twist	45 seconds
Swing-Step Forward	30 seconds
Side Flex	45 seconds
Free Jumping	30 seconds
Sit and Stretch	45 seconds

DPE p. 303

Use scatter formation.

Taped intervals of music and no music can be used to signal rope jumping (with music) and performing exercises (without music).

A number of enjoyable chants can be used (e.g., "Physical Education" followed by a two-count response and repetition "is fun!").

Allow students to adjust the work load to their fitness level. This implies resting if the rope jumping is too strenuous.

PM.—The student will be able to perform all activities at the increased load level.

Cog.—The student will be able to verbalize in her own words the fact that regular exercise strengthens muscles and helps prevent joint and muscle injury.

MOVEMENT EXPERIENCE— CONTENT	ORGANIZATION AND TEACHING HINTS	EXPECTED STUDENT OBJECTIVES AND OUTCOMES

LESSON FOCUS (15 – 20 MINUTES)

Tumbling, Stunts, and Animal Movements (1)

Six groups of activities in this lesson ensure that youngsters receive a variety of experiences. Pick a few activities from each group and teach them alternately. For example, teach one or two animal movements, then a tumbling and inverted balance, followed by a balance stunt, etc. Give equal time to each group of activities

1. Animal Movements
   a. Cricket Walk
   b. Frog Jump
   c. Seal Crawl
   d. Reverse Seal Crawl
2. Tumbling and Inverted Balances
   a. Forward Roll to a Walkout
   b. Backward Roll (Inclined)
   c. Backward Roll (Handclasp)
   d. Headstand
   e. Climb Up
3. Balance Stunts
   a. One-Leg Balance Reverse
   b. Tummy Balance
   c. Leg Dip
4. Individual Stunts
   a. Reach Under
   b. Stiff Person Bend
   c. Coffee Grinder
   d. Scooter
   e. Hip Walk
   f. Long Bridge
5. Partner and Group Stunts
   a. Partner Hopping
   b. Partner Twisting
   c. Partner Pull-Up
   d. Back to Back Get-Up
6. Partner Support Stunts
   a. Double Bear
   b. Table

DPE pp. 507 – 526

Scatter as many tumbling mats as possible throughout the area in order to avoid waiting lines.

Do not perform many repetitions of tumbling and inverted balances. For most children, limiting the number of forward or backward roll repetitions to four or five will prevent fatigue and injury.

There is usually a wide range of ability among youngsters in this lesson. If necessary, start at a lower level than listed here to assure students find success.

A major concern for safety is the neck and back region. Overweight children are at greater risk and might be allowed to avoid tumbling and inverted balances.

Teach youngsters to stand on the hips and shoulders when doing partner-support stunts.

PM.—The student will be able to perform a forward and a backward roll.

PM.—The student will be able to perform the basic headstand.

PM.—The student will be able to balance her body in the balance stunts and manage it easily in the individual stunts.

Cog.—The student will be able to state the key points necessary to spot the headstand.

Aff.—Tumbling is an excellent activity as it teaches children to control their bodies in various situations. Discuss the courage and perseverance gymnasts must have to meet success.

Cog.—Wellness refers to taking care of one's self for better health. It places the responsibility for good health on the individual rather than a doctor. Discuss various facets of wellness and making responsible decisions for better health.

Cog.—The student will be able to recite the stress points necessary to know in performing the forward and backward rolls.

Cog.—Stability and balance can be increased by (1) keeping the body weight over the base of support, (2) increasing the size of the base of support, and (3) lowering the center of gravity. Identify this process being performed in the stunts and tumbling exercises.

MOVEMENT EXPERIENCE— CONTENT	ORGANIZATION AND TEACHING HINTS	EXPECTED STUDENT OBJECTIVES AND OUTCOMES

GAME (5 – 7 MINUTES)

Whistle Mixer—*DPE*, p. 580

Supplies: A whistle

Skills: All basic locomotor movements

Children are scattered throughout the area. To begin, they walk around in any direction they wish. The teacher blows a whistle a number of times in succession with short, sharp blasts. Children then form small circles with the number in the circles equal to the number of whistle blasts. If there are four blasts, children form circles of four—no more, no less. The goal is not to be left out or caught in a circle with the incorrect number of students. Children should be encouraged to move to the center of the area and raise their hands to facilitate finding others without a group.

After the circles are formed, the teacher calls "Walk," and the game continues. In walking, children should move in different directions.

Variation: A fine version of this game is done with the aid of a tom-tom. Different beats indicate different locomotor movements—skipping, galloping, slow walking, normal walking, running. The whistle is still used to set the number for each circle.

Competitive Circle Contests—*DPE*, p. 573

Supplies: Volleyballs or 8-in. foam rubber balls, two bowling pins

Skills: Throwing, catching

Two teams arranged in independent circles compete against each other. The circles should be of the same size; lines can be drawn on the floor to ensure this. The players of each team are numbered consecutively so that each player in one circle corresponds to a player in the other circle. The numbered players, in sequence, go to the center of the opponents' circle to compete for their team in either of the following activities.

1. Circle Club Guard. The center player guards a bowling pin. The circle that knocks down the club first wins a point. The ball should be rolled at the club.

2. Touch Ball. The circle players pass the ball from one to another while the center player tries to touch it. The center player who touches the ball first wins a point for the respective team. In case neither player is able to touch the ball in a reasonable period of time, the action should be cut off without awarding a point.

After all players have competed, the team with the most points wins. For Circle Club Guard, there must be three passes to different people before the ball can be thrown at the center. Establishing circle lines may be necessary to regulate throwing distance.

Alaska Baseball—*DPE*, p. 570

Supplies: A volleyball or soccer ball

Skills: Kicking, batting, running, ball handling

The players are organized in two teams, one of which is at bat while the other is in the field. A straight line provides the only out-of-bounds line, and the team at bat is behind this line at about the middle. The other team is scattered around the fair territory.

One player propels the ball, either batting a volleyball or kicking a stationary soccer ball. His teammates are in a close file behind him. As soon as the batter sends the ball into the playing area, he starts to run around his own team. Each time the runner passes the head of the file, the team gives a loud count.

There are no outs. The first fielder to get the ball stands still and starts to pass the ball back overhead to the nearest teammate, who moves directly behind to receive it. The remainder of the team in the field must run to the ball and form a file behind it. The ball is passed back overhead, with each player handling the ball. When the last field player in line has a firm grip on it, she shouts "Stop." At this signal, a count is made of the number of times the batter ran around his own team. To score more sharply, half rounds should be counted.

Five batters or half of the team should bat; then the teams should change places. This is better than allowing an entire team to bat before changing to the field, because players in the field tire from many consecutive runs.

Variation: Regular bases can be set up, and the batter can run the bases. Scoring can be in terms of a home run made or not; or the batter can continue around the bases, getting a point for each base.

DYNAMIC PHYSICAL EDUCATION LESSON PLAN
Rhythmic Movement (Lesson 2)
Level II

Supplies and Equipment Needed:
- Tape player
- Jump ropes
- Music for rhythms
- Bowling pins

Dances Taught:
- Wild Turkey Mixer
- Bingo
- Oh Susanna
- Patty Cake Polka
- Polly Wolly Doodle
- Ve David
- Troika
- Jingle Bells (Var. 2)

MOVEMENT EXPERIENCE— CONTENT	ORGANIZATION AND TEACHING HINTS	EXPECTED STUDENT OBJECTIVES AND OUTCOMES

INTRODUCTORY ACTIVITY (2 – 3 MINUTES)

Following Activity

One partner leads and performs various kinds of movements. The other partner follows and performs the same movements. This can also be used with squad organization with the squad following a leader.

DPE p. 257

The leaders should be changed often. Use a whistle to signal the change of roles.

Partner or squad formation.

Encourage good reproduction of the leader's movements.

PM.—Be able to follow and accurately reproduce the movements of the leader.

Aff.—People must be able to lead as well as follow at times. Briefly discuss the need for cooperation between people.

FITNESS DEVELOPMENT ACTIVITY (7 – 8 MINUTES)

Continuity Drills

Students alternate jump rope activity with exercises done in two-count fashion. Exercises are done with the teacher saying "Ready;" the class answers "One-two" and performs a repetition of exercise. In activities like Push-Ups and Curl-Ups, students can pick any challenge activity (*DPE*, 281–283) they choose. Teachers or students can lead.

Rope Jumping - Forward	30 seconds
Double Crab Kick	45 seconds
Rope Jumping - Backward	30 seconds
Knee Touch Curl-Up	45 seconds
Jump and Slowly Turn Body	30 seconds
Push-Up Challenges	45 seconds
Rocker Step	30 seconds
Sit and twist	45 seconds
Swing-Step Forward	30 seconds
Side Flex	45 seconds
Free Jumping	30 seconds
Sit and Stretch	45 seconds

DPE p. 303

Use scatter formation.

Taped intervals of music and no music can be used to signal rope jumping (with music) and performing exercises (without music).

A number of enjoyable chants can be used (e.g., "Physical Education" followed by a two-count response and repetition "is fun").

Allow students to adjust the work load to their fitness level. This implies resting if the rope jumping is too strenuous.

Cog.—Continuity Drills are a balanced routine that exercises all parts of the body. For the conditioning effect to take place, the pulse rate should be elevated. Use a stop watch and have students check their pulse rate.

Cog.—A study showed that regular cigarette smoking reduced average life spans by 7 years. Discuss how smoking is not a responsible choice on the pathway to wellness.

173

MOVEMENT EXPERIENCE— CONTENT	ORGANIZATION AND TEACHING HINTS	EXPECTED STUDENT OBJECTIVES AND OUTCOMES

LESSON FOCUS (15 – 20 MINUTES)

Rhythmic Movement (2)

Begin each lesson with a dance the children know and enjoy. Then review dances from the unit as needed before teaching new ones.

When teaching a dance, use the following steps:
1. Tell about the dance and listen to the music.
2. Clap the beat and learn the verse.
3. Practice the dance steps without the music and with verbal cues.
4. Practice the dance with the music.

1. Listen to the music, clapping the rhythms and pointing out where changes occur.
2. Teach the basic skills used in the dance.

Make dances easy for students to learn by using some of the following ideas:
1. Teach the dances without partners.
2. Allow youngsters to move in any direction—avoid the left–right orientation.
3. Use scattered formation instead of circles—it helps avoid embarrassment.
4. Emphasize strong movements such as clapping and stomping to encourage involvement.
5. Tape the music at a slower speed when first learning the dance.

Rhythms should be taught like other sport skills. Avoid expecting perfection when teaching rhythms. Teach a variety of dances rather than one or two in depth. Youngsters will enjoy rhythms if they know it is acceptable to make mistakes without being ridiculed.

a. Wild Turkey Mixer (*DPE*, p 380)

An American dance.

Basic dance skills:
1. Walking
2. Elbow swing
In lines of three facing CCW.

The center person is the "Wild Turkey."

As a mixer, the "Wild Turkey" moves forward to join the next group.

Aff.—The student will be courteous when accepting a new partner.

b. Patty Cake Polka (Heel and Toe Polka) (*DPE*, p. 381)

This is an international dance.

Basic dance skills:
1. Heel and toe step
2. Slide
3. Elbow swing
Double circle, partners facing, boy in inner circle with back to the center.

Boy begins with the left foot free, girl with the right foot free.

Practice the partner change until the class is able to perform it smoothly before adding the music.

PM.—The students will learn the heel and toe step and be able to transfer the step to other dances.

PM.—The student will participate in the dance successfully with others.

Aff.—The student will accept a new partner graciously.

MOVEMENT EXPERIENCE— CONTENT	ORGANIZATION AND TEACHING HINTS	EXPECTED STUDENT OBJECTIVES AND OUTCOMES

c. Polly Wolly Doodle (*DPE*, p. 381)	An American dance.
	
	Basic dance skills:
	  1. Slide
	  2. Turn solo
	  3. Walk
	  4. Swing
	  5. "Polly" stamp
	Double circle of dancers, partners facing, boys with back to center of circle.
	
	This dance involves a change of partners.
	
	It may be helpful to teach the dance without the partner change, practice it with the music, and then add the partner change as a progression.
		PM.—The student will be able to perform the "Polly" stamp in time to the music.

d. Bingo (*DPE*, p. 382)	An American dance.
	
	Basic dance skills:
	  1. Walking
	  2. Grand right and left
	This dance may be performed using a parachute.
		Cog.—The student will learn what a right-and-left grand is.

e. Jingle Bells (var. 2) (*DPE*, p. 384)	Basic dance skills:
	  1. Skipping
	  2. Skater's position
	  3. Sliding
	  4. Elbow swing
	Circle of partners facing CCW.
	
	Begin with slow tempo and gradually increase to normal tempo.
		PM.—The student will be able to go through the entire dance without difficulty.

f. Ve David (*DPE*, p. 385)	An Israeli dance.
	
	Basic dance skills:
	  1. Walk
	  2. Pivot
	  3. Buzz-step turn
	Circle of couples facing counterclockwise.
		Aff.—The student will gain some appreciation for the culture of Israel.
		
		PM.—The student will be able to successfully perform the "buzz" step.

g. Oh Susanna (*DPE*, p. 386)	An American dance.
	
	Basic dance skills:
	  1. Walking
	  2. Right-and-left grand
	  3. Skater's position (while walking)
	Any two students may be partners. Boy–girl partners are not necessary. Students may be identified as "pinnie" and "nonpinnie."
	
	Students continue the right-and-left grand until they reach the seventh person, who then becomes their new partner.
		Cog.—Students will learn the right-and-left grand, and will be able to state it in their own words.
		
		PM.—The student will learn the right-and-left grand for this dance, and be able to apply the learning to other dances.

MOVEMENT EXPERIENCE— CONTENT	ORGANIZATION AND TEACHING HINTS	EXPECTED STUDENT OBJECTIVES AND OUTCOMES
h. Troika (*DPE*, p. 387)	A Russian dance. Basic dance skills: 1. Running step 2. Turning under Trios in lines, facing counterclockwise. This dance may also be done with the groups of threes scattered in the gym. As a mixer, the center dancer releases joined hands and moves to a new pair to begin the dance again.	Aff.—The student will gain an appreciation of the Russian culture. PM.—The student will have sufficient endurance to perform this dance without becoming fatigued.

GAME (5 – 7 MINUTES)

Fox Hunt—*DPE*, p. 575
    Supplies: None
    Skills: Running, dodging
    Two players form trees by facing each other and holding hands. The third member of the group is a fox and stands between the hands of the trees. Three players are identified as foxes without trees and three players are designated as hounds. The hounds try to tag foxes who are not in trees. The extra foxes may move to a tree and displace the fox who is standing in the tree. In addition, the foxes in trees may leave the safety of their trees at any time. If the hound tags a fox, their roles are reversed immediately, the fox becoming the hound.
    The game should be stopped at regular intervals to allow the players who are trees to change places with the foxes and hounds. Different locomotor movements can be specified to add variety to the game.

Steal the Treasure—*DPE*, p. 579
    Supplies: A bowling pin
    Skill: Dodging
    A playing area 20 ft square is outlined, with a small circle in the center. A bowling pin placed in the circle is the treasure. A guard is set to protect the treasure. Players then enter the square and try to steal the treasure without getting caught. The guard tries to tag them. Anyone tagged must retire and wait for the next game. The player who gets the treasure is the next guard. Teaching suggestion: If getting the treasure seems too easy, the child can be required to carry the treasure to the boundary of the square without being tagged.
    Variation: Bear and Keeper. Instead of a treasure, a bear (seated cross-legged on the ground) is protected by a keeper. Anyone who touches the bear without being tagged becomes the new keeper, with the old keeper becoming the bear.

Addition Tag—*DPE*, p. 570
    Supplies: None
    Skills: Running, dodging
    Two couples are it, and each stands with inside hands joined. These are the taggers. The other children run individually. The couples move around the playground, trying to tag with the free hands. The first person tagged joins the couple, making a trio. The three then chase until they catch a fourth. Once a fourth person is caught, the four divide and form two couples, adding another set of taggers to the game. This continues until all children are tagged.
    Teaching suggestions: Some limitation of area should be established to enable the couples to catch the runners; otherwise, the game moves slowly and is fatiguing. The game moves faster if started with two couples. A tag is legal only when the couple or group of three keeps their hands joined. The game can be used as an introductory activity, since all children are active.

DYNAMIC PHYSICAL EDUCATION LESSON PLAN
Fundamental Skills Using Benches
Level II

Supplies and Equipment Needed:
 Balance-beam benches
 Tumbling mats
 Cageball
 Cones
 Pinnies

MOVEMENT EXPERIENCE— CONTENT	ORGANIZATION AND TEACHING HINTS	EXPECTED STUDENT OBJECTIVES AND OUTCOMES

INTRODUCTORY ACTIVITY (2 – 3 MINUTES)

Leapfrog

Two, three or four children are used for this group activity. They form a straight or curved line, with all except the last child in line taking the low leapfrog position. The last child moves or leaps over the other children in turn and, after going over the last child, gets down in position so that the others can leap him or her. Variations:
1. Increase the distance between the youngsters in the leapfrog position.
2. Add some locomotor movements or stunts that the youngster on the move must perform between leaps over each child.

DPE p. 258

Lines should curve to avoid running into other jumpers.

Stress good form on the jump.

Encourage, but don't force, youngsters to try the jump. If they are reticent, allow them to be in the down position and run around each student when it is their turn to jump.

PM.—The student will be able to crouch jump over the students in the down position.

Cog.—The student will be able to identify the elements necessary to land softly after jumping over another student.

Cog.—Reciprocal innervation is a dual set of messages to the muscles which tells one set to contract and the opposing set to relax. Discuss the importance of this process for efficient movement.

FITNESS DEVELOPMENT ACTIVITY (7 – 8 MINUTES)

Aerobic Fitness and Partner Resistance Exercises

Tape alternating segments of silence and music to signal duration of exercise. Music segments indicate aerobic activity while intervals of silence announce flexibility and strength development activities.

Bounce and Clap	25 seconds
Arm Curl-Up	45 seconds
Jumping Jack variations	25 seconds
Camelback	45 seconds
Lunge variations	25 seconds
Fist Pull apart	45 seconds
Directional Runs	25 seconds
Scissors	45 seconds
Rhythmic Running	25 seconds
Butterfly	45 seconds
Bounce with Body Twist	25 seconds
Resistance Push-Up	45 seconds

Walk, stretch, and relax for a minute or two.

DPE pp. 305 – 307 lists aerobic fitness activities.

DPE pp. 297 – 299 describes partner resistance exercises.

During the time allowed for partner resistance exercises, both students should have the opportunity to exercise.

Exercises should be done through the full range of motion.

Youngsters should take 6–10 seconds to move through the full range of motion while their partner applies resistance.

A sign with aerobic activities on one side and partner resistance exercises on the other aids instruction. The signs can be held upright by cones and shared by 2 to 4 students.

PM.—The student will be able to perform all the exercises.

Cog.—The student will be able to recite the fact that resistance should be offered throughout the full range of motion for maximum benefit.

MOVEMENT EXPERIENCE—CONTENT	ORGANIZATION AND TEACHING HINTS	EXPECTED STUDENT OBJECTIVES AND OUTCOMES

LESSON FOCUS (15 – 20 MINUTES)

Fundamental Skills Using Benches

1. Animal movements on bench.
   a. Seal Crawl
   b. Cat Walk
   c. Lame Dog Walk
   d. Rabbit Jump
   e. Crab Walk
2. Locomotor movements.
   a. Skip on the bench.
   b. Gallop on the bench.
   c. Step on and off the bench.
   d. Jump on and off the bench.
   e. Hop on and off the bench.
   f. Jump or hop over the bench.
   g. Jump on and off the bench. (Jump down with legs in a straddle position.)
3. Pulls—pull body along the bench in various positions.
   a. Prone position—head first, feet first.
   b. Supine position—head first, feet first.
   c. Side position—head first, feet first.
4. Pushes—same as above activity except push with the arms in all positions.
5. Movements alongside the benches—proceed alongside the bench in the following positions.
   a. Prone position—hands on bench.
   b. Supine position—hands on bench.
   c. Turn over—proceed along bench changing from prone to supine positions with hands on bench.
   d. All of the above positions performed with the feet on the bench.
6. Scooter movements—sit on bench and proceed along bench without using hands.
   a. Regular scooter—feet leading.
   b. Reverse scooter—legs trailing.
   c. Seat walk—walk on the buttocks.
7. Crouch jumps.
   a. Straddle jump
   b. Regular jump
   c. One hand, two feet.
   d. One hand, one foot
8. Jump dismounts.
   a. Single jump—forward or backward
   b. Jump with turns—½, ¾, or full
   c. Pike
   d. Straddle
   e. Heel or knee slap

DPE pp. 469 – 472

Six benches, one group behind each bench.

Place a mat at end of bench for dismounts.

Use a dismount at the end of each activity. See items 8 and 9 for suggestions.

Have the next person in line begin when the person in front of him is halfway across the bench.

Have the youngsters perform a return activity on the way back to their line. Place return activity signs on cones to stimulate and signal movements.

Speed is not the goal. Move deliberately across the bench.

Keep the limbs on the floor as far away as possible from the bench to achieve maximum developmental effect.

Allow students time to develop their own routines on the benches including dismounts and return activities.

Use the dismounts to add variety to each of the previous activities. Proper dismounting should be encouraged and can be associated with gymnastic routines.

PM.—The student will be able to perform all the animal walks across the bench.

PM.—The student will be able to perform the locomotor movements across the bench.

Cog.—The student will be able to identify which bench activities develop arm and shoulder girdle strength.

Cog.—The student will be able to describe why quality of movement is necessary on the benches to ensure beneficial results.

Cog.—Increased fat causes the heart to have to work harder. The resting pulse rate of an obese person is often 10 beats per minute faster than a normal-weight individual. This amounts to approximately 14,000 extra beats per day due to excessive fat.

Aff.—Satisfaction is increased from attaining goals that are realistic. Discuss the importance of setting goals based upon individual characteristics and abilities.

Cog.—Flexing at the ankles, knees, and hips is important when landing after a dismount. This increases the time over which the force is absorbed. Students should understand the importance of absorbing force for a stable landing and minimizing the risk of injury.

MOVEMENT EXPERIENCE— CONTENT	ORGANIZATION AND TEACHING HINTS	EXPECTED STUDENT OBJECTIVES AND OUTCOMES

9. Jump followed by a stunt.
   a. Jump, forward roll
   b. Back jump, back roll
   c. Side jump, side roll
   d. Shoulder roll
   e. Cartwheel.

GAME (5 – 7 MINUTES)

Cageball Kick-Over—*DPE*, p. 573
  Supplies: A cageball, 24- or 30-inch size
  Skill: Kicking
  Players are divided into two teams and sit facing each other, with legs outstretched and soles of the feet about 3 to 6 ft apart. While maintaining the sitting position, each player supports her weight on the hands, which are placed slightly to the rear.
  The teacher rolls the cageball between the two teams. The object of the game is to kick the ball over the other team, thereby scoring a point. After a point is scored, the teacher rolls the ball into play again. A good system of rotation is to have the player on the left side of the line take a place on the right side after a point is scored, thus moving all the players one position to the left. When the ball is kicked out at either end, no score results, and the ball is put into play again by the teacher.
  Variation: Children can be allowed to use their hands to stop the ball from going over them.

  Squad Tag—*DPE*, p. 579
  Supplies: Pinnies or markers for one squad, stopwatch
  Skills: Running, dodging
  An entire squad acts as taggers. The object is to see which squad can tag the remaining class members in the shorter time. The tagging squad should be marked. They stand in a football huddle formation in the center of the area. Their heads are down, and their hands are joined in the huddle. The remainder of the class is scattered as they wish throughout the area. On signal, the tagging squad scatters and tags the other class members. When a class member is tagged, she stops in place and remains there. Time is recorded when the last person is tagged. Each squad gets a turn at tagging.
  Teaching suggestion: Children should be cautioned to watch for collisions, because there is much chasing and dodging in different directions. Definite boundaries are needed.

DYNAMIC PHYSICAL EDUCATION LESSON PLAN
Basketball-Related Activities (Lesson 1)
Level II

Supplies and Equipment Needed:
One junior basketball or playground ball per student
Hoops or individual mats

MOVEMENT EXPERIENCE— CONTENT	ORGANIZATION AND TEACHING HINTS	EXPECTED STUDENT OBJECTIVES AND OUTCOMES

INTRODUCTORY ACTIVITY (2 – 3 MINUTES)

Bridges by Three

Children work in groups of three, with two of the children making bridges and the third moving under them. As soon as the third person has moved under the others, she makes a bridge. Each child in turn goes under the bridge of the other two students.

DPE p. 258

Groups of three.

Different challenges can be tried by specifying different types of bridges, having the moving child perform different movements and tasks, or increasing the distance between bridges.

PM.—The student will be able to make at least five different bridges.

Cog.—The student will identify the isometric exercises (bridging) as well as the isotonic exercises (moving).

FITNESS DEVELOPMENT ACTIVITY (7 – 8 MINUTES)

Aerobic Fitness and Partner Resistance Exercises

Tape alternating segments of silence and music to signal duration of exercise. Music segments indicate aerobic activity while intervals of silence announce flexibility and strength development activities.

Bounce and Clap	30 seconds
Arm Curl-Up	45 seconds
Jumping Jack variations	30 seconds
Camelback	45 seconds
Lunge variations	30 seconds
Fist Pull Apart	45 seconds
Directional Runs	30 seconds
Scissors	45 seconds
Rhythmic Running	30 seconds
Butterfly	45 seconds
Bounce with Body Twist	30 seconds
Resistance Push-Up	45 seconds

Walk, stretch and relax for a minute or two.

DPE pp. 305 – 307 lists aerobic fitness activities.

DPE pp. 297 – 299 describes partner resistance exercises.

During the time allowed for partner resistance exercises, both students should have the opportunity to exercise.

Exercises should be done through the full range of motion.

Youngsters should take 6–10 seconds to move through the full range of motion while their partner applies resistance.

A sign with aerobic activities on one side and partner resistance exercises on the other aids instruction. The signs can be held upright by cones and shared by 2 to 4 students.

Cog.—Sweating occurs when the body is overheated due to stress in an attempt to maintain a constant body temperature. The student will be able to explain why the body sweats.

Cog.—The student will be able to explain that maximum effort must be exerted if the exercise is going to be of any value.

PM.—The student will be able to demonstrate one new partner resistance exercise to the class.

LESSON FOCUS (15 – 20 MINUTES)

Basketball-Related Activities (1)
Chest (Push) Pass (two-handed)

1. Ball at chest level, face partner.
2. Fingers spread above center of ball.
3. Step toward partner and extend arms.
4. Throw to chest level.
5. Catching.
6. Thumbs together for high pass.
7. Little fingers together for low pass.

DPE pp. 615 – 620

Organize by partners.

Explain that this is one of the basic passes and must be mastered.

Get the "push" first, then later stress the finger action.

PM.—The student will be able to perform the following skills adequately:
1. Push, baseball, underhand, and one-hand passes
2. Dribbling—right and left hands while moving
3. Shooting—one-handed shot
4. Catching—high and low passes

MOVEMENT EXPERIENCE—CONTENT	ORGANIZATION AND TEACHING HINTS	EXPECTED STUDENT OBJECTIVES AND OUTCOMES
8. Hands relaxed, provide a little "give." 9. Practice on the fly. 10. Add the bounce pass—same technique. 11. Avoid forward spin. **Basketball (One Hand) Pass** 1. Side toward catcher. 2. Ball back with both hands to side of head or above shoulder. Fingers spread, one hand directly behind the ball. 3. Release the forward hand and throw with a wrist snap. 4. Practice both right and left. **Underhand Pass (two-handed)** 1. Use both hands. 2. Side toward catcher, arms almost fully extended with the ball between the hands, fingers spread, and little fingers fairly close. 3. Step with the forward foot and deliver the ball. Practice both right and left.	Encourage the students to throw at different levels in order to challenge their catching skills as well as throwing accuracy. Bounce the ball just beyond the halfway mark. Try "Keep-away" drills in groups of three using basketball passes and dribbling. Step is short.	Cog.—The student will be able to recite the basic rules of basketball in the following areas: 1. Dribbling 2. Traveling 3. Out of bounds 4. Jump ball Cog.—A spinning object will rebound from the floor in the direction of its spin. Discuss how spin can be applied to a basketball (by applying force off-center) and be used to advantage.
One-Handed Passing (by partners) 1. Left hand in front, right hand in back. 2. Push to partner with one hand. 3. Raise the ball in an arc. **Use all the passes learned above in a passing drill. (DPE, pp. 621–627)** **Birdie in the Cage** 1. Form circle of 7 or 8 children. 2. Pass ball among the circle for practice. Be sure everyone handles the ball. 3. Select "Birdie," put in center. Must stay in center until he touches the ball, or there is a loose ball leaving the circle. **Dribbling (each has a ball)** 1. Explain rules: traveling, double dribbles. 2. Explain technique: wrist action, finger control, eyes ahead. 3. Dribble in different directions. Use right and left in turn. 4. Use whistle dribble. Stop on whistle. 5. Dribble under leg, or around back. 6. Dribble with eyes closed (in place).	Start passing with partners 10–15 ft apart and gradually increase the distance. Encourage short quick passes. Try not to "telegraph" the pass by looking at the target. Let children call the fault. Watch for collisions. Loose balls—stop the ball or just return it.	PM.—The student will be able to play Birdie in the Cage successfully both as a passer and as "Birdie." Cog.—Ligaments are inelastic and do not contract. Joint injuries usually damage ligaments. When ligaments are stretched, they do not grow back to their regular length. Discuss the need for surgery to repair ligament damage. Cog.—Many backaches occur from weak abdominal muscles. This occurs due to the strength of psoas tilting the pelvis forward and creating excessive back arch. Discuss how back muscles are developed by walking and running, whereas the abdominal muscles must be strengthened using curl-ups, rowing, and other abdominal exercises.

MOVEMENT EXPERIENCE— CONTENT	ORGANIZATION AND TEACHING HINTS	EXPECTED STUDENT OBJECTIVES AND OUTCOMES

Shuttle Dribbling

Shuttle dribbling begins at the head of a file. The head player dribbles across to another file and hands the ball off to the player at the head of the second file. He then takes a place at the end of that file. The player receiving the ball dribbles back to the first file. A number of shuttles can be arranged for dribbling crossways over a basketball court.

1 dribbles to 2, who returns the ball by dribbling to 3, who dribbles to 4, and so on back to 1. This can also be done with three players.

Aff.—Basketball is a team sport demanding contribution from all members of the team. Discuss the importance of using all players without prejudice when developing plays and strategy.

Play Dribblerama

One-Handed shot

1. Raise ball up to eye level, sight and shoot (demonstrate).
2. Shoot from close position around the basket with partners alternating.
3. Add a short dibble and a shot.

If too many balls, alternate with dribbling or reduce the number of balls.

Each can take two shots.

This is preliminary to lay-up practice later.

Play Captain Ball

1. Lay out the court(s).
2. Select teams (seven on a side).
3. Put one team in place and show scoring.
4. Put second team in and practice scoring.
   a. One point from forward to captain.
   b. Two points for circuit and then captain.
5. Explain center jump, free throw, fouling the captain scores a point.
6. Show how to get the ball in to the forwards.
7. Play and then rotate the other teams or the substitutes.

Cog.—The student will be able to explain the rules of Captain Ball.

PM.—The student will be able to play all positions in Captain Ball.

Cog.—Skill can be improved with practice. However, readiness will determine when the fastest improvement will occur. This indicates that students will develop their skills at different times, regardless of chronological age. Discuss the need to understand individual growth patterns.

Play Basketball Tag

Play without defenders so students can concentrate on passing.

GAME (5 – 7 MINUTES)

Basketball Lead-Up Games

Birdie in the Cage—*DPE*, p. 628
   Supplies: A soccer ball, basketball, or volleyball
   Skills: Passing, catching, intercepting
   Players are in circle formation with one child in the middle. The object of the game is for the center player to try to touch the ball. The ball is passed from player to player in the circle, and the center player attempts to touch the ball on one of these passes. The player who threw the ball that was touched takes the place in the center. In case of a bad pass resulting in the ball's leaving the circle area, the player who caused the error can change to the center of the ring.
Teaching suggestions: The ball should move rapidly. Passing to a neighboring player is not allowed. If touching the ball proves difficult, a second center may join the first. Play can be limited to a specific type of pass (bounce, two-hand, push).
Variation: As few as three children can play, with two children passing the ball back and forth between them while a third tries to touch it. An excellent version of this game calls for four players, with three forming a triangle and positioning themselves about 15 ft apart.

MOVEMENT EXPERIENCE— CONTENT	ORGANIZATION AND TEACHING HINTS	EXPECTED STUDENT OBJECTIVES AND OUTCOMES

Dribblerama—*DPE*, p. 628

Supplies: One basketball for each player

Skills: Dribbling and protecting the ball

The playing area is a large circle or square, clearly outlined. All players dribble within the area. The game is played on two levels.

Level 1: Each player dribbles throughout the area, controlling the ball so that it does not touch another ball. If a touch occurs, both players go outside the area and dribble counterclockwise around the area. Once youngsters have completed dribbling one lap around the path, they can reenter the game.

Level 2: While dribbling and controlling the ball, each player attempts to cause another player to lose control of the ball. When control is lost, that player takes the ball and dribbles around the perimeter of the area. Play continues until only two or three players who have not lost control of their ball are left. These are declared the winners. Bring all players back into the game and repeat.

Captain Ball—*DPE*, p. 628

Supplies: A basketball, pinnies, eight hoops or individual mats

Skills: Passing, catching, guarding

Two games can be played crosswise on a basketball court. A centerline is needed and the normal out-of-bounds lines can be used. Hoops or individual mats can provide the markers for the forwards and the captains. Captain Ball is a very popular game that is played with many variations. In this version, a team is composed of a captain, three forwards, and three guards. The guards throw the ball to their captain. The captain and the three forwards are each assigned to respective circles and must always keep one foot inside the circle. Guarding these four circle players are three guards.

The game is started by a jump at the centerline by two guards from opposing teams. The guards can rove in their half of the court but must not enter the circles of the opposing players. The ball is put into play after each score in much the same manner as in regular basketball. The team scored on puts the ball into play by a guard throwing the ball in bounds from the side of the court.

As soon as a guard gets the ball, he throws it to one of the forwards, who must maneuver to be open. The forward then tries to throw it to the other forwards or in, to the captain. Two points are scored when all three forwards handle the ball and then it is passed to the captain. One point is scored when the ball is passed to the captain but has not been handled by all three forwards.

Stepping over the centerline is a foul. It is also a foul if a guard steps into a circle or makes personal contact with a circle player. The penalty for a foul is a free throw.

For a free throw, the ball is given to an unguarded forward, who has 5 seconds to get the ball successfully to the guarded captain. If the throw is successful, one point is scored. If it is not successful, the ball is in play. Successive fouls rotate free throws among the forwards.

As in basketball, when the ball goes out-of-bounds, it is awarded to the team that did not cause it to go out. If a forward or a captain catches a ball with both feet out of her circle, the ball is taken out-of-bounds by the opposing guard. For violations such as traveling or kicking the ball, the ball is awarded to an opposing guard out-of-bounds. No score may be made from a ball that is thrown in directly from out-of-bounds.

Teaching suggestions: Some instruction is necessary for children to absorb the basic strategy of the game. An effective offensive formation is to space the guards along the centerline. Only the offensive team is diagrammed. By passing the ball back and forth among the guards, the forwards have more opportunity to be open, since the passing makes the guards shift position. The guards may dribble, but this should be held to a minimum and used for advancing the ball only when necessary. Otherwise, dribbling accomplishes little.

The forwards and the captain should learn to shift back and forth to become open for passes. Considerable latitude is available, since they need keep only one foot in the hoop. Short and accurate passing uses both high and bounce passes. Circle players may jump for the ball but must come down with one foot in the circle.

Variations:

1. Four guards can be used, but scoring is then more difficult.

2. A five-circle formation can be used, forming a five spot like that on a die. Nine players are needed on each team: four forwards, four guards, and one captain.

3. A platform 6 to 8 in. high and 20 in. square can elevate the captain to make reception of the ball easier.

Basketball Tag—*DPE*, p. 627

Supplies: A foam rubber basketball, pinnies

Skills: Catching, passing, dribbling, guarding

Two versions of this game can be played. The simpler version is to designate three to five students to be it and wear a pinnie. The rest of the class passes the ball and tries to tag one of the students who is it with the ball. If desired, more than one ball can be used.

A more difficult version of the game allows tagging. A player from each team is designated to be it and wears a pinnie. The object of the game is to tag the other team's target player with the ball. The player who is it may move only by walking. Players can move the ball by dribbling or by passing the ball to teammates. The player who is it tries to avoid moving near the ball, while others try to pass, dribble, and move near the roving it. The team without the ball plays defense and tries to intercept the ball.

Variation: More than one ball can be used and more than one player per team can be identified as it.

DYNAMIC PHYSICAL EDUCATION LESSON PLAN
Basketball-Related Activities (Lesson 2)
Level II

Supplies and Equipment Needed:
  One basketball or playground ball per student
  Apparatus for the Challenge Course
  Hoops or individual mats
  Balance-beam bench
  Jumping box

MOVEMENT EXPERIENCE— CONTENT	ORGANIZATION AND TEACHING HINTS	EXPECTED STUDENT OBJECTIVES AND OUTCOMES

INTRODUCTORY ACTIVITY (2 – 3 MINUTES)

Jumping and Hopping Patterns

Many combinations can be devised with the basic idea being to work combinations so one returns to home place. An example is: Jump in all directions and hop back to place; or three jumps forward and a half twist, three jumps back to place and a half twist.

DPE p. 255

Students should devise their own combinations of movement.

Pick out a few students and have them demonstrate their ideas to the rest of the class.

PM.—The student will be able to create and perform five different movement combinations utilizing jumping and hopping.

FITNESS DEVELOPMENT ACTIVITY (7 – 8 MINUTES)

Challenge Course Fitness

Design a course around the perimeter of the area using the following ideas:
  1. Step on jumping box, dismount to tumbling mat, and do a forward roll.
  2. Run and weave through four wands held upright by cones.
  3. Handwalk across a horizontal ladder or do a flexed-arm hang from a climbing rope for 5 seconds.
  4. Step on and off three jumping boxes (small-large-small).
  5. Agility run through hoops.
  6. Perform jump turns.
  7. Leap over a magic rope held taut with two chairs or jumping boxes.
  8. Hop on one foot.
  9. Do a Log Roll across a tumbling mat.
  10. Alternate going over and under six obstacles (cones and wands or hoops).
  11. Crouch jump or scooter movements the length of a balance-beam bench.
  12. Slide through a parallel tumbling mat maze (mats stood on their sides).

DPE pp. 304 – 305

Design a Challenge Course that exercises all body parts.

Emphasize moving through the Challenge Course with quality movements. The goal is fitness, not how fast youngsters can move through the course.

Distribute youngsters throughout the course rather than lining them up to start at one point. Faster moving youngsters can pass a station one time only.

Stop the class at regular intervals to perform flexibility and strength development activities for the shoulder girdle and abdominal region.

Change directions periodically. This will help prevent a build-up of students at slower moving stations.

Cog.—The student will be able to design a Challenge Course that exercises all parts of the body.

PM.—The student will be able to accomplish all the challenges successfully.

Aff.—Many different methods for developing and maintaining physical fitness are used in this curriculum. Discuss the importance of people analyzing their likes and dislikes as they find an approach to fitness that best suits them.

MOVEMENT EXPERIENCE— CONTENT	ORGANIZATION AND TEACHING HINTS	EXPECTED STUDENT OBJECTIVES AND OUTCOMES

LESSON FOCUS (15 – 20 MINUTES)

Basketball-Related Activities (2)

1. Review and use different drills such as figure-eight drill, file dribbling drill, dribble and pass drill, and set-shot formations to practice previously introduced skills. Skills that should be reviewed are:
   a. Chest pass and bounce pass
   b. One-handed and under-handed passes
   c. Dribbling
   d. One-hand set shot
2. Introduce the lay-up shot. Use the lay-up drill to practice. Practice without a ball so that children can practice taking off on the correct foot and using the proper number of steps.
3. Introduce guarding. Emphasis should be placed on the following points:
   a. Slide feet, don't cross them.
   b. Keep one or both hands up.
   c. Stay loose, not flat-footed.
4. Integrate the following lead-up games into each day's lesson focus:
   a. Captain Ball
   b. Five Passes
   c. Around the Key

DPE pp. 615 – 620

Try to organize the lesson focus period so that half of the time is spent practicing skills and half playing lead-up or skill-related games.

Don't turn every drill into a relay. Competition will force children to think more about winning than polishing their skills.

It takes a long time to learn basic skills. Don't be in a hurry to teach all activities, and allow plenty of review time.

Stress:
1. Take off on the left foot when shooting with the right hand, and vice versa.
2. Carry the ball in both hands until just before shooting.
3. Aim at a spot on the backboard above the basket.
4. Shoot with right hand when approaching the basket from the right side, and vice versa.

When playing lead-up games, encourage person-to-person guarding so that youngsters learn to stay with their opponent, rather than chasing the ball.

Cog.—Blood pressure measurements are recorded using two numbers. When your heart contracts, the pressure in the arteries is called systolic pressure. When the heart is relaxed and filling with blood, the diastolic pressure is recorded. Discuss how blood pressure is measured and what constitutes high blood pressure.

Cog.—The reason backspin is put on a basketball when it is shot is that the spin opposite to the direction of flight will cause the ball to remain closer to the backboard and increase the possibility of its dropping in. Discuss the effects of spin in the direction of flight and when it is used to advantage.

Cog.—Muscle fatigue occurs when muscles will no longer contract. Training will delay the onset and severity of fatigue. Discuss the effects of fatigue on athletic play and the importance of maintaining a high level of fitness.

GAME (5 – 7 MINUTES)

Basketball Lead-Up Games

Captain Ball—*DPE*, p. 628
Supplies: A basketball, pinnies, eight hoops or individual mats
Skills: Passing, catching, guarding

Two games can be played crosswise on a basketball court. A centerline is needed and the normal out-of-bounds lines can be used. Hoops or individual mats can provide the markers for the forwards and the captains. Captain Ball is a very popular game that is played with many variations. In this version, a team is composed of a captain, three forwards, and three guards. The guards throw the ball to their captain. The captain and the three forwards are each assigned to respective circles and must always keep one foot inside the circle. Guarding these four circle players are three guards.

The game is started by a jump at the centerline by two guards from opposing teams. The guards can rove in their half of the court but must not enter the circles of the opposing players. The ball is put into play after each score in much the same manner as in regular basketball. The team scored on puts the ball into play by a guard throwing the ball in bounds from the side of the court.

As soon as a guard gets the ball, he throws it to one of the forwards, who must maneuver to be open. The forward then tries to throw it to the other forwards or in, to the captain. Two points are scored when all three forwards handle the ball and then it is passed to the captain. One point is scored when the ball is passed to the captain but has not been handled by all three forwards.

Stepping over the centerline is a foul. It is also a foul if a guard steps into a circle or makes personal contact with a circle player. The penalty for a foul is a free throw.

For a free throw, the ball is given to an unguarded forward, who has 5 seconds to get the ball successfully to the guarded captain. If the throw is successful, one point is scored. If it is not successful, the ball is in play. Successive fouls rotate free throws among the forwards.

As in basketball, when the ball goes out-of-bounds, it is awarded to the team that did not cause it to go out. If a forward or a captain catches a ball with both feet out of her circle, the ball is taken out-of-bounds by the opposing guard. For violations such as traveling or kicking the ball, the ball is awarded to an opposing guard out-of-bounds. No score may be made from a ball that is thrown in directly from out-of-bounds.

MOVEMENT EXPERIENCE— CONTENT	ORGANIZATION AND TEACHING HINTS	EXPECTED STUDENT OBJECTIVES AND OUTCOMES

Teaching suggestions: Some instruction is necessary for children to absorb the basic strategy of the game. An effective offensive formation is to space the guards along the centerline. Only the offensive team is diagrammed. By passing the ball back and forth among the guards, the forwards have more opportunity to be open, since the passing makes the guards shift position.

The guards may dribble, but this should be held to a minimum and used for advancing the ball only when necessary. Otherwise, dribbling accomplishes little.

The forwards and the captain should learn to shift back and forth to become open for passes. Considerable latitude is available, since they need keep only one foot in the hoop. Short and accurate passing uses both high and bounce passes. Circle players may jump for the ball but must come down with one foot in the circle.

Variations:

1. Four guards can be used, but scoring is then more difficult.

2. A five-circle formation can be used, forming a five spot like that on a die. Nine players are needed on each team: four forwards, four guards, and one captain.

3. A platform 6 to 8 in. high and 20 in. square can elevate the captain to make reception of the ball easier.

Five Passes—*DPE*, p. 630

Supplies: A basketball; colored shirts, markers, or pinnies

Skills: Passing, guarding

Two teams play. The object of the game is to complete five consecutive passes, which scores a point. On one basketball floor, two games can proceed at the same time, one in each half.

The game is started with a jump ball at the free-throw line. The teams observe regular basketball rules in ball handling and with regard to traveling and fouling. Five consecutive passes must be made by a team, who count out loud as the passes are completed.

The ball must not be passed back to the person from whom it was received. No dribbling is allowed. If for any reason the ball is fumbled and recovered or improperly passed, a new count is started. After a successful score, the ball can be thrown up again in a center jump at the free-throw line. A foul draws a free throw, which can score a point. Teams should be well marked to avoid confusion.

Variations:

1. After each successful point (five passes), the team is awarded a free throw, which can score an additional point.

2

After a team has scored a point, the ball can be given to the other team out-of-bounds to start play again.

3. Passes must be made so that all players handle the ball.

Around the Key—*DPE*, p. 629

Supplies: A basketball

Skill: Shooting

Spots are arranged for shooting around the key. A player begins at the first spot and continues until a miss. When a miss occurs, the player can stop and wait for her next opportunity and begin from the point where the miss occurred, or she can "risk it" and try another shot immediately from the point where the first try was missed. If the shot is made, the player continues. If the shot is missed, the player must start over on the next turn. The winner is the player who completes the key first or who makes the most progress.

Variations:

1. Each child shoots from each spot until a basket is made. A limit of three shots from any one spot should be set. The child finishing the round of eight spots with the lowest number of shots taken is the winner.

2. The order of the spots can be changed. A player can start on one side of the key and continue back along the line, around the free-throw circle, and back down the other side of the key.

DYNAMIC PHYSICAL EDUCATION LESSON PLAN
Recreational Activities
Level II

Supplies and Equipment Needed:
Fleece balls—one for each child
Apparatus for Challenge Course
Equipment for recreational activities

MOVEMENT EXPERIENCE—CONTENT	ORGANIZATION AND TEACHING HINTS	EXPECTED STUDENT OBJECTIVES AND OUTCOMES

INTRODUCTORY ACTIVITY (2 – 3 MINUTES)

Fleece Ball Fun

Each child has a fleece ball. Allow students to kick, throw or move with the ball for a designated time (e.g., one minute).

On signal, place the balls on the floor and perform movements around, between and over the balls.

DPE p. 258

This activity works best when students have enough room to move freely.

Movement patterns can be designated, such as rectangular, circular, and figure eight.

Beanbags may be substituted for fleece balls.

PM.—The students will be able to demonstrate the ability to kick and throw their fleece balls without running into other people.

FITNESS DEVELOPMENT ACTIVITIES (7 – 8 MINUTES)

Challenge Course Fitness

Design a course around the perimeter of the area using the following ideas:
1. Step on jumping box, dismount to tumbling mat, and do a forward roll.
2. Run and weave through four wands held upright by cones.
3. Handwalk across a horizontal ladder or do a flexed-arm hang from a climbing rope for 5 seconds.
4. Step on and off three jumping boxes (small-large-small).
5. Agility run through hoops.
6. Perform jump turns.
7. Leap over a magic rope held taut with two chairs or jumping boxes.
8. Hop on one foot.
9. Do a Log Roll across a tumbling mat.
10. Move through a tunnel made with jumping boxes covered by a tumbling mat.
11. Crouch jump or scooter movements the length of a balance-beam bench.
12. Slide through a parallel tumbling mat maze (mats stood on their sides).

DPE pp. 304 – 305

Design a Challenge Course that exercises all body parts. Allow students an opportunity to develop new challenge ideas.

Emphasize moving through the Challenge Course with quality movements. The goal is fitness, not how fast youngsters can move through the course.

Distribute youngsters throughout the course rather than lining them up to start at one point. Faster moving youngsters can pass a station one time only.

Stop the class at regular intervals to perform flexibility and strength development activities for the shoulder girdle and abdominal region.

Change directions periodically. This will help prevent a build-up of students at slower moving stations.

Cog.—Challenge Courses were a common way of developing fitness in the armed services.

PM.—All students should be able to run the Challenge Course three times.

Aff.—There is no easy way to fitness. It demands self-discipline. Discuss the importance of possessing a positive attitude toward activity in later life.

MOVEMENT EXPERIENCE—CONTENT	ORGANIZATION AND TEACHING HINTS	EXPECTED STUDENT OBJECTIVES AND OUTCOMES

LESSON FOCUS AND GAME (15 – 20 MINUTES)

Recreational Activities

The purpose of the recreation is to teach children activities that they can play during leisure time.

Suggested activities are:
1. Shuffleboard
2. Four Square
3. Hopscotch
4. Beanbag Horseshoes
5. Jacks
6. Marbles
7. Sidewalk Tennis
8. Rope Quoits
9. Deck Tennis
10. Tetherball
11. Tennis Volleyball

Emphasis should be placed on teaching the rules of the activities so children can enjoy them on their own time.

Three or four activities may be set up in each of four quadrants. Students work on any activity in their quadrant until signaled to move to the next quadrant.

If you know a traditional game played by children in your area for many years, now is a good time to teach it.

PM.—The student will be able to play at least four of the given activities.

Cog.—The student will be able to recite the rules for playing four or more of the activities.

Aff.—Recreational activities can be an excellent release for reducing stress. Relaxation demands playing for enjoyment and personal pleasure. Adults spend millions of dollars searching for activities that are relaxing and rewarding.

DYNAMIC PHYSICAL EDUCATION LESSON PLAN
Fundamental Skills Using Balance Beams
Level II

Supplies and Equipment Needed:
Beanbags, wands, hoops, and jump ropes
Balance-beam benches
Apparatus for Challenge Course
Cones
Playground ball for each student
Targets

MOVEMENT EXPERIENCE—CONTENT	ORGANIZATION AND TEACHING HINTS	EXPECTED STUDENT OBJECTIVES AND OUTCOMES

INTRODUCTORY ACTIVITY (2 – 3 MINUTES)

Ball Activities

Each student has an 8-½" playground ball. The balls can be dribbled as in basketball or as in soccer. On signal, students stop, balance on one leg, pass the ball under other leg and around back and overhead, maintaining control and balance.

Variations:

1. Toss ball up in place or dibble.
2. Play catch with a friend while moving.
3. Have a leader challenge the class to try different stunts and manipulative actions.

DPE p. 256

Emphasis should be on movement rather than ball skill activities.

Spread the playground balls throughout the area so the time needed to secure and put away equipment is minimized.

Cog.—The student will explain the concept of making a toss that leads the catcher so she can move into the path of the ball.

PM.—The students will be able to toss the balls in front of themselves so movements are not interrupted.

FITNESS DEVELOPMENT ACTIVITIES (7 – 8 MINUTES)

Challenge Course Fitness

Design a course around the perimeter of the area using the following ideas:
1. Step on jumping box, dismount to tumbling mat, and do a forward roll.
2. Run and weave through four wands held upright by cones.
3. Handwalk across a horizontal ladder or do a flexed-arm hang from a climbing rope for 5 seconds.
4. Step on and off three jumping boxes (small-large-small).
5. Agility run through hoops.
6. Perform jump turns.
7. Leap over a magic rope held taut with two chairs or jumping boxes.
8. Hop on one foot.
9. Do a Log Roll across a tumbling mat.
10. Move through a tunnel made with jumping boxes covered by a tumbling mat.
11. Crouch jump or scooter movements the length of a balance-beam bench.

DPE pp. 304 – 305

Change some of the challenges and add new ones designed by students.

Emphasize moving through the Challenge Course with quality movements. The goal is fitness, not how fast youngsters can move through the course.

Distribute youngsters throughout the course rather than lining them up to start at one point. Faster moving youngsters can pass a station one time only.

Stop the class at regular intervals to perform flexibility and strength development activities for the shoulder girdle and abdominal region.

Change directions periodically. This will help prevent a build-up of students at slower moving stations.

Cog.—The student will be able to explain that in order to support stronger muscles, larger bones are developed. Muscles grow when exercised regularly and bones become stronger in response to the increased stress.

PM.—The student will be able to go through the Challenge Course four times.

MOVEMENT EXPERIENCE— CONTENT	ORGANIZATION AND TEACHING HINTS	EXPECTED STUDENT OBJECTIVES AND OUTCOMES

12. Slide through a parallel tumbling mat maze (mats stood on their sides).

LESSON FOCUS (15 – 20 MINUTES)

Fundamental Skills Using Balance Beams

Practice walking on lines to establish qualities on controlled movement and not looking at feet.
1. Walk length of beam and dismount correctly.
    a. Walk forward.
    b. Walk backward.
    c. Walk sideways—lead with both left and right sides of body.
2. Walk different directions and vary arm and body positions.
    a. Hands on hips.
    b. Hands on head.
    c. Hands folded across chest.
    d. Lean to one side or the other.
    e. Body bent forward or backward.
    f. Hands on knees or feet.
    g. Exploratory activity.
3. Balance objects such as beanbags, erasers or wands while walking across beam. (Exploratory approach)
4. Move across the beam in various directions using the following movements:
    a. Slide
    b. Heel and toe
    c. Tiptoes
    d. Grapevine
    e. Dip step
    f. Student choice
5. Use various equipment:
    a. Play catch with beanbags. Try different throws and movements.
    b. Bounce a playground ball and catch it, dribble it, play catch with a partner.
    c. Step over a wand, go under a wand, change directions.
    d. Go through a hoop.
6. Allow a few minutes for student exploration of ideas.

DPE pp. 467 – 469

Use at least six beams with equal number of students at each beam.

Use a mat at the finishing end of the beam for students to perform their dismounts.

Assign a return activity for students so they are busy off as well as on the beam.

Stress quality of movement across the beam as well as during the dismount.

If a child falls, have him step back on the beam and continue. This will ensure him of the same amount of practice that the gifted child receives.

Make sure each student performs a dismount. The dismount will discourage the student from running across the beam and will closely simulate the competitive balance-beam event.

Stress student choice and exploration.

Place a target on the wall in front of the beams. Ask students to visually focus on the targets while walking on the beams.

PM.—The students will be able to balance themselves while walking across beam. A desirable goal would be for the child to walk across the beam without falling.

Cog.—Balance is a learned activity. The student will be able to explain that balance and concentration are necessary for improvement.

Cog.—The student will be able to explain how changing arm and leg positions or direction of movement creates a new balance task for the body.

Cog.—Balance activities are best performed when performers are relaxed. Increased leg strength also plays an important part in balance. Encourage practice at home where there is little fear of falling and embarrassment.

Cog.—For increased balance control, widen the base of support and lower the center of gravity. Discuss the impact of the narrow base of support found on balance beams.

MOVEMENT EXPERIENCE— CONTENT	ORGANIZATION AND TEACHING HINTS	EXPECTED STUDENT OBJECTIVES AND OUTCOMES

GAME (5 – 7 MINUTES)

Fly Trap—*DPE*, p. 574
Supplies: None
Skills: Fundamental locomotor movements
Half of the class is scattered around the playing area, sitting on the floor in cross-legged fashion. These children form the trap. The other children are the flies, and they buzz around the seated children. When a whistle is blown, the flies must freeze where they are. If any of the trappers can touch a fly, that fly sits down at that spot and becomes a trapper. The trappers must keep their seats glued to the floor.

The game continues until all of the flies are caught. Some realism is given to the game if the flies make buzzing sounds and move their arms as wings.

Teaching suggestion: Some experience with the game enables the teacher to determine how far apart to place the seated children. After all (or most) of the flies have been caught, the groups trade places. The method of locomotion should be changed occasionally also.

Nonda's Car Lot—*DPE*, p. 578
Supplies: None
Skills: Running, dodging
One player is it and stands in the center of the area between two lines established about 50 ft apart. The class selects four brands of cars (e.g., Honda, Corvette, Toyota, Cadillac). Each student then selects a car from the four but does not tell anyone what it is.

The tagger calls out a car name. All students who selected that name attempt to run to the other line without getting tagged. The tagger calls out the cars until all students have run. When a child (car) gets tagged, she must sit down at the spot of the tag. She cannot move but may tag other students who run too near her. When the one who is it calls out "Car lot," all of the cars must go. The game is played until all students have been tagged.

DYNAMIC PHYSICAL EDUCATION LESSON PLAN
Stunts and Tumbling Skills (Lesson 2)
Level II

Supplies and Equipment Needed:
  Tape player and tapes
  Tumbling mats

MOVEMENT EXPERIENCE— CONTENT	ORGANIZATION AND TEACHING HINTS	EXPECTED STUDENT OBJECTIVES AND OUTCOMES

INTRODUCTORY ACTIVITY (2 – 3 MINUTES)

Moving to Music

Use a different music to stimulate various locomotor and non-locomotor movements. Different dance steps such as polka, two-step and schottische could be practiced.

DPE p. 256

Emphasis should be placed on creating a movement that is synchronized to the music.

If youngsters have difficulty sensing the rhythm, use a tom-tom to aid them.

PM.—The student will be able to move, in time with the music, to five different rhythms.

Cog.—The student will be able to identify the difference between 3/4 and 4/4 rhythm.

FITNESS DEVELOPMENT ACTIVITIES (7 – 8 MINUTES)

Aerobic Fitness

1. Rhythmic run with clap.
2. Bounce turn and clap.
3. Rhythmic 4-count curl-ups (knees, toes, knees, back).
4. Rhythmic Crab Kicks (slow time).
     Repeat steps 1–4 three times.
5. Jumping Jack combination.
6. Double knee lifts.
7. Lunges (right, left, forward) with single-arm circles (on the side lunges) and double-arms circles (on the forward lunge).
8. Rhythmic trunk twists.
     Repeat steps 5–8 three times.
9. Directional run (forward, backward, side, turning).
10. Rock side to side with clap.
11. Side leg raises (alternate legs).
12. Rhythmic 4-count push-ups. (If these are too difficult for students, substitute single-arm circles in the push-up position.)
     Repeat steps 9–12 three times.

DPE pp. 305 – 307

Perform the routine for 7 minutes. Increase by 30 seconds per week.

Alternate bouncing and running movements with flexibility and strength development movements.

Do not use confusing steps and combinations.

Make the routine easy to follow.

Select music that has a definite beat.

Posters may be used to list the steps as an aid for students.

Help students become interested in aerobic dance and in fitness activities by making the routine enjoyable.

Monitor heart rate to check to see how this activity raises the heart rate into the training zone.

Try adding rhythmic bounces or jogging between steps to allow students to regroup.

Don't stress or expect perfection. The routine should be for fitness development.

Cog.—It is interesting to measure the breathing rate at rest as well as during and after exercise. Why does breathing rate vary?

Aff.—Many experts feel people are overweight due to lack of activity rather than eating too much. Discuss why this might be true.

MOVEMENT EXPERIENCE— CONTENT	ORGANIZATION AND TEACHING HINTS	EXPECTED STUDENT OBJECTIVES AND OUTCOMES

LESSON FOCUS (15 – 20 MINUTES)

Tumbling, Stunts, and Animal Movements (2)

Six groups of activities in this lesson ensure that youngsters receive a variety of experiences. Pick a few activities from each group and teach them alternately. For example, teach one or two animal movements, then a tumbling and inverted balance, followed by a balance stunt, etc. Give equal time to each group of activities

1. Animal Movements
    a. Elbow Crawl
    b. Measuring Worm
    c. Mule Kick
    d. Walrus Walk
2. Tumbling and Inverted Balances
    a. Headstand Kick-Up
    b. Frog Handstand
    c. Half Teeter-Totter
    d. Cartwheel
    e. Forward Roll - Pike Position
3. Balance Stunts
    a. Leg Dip
    b. Balance Jump
    c. Seat Balance
4. Individual Stunts
    a. Heelstand
    b. Wicket Walk
    c. Knee Jump to Standing
    d. Kneel Drop
    e. Forward Drop
5. Partner and Group Stunts
    a. Rowboat
    b. Leapfrog
    c. Wheelbarrow
    d. Wheelbarrow Lifting
6. Partner Support Stunts
    a. Table
    b. Statue

DPE pp. 507 – 526

Scatter as many tumbling mats as possible throughout the area in order to avoid waiting lines.

Do not perform many repetitions of tumbling and inverted balances. For most children, limiting the number of forward or backward roll repetitions to four or five will prevent fatigue and injury.

If necessary, start at a lower level than listed here to assure students find success.

After students learn the basic activities, emphasize three phases of correct performance:
1. Starting position
2. Execution
3. Finishing position

Teach youngsters to stand on the hips and shoulders when doing partner support stunts.

Cog.—Momentum needs to be developed and applied when performing rolls. The student will be able to name three ways of developing momentum (i.e., tucking, starting from a higher point, preliminary raising of the arms).

Cog.—The center of weight must be positioned over the center of support in balance stunts. The student will be able to describe and demonstrate this in his own fashion.

P.M.—The student will be able to perform at least two of the activities in each of the groups.

Aff.—Tumbling and stunts are activities in which there is a wide range of student ability which is evident to others. Discuss the sensitivity of the situation and the need to understand the shortcomings of others.

Cog.—Certain sports and activities offer a greater degree of aerobic conditioning. Contrast activities such as basketball, jogging, bicycling, rope jumping, and swimming with bowling, golf, softball, and football.

Aff.—Many people take drugs to help them handle stress. Unfortunately, they avoid dealing with the cause of stress. Drugs are short-term solutions and ultimately cause more problems than they solve. Discuss how drugs can cause physiological and psychological changes and addiction.

MOVEMENT EXPERIENCE— CONTENT	ORGANIZATION AND TEACHING HINTS	EXPECTED STUDENT OBJECTIVES AND OUTCOMES

GAME (5 – 7 MINUTES)

Partner Stoop—*DPE*, p. 578
  Supplies: Music
  Skills: Marching rhythmically
  The game follows the same basic principle of stooping as in Circle Stoop, but it is played with partners. The group forms a double circle, with partners facing counterclockwise, which means that one partner is on the inside and one is on the outside. When the music begins, all march in the line of direction. After a short period of marching, a signal (whistle) is sounded, and the inside circle reverses direction and marches the other way—clockwise. The partners are thus separated. When the music stops, the outer circle stands still, and the partners making up the inner circle walk to rejoin their respective outer circle partners. As soon as a child reaches her partner, they join inside hands and stoop without losing balance. The last couple to stoop and those who have lost balance go to the center of the circle and wait out the next round.
  Insist that players walk when joining their partner. This avoids the problem of stampeding and colliding with others.

Crows and Cranes—*DPE*, p. 574
  Supplies: None
  Skills: Running, dodging
  Two goal lines are drawn about 50 ft apart. Children are divided into two groups—the crows and the cranes. The groups face each other at the center of the area, about 5 ft apart. The leader calls out either "Crows" or "Cranes," using a cr-r-r-r-r sound at the start of either word to mask the result. If "Crows" is the call, the crows chase the cranes to the goal line. If "Cranes" is the call, then the cranes chase. Any child caught goes over to the other side. The team that has the most players when the game ends is the winner.
  Variations:
  1. Instead of facing each other, children stand back to back, about a foot apart, in the center.
  2. The game can be played with the two sides designated as red and blue. A piece of plywood painted red on one side and blue on the other can be thrown into the air between the teams, instead of having someone give calls. If red comes up, the red team chases, and vice versa.
  3. Blue, black, and baloney. On the command "Blue" or "Black," the game proceeds as described. On the command "Baloney," no one is to move. The caller should draw out the bl-l-l-l sound before ending with one of the three commands.
  4. Another variation of the game is to have a leader tell a story using as many words beginning with cr- as possible. Words that can be incorporated into a story might be crazy, crunch, crust, crown, crude, crowd, crouch, cross, croak, critter. Each time one of these words is spoken, the beginning of the word is lengthened with a drawn out cr-r-r sound. No one may move on any of the words except crows or cranes.

DYNAMIC PHYSICAL EDUCATION LESSON PLAN
Manipulative Skills Using Wands
Level II

Supplies and Equipment Needed:
  One wand per child
  Tom-tom
  Record player and records
  Poster for aerobic routines
  Deck tennis rings

MOVEMENT EXPERIENCE—CONTENT	ORGANIZATION AND TEACHING HINTS	EXPECTED STUDENT OBJECTIVES AND OUTCOMES

INTRODUCTORY ACTIVITY (2 – 3 MINUTES)

European Rhythmic Running with Variations

Students clap to the beat of the drum and run in single-file formation. Practice some of the following variations:
1. Run lightly counterclockwise.
2. Clap hands on every fourth beat.
3. Stamp foot on every second beat.
4. Stamp every second beat and clap every fourth.
5. On signal, make a complete turn, using four running steps.
6. On signal, stop, pivot and move in the opposite direction.
7. Appoint a student to lead the class through various formations.

DPE pp. 252 – 253

Variations should be tried after the class has mastered the quality requirements of rhythm, spacing, and staying in line.

At times, stop the drum beat and have the class continue running. The patter of their feet is a good measure of their success in this activity.

Cog.—Skilled runners do not need the beat of the tom-tom, but can keep time with a leader.

PM.—The student will be able to perform the variation and maintain the proper rhythm at the same time.

FITNESS DEVELOPMENT ACTIVITY (7 – 8 MINUTES)

Aerobic Fitness

1. Rhythmic run with kicks.
2. Bounce forward and backward with clap.
3. Rhythmic 4-count curl-ups.
4. Crab Kick combinations.
    Repeat steps 1–4 three times.
5. Jumping Jack variations.
6. Knee lifts, turning.
7. Side bends.
8. Leg extensions (seated).
    Repeat steps 5–8 three times.
9. Directional run (changing formations).
10. Bounce with body twist.
11. Side leg raises (alternate legs).
12. Rhythmic Push-Up Challenges.
    Repeat steps 9–12 three times.

DPE pp. 305 – 307

Perform the routine for 7 1/2 minutes.

May be done in scattered formation or in a circle.

A follow-the-leader approach is excellent.

Use music that stimulates students to exercise.

Alternate bouncing and running movements with flexibility and strength development movements.

While performing rhythmic running movements, students can move into different formations.

Place poster with cues on the wall that list steps, number of repetitions, and "cue words."

Smile and have a good time—students will believe you enjoy fitness activity.

Variations may be made in the suggested routines.

PM.—The student will be able to perform all of the exercises in time to the music by the end of the week.

Cog.—The student will be able to recognize all of the exercises by name by the end of the week.

Cog.—The blood is transported back to the lungs in the veins. This system is called the circulatory system.

195

MOVEMENT EXPERIENCE— CONTENT	ORGANIZATION AND TEACHING HINTS	EXPECTED STUDENT OBJECTIVES AND OUTCOMES

LESSON FOCUS (15 – 20 MINUTES)

Manipulative Skills Using Wands

Select activities from each of the three groups: Exercises, Stunts and Partner Activities.

Exercises Using Wands

1. Standing isometrics
   a. Push hands together; chest high, overhead, behind seat.
   b. Pull hands apart; chest high, overhead, behind sea.
2. Wand overhead, with straight arms
   a. Bend right, left, forward.
3. Body twist
   a. Twist right, left.
   b. Bend right, left.
4. Long sitting, want overhead
   a. Touch toes with wand.

Wand Stunts

1. Wand catch
   a. Practice different combinations.
   b. Do four-way routine.
2. Thread needle—V-Seat
   a. Legs crossed
   b. Legs together
   c. Combination
3. Thread needle—standing
   a. Front-back, reverse, side to side
   b. Add shoulder dislocate
4. Grapevine
   a. 1st stage
   b. 2nd stage—stepout
   c. Reverse
5. Back Scratcher
   a. 1st stage—down back.
   b. 2nd stage—down over seat.
6. Wand whirl
   a. Practice standing wand.
   b. Grab with hand, grab with one finger.
   c. Do right and left turns
7. Twist under
   a. Right hand, left hand.
   b. Twist right, left. Reverse.
8. Jump stick
9. Wand balances
   a. Student choice—back of hand, shift to front of hand, change hands, sit down, get up. Try balancing on foot.
10. Crab Leap
   a. Alternating feet.
11. Long reach
   a. Perform with the wand in both the left and right hand in turn.

DPE pp. 427 – 431

Watch posture. Stress good effort. Hold for 8 seconds.

Stress full bends. Reach beyond toes.

Do one each way. Keep balance.

Stress not touching.

Hold wand in fingertips.

Allow kneeling, may be better for some. Use demonstration.

Crossed-hands position, palms up. Use demonstration.

Secure some skill in standing wand.

Stick will slip. Must control.

Do not reverse jump. Get height. Practice without stick.

Aff.—Wand stunts demand a great deal of flexibility. Often, girls are more successful at flexibility activities than boys. This is an opportune time to discuss individual differences as well as ability differences between sexes.

Cog.—The students will be able to explain in their own words that frequent stretching makes possible a wider range of motion and conserves energy.

Cog.—It appears to be impossible to improve reaction time. Reaction time is the time it takes to initiate a response to a signal. However, movement time can be improved through increasing strength, shortening the length of a lever, and decreasing the distance to be moved. Movement time is the time it takes to move a certain distance. Discuss a skill and what could be modified to improve movement time.

Cog.—Knowledge of results is important when learning motor skills. Performers can evaluate their movements and make modifications for improvement. Discuss various aspects of a skill students should analyze to improve their skills.

Cog.—Teaching a skill in parts is effective when the skill is complex and contains many individual skills, and the learner has limited memory span. Explain and demonstrate to youngsters how skills can be taught in parts and then put together as a complete task.

PM.—The student will be able to perform 6 of the 11 wand stunts.

Cog.—Practice sessions should be short when tasks are difficult and performers young. Also, when excessive repetition is demanded, sessions should be kept short. Students will understand the need for short practice sessions, distributed evenly over a long period of time.

MOVEMENT EXPERIENCE— CONTENT	ORGANIZATION AND TEACHING HINTS	EXPECTED STUDENT OBJECTIVES AND OUTCOMES
Partner Activities		Aff.—Goals should be set based on a person's capability. Discuss some types of goals students might set to maintain physical fitness. Some examples might be:
1. Partner Catch	Keep distances short.	
a. One wand, two wands.		
2. Partner Change	Distances short, use one step.	1. Jog daily.
a. Simple exercise.		2. Do pull-ups daily.
b. Spin.		3. Jump-rope daily.
3. Partner Rowing		4. Play basketball every day for 30 minutes.
a. Seated, legs spread, feet against feet.	Hold wand instead of hands.	5. Do sit-ups daily.
b. Overhand grip, row back and forth.		
4. Stick Twist	Try to get opponent to shift grip.	
a. Facing partner, arms overhead, overhand grip.	Complete descriptions in *DPE,* Chapter 21.	
5. Wand Wrestle	Try to wrestle stick away.	
a. One hand outside.		
6. Partner Pull-Up	Stress equal start.	
a. Sit, facing, knees straight, soles against soles.		
b. Bend forward, grasp wand.	Both hands either inside or out.	
7. Turn the Dishrag		
8. Ring toss with deck tennis rings.	Keep distances short at first.	
a. Alternate back and forth.		

GAME (5 – 7 MINUTES)

Home Base—*DPE,* p. 576

   Supplies: Cones to delineate the area, four pinnies

   Skills: Reaction time, locomotor movements, body management

   The area is divided into four quadrants with cones or floor lines. Each quadrant is the home base for one of the squads. The captain of the squad wears a pinnie for easy identification. The teams begin in a straight line sitting on the floor. The teacher calls out a locomotor movement which the players use to move throughout the area. When the teacher calls "Home base," the students return to their quadrant and return to the starting position behind their captain. The first team to return to proper position (sitting in a straight line) is awarded 2 points. Second place receives 1 point.

   Teaching suggestion: Avoid calling "Home base" until the students have left the area of their quadrant. A number of different formations can be specified which students must assume upon return to their home base.

Indianapolis 500—*DPE,* p. 577

   Supplies: None

   Skills: Running, tagging

   Children start in a large circle and are numbered off in threes or fours. A race starter says "Start your engines," and then calls out a number. Those children with the corresponding number run clockwise around the circle and try to tag players in front of them. If the leader yells "Pit stop," all runners have to stop and return to their original position. If "Accident" is called by the leader, all runners must change direction and proceed counterclockwise. Change the starter often.

Nine Lives—*DPE,* p. 577

   Supplies: Fleece balls

   Skills: Throwing, dodging

   Any number of fleece balls can be used—the more the better. At a signal, players get a ball and hit as many people below waist level as possible. When a player counts that she has been hit nine times, she leaves the game and stands out of bounds until she has counted to 25. A player may run anywhere with a ball or to get a ball, but he may possess only one ball at a time. Players must not be hit in the head. This puts the thrower out.

   Teaching suggestion: Children often cheat about the number of times they have been hit. A few words about fair play may be necessary, but a high degree of activity is the important game element.

   Variations:

   1. For a ball caught on the fly, a designated number of hits may be taken away.

   2. Either left- or right-hand throwing can be specified.

DYNAMIC PHYSICAL EDUCATION LESSON PLAN
Rhythmic Movement (Lesson 3)
Level II

Supplies and Equipment Needed:
Tape player
Music
Tinikling poles
Indian clubs
Beach balls

Dances Taught:
E-Z Mixer
Irish Washerwoman
Gustaf's Skoal
Tinikling

MOVEMENT EXPERIENCE— CONTENT	ORGANIZATION AND TEACHING HINTS	EXPECTED STUDENT OBJECTIVES AND OUTCOMES

INTRODUCTORY ACTIVITY (2 – 3 MINUTES)

Tortoise and Hare

When the leader calls out the word "tortoise," students run in place slowly. On the word "hare," they change to a rapid run.

Variations:
1. Perform to music.
2. Move throughout the area.
3. Perform various stretching activities on command.
4. Move in different directions.

DPE p. 253

Encourage good knee lift.

Scatter formation.

Have students lift their knees to their hands, which are held in front of the body at waist level.

PM.—The student will be able to maintain a steady rhythm at both slow and fast speeds.

Cog.—People need to psychologically warm up so they "feel" like moving. Discuss the importance of movement in setting the right frame of mind for fitness development activity.

FITNESS DEVELOPMENT ACTIVITY (7 – 8 MINUTES)

Aerobic Fitness (suggested routine)

1. Bounce and do arm circles.
2. Grapevine step with clap.
3. Curl-Up variations.
4. Treadmill combinations.
   Repeat steps 1–4 three times.
5. Forward and side stride hops.
6. Knee list and kick combinations.
7. Rhythmic windmills.
8. Leg extensions (seated).
   Repeat steps 5–8 three times.
9. Rhythmic rum with knee lift on every 4th beat.
10. Rock side to side with double bounce on each side.
11. Rhythmic Push-Up Challenges (try them in the reverse position!).
12. Bear hugs.
    Repeat steps 9–12 three times.

DPE pp. 305 – 307

Perform the routine for 8 minutes.

This is the final week of aerobic dance.

Students should be given the opportunity to lead.

Groups of four to six may be formed to create aerobic dance routines.

Use music that stimulates students to exercise.

Smile and have a good time—students will get a positive feeling about fitness activities.

Aff.—Leadership demands an increase in responsibility. Leaders must be concerned for the welfare of others as well as themselves. Discuss how the leaders determine the work load for the rest of the group.

PM.—The student will be able to perform the exercises at an increased work load (longer duration) than the previous week.

Cog.—One method often used to measure fitness is to count the pulse rate after exercise within 2 or 3 minutes. It might be interesting to measure pulse rate at various intervals after exercise. The more fit one is, the faster pulse rate returns to normal.

Aff.—A well-balanced diet provides fuel for physical activity. Discuss the basics of a good diet and the need for such.

PM.—The students will be able to work in small groups and create aerobic dance routines by the end of the week.

MOVEMENT EXPERIENCE— CONTENT	ORGANIZATION AND TEACHING HINTS	EXPECTED STUDENT OBJECTIVES AND OUTCOMES

LESSON FOCUS (15 – 20 MINUTES)

Rhythmic Movement (3)

When teaching a dance, use the following steps:
1. Tell about the dance and listen to the music.
2. Clap the beat and learn the verse.
3. Practice the dance steps without the music and with verbal cues.
4. Practice the dance with the music.

Make dances easy for students to learn by using some of the following ideas:
1. Teach the dances without partners.
2. Allow youngsters to move in any direction—avoid the left–right orientation.
3. Use scattered formation instead of circles—it helps avoid embarrassment.
4. Emphasize strong movements such as clapping and stomping to encourage involvement.
5. Tape the music at a slower speed when first learning the dance.

Rhythms should be taught like other sport skills. Avoid expecting perfection when teaching rhythms. Teach a variety of dances rather than one or two in depth. Youngsters will enjoy rhythms if they know it is acceptable to make mistakes without being ridiculed.

1. E-Z Mixer (*DPE*, p. 385)

An American dance.

Circle of partners facing CCW.

Basic dance skills:
1. Walking
2. Elbow swing
3. Pivot (and move to new partner)

PM.—The student will develop the proper rhythm needed to perform this dance successfully.

Aff.—The student will accept new partners graciously.

2. Irish Washerwoman (*DPE*, p. 385)

Basic dance steps:
1. Walk
2. Swing
3. Promenade
Review the terms:
1. Partner
2. Corner
Single circle, couples facing center, girl (or "pinnie" person) to the right side of partner.

Spend some time practicing moving smoothly from a swing into a promenade position.

Aff.—The student will be courteous when accepting a new partner.

PM.—The student will be able to go through the entire dance without difficulty.

3. Gustaf's Skoal (*DPE*, p. 387)

A Swedish dance.

Basic dance skills:
1. Stately walking
2. Skipping
3. Turning
4. Forming arches

Review the terms:
1. Head couples
2. Side couples

Aff.—The student will appreciate that this dance begins in a stately, dignified manner.

PM.—The student will be able to master the maneuvers in this dance without difficulty.

MOVEMENT EXPERIENCE— CONTENT	ORGANIZATION AND TEACHING HINTS	EXPECTED STUDENT OBJECTIVES AND OUTCOMES

MOVEMENT EXPERIENCE—CONTENT

4. Tinikling (*DPE*, p. 389)
   1. Teach the Dance Rhythm
      a. Teach the basic step rhythms using two parallel chalked lines or jump ropes.
      b. Practice a two-count weight transfer rocking sideways on the left and right feet.
      c. When students can shift the weight from side to side, introduce the uneven rhythm. This is a similar rocking motion where one hop is done on the left foot and two on the right.
      d. Practice the uneven rhythm moving in and out of the ropes, lines on the floor, or stationary poles.
   2. Teach the Pole Rhythm
      a. Teach the pole rhythm by practicing a three-count clapping rhythm cued by the teacher with a tom-tom. The rhythm is clap (hands together); down (slap top of legs); down (same as previous).
      b. Clap the rhythm to the record. Slow the music down in the early learning stages.
      c. Allow everyone to practice the rhythm with the poles and no dances.
      d. Add dancers doing the basic step.
   3. Practice other steps and the circling movement:
      a. Crossover step
      b. Rocker step
      c. Circle the poles
      d. Cross step
   4. Formation dancing
      a. Line of poles, individually or with a partner
      b. Square formation

ORGANIZATION AND TEACHING HINTS

Small-group formations.

Make sure the sticks go together on the *down* beat, as this is an auditory cue for the dancer.

This dance takes some time to learn. Don't be impatient, and allow class enough time to practice.

Make sure that the people handling the sticks are rotated often.

The sticks should be kept low or the dancer's legs may be caught.

The initial step is used only to get the dance under way.

Eyes should be up, not looking at feet or poles.

Partners face, holding hands with the side to the poles. Begin with the foot nearest the poles.

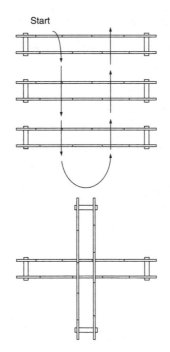

Signs listing the Tinikling steps in progression allows students to learn at individual rates.

EXPECTED STUDENT OBJECTIVES AND OUTCOMES

Cog.—The student will know the origin of the dance.

PM.—The student will be able to perform the basic tinikling step as well as move the sticks to the proper rhythm.

Aff.—Dancing is an activity that has been done for many years, in many cultures. Discuss the possibilities as to why this occurs.

Aff.—One of the important facets to positive social adjustment is accepting individual differences. Discuss the importance of accepting others as they are and avoiding comparing, judging, and disapproving of others' performances.

MOVEMENT EXPERIENCE— CONTENT	ORGANIZATION AND TEACHING HINTS	EXPECTED STUDENT OBJECTIVES AND OUTCOMES

GAME (5 – 7 MINUTES)

Jump the Shot—*DPE*, p. 577
    Supplies: A jump-the-shot rope
    Skill: Rope jumping
    The players stand in circle formation. One player with a long rope stands in the center. A soft object is tied to the free end of the rope to give it some weight. An old, deflated ball or beanbag makes a good weight (tie the rope to it and use duct tape to keep it from becoming untied). The center player turns the rope under the feet of the circle players, who must jump over it. A player who touches the rope with the feet must move up to the next group.
    Variation: Change the center player after one or two misses. The center player should be cautioned to keep the rope along the ground. The rope speed can be varied. A good way to turn the rope is to sit cross-legged and turn it over the head. Different tasks can be performed such as hopping, jumping and turning, or jumping and clapping.
    Variations:
    1. Squads line up in spoke formation. Each member does a specified number of jumps (from three to five) and then exits. The next squad member in line must come in immediately without missing a turn of the rope. A player scores a point for the squad when he comes in on time, jumps the prescribed number of turns, and exits successfully. The squad with the most points wins.
    2. Couples line up in the same formation. They join inside hands and stand side by side when jumping.

Beachball Batball—*DPE*, p. 571
    Supplies: Four to six beachballs
    Skills: Batting, tactile handling
    Two games are played across the gymnasium area. The teams are scattered throughout the area without restriction as to where they may move. To begin the game, the balls are placed on the centerline dividing the court area. Four to six beachballs are in play at the same time. A score occurs when the beachball is batted over the end line. Once the ball moves across the end line it is dead. Players concentrate on the remaining balls in play.
    If a ball is on the floor, it is picked up and batted into play. At no time may a ball be carried. After all four balls are scored, the game ends. A new game is started after teams switch goals.

Club Guard—*DPE*, p. 573
    Supplies: A juggling club or bowling pin and foam rubber ball
    Skill: Throwing
    A circle about 15 ft in diameter is drawn. Inside the circle at the center, an 18-in. circle is drawn. The club is put in the center of the small circle. One child guards the club. The other children stand outside the large circle, which is the restraining line for them.
    The circle players throw the ball at the club and try to knock it down. The guard tries to block the throws with the legs and body. She must, however, stay out of the small inner circle. The outer circle players pass the ball around rapidly so that one of the players can get an opening to throw, since the guard needs to maneuver to protect the club. Whoever knocks down the club becomes the new guard. If the guard steps into the inner circle, she loses the place to whoever has the ball at that time.
    Teaching suggestion: A small circle cut from plywood (or a hula hoop or similar object) makes a definite inner circle so that determining whether the guard steps inside is easier. The outer circle should also be definite.
    Variation: More than one club can be in the center.

DYNAMIC PHYSICAL EDUCATION LESSON PLAN
Volleyball-Related Skills
Level II

Supplies and Equipment Needed:
  Tambourine
  Beach ball for each child
  Hoops
  Volleyball net (6 ft height)
  Tape player
  Music

MOVEMENT EXPERIENCE— CONTENT	ORGANIZATION AND TEACHING HINTS	EXPECTED STUDENT OBJECTIVES AND OUTCOMES

INTRODUCTORY ACTIVITY (2 – 3 MINUTES)

Bend, Stretch and Shake

Students should alternate between various bending and stretching activities. On signal, students shake and relax various body parts. Teach a wide variety of bending and stretching activities.

DPE p. 259

Strike a tambourine to signal changes in bending and stretching and then shake it to signal shaking movements.

Encourage shaking of all body parts. If necessary, start by shaking and adding one body part at a time.

Cog.—Exercise, if demanding enough, will cause the training effect to occur in a short period of time. Discuss the fact that 10 minutes of rope jumping is equal to 30 minutes of jogging.

FITNESS DEVELOPMENT ACTIVITY (7 – 8 MINUTES)

Astronaut Drills

Tape alternating segments of silence and music to signal duration of exercise. Music segments indicate aerobic activity while intervals of silence announce flexibility and strength development activities.

Walk while doing	
Arm circles	30 seconds
Crab Alternate-Leg	
Extension	35 seconds
Skip	30 seconds
Body Twist	35 seconds
Slide	30 seconds
Jumping Jack variations	35 seconds
Crab Walk to center and	
back	30 seconds
Abdominal Challenges	35 seconds
Hop to center and back	30 seconds
Push-Up Challenges	35 seconds
Gallop	30 seconds
Bear Hugs	35 seconds
Pogo Stick Jump	30 seconds

Cool down with stretching for 1–2 minutes.

DPE p. 304

Use circle or scatter formation with ample space between youngsters. If a circle formation is used, establish a "passing lane" to the outside for faster students.

Change directions occasionally to keep students spread out.

To vary the work load while moving, less able students can move toward the center of the area if a circle is being used.

PM.—The student will be able to demonstrate five or more styles of bending and stretching.

Aff.—Warming up the body before exercise is an important step in preparation for activity as it prepares all the body systems for stress. Discuss how the need for warm-up becomes more important as one grows older.

MOVEMENT EXPERIENCE— CONTENT	ORGANIZATION AND TEACHING HINTS	EXPECTED STUDENT OBJECTIVES AND OUTCOMES

LESSON FOCUS (15–20 MINUTES)

Volleyball-Related Skills
Individual Skills

1. Practice wall rebounding: Stand 6 feet away from a wall. Pass the ball against the wall and catch it.
2. From a spot 6 feet from the wall, throw the ball against the wall and alternate an overhand pass with a forearm pass.
3. Throw the ball to one side (right or left) and move to the side to pass the ball to the wall. Catch the rebound.
4. Pass the ball directly overhead and catch it. Try making two passes before catching the ball. Later, alternate an overhand pass with a forearm pass and catch the ball. This is a basic drill and should be mastered before proceeding to others.
5. Pass the ball 3 feet or so to one side, move under the ball, and pass it back to the original spot. The next pass should be to the other side.
6. Pass the ball directly overhead. On the return, jump as high as possible and make a second pass. Continue.
7. Stand with one foot in a hoop. Pass the ball overhead and attempt to continue passing while keeping one foot in the hoop. Try with both feet in the hoop.

Partner Work (Passing)

1. Players are about 10 feet apart. Play A tosses the ball (controlled toss) to player B, who passes the ball back to A, who catches the ball. Continue for several exchanges and then change throwers.
2. Two players are about 15 feet apart. Player a passes to themselves first and then makes a second pass to player B, who catches the ball and repeats. Follow with a return by B.
3. Players A and B try to keep the ball in the air continuously.
4. Players are about 15 feet apart. Player A remains stationary and passes in such a fashion that player B must move from side to side. An option is to have player B move forward and backward.
5. Players are about 10 feet apart. Both have hoops and attempt to keep one foot in the hoop while passing. Try keeping both feet in the hoop.

DPE pp. 719 – 721

Beach balls are preferred for learning volleyball skills at this age. The slow-moving beach ball allows youngsters to learn proper footwork by moving into position instead of reaching for the ball.

If beach balls are not available, 8" foam gray balls can be substituted. Volleyball trainer balls are also on the market, but are quite expensive. They are larger and lighter than regulation volleyballs and will prevent youngsters from injury.

If wall space is not available, work in partners and have one player toss the ball to the passer.

Emphasis should be placed on correctly volleying the ball rather than seeing how high it can be hit.

Discourage striking the ball with one hand. This practice leads to uncontrolled swinging at the ball. If the ball can be reached with only one hand, youngsters should be encouraged to start over.

Partner drills are effective only if the set-up toss is accurate. It might be useful to have students practice tossing to each other before proceeding to the tossing and passing drill.

Rule out passing the volleyball with a fist. This is always a result of students' being out of position.

Emphasize moving the feet and keeping the body weight on the balls of the feet. If students are not doing well with footwork, place the balls on the floor and practice moving the feet in different directions.

Hoops or individual mats can be used to restrict movement and emphasize accuracy. If students are having difficulty with accuracy, reduce the distance between them.

PM.—The student will be able to perform the following skills adequately:
1. Underhand serve
2. Overhand pass

Cog.—The student will be able to explain the importance of moving the feet into proper position before passing the ball.

Cog.—The student will be able to explain why the fist should not be used for passing the ball.

Cog.—The student will be able to explain the most basic rules of volleyball, including:
1. Only the serving team scores.
2. The ball may not be caught.
3. Passing is actually a batting of the ball, not a throw.
4. Only three volleys are allowed before the ball is returned over the net.

Aff.—Cooperation is necessary if students are going to learn volleyball skills. Review the need for helping others in practice situations.

PM.—The student will be able to accurately toss the ball to a partner.

PM.—The student will be able to accurately pass the ball to a partner.

MOVEMENT EXPERIENCE—CONTENT	ORGANIZATION AND TEACHING HINTS	EXPECTED STUDENT OBJECTIVES AND OUTCOMES
6. Player A passes to player B and does a complete turnaround. B passes back to A and also does a full turn. Other stunts can be used.		

Partner Work (Serving)

1. Partners are about 20 feet apart. Partner A serves to partner B, who catches the ball and returns the serve to A. 2. Partner A serves to partner B, who makes a pass back to A. Change roles.	Develop proper serving form rather than concern for how far the serve travels. If youngsters do not have to worry about getting the ball over a net, they will be less concerned with how much power they generate on the serve.	Cog.—The student will be able to explain the importance of passing the ball with accuracy rather than hitting it for distance.
3. Play Service One-Step. Partners begin about 10 feet apart. Partner A serves to partner B, who catches the serve. B now serves to A, who must catch the serve. Each time the serve is caught, both players take one step back. If a serve is not caught, the players revert to the original distance of 10 feet and start over.	Emphasize process rather than product. Students should be encouraged to help each other learn proper technique rather than worry about the product (distance, height, etc.).	Cog.—The student will be able to describe the importance of proper form rather than the outcome of the skill.

GAMES (5 – 7 MINUTES)

Volleyball Lead-Up Games

Beach Ball Volleyball—*DPE*, p. 724
   Supplies: A beach ball 12 to 16 in. in diameter
   Skills: Most passing skills, modified serving
   The players of each team are in two lines on their respective sides of the net. Serving is done, as in regulation volleyball, by the player on the right side of the back line. The distance is shortened, however, because serving a beach ball successfully from the normal volleyball serving distance is difficult. The player serves from the normal playing position on the court in the right back position. Scoring is as in regulation volleyball. Play continues until the ball touches the floor.
   A team loses a point to the other team when it fails to return the ball over the net by the third volley or when it returns the ball over the net but the ball hits the floor out-of-bounds without being touched by the opposing team. The server continues serving as long as she scores. Rotation is as in regulation volleyball.
   Teaching suggestion: The server must be positioned as close to the net as possible while still remaining in the right back position on the court. Successful serving is an important component of an enjoyable game.
   Variations:
   1. In a simplified version of Beach Ball Volleyball, the ball is put into play by one player in the front line, who throws the ball into the air and then passes it over the net. Play continues until the ball touches the floor, but the ball may be volleyed any number of times before crossing the net. When either team has scored 5 points, the front and back lines of the respective teams change. When the score reaches 10 for the leading team, the lines change back. Game is 15.
   2. Any player in the back line may catch the ball as it comes initially from the opposing team and may immediately make a little toss and pass the ball to a teammate. The player who catches the ball and bats it cannot send it across the net before a teammate has touched it.

Informal Volleyball—*DPE*, p. 725
   Supplies: A trainer volleyball
   Skills: Passing
   This game is similar to regulation volleyball, but there is no serving. Each play begins with a student on one side tossing to herself and passing the ball high over the net. Points are scored for every play, as there is no "side out." As soon as a point is scored, the nearest player takes the ball and immediately puts it into play. Otherwise, basic volleyball rules govern the game. Rotation occurs as soon as a team has scored 5 points, with the front and back lines changing place. Action is fast, and the game moves rapidly since every play scores a point for one team or the other.

MOVEMENT EXPERIENCE— CONTENT	ORGANIZATION AND TEACHING HINTS	EXPECTED STUDENT OBJECTIVES AND OUTCOMES

Shower Service Ball—*DPE*, p. 725

Supplies: Four to six trainer volleyballs

Skills: Serving, catching

A line parallel to the net is drawn through the middle of each court to define the serving area. Players are scattered in no particular formation. The game involves the skills of serving and catching. To start the game, two or three volleyballs are given to each team and are handled by players in the serving area.

Balls may be served at any time and in any order by a server who must be in the back half of the court. Any ball served across the net is to be caught by any player near the ball. The person catching or retrieving a ball moves quickly to the serving area and serves. A point is scored for a team whenever a served ball hits the floor in the other court or is dropped by a receiver. Two scorers are needed, one for each side.

Teaching suggestion: As children improve, all serves should be made from behind the baseline.

DYNAMIC PHYSICAL EDUCATION LESSON PLAN
Manipulative Skills Using Hoops
Level II

Supplies and Equipment Needed:
  One hoop per child
  Cageball
  Tape player
  Music

MOVEMENT EXPERIENCE—CONTENT	ORGANIZATION AND TEACHING HINTS	EXPECTED STUDENT OBJECTIVES AND OUTCOMES

INTRODUCTORY ACTIVITY (2 – 3 MINUTES)

Move, Perform Task

Do a locomotor movement; on signal, stop and perform a task such as an exercise or stunt.

Suggested activities:
1. Heel Click
2. Push-Up
3. Turnover
4. Top
5. Stork Stand
6. Coffee Grinder

DPE p. 254

Many individual stunts, such as the heel click, heel slap, or jump turn, can be performed. These add challenge and excitement to the activity.

Vary the locomotor movements by adding quality words (i.e., slow–fast, high–low).

PM.—The student will be able to perform the basic locomotor movement variations as well as the designated stunts or exercises.

Aff.—The body should be gradually warmed up, rather than moving into demanding activity immediately. Discuss this with the class with regard to a need to self-pace and gradually work toward maximum output. Incorporate this principle into your teaching by demanding more as the introductory and fitness work progress.

FITNESS DEVELOPMENT ACTIVITY (7 – 8 MINUTES)

Astronaut Drills

Tape alternating segments of silence and music to signal duration of exercise. Music segments indicate aerobic activity while intervals of silence announce flexibility and strength development activities.

Walk while doing	
Arm circles	30 seconds
Crab Alternate-Leg	
Extension	35 seconds
Skip	30 seconds
Body Twist	35 seconds
Slide	30 seconds
Jumping Jack variations	35 seconds
Crab Walk to center and	
back	30 seconds
Abdominal Challenges	35 seconds
Hop to center and back	30 seconds
Push-Up Challenges	35 seconds
Gallop	30 seconds
Bear Hugs	35 seconds
Pogo Stick Jump	30 seconds

Cool down with stretching and walking or jogging for 1–2 minutes.

DPE p. 304

Use circle or scatter formation with ample space between youngsters. If a circle formation is used, establish a "passing lane" to the outside for faster students.

Change directions occasionally to keep students spread out.

To vary the work load while moving, less able students can move toward the center of the area if a circle is being used.

Cog.—When a person exercises regularly, additional capillaries form in the muscle tissue so that the muscle cells are better supplied with blood. The student will be able to describe this occurrence in his or her own words.

MOVEMENT EXPERIENCE— CONTENT	ORGANIZATION AND TEACHING HINTS	EXPECTED STUDENT OBJECTIVES AND OUTCOMES

LESSON FOCUS (15 – 20 MINUTES)

Manipulative Skills Using Hoops

1. Hula-hoop using various body parts such as waist, neck, knees, arms and fingers.
   a. While hula-hooping on the arms, try to change the hoop from one arm to the other.
   b. Change hoop from one partner to another while hula-hooping.
   c. Try leg-skippers—hula-hoop with one leg and jump the hoop with the other leg.
2. Jump-rope with the hoop—forward, sideways, and backward. Begin with a back-and-forth swing.
3. Roll hoop and run alongside it. Run in front of it.
4. Roll hoop with a reverse spin to make it return to the thrower.
5. Roll with a reverse spin and see how many times partner can go through it.
6. Roll with a reverse spin, jump the hoop, and catch it as it returns.
7. Roll with a reverse spin, kick into the air, and catch.
8. Balance the hoop on your head, try to walk through it ("thread the needle") forward, backward and sideways.
9. Use the hoop as a cowboy lasso, standing, sitting or lying down.
10. Try partner activities:
    a. Play catch with hoop.
    b. Hula-hoop on one arm, toss to partner who catches it on one arm.
    c. Use two hoops for catching.
    d. Hoop with one hoop and play catch with other.
    e. Move through a hoop held by a partner.

DPE pp. 431 – 433

Scatter formation.

Hula-hooping demands that body parts are moved back and forth, *not* in a circle.

Have the class drop their hoops when you desire their attention.

When they jump through hoops, children should be encouraged to hold them loosely to prevent falls.

Use the hoops as a home area for children. This will keep them in a designated area.

The reverse spin must be taught and practiced. Many students find it to be a difficult skill.

When throwing and catching two hoops, each partner should throw one and then progress to both hoops being thrown at the same time by one partner.

PM.—The students will be able to hula-hoop on at least one part of their bodies.

PM.—The student will be able to jump rope for 20 seconds without missing in at least one of the sessions.

PM.—The students will be able to place a reverse spin on the hoop, causing it to return to them.

Aff.—Many students will not immediately be able to hula-hoop or apply the reverse spin. Discuss the value of continued practice versus the alternative of quitting and never learning the skill.

Aff.—Discuss the value of learning a skill simply for one's own enjoyment and satisfaction.

Cog.—The body adapts rapidly to hot, humid conditions. Within two weeks of practice and training in heat, the body will adapt and become more efficient. Primarily, the body sweats more rapidly and to a greater extent. The evaporation of sweat effectively cools the body. Discuss adaptation and the important role of sweating to maintain a constant body temperature.

Cog.—Aerobic training increases maximal oxygen uptake. A large part of the increase is due to increased stroke volume of the heart. More blood is pumped per heart beat due to increased capacity of the heart and stronger contractions. How is the heart strengthened?

GAME (5 – 7 MINUTES)

Hand Hockey—*DPE*, p. 576
   Supplies: 8-inch gray foam balls
   Skills: Striking, volleying
   The players are on two teams. Half of the players on each team are guards and are stationed on the goal line as defenders. The other half are active players and are scattered throughout the playing area in front of their goal line.
   The object of the game is to bat or push the ball with either hand so that it crosses the goal line that the other team is defending. Players may move the ball as in hockey but may not throw, hoist, or kick it. The defensive goal line players are limited to one step into the playing field when playing the ball.
   The ball is put into play by being rolled into the center of the field. After a goal has been scored or after a specified period, guards become active players, and vice versa. An out-of-bounds ball goes to the opposite team and is put into play by being rolled from the sidelines into the playing area. If the ball becomes entrapped among players, play is stopped, and the ball is put into play again by a roll from the referee.

MOVEMENT EXPERIENCE— CONTENT	ORGANIZATION AND TEACHING HINTS	EXPECTED STUDENT OBJECTIVES AND OUTCOMES

Players must play the ball and not resort to rough tactics. A player who is called for unnecessary roughness or for illegally handling the ball must go to the sidelines (as in hockey) and remain in the penalty area until the players change positions. Players should scatter and attempt to pass to each other rather than bunch around the ball.

Once youngsters learn the game, introduce more than one ball to increase the amount of activity.

Variation: Scooter Hockey. The active center players from each team are on gym scooters. The position that each child takes on the gym scooter can be specified or can be a free choice. Possible positions are kneeling, sitting, or balancing on the tummy. A hard surface is needed. This game version is usually played indoors on a basketball court.

Cageball Kick-Over—*DPE*, p. 573

Supplies: A cageball, 18-, 24-, or 30-in. size

Skill: Kicking

Players are divided into two teams and sit facing each other, with legs outstretched and soles of the feet about 3 to 6 ft apart. While maintaining the sitting position, each player supports her weight on the hands, which are placed slightly to the rear.

The teacher rolls the cageball between the two teams. The object of the game is to kick the ball over the other team, thereby scoring a point. After a point is scored, the teacher rolls the ball into play again. A good system of rotation is to have the player on the left side of the line take a place on the right side after a point is scored, thus moving all the players one position to the left. When the ball is kicked out at either end, no score results, and the ball is put into play again by the teacher.

Variation: Children can be allowed to use their hands to stop the ball from going over them.

DYNAMIC PHYSICAL EDUCATION LESSON PLAN
Manipulative Skills Using Paddles and Balls
Level II

Supplies and Equipment Needed:
One paddle and ball per child
One individual jump rope per child
Fleece balls (optional)
Tape player
Music
Bowling pins

MOVEMENT EXPERIENCE— CONTENT	ORGANIZATION AND TEACHING HINTS	EXPECTED STUDENT OBJECTIVES AND OUTCOMES

INTRODUCTORY ACTIVITY (2 – 3 MINUTES)

Tag Games

1. Addition Tag (*DPE*, p. 570)
2. Squad Tag, (*DPE*, p. 579)
3. Wolfe's Beanbag Exchange Tag, (*DPE*, p. 581)

Children should know the games so that little instruction is needed.

Vary the type of locomotor movement the class can use to chase or flee.

PM.—The student will be able to dodge or evade quickly and without falling.

FITNESS DEVELOPMENT ACTIVITY (7 – 8 MINUTES)

Continuity Drills

Students alternate jump rope activity with exercises done in two-count fashion. Exercises are done with the teacher saying "Ready;" the class answers "One-two" and performs a repetition of exercise. In activities like Push-Ups and Curl-Ups, students can pick any challenge activity (*DPE, pp. 281–283*) they choose. Teachers or students can lead.

Rope Jumping - Forward	30 seconds
Double Crab Kick	45 seconds
Rope Jumping - Backward	30 seconds
Knee Touch Curl-Up	45 seconds
Jump and Slowly Turn Body	30 seconds
Push-Up Challenges	45 seconds
Rocker Step	30 seconds
Bend and Twist	45 seconds
Swing-Step Forward	30 seconds
Side Flex 45 seconds	
Free Jumping	30 seconds
Sit and Stretch	45 seconds

DPE p. 303

Use scatter formation.

Other exercises can be substituted to add variation to the activity.

Allow students to adjust the work load to their fitness level. This implies resting if the rope jumping is too strenuous.

PM.—The student will be able to jump-rope for 20 seconds without missing.

Aff.—Lack of exercise is one of the key factors in heart disease. Symptoms of heart disease are often found in young people, and thus fitness activities may help retard this health problem. Discuss heart disease and the role of exercise.

LESSON FOCUS (15 – 20 MINUTES)

Manipulative Skills Using Paddles and Balls

1. Introduce proper method of holding paddle: forehand and backhand grip.

DPE pp. 423 – 425

Scatter formation.

Ping pong paddles and old tennis balls with holes punched in them work well. Also, one can use the children's hands as paddles and a fleece ball can be used.

Cog.—The student will be able to name five sports in which paddle skills are used.

PM.—The student will be able to control the paddle and ball in a variety of situations.

MOVEMENT EXPERIENCE—CONTENT	ORGANIZATION AND TEACHING HINTS	EXPECTED STUDENT OBJECTIVES AND OUTCOMES
2. Place ball on paddle and attempt to roll it around the edge of the paddle without allowing it to fall off the paddle. Flip the paddle over and roll ball.	This is a limited-movement activity; thus, break the activity into two parts separated by some running, rope-jumping, or similarly physically demanding activity.	Aff.—One way to improve skills is to experiment with different ways of performing them. Discuss the value of trying new activities rather than always practicing areas in which we are already skilled.
3. Balance the ball on the paddle using both right and left hands, as well as both grips while trying the following challenges: a. Touch the floor with hand. b. Move to knees and back to feet. c. Sit down and get back on feet. d. Lie down and get back on feet. e. Skip, gallop or any other locomotor movement. f. Choice activity.	Concentrate on control of the ball and quality of movement. Take your time going through activities. Use left hand as well as right in developing the paddle skills.	Cog.—The length of a lever determines, in part, the amount of force that can be developed in a striking implement. Understand how paddles are an extension of the arm and increase the force generated for striking. Cog.—Firmness of the grip on a paddle is important when generating force. Force can be lost upon impact if the racket slips.
4. Bounce the ball in the air using the paddle. a. See how many times it can be bounced without touching the floor. b. Bounce it off the paddle into the air and catch it with the other hand. c. Increase the height of the bounce. d. Kneel, sit down, other positions (student choice). e. Bounce ball off paddle, do a full turn and continue bouncing or balance ball on paddle. f. Bounce ball in the air, switch paddle to the other hand.	If students have a difficult time controlling the ball, it might be helpful to use fleece balls. Allow time for student choice. "Give" with the paddle. Change the paddle from hand to hand while the ball is in the air.	Cog.—The angle of the paddle when the ball is struck will determine the direction that the ball will travel. Cog.—A paddle will give the student a longer lever with which to strike the ball, and thus more force can be applied to the ball, which in turn will increase its speed.
5. Dribble ball with the paddle. a. From a kneeling position. b. From a sitting position. c. From a standing position. d. Move in different directions—forward, sideways, circle. e. Move using different locomotor movements. f. Exploratory activity.		
6. Alternate bouncing the ball in the air and on the floor.		
7. Bounce ball of the paddle into the air and "catch" it with the paddle. a. Increase the height of the bounce. b. Perform a heel click, full turn or similar activity and catch the ball.		
8. Bounce the ball continuously off the paddle into the air. a. Bounce the ball on the side of the paddle. b. Alternate sides of the paddle.		
9. Place ball on the floor. a. Scoop it up with the paddle. b. Roll the ball and scoop it up with the paddle. c. Start dribbling the ball without touching it with hands.		

MOVEMENT EXPERIENCE—CONTENT	ORGANIZATION AND TEACHING HINTS	EXPECTED STUDENT OBJECTIVES AND OUTCOMES

10. Partner Activities.
  a. Begin partner activities with controlled throwing (feeding) by one partner and the designated stroke return by the other.
  b. Bounce ball back and forth. How many times can you bounce it back and forth to your partner without missing it?
  c. Increase the distance between partners and the height of the ball.
  d. Catch the ball on your paddle after throw from your partner, then return throw.
  e. Perform stunts while ball is in the air, such as catch ball behind back, under leg, above head, clap hands, heel clicks, full turns, etc.
  f. Use two balls.
  g. Move and keep the balls going; try skipping, hopping, jumping, sliding.
  h. Play Volley Tennis.
	Stress the importance of accurate throws.	PM.—The student will be able to perform three partner activities.
		
		Aff.—People practice activities in which they are rewarded and praised. Discuss the importance of praising others and encouraging them to practice.
		
		Cog.—A balanced diet is important for good nutrition. Foods should be regularly selected from the following four groups:
		  1. Milk and milk products
		  2. Meat and protein
		  3. Fruits and vegetables
		  4. Breads and cereals
		
		Discuss the need for a balanced diet when one is involved in strenuous and demanding activity.

GAME (5 – 7 MINUTES)

Steal the Treasure—*DPE*, p. 579

  Supplies: A bowling pin

  Skill: Dodging

A playing area 20 ft square is outlined, with a small circle in the center. A bowling pin placed in the circle is the treasure. A guard is set to protect the treasure. Players then enter the square and try to steal the treasure without getting caught. The guard tries to tag them. Anyone tagged must retire and wait for the next game. The player who gets the treasure is the next guard. Teaching suggestion: If getting the treasure seems too easy, the child can be required to carry the treasure to the boundary of the square without being tagged.

  Variation: <u>Bear and Keeper</u>. Instead of a treasure, a bear (seated cross-legged on the ground) is protected by a keeper. Anyone who touches the bear without being tagged becomes the new keeper, with the old keeper becoming the bear.

Trees—*DPE*, p. 580

  Supplies: None

  Skills: Running, dodging

Two parallel lines are drawn 60 ft apart. All players, except the one who is it, are on one side of the area. On the signal "Trees," the players run to the other side of the court. The tagger tries to tag as many as possible. Any player tagged becomes a tree, stopping where tagged and keeping both feet in place. He cannot move the feet but can tag any runners who come close enough. The child who is it continues to chase the players as they cross on signal until all but one are caught. This player becomes it for the next game.

  To speed up the action, two or more taggers may be chosen. Children cross from side to side only on the signal "Trees."

DYNAMIC PHYSICAL EDUCATION LESSON PLAN
Stunts and Tumbling Skills (Lesson 3)
Level II

Supplies and Equipment Needed:
  One jump rope for each student
  Tumbling mats
  Beach balls
  Tape player
  Music

MOVEMENT EXPERIENCE— CONTENT	ORGANIZATION AND TEACHING HINTS	EXPECTED STUDENT OBJECTIVES AND OUTCOMES

INTRODUCTORY ACTIVITY (2 – 3 MINUTES)

Combination Movement Patterns

Explore some of the following combinations:
  1. Run, leap and roll.
  2. Run, collapse and roll.
  3. Hop, turn around and shake.
  4. Run, change direction and collapse.
  5. Kneel and balance.
  6. Hop, make a shape in the air and balance.
  7. Twist and untwist.
  8. Click heels in different ways.
  9. Students' choice.

DPE p. 254

Encourage variety of responses.

Praise children who attempt new and different movements.

Try having students work in pairs and critique each other's movements.

PM.—The student will be able to perform the movement combinations and create three new patterns.

Cog.—The student will be able to distinguish between a nonlocomotor and a locomotor movement.

FITNESS DEVELOPMENT ACTIVITY (7 – 8 MINUTES)

Continuity Drills

Students alternate jump rope activity with exercises done in two-count fashion. Exercises are done with the teacher saying "Ready;" the class answers "One-two" and performs a repetition of exercise. In activities like Push-Ups and Curl-Ups, students can pick any challenge activity (*DPE, pp. 281–283*) they choose. Teachers or students can lead.

Rope Jumping - forward	30 seconds
Double Crab Kick	45 seconds
Rope Jumping - Backward	30 seconds
Knee Touch Curl-Up	45 seconds
Jump and Slowly Turn Body	30 seconds
Push-Up Challenges	45 seconds
Rocker Step	30 seconds
Bend and Twist	45 seconds
Swing-Step Forward	30 seconds
Side Flex	45 seconds
Free Jumping	30 seconds
Sit and Stretch	45 seconds

DPE p. 303

Use scatter formation.

Taped intervals of music and no music can be used to signal rope jumping (with music) and performing exercises (without music).

Other exercises can be substituted to add variation to the activity.

Allow students to adjust the work load to their fitness level. This implies resting if the rope jumping is too strenuous.

PM.—The student will be able to jump-rope continuously without a miss for 30 seconds.

Aff.—Contrary to popular belief, girls can become stronger through exercise and weight training without fear of developing huge, unattractive muscles. Discuss testosterone and the impact it has on muscle development. It might be helpful to bring pictures of various girls as examples of fitness.

MOVEMENT EXPERIENCE— CONTENT	ORGANIZATION AND TEACHING HINTS	EXPECTED STUDENT OBJECTIVES AND OUTCOMES

LESSON FOCUS (15 – 20 MINUTES)

Tumbling, Stunts, and Animal Movements (3)

Six groups of activities in this lesson ensure that youngsters receive a variety of experiences. Pick a few activities from each group and teach them alternately. For example, teach one or two animal movements, then a tumbling and inverted balance, followed by a balance stunt, etc. Give equal time to each group of activities

1. Animal Movements
   a. Double Lame Dog
   b. Turtle
   c. Walrus Slap
   d. Reverse Walrus Slap
2. Tumbling and Inverted Balances
   a. Forward Roll combinations
   b. Backward Roll combinations
   c. Headstand Variations
   d. Teeter-Totter
   e. Handstand
3. Balance Stunts
   a. Seat Balance
   b. Face-to-Knee Touch
   c. Finger Touch
4. Individual Stunts
   a. Dead Body Fall
   b. Stoop and Stretch
   c. Tanglefoot
   d. Egg Roll
   e. Toe Touch Nose
   f. Toe Tug Walk
5. Partner and Group Stunts
   a. Camel Lift and Walk
   b. Dump the Wheelbarrow
   c. Dromedary Walk
   d. Centipede
   e. Double Wheelbarrow
6. Partner Support Stunts
   a. Lighthouse
   b. Hip-Shoulder Stand

DPE pp. 463 – 481

Scatter as many tumbling mats as possible throughout the area in order to avoid waiting lines.

Do not perform many repetitions of tumbling and inverted balances. For most children, limiting the number of forward or backward roll repetitions to four or five will prevent fatigue and injury.

As activities become more difficult, the range of skill ability becomes obvious. Allow for individual differences and offer more personalized help.

A major concern for safety is the neck and back region. Overweight children are at greater risk and might be allowed to avoid tumbling and inverted balances.

Whenever youngsters have difficulty, review previously learned activities.

Teach youngsters to stand on the hips and shoulders when doing partner support stunts.

PM.—The student will be able to perform at least two activities from each of the categories.

Cog.—The student will be able to describe proper positioning of the hands and knees in partner support and pyramid activities.

Cog.—The student will be able to name at least three safety principles that are important in tumbling and inverted balance activities.

Aff.—Tumbling is an excellent activity for overcoming personal fear of harm from the activities. Discuss how many athletes must conquer various fears and take risks in order to succeed.

Cog.—When a forward roll is started, the center of gravity is moved outside the base of support. This causes momentum to be developed in the direction of the roll. What skills demand that the performer move into an unstable position?

PM.—The student and his partner will be able to originate and demonstrate two partner support activities.

GAME (5 – 7 MINUTES)

Trades—*DPE*, p. 579
   Supplies: None
   Skills: Imagery, running, dodging
   The class is divided into two teams of equal number, each of which has a goal line. One team, the chasers, remains behind its goal line. The other team, the runners, approaches from its goal line, marching to the following dialogue:
   Runners: Here we come.
   Chasers: Where from?
   Runners: New Orleans.
   Chasers: What's your trade?
   Runners: Lemonade.
   Chasers: Show us some.

MOVEMENT EXPERIENCE— CONTENT	ORGANIZATION AND TEACHING HINTS	EXPECTED STUDENT OBJECTIVES AND OUTCOMES

Runners move up close to the other team's goal line and proceed to act out an occupation or a specific task that they have chosen previously. The opponents try to guess what the pantomime represents. On a correct guess, the running team must run back to its goal line chased by the others. Any runner tagged must join the chasers. The game is repeated with roles reversed. The team ending with the greater number of players is the winner.

Teaching suggestion: If a team has trouble guessing the pantomime, the other team should provide hints. Teams also should be encouraged to have a number of activities selected so that little time is consumed in choosing the next activity to be pantomimed.

Beachball Batball—*DPE*, p. 571

Supplies: Four to six beachballs

Skills: Batting, tactile handling

Two games are played across the gymnasium area. The teams are scattered throughout the area without restriction as to where they may move. To begin the game, the balls are placed on the centerline dividing the court area. Four to six beachballs are in play at the same time. A score occurs when the beachball is batted over the end line. Once the ball moves across the end line it is dead. Players concentrate on the remaining balls in play.

If a ball is on the floor, it is picked up and batted into play. At no time may a ball be carried. After all four balls are scored, the game ends. A new game is started after teams switch goals.

DYNAMIC PHYSICAL EDUCATION LESSON PLAN
Fundamental Skills Using Tug-of-War Ropes and Relays
Level II

Supplies and Equipment Needed:
  15–18 partner tug-of-war ropes
  Relay supplies
  Exercise-to-music tape and tape player
  Tom-tom
  Beanbags or balls
  Relay equipment
  Jump ropes

MOVEMENT EXPERIENCE— CONTENT	ORGANIZATION AND TEACHING HINTS	EXPECTED STUDENT OBJECTIVES AND OUTCOMES

INTRODUCTORY ACTIVITY (2 – 3 MINUTES)

European Rhythmic Running with Equipment

Review European Rhythmic Running and emphasize the following points:
  1. Move to the rhythm.
  2. Lift the knees and prance.
  3. Maintain proper spacing between each other.
After the review, give each child a beanbag or playground ball. Every fourth step, they can toss up the bag or bounce the ball. Other variations can be tried using different beats of the rhythm.

DPE pp. 252 – 253

Use tom-tom to accentuate the rhythm.

Encourage the students to try different challenges with their beanbag or ball.

PM.—The student will be able to toss the beanbag into the air and catch it while doing European Running.

PM.—The student will be able to create three activities with the beanbag or ball while doing European Running.

FITNESS DEVELOPMENT ACTIVITIES (7 – 8 MINUTES)

Exercises to Music

Side Flex (switch sides)	40 seconds
Trunk Twister	25 seconds
Abdominal Challenges	40 seconds
Slide/Skip	25 seconds
Jumping Jack variations	40 seconds
Triceps Push-Ups	25 seconds
Curl-Up Challenges	40 seconds
Gallop	25 seconds
Push-Up challenges	40 seconds
Aerobic Bouncing and Clapping	25 seconds
Leg Extensions	40 seconds
Walking to cool down	25 seconds

DPE p. 300

Student should know the exercises before trying to do them rhythmically.

The exercise music should be taped prior to the routine. This frees the teacher to move and help students.

Voice instructions can be dubbed onto the tape to tell students when to change to a new exercise.

Aff.—Regular exercise strengthens muscles, thus minimizing the tendency for joint and muscular injury. Discuss that one of the major reasons for the conditioning of athletes is to prevent any injury.

LESSON FOCUS (15 – 20 MINUTES)

Fundamental Skills Using Partner Tug-of-War Ropes

Alternate tug-of-war rope activities with relays for complete physical development. The relays stimulate the cardiovascular system while the tug-of-war activities develop the muscular system.

DPE pp. 433 – 435

PM.—The student will develop sufficient strength to hold her own with partner of equal size.

Cog.—The student will be able to recite what tug-of-war ropes do for body development.

215

MOVEMENT EXPERIENCE— CONTENT	ORGANIZATION AND TEACHING HINTS	EXPECTED STUDENT OBJECTIVES AND OUTCOMES

Isometric Exercises

Make sure joints are bent and students aren't leaning.
1. Standing—use ends of ropes only and try to stretch the handle apart.
   a. Use different hand positions and arm positions.
2. Partner resistance Exercises—start and stop on signal.
   a. Standing—sides facing each other and use both arms, as well as right and left individually.
   b. Standing facing—use arms at various levels: above, below head, etc.
   c. Seated—sides facing, back to back, facing, legs elevated, etc. Also, hook on feet, knees; tug.
   d. Prone position—feet touching, heads toward each other, pull on ankle, push-up position pull, etc.
   e. On back—pull with feet, knees, arms.
   f. Develop other areas. Pupil choice.

Make sure they hold their *maximum* effort for 8–10 seconds.

Encourage gradual pulling to maximum effort rather than jerking.

When signal is given, place tug-of-war ropes on floor, ready for the next activity.

Pull through full range of motion.

Aff.—Even though tug-of-war ropes are competitive, cooperation is necessary to ensure an equal start and contest. Discuss the necessity of cooperation in all major sports.

Cog.—The student will explain that maximum effort is required for best results in strength development.

Cog.—Oxygen debt occurs when the muscles need more oxygen than is being supplied. Anaerobic exercise usually creates an oxygen debt. Students should be able to distinguish anaerobic from aerobic activities.

Tug-of-War Activities

1. Right, left and both hands.
2. Leg pulls, elbows, pull between legs.
3. Tug with three body parts, on all fours.
4. Crab position, seal walk pull.
5. Line touch tug (pull until you can touch the line behind you.
6. Partners facing; on signal, pick up partner's end of rope and pull.
   a. Begin in a push-up position.
   b. Start sitting crossed-leg fashion with hands on head.
   c. Touch a specified line before grabbing partner's end of rope.

Establish goals to cross in order to win.

Start and stop on signal.

If grip is slipping—stop, renew grip, and proceed.

Rotate partners often.

Place partners on two parallel lines. When one partner is pulled across the opponent's line, the contest is immediately stopped.

Aff.—A sense of fairness should be encouraged during this highly competitive activity. Take time to discuss the importance of fair play.

Cog.—Arteries, arterioles, and capillaries carry oxygenated blood to the muscles. Capillaries are so small and thin that oxygen passes right through the walls. At the same time, carbon dioxide is transferred from the body cells to the blood cells and carried back to the lungs to be expelled. The blood is transported back to the lungs in the veins. This system is called the circulatory system.

Tug-of-War Games

1. Four-way pull.
2. Two against two pull.
3. Frozen Tug-of-War.
4. Hawaiian Tug-of-War.

It might be a good idea to try a change-of-pace activity in the middle of the tug-of-war activities to pick up the tempo of the lesson. Suggested activities are jogging, beanbags, hoops, or jump ropes.

Relays

Introduce a variety of relays. The following are listed in sequence from easy to difficult.
1. Partner Relays, (*DPE,* p. 595)
2. Carry and Fetch Relay, (*DPE,* p. 595)
3. Attention Relay, (*DPE,* p. 601)
4. Corner Fly Relay, (*DPE,* p. 599)
5. Pass and Squat Relay, (*DPE,* p. 599)
6. Rescue Relay, (*DPE,* p. 600)

Teach relays with learning to understand the concept of cooperation, competition, playing under stress, and abiding by certain rules in mind, rather than teaching various skills.

Teams should contain four to eight members. Change leaders often.

Rotate students into different squads so the makeup of each squad changes.

PM.—The student will be able to participate in the relays at an adequate level.

Aff.—Relays involve performing under stress. Explain what happens to athletic performance when stress is too great. Mention the fear of looking stupid and being embarrassed.

MOVEMENT EXPERIENCE—CONTENT	ORGANIZATION AND TEACHING HINTS	EXPECTED STUDENT OBJECTIVES AND OUTCOMES
7. Circular Attention relay, (*DPE*, p. 601) 8. Potato Relay, (*DPE*, p. 596) 9. Tadpole Relay, (*DPE*, p. 600) 10. Three Spot Relay, (*DPE*, p. 596) 11. Jack Rabbit Relay, (*DPE*, p. 598)	Have the children sit down when they are finished. Put the least talented students in the middle of the squad so they do not stand out. Emphasis should be on student enjoyment rather than winning at all costs.	Cog.—The importance of winning sometimes supersedes the reasons for participating in competitive activities. Discuss participating for enjoyment, skill development, and fitness maintenance.

GAME (5 – 7 MINUTES)

Wolfe's Beanbag Exchange—*DPE*, p. 581
Supplies: One beanbag per child
Skills: Running, dodging, tossing, catching
Five or six children are identified as taggers. The remaining children start scattered throughout the area, each with a beanbag in hand. The taggers chase the players with beanbags. When a tag is made, the tagged player must freeze, keeping her feet still and beanbag in hand. To unfreeze a player, a non-frozen player can exchange his beanbag for a beanbag held by a frozen player. If two frozen players are within tossing distance, they can thaw each other by exchanging their beanbags through the air using a toss and catch. **Both** tosses have to be caught or the beanbags must be retrieved and tried again.
Variation: After students have learned the game, tell the taggers that they may interfere with the tossing of beanbags between two frozen players by batting them to the floor. This forces the toss to be tried again and the players remain frozen until successful catches are made by both players.

Arches—*DPE*, p. 571
Supplies: Music
Skills: Moving rhythmically
The game is similar to London Bridge. An arch is placed in the playing area. (To form an arch, two players stand facing one another with hands joined and arms raised.) When the music starts, the other players move in a circle, passing under the arch. Suddenly, the music stops, and the arch is brought down by dropping the hands. All players caught in an arch immediately pair off to form other arches, keeping in a general circle formation. If a caught player does not have a partner, he waits in the center of the circle until one is available. The last players caught (or left) form arches for the next game.
The arches should be warned not to bring down their hands and arms too forcefully so that children passing under are not pummeled.
Variation: Different types of music can be used, and children can move according to the pattern of the music.

DYNAMIC PHYSICAL EDUCATION LESSON PLAN
Rhythmic Movement with Equipment (Lesson 4)
Level II

Supplies and Equipment Needed:
  Playground balls or equivalent
  Jump ropes (individual)
  Tape player and music
  Exercise-to-music tape
  Lummi sticks
  Hoops
  Cageball

MOVEMENT EXPERIENCE—CONTENT	ORGANIZATION AND TEACHING HINTS	EXPECTED STUDENT OBJECTIVES AND OUTCOMES

INTRODUCTORY ACTIVITY (2 – 3 MINUTES)

Marking

Each child has a partner who is somewhat equal in ability. Under control, one partner runs, dodges, and tries to lose the other, who tries to stay within 3 ft of the runner. On signal, both freeze. The chaser must be close enough to touch her partner to say that they have marked (scored a point) them. Partners then reverse roles.

Variations:
  1. Use different locomotor movements.
  2. Use positions such as Crab Walk, Puppy Dog Walk, etc.
  3. Allow a point to be scored only when they touch a specified body part (i.e., knee, elbow, left hand).

DPE p. 257

Encourage students to "watch where they are going" so they won't run into each other.

Partners should be somewhat equal in ability.

Change partners once or twice.

PM.—The students will be able to move with enough agility and quickness to allow them to catch as well as evade their partners.

Cog.—The student will be able to verbalize a simple reason for warm-up prior to strenuous activity.

FITNESS DEVELOPMENT ACTIVITIES (7 – 8 MINUTES)

Exercises to Music

Side Flex (switch sides)	40 seconds
Trunk Twister	25 seconds
Abdominal Challenges	40 seconds
Slide/Skip	25 seconds
Jumping Jack variations	40 seconds
Triceps Push-Ups	25 seconds
Curl-Up Challenges	40 seconds
Gallop	25 seconds
Push-Up challenges	40 seconds
Aerobic Bouncing and Clapping	25 seconds
Leg Extensions	40 seconds
Walking to cool down	25 seconds

DPE p. 300

Student should know the exercises before trying to do them rhythmically.

The exercise music should be taped prior to the routine. This frees the teacher to move and help students.

Voice instructions can be dubbed onto the tape to tell students when to change to a new exercise.

Cog.—The body starts to perspire in an attempt to maintain a constant temperature. The student will verbalize this in his own words.

PM—The student will be able to perform the fitness activities.

Aff.—Regulation of body temperature is essential for comfort and safety. Discuss the many ways we attempt to regulate this temperature—more or fewer clothes, perspiring, swimming, fires.

MOVEMENT EXPERIENCE—CONTENT	ORGANIZATION AND TEACHING HINTS	EXPECTED STUDENT OBJECTIVES AND OUTCOMES

LESSON FOCUS (15 – 20 MINUTES)

Rhythmic Movement with Equipment (4)
Rope Jumping to Music

1. Perform the slow-time and fast-time rhythm with the rope held in one hand and turned.
2. Jump the rope and practice changing back and forth from slow to fast time.
3. Introduce a few basic steps that you plan to use in your routine, for instance, two-foot basic step, swing step forward and sideways, and crossing arms forward.
4. Try a rope jumping routine. The following routine is based on a schottische record and can serve the dual purpose of enhancing both rope jumping and the schottische step.

1st Verse Part: Two-foot basic jump—slow time.

Chorus: Two-foot basic jump—fast time.

2nd Verse Part: alternate basic foot step—slow time.

Chorus: Alternate basic foot step—fast time.

3rd Verse Part: Swing Step Forward—slow time.

Chorus: Swing Step Forward—fast time.

4th Verse Part: Swing Step Sideways—slow time.

Chorus: Swing Step Sideways—slow time.

DPE pp. 451 – 458

Use music that possesses a rhythm that is steady, unchanging, and easy to hear.

Music that has a two-part format (a verse and chorus) is excellent as it gives students a natural break at which to change their routine.

Turn up the amplifier so the music is loud and easy to hear.

It may be necessary to take a short break and work with something like beanbags or play an inactive game, as children will tire easily in this activity.

Double Dutch activities can be used for developing a long-jump rope rhythmic routine.

Be patient. Some students will have more difficulty jumping to the rhythm than others.

PM—The student will be able to jump-rope to the rhythm of the music.

PM.—The student will be able to perform the routine to the schottische with the jump rope.

Cog.—The students will recognize the basic underlying beat and clap their hands to the rhythm after listening to a variety of records.

Aff.—The student will learn the value of overlearning a skill. Here is a chance to discuss the overlearning principle and explain that it is hard to listen for the rhythm if you haven't overlearned the skill of rope jumping. If you *have* overlearned rope jumping, you can easily listen to the music *without* thinking about rope jumping.

Cog.—The development of aerobic capacity involves basic elements: intensity, duration, and frequency of exercise. Students will understand each of the elements and how each can be manipulated to enhance fitness level.

Ball Skills to Music

1. Perform the following skills to the rhythm of the music:
   a. Bounce and catch.
   b. Bounce, clap, catch; bounce, turn, catch—also use toss.
   c. Dribble continuously in place and while moving.
   d. Work with a partner or in groups, passing one or more balls from one another in rhythm.
   e. Develop a routine utilizing the skills above.

DPE, pp. 413 – 417

Bounce a certain number of times and catch. Combine the bounces with various locomotor movements.

Form circles, triangles, and other patterns. Dribble forward, backward, sideward, stop and go.

Vary with bounce passes.

Hula hoops may also be used if more variety is desired.

PM.—The student will be able to bounce, pass, and catch the ball in rhythm to the music.

PM—The students will be able to develop creative routines utilizing themselves and partners.

Cog.—Rhythm and timing are important elements in motor skill performance. Discuss the need for learning rhythmic activities through correct practice and repetition.

MOVEMENT EXPERIENCE—CONTENT	ORGANIZATION AND TEACHING HINTS	EXPECTED STUDENT OBJECTIVES AND OUTCOMES

Lummi Sticks
 	
1. Without sticks, lean the chant.
2. Issue sticks. Show: vertical taps, tap together. Work out a three-count routine: (1) vertical tap, (2) tap together, (3) rest beat. Sing the chant to this rhythm.
3. Organize by partners. Children sit cross-legged, facing, at a distance of 18–20". Work out the following routines:
  a. Vertical tap, tap together, partner tap right; vertical tap, tap together, partner tap left.
  b. Vertical tap, tap together, pass right stick; vertical tap, tap together, pass left stick.
  c. Vertical tap, tap together, toss right stick; vertical tap, tap together, toss left stick.
  d. Repeat a, b, c, except substitute an end tap and flip for the vertical tap and tap together (i.e., end tap, flip, partner tap right, end tap, flip, partner tap left).
  e. Vertical tap, tap together, pass right and left quickly; repeat.
  f. End tap, flip, toss right and left quickly, repeat.
  g. Right flip side, left flip in front, vertical tap in place, partner tap right; left flip side, right flip front, vertical tap in place, tap left.
  h. End tap in front, flip, vertical tap, tap together, toss right, toss left.
  i. Vertical tap, tap together, right stick to partner's left hand and left stick to own right hand. Repeat.
  j. Repeat previous routines, but reverse the circle.
  k. Devise own routines.
	DPE, p. 388
	
	Most commercially available lummi stick music is written in measures of four beats (4/4). However, the traditional way is a three-beat measure (3/4) as described here. If a 4/4 rhythm is used, a pause or additional movement will have to be added to the routines listed.
	
	The traditional chant is listed in the text. If using the chant, establish it early as it must carry the activity.
	
	Hold stick with thumb and fingers (not the first) at the bottom third of the stick.
	
	Stress relaxed and light tapping.
	
	Partners provide their own chanting. Two or three sets of partners can work in unison.
		PM.—The student will get accustomed to the proper grip so it becomes automatic.
		
		PM.—The student will be able to do the following: vertical tap, tap together, partner tap right (left), pass right (left), toss right (left), end tap, flip, toss right and left quickly; and he will put these together in rhythm to the chant.
		
		Cog.—Water accounts for 70% of the body's weight. At least a quart of water must be ingested per day. Discuss how a great deal more must be ingested when one is involved in strenuous exercise. What problems arise when one doesn't drink enough water?
		
		Cog.—Practicing skills incorrectly can make it difficult to learn them correctly later. Discuss the need for patience with one's self when learning new rhythmic activities. This prevents learning them incorrectly due to fear of failure and resultant peer pressure.
		
		Cog.—All activities in sports involve rhythm. Most movements can be classified into even or uneven rhythm. Identify various sport skills and the underlying rhythm involved when they are performed correctly.
		
		Aff.—People feel part of a group when they can perform mutual skills. Discuss how learning various physical skills allows people to interact with friends and people with similar interests.

GAME (5 – 7 MINUTES)

Alaska Baseball—*DPE*, p. 570

Supplies: A volleyball or soccer ball

Skills: Kicking, batting, running, ball handling

The players are organized in two teams, one of which is at bat while the other is in the field. A straight line provides the only out-of-bounds line, and the team at bat is behind this line at about the middle. The other team is scattered around the fair territory.

One player propels the ball, either batting a volleyball or kicking a stationary soccer ball. His teammates are in a close file behind him. As soon as the batter sends the ball into the playing area, he starts to run around his own team. Each time the runner passes the head of the file, the team gives a loud count.

There are no outs. The first fielder to get the ball stands still and starts to pass the ball back overhead to the nearest teammate, who moves directly behind to receive it. The remainder of the team in the field must run to the ball and form a file behind it. The ball is passed back overhead, with each player handling the ball. When the last field player in line has a firm grip on it, she shouts "Stop." At this signal, a count is made of the number of times the batter ran around his own team. To score more sharply, half rounds should be counted.

Five batters or half of the team should bat; then the teams should change places. This is better than allowing an entire team to bat before changing to the field, because players in the field tire from many consecutive runs.

Variation: Regular bases can be set up, and the batter can run the bases. Scoring can be in terms of a home run made or not; or the batter can continue around the bases, getting a point for each base.

MOVEMENT EXPERIENCE—CONTENT	ORGANIZATION AND TEACHING HINTS	EXPECTED STUDENT OBJECTIVES AND OUTCOMES

Addition Tag—*DPE*, p. 570

Supplies: None

Skills: Running, dodging

Two couples are it, and each stands with inside hands joined. These are the taggers. The other children run individually. The couples move around the playground, trying to tag with the free hands. The first person tagged joins the couple, making a trio. The three then chase until they catch a fourth. Once a fourth person is caught, the four divide and form two couples, adding another set of taggers to the game. This continues until all children are tagged.

Teaching suggestions: Some limitation of area should be established to enable the couples to catch the runners; otherwise, the game moves slowly and is fatiguing. The game moves faster if started with two couples. A tag is legal only when the couple or group of three keeps their hands joined. The game can be used as an introductory activity, since all children are active.

DYNAMIC PHYSICAL EDUCATION LESSON PLAN
Track and Field–Related Activities (Lesson 1)
Level II

Supplies and Equipment Needed:
  Two stopwatches with neck lanyards (box for these for safety in the field)
  Measuring boards for the four jumps
  Starter (p. 716)
  Pits for the jumps with takeoff boards
  8–12 hurdles
  Rope crossbar for high jump (p. 710)
  High jump standards
  Technique hints for each station (on poster boards)
  Eight batons
  Four sets of boxes and blocks for potato relay

MOVEMENT EXPERIENCE—CONTENT	ORGANIZATION AND TEACHING HINTS	EXPECTED STUDENT OBJECTIVES AND OUTCOMES

INTRODUCTORY ACTIVITY AND FITNESS DEVELOPMENT ACTIVITIES (9 – 11 MINUTES)

Stretching and Jogging

Combine the introductory and fitness activities during the track and field unit. This will help students understand how to stretch and warm up for demanding activity such as track and field.

Jog	1–2 minutes
Standing Hip Bend	30 seconds
Sitting Stretch	30 seconds
Partner Rowing	60 seconds
Bear Hug (20 seconds each leg)	40 seconds
Side Flex (20 seconds each leg)	40 seconds
Trunk Twister	30 seconds
Jog	3–4 minutes

DPE pp. 289 – 291

To prepare for strenuous activity, students should learn to warm up their body by walking or jogging, stretching, and finishing with jogging.

Cog.—The student will be able to explain why stretching exercises and warm-ups are essential to track and field work.

PM.—The student will demonstrate the ability to put proper stress on muscles in stretching.

LESSON FOCUS (15 – 20 MINUTES)

Track and Field-Related Activities Orientation

1. Goal is self-improvement and developing proper techniques.
2. Each must accept responsibility for self-directed work. Try all activities.
3. Learn from the general sessions and from the technique hints that are given at each station.
4. You should rotate through two stations each day. The following period, you will participate in two other station activities. Please stay at your stations until the time is signaled for rotation.
5. To measure the long jumps and the hop-step-and-jump, use the measuring tapes.

DPE pp. 704 – 710

Establish a signal which brings all students to a central instructional area. This allows the teacher to stop station work and give instruction to the entire class.

Develop signs for all stations. The signs should include appropriate performance techniques, what is to be done at each station, and appropriate safety precautions.

Emphasize care for the watches. Show how they work and emphasize no winding.

Explain that height is a factor and that this is one reason the groups are formed. They are important particularly in the high jump.

Aff.—To succeed in track and field, one must work diligently and independently. Discuss the need for self-discipline in training.

Aff.—It is important to concentrate on good techniques, rather than performance, at this point. Discuss the importance of learning proper technique before worrying about maximum effort.

PM.—The student will demonstrate the ability to use the measuring tapes accurately.

Cog.—The student will be able to explain how a stopwatch operates.

Aff.—Acceptance of responsibility for care of equipment.

MOVEMENT EXPERIENCE— CONTENT	ORGANIZATION AND TEACHING HINTS	EXPECTED STUDENT OBJECTIVES AND OUTCOMES

6. Use care with the stopwatches. They are expensive to purchase and also to repair. Put the lanyard around your neck when using stopwatches.
7. Announce the four groups. (Form groups according to formula on *DPE,* p. 710)

Group Drills

1. Explain starting:
   a. Standing start
   b. Norwegian start
   c. Sprint start
2. Starting practice by groups.
3. Explain striding.
4. Stride practice.

Station (Small Group) Instruction

Divide the group into small groups and send an equal number of students to each station.

Station 1 - Starting and Sprinting

1. Front foot 4–12" behind line.
2. Thumb and first finger behind line, other fingers support.
3. Knee of other leg placed just opposite front foot.
4. On "get set," seat is raised, the down knee comes up a little, and the shoulders move forward over the hands.
5. On "go," push off sharply and take short, driving steps.

Hop-Step-and-Jump

1. Important to get the sequence and rhythm first, then later try for distance.
2. Sprinting.

Station 2 - Running High Jump

1. Place bar low enough (30 in.) so all can practice.
2. Approach at 45°.
3. Good kick-up and arm action.

Baton Passing

1. Decide on method of passing.
2. Incoming runner passes with left hand to right hand of receiver.
3. After receiving, change to the left hand.
4. Estimate how fast to take off with respect to the incoming runner.

Station 3 - Running Long Jump

1. Decide on jumping foot.
2. Establish check point.
3. Control last four steps.
4. Seek height.

Standing Long Jump or the Potato Shuttle Race

Organization and Teaching Hints:

Use an entire group at one time.

Stride about 70 yd and return to start. Repeat several times.

Sprint 25 to 30 yd or so. Have one child use the starter and count out the rhythm of the start.

Should be a gradual rise of the shoulders.

Foul rule applies.

The runner can sprint forward and then take a jump as a return activity.

Can begin with the scissors style.

Use only two heights in beginning practice.

No contest for height.

Space runners.

Change baton promptly.

Avoid "blind" exchange.

Stress the foul rule.

Hit with the jumping foot.

Use either activity.

Expected Student Objectives and Outcomes:

Aff.—Acceptance by students of the group division is necessary if this approach is to work. Take time to discuss grouping, if deemed necessary.

PM.—The student will demonstrate improvement in form, technique, and performance of:
   Starting
   Sprinting
   Striding
   Hop-step-and-jump
   High jump
   Relay and baton passing
   Standing Long Jump (optional)
   Potato Shuttle Race
   Running Long Jump
   Hurdling

Cog.—The student will demonstrate knowledge about the points of technique of the above.

Cog.—When sprinting, initial contact is made with the ball of the foot as compared with the heel or flat-footed contact made when running long distance. Discuss this and arm carry difference between sprinters and distance runners.

Cog.—Gravity and air resistance limit performances in the jumping events. Identify these factors and why altitude (Mexico City Olympics) has a positive impact on long jump performances.

Cog.—The ratio of fast twitch versus slow twitch fibers is genetically determined. Fast twitch fibers contract rapidly and are useful in activities demanding speed and explosive power. Slow twitch fibers contract less quickly and are excellent for aerobic endurance activities. People are born with varying ratios and thus have a predisposition to succeed in activities in line with their given muscle fiber ratio.

MOVEMENT EXPERIENCE— CONTENT	ORGANIZATION AND TEACHING HINTS	EXPECTED STUDENT OBJECTIVES AND OUTCOMES

Station 4 - Hurdling

1. At beginning, use one or two hurdles.
2. Leading foot is directly forward.

Striding for Distance

1. Repeat three to four times.
2. Run 110 yards, walk 110 yards.

Succeeding Meetings for the First Week

1. Same introductory and fitness activity. Omit the orientation.
2. Repeat the group drills—starting and striding. Make them shorter.
3. Each group visits only two stations each meeting and the other two the next meeting.
4. Finish with interval training.

Work for form.

Keep in the infield, keeping track clear.

Begin in straightaway and stride around curve.

Best around the track.

Cog.—Knowledge of what interval training is and can do for performance.

GAME ACTIVITY (5 – 7 MINUTES)

Potato Shuttle Relay—*DPE*, p. 596

A small box about a foot square is placed 5 ft in front of each lane. Four 12-in. circles are drawn at 5-ft intervals beyond the box. This makes the last circle 25 ft from the starting point. Four blocks or beanbags are needed for each team.

To start, the blocks are placed in the box in front of each team. The first runner goes to the box, takes a single block, and puts it into one of the circles. She repeats this performance until there is a block in each circle; then she tags off the second runner. This runner brings the blocks back to the box, one at a time, and tags off the third runner, who returns the blocks to the circles, and so on.

Using a box to receive the blocks makes a definite target. When the blocks are taken to the circles, some rules must be made regarding placement. The blocks should be considered placed only when they are inside or touching a line. Blocks outside need to be replaced before the runner can continue. Paper plates or pie plates can be used instead of circles drawn on the floor.

Variation: The race can also be done with bowling pins. Instead of being placed in a box, they are in a large circle at the start.

Shuttle Relays—*DPE*, p. 706

Since children are running toward each other, one great difficulty in running shuttle relays is control of the exchange. In the excitement, the next runner may leave too early, and the tag or exchange is then made ahead of the restraining line. A high-jump standard or cone can be used to prevent early exchanges. The next runner awaits the tag with an arm around the standard or a hand on a cone.

One on One Contests

Allow students to find a friend and have a number of personal contests in track and field events such as sprints, hurdling, high jump, and standing long jump.

DYNAMIC PHYSICAL EDUCATION LESSON PLAN
Track and Field–Related Activities (Lesson 2)
Level II

Supplies and Equipment Needed:
  Four stopwatches with neck lanyards (box for these for safety in the field)
  Measuring boards for the four jumps
  Starter (p. 716)
  Pits for the jumps with takeoff boards
  8–12 hurdles
  Stretch rope crossbar for high jump (p. 710)
  High jump standards
  Technique hints for each station (on poster boards)
  Eight batons
  Four sets—boxes and blocks for potato relay
  Clipboards and pencils
  Recording sheets for each group

MOVEMENT EXPERIENCE— CONTENT	ORGANIZATION AND TEACHING HINTS	EXPECTED STUDENT OBJECTIVES AND OUTCOMES

INTRODUCTORY ACTIVITY AND FITNESS DEVELOPMENT ACTIVITIES (9 – 11 MINUTES)

Stretching and Jogging

Combine the introductory and fitness activities during the track and field unit. This will help students understand how to stretch and warm up for demanding activity such as track and field.

Jog	1–2 minutes
Standing Hip Bend	30 seconds
Sitting Stretch	30 seconds
Partner Rowing	60 seconds
Bear Hug (20 seconds each leg)	40 seconds
Side Flex (20 seconds each leg)	40 seconds
Trunk Twister	30 seconds
Jog	3–4 minutes

DPE pp. 289 – 291

To prepare for strenuous activity, students should learn to warm up their body by walking or jogging, stretching, and finishing with jogging.

Cog.—The student will be able to explain why stretching exercises and warm-ups are essential to track and field work.

PM.—The student will demonstrate the ability to put proper stress on muscles in stretching.

LESSON FOCUS (15 – 20 MINUTES)

Track and Field-Related Activities

Continue the same rotation plan as in week 1. Each group participates in two stations each meeting. Next meeting, visit the other two stations. At each station, students allow students to record their performances.

Station 1 - Sprinting

1. 50-yard distance
2. 70-yard distance
3. Two trials

Hop-Step-and-Jump

1. Three trials
2. Record all three, circle best

DPE pp. 704 – 710

Develop signs for all stations. The signs should included appropriate performance techniques, what is to be done at each station, and appropriate safety precautions.

One watch.

Run individually.

Take best time.

Use starter.

PM.—The student will be able to perform creditably in the various events.

Cog.—Red blood cells pick up oxygen as they pass through the lungs. When exercising, a person breathes faster to bring more oxygen into the lungs. The heart beats faster to move more blood and transport oxygen to the muscles.

MOVEMENT EXPERIENCE—CONTENT	ORGANIZATION AND TEACHING HINTS	EXPECTED STUDENT OBJECTIVES AND OUTCOMES

Station 2 - High Jump

1. Begin at 30 in., raise 3" at a time
2. Two trials
3. Record best height made

Baton Passing

Practice while waiting for high jump turn or when "out."

Station 3 - Running Long Jump

1. Three trials
2. Record all three, circle best

Standing Long Jump

1. Three trials
2. Record all three, circle best

Shuttle Relay

One trial, run two races at a time.

Station 4 - Hurdling

1. Set up 60-yard hurdle course
2. Give two trials
3. Take best time

Striding

Striding practice can be done while waiting for turns.

Organization and Teaching Hints column:

This increment keeps things moving.

Use a magic rope (elastic shock cord) for a crossbar to eliminate the fear of getting hurt.

Use foul rule.

Watch for falling backward.

Two watches.

This can be omitted.

Expected Student Objectives and Outcomes column:

Cog.—Smoking causes the heart rate to jump 10–20 beats per minute. The blood vessels constrict and the heart must pump harder to get blood through them. Discuss how this can be a detriment to good health.

GAME (5 – 7 MINUTES)

Circular (Pursuit) Relays—*DPE*, p. 706

   Circular relays make use of the regular circular track. The baton exchange technique is important, and practice is needed. On a 220-yd or 200-m track, relays can be organized in a number of ways, depending on how many runners are spaced for one lap. Four runners can do a lap, each running one quarter of the way; two can do a lap, each running one half of the distance; or each runner can complete a whole lap. In these races, each member of the relay team runs the same distance. Relays can also be organized so that members run different distances.

Shuttle Relays—*DPE*, p. 706

   Since children are running toward each other, one great difficulty in running shuttle relays is control of the exchange. In the excitement, the next runner may leave too early, and the tag or exchange is then made ahead of the restraining line. A high-jump standard or cone can be used to prevent early exchanges. The next runner awaits the tag with an arm around the standard or a hand on a cone.

One on One Contests

   Allow students to find a friend and have a number of personal contests in track and field events such as sprints, hurdling, high jump, and standing long jump.

DYNAMIC PHYSICAL EDUCATION LESSON PLAN
Fundamental Skills Using Parachute Activity
Level II

Supplies and Equipment Needed:
  Parachute
  Cones
  Beanbags
  Jump ropes
  Basketballs or cageballs

MOVEMENT EXPERIENCE—CONTENT	ORGANIZATION AND TEACHING HINTS	EXPECTED STUDENT OBJECTIVES AND OUTCOMES

INTRODUCTORY ACTIVITY (2 – 3 MINUTES)

Creative Routine

Each student should develop his own warm-up routine. Youngsters should be encouraged to use a combination of locomotor activities and stretching activities.

DPE pp. 258 – 259

It might be necessary to point out some activities to stimulate some of the youngsters.

Charts on the walls could be used to describe various warm-up activities.

PM.—The students will be able to physically warm themselves up in preparation for fitness activities.

FITNESS DEVELOPMENT ACTIVITY (7 – 8 MINUTES)

Hexagon Hustle

Outline a large hexagon with six cones. Place signs with directions on both sides of the cones. The signs identify the hustle activity students are to perform as they approach a cone. Tape alternating segments of silence and music to signal duration of exercise. Music segments indicate aerobic activity while intervals of silence announce flexibility and strength development activities.

Hustle	20 seconds
Push-Up from Knees	30 seconds
Hustle	20 seconds
Bend and Twist (8 counts)	30 seconds
Hustle	20 seconds
Jumping Jacks (4 counts)	30 seconds
Hustle	20 seconds
Curl-Up Challenges	
(2 counts)	30 seconds
Hustle	20 seconds
Double Leg Crab Kick	30 seconds
Hustle	20 seconds
Sit and Stretch (8 counts)	30 seconds
Hustle	20 seconds
Power Jumper	30 seconds
Hustle	20 seconds
Squat Thrust (4 counts)	30 seconds

DPE pp. 303 – 304

Examples of hustle activities that can be listed on signs are:
1. Jogging
2. Skipping and galloping
3. Hopping or jumping
4. Sliding
5. Running and leaping
6. Animal movements
7. Sport movements such as defensive sliding, running backwards, and carioca step.

During the hustle, faster moving students can pass to the outside of the hexagon.

Change directions regularly to keep students spaced evenly along the hexagon.

During the hustle, quality movement rather than speed is the goal.

Cog.—The student will be able to identify five exercises that stretch different body parts.

PM.—The student will be able to perform exercises to stretch the body.

Aff.—The student will be able to explain that stretching should be done slowly and with gradual force, rather than strong bouncing movements.

MOVEMENT EXPERIENCE— CONTENT	ORGANIZATION AND TEACHING HINTS	EXPECTED STUDENT OBJECTIVES AND OUTCOMES

LESSON FOCUS (15 – 20 MINUTES)

Fundamental Skills Using Parachute Activity

1. Shaking the Rug and Making Waves—Shaking the Rug should involve small, rapid movement, whereas Making Waves is large movements.
2. Circular movements—Move utilizing the basic locomotor movements and holding the chute at various levels.
3. Making a Dome—Parachute should be on the floor and held with both hands. Make a dome by standing up and rapidly lifting the chute overhead.
   a. Punching Bag—Make a dome, stand on edge, and punch the air out.
   b. Make a Dome—Stand on the edge, and in a circular fashion, push the air around the parachute.
4. Mushroom—similar to the Dome except three or four steps toward the center are taken by each student.
   a. Mushroom Release—All students release the chute at its peak of inflation.
   b. Mushroom Run—Make a mushroom, call out the names of a few students who release the chute and move to a vacant position.
5. Activities with balls and beanbags
   a. Ball Circle—Use a basketball or cageball and make it circle around the outside of the chute. Add a second ball.
   b. Popcorn—Place six to ten beanbags on the chute and shake them into the air.
   c. Poison Snake—Place six to ten jump ropes on the chute. Divide the players in half. Try to shake the ropes so they touch a player on the opposing team.
   d. Cannon Ball—Use a 24" cageball on the chute. On the command "load," lower the chute to the ground. On "fire," lift the chute and fire the ball into the air.

DPE pp. 477 – 482

Teach the proper terminology so students can identify the various activities.

Perform the activities with different grips.

Various patterns can be made by having the class work in small groups around the chute.

Try making a dome while moving in a circle.

Teach the proper technique of standing and lifting the parachute to avoid back strain.

Work for precision so that all students are together in their movement.

Proper care of the chute should be taught so that it is not ripped.

Many routines to music can be developed and incorporated with the various chute activities. Many folk dances can be done utilizing parachute activities which increases motivation for students.

Cog.— The student will be able to identify the various parachute activities by name.

Aff.—The parachute requires group cooperation for successful implementation of the activities. Discuss the importance of working together to improve everybody's welfare.

PM.—The student will be able to cooperatively perform the following activities:
1. Making Waves.
2. Making a Dome.
3. Popcorn.
4. Ball Circles.

PM.—The student will be able to perform a simple folk dance incorporating the parachute.

Cog.—When exercising in hot weather, the amount of clothes worn should be minimized. This is due to the fact that clothes prevent sweat from evaporating and cooling the body. On the other hand, when it is cold outside, the body should be clothed so body heat will be maintained.

MOVEMENT EXPERIENCE— CONTENT	ORGANIZATION AND TEACHING HINTS	EXPECTED STUDENT OBJECTIVES AND OUTCOMES

GAME (5 – 7 MINUTES)

Nonda's Car Lot—*DPE*, p. 578
 Supplies: None
 Skills: Running, dodging
 One player is it and stands in the center of the area between two lines established about 50 ft apart. The class selects four brands of cars (e.g., Honda, Corvette, Toyota, Cadillac). Each student then selects a car from the four but does not tell anyone what it is.
 The tagger calls out a car name. All students who selected that name attempt to run to the other line without getting tagged. The tagger calls out the cars until all students have run. When a child (car) gets tagged, she must sit down at the spot of the tag. She cannot move but may tag other students who run too near her. When the one who is it calls out "Car lot," all of the cars must go. The game is played until all students have been tagged.

Box Ball—*DPE*, p. 572
 Supplies: A sturdy box, 2 ft square and about 12 in. deep; four volleyballs (or similar balls)
 Skills: Running, ball handling
 The class is divided into four even teams, with six to ten players per team. Each team occupies one side of a hollow square at an equal distance from the center. Players face inward and number off consecutively from right to left.
 A box containing four balls is put in the center. The instructor calls a number, and the player from each team who has that number runs forward to the box, takes a ball, and runs to the head of his line, taking the place of player 1. In the meantime, the players in the line have moved to the left just enough to fill in the space left by the runner. On reaching the head of the line, the runner passes the ball to the next person and so on down the line to the end child. The last child runs forward and returns the ball to the box. The first team to return the ball to the box scores a point.
 The runner must not pass the ball down the line until he is in place at the head of the line. The ball must be caught and passed by each child. Failure to conform to these rules results in team disqualification. Runners stay at the head of the line, retaining their original number. Keeping the lines in consecutive number sequence is not important.

DYNAMIC PHYSICAL EDUCATION LESSON PLAN
Manipulative Skills Using Frisbees (Flying Discs)
Level II

Supplies and Equipment Needed:
   Cones
   One Frisbee per child
   Hoops
   Signs
   Bowling pins

MOVEMENT EXPERIENCE— CONTENT	ORGANIZATION AND TEACHING HINTS	EXPECTED STUDENT OBJECTIVES AND OUTCOMES

INTRODUCTORY ACTIVITY (2 – 3 MINUTES)

Four-Corners Movement

Lay out a square with a cone at each corner. As the child passes each corner, he changes to a different locomotor movement.

Challenge the students by declaring various qualities of movement (i.e., soft, heavy, slow, fast).

DPE p. 287

Students do not have to stay in line but can pass if they are doing a faster moving movement.

Encourage variety of movements and performing some movements that require placing body weight on the hands.

PM.—The student will be able to perform light locomotor movements using three different qualities.

FITNESS DEVELOPMENT ACTIVITY (7 – 8 MINUTES)

Hexagon Hustle

Outline a large hexagon with six cones. Place signs with directions on both sides of the cones. The signs identify the hustle activity students are to perform as they approach a cone. Tape alternating segments of silence and music to signal duration of exercise. Music segments indicate aerobic activity while intervals of silence announce flexibility and strength development activities.

Hustle	25 seconds
Push-Up from Knees	30 seconds
Hustle	25 seconds
Bend and Twist (8 counts)	30 seconds
Hustle	25 seconds
Jumping Jacks (4 counts)	30 seconds
Hustle	25 seconds
Abdominal Challenges (2 counts)	30 seconds
Hustle	25 seconds
Double Leg Crab Kick	30 seconds
Hustle	25 seconds
Sit and Stretch (8 counts)	30 seconds
Hustle	25 seconds
Power Jumper	30 seconds
Hustle	25 seconds
Squat Thrust (4 counts)	30 seconds

DPE pp. 303 – 304

Examples of hustle activities that can be listed on signs are:
   1. Jogging
   2. Skipping and galloping
   3. Hopping or jumping
   4. Sliding
   5. Running and leaping
   6. Animal movements
   7. Sport movements such as defensive sliding, running backwards, and carioca step.

During the hustle, faster moving students can pass to the outside of the hexagon.

Change directions regularly to keep students spaced evenly along the hexagon.

During the hustle, quality movement rather than speed is the goal.

Cog.—The student will be able to identify five exercises that stretch different body parts.

PM.—The student will be able to perform exercises to stretch her body.

Aff.—The student will be able to explain that stretching should be done slowly and with gradual force, rather than strong bouncing movements.

MOVEMENT EXPERIENCE— CONTENT	ORGANIZATION AND TEACHING HINTS	EXPECTED STUDENT OBJECTIVES AND OUTCOMES

LESSON FOCUS (15 – 20 MINUTES)

Manipulative Skills Using Frisbees

1. Skills:
   a. Backhand Throw
   b. Underhand Throw
   c. Thumbs-Down Catch
   d. Thumbs-Up Catch

Practice the throwing and catching skills so youngsters can practice the following activities.

2. Activities:
   a. Throw the Frisbee at different levels to partner.
   b. Throw a curve—to the left, right and upward. Vary the speed of the curve.
   c. Throw a bounce pass—try a low and a high pass.
   d. Throw the disc like a boomerang. Must throw at a steep angle into the wind.
   e. Throw the Frisbee into the air, run and catch. Increase the distance of the throw.
   f. Throw the Frisbee through a hoop held by a partner.
   g. Catch the Frisbee under your leg. Catch it behind your back.
   h. Throw the Frisbees into hoops that are placed on the ground as targets. Different-colored hoops can be given different values. Throw through your partner's legs.
   i. Frisbee bowling—One partner has a bowling pin which the other partner attempts to knock down by throwing the Frisbee.
   j. Play catch while moving. Lead your partner so he doesn't have to break stride.
   k. See how many successful throws and catches you can make in 30 seconds.
   l. Frisbee Baseball Pitching—Attempt to throw the Frisbee into your partner's "Strike Zone."

DPE pp. 425 – 427

Partner formation.

Throw and catch with a partner—begin with short distances and gradually move apart as skill improves.

Give students plenty of room—their lack of skill will result in many inaccurate throws.

Offer a helping station for those students who have difficulty learning the basic throws.

Emphasize accuracy rather than distance in the early stages of throwing the Frisbee.

Use both dominant and nondominant hands.

For a straight throw, the disc should be parallel to the ground on release.

Remind students to focus their eyes on the disc as long as possible.

Encourage students to try different activities of their own creation.

PM.—The student will be able to perform the following skills:
   a. Backhand Throw.
   b. Underhand Throw.
   c. Thumbs-Down Catch.
   d. Thumbs-Up Catch.

Cog.—The student will be able to explain the effect that the angle of the disc upon release will have on its flight.

Cog.—Age plays a role on pulse rate. At birth, the heart rate is 130–140 beats per minute at rest. At maturity, the heart rate will have gradually slowed to a rate of 68–84 beats per minute.

PM.—The student will be able to catch the Frisbee five out of eight times.

Aff.—Frisbees are a recreational activity. Discuss the importance of learning leisure-time skills for the future.

GAME (5 – 7 MINUTES)

Frisbee Keep Away
   Supplies: Frisbees
   Skills: Throwing and catching Frisbees
   Students break into groups of three. Two of the players in the group try to keep the other player from touching the Frisbee while they are passing it back and forth. If the Frisbee is touched by the defensive player, the person who through the Frisbee becomes the defensive player. Begin the game by asking students to remain stationary while throwing and catching. Later, challenge can be added by allowing all players in the group move.

MOVEMENT EXPERIENCE— CONTENT	ORGANIZATION AND TEACHING HINTS	EXPECTED STUDENT OBJECTIVES AND OUTCOMES

Frisbee Golf—*DPE*, p. 589

Supplies: One Frisbee per person, hoops for hole markers, cones

Skills: Frisbee throwing for accuracy

Frisbee Golf or disk golf is a favorite game of many students. Boundary cones with numbers can be used for tees, and holes can be boxes, hula hoops, trees, tires, garbage cans, or any other available equipment on the school grounds. Draw a course on a map for students and start them at different holes to decrease the time spent waiting to tee off. Regulation golf rules apply. The students can jog between throws for increased activity.

Disk golf is played like regular golf. One stroke is counted for each time the disk is thrown and when a penalty is incurred. The object is to acquire the lowest score. The following rules dictate play:

Tee-throws: Tee-throws must be completed within or behind the designated tee area.

Lie: The lie is the spot on or directly underneath the spot where the previous throw landed.

Throwing order: The player whose disk is the farthest from the hole throws first. The player with the least number of throws on the previous hole tees off first.

Fairway throws: Fairway throws must be made with the foot closest to the hole on the lie. A run-up is allowed.

Dog leg: A dog leg is one or more designated trees or poles in the fairway that must be passed on the outside when approaching the hole. There is a two-stroke penalty for missing a dog leg.

Putt throw: A putt throw is any throw within 10 ft of the hole. A player may not move past the point of the lie in making the putt throw. Falling or jumping putts are not allowed.

Unplayable lies: Any disk that comes to rest 6 ft or more above the ground is unplayable. The next throw must be played from a new lie directly underneath the unplayable lie (one-stroke penalty).

Out-of-bounds: A throw that lands out-of-bounds must be played from the point where the disk went out (one-stroke penalty).

Course courtesy: Do not throw until the players ahead are out of range.

Completion of hole: A disk that comes to rest in the hole (box or hoop) or strikes the designated hole (tree or pole) constitutes successful completion of that hole.

DYNAMIC PHYSICAL EDUCATION LESSON PLAN
Softball-Related Activities (Lesson 1)
Level II

Supplies and Equipment Needed:
  Station 1: 2 batting tees, 4 balls, 2 bats (whiffle balls and bats preferred)
  Station 2: 1 ball for each 2 children (can use fleece balls or whiffle balls)
  Station 3: 4 bases (home plates), 4 balls
  Station 4: 2 balls, 2 bats
  28-ft. parachute and 10–12 long jump ropes

MOVEMENT EXPERIENCE—CONTENT	ORGANIZATION AND TEACHING HINTS	EXPECTED STUDENT OBJECTIVES AND OUTCOMES

INTRODUCTORY ACTIVITY (2 – 3 MINUTES)

Long-Rope Routine

Have the squad form a loose column and hold a long jump rope in the right hand.
On the first signal: Run in a column with one child leading the way.
Second signal: Shift the rope overhead from right hand to left hand without stopping.
Third signal: Two inside children let go of rope, outside children begin turning the rope for the two who have released the rope. They continue jumping the rope until the next signal.
Fourth signal: The outside youngsters move to the inside positions and vice-versa. The sequence is then repeated.

DPE, p. 256

Group youngsters by fours.

The sequence should be smooth with very little hesitation.

Youngsters can think of other activities to perform with the rope on the second signal.

May want to have students carry two long ropes and work on Double Dutch on the third and fourth signals.

PM.—The student will be able to jump the long rope ten times consecutively without a miss.

Cog.—The student will be able to develop one new idea to be used by his or her group on the second signal.

FITNESS DEVELOPMENT ACTIVITY (7 – 8 MINUTES)

Parachute Fitness

1. Jog in circle with chute held in left hand. Reverse directions and hold with right hand.
2. Standing, raise the chute overhead, lower to waist, lower to toes, raise to waist, etc.
3. Slide to the right; return slide to the left.
4. Sit and perform Abdominal Challenges - 30 seconds.
5. Skip for 20 second.
6. Freeze; face the center, and stretch the chute tightly with bent arms. Hold for 8–12 seconds. Repeat five to six times.
7. Run in place, hold the chute at waist level and hit the chute with lifted knees.
8. Sit with legs under the chute. Do a seat walk toward the center. Return to the perimeter. Repeat four to six times.

DPE, p. 285

Evenly space youngsters around the chute.

Use different grips to add variation to the activities.

Develop group morale by encouraging students to move together.

Use music to motivate youngsters.

PM.—The students will be able to perform the exercises together.

Aff.—There are many approaches and activities used to develop fitness. Discuss the need for variety in developing fitness programs. This is a good time to discuss the reasons we teach a broad range of activities with the class.

MOVEMENT EXPERIENCE— CONTENT	ORGANIZATION AND TEACHING HINTS	EXPECTED STUDENT OBJECTIVES AND OUTCOMES

9. Place the chute on the ground. Jog away from the chute and return on signal. Repeat for 30 seconds.
10. On sides with legs under the chute, perform Side Flex and lift chute with legs.
11. Lie on back with legs under the chute. Shake the chute with the feet.
12. Hop to the center of the chute and return. Repeat for 20 seconds.
13. Assume the push-up position with the legs aligned away from the center of the chute. Shake the chute with one arm while the other arm supports the body.
14. Sit with feet under the chute. Stretch by touching the toes with the chute. Relax with other stretches while sitting.
15. If desired, cool down by performing parachute stunts like the Dome or Mushroom.

LESSON FOCUS (15 – 20 MINUTES)

Softball-Related Activities

Station (Small Group) Instruction

DPE pp. 639 – 657

Squad formation.

Have signs at each of the stations giving both direction and skill hints.

Captain gathers equipment in designated spot before changing to next station.

Aff.—Willingness to cooperate at each station is crucial to the success of the lesson. Discuss and emphasize the importance of cooperation among peers.

Station 1 - Batting

1. Weight on both feet.
2. Bat pointed over right shoulder.
3. Trademark up on swing.
4. Elbows up and away from body.
5. Begin with hip roll and short step.
6. Swing level.
7. Follow through.
8. Eyes on ball.

Batting from Tee

1. Stand back (3 feet) from tee, so when stepping forward, ball is hit in front.
2. Show three types of grips.

Divide squad—with one batter, a catcher (next batter), and one or more fielders.

Points to avoid:
1. Lifting the front foot high off the ground
2. Stepping back with the rear foot
3. Dropping the rear shoulder
4. Chopping down on the ball (golfing)
5. Dropping the elbows

For safety, whiffle balls and plastic bats are suggested when working in stations.

PM.—The student will be able to meet the ball squarely on the tee.

Cog.—The student will know the different points in good batting.

Cog.—Strenuous exercise causes blood pressure to go up. This occurs because the heart beats faster and more blood is trying to push its way through the vessels. Why do some people have high blood pressure even at rest?

Station 2 - Throwing and Catching

1. Show grips.
2. How to catch—Stress "give," eyes on the ball.

Practice Throwing

1. Overhand.
2. Side arm.
3. Underhand toss.

One ball for each two players. Partners stand about 10 yd apart.

Suggest spacing to conform to skill.

Use "soft" softballs.

PM.—The students will be able to increase their catching potential and increase their accuracy in throwing (three styles).

Cog.—The student will be able to define and recognize good points of throwing and catching.

MOVEMENT EXPERIENCE— CONTENT	ORGANIZATION AND TEACHING HINTS	EXPECTED STUDENT OBJECTIVES AND OUTCOMES
Station 3 - Pitching Rules 1. Face the batter, both feet on the rubber and the ball held in front with both hands. One step is allowed, and the ball must be delivered on that step. 2. Ball must be pitched underhanded. 3. No motion or fake toward the plate can be made without delivering the ball. 4. No quick return is permitted, nor can the ball be rolled or bounced toward the batter. 5. Practice both regular and windmill pitching motions.	Divide squad into two groups. Each has a catcher, pitcher, and "batter," who just stands in position. A home plate and pitching rubber are helpful. Stress legal preliminary position before taking one hand off the ball to pitch.	PM.—The student will be able to pitch in observance with the rules. Cog.—The student will know the rules governing pitching. PM.—The student will be able to pitch 50% of the balls into the strike zone. Cog.—Softball is not a very effective sport for exercising the cardiovascular system. Most of the time is spent sitting or standing. Therefore, there is little, if any, aerobic activity.
Station 4 - Throwing or Batting Fly Balls 1. Begin with high throwing from the "batter." 2. Have the fielders return the ball with a one-bounce throw to the "batter." 3. Show form for high and low catch. Show sure stop for outfielders.	Divide squad into two groups.	PM.—The student will begin to handle (catch) easy fly balls with confidence. PM.—The fielders will improve in estimating flight of the ball and getting under it in time.

GAMES (5 – 7 MINUTES)

Softball Lead-Up Games

Throw It and Run—*DPE*, p. 695
Supplies: A softball or similar ball
Skills: Throwing, catching, fielding, base running
Throw-It-and-Run Softball is played like regular softball with the following exception. With one team in the field at regular positions, the pitcher throws the ball to the batter, who, instead of batting the ball, catches it and immediately throws it into the field. The ball is then treated as a batted ball, and regular softball rules prevail. No stealing is permitted, however, and runners must hold bases until the batter throws the ball. A foul ball is an out.
Variations:
1. Under-Leg Throw. Instead of throwing directly, the batter can turn to the right, lift the left leg, and throw the ball under the leg into the playing field.
2. Beat-Ball Throw. The fielders, instead of playing regular softball rules, throw the ball directly home to the catcher. The batter, in the meantime, runs around the bases. A point is scored for each base that she touches before the catcher receives the ball. A ball caught on the fly would mean no score. Similarly, a foul ball would not score points but would count as a turn at bat.

Two-Pitch Softball—*DPE*, p. 695
Supplies: A softball, a bat
Skills: Most softball skills, except regular pitching
Two-Pitch Softball is played like regular softball with the following changes.
1. A member of the team at bat pitches. A system of rotation should be set up so that every child takes a turn as pitcher.
2. The batter has only two pitches in which to hit the ball, and he must hit a fair ball on one of these pitches or he is out. The batter can foul the first ball, but if he fouls the second, he is out. There is no need to call balls or strikes.
3. The pitcher does not field the ball. A member of the team in the field acts as the fielding pitcher.
4. If the batter hits the ball, regular softball rules are followed. No stealing is permitted, however.
Teaching suggestion: Since the pitcher is responsible for pitching a ball that can be hit, the pitching distance can be shortened to give the batter ample opportunity to hit the ball. The instructor can act as the pitcher.
Variation: <u>Three Strikes</u>: In this game, the batter is allowed three pitches (strikes) to hit the ball. Otherwise, the game proceeds as in Two-Pitch Softball.

MOVEMENT EXPERIENCE— CONTENT	ORGANIZATION AND TEACHING HINTS	EXPECTED STUDENT OBJECTIVES AND OUTCOMES

Hit and Run—*DPE*, p. 696

Supplies: A volleyball or soccer ball or playground ball, home plate, base markers

Skills: Catching, throwing, running, dodging

One team is at bat, and the other is scattered in the field. Boundaries must be established, but the area does not have to be shaped like a baseball diamond. The batter stands at home plate with the ball. In front of the batter, 12 ft away, is a short line over which the ball must be hit to be in play. In the center of the field, about 40 ft away, is the base marker.

The batter bats the ball with the hands or fists so that it crosses the short line and lands inside the area. She then attempts to run down the field, around the base marker, and back to home plate without being hit by the ball. The members of the other team field the ball and throw it at the runner. The fielder may not run or walk with the ball but may throw to a teammate who is closer to the runner.

A run is scored each time a batter runs around the marker and back to home plate without getting hit by the ball. A run also is scored if a foul is called on the fielding team for walking or running with the ball.

The batter is out in any of the following circumstances.

1. A fly ball is caught.

2. He is hit below the shoulders with the ball.

3. The ball is not hit beyond the short line.

4. The team touches home plate with the ball before the runner returns. (This out is used only when the runner stops in the field and does not continue.)

The game can be played in innings of three outs each, or a change of team positions can be made after all members of one team have batted.

Teaching suggestion: The distance the batter runs around the base marker may have to be shortened or lengthened, depending on player's ability.

Variation: <u>Five Passes</u>: The batter is out when a fly ball is caught or when the ball is passed among five different players of the team in the field, with the last pass to a player at home plate beating the runner to the plate. The passes must not touch the ground.

DYNAMIC PHYSICAL EDUCATION LESSON PLAN
Softball-Related Activities (Lesson 2)
Level II

Supplies and Equipment Needed:
Station 1: 2 bats, 2 softballs (whiffle balls and bats are preferred)
Station 2: 2 plates, 2 softballs
Station 3: 4 bases (regular diamond), ball, bat (optional)
Station 4: 2 bats, 2 balls, home plates (optional)
Parachute
Tape player
Music

MOVEMENT EXPERIENCE—CONTENT	ORGANIZATION AND TEACHING HINTS	EXPECTED STUDENT OBJECTIVES AND OUTCOMES

INTRODUCTORY ACTIVITY (2 – 3 MINUTES)

Squad Leader Movement

Squads move around the area, following a leader. When a change is signaled, the last person goes to the head of the line and becomes the leader.

DPE p. 258

Encourage leaders to keep the squads moving and to offer challenging movements.

PM.—Each leader will be able to take her squad through at least two different movements.

FITNESS DEVELOPMENT ACTIVITY (7 – 8 MINUTES)

Parachute Fitness

1. Jog in circle with chute held in left hand. Reverse directions and hold with right hand.
2. Standing, raise the chute overhead, lower to waist, lower to toes, raise to waist, etc.
3. Slide to the right; return slide to the left.
4. Sit and perform Abdominal Challenges - 30 seconds.
5. Skip for 25 seconds.
6. Freeze; face the center, and stretch the chute tightly with bent arms. Hold for 8–12 seconds. Repeat five to six times.
7. Run in place, hold the chute at waist level, and hit the chute with lifted knees.
8. Sit with legs under the chute. Do a seat walk toward the center. Return to the perimeter. Repeat four to six times.
9. Place the chute on the ground. Jog away from the chute and return on signal. Repeat for 35 seconds.
10. On sides with legs under the chute, perform Side Flex and lift chute with legs.
11. Lie on back with legs under the chute. Shake the chute with the feet.
12. Hop to the center of the chute and return. Repeat for 25 seconds.

DPE, p. 285

Evenly space youngsters around the chute.

Use different grips to add variation to the activities.

Develop group morale by encouraging students to move together.

Use music to motivate youngsters.

PM.—The student will be able to perform all the parachute exercises.

Cog.—The student will be able to state which parachute exercises are isometric and which are isotonic.

Aff.—Society rewards individuals who are fit. Bring some advertisements from magazines and show how companies try to sell their product using a physically fit model.

MOVEMENT EXPERIENCE—CONTENT	ORGANIZATION AND TEACHING HINTS	EXPECTED STUDENT OBJECTIVES AND OUTCOMES
13. Assume the push-up position with the legs aligned away from the center of the chute. Shake the chute with one arm while the other arm supports the body. 14. Sit with feet under the chute. Stretch by touching the toes with the chute. Relax with other stretches while sitting. 15. If desired, cool down by performing parachute stunts like the Dome or Mushroom.		

LESSON FOCUS (15 – 20 MINUTES)

MOVEMENT EXPERIENCE—CONTENT	ORGANIZATION AND TEACHING HINTS	EXPECTED STUDENT OBJECTIVES AND OUTCOMES
Softball-Related Activities **Station (Small Group) Instruction** **Station 1 - Game of Pepper**	*DPE* pp. 639 – 657 For safety, whiffle balls and plastic bats should be used when teaching softball with the station format. Divide squad into two groups. Change batters every six swings.	Aff.—Each player will work at the designated skill and attempt to improve her skill. Discuss the importance of practicing both strengths and weaknesses. PM.—The players will be able to play this game successfully in order to develop throwing, catching, and striking skills.

Station 2 - Pitching and Umpiring
 	
1. Teach umpiring (by catcher)
  a. Right hand—strike
  b. Left hand—ball
	Stress easy underhand pitching.
	
	Need catcher and pitcher.
	
	Pitch to three batters and then rotate.
		PM.—The student will be able to "strike out" two out of three batters.
		
		PM.—Umpires will gain in increased skill.
		
		PM.—The student will be able to demonstrate proper umpiring techniques in calling balls and strikes.

Station 3 - Infield Practice 1. Throw around the bases clockwise and counterclockwise. 2. Roll ball to infielders and make the play at first. After each play, throw around the infield. 3. If enough skill, bat the ball to the infielders in turn.	Set up regular infield, staffed by squad. Rotate where needed.	PM.—The infielders will gain in skill in infield play. PM.—The infielders will learn to "play" the grounder at the most advantageous spot.
Station 4 - Batting Practice Each batter takes six swings and then rotates to the field. Catcher becomes batter and pitcher moves up to catcher. Review stress points for batting.	Use the squad. Have hitter, catcher, pitcher, and fielders. Use two softballs to keep things moving. Pitcher must be able to serve up good pitches. Use a shorter distance for pitching.	

MOVEMENT EXPERIENCE— CONTENT	ORGANIZATION AND TEACHING HINTS	EXPECTED STUDENT OBJECTIVES AND OUTCOMES

GAME (5 – 7 MINUTES)

Softball Lead-Up Games

Kick Softball.—*DPE*, p. 696

Supplies: A soccer ball or another ball to be kicked

Skills: Kicking a rolling ball, throwing, catching, running bases

The batter stands in the kicking area, a 3-ft-square home plate. The batter kicks the ball rolled on the ground by the pitcher. The ball should be rolled at moderate speed. An umpire calls balls and strikes. A strike is a ball that rolls over the 3-ft square. A ball rolls outside this area. Strikeouts and walks are called the same as in regular softball. The number of foul balls allowed should be limited. No base stealing is permitted. Otherwise, the game is played like softball.

Variations:

1. The batter kicks a stationary ball. This saves time, since there is no pitching.
2. Punch Ball. The batter can hit a volleyball as in a volleyball serve or punch a ball pitched by the pitcher.

In a Pickle—*DPE*, p. 697

Supplies: A softball, two bases 45 to 55 ft apart

Skills: Throwing, catching, running down a base runner, tagging

When a base runner gets caught between two bases and is in danger of being run down and tagged, she is "in a pickle." To begin, both fielders are on bases, one with a ball. The runner is positioned in the base path 10 to 15 ft away from the fielder with the ball. The two fielders throw the ball back and forth in an attempt to run down the runner between the bases and tag her. If the runner escapes and secures a base, she gets to try again. Otherwise, a system of rotation is established, including any sideline (waiting) players. No sliding is permitted.

Beat Ball—*DPE*, p. 697

Supplies: Soft softball, bat, batting tee (optional)

Skills: All softball skills

One team is at bat and the other team in the field. The object of the game is to hit the ball and run around the bases before the fielding team can catch the ball, throw it to first base, and then throw it to the catcher at home plate. If the ball beats the hitter home or a fly ball is caught, it is an out. If the hitter beats the ball to home plate, a run is scored. All players on a team bat once before switching positions with the fielding team. The ball must be hit into fair territory before the hitter can run. Only three pitches are allowed each hitter.

Variations:

1. Depending on the maturity of the players, a batting tee may be used. The hitter can be allowed the option of using the batting tee or hitting a pitched ball.
2. The pitcher can be selected from the batting team. This assures that an attempt will be made to make pitches that can be hit.
3. The distance can be varied so that hitters have a fair opportunity to score. If hitters score too easily, another base can be added.

DYNAMIC PHYSICAL EDUCATION LESSON PLAN—
ALTERNATE
Football-Related Activities (Lesson 1)
Level II

Supplies and Equipment Needed:
  8 footballs or foam rubber footballs
  4 soccer balls or foam rubber balls
  12 cones (for boundaries)
  16 flags
  16 pinnies

MOVEMENT EXPERIENCE—CONTENT	ORGANIZATION AND TEACHING HINTS	EXPECTED STUDENT OBJECTIVES AND OUTCOMES

INTRODUCTORY AND FITNESS DEVELOPMENT ACTIVITIES

This lesson may be substituted for any of the previous lessons. Use the introductory and fitness development activities given in the sequenced lesson plans.

LESSON FOCUS (15 – 20 MINUTES)

Football-Related Activities

Station (Small Group) Instruction

Station 1 - Stance Drills

1. Offensive stance (3 point)
   a. Feet shoulder width apart.
   b. Toes point ahead.
   c. Heel-toe relationship.
   d. One hand down.
   e. Look ahead.
2. Defensive stance
   a. Four-point stance.
   b. Toes pointed ahead.
   c. Look ahead.
   d. Move rapidly forward.

Punting

1. Use soccer balls or foam rubber footballs.
2. Technique:
   a. Kicking foot forward.
   b. Short step with that foot.
   c. Long step with other foot.
   d. Good knee flexion.
   e. Keep an eye on the ball.

Station 2 - Centering

1. Use three footballs.
2. Technique:
   a. Feet well spread.
   b. Toes pointed ahead.
   c. Proper hand and finger position.
   d. Send to receiver about waist high.

DPE pp. 636 – 641

Emphasize that stance is important.

Use stance drill with entire squad at one time; squads go in succession.

Go through four or five repetitions.

One ball for each two students.

Squad divides into partner activity.

Concentrate on form with a moderate distance.

It is easier to concentrate on form when using a soccer ball.

Cog.—The student will be able to describe why a good football player employs the proper stance. How does a stance affect stability and balance?

PM.—The student will demonstrate the ability to use the two-step punting form.

Cog.—The student will be able to tell when a punt is used in a football game and why it is used.

Cog.—Every play starts with a center pass. The student will be able to express the importance of accuracy to prevent fumbles and loose balls.

PM.—The student will demonstrate the ability to center the ball so that centering does not interfere with the play.

MOVEMENT EXPERIENCE—CONTENT	ORGANIZATION AND TEACHING HINTS	EXPECTED STUDENT OBJECTIVES AND OUTCOMES

Station 3 - Passing and Receiving

1. Use three footballs.
2. Technique (passing):
   a. Comfortable grip.
   b. Point foot in direction of pass.
   c. Turn partially sideways.
   d. Overhand motion.
3. Technique (catching):
   a. Relax fingers and hands.
   b. Bring ball into body.
   c. Little fingers together.

Station 4 - Ball Carrying

Divide squad into defensive and offensive players.

1. Use two footballs.
2. Each player has two flags. Show proper method of carrying ball.

Wait until player is completely through area before next player runs.

GAME (7 – 10 MINUTES)

Football Lead-Up Games

Football End Ball—*DPE*, p. 643
 Supplies: Footballs
 Skills: Passing, catching
 The court is divided in half by a centerline. End zones are marked 3 ft wide, completely across the court at each end. Players on each team are divided into three groups: forwards, guards, and ends. The object is for a forward to throw successfully to one of the end-zone players. End-zone players take positions in one of the end zones. Their forwards and guards then occupy the half of the court farthest from this end zone. The forwards are near the centerline, and the guards are back near the end zone of their half of the court.
 The ball is put into play with a center jump between the two tallest opposing forwards. When a team gets the ball, the forwards try to throw over the heads of the opposing team to an end-zone player. To score, the ball must be caught by an end-zone player with both feet inside the zone. No moving with the ball is permitted by any player. After each score, play is resumed by a jump ball at the centerline.
 A penalty results in loss of the ball to the other team. Penalties are assessed for the following.
 1. Holding a ball for more than 5 seconds
 2. Stepping over the end line or stepping over the centerline into the opponent's territory
 3. Pushing or holding another player
 In case of an out-of-bounds ball, the ball belongs to the team that did not cause it to go out. The nearest player retrieves the ball at the sideline and returns it to a player of the proper team.
 Teaching suggestions: Fast, accurate passing is to be encouraged. Players in the end zones must practice jumping high to catch the ball while still landing with both feet inside the end-zone area. A system of rotation is desirable. Each time a score is made, players on that team can rotate one person.
 To outline the end zones, some instructors use folding mats (4 by 7 ft or 4 by 8 ft). Three or four mats forming each end zone make a definite area and eliminate the problem of defensive players (guards) stepping into the end zone.

Five Passes—*DPE*, p. 643
 Supplies: A football, pinnies or other identification
 Skills: Passing, catching
 Players scatter on the field. The object of the game is for one team to make five consecutive passes to five different players without losing control of the ball. This scores 1 point. The defense may play the ball only and may not make personal contact with opposing players. No player can take more than three steps when in possession of the ball. More than three steps is called traveling, and the ball is awarded to the other team.
 The ball is given to the opponents at the nearest out-of-bounds line for traveling, minor contact fouls, after a point has been scored, and for causing the ball to go out-of-bounds. No penalty is assigned when the ball hits the ground. It remains in play, but the five-pass sequence is interrupted and must start again. Jump balls are called when the ball is tied up or when there is a pileup. The official should call out the pass sequence.

DYNAMIC PHYSICAL EDUCATION LESSON PLAN— ALTERNATE
Football-Related Activities (Lesson 2)
Level II

Supplies and Equipment Needed:
8 footballs
16 pinnies
24 cones for marking boundaries (or substitutes)
4 folding mats for the box ball
Flags

MOVEMENT EXPERIENCE— CONTENT	ORGANIZATION AND TEACHING HINTS	EXPECTED STUDENT OBJECTIVES AND OUTCOMES

INTRODUCTORY AND FITNESS DEVELOPMENT ACTIVITIES

This lesson may be substituted for any of the previous lessons. Use the introductory and fitness development activities given in the sequence plans.

LESSON FOCUS (15 – 20 MINUTES)

Football-Related Activities	*DPE* pp. 636 – 641	
Station (Small Group) Instruction	Each has two footballs.	Cog.—The students will be able to verbalize the rules of football.
First Day **Orientation**	Select a good kicker for punting.	Aff.—The student will be able to accept the abilities of all in conducting the drills.
1. Review passing, catching, and centering skills.		
2. Show combination drill.		PM.—The student will be able to reach the level of skill so that football-type games can be played with success.
3. Show punt return drill.		
Station Instruction		PM.—The student will have the ability to catch and pass to the extent that this game can be played successfully and pleasurably.
1. Squads 1 and 2 to combination drill.		
2. Squads 3 and 4 to punt return drill.	Exchange positions.	
3. Rotate after 7 or 8 minutes.		Cog.—The student will show improvement in strategic maneuvering.
Second Day **Station (Small Group) Instruction**		Aff.—The students will be able to accept whatever role the captain assigns them in team play.
1. Squads 1 and 2 to punt return.		
2. Squads 3 and 4 to combination drill.	Two balls for each squad.	
3. Exchange positions after 6 or 7 minutes.		

LESSON FOCUS (15 – 20 MINUTES)

Football Lead-Up Games

Football Box Ball—*DPE*, p. 645
Supplies: A football, team colors
Skills: Passing, catching
Five yards beyond each goal is a 6-by-6-ft square, which is the box. The teams should be marked so that they can be distinguished. The game is similar to End Ball in that the teams try to make a successful pass to the captain in the box.
To begin the play, players are onside, which means that they are on opposite ends of the field. One team, losing the toss, kicks off from its own 10-yd line to the other team. The game then becomes a kind of keep-away, with either team trying to secure or retain possession of the ball until a successful pass can be made to the captain in the box. The captain must catch the ball on the fly and still keep both feet in the box. This scores a touchdown.
A player may run sideward or backward when in possession of the ball. Players may not run forward but are allowed momentum (two steps) if receiving or intercepting a ball. The penalty for illegal forward movement while in possession of the ball is loss of the ball to the opponents, who take it out-of-bounds.

242

MOVEMENT EXPERIENCE— CONTENT	ORGANIZATION AND TEACHING HINTS	EXPECTED STUDENT OBJECTIVES AND OUTCOMES

LESSON FOCUS (15 – 20 MINUTES)

The captain is allowed only three attempts to score or one goal. If either occurs, another player is rotated into the box. On any incomplete pass or failed attempt to get the ball to the captain, the team loses the ball. If a touchdown is made, the team brings the ball back to its 10-yd line and kicks off to the other team. If the touchdown attempt is not successful, the ball is given out-of-bounds on the end line to the other team.

Any out-of-bounds ball is put into play by the team that did not cause the ball to go out-of-bounds. No team can score from a throw-in from out-of-bounds.

In case of a tie ball, a jump ball is called at the spot. The players face off as in a jump ball in basketball.

Players must play the ball and not the individual. For unnecessary roughness, the player is sidelined until a pass is thrown to the other team's captain. The ball is awarded to the offended team out-of-bounds.

On the kickoff, all players must be onside, that is, behind the ball when it is kicked. If the kicking team is called offside, the ball is awarded to the other team out-of-bounds at the centerline. After the kickoff, players may move to any part of the field. On the kickoff, the ball must travel 10 yd before it can be recovered by either team. A kickoff outside or over the end line is treated as any other out-of-bounds ball.

A ball hitting the ground remains in play as long as it is in bounds. Players may not bat or kick a free ball. The penalty is loss of the ball to the other team out-of-bounds. Falling on the ball also means loss of the ball to the other team.

Teaching suggestion: A 4-by-7-ft or a 4-by-8-ft folding tumbling mat can be used to define the box where the captain must stand to catch the ball for a score.

Speed Football—*DPE*, p. 643

Supplies: Football, flag for each player

Skills: Passing, catching, running with ball

The ball can be kicked off or started at the 20-yd line. The object is to move the ball across the opponent's goal by running or passing. If the ball drops to the ground or a player's flag is pulled when carrying the ball, it is a turnover and the ball is set into play at that spot. Interceptions are turnovers and the intercepting team moves on offense. Teams must make at least four complete passes before they are eligible to move across the opponent's goal line. No blocking is allowed.

Variation: Playing more than one game at a time on smaller fields will allow more students to be actively involved in the game. This is also an enjoyable game when played with Frisbees.

DYNAMIC PHYSICAL EDUCATION LESSON PLAN— ALTERNATE
Softball-Related Activities (Lesson 3)
Level II

Supplies and Equipment Needed:
Station 1: 2 bats, 2 balls, 2 tees
Station 2: 2 bases, 1 bat, 1 ball
Station 3: 2 pitching targets, 2 balls
Station 4: 1 bat, 2 balls

MOVEMENT EXPERIENCE— CONTENT	ORGANIZATION AND TEACHING HINTS	EXPECTED STUDENT OBJECTIVES AND OUTCOMES

INTRODUCTORY AND FITNESS DEVELOPMENT ACTIVITIES (2 – 3 MINUTES)

This lesson may be substituted for any of the previous lessons. Use the introductory and fitness development activities given in the sequence plans.

LESSON FOCUS (15 – 20 MINUTES)

Softball-Related Activities

DPE pp. 684 – 694

Station (Small Group) Instruction
Station 1 - Catching Fly Balls

1. Students take turns hitting fly balls to fielders.
2. Try different catching techniques.

Station 2 - Bunting techniques

1. Square around.
2. Run the upper hand up the bat halfway.
3. Hold the bat level.
4. Just meet the ball.
5. Direct the ball down either foul line.

Station 3 - Pitching to Targets

1. Set up normal (35') pitching distance.
2. Each pitcher gets to pitch to three batters.
3. Score either walk or strikeout.
4. Review pitching rules.

Station 4 - Hitting Practice

1. Need pitcher, batter, catcher, and fielders. Each batter gets six swings.
2. Review stress points for hitting.

Squads form the basis for rotative activity.

Need a batter and fielders. If more than six on a squad, divide into two groups.

Use full squad—pitcher, catcher, first baseman, and the rest infielders. One batter is up. He gets three bunts. On the third bunt, he runs to first base. He then becomes a fielder. Establish a system of rotation.

Divide into two groups. Need batter, retriever, and scorer.

Full squad activity.

Controlled pitching is important. See that the batter has a good chance to hit.

Use two softballs.

Aff.—The student will be able to cooperate in practicing designated skills at the respective stations.

PM.—The student will develop enough skill to play Hit the Bat successfully.

Cog.—The student will be able to verbalize proper strategy in playing the ball with respect to the game.

PM.—The student will develop reasonable skill in bunting.

PM.—The student, as a pitcher, will be able to strike out two of three batters.

PM.—Out of six swings, the student will be able to hit solidly four times.

Cog.—The student will be able to recount the important stress points in hitting techniques.

GAME (5 – 7 MINUTES)

Softball Lead-Up Games

Beat Ball—*DPE*, p. 697
Supplies: Soft softball, bat, batting tee (optional)
Skills: All softball skills
One team is at bat and the other team in the field. The object of the game is to hit the ball and run around the bases before the fielding team can catch the ball, throw it to first base, and then throw it to the catcher at home plate. If the ball beats the hitter home or a fly ball is caught, it is an out. If the hitter beats the ball to home plate, a run is scored. All players on a team bat once before switching positions with the fielding team. The ball must be hit into fair territory before the hitter can run. Only three pitches are allowed each hitter.

MOVEMENT EXPERIENCE— CONTENT	ORGANIZATION AND TEACHING HINTS	EXPECTED STUDENT OBJECTIVES AND OUTCOMES

Variations:

1. Depending on the maturity of the players, a batting tee may be used. The hitter can be allowed the option of using the batting tee or hitting a pitched ball.

2. The pitcher can be selected from the batting team. This assures that an attempt will be made to make pitches that can be hit.

3. The distance can be varied so that hitters have a fair opportunity to score. If hitters score too easily, another base can be added.

Kick Softball—*DPE*, p. 696

Supplies: A soccer ball or another ball to be kicked

Skills: Kicking a rolling ball, throwing, catching, running bases

The batter stands in the kicking area, a 3-ft-square home plate. The batter kicks the ball rolled on the ground by the pitcher. The ball should be rolled at moderate speed. An umpire calls balls and strikes. A strike is a ball that rolls over the 3-ft square. A ball rolls outside this area. Strikeouts and walks are called the same as in regular softball. The number of foul balls allowed should be limited. No base stealing is permitted. Otherwise, the game is played like softball.

Variations:

1. The batter kicks a stationary ball. This saves time, since there is no pitching.

2. Punch Ball. The batter can hit a volleyball as in a volleyball serve or punch a ball pitched by the pitcher.

Two-Pitch Softball—*DPE*, p. 695

Supplies: A softball, a bat

Skills: Most softball skills, except regular pitching

Two-Pitch Softball is played like regular softball with the following changes.

1. A member of the team at bat pitches. A system of rotation should be set up so that every child takes a turn as pitcher.

2. The batter has only two pitches in which to hit the ball, and he must hit a fair ball on one of these pitches or he is out. The batter can foul the first ball, but if he fouls the second, he is out. There is no need to call balls or strikes.

3. The pitcher does not field the ball. A member of the team in the field acts as the fielding pitcher.

4. If the batter hits the ball, regular softball rules are followed. No stealing is permitted, however.

Teaching suggestion: Since the pitcher is responsible for pitching a ball that can be hit, the pitching distance can be shortened to give the batter ample opportunity to hit the ball. The instructor can act as the pitcher.

Variation: Three Strikes: In this game, the batter is allowed three pitches (strikes) to hit the ball. Otherwise, the game proceeds as in Two-Pitch Softball.

DYNAMIC PHYSICAL EDUCATION LESSON PLAN— ALTERNATE
Fundamental Skills Using Balance Beams and Manipulative Equipment

Supplies and Equipment Needed:
  Balance-beam benches, mats for landing
  12 beanbags, hoops, wands, and playground balls
  Jump ropes

MOVEMENT EXPERIENCE— CONTENT	ORGANIZATION AND TEACHING HINTS	EXPECTED STUDENT OBJECTIVES AND OUTCOMES

INTRODUCTORY AND FITNESS DEVELOPMENT ACTIVITIES (2 – 3 MINUTES)

This lesson may be substituted for any of the previous lessons. Use the introductory and fitness development activities given in the sequenced lesson plans.

LESSON FOCUS ACTIVITY (15 – 20 MINUTES)

Fundamental Skills Using Balance Beams and Manipulative Equipment

Balance Beam Activities with Beanbags and Balls

1. Use one or two beanbags and toss to self in various fashions—around the body, under the legs, etc.
2. Use a playground ball and toss to self.
3. Bounce the ball on the floor and on the beam. Dribble the ball.
4. Play catch with a partner.
5. Balance a beanbag on various body parts. Use more than one bag.
6. Student's choice.

Balance Beam Activities with Wands and Hoops

1. Carry a wand or hoop. Step over the wand or through the hoop in various fashions—forward, sideways, backward.
2. Step over or go under wands or hoops held by a partner.
3. Hula-hoop on various body parts while moving across the beam.
4. Balance a wand on various body parts while moving across the beam.
5. Balance a wand in one hand and twirl a hoop in the other hand and proceed across the beam.
6. Student's choice.

Challenge Activities

1. Hop the length of the beam.
2. Walk the beam with the eyes closed. Spot the performer.
3. Perform some animal walks across the beam (i.e., Cat Walk, Lame Dog Walk and Crab Walk).
4. Walk to center of beam and do a complete body turn on one foot.

DPE pp. 467 – 469

Move deliberately, catching their balance after each step. Speed is not a goal.

Mats should be placed at the end of each beam to cushion the dismount and allow selected rolls and stunts.

Encourage quality dismounts. Students should pause at the end of the beam before dismounting.

Both sides of the body should receive equal treatment. If students walk with the left side leading, they should also walk with the right leading.

If the student steps off the beam, he should step back on at that point and continue to the end of the beam.

Students should look ahead at eye level, rather than at their feet.

Challenge the students to develop some of their own ideas and give them time to implement them.

Use return activities so students accomplish something on their way back to the beam.

PM.—The student will be able to walk the beam forward and backward while manipulating a piece of equipment.

Cog.—The student will be able to name five activities where balance is the major factor.

Aff.—Balance is affected a great deal by the auditory and visual senses. Experiment by trying various balance activities and eliminating some of the senses.

PM.—The student will be able to perform a full turn on the beam while balancing a wand on some body part.

246

MOVEMENT EXPERIENCE—CONTENT	ORGANIZATION AND TEACHING HINTS	EXPECTED STUDENT OBJECTIVES AND OUTCOMES

5. Partners start on opposite ends of the beam and attempt to pass catch other without losing their balance.

GAME (5 – 7 MINUTES)

Hand Hockey—*DPE*, p. 576

Supplies: 8-inch gray foam balls

Skills: Striking, volleying

The players are on two teams. Half of the players on each team are guards and are stationed on the goal line as defenders. The other half are active players and are scattered throughout the playing area in front of their goal line.

The object of the game is to bat or push the ball with either hand so that it crosses the goal line that the other team is defending. Players may move the ball as in hockey but may not throw, hoist, or kick it. The defensive goal line players are limited to one step into the playing field when playing the ball.

The ball is put into play by being rolled into the center of the field. After a goal has been scored or after a specified period, guards become active players, and vice versa. An out-of-bounds ball goes to the opposite team and is put into play by being rolled from the sidelines into the playing area. If the ball becomes entrapped among players, play is stopped, and the ball is put into play again by a roll from the referee.

Players must play the ball and not resort to rough tactics. A player who is called for unnecessary roughness or for illegally handling the ball must go to the sidelines (as in hockey) and remain in the penalty area until the players change positions. Players should scatter and attempt to pass to each other rather than bunch around the ball.

Once youngsters learn the game, introduce more than one ball to increase the amount of activity.

Variation: <u>Scooter Hockey</u>. The active center players from each team are on gym scooters. The position that each child takes on the gym scooter can be specified or can be a free choice. Possible positions are kneeling, sitting, or balancing on the tummy. A hard surface is needed. This game version is usually played indoors on a basketball court.

Nine Lives—*DPE*, p. 577

Supplies: Fleece balls

Skills: Throwing, dodging

Any number of fleece balls can be used—the more the better. At a signal, players get a ball and hit as many people below waist level as possible. When a player counts that she has been hit nine times, she leaves the game and stands out of bounds until she has counted to 25. A player may run anywhere with a ball or to get a ball, but he may possess only one ball at a time. Players must not be hit in the head. This puts the thrower out.

Teaching suggestion: Children often cheat about the number of times they have been hit. A few words about fair play may be necessary, but a high degree of activity is the important game element.

Variations:

1. For a ball caught on the fly, a designated number of hits may be taken away.
2. Either left- or right-hand throwing can be specified.

DYNAMIC PHYSICAL EDUCATION LESSON PLAN— ALTERNATE
Fundamental Skills Using Climbing Ropes
Level II

Supplies and Equipment Needed:
16 climbing ropes
Tumbling mats

MOVEMENT EXPERIENCE—CONTENT	ORGANIZATION AND TEACHING HINTS	EXPECTED STUDENT OBJECTIVES AND OUTCOMES

INTRODUCTORY AND FITNESS DEVELOPMENT ACTIVITIES (2 – 3 MINUTES)

This lesson may be substituted for any of the previous lessons. Use the introductory and fitness development activities given in the sequenced lesson plans.

LESSON FOCUS (15 – 20 MINUTES)

Fundamental Skills Using Climbing Ropes

Supported Pull-Ups

1. Kneel and pull to feet. Return.
2. Sit, pull to feet and back to seat.
3. Stand, keep body straight while lowering body to the floor.

Hangs

1. Sit, pull body off floor except for feet and hold.
2. Jump up, grasp the rope and hand.
3. Jump up, grasp the rope, and hang and perform the following leg movements:
   a. One or both knees up
   b. Bicycling movement
   c. Half-lever
   d. Choice movement

Swinging and Jumping.

To take off, the child reaches high and jumps to a bent-arm position. Landing should be with bent knees.

1. Swing and jump. Add half turns and full turns.
2. Swing and return to the perch. Add single- and double-knee bends.
3. Jump for distance, over a high-jump bar or through a hoop.
4. Swing and pick up a bowling pin and return to the perch.
5. Carry objects (e.g., beanbags, balls, deck tennis rings). A partner, standing to the side away from the takeoff bench, can put articles to be carried back on the takeoff perch by placing each article between her knees or feet.
6. Not using a takeoff device, run toward a swinging rope, grasp it, and gain momentum for swinging.

DPE pp. 460 – 464

Place tumbling mats under all the climbing apparatus.

Caution students not to slide quickly down the rope to prevent rope burns.

Swinging on the ropes is motivating and should be done with bent arms.

The pull-up and hang activities are excellent lead-ups for students who are not strong enough to climb the rope.

PM.—The student will be able to demonstrate proper techniques in the following activities:
1. Climbing with the scissors grip
2. Leg round rest
3. Reverse scissors grip
4. Instep squeeze

248

MOVEMENT EXPERIENCE—CONTENT	ORGANIZATION AND TEACHING HINTS	EXPECTED STUDENT OBJECTIVES AND OUTCOMES

Climbing Activities

1. Scissors grip:
   Place the rope inside the knees and outside the foot. Climb halfway up and practice descending using the reverse scissors grip before climbing to the top of the rope.
2. Leg around rest:
   Wrap the left leg around the rope and over the instep of the left foot from the outside. Stand on the rope and instep with right foot.

Descending Techniques

1. Reverse scissors grip
2. Leg around rest.
3. Instep squeeze: The rope is squeezed between the insteps by keeping the heels together.

Activities Using Two Ropes

1. Straight arm hand: Jump up, grasp rope and hand.
2. Arms with different leg positions.
   a. Single and double knee lifts
   b. Half lever
   c. Full lever
   d. Bicycle—pedal feet like bicycle
3. Pull-ups
   Same as pull-up on a single rope.
4. Inverted hands
   a. With feet wrapped around the ropes.
   b. with feet against the inside of the ropes.
   c. With the toes pointed and the feet not touching the ropes.

Students should be encouraged to learn the various techniques of climbing and descending.

If there are only a few climbing ropes, it would be a good teaching technique to have the nonclimbing students work on another unit. Some good units are beanbags, hoops, wands, and/or playground balls.

Rope climbing is a very intense and demanding activity. A good idea is to break up the lesson focus with a game or relay. This will also offer leg development activity.

If other climbing equipment is available such as a horizontal ladder and/or exercise bar, many activities are offered in *DPE* pp. 465 – 466.

Two ropes, hanging close together, are needed.

Spotting should be done when students are performing inverted hangs on two ropes.

Cog.—The student will be able to describe the safety rules necessary when climbing ropes.

Aff.—Rope climbing demands a great deal of upper body strength. Discuss how muscular strength develops through overloading and increasing the demands placed on the body.

Cog.—Rope climbing is excellent for developing upper body strength. Discuss the major muscle groups that are used and developed when climbing ropes.

Cog.—The larger the diameter of the muscle, the greater the amount of force that can be generated. Identify various muscles of the body and their relative size.

PM.—The student will be able to perform the following two-rope activities:
1. Straight-arm hang
2. Hangs with different leg positions
3. Pull-ups
4. Inverted hangs

Aff.—Rope climbing favors those students who are small and carry little body fat. Discuss individual differences and how different sports favor certain types of body build.

GAME (5 – 7 MINUTES)

Nonda's Car Lot—*DPE*, p. 578
   Supplies: None
   Skills: Running, dodging
   One player is it and stands in the center of the area between two lines established about 50 ft apart. The class selects four brands of cars (e.g., Honda, Corvette, Toyota, Cadillac). Each student then selects a car from the four but does not tell anyone what it is.
   The tagger calls out a car name. All students who selected that name attempt to run to the other line without getting tagged. The tagger calls out the cars until all students have run. When a child (car) gets tagged, she must sit down at the spot of the tag. She cannot move but may tag other students who run too near her. When the one who is it calls out "Car lot," all of the cars must go. The game is played until all students have been tagged.

Indianapolis 500—*DPE*, p. 577
   Supplies: None
   Skills: Running, tagging
   Children start in a large circle and are numbered off in threes or fours. A race starter says "Start your engines," and then calls out a number. Those children with the corresponding number run clockwise around the circle and try to tag players in front of them. If the leader yells "Pit stop," all runners have to stop and return to their original position. If "Accident" is called by the leader, all runners must change direction and proceed counterclockwise. Change the starter often.

DYNAMIC PHYSICAL EDUCATION LESSON PLAN— ALTERNATE
Fundamental Skills Using Magic Ropes
Level II

Supplies and Equipment Needed:
  6–10 magic ropes per class
  Balls
  Beanbags

MOVEMENT EXPERIENCE— CONTENT	ORGANIZATION AND TEACHING HINTS	EXPECTED STUDENT OBJECTIVES AND OUTCOMES

INTRODUCTORY AND FITNESS DEVELOPMENT ACTIVITIES (2 – 3 MINUTES)

This lesson may be substituted for any of the previous lessons. Use the introductory and fitness development activities given in the sequenced lesson plans.

LESSON FOCUS (15 – 20 MINUTES)

Fundamental Skills Using Magic Ropes

Single-Rope Activities

1. Jump back and forth, feet uncrossed.
2. Jump back and forth, feet crossed and uncrossed alternately.
3. Jump back and forth, feet crossed.
4. Hop back and forth over rope using both right and left foot in turn.
5. Jump the rope and perform various body turns while jumping.
6. Change body shapes and sizes while jumping.
7. Crawl or slide under the rope.
8. Alternate going over and under the rope.
9. Crouch jump over the rope.
10. Run and high jump (scissors kick) over rope.
11. Choice—exploratory activity.

Double Rope Activities

1. Ropes parallel to each other:
   a. Jump in one side, out other.
   b. Hop in one side, out other.
   c. Crouch jump in and out.
   d. Perform various animal walks in and out.
   e. Exploratory activity.
2. Ropes crossed at right angles to each other:
   a. Perform various movements from one to the other.
   b. Jump into one area, crawl out other.
3. One rope above other, create "barbed wire fence" effect:
   a. Step through ropes without touching.
   b. Crouch jump through.
   c. Vary height and distance apart in which ropes are placed.

DPE pp. 474 – 475

Divide the class into small groups of five or six members.

Start activities with the rope at a 6" height and progressively raise it to increase the challenge.

Emphasize the point that students are *not* supposed to touch the rope. The objective is body management and learning to control the body in space.

Rotate the rope holders.

Students should approach the rope from one end and perform their activities to the other end of the rope.

The child next in turn should begin movement when performing child is near the end of the rope.

Try holding one end near the floor and the other end 2–3 ft. high. Children then progress from the low end to the high and more difficult end.

PM.—The student will be able to hop back and forth from one end of the rope to the other without touching the rope at a height of 10".

Cog.—The student will understand and be able to recite why magic ropes are used in the program—to develop body management skills.

Aff.—Carbon monoxide in tobacco smoke reduces the physical endurance of the smoker. Discuss the detrimental effects of this habit.

MOVEMENT EXPERIENCE—CONTENT	ORGANIZATION AND TEACHING HINTS	EXPECTED STUDENT OBJECTIVES AND OUTCOMES

4. Miscellaneous—Perform the activities while balancing a beanbag on top of head or while bouncing a ball.
5. Choice—exploratory activity.

GAME (5 – 7 MINUTES)

Busy Bee—*DPE*, p. 572

Supplies: None

Skills: Fundamental locomotor movements

Half of the children form a large circle, facing in, and are designated the stationary players. The other children seek partners from this group, and stand in front of the stationary players. An extra child in the center is the busy bee. The bee calls out directions such as "Back to back," "Face to face," "Shake hands," "Kneel on one knee [or both]," and "Hop on one foot." The other children follow these directions.

The center child then calls out, "Busy bee." Stationary players stand still, and their partners seek other partners while the center player also tries to get a partner. The child without a partner becomes the new busy bee.

Teaching suggestions: Children should be instructed to think about the different movements that they might have the class do if they become the busy bee. In changing partners, children must select a partner other than the stationary player next to them. After a period of time, the active and stationary players are rotated. Different methods of locomotion should also be used when children change partners.

Variations:

1. All children who have not repeated any partner during a specified number of exchanges (say, ten) and who have not been caught as the busy bee are declared winners.

2. Instead of standing back to back, children lock elbows and sit down. After they sit down and are declared safe, they can get up, and the game proceeds as described.

Box Ball—*DPE*, p. 572

Supplies: A sturdy box, 2 ft square and about 12 in. deep; four volleyballs (or similar balls)

Skills: Running, ball handling

The class is divided into four even teams, with six to ten players per team. Each team occupies one side of a hollow square at an equal distance from the center. Players face inward and number off consecutively from right to left.

A box containing four balls is put in the center. The instructor calls a number, and the player from each team who has that number runs forward to the box, takes a ball, and runs to the head of his line, taking the place of player 1. In the meantime, the players in the line have moved to the left just enough to fill in the space left by the runner. On reaching the head of the line, the runner passes the ball to the next person and so on down the line to the end child. The last child runs forward and returns the ball to the box. The first team to return the ball to the box scores a point.

The runner must not pass the ball down the line until he is in place at the head of the line. The ball must be caught and passed by each child. Failure to conform to these rules results in team disqualification. Runners stay at the head of the line, retaining their original number. Keeping the lines in consecutive number sequence is not important.

Lesson Plans for the School Year
Developmental Level III

WEEK	INTRODUCTORY ACTIVITY	FITNESS DEVELOPMENT ACTIVITY	LESSON FOCUS ACTIVITY	GAME ACTIVITY	PAGE
1	Move and Freeze on Signal	Teacher Leader Exercises	Orientation	Class Management Games	255
2	Fastest Tag in the West	Teacher-Leader Exercises	Soccer Skills(1)	Soccer Related	257
3	Move and Freeze	Teacher-Leader Exercises	Soccer Skills(1)	Soccer Related	260
4	Pop-Up	Hexagon Hustle	Soccer Skills(3)	Soccer Related	264
5	Run, Stop, and Pivot	Hexagon Hustle	Rhythmic Movement(1)	Triplet Stoop Pacman	266
6	European Running	Hexagon Hustle	Rhythmic Movement(2)	Cageball Target Throw Chain Tag	270
7	Hospital Tag	Circuit Training	Racquet Sport Skills	Volley Tennis One Wall Racquetball and Handball	273
8	Medic Tag	Circuit Training	Football Skills(1)	Football Related	276
9	Pyramid Power	Circuit Training	Football Skills(2)	Football Related	279
10	Stretching	Jogging	Walking and Jogging Skills	Recreational Activities	283
11	Stretching	Jogging	Cross-Country Running/Walking	Recreational Activities	285
12	Partner Over and Under	Exercises to Music	Individual Rope Jumping Skills(1)	Right Face One Base Tagball	287
13	Move and Manipulate	Exercises to Music	Tug-of-War Ropes and Frisbee Skills	Frisbee Games	290
14	New Leader	Exercises to Music	Hockey Skills(1)	Hockey Related	294
15	Group Over and Under	Exercises to Music	Hockey Skills(2)	Hockey Related	297
16	Four Corners Sport Movement	Astronaut Drills	Basketball Skills(1)	Basketball Related	300
17	Beanbag Touch and Go	Astronaut Drills	Basketball Skills(2)	Basketball Related	304
18	Leapfrog	Astronaut Drills	Basketball Skills(3)	Basketball Related	307
19	Living Obstacles	Partner Aerobic Fitness and Resistance Exercises	Recreational Activities	Recreational Activities	309
20	Barker's Hoopla	Partner Aerobic Fitness and Resistance Exercises	Gymnastics and Climbing Rope Skills	Star Wars Flag Chase	311
21	Following Activity	Parachute Fitness	Gymnastics and Juggling Skills	Team Handball Octopus Bomb the Pins	315
22	Ball Activities	Parachute Fitness	Gymnastics and Bench Skills	Pin Knockout Over the Wall	320

WEEK	INTRODUCTORY ACTIVITY	FITNESS DEVELOPMENT ACTIVITY	LESSON FOCUS ACTIVITY	GAME ACTIVITY	PAGE
23	Rubber Band	Aerobic Fitness	Gymnastics and Balance Beam Skills	Octopus Fast Pass	324
24	Moving to Music	Aerobic Fitness	Manipulative Skills Using Wands and Hula Hoops	Jollyball Circle Touch Galactic Empire and Rebels	327
25	Vanishing Beanbags	Challenge Course	Volleyball Skills(1)	Volleyball Related	332
26	Marking	Challenge Course	Volleyball Skills(2)	Volleyball Related	336
27	European Running with Variations	Challenge Course	Rhythmic Movement(3)	Whistle Ball Jump the Shot Variations	339
28	Pop-Up	Continuity Drills	Rhythmic Movement(4)	Scooter Kickball Touchdown Chain Tag	343
29	Move, Exercise on Signal	Continuity Drills	Juggling Skills and Pyramids	Pyramid Building	347
30	Long Rope Routine	Continuity Drills	Relay Activities	Relays	351
31	Stretching	Jogging	Track and Field Skills(1)	Shuttle/Circular Relays One on One Contests	353
32	Stretching	Jogging	Track and Field Skills(2)	Shuttle/Circular Relays One on One Contests	356
33	Stretching	Jogging	Track and Field Skills(3)	Shuttle/Circular Relays One on One Contests	358
34	Personal Choice	Squad Leader Exercises with Task Cards	Long Rope Jumping Skills	Cageball Target Throw Sunday	360
35	Personal Choice	Squad Leader Exercises with Task Cards	Softball Skills(1)	Softball Related	363
36	Personal Choice	Squad Leader Exercises with Task Cards	Softball Skills(2)	Softball Related	367
Alternate Lesson Plans					
A	Substitute	Substitute	Rhythmic Movement(5)	Scooter Kickball	370
B	Substitute	Substitute	Rhythmic Gymnastics	Touchdown Circle Touch Cageball Target Throw	372
C	Substitute	Substitute	Climbing Rope Skills	Whistle Mixer Touchdown Chain Tag	376

DYNAMIC PHYSICAL EDUCATION LESSON PLAN
Orientation and Class Management Games
Level III

Orientation Lesson Plan

The first week of school should be used to teach students the system you are going to use throughout the year. The following are reminders you might find useful in establishing your expectations and routines.

1. Establish rules and expectations. Discuss your expectations with the class to assure students understand reasons for your guidelines. Explain what the consequences are when rules are not followed. Show where time-out boxes are located and how they will be used.
2. Explain to the class the method you will use to learn names. It might be helpful to ask classroom teachers to have students put their name on a piece of masking tape (name tag). Tell students that you will ask them their names on a regular basis until it is learned.
3. Develop entry and exit behaviors for students coming and leaving physical education classes. Students should know how to enter the instructional area and to leave equipment alone until told to use it. If squads are used for instruction, place students into squads and practice moving into formation on signal.
4. Decide how excuses for non-participation will be handled. If possible, set up a routine where the school nurse determines which students are excused for health reasons.
5. Safety is important. Children should receive safety rules to be followed on apparatus and playground equipment. Safety procedures to be followed in physical education classes should be discussed.
6. Illustrate how you will stop and start the class. In general, a whistle (or similar loud signal) and a raised hand is effective for stopping the class. A voice command should be used to start the class. Telling the class when before what (*DPE*, Chapter 6) will assure they do not begin before instructions are finished.
7. Discuss the issue, distribution, and care of equipment. Make students responsible for acquiring a piece of equipment and returning it at the end of the lesson. Place equipment around the perimeter of the teaching area to reduce the chance of students fighting over a piece of equipment.
8. Explain to the class that the format of the daily lesson will include an introductory activity, fitness development, lesson focus, and finish with a game activity.
9. Practice various teaching formations such as open-squad formation and closed-squad formation. Practice moving into a circle while moving (fall-in). Transitions between formations should be done while moving, i.e., jogging from scatter formation into a circular formation.
10. Refer to Chapters 5, 6, and 7 in *DPE* for detailed information about planning, developing an effective learning environment, and class management strategies.

INTRODUCTORY ACTIVITY (2–3 MINUTES)

Move and Freeze on Signal
Have students move throughout the area using a variety of locomotor movements. On signal (whistle), they quickly freeze. Try to reduce the response latency by reinforcing students who stop quickly on signal. The primary objective should be to teach students the importance of moving under control (without bumping others or falling down) and quickly freezing, ready to listen to upcoming instructions.

FITNESS DEVELOPMENT ACTIVITIES (7–8 MINUTES)

Teacher Leader Exercises

Arm Circles	30 seconds
Push-Up Challenges	30 seconds
Bend and Twist	30 seconds
Treadmill	30 seconds
Abdominal Challenges	40 seconds
Single-Leg Crab Kick	30 seconds
Reverse Curl	40 seconds

Run in Place	35 seconds
Standing Hip Bend	30 seconds

Conclude the routine with 2–4 minutes of walking/jogging, rope jumping or other aerobic activity.

Increase the duration of exercises by 10–20% over the previous week.

LESSON FOCUS (15–20 MINUTES)

Since much time during the first week is used for orientation procedures and management, no lesson focus activity is scheduled.

GAME (5–7 MINUTES)

Play one or two management games to teach students how to move into partner and small group formation. The following games can be used to teach students such management goals in an enjoyable and efficient manner.

Back to Back—*DPE, p. 556*
Supplies: None
Skills: Fundamental locomotor movements
Students move under control throughout the area using a variety of locomotor movements. On signal, each child stands back to back (or toe to toe) with another child. If one child ends up without a partner, the teacher takes this student as a partner. Youngsters who do not find a partner nearby run to a designated spot in the center of the area. This helps assure that students do not run around looking for a partner or feel left out. Students who move to the center spot quickly find a partner and move out of the area (to avoid crowding around the center spot). Emphasis should be placed finding a partner near them, not searching for a friend, and taking a different partner each time.

Whistle Mixer—*DPE, p. 580*
Supplies: None
Skills: All basic locomotor movements
Children are scattered throughout the area. To begin, they move in any direction they wish. The teacher whistles a number of times in succession and raises the same number of fingers above their head to signal the group size. Children then form small groups with the number in each group equal to the number of whistles. For example, if there are four short whistles, children form circles of four—no more, no less. The goal is to find the correct number of students as quickly as possible. As soon as a group has the desired number, they sit down to signal that other may not join the group. Children who cannot find a group nearby should be encouraged to move to the center of the area and raise their hands to facilitate finding others without a group.

DYNAMIC PHYSICAL EDUCATION LESSON PLAN
Soccer Skills (Lesson 1)
Level III

Supplies and Equipment Needed:
  One ball per student (8" foam rubber balls or junior soccer balls)
  Cones for marking areas for lead-up activities
  Pinnies for soccer lead-up games
  Jump ropes

MOVEMENT EXPERIENCE— CONTENT	ORGANIZATION AND TEACHING HINTS	EXPECTED STUDENT OBJECTIVES AND OUTCOMES

INTRODUCTORY ACTIVITY (2 – 3 MINUTES)

Fastest Tag in the West

All students are it. On signal, they try to tag each other. If they are tagged, they must freeze, but they are eligible to tag other students who pass near them. If two or more players tag each other simultaneously, they are both/all "frozen."

DPE p. 257

An area at least 30 ft. by 50 ft. is recommended.

Restart the game frequently.

Vary the type of locomotor movement the class can use to chase and flee, or the part of the body that is tagged.

PM.—The student will be able to dodge/elude quickly without falling or colliding with another student.

Aff.—Fair play is of paramount importance in game activities. Discuss the importance of students' being their own referees in many games.

FITNESS DEVELOPMENT ACTIVITIES (7 – 8 MINUTES)

Teacher Leader Exercises

Tape alternating segments of silence (10 seconds) to signal a change of exercise and music to signal the duration of exercise (30 seconds).

Arm Circles	30 seconds
Push-Up Challenges	30 seconds
Bend and Twist	30 seconds
Treadmill	30 seconds
Sit-Up Challenges	30 seconds
Single-Leg Crab Kick	30 seconds
Knee to Chest Curl	30 seconds
Run in Place	30 seconds
Standing Hip Bend	30 seconds

Conclude the routine with 2–4 minutes of jogging, rope jumping or other aerobic activity.

Increase the duration of exercises by 10–20% over the previous week.

DPE pp. 289 – 299

Scatter formation.

Allow students to adjust the work load to their ability and fitness level. This implies that some students will perform more repetitions in the same amount of time.

Emphasize proper form and technique.

Rotate to different parts of the teaching area and help motivate students.

Cog.—Know why it is necessary to increase the number of repetitions (overload principle).

PM.—The student will be able to perform all activities.

Aff.—A positive attitude toward exercise and its value to people.

LESSON FOCUS (15 – 20 MINUTES)

Soccer Skill (1)

Skills

1. Instep kick: approach at 45° angle, top of instep meets ball. Place non-kicking foot alongside ball.
2. Side of foot kick: Short distance kick; keep toe down. Use both the inside and outside of the foot.

DPE pp. 663 – 665

Description of kicks and traps.

Partner or triangle formation, one ball for two or three children.

Keep head down, eyes on ball, follow through.

8" foam rubber training balls are excellent substitutes as they remove the fear of being hurt by a kicked soccer ball.

PM.—The student will be able to pass, kick, and trap the ball successfully at the end of the week.

Cog.—The student will be able to state two reasons why, in soccer activities, accuracy is much preferred over raw power and lack of control.

MOVEMENT EXPERIENCE— CONTENT	ORGANIZATION AND TEACHING HINTS	EXPECTED STUDENT OBJECTIVES AND OUTCOMES
3. Sole of the foot trap: Use sole of foot to stop ball; make sure weight is placed on the non-receiving foot. 4. Foot trap: Use side of foot, learn to "give" with leg so ball doesn't ricochet off foot.	If short of gray foam balls, substitute 8 1/2" playground balls or soccer balls. Partially deflate the balls so they move more slowly and allow for increased success. Make sure students handle the ball with their feet, not the hands. They should retrieve and move the balls with feet only.	Aff.—Even in basic lead-up games, teamwork is necessary for success and enjoyment by all. Cog.—The student will be able to state the basic rules necessary for soccer lead-up games.

Drills
 	
1. Ball juggling
  a. Alternate feet
  b. Twice with one foot, then other foot
2. Dribbling, marking and ball recovery
3. Body control (trapping)
  a. Inside of thigh
  b. Chest
4. Dribbling and passing
	DPE pp. 668 – 674
	
	Individual work; let ball bounce once when changing feet.
	
	Pairs scattered; one has a soccer ball.
	
	Groups of two or three; one acts as a feeder (rotate feeders); girls should fold arms across chest for protection.
	
	Three-player shuttle drill.
	
	The grid system described in DPE, pp. 669–673 is an excellent way to keep many children simultaneously involved in learning soccer skills and drills.
		Aff.—The student will learn to appreciate individual differences and show concern for the welfare of others.
		
		Aff.—Cooperation needs to be learned before students can compete with others. Discuss how it is impossible to have a competitive game if others choose not to cooperate and follow rules.

GAME (5 – 7 MINUTES)

Soccer Lead-Up Games

Dribblerama—*DPE*, p. 675
  Supplies: One soccer ball for each player
  Skills: Dribbling, protecting the ball
  The playing area is a large circle or square, clearly outlined. All players dribble within the area. The game is played on two levels.
    Level 1: Each player dribbles throughout the area, controlling the ball so that it does not touch another ball. If a touch occurs, both players go outside the area and dribble counterclockwise around the area. Once youngsters have completed dribbling one lap of the counterclockwise path, they may reenter the game.
    Level 2: While dribbling and controlling the ball, each player attempts to kick any other ball out of the area. When a ball is kicked out, the player owning that ball takes it outside and dribbles around the area. Play continues until only two or three players who have not lost control of their ball are left. These are declared the winners. Bring all players back into the game and repeat.

Sideline Soccer—*DPE*, p. 676
  Supplies: A soccer ball, four cones, pinnies (optional)
  Skills: Most soccer skills, competitive play
  The teams line up on the sidelines of the rectangle. Three or four active players from each team are called from the end of the team line. These players remain active until a point is scored; then they rotate to the other end of the line.
  The object is to kick the ball between cones that define the scoring area. The active players on each team compete against each other, aided by their teammates on the sidelines.
  To start play, a referee drops the ball between two opposing players at the center of the field. To score, the ball must be kicked last by an active player and must go through the goal at or below shoulder height. A goal counts one point. Sideline players may pass to an active teammate, but a sideline kick cannot score a goal.
  Regular rules generally prevail, with special attention to the restrictions of no pushing, holding, tripping, or other rough play. Rough play is a foul and causes a point to be awarded to the other team. For an out-of-bounds ball, the team on the side of the field where the ball went out-of-bounds is awarded a free kick near that spot. No score can result from a free kick. Violation of the touch rule also results in a free kick.
  Teaching suggestions: A system of rotation in which active players move to the opposite end of the sideline and new players come forth is necessary. More active players can be added when the class is large, and the distance between goals can be increased. After some expertise is acquired, the cones should be moved in to narrow the goal area. If the ball goes over the end line but not through the goal area, the ball is put into play by a defender with a kick.

MOVEMENT EXPERIENCE— CONTENT	ORGANIZATION AND TEACHING HINTS	EXPECTED STUDENT OBJECTIVES AND OUTCOMES

Line Soccer—*DPE*, p. 678

Supplies: A soccer ball, four cones, pinnies

Skills: Most soccer skills, competitive play

Two goal lines are drawn 80 to 120 ft apart. A restraining line is drawn 15 ft in front of and parallel to each goal line. Field width can vary from 50 to 80 ft. Each team stands on one goal line, which it defends. The referee stands in the center of the field and holds a ball. At the whistle, three players (more if the teams are large) run from the right side of each line to the center of the field and become active players. The referee drops the ball to the ground, and the players try to kick it through the other team defending the goal line. The players in the field may advance by kicking only.

A score is made when an active player kicks the ball through the opposing team and over the end line (provided that the kick was made from outside the restraining line). Cones should be put on field corners to define the goal line. A system of player rotation should be set up.

Line players act as goalies and are permitted to catch the ball. Once caught, however, the ball must be laid down immediately and either rolled or kicked. It cannot be punted or drop-kicked.

One point is scored when the ball is kicked over the opponent's goal line below shoulder level. One point is also scored in case of a personal foul involving pushing, kicking, tripping, and the like.

Mini-Soccer—*DPE*, p. 679

Supplies: A soccer ball, pinnies or colors to mark teams, four cones for the corners

Skills: All soccer skills

Each end of the field has a 21-ft-wide goal marked by jumping standards. A 12-yd semicircle on each end outlines the penalty area. The center of the semicircle is at the center of the goal.

The game follows the general rules of soccer, with one goalie for each side. One new feature, the corner kick, needs to be introduced. This kick is used when the ball, last touched by the defense, goes over the end line but not through the goal. The ball is taken to the nearest corner for a direct free kick, and a goal can be scored from the kick. In a similar situation, if the attacking team last touched the ball, the goalkeeper kick is awarded. The goalie puts the ball down and placekicks it forward.

The players are designated as center forward, outside right, outside left, right halfback, left halfback, fullback, and goalie. Players should rotate positions. The forwards play in the front half of the field, and the guards in the back half. Neither position, however, is restricted to these areas entirely, and all may cross the centerline without penalty.

A foul by the defense within its penalty area (semicircle) results in a penalty kick, taken from a point 12 yd distant, directly in front of the goal. Only the goalie is allowed to defend. The ball is in play, with others waiting outside the penalty area.

Teaching suggestion: Position play should be emphasized. The lines of three should be encouraged to spread out and hold reasonable position.

Variation: The number of players can vary, with some games using as few as three on a side in a more restricted area. If teams have more than seven players, the seven-player game should be maintained but with frequent substitutions.

DYNAMIC PHYSICAL EDUCATION LESSON PLAN
Soccer Skills (Lesson 2)
Level III

Supplies and Equipment Needed:
   One soccer ball per student (8" foam rubber balls or junior soccer balls)
   Cones for marking areas for lead-up activities
   Pinnies for soccer lead-up games
   Tom-toms
   Jump ropes

MOVEMENT EXPERIENCE—CONTENT	ORGANIZATION AND TEACHING HINTS	EXPECTED STUDENT OBJECTIVES AND OUTCOMES

INTRODUCTORY ACTIVITY (2 – 3 MINUTES)

Move and Freeze

1. Review the run, walk, hop, jump, leap, slide, gallop and skip with proper stopping.
2. Practice moving and stopping correctly—emphasize basics of proper movement.
3. Add variety to the movements by asking students to respond to the following factors:
   a. Level—low, high, in-between.
   b. Direction—straight, zigzag, circular, curved, forward, backward, upward, downward.
   c. Size—large, tiny, medium movement.
   d. Patterns—forming squares, diamonds, triangles, circles, figure eights.

DPE p. 253

Scatter formation.

A tom-tom can be used. Otherwise, use a whistle to signal the stop.

Emphasize and reinforce creativity.

Change the various factors often and take time to explain the concepts the words describe if children cannot interpret them.

PM.—The student will be able to stop quickly under control.

Cog.—Know the elements involved in stopping quickly.

PM.—The student will be able to execute the various locomotor movements.

Cog.—The student will be able to interpret the concepts the words describe by moving the body in a corresponding manner.

PM.—The student will be able to move the body with ease throughout the range of movement varieties.

FITNESS DEVELOPMENT ACTIVITIES (7 – 8 MINUTES)

Teacher Leader Exercises

Tape alternating segments of silence (10 seconds) to signal a change of exercise and music to signal the duration of exercise (35 seconds).

Sitting Stretch	35 seconds
Push-Up Challenges	35 seconds
Power Jumper	35 seconds
Jumping Jacks	35 seconds
Sit-Up Challenges	35 seconds
Single-Leg Crab Kick	35 seconds
Knee to Chest Curl	35 seconds
Windmill	35 seconds
Trunk Twister	35 seconds

Conclude the routine with 2–4 minutes of jogging, rope jumping or other aerobic activity.

Increase the duration of exercises by 10–20% over the previous week.

DPE pp. 289 – 299

Scatter formation.

Allow students to adjust the work load to their ability and fitness level. This implies that some students will perform more repetitions in the same amount of time.

Emphasize proper form and technique.

Rotate to different parts of the teaching area and help motivate students.

Student leaders can be added this week. Instructional signs with pictures of each exercise help leaders and free the teacher to give individual help to students.

Cog.—The student will be able to explain verbally why correct form is important when performing fitness activities.

PM.—The student will be able to perform all activities.

MOVEMENT EXPERIENCE—CONTENT	ORGANIZATION AND TEACHING HINTS	EXPECTED STUDENT OBJECTIVES AND OUTCOMES

LESSON FOCUS (15 – 20 MINUTES)

Soccer Skills

Soccer

The soccer lesson works well in a circuit of instructional stations. Divide the skills into four to six stations and place the necessary equipment and instructions at each.

DPE pp. 663 – 665

PM.—The student will be able to kick, dribble, trap, and pass the soccer ball by the end of the week.

Skills

1. Outside foot kick: Use the outside of the foot. More of a push than a kick.
2. Dribbling: Move the ball with a series of taps. Start slowly and don't kick the ball too far away from the player.
3. Passing: Start passing the ball from a stationary position and then progress to moving while passing.
4. Goalkeeping/shooting: One player dribbles the ball 15–20 yards and shoots for a goal against a goalie from 15–20 yards away. The goalie, after stopping or retrieving the shot, becomes the dribbler/shooter, with the other player becoming the goalie on his end of the practice area.

One ball per two children—or triangle formation, one ball for each group of three children.

8" foam rubber training balls are useful for learning proper form in soccer activities.

Start expecting quality and accuracy in the kicks, passes, and traps.

Outside foot kick is used for short distances only.

Review the skills taught last lesson and integrate them into this lesson. Proper motor patterns can be learned only when they are reviewed and practiced many times.

Two beanbags spread 15–20 ft. apart on each side of the area for each pair of players; if the groups have three students, the third person can back up the goalie and rotate in after each shot on goal.

Cog.—The student will be able to describe the situations in which the outside foot kick should be used.

Aff.—When soccer is taught in a coed situation, students must appreciate individual differences.

Cog.—Flexibility is the range of motion at a joint. Flexibility is important in kicking activities as more force can be generated over a greater range of motion. Discuss the importance of stretching in order to lengthen connective tissue.

Drills

1. Ball Juggling
   a. Review Week 1
   b. Thigh—start with catch; add successive thigh volleys.
   c. Juggle with foot, thigh, head, thigh and foot and catch.
2. Dribbling, moving and passing drill.
3. Heading, volleying and controlling drill.
4. Passing, guarding and tackling drill.

DPE pp. 623 – 628

Individual work. Be patient with these skills, as varying ability levels will appear.

Let students progress at their own rate.

Partner work: both partners repeat same maneuvers.

Groups of two to three: One player "feeds" the other two with soft underhand tosses; rotate feeders often.

Groups of four: Players need to learn to pass with both right and left feet. Defender should watch the ball, not the passer's feet.

Aff.—Good passes can be easily handled by a teammate. Praise passes and teamwork.

Aff.—Teammates appreciate "soft tosses" when learning to execute chest and thigh traps, volleys, and heading.

PM.—The student will be able to pass without "telegraphing" his pass to a teammate.

MOVEMENT EXPERIENCE— CONTENT	ORGANIZATION AND TEACHING HINTS	EXPECTED STUDENT OBJECTIVES AND OUTCOMES

GAME (5 – 7 MINUTES)

Soccer Lead-Up Games

Bull's-Eye—*DPE*, p. 675
  Supplies: One soccer ball per player
  Skills: Dribbling, protecting the ball
  The playing area is a large outlined area—circle, square, or rectangle. One player holds a ball in her hands, which serves as the bull's-eye. The other players dribble within the area. The player with the bull's-eye attempts to throw her ball (basketball push shot) at any other ball. The ball that is hit now becomes the new bull's-eye. The old bull's-eye becomes one of the dribblers. A new bull's-eye cannot hit back immediately at the old bull's-eye. A dribbler should protect the ball with her body. If the group is large, have two bull's-eyes. No score is kept and no one is eliminated.

Line Soccer—*DPE*, p. 678
  See the Lesson Plan, Soccer Skills (Lesson 1) for a complete game description.

Mini-Soccer—*DPE*, p. 679
  See the Lesson Plan, Soccer Skills (Lesson 1) for a complete game description.

Regulation Soccer.—*DPE*, p. 679
  Supplies: A soccer ball, pinnies
  Skills: All soccer skills
  A team usually consists of three forwards, three midfield players, four backline defenders, and one goalkeeper. Forwards are the main line of attack. They need to develop good control, dribbling, and shooting skills, and they must have a strong desire to score. They should be encouraged to shoot frequently. Midfield players tend to be the powerhouse of the team. They need good passing and tackling skills as well as a high level of cardiovascular fitness. Defenders should work well together and know when to tackle. They should play safely by clearing the ball away from their own penalty area, and not risk dribbling or passing toward their own goal unless it is absolutely safe to do so. Goalkeepers must be quick and agile, be good decision makers, and have ball-handling skills.
  On the toss of the coin, the winning team gets its choice of kicking off or selecting which goal to defend. The loser exercises the option not selected by the winner.
  On the kickoff, the ball must travel forward about 1 yd, and the kicker cannot touch it again until another player has kicked it. The defensive team must be 10 yd away from the kicker. After each score, the team not winning the point gets to kick off. Both teams must be onside at the kickoff. The defensive team must stay onside and out of the center circle until the ball is kicked. Regular soccer rules call for scoring by counting the number of goals made.
  Elementary school children usually play 6-minute quarters. There should be a rest period of 1 minute between quarters and 10 minutes between halves.
  When the ball goes out-of-bounds on the sideline, it is put into play with a throw-in from the spot where it crossed the line. No goal may be scored, nor may the thrower play the ball a second time until it has been touched by another player. All opponents are to be 10 yd back at the time of the throw.
  If the ball is caused to go out-of-bounds on the end line by the attacking team, a goal kick is awarded. The ball is placed in the goal area and kicked beyond the penalty area by a defending player, who may not touch the ball twice in succession. If the ball is touched by a player before it goes out of the penalty area, it is not yet in play and should be kicked again.
  If the defensive team causes the ball to go out-of-bounds over the end line, a corner kick is awarded. The ball is placed 1 yd from the corner of the field and kicked into the field of play by an attacking player. The 10-yd restriction also applies to defensive players.
  If the ball is touched by two opponents at the same time and caused to go out-of-bounds, a drop ball is called. The referee drops the ball between two opposing players, who cannot kick it until it touches the ground. A drop ball also is called when the ball is trapped among downed players.
  If a player is closer to the opponent's goal line than to the ball at a time when the ball is played in a forward direction, it is an offside infraction. Exceptions exist, and a player is not offside when she is in her half of the playing field, when two opponents are nearer their goal line than the attacking player at the moment when the ball is played, or when the ball is received directly from a corner kick, a throw-in, or a goal kick.
  Personal fouls involving unnecessary roughness are penalized. Tripping, striking, charging, holding, pushing, and jumping an opponent intentionally are forbidden.
  It is a foul for any player, except the goalkeeper, to handle the ball with the hands or arms. The goalkeeper is allowed only four steps and must then get rid of the ball. After the ball has left her possession, the goalkeeper may not pick it up again until another player has touched it. Players are not allowed to screen or obstruct opponents, unless they are in control of the ball.

MOVEMENT EXPERIENCE— CONTENT	ORGANIZATION AND TEACHING HINTS	EXPECTED STUDENT OBJECTIVES AND OUTCOMES

Penalties are as follows:

1. A direct kick is awarded for all personal fouls and handballs. A goal can be scored from a direct free kick. Examples of infringements are pushing, tripping, kicking a player, and holding.

2. A penalty kick is awarded if direct free-kick infringements are committed by a defender in his own penalty area.

3. An indirect free kick is awarded for offsides, obstruction, dangerous play such as high kicking, a goalkeeper's taking more than four steps or repossessing the ball before another player has touched it, and playing the ball twice after a dead-ball situation. The ball must be touched by a second player before a goal can be scored. The referee should signal if the kick is indirect by pointing one arm upward vertically.

Teaching suggestions: Players should be encouraged to use the space on the field to the best advantage. When a team is in possession of the ball, players should attempt to find a position from which they can pass either behind the player with the ball to give support, or toward the goal to be in a better position to shoot. When a team is forced into defense, the defenders should get "goalside" of attackers (between the attackers and their own goal) to prevent them from gaining an advantage.

From an early stage, players should be taught to give information to each other during the game, especially when they have possession of the ball. Valuable help can be given by shouting instructions such as "Man on," "You have time," or "Player behind," and also by calling for the ball when in a good position to receive a pass.

DYNAMIC PHYSICAL EDUCATION LESSON PLAN
Soccer Skills (Lesson 3)
Level III

Supplies and Equipment Needed:
  One soccer ball per student (8" foam rubber balls or junior soccer balls)
  Cones for marking areas for lead-up activities
  Pinnies for soccer lead-up games

MOVEMENT EXPERIENCE— CONTENT	ORGANIZATION AND TEACHING HINTS	EXPECTED STUDENT OBJECTIVES AND OUTCOMES

INTRODUCTORY ACTIVITY (2 – 3 MINUTES)

Popcorn

Students pair up with one person on the floor in push-up position and the other standing ready to move. On signal, the standing students move over and under the persons on the floor. The person on the floor changes from a raised to a lowered push-up position each time the partner goes over or under them. On signal, reverse positions.

DPE p. 258

Partner formation.

Encourage students to move as quickly as possible.

Challenge them to see how many times they can go over and under each other.

PM.—The student will be able to move quickly over, under, and around her partner.

Aff.—Warm-up activities only work when an individual motivates himself to move quickly and with intensity.

FITNESS DEVELOPMENT ACTIVITIES (7 – 8 MINUTES)

Hexagon Hustle

Outline a large hexagon with six cones. Place signs with directions on both sides of the cones. The signs identify the hustle activity students are to perform as they approach a cone. Tape alternating segments of silence and music to signal duration of exercise. Music segments indicate aerobic activity while intervals of silence announce flexibility and strength development activities.

Hustle	25 seconds
Push-Up from Knees	30 seconds
Hustle	25 seconds
Bend and Twist (8 counts)	30 seconds
Hustle	25 seconds
Jumping Jacks (4 counts)	30 seconds
Hustle	25 seconds
Curl-Ups (2 counts)	30 seconds
Hustle	25 seconds
Crab Kick (2 counts)	30 seconds
Hustle	25 seconds
Sit and Stretch (8 counts)	30 seconds
Hustle	25 seconds
Power Jumper	30 seconds
Hustle	25 seconds
Squat Thrust (4 counts)	30 seconds

Conclude the Hexagon Hustle with a slow jog or walk.

DPE pp. 303 – 304

Examples of hustle activities that can be listed on signs are:
  1. Jogging
  2. Skipping or galloping
  3. Hopping or jumping
  4. Sliding
  5. Running and leaping
  6. Animal movements
  7. Sport movements such as defensive sliding, running backwards, and carioca step

During the hustle, faster moving students can pass to the outside of the hexagon.

Change directions regularly to keep students spaced evenly along the hexagon.

During the hustle, quality movement rather than speed is the goal.

Cog.—It is necessary to increase the number of repetitions of activity to provide additional stress on the body and increase fitness levels.

PM.—The student will be able to perform one to two more repetitions of each exercise than he was capable of two weeks ago.

Aff.—Physically fit people are rewarded by society. Teachers, parents, and peers respond much more favorably to those fit and attractive.

MOVEMENT EXPERIENCE—CONTENT	ORGANIZATION AND TEACHING HINTS	EXPECTED STUDENT OBJECTIVES AND OUTCOMES

LESSON FOCUS (15 – 20 MINUTES)

Soccer Skills

Since this is the third lesson of soccer, much emphasis should be placed on playing regulation soccer. Teach and/or review the following skills and devote the rest of the time to the game of soccer

Skills

1. Punting—Hold ball in both hands in front of the body and kick the ball on the instep of the foot.
2. Volleying—Practice using different parts of the body.
3. Heading—Keep the eyes on the ball as long as possible before impact. Contact the ball with the forehead.
4. Review any past rules and drills you find necessary for the success of the game activity.

DPE pp. 663 – 665

Students can work in pairs and practice kicking for accuracy to their partner.

Work in pairs and have a partner throw the ball toward different body parts to volley.

Use foam rubber balls for volleying and heading, as they are lighter and more comfortable for the students.

Cog.—In kicking activities, the swinging arc must be flattened. This can be accomplished by transferring the weight, moving ahead over a bent front knee, and reaching out during follow-through. Discuss how the arc should be flattened when kicking is performed.

PM.—The student will be able to punt the ball successfully five times.

PM.—The student will be able to volley and head the ball to a partner who is tossing the ball.

Cog.—The student will be able to state when volleying and heading are used in game situations.

Aff.—Soccer demands that players maintain their positions, rather than all chase the ball. Discuss the need for teamwork and the importance of all positions in the game.

Cog.—The angle of the rebound surface affects the rebound direction of the ball. Illustrate the necessity of adjusting the angle of the rebound surface to develop accuracy in kicking.

GAME (5 – 7 MINUTES)

Soccer Lead-Up Games

Use the Soccer Lead-Up games from previous lessons. See the Lesson Plan, Soccer Skills (Lessons 1 and 2) for complete game descriptions.

DYNAMIC PHYSICAL EDUCATION LESSON PLAN
Rhythmic Movement (Lesson 1)
Level III

Supplies and Equipment Needed:
Tom-tom
Cones
Tape player
Music for rhythms
Hexagon Hustle signs

Dances Taught:
Inside-Out Mixer
Comin' Round the Mountain
Jessie Polka
Cotton-Eyed Joe
Virginia Reel
D'Hammerschmiedsgselln

MOVEMENT EXPERIENCE—CONTENT	ORGANIZATION AND TEACHING HINTS	EXPECTED STUDENT OBJECTIVES AND OUTCOMES

INTRODUCTORY ACTIVITY (2 – 3 MINUTES)

Run, Stop and Pivot

The class runs, stops on signal and pivots. Vary the activity by pivoting on the left foot or the right foot, increasing the circumference, and performing pivots in quick succession. Teach both the stride stop and the jump stop prior to the pivot.

Students should continue running after the pivot. Movement should be continuous.

DPE p. 254

Emphasize correct form in stopping and absorbing force.

Make sure that students do not cross legs or lose balance while pivoting.

Allow a few moments for free practice.

Cog.—The student will be able to name sports such as basketball and baseball in which the pivot is used.

PM.—The student will be able to perform the pivot smoothly and correctly.

FITNESS DEVELOPMENT ACTIVITY (7 – 8 MINUTES)

Hexagon Hustle

Outline a large hexagon with six cones. Place signs with directions on both sides of the cones. The signs identify the hustle activity students are to perform as they approach a cone. Tape alternating segments of silence and music to signal duration of exercise. Music segments indicate aerobic activity while intervals of silence announce flexibility and strength development activities.

Hustle	30 seconds
Push-Up from Knees	30 seconds
Hustle	30 seconds
Bend and Twist (8 counts)	30 seconds
Hustle	30 seconds
Jumping Jacks (4 counts)	30 seconds
Hustle	30 seconds
Curl-Ups (2 counts)	30 seconds
Hustle	30 seconds
Crab Kick (2 counts)	30 seconds
Hustle	30 seconds
Sit and Stretch (8 counts)	30 seconds
Hustle	30 seconds
Power Jumper	30 seconds
Hustle	30 seconds
Squat Thrust (4 counts)	30 seconds

Conclude the Hexagon Hustle with a slow jog or walk.

DPE pp. 303 – 304

Examples of hustle activities that can be listed on signs are:
1. Jogging
2. Skipping and galloping
3. Hopping or jumping
4. Sliding
5. Running and leaping
6. Animal movements
7. Sport movements such as defensive sliding, running backwards, and carioca step

During the hustle, faster moving students can pass to the outside of the hexagon.

Change directions regularly to keep students spaced evenly along the hexagon.

During the hustle, quality movement rather than speed is the goal.

Cog.—The student will be able to accurately describe how overload is achieved (by increasing the length of activity at each station and decreasing the rest between stations).

266

MOVEMENT EXPERIENCE— CONTENT	ORGANIZATION AND TEACHING HINTS	EXPECTED STUDENT OBJECTIVES AND OUTCOMES

LESSON FOCUS (15 – 20 MINUTES)

Rhythmic Movement (1)

Begin each lesson with a dance or two students know and enjoy.

1. Listen to the music, clapping the rhythms and pointing out where changes occur.
2. Teach the basic skills used in the dance.
3. Practice the dance steps in sequence.
4. Practice with the music.

Make the rhythms unit an enjoyable one for students. Be enthusiastic when teaching rhythms.

1. Virginia Reel (*DPE*, p. 393)

An American dance.

The reel is a carryover from the colonial days.

It has many different forms.

Basic dance steps:
1. The "reel"
2. Sashay

The longways set should have not more than six couples.

Each maneuver must be completed in eight counts. The eighth count in each series is actually a stop so the student can be in time for the next figure.

Begin with slow tempo and gradually increase to normal tempo as students master the dance.

Aff.—Some appreciation of older American dances and culture will be acquired by the student.

Cog.—The student will understand the need for correct timing.

PM.—The student will be able to do the various figures and keep to reasonable time.

PM.—The student will react to the call with the proper movement.

PM.—The student will be able to perform the reel correctly.

2. Comin' Round the Mountain (*DPE*, p. 396)

An American dance

Basic dance skills:
1. Touch step
2. Step hop
3. Back-side-together

Circle of lines of three facing CCW.

As a change-of-pace activity, a simple game may be taught between dances.

PM.—The student will be able to put the parts of the dance together and perform it successfully.

3. Jessie Polka (*DPE*, p. 397)

An American dance

Basic dance skills:
1. Two-step or polka step
2. Heel step
3. Touch step

Begin teaching the dance with students working individually.

As students grasp the dance sequence, suggest that they form groups of two or more in a conga line (one behind the other).

The person at the end of the line rushes to the front of the line on the last two two-steps (or polka steps).

Do not demand perfection when teaching dances. Children can be expected to make mistakes similar to learning any other physical skill.

PM.—The student will master the two-step (or polka step) and be able to apply it to other dances.

Aff.—Some appreciation of older American dances and culture will be acquired by the student.

Aff.—The students will accept a new group leader with good grace.

MOVEMENT EXPERIENCE— CONTENT	ORGANIZATION AND TEACHING HINTS	EXPECTED STUDENT OBJECTIVES AND OUTCOMES

4. Inside-Out Mixer (*DPE*, p. 398)	May use any record with a pronounced beat that has a moderate speed for walking.
	
	Basic skills:
	  1. Walking
	  2. Inside-out circle
	Circle of partners facing CCW.
	
	Begin with a slow tempo and gradually increase to normal speed.
	
	Center student may wear a pinnie for ease of identification.
	
	Mixers provide quick and easy accomplishment, thus reinforcing success through dance.
		Cog.—The student will be able to recognize that dancing provides an enjoyable means of socialization.

5. D'Hammerschmiedsgselln ("The Journey Blacksmith") (*DPE*, p. 398)	A Bavarian dance
	
	Basic dance skills:
	  1. Clapping pattern
	  2. Step hops
	  3. Stars
	Play the music, pointing out where changes occur. Right and left hand stars are done while performing step hops.
	
	Begin by teaching the dance in partners. Practice the dance with the music.
	
	When students have grasped the dance sequence, groups of four may be formed.
	
	Vary the dance by performing it as a mixer.
		PM.—The student will be able to add each part in turn and perform the dance successfully.
		
		Aff.—The student will enjoy dances he knows.
		
		Cog.—The student will be able to recognize and react to the changes as indicated in the music.

6. Cotton-Eyed Joe (*DPE*, p. 400)	An American dance
	
	Basic dance skills:
	  1. Heel and toe step
	  2. Two-step
	  3. Two-step turning
	May want to teach the steps with the students scattered individually in the gym. After performing the dance steps to the music individually, progress to performing the dance in couples arranged in one large circle with the boys' (nonpinnie's) back to the center.
	
	Two-steps turning may be done solo.
		PM.—The students will improve their technique in the two-step.
		
		Aff.—Students will take pride in doing dances properly.

GAME (5 – 7 MINUTES)

Triplet Stoop—*DPE*, p. 588
  Supplies: Music
  Skill: Moving rhythmically
  The game is played in groups of three with the three youngsters holding hands and marching abreast, counterclockwise. On signal, the outside player of the three continues marching in the same direction. The middle player of the three stops and stands still. The inside player reverses direction and marches clockwise. When the music stops, the groups of three attempt to reunite at the spot where the middle player stopped. The last three to join hands and stoop are put into the center for the next round.

MOVEMENT EXPERIENCE— CONTENT	ORGANIZATION AND TEACHING HINTS	EXPECTED STUDENT OBJECTIVES AND OUTCOMES

Pacman—*DPE*, p. 585

    Supplies: Markers in the shape of Pacman

    Skills: Fleeing, reaction time

    Three students are it and carry the Pacman marker. The remainder of the class is scattered throughout the area, standing on a floor line. Movement can only be made on a line.

    Begin the game by placing the three taggers at the corners of the perimeter lines. Play is continuous; a player who is tagged takes the marker and becomes a new tagger. If a player leaves a line to escape being tagged, that player must secure a marker and become an additional tagger.

DYNAMIC PHYSICAL EDUCATION LESSON PLAN
Rhythmic Movement (Lesson 2)
Level III

Supplies and Equipment Needed:
  Tom-tom
  Cones
  Cageball
  15 playground balls
  Tape player
  Music for rhythms
  Pinnies
  Hexagon Hustle Signs

Dances Taught:
  Alley Cat
  Hora
  Hot Time in the Old Town Tonight
  Teton Mountain Stomp
  Kalvelis
  Limbo Rock

MOVEMENT EXPERIENCE— CONTENT	ORGANIZATION AND TEACHING HINTS	EXPECTED STUDENT OBJECTIVES AND OUTCOMES

INTRODUCTORY ACTIVITY (2 – 3 MINUTES)

European Running

Develop the ability to follow the leader, maintain proper spacing, and move to the rhythm of the tom-tom. Stop on a double beat of the tom-tom.

Variation:
Have the leader move in different shapes and designs. Have class freeze and see if they can identify the shape or formation.

DPE pp. 252 – 253

Single file formation with a leader.

Move in time to the beat of the tom-tom. Add clapping hands. Other movements may be added. The beat must be fast enough so students move at a fast trot with knees up.

PM.—The student will be able to move rhythmically with the beat of the tom-tom.

Cog.—The student will describe six sport and recreational activities in which the body moves rhythmically.

FITNESS DEVELOPMENT ACTIVITIES (7 – 8 MINUTES)

Hexagon Hustle

Outline a large hexagon with six cones. Place signs with directions on both sides of the cones. The signs identify the hustle activity students are to perform as they approach a cone. Tape alternating segments of silence and music to signal duration of exercise. Music segments indicate aerobic activity while intervals of silence announce flexibility and strength development activities.

Hustle	35 seconds
Push-Up from Knees	30 seconds
Hustle	35 seconds
Bend and Twist (8 counts)	30 seconds
Hustle	35 seconds
Jumping Jacks (4 counts)	30 seconds
Hustle	35 seconds
Curl-Ups (2 counts)	30 seconds
Hustle	35 seconds
Crab Kick (2 counts)	30 seconds
Hustle	35 seconds
Sit and Stretch (8 counts)	30 seconds
Hustle	35 seconds
Power Jumper	30 seconds
Hustle	35 seconds
Squat Thrust (4 counts)	30 seconds

Conclude the Hexagon Hustle with a slow jog or walk.

DPE pp. 303 – 304

Examples of hustle activities that can be listed on signs are:
  1. Jogging
  2. Skipping or galloping
  3. Hopping or jumping
  4. Sliding
  5. Running and leaping
  6. Animal movements
  7. Sport movements such as defensive sliding, running backwards, and carioca step

During the hustle, faster moving students can pass to the outside of the hexagon.

Change directions regularly to keep students spaced evenly along the hexagon.

During the hustle, quality movement rather than speed is the goal.

PM.—The student will be able to perform all exercises.

Aff.—Most fitness gains are made when the body is exercised past the point of initial fatigue. Briefly discuss the value of pushing one's self past the first signs of tiring.

MOVEMENT EXPERIENCE— CONTENT	ORGANIZATION AND TEACHING HINTS	EXPECTED STUDENT OBJECTIVES AND OUTCOMES
	LESSON FOCUS (15 – 20 MINUTES)	
Rhythmic Movement (2) Begin each lesson with a dance or two students know and enjoy.	1. Listen to the music, clapping the rhythms and pointing out where changes occur. 2. Teach the basic skills used in the dance. 3. Practice the dance steps in sequence. 4. Practice with the music.	

1. Hora (*DPE*, p. 393)	Regarded as the national dance of Israel. It is a simple dance designed to express joy.
	
	There are two versions done in Israel, the Old Hora and the New Hora. The New Hora is more energetic.
	
	Basic dance steps:
	  1. Grapevine
	  2. Swing step
	Circle formation, hands joined (may be taught in a scattered formation first).
	
	Present both versions of the Hora. Master one before presenting the other.
	
	As a change of activity, a simple game may be taught between dances.
		Aff.—The student will appreciate the culture of Israel as exemplified by this dance.
		
		PM.—The student will be able to do the Hora alone, in a circle, or in a line.
		
		PM.—The basic step will be mastered by the student so that it can be done automatically.

2. Alley Cat (*DPE*, p. 395)	An American dance
	
	Basic dance steps:
	  1. Grapevine
	  2. Knee lifts
	All students should be scattered and face the same direction during instruction.
	
	When the routine has been repeated three times, the dancer should be facing the original direction.
		PM.—The students will improve their techniques in the grapevine step to the point of utility in this dance.
		
		PM.—The dancer will be able to transfer the grapevine step learned in previous dances to this dance.

3. Limbo Rock (*DPE*, p. 396)	An American dance
	
	Basic dance skills:
	  1. Touch step
	  2. Swivel step
	  3. Jump clap step
	Begin by teaching the steps with students scattered individually. Progress to a single circle of partners, or scattered with partners.
		PM.—The student will develop the proper rhythm to perform this dance successfully.

4. Hot Time in the Old Town Tonight (*DPE*, p. 397)	An American dance
	
	Basic dance skills:
	  1. Two-step
	  2. Directional walking
	Single circle facing center.
	
	Begin with music at slow speed and gradually increase to normal speed.
		Aff.—The student will take pride in doing dances correctly.

MOVEMENT EXPERIENCE— CONTENT	ORGANIZATION AND TEACHING HINTS	EXPECTED STUDENT OBJECTIVES AND OUTCOMES
5. Kalvelis ("Little Blacksmith") (*DPE*, p. 399)	A Lithuanian dance Basic dance steps: 1. Polka step 2. Swing 3. Clapping pattern 4. Grand right and left The formation is a single circle, with partners facing the center. Use the polka step when performing the grand right and left in this dance. A new partner will be met at the completion of each grand right and left pattern.	PM.—The student will be able to transfer the polka step from previous dances to the present dance. PM.—The student will be able to put the parts of the dance together and make the partner change properly. Aff.—The student will accept new partners graciously.
6. Teton Mountain Stomp (*DPE*, p. 401)	An American dance Basic dance skills: 1. Step, close, step, stomp 2. Two-step 3. Banjo position 4. Sidecar position The banjo position resembles a swing position, with both hands joined and right hips adjacent. The sidecar position is the reverse of the banjo position, with left hips adjacent.	PM.—The student will be able to make smooth transitions from walking with a partner, to the banjo position, and then into the sidecar position.

GAME (5 – 7 MINUTES)

Cageball Target Throw—*DPE*, p. 582
   Supplies: A cageball (18- to 30-in.), 12 to 15 smaller balls of various sizes
   Skill: Throwing
   An area about 20 ft wide is marked across the center of the playing area, with a cageball in the center. The object of the game is to throw the smaller balls against the cageball, thus forcing it across the line in front of the other team. Players may come up to the line to throw, but they may not throw while inside the cageball area. A player may enter the area, however, to recover a ball. No one is to touch the cageball at any time, nor may the cageball be pushed by a ball in the hands of a player.
   Teaching suggestion: If the cageball seems to roll too easily, it should be deflated slightly. The throwing balls can be of almost any size—soccer balls, volleyballs, playground balls, or whatever.
   Variation: Two rovers, one from each team, can occupy the center area to retrieve balls. These players cannot block throws or prevent a ball from hitting the target. They are there for the sole purpose of retrieving balls for their team.

Chain Tag—*DPE*, p. 582
   Supplies: None
   Skills: Running, dodging
   Two parallel lines are established about 50 ft apart. The center is occupied by three players who form a chain with joined hands. The players with free hands on either end of the chain do the tagging. All other players line up on one of the parallel lines.
   The players in the center call "Come," and children cross from one line to the other. The chain tries to tag the runners. Anyone caught joins the chain. When the chain becomes too long, it should be divided into several smaller chains.
   Variation: Catch of Fish. The chain catches children by surrounding them like a fishing net. The runners cannot run under or through the links of the net.

DYNAMIC PHYSICAL EDUCATION LESSON PLAN
Racquet Sport Skills
Level III

Supplies and Equipment Needed:
Racquets
Yarn balls or whiffle balls
Foam balls that bounce
Used tennis balls
Nets
Targets
Signs for circuit training
Jump rope

MOVEMENT EXPERIENCE—CONTENT	ORGANIZATION AND TEACHING HINTS	EXPECTED STUDENT OBJECTIVES AND OUTCOMES

INTRODUCTORY ACTIVITY (2 – 3 MINUTES)

Hospital Tag

Students run around the area. When tagged, they must cover the area of their body with one hand. Students may be tagged twice, but they must be able to hold both tagged spots and keep moving. When a student is tagged three times, he must freeze. Restart the game after all students have been frozen.

DPE p. 257

Scattered formation.

Three or four taggers.

May vary locomotor movements.

Students keep moving even after they have been tagged.

PM.—Students will be able to dodge taggers effectively without falling.

Aff.—Students will freeze graciously and display good sportsmanship when tagged.

FITNESS DEVELOPMENT ACTIVITIES (7 – 8 MINUTES)

Circuit Training

Tape alternating segments of silence and music to signal duration of exercise. Music segments (begin at 30 seconds) indicate activity at each station while intervals of silence (10 seconds) announce it is time to stop and move forward to the next station.
Rope Jumping
Triceps Push-Ups
Agility Run
Body Circles
Hula Hoops
Reverse Curls
Crab Walk
Tortoise and Hare
Bend and Twist

Conclude circuit training with 2–4 minutes of walking, jogging, rope jumping or other aerobic activity

DPE pp. 300 – 303

Start with 30 seconds of exercise followed by 10 seconds of time to move and prepare for the next station.

Use signals such as "start," "stop," and "move up" to ensure rapid movement to the next station.

Move randomly from station to station to offer help for students who are not using correct technique.

Cog.—The student will be able to explain the need to exercise the arm and shoulder girdle area to increase strength in that region of the body.

Cog.—Water accounts for 70% of the body's weight. At least a quart of water must be ingested per day. Discuss how a great deal more must be ingested when one is involved in strenuous exercise. What problems arise when one doesn't drink enough water?

PM.—The student will be able to perform exercises and movements at this level.

MOVEMENT EXPERIENCE— CONTENT	ORGANIZATION AND TEACHING HINTS	EXPECTED STUDENT OBJECTIVES AND OUTCOMES

LESSON FOCUS (15 – 20 MINUTES)

Racquet Sport Skills

The focus of this unit should be to give youngsters an introduction to tennis, badminton and racquetball. Give students two or three activities to practice so you have time to move and help youngsters. Alternate activities from each of the categories so students receive a variety of skills to practice.

1. Discuss the proper method of holding the racquet using the forehand and backhand grips.
2. Air dribble the ball and try the following challenges:
   a. How many bounces without touching the floor?
   b. Bounce it as high as possible. Perform a heel click (or other stunt) while the ball is in the air.
   c. Kneel, sit and lie down while air dribbling.
3. Dribble the ball on the floor with the racquet:
   a. Move in different directions—forward, backward, sideways.
   b. Move using different steps, such as skip, grapevine, gallop.
   c. Move to a kneeling, sitting and supine position while continuing the dribble. Return to a standing position.
4. Bounce the ball off the racquet and "catch" it with the racquet.
5. Place the ball on the floor:
   a. Scoop it up with the racquet.
   b. Roll the ball and scoop it up with the racquet.
   c. Start dribbling the ball without touching it with the hands.
6. Self-toss and hit to a fence, net or tumbling mat. This drill should be used to practice the forehand and backhand. The ball should be dropped so it bounces to waist level.
7. Partner activities:
   a. One partner feeds the ball to the other, who returns the ball with a forehand or backhand stroke.
   b. Stroke the ball back and forth to each other with one or more bounces between contact.
   c. Self-toss and hit. Drop the ball and stroke it to a partner 20–30 feet away. Partner does the same thing to return the ball.
   d. Partner throw and hit. One partner throws the ball to the other, who returns the ball by stroking it with the racquet.

DPE pp. 423 – 425

Scatter formation.

Racquets and old tennis balls with holes punched in them work well. Also, the children can use their hands as paddles, and a fleece ball can be used.

This is a limited-movement activity; thus, break the activity into two parts separated by some running, rope jumping, or similarly physically demanding activity.

Concentrate on control of the ball and quality of movement. Take your time going through activities.

Use left hand as well as right in developing the racquet skills.

Foam rubber balls that bounce are excellent for these skills.

Ask junior or senior high schools for their old tennis balls. They are "dead," which will be helpful in teaching some of these skills.

Focus on correct technique of strokes rather than accuracy. Students have to swing with velocity if they are to learn proper form.

If students have a difficult time controlling the ball, it might be helpful to use fleece balls.

Allow time for student choice.

"Give" with the paddle.

Change the racquet from hand to hand while the ball is in the air.

The foam balls are excellent, since they bounce but do not carry.

Cog.—The student will be able to name five sports in which racquet skills are used.

PM.—The student will be able to control the racquet and ball in a variety of situations.

Aff.—One way to improve skills is to experiment with different ways of performing them. Discuss the value of trying new activities rather than always practicing areas in which we are already skilled.

Cog.—The angle of the racquet when the ball is struck will determine the direction that the ball will travel.

Cog.—A racquet will give the student a longer lever with which to strike the ball, and thus more force can be applied to the ball which in turn will increase its speed.

PM.—The student will be able to perform three partner activities.

Aff.—People feel part of a group when they can perform mutual skills. Discuss how learning various physical skills allows people to interact with friends and people with similar interests.

MOVEMENT EXPERIENCE— CONTENT	ORGANIZATION AND TEACHING HINTS	EXPECTED STUDENT OBJECTIVES AND OUTCOMES

e. Wall volley: If a wall is available, partners can volley against it.

8. Serving:

a. Teach tennis serve without a racquet. Use a yarn ball and practice hitting it with the open hand. The serve is similar to the overhand throwing motion. The toss is a skill that will need to be mastered prior to learning the striking motion.

b. Teach the racquetball serve in similar fashion. The hard, driving serve is done using a side-underhand throwing motion. The striking hand should be raised on the backswing. A small foam (Nerf) ball that bounces should be dropped to the floor and struck on the rebound.

c. For a racquetball lob serve, the ball is bounced and hit with an underhand motion. The ball is hit high on the wall and bounces to the back wall.

d. The foam ball can be used for the badminton serve also. For this serve, the ball is dropped and hit with an underhand motion before it hits the floor.

e. Depending on facilities, racquets can be used after the basic motion has been learned.

GAME (5 – 7 MINUTES)

Volley Tennis—*DPE*, p. 592

Supplies: A volleyball

Skills: Most volleyball and tennis skills

The game can be played as a combination of volleyball and tennis. The net is put on the ground, as in tennis, and the ball is put into play with a serve. It may bounce once or can be passed directly to a teammate. The ball must be hit three times before going over the net. Spiking is common because of the low net. A point is scored when it cannot be returned over the net to the opposing team.

One-Wall Handball and Racquetball

Supplies: Racquetballs (or tennis balls) and racquets

Skills: Racquet skills

Two players find a wall and volley the ball back and forth off the wall. Rules can be developed by players for the serve style and what constitutes out of bounds. The basic rule is that the ball can only bounce once on its return from the wall. When a player returns the ball to the wall, it cannot touch the floor before it hits the wall. Any of these rules can be modified by agreement of the players.

DYNAMIC PHYSICAL EDUCATION LESSON PLAN
Football Skills (Lesson 1)
Level III

Supplies and Equipment Needed:
  Signs for circuit training
  4–6 individual jump ropes (circuit training)
  8–12 junior footballs or foam rubber footballs
  4 soccer balls or foam rubber balls
  Audio player for circuit training
  12 cones (for boundaries)
  1 flag belt with flags per student
  1 pinnie per student (optional)
  Flag belts and flags

MOVEMENT EXPERIENCE—CONTENT	ORGANIZATION AND TEACHING HINTS	EXPECTED STUDENT OBJECTIVES AND OUTCOMES

INTRODUCTORY ACTIVITY (2 – 3 MINUTES)

Medic Tag

Three or four students are designated as "taggers." They try to tag the others; when tagged, a student kneels down as if injured. Another student (not one of the taggers) can "rehabilitate" the injured player, enabling her to reenter play.

DPE p. 257

Pinnies can be used to identify "taggers."

An area at least 30 ft by 50 ft is recommended.

Teacher designates means of "rehabilitation" (i.e., touching right shoulder and left knee; touching head—whereupon the injured must Crab Walk three steps).

Vary the types of locomotor movement the class can use to chase or flee.

Aff.—Self-responsibility is an integral part of many game activities. Discuss the importance of playing by the rules for the welfare of the entire class.

PM.—The student will be able to dodge/elude quickly without falling or colliding with another student.

FITNESS DEVELOPMENT ACTIVITIES (7 – 8 MINUTES)

Circuit Training

Tape alternating segments of silence and music to signal duration of exercise. Music segments (begin at 30 seconds) indicate activity at each station while intervals of silence (10 seconds) announce it is time to stop and move forward to the next station.
Rope Jumping
Triceps Push-Ups
Agility Run
Body Circles
Hula Hoops
Reverse Curls
Crab Walk
Tortoise and Hare
Bend and Twist

Conclude circuit training with 2–4 minutes of walking, jogging, rope jumping or other aerobic activity.

DPE pp. 300 – 303

Emphasize quality of movement rather than quantity and lack of technique.

Cog.—Muscles atrophy without exercise and grow stronger with use. The student will be able to describe in his own words the need for exercises.

PM.—All students will be able to move and exercise through the circuit.

MOVEMENT EXPERIENCE—CONTENT	ORGANIZATION AND TEACHING HINTS	EXPECTED STUDENT OBJECTIVES AND OUTCOMES

LESSON FOCUS (15 – 20 MINUTES)

Football Skills

Skills and Drills

Station (Small Group) Instruction

The teacher should instruct at a different station each day. Start at the station that demands the most instruction. Set up a system of rotation that assures all stations will be covered during the unit.

DPE pp. 636 – 642

Focus on the basic fundamentals. Offer brief explanation for the skills and allow time for practice.

Place critical points of technique on task cards at each station. Encourage students to analyze each other's technique.

Use foam rubber footballs during the first part of the drill so students learn proper technique without worrying about being hurt by the football.

Station 1 - Stance and Blocking

Offensive players use a 3-point stance with toes pointed forward and head up.

Defensive players use a 4-point stance with more weight on hands.

Blockers should avoid falling and should stay on toes and in front of defensive player

Use the Stance Drill with one student calling signals.

Once the stance is learned, practice blocking with emphasis on maintaining contact with the defensive player.

Cog.—The student will be able to describe why a good football player employs the proper stance. How does a stance affect stability and balance?

PM.—The student will be able to demonstrate correct blocking technique.

Station 2 - Centering and Carrying the Ball

Teach proper technique for long centering and T-formation centering.

Practice centering to a quarterback in the shotgun formation. The quarterback then practices carrying the ball.

Long centering is used for the shotgun formation and punting. When the football is centered to the quarterback in the T-formation, only one hand is used.

Use the Combination Drill to practice short and long centering.

Cog.—Every play starts with a center snap. The student will be able to express the importance of accuracy to prevent fumbles and loose balls.

PM.—The student will be able to center the ball to the quarterback (or punter) five consecutive times without a fumble.

Station 3 - Passing and Receiving

Begin practice with short passes to a stationary receiver.

Practice throwing to moving receivers, placing emphasis on leading the receiver with the pass.

Use the Combination Drill with emphasis placed on leading the receiver.

Practice throwing from under the center with a three-step drop.

Practice passing from the shotgun formation.

Rotate the center, quarterback, receiver, and ball chaser every five passes.

Aff.—Students will be able to understand the individual differences of others when participating in sport activities.

PM.—The student will be able to explain the importance of leading the receiver.

Station 4 - Punting

Concentrate on technique rather than distance when teaching punting. Emphasize keeping the head down with the eyes on the ball. Drop the football rather than tossing it upward prior to the kick.

For beginning punters, using a round foam rubber ball will be easier than kicking a football. The foam rubber footballs can be used after the basic components of kicking are learned.

Cog.—Students will be able to explain when and why punting is used in football.

PM.—The student will demonstrate the ability to use the two-step punting technique.

MOVEMENT EXPERIENCE— CONTENT	ORGANIZATION AND TEACHING HINTS	EXPECTED STUDENT OBJECTIVES AND OUTCOMES

GAME (5 – 7 MINUTES)

Football Lead-Up Games

Football End Ball—*DPE*, p. 643
 Supplies: Footballs
 Skills: Passing, catching
 The court is divided in half by a centerline. End zones are marked 3 ft wide, completely across the court at each end. Players on each team are divided into three groups: forwards, guards, and ends. The object is for a forward to throw successfully to one of the end-zone players. End-zone players take positions in one of the end zones. Their forwards and guards then occupy the half of the court farthest from this end zone. The forwards are near the centerline, and the guards are back near the end zone of their half of the court.
 The ball is put into play with a center jump between the two tallest opposing forwards. When a team gets the ball, the forwards try to throw over the heads of the opposing team to an end-zone player. To score, the ball must be caught by an end-zone player with both feet inside the zone. No moving with the ball is permitted by any player. After each score, play is resumed by a jump ball at the centerline.
 A penalty results in loss of the ball to the other team. Penalties are assessed for the following.
 1. Holding a ball for more than 5 seconds
 2. Stepping over the end line or stepping over the centerline into the opponent's territory
 3. Pushing or holding another player
 In case of an out-of-bounds ball, the ball belongs to the team that did not cause it to go out. The nearest player retrieves the ball at the sideline and returns it to a player of the proper team.
 Teaching suggestions: Fast, accurate passing is to be encouraged. Players in the end zones must practice jumping high to catch the ball while still landing with both feet inside the end-zone area. A system of rotation is desirable. Each time a score is made, players on that team can rotate one person.
 To outline the end zones, some instructors use folding mats (4 by 7 ft or 4 by 8 ft). Three or four mats forming each end zone make a definite area and eliminate the problem of defensive players (guards) stepping into the end zone.

Five Passes—*DPE*, p. 643
 Supplies: A football, pinnies or other identification
 Skills: Passing, catching
 Players scatter on the field. The object of the game is for one team to make five consecutive passes to five different players without losing control of the ball. This scores 1 point. The defense may play the ball only and may not make personal contact with opposing players. No player can take more than three steps when in possession of the ball. More than three steps is called traveling, and the ball is awarded to the other team.
 The ball is given to the opponents at the nearest out-of-bounds line for traveling, minor contact fouls, after a point has been scored, and for causing the ball to go out-of-bounds. No penalty is assigned when the ball hits the ground. It remains in play, but the five-pass sequence is interrupted and must start again. Jump balls are called when the ball is tied up or when there is a pileup. The official should call out the pass sequence.

Speed Football—*DPE*, p. 643
 Supplies: Football, flag for each player
 Skills: Passing, catching, running with ball
 The ball can be kicked off or started at the 20-yd line. The object is to move the ball across the opponent's goal by running or passing. If the ball drops to the ground or a player's flag is pulled when carrying the ball, it is a turnover and the ball is set into play at that spot. Interceptions are turnovers and the intercepting team moves on offense. Teams must make at least four complete passes before they are eligible to move across the opponent's goal line. No blocking is allowed.
 Variation: Playing more than one game at a time on smaller fields will allow more students to be actively involved in the game. This is also an enjoyable game when played with Frisbees.

Kick-Over—*DPE*, p. 644
 Supplies: A football
 Skills: Kicking, catching
 Teams are scattered on opposite ends of the field. The object is to punt the ball over the other team's goal line. If the ball is caught in the end zone, no score results. A ball kicked into the end zone and not caught scores a goal. If the ball is kicked beyond the end zone on the fly, a score is made regardless of whether the ball is caught.
 Play is started by one team with a punt from a point 20 to 30 ft in front of its own goal line. On a punt, if the ball is not caught, the team must kick from the spot of recovery. If the ball is caught, three long strides are allowed to advance the ball for a kick.
 Teaching suggestion: The player kicking next should move quickly to the area from which the ball is to be kicked. Players should be numbered and should kick in rotation. If the players do not kick in rotation, one or two aggressive players will dominate the game.
 Variation: Scoring can be made only by a dropkick across the goal line.

DYNAMIC PHYSICAL EDUCATION LESSON PLAN
Football Skills (Lesson 2)
Level III

Supplies and Equipment Needed:
  Signs for circuit training
  4–6 individual jump ropes
  8 junior footballs or foam rubber footballs
  4 soccer balls or foam rubber balls
  12 cones
  1 flag belt with flags per student
  1 pinnie per student (optional)
  Audio player (circuit training)

MOVEMENT EXPERIENCE—CONTENT	ORGANIZATION AND TEACHING HINTS	EXPECTED STUDENT OBJECTIVES AND OUTCOMES

INTRODUCTORY ACTIVITY (2 – 3 MINUTES)

Pyramid Power

Students move throughout the area. On signal, they find a partner and build a simple partner support stunt or pyramid (i.e., double bear, table, hip-shoulder stand, statue). On the next signal, pyramids are quickly and safely dismantled and students move again.

Circuit Training

DPE p. 258

Students should select a partner of similar size.

Remind students to stand on the proper points of support.

Prerecorded music with blank intervals works well here.

Aff.—Cooperation and consideration are integral components of all partner activities. Discuss the need to cooperate with and have compassion for others.

PM.—The student will be able to form two different pyramids.

Cog.—The student will know the proper points of support when forming pyramids.

FITNESS DEVELOPMENT ACTIVITIES (7 – 8 MINUTES)

Tape alternating segments of silence and music to signal duration of exercise. Music segments (begin at 35 seconds) indicate activity at each station while intervals of silence (10 seconds) announce it is time to stop and move forward to the next station.
Rope Jumping
Push-Ups
Agility Run
Lower Leg Stretch
Juggling Scarves
Curl-Ups with Twist
Alternate Leg Extension
Tortoise and Hare
Bear Hug

Conclude circuit training with 2–4 minutes of walking, jogging, rope jumping or other aerobic activity

DPE pp. 300 – 303

Hula hoops and juggling scarves placed at a station allow youngsters a chance to rest and are motivating activities.

This is the last week of circuit training. Encourage improvement of performance and technique.

Aff.—Most fitness gains are made when the body is exercised past the point of initial fatigue. Thus, briefly discuss the value of pushing one's self past the initial signs of fatigue.

PM.—The student will be able to complete each station with minimal resting.

MOVEMENT EXPERIENCE— CONTENT	ORGANIZATION AND TEACHING HINTS	EXPECTED STUDENT OBJECTIVES AND OUTCOMES

LESSON FOCUS (15 – 20 MINUTES)

Football Skills

Skills and Drills

Station (Small Group) Instruction

The teacher should instruct at a different station each day. Start at the station that demands the most instruction. Set up a system of rotation that assures all stations will be covered during the unit.

Station 1 - Stance and Blocking

Offensive players use a 3-point stance with toes pointed forward and head up.

Defensive players use a 4-point stance with more weight on hands.

Blockers should avoid falling and should stay on toes and in front of defensive player.

Station 2 - Centering and Carrying the Ball

Teach proper technique for long centering and T-formation centering.

Practice centering to a quarterback in the shotgun formation. The quarterback then practices carrying the ball.

Station 3 - Passing and Receiving

Begin practice with short passes to a stationary receiver.

Practice throwing to moving receivers, placing emphasis on leading the receiver the pass.

Use the Combination drill with emphasis placed on leading the receiver.

Station 4 - Punting

Concentrate on technique rather than distance when teaching punting. Emphasize keeping the head down with the eyes on the ball. Drop the football rather than tossing it upward prior to the kick.

DPE pp. 636 – 642

Place critical points of technique on task cards at each station. Encourage students to analyze each other's technique.

Use the Stance Drill with one student calling signals.

Once the stance is learned, practice blocking with emphasis on maintaining contact with the defensive player.

Long centering is used for the shotgun formation and punting. When the football is centered to the quarterback in the T-formation, only one hand is used.

Use the Combination Drill to practice short and long centering.

Practice passing after moving from under the center with a three-step drop.

Practice passing from the shotgun formation.

Rotate the center, quarterback, receiver, and ball chaser every five passes.

For beginning punters, using a round foam rubber ball will be easier than kicking a football. The foam rubber footballs can be used after the basic components of kicking are learned.

Aff.—Students will be able to evaluate the skill technique of peers after reviewing task cards.

Cog.—The student will be able to describe why a good football player employs the proper stance. How does a stance affect stability and balance?

PM.—The student will be able to demonstrate correct blocking technique.

Cog.—Every play starts with a center snap. The student will be able to express the importance of accuracy to prevent fumbles and loose balls.

PM.—The student will be able to center the ball to the quarterback (or punter) five consecutive times without a fumble.

Aff.—Students will be able to understand the individual differences of others when participating in sport activities.

PM.—The student will be able to explain the importance of leading the receiver.

Cog.—Students will be able to explain simple elements of football strategy.

PM.—The student will demonstrate the ability to use the two-step punting technique.

GAME ACTIVITY (5–7 MINUTES)

Football Lead-Up Games

Speed Football—*DPE*, p. 643
See the Lesson Plan, Football Skills (Lesson 1) for a complete game description.

Fourth Down—*DPE*, p. 644
Supplies: A football
Skills: Most football skills, except kicking and blocking
Every play is a fourth down, which means that the play must score or the team loses the ball. No kicking is permitted, but players may pass at any time from any spot and in any direction. There can be a series of passes on= any play, either from behind or beyond the line of scrimmage.

MOVEMENT EXPERIENCE— CONTENT	ORGANIZATION AND TEACHING HINTS	EXPECTED STUDENT OBJECTIVES AND OUTCOMES

The teams line up in an offensive football formation. To start the game, the ball is placed into the center of the field, and the team that wins the coin toss has the chance to put the ball into play. The ball is put into play by centering. The back receiving the ball runs or passes to any of his teammates. The one receiving the ball has the same privilege. No blocking is permitted. After each touchdown, the ball is brought to the center of the field, and the team against which the score was made puts the ball into play.

To down a runner or pass receiver, a two-handed touch above the waist is made. The back first receiving the ball from the center has immunity from tagging, provided that he does not try to run. All defensive players must stay 10 ft away unless he runs. The referee should wait for a reasonable length of time for the back to pass or run. If the ball is still held beyond that time, the referee should call out, "Ten seconds." The back must then throw or run within 10 seconds or be rushed by the defense.

The defensive players scatter to cover the receivers. They can use a one-on-one defense, with each player covering an offensive player, or a zone defense.

Since the team with the ball loses possession after each play, the following rules are used to determine where the ball should be placed when the other team takes possession.

1. If a ball carrier is tagged with two hands above the waist, the ball goes to the other team at that spot.

2. If an incomplete pass is made from behind the line of scrimmage, the ball is given to the other team at the spot where the ball was put into play.

3. Should an incomplete pass be made by a player beyond the line of scrimmage, the ball is brought to the spot from which it was thrown.

Teaching suggestion: The team in possession should be encouraged to pass as soon as is practical, because children tire from running around to become free for a pass. The defensive team can score by intercepting a pass. Since passes can be made at any time, on interception the player should look down the field for a pass to a teammate.

Variation: The game can be called Third Down, with the offensive team having two chances to score.

Flag Football—*DPE,* p. 645

Supplies: A football, two flags per player (about 3 in. wide and 24 in. long)

Skills: All football skills

The field is divided into three zones by lines marked off at 20-yd intervals. There also should be two end zones, from 5 to 10 yd in width, defining the area behind the goal in which passes may be caught. Flag Football is played with two flags on each player. The flag is a length of cloth that is hung from the side at the waist of each player. To down (stop) a player with the ball, one of the flags must be pulled.

Flag Football should rarely, if ever, be played with 11 players on a side. This results in a crowded field and leaves little room to maneuver. If six or seven are on a team, four players are required to be on the line of scrimmage. For eight or nine players, five offensive players must be on the line.

The game consists of two halves. A total of 25 plays makes up each half. All plays count in the 25, except the try for the point after a touchdown and a kickoff out-of-bounds.

The game is started with a kickoff. The team winning the coin toss has the option of selecting the goal it wishes to defend or choosing to kick or receive. The loser of the toss takes the option not exercised by the first team. The kickoff is from the goal line, and all players on the kicking team must be onside. The kick must cross the first zone line or it does not count as a play. A kick that is kicked out-of-bounds (and is not touched by the receiving team) must be kicked again. A second consecutive kick out-of-bounds gives the ball to the receiving team in the center of the field. The kickoff may not be recovered by the kicking team unless caught and then fumbled by the receivers.

A team has four downs to move the ball into the next zone or they lose the ball. If the ball is legally advanced into the last zone, then the team has four downs to score. A ball on the line between zones is considered in the more forward zone.

Time-outs are permitted only for injuries or when called by the officials. Unlimited substitutions are permitted. Each must report to the official.

The team in possession of the ball usually huddles to make up the play. After any play, the team has 30 seconds to put the ball into play after the referee gives the signal.

Blocking is done with the arms close to the body. Blocking must be done from the front or side, and blockers must stay on their feet.

A player is down if one of her flags has been pulled. The ball carrier must make an attempt to avoid the defensive player and is not permitted to run over or through the defensive player. The tackler must play the flags and not the ball carrier. Good officiating is needed, because defensive players may attempt to hold or grasp the ball carrier until they are able to remove one of her flags.

All forward passes must be thrown from behind the line of scrimmage. All players on the field are eligible to receive and intercept passes.

All fumbles are dead at the spot of the fumble. The first player who touches the ball on the ground is ruled to have recovered the fumble. When the ball is centered to a back, she must gain definite possession of it before a fumble can be called. She is allowed to pick up a bad pass from the center when she does not have possession of the ball.

All punts must be announced. Neither team can cross the line of scrimmage until the ball is kicked. Kick receivers may run or use a lateral pass. They cannot make a forward pass after receiving a kick.

A pass caught in an end zone scores a touchdown. The player must have control of the ball in the end zone. A ball caught beyond the end zone is out-of-bounds and is considered an incomplete pass.

MOVEMENT EXPERIENCE— CONTENT	ORGANIZATION AND TEACHING HINTS	EXPECTED STUDENT OBJECTIVES AND OUTCOMES

A touchdown scores 6 points, a completed pass or run after touchdown scores 1 point, and a safety scores 2 points. A point after touchdown is made from a distance of 3 ft from the goal line. One play (pass or run) is allowed for the extra point. Any ball kicked over the goal line is ruled a touchback and is brought out to the 20-yd line to be put into play by the receiving team. A pass intercepted behind the goal line can be a touchback if the player does not run it out, even if she is tagged behind her own goal line.

A penalty of 5 yd is assessed for the following:
1. Being offside
2. Delay of game (too long in huddle)
3. Failure of substitute to report
4. Passing from a spot not behind line of scrimmage (This also results in loss of down.)
5. Stiff-arming by the ball carrier, or not avoiding a defensive player
6. Failure to announce intention to punt
7. Shortening the flag in the belt, or playing without flags in proper position
8. Faking the ball by the center, who must center the pass on the first motion

The following infractions are assessed a 15-yd loss:
1. Holding, illegal tackling
2. Illegal blocking
3. Unsportsmanlike conduct (This also can result in disqualification.)

Teaching suggestions: Specifying 25 plays per half eliminates the need for timing and lessens arguments about a team's taking too much time in the huddle. Using the zone system makes the first-down yardage point definite and eliminates the need for a chain to mark off the 10 yd needed for a first down.

DYNAMIC PHYSICAL EDUCATION LESSON PLAN
Walking and Jogging Skills
Level III

Supplies and Equipment Needed:
  Manipulative equipment for jogging (as needed)
  Recreational and individual equipment as desired

MOVEMENT EXPERIENCE—CONTENT	ORGANIZATION AND TEACHING HINTS	EXPECTED STUDENT OBJECTIVES AND OUTCOMES

INTRODUCTORY AND FITNESS ACTIVITIES (9 – 11 MINUTES)

Stretching and Jogging

Combine the introductory and fitness activities during the track and field unit. This workout helps students learn to stretch and warm up for demanding activity such as walking and jogging.

Jog for 1–2 minutes

Standing Hip Bend	30 seconds
Sitting Stretch	30 seconds
Partner Rowing	60 seconds
Bear Hug (do each leg)	40 seconds
Side Flex (do each leg)	40 seconds
Trunk Twister	30 seconds

Jog for 2–3 minutes

DPE pp. 289 – 291

To prepare for strenuous activity, students should learn to warm up their body by walking or jogging, stretching, and finishing with jogging.

Avoid bouncing during the stretching activities. All stretching should be smooth and controlled movements.

Allow students to direct their warm- up activity. It is important that students be able to warm up without teacher direction.

Cog.—Static stretching involves stretching without bouncing. Stretches should be held for 15–30 seconds for maximum benefit.

Cog.—The student will be able to explain why stretching exercises and warm-ups are essential to track and field work.

PM.—The student will demonstrate the ability to put proper stress on muscles in stretching.

Cog.—The term *isometric* refers to maximum muscular effort exerted by pushing or pulling an immovable object.

LESSON FOCUS (15 – 20 MINUTES)

Walking and Jogging Skills

The walking and jogging lesson should be a relaxed lesson with emphasis on developing activity patterns that can be used outside of the school environment. An educational approach to this lesson can teach students that walking and jogging is done without equipment and offers excellent health benefits. It is an activity that can literally be done for a lifetime. The following are suggestions for implementing this unit of instruction:

1. Youngsters should be allowed to find a friend with whom they want to jog or walk. The result is usually a friend of similar ability level. A way to judge correct pace is to be able to talk with a friend without undue stress. If students are too winded to talk, they are probably running too fast. A selected friend will encourage talking and help assure that the experience is positive and within the student's aerobic capacity. *Pace, not race* is the motto.

DPE pp. 309 – 310

Teach children the proper style of running and walking.

Start students at a short distance so they will not become discouraged.

Concentrate on teaching the values of jogging and walking and encouraging students to start their own jogging program.

"Train, don't strain."

PM.—The student will be able to demonstrate proper jogging and walking style.

PM.—The student will be able to jog or walk 220 yd nonstop.

Aff.—Jogging and walking are excellent activities for developing cardiovascular endurance. Discuss the value of jogging and walking for personal health.

Cog.—The student will be able to list three chronic effects jogging and walking has on the body.

MOVEMENT EXPERIENCE— CONTENT	ORGANIZATION AND TEACHING HINTS	EXPECTED STUDENT OBJECTIVES AND OUTCOMES

2. Jogging and walking should be done in any direction so people are unable to keep track of the distance covered. Doing laps on a track is one of the surest ways to discourage less able youngsters. They always finish last and are open to chiding by the rest of the class.

3. Jogging and walking should be done for a specified time rather than a specified distance. All youngsters should not have to run the same distance. This goes against the philosophy of accompanying individual differences and varying aerobic capacities. Running or walking for a set amount of time will allow the less able child to move without fear of ridicule.

4. Teachers should not be concerned about foot action, since the child selects naturally the means that is most comfortable. Arm movement should be easy and natural, with elbows bent. The head and upper body should be held up and back. The eyes look ahead. The general body position in walking and jogging should be erect but relaxed. Jogging on the toes should be avoided.

5. Jogging and walking should not be a competitive, timed activity. Each youngster should move at a self-determined pace. Racing belongs in the track program. Another reason to avoid speed is that racing keeps youngsters from learning to pace themselves. For developing endurance and gaining health benefits, it is more important to move for a longer time at a slower speed than to run at top speed for a shorter distance.

6. It can be motivating for youngsters if they run with a piece of equipment, i.e., beanbag or jump rope. They can play catch with a beanbag or roll a hoop while walking or jogging.

"Pace, not race."

Don't praise the first few people leading the run if you are working on pace. The praise will cause the class to concentrate on winning rather than running for pace.

Bring in high school track or cross-country runners to talk about their training.

GAME: INDIVIDUAL OR RECREATIONAL ACTIVITY

Individual or Recreational Activities

When youngsters are finished walking and jogging, allow them the opportunity to participate in a choice of individual or recreational activities.

DYNAMIC PHYSICAL EDUCATION LESSON PLAN
Cross-Country Running/Walking
Level III

Supplies and Equipment Needed:
  Recreational and individual equipment as needed
  8–12 cones for cross-country "funnel" (meet)
  1 pinnie per student for meet (optional)

MOVEMENT EXPERIENCE— CONTENT	ORGANIZATION AND TEACHING HINTS	EXPECTED STUDENT OBJECTIVES AND OUTCOMES

INTRODUCTORY AND FITNESS DEVELOPMENT ACTIVITIES (9 – 11 MINUTES)

Stretching and Jogging

Combine the introductory and fitness activities during the cross country unit.

Jog for 1–2 minutes

Standing Hip Bend	30 seconds
Sitting Stretch	30 seconds
Partner Rowing	60 seconds
Bear Hug (do each leg)	40 seconds
Side Flex (do each leg)	40 seconds
Trunk Twister	30 seconds

Jog for 2–3 minutes

DPE pp. 289 – 291

To prepare for strenuous activity, students should learn to warm up their body by walking or jogging, stretching, and finishing with jogging.

Avoid bouncing during the stretching activities. All stretching should be smooth and controlled movements.

Allow students to direct their warm-up activity. It is important that students be able to warm up without teacher direction.

Cog.—The student will be able to explain why stretching exercises are essential to track and field work.

PM.—The student will demonstrate the ability to put the proper stress on muscles in stretching.

Cog.—Flexors decrease the angle of a joint and extensors cause the return from flexion. Identify different flexor and extensor muscle groups and the joint they affect.

LESSON FOCUS (15 – 20 MINUTES)

Cross-Country Running/Walking

1. Discuss the sport of cross-country running and how it is scored.
   a. Seven members to a team.
   b. Lowest score wins.
   c. Total points for each team based on places finished in race.
2. Divide the class into equal teams by recording times for all members of the class regardless of whether they walked or ran. Create teams of equal ability by dividing students to that the total elapsed time (for all team members) is equal.
3. Depending on the age of youngsters, as well as their ability, teams can run different length courses. The following lengths are suggested:
   a. Beginning—3/4 mile
   b. Intermediate—1-1/2 miles
   c. Advanced—2 miles

DPE pp. 713 – 715

Reinforce proper running style.

Intersperse the cognitive material with running and team practice. Don't sit for long (more than 2 minutes) without activity.

The number of students on each team should be equal, but seven are not necessary.

Time trials (informal) could be held so teams could be developed equally. A reasonable estimate of their distance running ability could be predicted by timing them over a short distance (50 yd). This distance should be covered in an all-out sprint.

Cog.—The students will understand how to score a cross-country meet.

PM.—The student will be able to complete a run-walk over the cross-country course.

Aff.—Cross-country running places a burden on each member of the team to do her best, regardless of ability. Discuss the importance of self-competition as compared with competing against others of greater or lesser ability.

Cog.—The student will understand the importance of and need for "warming down" after strenuous activity.

MOVEMENT EXPERIENCE— CONTENT	ORGANIZATION AND TEACHING HINTS	EXPECTED STUDENT OBJECTIVES AND OUTCOMES
4. Practice pace running by having students run 100 yards in different amounts of time (see chart, *DPE,* p. 714) 5. Explain how to "warm down" after each course run. 6. Have a "mini" cross-country meet.	This is a team sport, rather than individual activity; thus, the slowest runner on the team is as important as the fastest. If walking is necessary, it should be done briskly.	Aff.—Students who excel in cross-country running may be different from those who excel in team sports. Discuss individual differences regardless of the activity being analyzed. Cog.—Students will understand how to score a cross-country meet.

GAME (INDIVIDUAL OR RECREATIONAL ACTIVITY)

Recreational Activities

When youngsters are finished with cross-country running, allow them the opportunity to participate in a choice of individual or recreational activities.

DYNAMIC PHYSICAL EDUCATION LESSON PLAN
Individual Rope Jumping Skills (Lesson 1)
Level III

Supplies and Equipment Needed:
Individual jump ropes
Exercise-to-music tape
Cassette tape player
Balls

MOVEMENT EXPERIENCE—CONTENT	ORGANIZATION AND TEACHING HINTS	EXPECTED STUDENT OBJECTIVES AND OUTCOMES

INTRODUCTORY ACTIVITY (2 – 3 MINUTES)

Partner Over and Under

Students pair up with one person on the floor and the other standing ready to move. On signal, the standing students move over, under and/or around the person on the floor. On signal, reverse positions. Students on the floor can also alternate between positions such as curl, stretch and bridge.

DPE p. 257

Partner formation.

Encourage students to move as quickly as possible.

Challenge them to see how many times they can go over and under each other.

As an additional challenge, bridges may move as long as they remain in a bridge position.

PM.—The student will be able to move quickly over, under, and around her partner.

Aff.—Warm-up activities only work when an individual motivates himself to move quickly and with intensity.

FITNESS DEVELOPMENT ACTIVITIES (7 – 8 MINUTES)

Exercises to Music

Forward Lunges	40 seconds
Alternate Crab Kicks	25 seconds
Windmills	40 seconds
Walk and do Arm Circles	25 seconds
Abdominal Crunchers	40 seconds
Side Flex	25 seconds
Triceps Push-Ups	40 seconds
Two-Step or Gallop	25 seconds
Jumping Jack variations	40 seconds
Aerobic Jumping	25 seconds
Leg Extensions	40 seconds
Push-Ups	25 seconds
Walking to cool down	40 seconds

DPE p. 300

Students should know the exercises before trying to do them rhythmically.

The exercise music should be taped prior to the routine. This frees the teacher to move and help students.

Voice instructions can be dubbed onto the tape to tell students when to change to a new exercise.

Cog.—The body starts to perspire in an attempt to maintain a constant temperature. The student will verbalize this in her own words.

PM.—The student will be able to perform all of the fitness activities.

Aff.—Regulation of body temperature is essential for comfort and safety. Discuss the many ways we attempt to regulate this temperature—more or fewer clothes, perspiring, swimming, fires.

LESSON FOCUS (15 – 20 MINUTES)

Individual Rope-Jumping Skills (1)

1. Introduce the two basic jumps:
   a. Slow time.
   b. Fast time.
2. Introduce some of the basic step variations:
   a. Alternate foot basic step.
   b. Swing step forward.
   c. Swing step sideways.
   d. Rocker step.
   e. Spread legs, forward and backward.
   f. Toe touch, forward and backward.
   g. Shuffle step.

DPE pp. 451 – 458

Slow time—use a double rebound between each turn of the rope.

Fast time—one bounce for each turn of the rope.

Allow students to progress at their own rate. It is good to show the better jumpers some of the more difficult variations and allow them to practice by themselves.

PM.—Youngsters will be able to jump-rope to slow and fast time rhythm for 30–60 seconds.

Cog.—High-density lipoproteins (HDL) can slow the deposit of fat in arteries. The ratio of HDL to low-density lipoproteins (LDL) can be enhanced through exercise.

MOVEMENT EXPERIENCE—CONTENT	ORGANIZATION AND TEACHING HINTS	EXPECTED STUDENT OBJECTIVES AND OUTCOMES

   h. Cross arms, forward, backward
   i. Double jump
3. Work out combinations—add cross-hands.
4. Teach how to go from rope turning forward to rope turning backward without stopping the rope.
5. Using an individual rope with one partner holding each end. Each partner turns, partners take turns jumping in while turning.
6. One partner holds and turns rope. Second partner jumps with partner.
7. With a partner, do "the wheel" using both individual ropes. Both partners jump.
8. Attempt combinations of jump rope variations.
9. Put combinations to music.

All of the variations can be done with the turning in a forward or backward direction.

Partner A holds one of his rope handles in his left hand and one of Partner B's handles in his right hand. Partner B holds one of her rope handles in her right hand and one of Partner A's in her left hand.

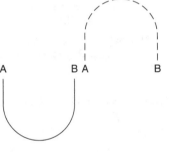

Aff.—Stress can be detrimental to a person's health. Discuss various situations that create stress among students. Discuss ways of coping with the stress.

Cog.—Some doctors estimate that young people eat 150–200 lb of sugar per year. Sugar offers "empty calories"—calories but no nutritional value. Eating too much sugar releases insulin to handle the extra sugar and soon depresses the blood sugar level to make you feel sluggish. Discuss the importance of reducing raw sugar intake.

Cog.—Students will understand that 10 minutes of rope jumping is equal to 30 minutes of jogging.

Aff.—Rope jumping is neither a male nor a female activity. It is performed by boxers, football players, and dancers for fitness development.

GAME (5 – 7 MINUTES)

Right Face, Left Face (Maze Tag)—*DPE*, p. 586
   Supplies: None
   Skills: Running, dodging
   Children stand in rows that are aligned both from front to rear and from side to side. A runner and a chaser are chosen. Children all face the same way and join hands with the players on each side. The chaser tries to tag the runner, who runs between the rows with the restriction that he cannot break through or under the arms. The teacher can help the runner by calling "Right face" or "Left face" at the proper time. On command, the children drop hands, face the new direction, and grasp hands with those who are then on each side, thus making new passages available. When the runner is caught or when children become tired, a new runner and chaser are chosen.
   Variations:
   1. Directions (north, south, east, west) can be used instead of the facing commands.
   2. Streets and Alleys. The teacher calls, "Streets," and the children face in one direction. The call "Alleys" causes them to face at right angles.
   3. The command "Air raid" can be given, and children drop to their knees and make themselves into small balls, tucking their heads and seats down.
   4. Having one runner and two chasers speeds up the action.

One Base Tagball—*DPE*, p. 584
   Supplies: A base (or standard), a volleyball (8-in. foamball for younger children)
   Skills: Running, dodging, throwing
   A home line is drawn at one end of the playing space. A base or standard is placed about 50 ft in front of the home line. Two teams are formed. One team is scattered around the fielding area, the boundaries of which are determined by the number of children. The other team is lined up in single file behind the home line.
   The object of the game is for the fielding team to tag the runners with the ball. Two runners at a time try to round the base and head back for the home line without being tagged. The game is continuous, meaning that as soon as a running team player is tagged or crosses the home line, another player starts immediately.

MOVEMENT EXPERIENCE— CONTENT	ORGANIZATION AND TEACHING HINTS	EXPECTED STUDENT OBJECTIVES AND OUTCOMES

The fielding team may run with the ball and pass it from player to player, trying to tag one of the runners. The running team scores a point for each player who runs successfully around the base and back to the home line.

At the start of the game, the running team has two players ready at the right side of the home line. The others on the team are in line, waiting for a turn. The teacher throws the ball anywhere in the field, and the first two runners start toward the base. They must run around the base from the right side. After all of the players have run, the teams exchange places. The team scoring the most points wins.

Teaching suggestions: To facilitate tagging a runner, players on the fielding team should make passes to a person close to the runner. They must be alert, because two children at a time are running. The next player on the running team must watch carefully in order to start the instant one of the two preceding runners is back safely behind the line or has been hit.

DYNAMIC PHYSICAL EDUCATION LESSON PLAN
Tug-of-War Rope and Frisbee Skills
Level III

Supplies and Equipment Needed:
  Team tug-of-war rope
  Partner tug-of-war ropes
  Frisbees
  Music (for the exercise routine)
  Record player or cassette tape player
  Manipulative equipment
  Hoops
  Bowling pins

MOVEMENT EXPERIENCE—CONTENT	ORGANIZATION AND TEACHING HINTS	EXPECTED STUDENT OBJECTIVES AND OUTCOMES

INTRODUCTORY ACTIVITY (2 – 3 MINUTES)

Move and Manipulate

Each student is given a piece of equipment and moves around the area using locomotor movements. Students toss and catch the equipment while moving. On signal, the equipment is dropped, and students move over and around equipment.

DPE p. 258

Scatter formation.

Beanbags, fleece balls (yarn balls), hula hoops, or balls may be used.

Add many challenges while moving to both the locomotor movements and manipulative activities.

PM.—The student will be able to toss and catch an object while moving.

Cog.—The student will recite the fact that it is easier to toss and catch an object while standing stationary than while moving.

FITNESS DEVELOPMENT ACTIVITIES (7 – 8 MINUTES)

Exercises to Music

Forward Lunges	40 seconds
Alternate Crab Kicks	25 seconds
Windmills	40 seconds
Walk, do Arm Circles	25 seconds
Abdominal Crunchers	40 seconds
Side Flex	25 seconds
Triceps Push-Ups	40 seconds
Two-Step or Gallop	25 seconds
Jumping Jack variations	40 seconds
Aerobic Jumping	25 seconds
Leg Extensions	40 seconds
Push-Ups	25 seconds
Walking to cool down	40 seconds

DPE p. 300

Students should know the exercises before trying to do them rhythmically.

The exercise music should be taped prior to the routine. This frees the teacher to move and help students.

Voice instructions can be dubbed onto the tape to tell students when to change to a new exercise.

Cog.—The student will know each exercise by name.

PM.—The student will be able to pick up the beat of the music and stay with the rhythm while performing the exercises.

Aff.—Compare performances with those of the preceding week. Discuss the attitude that self-improvement is self-rewarding and motivates the learner to continue the effort.

Cog.—Oxygen debt occurs when the muscles need more oxygen than is being supplied. Anaerobic exercise usually creates an oxygen debt. Students should be able to distinguish anaerobic from aerobic activities.

LESSON FOCUS (15 – 20 MINUTES)

Tug-of-War Rope and Frisbee Skills

Isometric Exercises

1. Standing—use the end of ropes only and try to stretch the handle apart.
   a. Use different hand positions and arm positions.

DPE pp. 433 – 435

Two parallel lines—this will allow you to start and stop them easily.

Make sure they hold their *maximum* effort for 8–10 seconds.

Force is applied to rope only, not partner.

MOVEMENT EXPERIENCE— CONTENT	ORGANIZATION AND TEACHING HINTS	EXPECTED STUDENT OBJECTIVES AND OUTCOMES

2. Partner Resistance Activities—
start and stop on signal.
  a. Standing—sides facing each
    other and use both arms, as well
    as right and left individually.
  b. Standing facing—use arms at
    various levels: above, below
    head, etc.
  c. Seated—sides facing, back to
    back, facing, legs elevated, etc.
    Also, hook on feet, knees—tug.
  d. Prone position—feet touching,
    heads toward each other, pull on
    ankle, push-up position pull, etc.
  e. On back—pull with feet, knees,
    arms.
  f. Develop other area. Student's
    choice.
	Start and stop on signal.
	
	Pull through the full range of motion.
	
	Rotate partners often.
		Cog.—Arteries, arterioles, and capillaries carry oxygenated blood to the muscles. Capillaries are so small and thin that oxygen passes right through the walls. At the same time, carbon dioxide is transferred from the body cells to the blood cells and carried back to the lungs to be expelled. The blood is transported back to the lungs in the veins. This system is called the circulatory system.
		
		PM.—The student will develop sufficient strength to hold her own with partner of equal size.
		
		Cog.—The student will be able to recite what tug-of-war ropes do for body development.

Tug-of-War Activities

1. Right, left and both hands.
2. Leg pulls, elbows, pull between legs.
3. Tug with three body parts; on all fours.
4. Crab position, seal walk pull.
5. Line touch tug—(pull until you can touch the line behind you).
6. Partners facing, on signal, pick up partner's end of rope and pull.
  a. Begin in a push-up position.
  b. Start sitting cross-leg fashion with hands on head.
  c. Touch a specified line before grabbing partner's end of rope.
7. Exploratory opportunity.

Tug-of-War Games

1. Four way pull
2. Two against two pull
3. Frozen Tug-of-War
4. Hawaiian Tug-of-War

The tug-of-war rope and Frisbee lesson has a dual lesson focus that may be approached in a variety of ways.
1. Alternate tug-of-war activities with Frisbee activities.
2. For each period, teach half of the lesson on tug-of-war ropes and half on Frisbees.
3. Teach 1 day of the week on tug-of-war ropes and the next day on Frisbees.
When signal is given, place tug-of-war ropes on floor, ready for the next activity.

Encourage gradual pulling to maximum effort rather than jerking.

If grip is slipping—stop, renew grip, and proceed.

Stress working safely with partner. Don't let go of the end of the tug-of-war rope abruptly.

Establish lines to cross in order to win the tug-of-war.

It might be a good idea to try a change-of-pace activity in the middle of the Tug-of-War lesson to pick up the tempo of the lesson. Try alternating tug-of-war ropes with Frisbee activities.

Aff.—Even though tug-of-war ropes are competitive, cooperation is necessary to ensure an equal start and contest. Discuss the necessity of cooperation in all major sports.

Cog.—The student will explain that maximum effort is required for best results in strength development.

Aff.—A sense of fairness should be encouraged during this highly competitive activity. Take time to discuss the importance of fair play.

Frisbees (Flying Discs)

1. Skills
  a. Backhand throw
  b. Underhand throw
  c. Thumbs-down catch
  d. Thumbs-up catch.
Practice the throwing and catching skills so youngsters will feel comfortable with the following activities.

DPE pp. 380 – 382

Partner formation.

Throw and catch with a partner. Begin with short distances and gradually move apart as skill improves.

PM.—The student will be able to perform the following skills:
1. Backhand throw
2. Underhand throw
3. Thumbs-down catch
4. Thumbs-up catch

MOVEMENT EXPERIENCE— CONTENT	ORGANIZATION AND TEACHING HINTS	EXPECTED STUDENT OBJECTIVES AND OUTCOMES

2. Activities
  a. Throw the Frisbee at different levels to partner.
  b. Throw a curve—to the left, right and upward. Vary the speed of the curve.
  c. Throw a bounce pass—try a low and high pass.
  d. Throw the Frisbee like a boomerang. Must throw at a steep angle into the wind.
  e. Throw the Frisbee into the air, run and catch. Increase the distance of the throw.
  f. Throw the Frisbee through a hoop held by a partner.
  g. Catch the Frisbee under your leg. Catch it behind your back.
  h. Throw the Frisbee into hoops that are placed on the ground as targets. Different colored hoops can be given different values. Throw through your partner's legs.
  i. Frisbee bowling—One partner has a bowling pin that the other partner attempts to knock down by throwing the Frisbee.
  j. Play catch while moving. Lead your partner so he doesn't have to break stride.
  k. See how many successful throws and catches you can make in 30 seconds.
  l. Frisbee Baseball Pitching—Attempt to throw the Frisbee into your partner's "Strike Zone."
	Give students plenty of room—their lack of skill will result in many inaccurate throws.
	
	Emphasize accuracy rather than distance in the early stages of throwing the Frisbee.
	
	Use both dominant and nondominant hand.
	
	For a straight throw, the disc should be parallel to the ground on release.
	
	Remind students to focus their eyes on the disc as long as possible.
	
	Encourage students to try different activities of their own creation.
	
	Offer a helping station for those students who have difficulty learning the basic throws.
		Cog.—The student will be able to explain the effect that the angle of the disc on release will have on its flight.
		
		Aff.—Frisbees are a recreational activity. Discuss the importance of learning leisure-time skills for the future.
		
		PM.—The student will be able to catch the Frisbee six out of eight times.

GAME (5 – 7 MINUTES)

Frisbee Keep Away
Supplies: Frisbees
Skills: Throwing and catching Frisbees
Students break into groups of three. Two of the players in the group try to keep the other player from touching the Frisbee while they are passing it back and forth. If the Frisbee is touched by the defensive player, the person who through the Frisbee becomes the defensive player. Begin the game by asking students to remain stationary while throwing and catching. Later, challenge can be added by allowing all players in the group move.

Frisbee Golf—*DPE*, p. 589
Supplies: One Frisbee per person, hoops for hole markers, cones
Skills: Frisbee throwing for accuracy
Frisbee Golf or disk golf is a favorite game of many students. Boundary cones with numbers can be used for tees, and holes can be boxes, hula hoops, trees, tires, garbage cans, or any other available equipment on the school grounds. Draw a course on a map for students and start them at different holes to decrease the time spent waiting to tee off. Regulation golf rules apply. The students can jog between throws for increased activity.
Disk golf is played like regular golf. One stroke is counted for each time the disk is thrown and when a penalty is incurred. The object is to acquire the lowest score. The following rules dictate play:
Tee-throws: Tee-throws must be completed within or behind the designated tee area.
Lie: The lie is the spot on or directly underneath the spot where the previous throw landed.
Throwing order: The player whose disk is the farthest from the hole throws first. The player with the least number of throws on the previous hole tees off first.
Fairway throws: Fairway throws must be made with the foot closest to the hole on the lie. A run-up is allowed.

MOVEMENT EXPERIENCE— CONTENT	ORGANIZATION AND TEACHING HINTS	EXPECTED STUDENT OBJECTIVES AND OUTCOMES

Dog leg: A dog leg is one or more designated trees or poles in the fairway that must be passed on the outside when approaching the hole. There is a two-stroke penalty for missing a dog leg.

Putt throw: A putt throw is any throw within 10 ft of the hole. A player may not move past the point of the lie in making the putt throw. Falling or jumping putts are not allowed.

Unplayable lies: Any disk that comes to rest 6 ft or more above the ground is unplayable. The next throw must be played from a new lie directly underneath the unplayable lie (one-stroke penalty).

Out-of-bounds: A throw that lands out-of-bounds must be played from the point where the disk went out (one-stroke penalty).

Course courtesy: Do not throw until the players ahead are out of range.

Completion of hole: A disk that comes to rest in the hole (box or hoop) or strikes the designated hole (tree or pole) constitutes successful completion of that hole.

DYNAMIC PHYSICAL EDUCATION LESSON PLAN
Hockey Skills (Lesson 1)
Level III

Supplies and Equipment Needed:
  Hockey sticks and pucks (indoors) or whiffle balls (outdoors)
  Beanbags, fleece balls (optional)
  Exercise-to-music tape
  Audiotape player
  Tumbling mats for goals

MOVEMENT EXPERIENCE— CONTENT	ORGANIZATION AND TEACHING HINTS	EXPECTED STUDENT OBJECTIVES AND OUTCOMES

INTRODUCTORY ACTIVITY (2 – 3 MINUTES)

New Leader

Squads move around the area, following the squad leader. On signal, the last person can move to the head of the squad and become the leader. Various types of locomotor movements and/or exercises should be used.

Variation:
Assign each squad a specific area if desired. Each area could include a piece of equipment to aid in the activity (beanbag, fleece ball, etc.).

DPE p. 258

Squad formation. Encourage students to keep moving unless an exercise or similar activity is being performed.

Cog.—The student will be able to give two reasons why warm-up is necessary prior to strenuous exercises.

Aff.—The student will be capable of leading as well as following. Discuss the necessity of both in our society.

FITNESS DEVELOPMENT ACTIVITIES (7 – 8 MINUTES)

Exercises to Music

Side Flex (switch sides)	40 seconds
Trunk Twister	30 seconds
Reverse Curls	40 seconds
Slide/Skip	30 seconds
Jumping Jack variations	40 seconds
Triceps Push-Ups	30 seconds
Abdominal Crunchers	40 seconds
Gallop	30 seconds
Push-Ups	40 seconds
Aerobic Jumping	30 seconds
Leg Extensions	40 seconds
Walking to cool down	30 seconds

DPE p. 300

Students should know the exercises before trying to do them rhythmically.

Students can lead the exercise-to-music routine while the instructor monitors student progress.

Voice instructions can be dubbed onto the tape to tell students when to change to a new exercise.

Cog.—The student will recognize the names of the activities and be able to demonstrate each one.

PM.—The student will be able to perform the exercises to the beat of the music on the tape.

LESSON FOCUS (15 – 20 MINUTES)

Hockey Skills

Skills

  1. Review Gripping/Carrying of stick.
  2. Quick Hit and Side Fielding on the move—The hit is a short pass, usually following the dribble. Fielding is "catching" the puck or ball with stick.

DPE pp. 652 – 655

Keep stick below waist level to ensure accuracy and safety.

Do not lift the stick too high, and hit through the ball. Strive for accuracy.

Good fielding requires learning to "give" with the stick.

Begin with movement; if skills are lacking, return to stationary practice (front field).

Cog.—The student will be able to describe the meaning of the following terms: grip, carry, dribble, field, dodge, tackle, and drive.

PM.—The student will be able to perform each of the skills listed.

MOVEMENT EXPERIENCE—CONTENT	ORGANIZATION AND TEACHING HINTS	EXPECTED STUDENT OBJECTIVES AND OUTCOMES

3. Controlled Dribble—A series of short taps used to move the ball or puck in desired direction; use both sides of the blade.
4. Tackling—an attempt to intercept the ball from an opponent.
5. Dodging—Maintaining control of the ball while evading a tackler. Hold the ball as long as possible until one can determine which direction the tackler is going to move—then pass the puck or ball.
6. Diving—Hitting the ball or puck for distance or trying to score a goal.
7. Goalkeeping—The goalie should practice moving in front of the ball and bringing the feet together; turn the stick sideways.

Drills

1. Dribbling
   a. Students in pairs—20 feet apart. One partner dribbles toward the other, goes around her and back to starting point. The first student then drives the ball to the second, who completes the same sequence.
   b. Student in threes—one student dribbles and dodges three cones spaced 10 feet apart; after clearing the last cone, "quick hit" to the next player, who fields and repeats in opposite direction.
2. Passing and Fielding—Downfield Drill—Two or three files of players start at one end of area. One player from each file proceeds downfield, passing to and fielding from others until reaching end. Shoot on goal at this point. A goalie may be used.
3. Dodging and Tackling—Pairs—One partner dribbles toward the other, who tries to tackle; reverse roles if tackle is successful.

Individual or partner work.

Use a plastic puck indoors and a whiffle ball outdoors.

Keep hands spread 10–14".

The proper time to tackle is when the ball is *off* the opponent's stick.

Assure students that it is impossible to make a successful tackle every time.

Pass the ball to one side of the tackler and move self around the opposite side.

The stick is raised higher (waist level) and the hands are brought together to give the player a longer lever.

The goalie may kick the puck, stop it with any body part, or allow it to rebound off any body part.

An 8-ft folding tumbling mat set on end makes an excellent goal.

DPE pp. 656 – 657

Students should also practice driving and fielding in this drill.

Shuttle-type formation with two players starting on one side and one player on the other side.

If two lines are used, have two or three drills going to decrease student "waiting" time.

When finished, return around the outside to avoid interfering with next group, and rotate to a new line.

Rotate goalies.

Practice this drill at a moderate speed in early stages.

Aff.—Safety and concern for others is important. Others can be hurt by wild swinging of the stick. Discuss the need for rules in all sports in order to protect the participants.

PM.—The student will be able to control the ball while moving.

Cog.—The distance over which a muscle contracts determines, in part, the amount of force to be generated. Various backswings and wind-ups are performed to increase the range of motion prior to contraction. Students will understand why preliminary movements are carried out in sports activities.

PM.—The student will be able to demonstrate the proper manner of blocking a shot on goal.

PM.—The student will be able to drive the ball or puck without bringing the blade of the stick above the waist on the backswing or follow-through.

Cog.—Hockey is a team game and passing is a needed skill. The student will be able to describe what factors make up a good pass.

Aff.—In fine motor control skills, much practice is needed to approach a desirable level. Discuss the need for drills and repeated practice.

MOVEMENT EXPERIENCE— CONTENT	ORGANIZATION AND TEACHING HINTS	EXPECTED STUDENT OBJECTIVES AND OUTCOMES

LESSON FOCUS (15 – 20 MINUTES)

Hockey Lead-Up Games

Lane Hockey—*DPE*, p. 657

Supplies: Hockey stick per player, puck, two goals

Skills: All hockey skills

The field is divided into eight lanes. A defensive and an offensive player are placed in each of the eight lanes. A goalkeeper for each team is also positioned in front of the goal area. Players may not leave their lane during play. A shot on goal may not be taken until a minimum of two passes have been completed. This rule encourages looking for teammates and passing to someone in a better position before a shot on goal is taken.

Players should be encouraged to maintain their spacing during play. The purpose of the lanes is to force them to play a zone rather than rushing to the puck. Rules used for regulation hockey (p. 659) enforce situations not described here. A free hit (unguarded) is awarded a team if a foul occurs. Players should be rotated after a goal is scored or at regular time intervals.

Variation: Increase the number of lanes to five or six. This involves a larger number of players. On a large playing area, the lanes may be broken into thirds rather than halves. Increase the number of passes that should be made prior to a shot on goal.

Goalkeeper Hockey—*DPE*, p. 658

Supplies: One stick per player, a puck or ball

Skills: Passing, fielding, goalkeeping

Each team occupies two adjacent sides of the square. Team members are numbered consecutively from left to right. Two or three numbers are called by the instructor. These players enter the playing area and attempt to capture the ball, which is placed in the center of the square, and to pass it through the opposing team. A point is scored when the ball goes through the opponent's side. Sideline players should concentrate on goalkeeping skills. When a score is made, the active players return to their positions, and new players are called.

Teaching suggestions: The teacher needs to keep track of the numbers called so that all players have an equal opportunity to play. Different combinations can be called.

Sideline Hockey.—*DPE*, p. 658

Supplies: One hockey stick per player, a puck or ball, two 4-by-8-ft folding tumbling mats

Skills: Most hockey skills, except goaltending

Each team is divided into two groups. Half of each team is on the court; these are the active players. The others stand on the sidelines. No goalkeeper is used. A face-off at the center starts the game and puts the ball into play after each score. Each team on the field, aided by the sideline players, attempts to score a goal. The sideline players help keep the ball in bounds and can pass it onto the court to the active players. Sideline players may pass only to an active player and not to each other.

Any out-of-bounds play on a sideline belongs to the team guarding that sideline and is put into play with a pass. An out-of-bounds over the end line that does not score a goal is put into play by the team defending the goal. The group of players on the field change places with the sideline players on their team as soon as a goal is scored or after a specified time period.

Illegal touching, sideline violations, and other minor fouls result in loss of the ball to the opposition. Roughing fouls and illegal striking should result in banishment to the sideline for the remainder of the competitive period.

Teaching suggestions: Some attention must be given to team play and passing strategies rather than having all players simply charge the ball. Teams should use the sideline players by passing to them and receiving passes from them in return. Teams can be rotated so that the same two teams do not face each other continually.

DYNAMIC PHYSICAL EDUCATION LESSON PLAN
Hockey Skills (Lesson 2)
Level III

Supplies and Equipment Needed:
  Hockey sticks and pucks or whiffle balls
  Tumbling mats for goals
  Cones
  Exercise-to-music tape
  Audiotape player

MOVEMENT EXPERIENCE— CONTENT	ORGANIZATION AND TEACHING HINTS	EXPECTED STUDENT OBJECTIVES AND OUTCOMES

INTRODUCTORY ACTIVITY (2 – 3 MINUTES)

Group Over and Under

One half of the class is scattered. Each is in a curled position. The other half of the class leaps or jumps over the down children. On signal reverse the group quickly. In place of a curl, the down children can bridge and the other go under. The down children can also alternate between curl and bridge, as well as move around the area while in bridge position.

DPE p. 257

Scatter formation.

Encourage the students to go over or under a specified number of classmates.

Vary the down challenges (i.e., bridge using two body parts, curl face down or on your side).

PM.—The student will be able to perform the activities of bridge, curl, leap, jump, and hop at a teacher-acceptable level.

Cog.—Warm-up loosens the muscles, tendons, and ligaments, decreasing the risk of injury. It also increases the flow of blood to the heart muscle.

FITNESS DEVELOPMENT ACTIVITIES (7 – 8 MINUTES)

Exercises to Music

Side Flex (switch sides)	40 seconds
Trunk Twister	30 seconds
Reverse Curls	40 seconds
Slide/Skip	30 seconds
Jumping Jack variations	40 seconds
Triceps Push-Ups	30 seconds
Abdominal Crunchers	40 seconds
Gallop	30 seconds
Push-Ups	40 seconds
Aerobic Jumping	30 seconds
Leg Extensions	40 seconds
Walking to cool down	30 seconds

DPE p. 300

Students should know the exercises before trying to do them rhythmically.

The exercise music should be taped prior to the routine. This frees the teacher to move and help students.

Voice instructions can be dubbed onto the tape to tell students when to change to a new exercise.

Cog.—The overload principle dictates that to increase strength, one must perform progressively larger work loads. Duration, frequency, and intensity can be modified to progressively overload the system. Students should be able to develop work loads that are meaningful to their fitness levels.

LESSON FOCUS (15 – 20 MINUTES)

Hockey Skills

Skills

Review skills taught in previous lesson:
  1. Quick hit/fielding
  2. Controlled dribble
  3. Tackling
  4. Dodging
  5. Driving
  6. Goalkeeping

DPE pp. 652 – 655

See previous hockey lesson plan for description and teaching hints.

PM.—The student will be able to perform the basic skills in hockey.

297

MOVEMENT EXPERIENCE— CONTENT	ORGANIZATION AND TEACHING HINTS	EXPECTED STUDENT OBJECTIVES AND OUTCOMES
Introduce new skills: 1. Face Off—The two players taking the face-off each face a sideline, with the right side facing the goal that they are defending. The players hit the ground and then each other's stick three times. Following the third stick hit, the ball/puck can be played. 2. Jab Shot—this maneuver is a one-sided poke that attempts to knock the ball/puck away from an opponent. The jab shot is used only when a tackle is not possible.	For safety purposes, keep the stick on the ground or floor when executing this skill.	Cog.—Wellness demands learning to cope with stressful situations. A study demonstrated that a 15-minute walk reduces tension more effectively than a tranquilizer. Students will understand the importance of exercise for stress reduction. Cog.—The student will be able to explain the importance of practicing and developing basic hockey skills before playing a regulation game.
Drills Review previously learned drills: 1. Student dribbling in pairs. 2. Dribbling and dodging through three cones with "quick hit" to next player. 3. Downfield Drill—passing, fielding and driving on the move. 4. Partner dodging and tackling drill. Practice jab shot, as well as tackling	*DPE* pp. 656 – 657 See previous hockey lesson plan for a description of the drills reviewed. Groups of three; shuttle-type formation. Two or three drills going on simultaneously; two or three lines per drill (have players rotate lines). Emphasize the importance of proper timing to facilitate a "clean" tackle. Tripping with the stick is illegal and should be avoided.	
Introduce following drills: 1. Three-on-Three Drill—Many goals can be set up and six students can work in small groups of three offensive and three defensive players. 2. Shooting Drill—Mats are set up as goals (three or four on each end of the floor). Half of class on each half of the floor. Each team attempts to hit pucks into opponents' goals without crossing center line of gym. Use a large number of pucks. 3. Face-Off Drill—groups of two. a. One stick per player, one puck or ball per group.	In the three-on-three drill, the offensive team should concentrate on passing, dribbling, and dodging and the defense-tackling and good body position. Use these drills as needed. One of the players may cue as follows: Floor—Stick Floor—Stick Floor—Stick Emphasize position play rather than everyone chasing the puck. Teach the basic rules first and then play the regulation game. As the game progresses, the more subtle rules can be introduced. In other words, don't sit the class down and discuss rules for 5–10 minutes. Play the game and introduce them as necessary.	PM.—The student will be able to successfully participate in the three-on-three drill. Aff.—Violence in sport is evident, particularly in hockey. Discuss the need for ethics in sport including self-discipline, accepting one's own and others' feelings, and the immorality of physical violence. PM.—The student will be able to play all positions in Regulation Elementary Hockey. Cog.—The student will be able to recite the basic rules of Regulation Elementary Hockey. Aff.—Teamwork and cooperation are important for a successful game of hockey. Discuss the importance of these two elements in all team sport activities.

MOVEMENT EXPERIENCE— CONTENT	ORGANIZATION AND TEACHING HINTS	EXPECTED STUDENT OBJECTIVES AND OUTCOMES

GAME (5 – 7 MINUTES)

Hockey Lead-Up Games

Sideline Hockey—*DPE*, p. 658

See the Lesson Plan, Hockey Skills (Lesson 1) for a complete game description.

Regulation Elementary Hockey—*DPE*, p. 659

Supplies: One stick per player, a puck or ball

Skills: All hockey skills

In a small gymnasium, the walls can serve as the boundaries. In a large gymnasium or on an outdoor field, the playing area should be delineated with traffic cones. The area should be divided in half, with a 12-ft restraining circle centered on the midline. This is where play begins at the start of the periods, after goals, or after foul shots. The official goal is 2 ft high by 6 ft wide, with a restraining area 4 ft by 8 ft around the goal to protect the goalie. Each team has a goalkeeper, who stops shots with her hands, feet, or stick; a center, who is the only player allowed to move full court and who leads offensive play (the center has her stick striped with black tape); two guards, who cannot go beyond the centerline into the offensive area and who are responsible for keeping the puck out of their defensive half of the field; and two forwards, who work with the center on offensive play and who cannot go back over the centerline into the defensive area.

A game consists of three periods of 8 minutes each, with a 3-minute rest between periods. Play is started with a face-off by the centers at midcourt. Other players cannot enter the restraining circle until the ball has been hit by the centers. The clock starts when the puck is put into play and runs continuously until a goal is scored or a foul is called. Substitutions can be made only when the clock is stopped. If the ball goes out-of-bounds, it is put back into play by the team that did not hit it last.

Whenever the ball passes through the goal on the ground, 1 point is scored. If, however, the ball crosses the goal line while in the air, it must strike against the mat or back wall to count for a score. Under no circumstances can a goal be scored on a foul. The puck can deflect off a player or equipment to score, but it cannot be kicked into the goal.

The goalkeeper may use her hands to clear the puck away from the goal, but she may not hold or throw it toward the other end of the playing area. She is charged with a foul for holding the puck. The goalkeeper may be pulled from the goal area but cannot go beyond the centerline. No other player may enter the restraining area without being charged with a foul.

The following are fouls and are penalized by loss of the puck at the spot of the foul.

1. Illegally touching the puck with the hands
2. Swinging the stick above waist height (called sticking)
3. Guards or forwards moving across the centerline
4. Player other than the goalie entering the restraining area
5. Goalie throwing the puck
6. Holding, stepping on, or lying on the puck

Defenders must be 5 yd back when the puck is put into play after a foul. If the spot where the foul occurred is closer than 5 yd to the goal, only the goalkeeper may defend. The puck is then put into play 5 yd directly out from the goal.

Personal fouls include any action or rough play that endangers other players. A player committing a personal foul must retire to the sidelines for 2 minutes. The following are personal fouls.

1. Hacking or striking with a stick
2. Tripping with either the foot or the stick
3. Pushing, blocking

DYNAMIC PHYSICAL EDUCATION LESSON PLAN
Basketball Skills (Lesson 1)
Level III

Supplies and Equipment Needed:
One basketball or playground ball for each student
Flags for Flag Dribble
Pinnies for lead-up games
Cones
Hoops or individual mats
Tape player
Music

MOVEMENT EXPERIENCE— CONTENT	ORGANIZATION AND TEACHING HINTS	EXPECTED STUDENT OBJECTIVES AND OUTCOMES

INTRODUCTORY ACTIVITY (2 – 3 MINUTES)

Four- Corners Sport Movement

Lay out a square with a cone at each corner. Each cone should have a sign on each side delineating one of the following movements from the list below. As the students pass each corner, they change to the movement on the sign. On signal, change directions and do the movements on the other side of the cone.

Challenge the students with some of the following agility movements:
1. Backward Running
2. Long Leaps
3. Carioca
4. Front Crossover
5. Back Crossover
6. High Knee/Fast Legs
7. Two slides, do a half turn, continue in the same direction leading with the other leg, etc.
8. Sprinting

DPE p. 255

Students do not have to stay in line but can pass if they are doing a faster moving movement.

Encourage variety of movements and performing some movements that require placing body weight on the hands.

It may be necessary to return to the basic locomotor movements with some classes (i.e., running, sliding, skipping).

Aff.—The student will display proper courtesy when passing other students.

PM.—The student will be able to perform five agility movements with quality.

PM.—The student will be able to perform light locomotor movements using three different qualities.

FITNESS DEVELOPMENT ACTIVITIES (7 – 8 MINUTES)

Astronaut Drills

Tape alternating segments of silence and music to signal duration of exercise. Music segments indicate aerobic activity while intervals of silence announce flexibility and strength development activities.

Walk, do Arm Circles	25 seconds
Crab Full-Leg Extension	30 seconds
Skip sideways	25 seconds
Body Twist	30 seconds
Slide; change lead leg	25 seconds
Jumping Jack variations	30 seconds
Crab Walk	25 seconds
Curl-Ups with Twist	30 seconds
Hop to center and back	25 seconds
Four Count Push-Ups	30 seconds
Gallop Backwards	25 seconds

DPE p. 304

Use circle or scatter formation with ample space between youngsters. If a circle formation is used, establish a "passing lane" to the outside for faster students.

Change directions occasionally to keep students spread out.

Emphasize quality movement over quantity. Allow students to adjust the work load pace. They should be able to move at a pace that is consistent with their fitness level.

Cog.—The student will be able to explain the need to exercise on all fours to increase arm and shoulder girdle strength.

PM.—The student will be able to perform the fitness activities at the beginning level.

Aff.—This routine is used by astronauts. They need to be fit, as fitness is extremely useful when unexpected demands are made on the body. Discuss some of these unexpected demands.

MOVEMENT EXPERIENCE—CONTENT	ORGANIZATION AND TEACHING HINTS	EXPECTED STUDENT OBJECTIVES AND OUTCOMES

Bear Hugs   30 seconds
Grapevine Step (Carioca)   25 seconds
Trunk Twisters   30 seconds
Power Jumper   25 seconds

Cool down with stretching and walking or jogging for 1–2 minutes.

LESSON FOCUS (15 – 20 MINUTES)

Basketball Skills

Skills

DPE pp. 569 – 591

Organize by partners.

Review previously learned passes:
1. Chest pass
2. Bounce pass
3. Baseball pass
4. Underhand pass
5. One-hand push pass

PM.—The student will be able to perform the following skills adequately:
1. Push, baseball, underhand, and one-hand passes
2. Dribbling—right and left hands while moving
3. Shooting—one-handed shot
4. Catching—high and low passes

Cog.—A spinning object will rebound from the floor in the direction of its spin. Discuss how spin can be applied to a basketball (by applying force off-center) and be used to advantage.

Introduce the two-handed overhead pass:

Remain in partner formation.

1. Fingers on the side of the ball, thumbs behind ball. The momentum comes from a forceful wrist and finger snap; ball takes slight downward path.

Cog.—The student will be able to recite the basic rules of basketball in the following areas:
1. Dribbling
2. Traveling
3. Out of bounds
4. Jump ball

Two-on-One Passing (game)

Groups of three.

1. Two players, spread out 15–20 feet apart.

Teach pivoting by player with ball to escape defensive pressure.

Rotate "ball chasers" frequently.

PM.—The student will be able to play Two-on-One Passing successfully as both a passer and a ball chaser.

2. A third player attempts to touch the ball while the other two pass it back and forth.

Chest pass gets little or no practice in this drill.

Cog.—Ligaments are inelastic and do not contract. Joint injuries usually damage ligaments. When ligaments are stretched, they do not grow back to their regular length. Discuss the need for surgery to repair ligament damage.

Dribbling (each has a ball)

1. Review rules—traveling, double dribble.
2. Review technique—wrist action, finger control, eyes ahead, knees bent.
3. Figure-Eight Dribbling Drill
   a. Three cones spaced 5 feet apart.
   b. Weave in and out of cones, changing hands so that the hand opposite the obstacle is always used.
4. Dribble-and-Pivot Drill
   a. Work in pairs.

Shuttle-type formation; three or four players per group.

Cog.—Many backaches occur from weak abdominal muscles. This occurs due to the strength of psoas tilting the pelvis forward and creating excessive back arch. Discuss how back muscles are developed by walking and running, whereas the abdominal muscles must be strengthened using curl-ups, rowing, and partial curl-ups.

MOVEMENT EXPERIENCE—CONTENT	ORGANIZATION AND TEACHING HINTS	EXPECTED STUDENT OBJECTIVES AND OUTCOMES

b. Three signals:
   Signal 1: dribble in any direction.
   Signal 2: stop and pivot back and forth.
   Signal 3: pass back to partner.
5. Practice fancy dribbling
   a. Behind back.
   b. Between legs.

For a parallel stop, player can pivot on either foot; for a stride stop, pivot must be made on back foot.

Use different types of passes.

One-Handed Shot

1. Raise ball up to eye level, sight and shoot (demonstrate).
2. Shoot from close position around the basket with partners alternating.
3. Add a short dribble and a shot.
4. Dribble and Shoot Drill
   a. Use this drill to introduce the lay-up shot.
   b. Have students practice with right and left hands.

If too many balls, alternate with dribbling or reduce the number of balls.

Each can take two shots.

This is preliminary to lay-up practice later.

DPE pp. 621 – 627

Stress points:
1. Take off on the left foot when shooting with the right hand, and vice versa.
2. Carry the ball in both hands until just before shooting.
3. Aim at a spot on the backboard above the basket.
4. Shoot with right hand when approaching the basket from the right side, and vice versa.

Group Defensive Drill *(DPE, p. 626)*

1. Students slide as commanded.
2. Ball dribbling by leader may be substituted for verbal commands.

Scatter formation.

Do not cross feet or bring them together. Keep sliding smooth (no bouncing).

Passing on the Move

Downfield Drill as described in hockey chapter *(DPE, p. 656)*

This serves as a good lead-up for the three-player weave drill.

Have two or three drills going on simultaneously to maximize practice opportunities.

Aff.—Basketball is a team sport demanding contribution from all members of the team. Discuss the importance of using all players without prejudice when developing plays and strategy.

Cog.—Skill can be improved with practice. However, readiness will determine when the fastest improvement will occur. This indicates that students will develop their skills at different times, regardless of chronological age. Discuss the need to understand individual growth patterns.

GAME (5 – 7 MINUTES)

Basketball Lead-Up Games

Flag Dribble.—*DPE*, p. 632
   Supplies: A basketball and a flag for each player
   Skill: Dribbling
   To play this game, children must have reasonable skill in dribbling. The object is to eliminate the other players while avoiding being eliminated. Players are eliminated if they lose control of the ball, if their flag is pulled, or if they go out-of-bounds. Keeping control of the ball by dribbling is interpreted to mean continuous dribbling without missing a bounce. A double dribble (both hands) is regarded as a loss of control.
   The game starts with players scattered around the area near the sidelines. Each has a ball and a flag tucked in the back of her belt. Extra players wait outside the area. On signal, each player begins to dribble in the area. While keeping control of the dribble and staying in bounds, they attempt to pull a flag from any other player's back. They can also knock aside any other player's ball to eliminate that player. As soon as the game is down to one player, that player is declared the winner. Sometimes two players lose control of their basketball at about the same time. In this case, both are eliminated. Sometimes, two players are left and the game results in a stalemate. In this case, both are declared winners and the game starts over.

MOVEMENT EXPERIENCE— CONTENT	ORGANIZATION AND TEACHING HINTS	EXPECTED STUDENT OBJECTIVES AND OUTCOMES

Variations:

1. If using flags is impractical, the game can be played without this feature. The objective then becomes to knock aside or deflect the other basketballs while retaining control of one's own ball.

2. Flag Dribble can be played by teams or squads. In this case, each squad or team should be clearly marked.

Captain Basketball.—*DPE*, p. 630

Supplies: A basketball, pinnies

Skills: All basketball skills except shooting

A captain's area is laid out by drawing a line between the two foul restraining lines 4 ft out from the end line. The captain must keep one foot in this area. Captain Basketball is closer to the game of basketball than Captain Ball is. The circle restrictions of Captain Ball limit movements of the forwards. Captain Basketball brings in more natural passing and guarding situations, and the game is played in much the same way as basketball.

A team normally is composed of three forwards, one captain, and four guards. The captain must keep one foot in his area under the basket. The game is started with a jump ball, after which the players advance the ball as in basketball. No player may cross the centerline, however. The guards must therefore bring the ball up to the centerline and throw it to one of their forwards. The forwards maneuver and attempt to pass successfully to the captain. A throw by one of the forwards to the captain scores 2 points; a free throw scores 1 point.

Fouls are the same as in basketball. In addition, stepping over the centerline or a guard stepping into the captain's area draws a foul.

In the case of a foul, the ball is given to a forward at the free-throw line. He is unguarded and has 5 seconds to pass successfully to the captain, who is guarded by one player. The ball is in play if the free throw is unsuccessful.

Teaching suggestions: A folding tumbling mat can be used to designate the captain's area at each end of the court. Use of a mat tends to discourage intrusion by guards into the captain's area.

While players are required to remain in their own half of the court, they should be taught to move freely within that area. Short, quick passes should be stressed, because long passes are not effective. This is also good practice for proper guarding techniques.

Sideline Basketball.—*DPE*, p. 631

Supplies: A basketball, pinnies

Skills: All basketball skills

The class is divided into two teams, each lined up along one side of the court, facing the other. The game is played by three or four active players from each team. The remainder of the players, who stand on the sideline, can catch and pass the ball to the active players. Sideline players may not shoot, nor may they enter the playing floor. They must keep one foot completely out-of-bounds at all times.

The active players play regular basketball, except that they may pass and receive the ball from sideline players. The game starts with the active players occupying their own half of the court. The ball is taken out-of-bounds under its own basket by the team that was scored upon. Play continues until one team scores or until a period of time (2 or 3 minutes) elapses. The active players then take places on the left side of their line and three new active players come out from the right. All other players move down three places in the line.

No official out-of-bounds on the sides is called. The players on that side of the floor simply recover the ball and put it into play by a pass to an active player without delay. Out-of-bounds on the ends is the same as in regular basketball. If one of the sideline players enters the court and touches the ball, it is a violation, and the ball is awarded out-of-bounds on the other side to a sideline player of the other team. Free throws are awarded when a player is fouled. Sideline players may not pass to each other but must pass back to an active player. Sideline players should be well spaced along the side.

DYNAMIC PHYSICAL EDUCATION LESSON PLAN
Basketball Skills (Lesson 2)
Level III

Supplies and Equipment Needed:
  Beanbags (one per student)
  Audiotape player for Astronaut Drills (optional)
  Pinnies for lead-up games
  1 basketball or playground ball per student

MOVEMENT EXPERIENCE— CONTENT	ORGANIZATION AND TEACHING HINTS	EXPECTED STUDENT OBJECTIVES AND OUTCOMES

INTRODUCTORY ACTIVITY (2 – 3 MINUTES)

Beanbag Touch and Go

Beanbags are spread throughout the area. On signal, students move and touch as many beanbags as possible. Different body parts can be specified for touching (i.e., "Touch five yellow beanbags with right knee").

DPE p. 256

Spread beanbags before class arrives, if possible.

Students may trace out a triangle, square, circle, etc., as they move around different bags.

PM.—The student will be able to perform challenges as designated by the teacher.

Cog.—Introductory activity should begin at a moderate level of intensity rather than an immediate all-out burst.

FITNESS DEVELOPMENT ACTIVITIES (7 – 8 MINUTES)

Astronaut Drills

Tape alternating segments of silence and music to signal duration of exercise. Music segments indicate aerobic activity while intervals of silence announce flexibility and strength development activities.

Walk, do Arm Circles	25 seconds
Crab Full-Leg Extension	30 seconds
Skip sideways	25 seconds
Body Twist	30 seconds
Slide; change lead leg	25 seconds
Jumping Jack variations	30 seconds
Crab Walk	25 seconds
Curl-Ups with Twist	30 seconds
Hop to center and back	25 seconds
Four Count Push-Ups	30 seconds
Gallop Backwards	25 seconds
Bear Hugs	30 seconds
Grapevine Step (Carioca)	25 seconds
Trunk Twisters	30 seconds
Power Jumper	25 seconds

Cool down with stretching and walking or jogging for 1–2 minutes.

DPE p. 304

Use circle or scatter formation with ample space between youngsters. If a circle formation is used, establish a "passing lane" to the outside for faster students.

Change directions occasionally to keep students spread out.

Emphasize quality movement over quantity. Allow students to adjust the work load pace. They should be able to move at a pace that is consistent with their fitness level.

Cog.—The training effect occurs when the heart rate is elevated above 150–160 beats per minute. To achieve this level, we keep moving without much rest.

Aff.—Very little resting time occurs in Astronaut Drills. When one exercises for a long period of time, without rest, muscular and cardiovascular endurance is developed.

LESSON FOCUS (15 – 20 MINUTES)

Basketball Skills

Skills

Review previously learned skills:
  1. Chest and bounce passes.
  2. Two-hand overhead pass.
  3. Dribbling and pivoting.
  4. One-hand set shot.
  5. Lay-up.
  6. Guarding

DPE pp. 615 – 620

Try to organize the lesson focus period so that half of the time is spent practicing skills and half playing lead-up or skill-related games.

Practice lay-ups with both right and left hands from both sides of the basket.

Cog.—Blood pressure measurements are recorded using two numbers. When your heart contracts, the pressure in the arteries is called systolic pressure. When the heart is relaxed and filling with blood, the diastolic pressure is recorded. Discuss how blood pressure is measured and what constitutes high blood pressure.

MOVEMENT EXPERIENCE— CONTENT	ORGANIZATION AND TEACHING HINTS	EXPECTED STUDENT OBJECTIVES AND OUTCOMES
Drills	*DPE* pp. 621 – 627	Cog.—The reason backspin is put on a basketball when it is shot is that spin opposite to the direction of flight will cause the ball to remain closer to the backboard and increase the possibility of its dropping in. Discuss the effects of spin in the direction of flight and when it is used to advantage.
Use some different drills such as the triangle passing drill, lay-up drill, file dribbling and pivoting drill, and the set-shot drill.	Don't turn every drill into a relay. Competition will often force children to think more about winning than polishing their skills.	
	It takes a long time to learn basic skills. Don't be in a hurry to teach all activities, and allow plenty of review time.	
Introduce the Three Lane Rush Drill	Three-player weave may develop slowly in initial stage.	
1. Use chest and/or bounce passes. 2. "Lead" the receiver with the pass. 3. Follow your pass, going behind the receiver; then cut for basket, awaiting receipt of a pass.	Cutting for the basket ensures short, accurate passes.	
Review guarding and introduce the "Give and Go."	Two groups can work at each basket (one per side). Rotate players after each shot.	Cog.—Muscle fatigue occurs when muscles will no longer contract. Training will delay the onset and severity of fatigue. Discuss the effects of fatigue on athletic play and the importance of maintaining a high level of fitness.
1. Offensive-defensive drill with a post a. An offensive player, being guarded by a defensive player, passes the ball to a stationary post player. b. The offensive player tries to maneuver around or past the defensive player for a return pass and shot.	Try this drill without a defensive player first. Game selection depends on skill level of class.	

GAME (5 – 7 MINUTES)

Basketball Lead-Up Games

Captain Basketball—*DPE*, p. 630
See the Lesson Plan, Basketball Skills (Lesson 1) for a complete game description.

Sideline Basketball—*DPE*, p. 631
See the Lesson Plan, Basketball Skills (Lesson 1) for a complete game description.

Twenty-One—*DPE*, p. 631
Supplies: A basketball
Skills: Shooting
Players are in file formation by teams. Each child is permitted a long shot (from a specified distance) and a follow-up shot. The long shot, if made, counts 2 points and the short shot counts 1 point. The follow-up shot must be made from the spot where the ball was recovered from the first shot. The normal one-two-step rhythm is permitted on the short shot from the place where the ball was recovered.
The first player scoring a total of 21 points is the winner. If the ball misses the backboard and basket altogether on the first shot, the second shot must be taken from the corner.
Variations:
1. A simpler game allows dribbling before the second shot.
2. Players can continue to shoot as long as every shot is made. This means that if he makes both the long and the short shot, a player goes back to the original position for a third shot. All shots made count, and the shooter continues until a miss.
3. The game works well as a team competition, with each player contributing to the team score.
4. Various combinations and types of shots may be used.

Lane Basketball—*DPE*, p. 631
Supplies: Basketball, pinnies, cones to mark zones
Skills: All basketball skills
The court is divided into six lanes. Players must stay in their lane and cannot cross the midcourt line. Regular basketball rules prevail with the exception that players cannot dribble more than four times. Play is started with a jump ball. At regular intervals, youngsters should rotate to the next lane to assure they get to play all positions.
A number of rule changes can be implemented to change the focus of the game. For example, three passes may be required before shooting may occur. Youngsters could be allowed to move the entire length of the floor within their lane.

MOVEMENT EXPERIENCE— CONTENT	ORGANIZATION AND TEACHING HINTS	EXPECTED STUDENT OBJECTIVES AND OUTCOMES

One-Goal Basketball—*DPE*, p. 632

Supplies: A basketball, pinnies (optional)

Skills: All basketball skills

If a gymnasium has four basketball goals, many children can be kept active with this game. If only two goals are available, a system of rotation can be worked out. The game is played by two teams according to the regular rules of basketball but with the following exceptions.

1. The game begins with a jump at the free-throw mark, with the centers facing the sidelines.

2. When a defensive player recovers the ball, either from the backboard or on an interception, the ball must be taken out beyond the foul-line circle before offensive play is started and an attempt at a goal is made.

3. After a basket is made, the ball is taken in the same fashion away from the basket to the center of the floor, where the other team starts offensive play.

4. Regular free-throw shooting can be observed after a foul, or some use can be made of the rule whereby the offended team takes the ball out-of-bounds.

5. If an offensive player is tied up in a jump ball, he loses the ball to the other team.

Fouls are something of a problem, because they are called on individuals by themselves. An official can be used, however.

Variations:

1. A system of rotation can be instituted whereby the team that scores a basket holds the floor and the losing team retires in favor of a waiting team. For more experienced players, a score of 3 or more points can be required to eliminate the opponents.

2. One-on-One. This variation differs from One-Goal Basketball primarily in the number of players. Only two play. Otherwise, the rules are generally the same. The honor system should be stressed since officials usually are not present and players call fouls on themselves. There is more personal contact in this game than in One-Goal Basketball. The game has value because of its backyard recreational possibilities. It is popular because it has been featured on television broadcasts of professional basketball players.

Basketball Snatch Ball—*DPE*, p. 633

Supplies: Two basketballs, two hoops

Skills: Passing, dribbling, shooting

Each of two teams occupies one side of a basketball floor. The players on each team are numbered consecutively and must stand in the numbered order. The two balls are placed inside two hoops, one on each side of the centerline. When the teacher calls a number, the player from each team whose number was called runs to the ball, dribbles it to the basket on her right, and tries to make the basket. As soon as a successful basket is made, she dribbles back and places the ball on the spot where she picked it up. The first player to return the ball after making a basket scores a point for her team. The teacher should use some system to keep track of the numbers so that all children have a turn. Numbers can be called in any order.

Teaching suggestion: In returning the ball, emphasis should be placed on legal dribbling or passing. In the hurry to get back, illegal traveling sometimes occurs.

Variations:

1. Players can run by pairs, with either a pair of players assigned the same number or the teacher calling two numbers. Three passes must be made before the shot is taken and before the ball is replaced inside the hoop.

2. Three players can run at a time, with the stipulation that the player who picks up the ball from the hoop must be the one who takes the first shot. All players must handle the ball on the way down and on the way back.

3. To make a more challenging spot for the return, use a deck tennis ring. This demands more critical control than placing the ball in a hoop. In either case, the ball must rest within the designated area to score.

4. A more demanding task calls for a single player to pass the ball to each of his teammates successively on the way down and on the way back. Teammates scatter themselves along the sideline after the number has been called.

DYNAMIC PHYSICAL EDUCATION LESSON PLAN
Basketball Skills (Lesson 3)
Level III

Supplies and Equipment Needed:
  Audiotape player for Astronaut Drills (optional)
  1 basketball or playground ball per student
  Pinnies for lead-up games
  Flags

MOVEMENT EXPERIENCE— CONTENT	ORGANIZATION AND TEACHING HINTS	EXPECTED STUDENT OBJECTIVES AND OUTCOMES

INTRODUCTORY ACTIVITY (2 – 3 MINUTES)

Leapfrog

Two, three or four children are used for this group activity. They form a curved line, with all except the last child in line taking the leapfrog position. The last child leaps over the other children in turn and, after going over the last child, gets down in position so that the others can leap him.

Variations:
  1. Change the height of the leapfrog position—low, medium, high.
  2. Increase the distance between the youngsters in the leapfrog position.
  3. Add some locomotor movements or stunts that the youngster on the move must perform between leaps over each child.

DPE p. 258

Lines should curve to avoid running into other jumpers.

Stress good form on the jump as well as holding the down position with the hands on the knees.

Encourage, but don't force, youngsters to try the jump. If they are reticent, allow them to be in the down position and run around each student when it is their turn to jump.

PM.—The student will be able to crouch jump over the students in the down position.

Cog.—The student will be able to identify the elements necessary to land softly after jumping over a student.

Cog.—Reciprocal innervation is a dual set of messages to the muscles which tell one set to contract and the opposing set to relax. Discuss the importance of this process for efficient movement.

FITNESS DEVELOPMENT ACTIVITY (7 – 8 MINUTES)

Astronaut Drills

Tape alternating segments of silence and music to signal duration of exercise. Music segments indicate aerobic activity while intervals of silence announce flexibility and strength development activities.

Walk, do Arm Circles	30 seconds
Crab Full-Leg Extension	30 seconds
Skip sideways	30 seconds
Body Twist	30 seconds
Slide; change lead leg	30 seconds
Jumping Jack variations	30 seconds
Crab Walk	30 seconds
Curl-Ups with Twist	30 seconds
Hop to center and back	30 seconds
Four Count Push-Ups	30 seconds
Gallop Backwards	30 seconds
Bear Hugs	30 seconds
Grapevine Step (Carioca)	30 seconds
Trunk Twisters	30 seconds
Power Jumper	30 seconds

Cool down with stretching and walking or jogging for 1–2 minutes.

DPE p. 304

Use circle or scatter formation with ample space between youngsters. If a circle formation is used, establish a "passing lane" to the outside for faster students.

Change directions occasionally to keep students spread out.

Emphasize quality movement over quantity. Allow students to adjust the work load pace. They should be able to move at a pace that is consistent with their fitness level.

PM.—The student will be able to perform all activities at the increased load level.

Cog.—The student will be able to verbalize in her own words the fact that regular exercise strengthens muscles and helps prevent joint and muscle injury.

MOVEMENT EXPERIENCE— CONTENT	ORGANIZATION AND TEACHING HINTS	EXPECTED STUDENT OBJECTIVES AND OUTCOMES

LESSON FOCUS (15 – 20 MINUTES)

Basketball Skills and Drills

This lesson should focus on skills and drills listed in the first two lessons that the teacher has not yet introduced, along with review.

Introduce skills and/or drills listed in Lessons 1 and 2 that have not yet been taught.

Review and use previously introduced drills to practice these skills:

1. Three Lane Rush
2. Guarding and "Give and Go."
3. Lay-up shot
4. One-handed set shot
   a. Introduce jump shot to those students who appear ready.
   b. Use the following games to teach shooting under pressure:
      — Freeze Out (*DPE*, p. 632)
      — Basketrama (*DPE*, p. 634)

DPE pp. 615 – 620

Try to organize the lesson so that half of the time is spent practicing skills and half playing lead-up to skill-related games.

DPE pp. 621 – 627

Offensive-defensive drill with a post (p. 583) works well here.

GAME (5 – 7 MINUTES)

Basketball Lead-Up Games

Sideline Basketball—*DPE*, p. 631
   See the Lesson Plan, Basketball Skills (Lesson 1) for a complete game description.

Flag Dribble—*DPE*, p. 632
   See the Lesson Plan, Basketball Skills (Lesson 1) for a complete game description.

One-Goal Basketball—*DPE*, p. 632
   See the Lesson Plan, Basketball Skills (Lesson 2) for a complete game description.

Basketball Snatch Ball—*DPE*, p. 633
   See the Lesson Plan, Basketball Skills (Lesson 2) for a complete game description.

Three-on-Three—*DPE*, p. 633
   Supplies: A basketball
   Skills: All basketball skills
   An offensive team of three stands just forward of the centerline, facing the basket. The center player has a basketball. Another team of three is on defense and awaits the offensive team in the area near the foul line. The remaining teams, waiting for their turn, stand beyond the end line.
   Regular basketball rules are used. At a signal, the offensive team advances to score. A scrimmage is over when the offensive team scores or when the ball is recovered by the defense. In either case, the defensive team moves to the center of the floor and becomes the offensive unit. A waiting team comes out on the floor and gets ready for defense. The old offensive team goes to the rear of the line of waiting players. Each of the teams should keep its own score. Two games can be carried on at the same time, one in each half of the court.
   Variations:
   1. If the offensive team scores, it remains on the floor, and the defensive team drops off in favor of the next team. If the defense recovers the ball, the offensive team rotates off the floor.
   2. If a team has a foul (by one of the players), that team rotates off the floor in favor of the next team.
   3. A team wins when it scores 3 points. The contest becomes a regular scrimmage in which the offensive team becomes the defensive team upon recovering the ball. When a team scores 3 points, the other team is rotated off the floor. Rules for One-Goal Basketball prevail.
   4. The game can be played with four against four.

DYNAMIC PHYSICAL EDUCATION LESSON PLAN
Recreational Activities
Level III

Supplies and Equipment Needed:
  Individual jump ropes
  Equipment for recreational activities

MOVEMENT EXPERIENCE—CONTENT	ORGANIZATION AND TEACHING HINTS	EXPECTED STUDENT OBJECTIVES AND OUTCOMES

INTRODUCTORY ACTIVITY (2 – 3 MINUTES)

Living Obstacles

Half of the class is scattered. Each is in a bridge position. The remaining half of the class moves under, over or around the obstacles. The bridges may move around the area while maintaining their bridged positions. On signal, reverse the group quickly.

DPE p. 257

Scatter formation.

Encourage students to go over, under, or around a specified number of "living obstacles."

Vary the down challenges (i.e., bridge using two body parts, do a side bridge).

PM.—The student will be able to move in a bridged formation.

Cog.—Warm-up loosens the muscles, tendons, and ligaments, decreasing the risk of injury. It also increases the flow of blood to the heart muscle.

FITNESS DEVELOPMENT ACTIVITY (7 – 8 MINUTES)

Partner Aerobic Fitness and Resistance Exercises

Students find a partner and lead each other in aerobic activities. Partners switch leader and follower roles after each partner resistance exercise. This routine assumes that students have previous aerobic fitness experience. If not, the aerobic activities will have to be led by the teacher. Tape alternating segments of silence and music to signal duration of exercise. Music segments indicate aerobic activity while intervals of silence announce flexibility and strength development activities.

Aerobic Fitness Activity	25 seconds
Arm Curl-Up	45 seconds
Aerobic Fitness Activity	25 seconds
Camelback	45 seconds
Aerobic Fitness Activity	25 seconds
Fist Pull Apart	45 seconds
Aerobic Fitness Activity	25 seconds
Scissors	45 seconds
Aerobic Fitness Activity	25 seconds
Butterfly	45 seconds
Aerobic Fitness Activity	25 seconds
Resistance Push-Up	45 seconds
Aerobic Fitness Activity	25 seconds
Knee Bender	45 seconds

Walk, stretch and relax for a minute or two.

DPE pp. 305 – 307 lists aerobic fitness activities.

DPE pp. 297 – 299 describes partner resistance exercises.

During the time allowed for partner resistance exercises, both students should have the opportunity to complete each exercise.

If youngsters can't think of an aerobic activity, ask them to copy another student.

Youngsters should take 6–10 seconds to move through the full range of motion while their partner applies resistance.

PM.—The student will be able to apply the correct amount of resistance for his partner to perform with maximum effort through the full range of motion.

PM.—The student will be able to do the aerobic conditioning activities.

Cog.—Cardiovascular endurance is developed though the use of aerobic conditioning activities.

Cog.—The student will understand that partner resistance exercises develop strength.

Cog.—Physical activity appears to change the state of mind in a positive direction. People on regular exercise programs are more productive and better able to cope with stress. Discuss the importance of regular exercise and acceptable types of exercise to cause the above effect.

Cog.—Exercise increases the diameter and density of bones. Why would this be important? Why do bones become stronger in response to exercise?

MOVEMENT EXPERIENCE— CONTENT	ORGANIZATION AND TEACHING HINTS	EXPECTED STUDENT OBJECTIVES AND OUTCOMES

LESSON FOCUS AND GAME (15 – 20 MINUTES)

Recreational Activities

The purpose of the recreation is to teach children activities that they can play during the time when school is not in session. Suggested activities are:
1. Shuffleboard
2. Four Square
3. Double Dutch rope jumping
4. Team Handball
5. Around the Key Basketball
6. Beach Ball Volleyball (2 on 2)
7. Jacks
8. Marbles
9. Sidewalk Tennis
10. Horseshoes
11. Rope Quoits
12. Tetherball
13. Tennis Volleyball

Emphasis should be placed on teaching the rules of the activities so children can enjoy them on their own time.

It might be useful to set up the activities at four different stations and rotate students from one station to the next.

If you know a traditional game played by children in your area for many years, now is a good time to teach it.

PM.—The student will be able to play at least four of the given activities.

Cog.—The student will be able to recite the rules for playing four or more of the activities.

Aff.—Recreational activities can be an excellent release for reducing stress. Relaxation demands playing for enjoyment and personal pleasure. Adults spend millions of dollars searching for activities that are relaxing and rewarding.

DYNAMIC PHYSICAL EDUCATION LESSON PLAN
Gymnastics and Climbing Rope Skills
Level III

Supplies and Equipment Needed:
  20–24 beanbags
  Hoops
  Tumbling mats
  Climbing ropes (as available)
  Other climbing apparatus (optional)
  Manipulative equipment (optional)
  4 Bowling pins
  One jump rope per child
  Flags

MOVEMENT EXPERIENCE—CONTENT	ORGANIZATION AND TEACHING HINTS	EXPECTED STUDENT OBJECTIVES AND OUTCOMES

INTRODUCTORY ACTIVITY (2 – 3 MINUTES)

Barker's Hoopla

Place on hoop in each of the four corners and the middle of a square playing area. A distance between hoops of 25–30 feet is challenging. Five or six beanbags are placed in each hoop. There are five teams, one beside each hoop (home base). The object is to steal beanbags from other hoops and return them to the hoop that is home base.

Variation:
Beanbags must be taken *out* of home base hoop and placed in other hoops.

DPE p. 581

Watch for collisions.

The type of locomotion used may be changed to add variety.

Only one bag at a time may be taken. Bag may be released only when hand is vertically over home base hoop.

Aff.—The student will develop an appreciation for playing by the rules without extrinsic motivation factors.

PM.—The student will be able to dodge or evade quickly without falling or colliding.

FITNESS DEVELOPMENT (7 – 8 MINUTES)

Partner Aerobic Fitness and Resistance Exercises

Students find a partner and lead each other in aerobic activities. Partners switch leader and follower roles after each partner resistance exercise. This routine assumes that students have previous aerobic fitness experience. If not, the aerobic activities will have to be led by the teacher. Tape alternating segments of silence and music to signal duration of exercise. Music segments indicate aerobic activity while intervals of silence announce flexibility and strength development activities.

Aerobic Fitness Activity	30 seconds
Arm Curl-Up	45 seconds
Aerobic Fitness Activity	30 seconds
Camelback	45 seconds
Aerobic Fitness Activity	30 seconds
Fist Pull Apart	45 seconds
Aerobic Fitness Activity	30 seconds
Scissors	45 seconds
Aerobic Fitness Activity	30 seconds
Butterfly	45 seconds
Aerobic Fitness Activity	30 seconds

DPE pp. 305 – 307 lists aerobic fitness activities.

DPE pp. 297 – 299 describes partner resistance exercises.

During the time allowed for partner resistance exercises, both students should have the opportunity to complete each exercise.

If youngsters can't think of an aerobic activity, ask them to copy another student.

Youngsters should take 6–10 seconds to move through the full range of motion while their partner applies resistance.

PM.—The student will be able to perform all the exercises.

Cog.—The student will be able to recite the fact that resistance should be offered throughout the full range of motion for maximum benefit.

Cog.—Partner resistance exercises are used to develop strength. Aerobic conditioning activities are needed for endurance development.

PM.—The student will be able to perform the aerobic conditioning activities.

MOVEMENT EXPERIENCE— CONTENT	ORGANIZATION AND TEACHING HINTS	EXPECTED STUDENT OBJECTIVES AND OUTCOMES

LESSON FOCUS (15 – 20 MINUTES)

Resistance Push-Up 45 seconds Aerobic Fitness Activity 30 seconds Knee Bender 45 seconds		

Walk, stretch and relax for a minute or two.

Gymnastics and Climbing Rope Skills

Gymnastics

Six groups of activities in this lesson ensure that youngsters receive a variety of experiences. Pick a few activities from each group and teach them alternately. For example, teach an individual stunt or two, then a tumbling skill or inverted balance, followed by a balance stunt, etc. Give equal time to each group of activities

1. Tumbling and Inverted Balances
   a. Forward and backward roll combinations
   b. Back Extension
   c. Headstand variations
   d. Handstand against a wall
2. Balance Stunts
   a. V-Up
   b. Push-Up variations
   c. Flip-Flop
3. Individual Stunts
   a. Wall Walk-up
   b. Skier's Sit
   c. Rocking Horse
   d. Heel Click (side)
4. Partner and Group Stunts
   a. Double Scooter
   b. Eskimo Roll (double roll)
   c. Tandem Bicycle
   d. Circle High Jump
5. Partner Support Stunts
   a. Back Layout
   b. Front Sit
   c. Flying Dutchman
6. Combatives
   a. Hand Wrestle
   b. Finger Fencing
   c. Touch Knees
   d. Grab the Flag
   e. Rooster Fight

DPE pp. 526 – 542

Scatter as many tumbling mats as possible throughout the area in order to avoid waiting lines.

Do not perform many repetitions of tumbling and inverted balances. For most children, limiting the number of forward or backward roll repetitions to four or five will prevent fatigue and injury.

There is usually a wide range of ability among youngsters in this lesson. If necessary, start at a lower level than listed here to assure students find success.

Teach youngsters to stand on the hips and shoulders when doing partner support stunts.

DPE pp. 543 – 547

Rotate partners to prevent one student from dominating another. For safety, use starting and stopping signals to ensure fair starts and fast stops.

PM.—The student will be able to perform a forward and a backward roll.

PM.—The student will be able to perform the basic headstand.

PM.—The student will be able to balance his body in the balance stunts and manage it easily in the individual stunts.

Cog.—The student will be able to recite the stress points necessary to know in performing the forward and backward roll.

Cog.—The student will be able to state the key points necessary to spot the headstand.

Aff.—Tumbling is an excellent activity as it teaches children to control their bodies in various situations. Discuss the courage and perseverance gymnasts must have to meet success.

Cog.—Wellness refers to taking care of one's self for better health. It places the responsibility for good health on the individual rather than a doctor. Discuss various facets of wellness and making responsible decisions for better health.

Cog.—Stability and balance can be increased by (1) keeping the body weight over the base of support, (2) increasing the size of the base of support, and (3) lowering the center of gravity. Identify this process being performed in the stunts and tumbling activities.

Aff.—Combatives are a good example of "one on one" competition. Discuss the need for self-control and good sportsmanship.

MOVEMENT EXPERIENCE—CONTENT	ORGANIZATION AND TEACHING HINTS	EXPECTED STUDENT OBJECTIVES AND OUTCOMES

Climbing Ropes

1. Supported Pull-Ups
   a. Kneel and pull to feet. Return
   b. Sit, pull to feet and back to seat.
   c. Stand, keep body straight while lowering body to the floor.
2. Hangs
   a. Sit, pull body off floor except for feet and hold.
   b. Jump up, grasp the rope, and hang.
   c. Jump up, grasp the rope and hang, and perform the following leg movements:
      — One or both knees up
      — Bicycling movement
      — Half lever
      — Choice movement
3. Swinging and Jumping
   Reach high and jump to a bent-arm position while swinging.
   a. Swing and jump. Add one-half and full turns.
   b. Swing and return.
   c. Swing and pick up a beanbag or bowling pin with the feet.
4. Climbing the rope
   a. Scissors grip
      Place the rope inside of the knee and outside the foot. Climb halfway up and practice descending using the reverse scissors grip before climbing to the top of the rope.
   b. Leg around rest
      Wrap the left leg around the rope and over the instep of the left foot from the outside. Stand on the rope and instep with right foot.
5. Descending the rope
   a. Reverse scissors grip
   b. Leg-around rest
   c. Instep squeeze—The rope is squeezed between the insteps by keeping the heels together.
6. Stunts Using Two Ropes
   a. Straight arm hand—Jump up, grasp rope and hang.
   b. arms with different leg positions.
      — Single and double knee lifts
      — Half lever
      — Full lever
      — Bicycle—pedal feet like bicycle.
   c. Pull-Ups — same as Pull-Up on a single rope.
   d. Inverted hangs
      — With feet wrapped around the ropes.
      — With feet against the inside of the ropes.
      — With the toes pointed and the feet not touching the ropes.

DPE pp. 460 – 464

Place tumbling mats under all the climbing apparatus.

Caution students not to slide quickly down the rope to prevent rope burns.

The pull-up and hang activities are excellent lead-ups for students who are not strong enough to climb the rope.

Swinging on the ropes should be done with bent arms and with knees tucked.

Caution the person waiting in line to wait out of the way until the person before her is completely finished.

Students should be encouraged to learn the various techniques of climbing and descending.

If there are only a few climbing ropes, it would be a good teaching technique to have the nonclimbing students work on another unit.

If such large apparatus is unavailable, other units that work well include hoops, wands, playground balls, and rope jumping.

Two ropes, hanging close together, are needed.

Spotting should be done when students are performing inverted hangs on two ropes.

PM.—The student will be able to demonstrate proper techniques in the following activities:
   1. Climbing with the scissors grip
   2. Leg around rest
   3. Reverse scissors grip
   4. Instep squeeze
Cog.—The student will be able to describe the safety rules necessary when climbing ropes.

Aff.—Rope climbing demands a great deal of upper body strength. Discuss how muscular strength develops through overloading and increasing the demands placed on the body.

Cog.—Rope climbing is excellent for developing upper body strength. Discuss the major muscle groups that are used and developed when climbing ropes.

Cog.—The larger the diameter of the muscle, the greater the amount of force that can be generated. Identify various muscles of the body and their relative size.

PM.—The student will be able to perform the following two-rope activities:
   1. Straight arm hang
   2. Hangs with different leg positions
   3. Pull-ups
   4. Inverted hangs

Aff.—Rope climbing favors those students who are small and carry little body fat. Discuss individual differences and how different sports favor certain types of body build.

MOVEMENT EXPERIENCE— CONTENT	ORGANIZATION AND TEACHING HINTS	EXPECTED STUDENT OBJECTIVES AND OUTCOMES

GAME (5 – 7 MINUTES)

Star Wars—*DPE*, p. 587
  Supplies: Four bowling pins
  Skill: Running
  A hollow square, about 10 yd on each side, is formed by four teams, each of which occupies one side, facing in. The teams should be even in number, and the members of each team should count off consecutively from right to left. This means that one person on each team has the same number as one child on each of the other three teams. Children are seated cross-legged.
  A number is called by the teacher. The four children with the number run to the right, all the way around the square, and through their own vacated space toward the center of the square. Near the center, in front of each team, stands a bowling pin. The first child to put the bowling pin down on the floor is the winner. The pins should be at an equal distance in front of the teams and far enough away from each other to avoid collisions in the center.
  Scoring is kept by the words Star Wars. The player who puts the pin down first gets to write two letters of the name. The player who is second gets to write one letter. The lettering can be done in a space in front of each team, where the name would be reasonably protected from the runners. The first team to complete the name is the winner.
  Teaching suggestion: In number games of this type, the numbers are not called in order. The teacher should keep a tally to make sure that every number is called.
  Variation: Instead of being seated, each child can take a prone position, as if ready to do a Push-Up. The teacher gives a preliminary command, such as "Ready," and each child comes up to a push-up position. The teacher then calls the number. Children with other numbers return to the prone position. Each child does a Push-Up every time a number is called.

Flag Chase—*DPE*, p. 583
  Supplies: Flags, stopwatch
  Skills: Running, dodging
  One team wears flags positioned in the back of the belt. The flag team scatters throughout the area. On signal, the object is for the chasing team to capture as many flags as possible in a designated amount of time. The flags are brought to the teacher or placed in a box. Players cannot use their hands to ward off a chaser. Roles are reversed. The team pulling the most flags is declared the winner.

DYNAMIC PHYSICAL EDUCATION LESSON PLAN
Gymnastics and Juggling Skills
Level III

Supplies and Equipment Needed:
  Parachute
  Scarves
  Balls for juggling
  Tumbling mats
  8 foam balls (8 1/2")
  Bowling pins
  Playground balls

MOVEMENT EXPERIENCE—CONTENT	ORGANIZATION AND TEACHING HINTS	EXPECTED STUDENT OBJECTIVES AND OUTCOMES

INTRODUCTORY ACTIVITY (2 – 3 MINUTES)

Following Activity

One partner leads and performs various kinds of movements. The other partner follows and performs the same movements. This can also be used with squad organization, with the squad following a leader.

DPE p. 257

The leaders should be changed often. Use a whistle to signal the changes of roles.

Partner or squad formation.

Encourage good reproduction of the leader's movements.

PM.—Be able to follow and accurately reproduce the movements of the leader.

Aff.—People must be able to lead as well as follow at times. Briefly discuss the need for cooperation between people.

FITNESS DEVELOPMENT (7 – 8 MINUTES)

Parachute Fitness

Tape alternating segments of silence and music to signal duration of exercise. Music segments indicate aerobic activity with the parachute while intervals of silence announce using the chute to enhance flexibility and strength development.
  1. Jog in circle with chute held in left hand. Reverse directions and hold with right hand.
  2. Standing, raise the chute overhead, lower to waist, lower to toes, raise to waist, etc.
  3. Slide to the right; return slide to the left.
  4. Sit and perform curl-ups with a twist— 40 seconds.
  5. Skip for 25 seconds.
  6. Freeze, face the center, and stretch the chute tightly with bent arms. Hold for 8–12 seconds. Repeat five to six times.
  7. Run in place, hold the chute at waist level, and hit the chute with lifted knees.
  8. Sit with legs under the chute. Do a seat walk toward the center. Return to the perimeter. Repeat four to six times.
  9. Place the chute on the ground. Jog away from the chute and return on signal. Repeat for 35 seconds.

DPE, p. 285

Evenly space youngsters around the chute.

Use different grips to add variation to the activities.

Develop group morale by encouraging students to move together.

Use music to motivate youngsters.

To cool down, allow youngsters a minute to perform parachute stunts like the Dome or Mushroom.

Cog.—The student will be able to explain that maximum effort must be exerted if the exercise is going to be of any value.

PM.—The student will be able to perform each aerobic conditioning activity.

Cog.—Sweating occurs when the body is overheated due to stress in an attempt to maintain a constant body temperature. The student will be able to explain why the body sweats.

MOVEMENT EXPERIENCE—CONTENT	ORGANIZATION AND TEACHING HINTS	EXPECTED STUDENT OBJECTIVES AND OUTCOMES

10. On sides with legs under the chute. Perform Side Flex and lift chute with legs.
11. Lie on back with legs under the chute. Shake the chute with the feet.
12. Hop to the center of the chute and return. Repeat for 25 seconds.
13. Assume the push-up position with the legs aligned away from the center of the chute. Shake the chute with one arm while the other arm supports the body.
14. Sit with feet under the chute. Stretch by touching the toes with the chute. Relax with other stretches while sitting.

LESSON FOCUS (15–20 MINUTES)

Gymnastics and Juggling Skills

Gymnastics

Six groups of activities in this lesson ensure that youngsters receive a variety of experiences. Pick a few activities from each group and teach them alternately. For example, teach an individual stunt or two, then a tumbling skill or inverted balance, followed by a balance stunt, etc. Give equal time to each group of activities

1. Tumbling and Inverted Balances
   a. Freestanding Handstand
   b. Cartwheel and Round-Off
   c. Judo Roll
   d. Advanced Forward and Backward Roll Combinations
   e. Gymnastic Routines
2. Balance Stunts
   a. Long Reach
   b. Toe Jump
   c. Handstand Stunts
3. Individual Stunts
   a. Walk-Through
   b. Jump-Through
   c. Circular Rope Jump
   d. Bouncer
4. Partner and Group Stunts
   a. Stick Carries
   b. Two-Way Wheelbarrow
   c. Partner Rising Sun
   d. Triple Roll
5. Partner Support Stunts
   a. Knee-and-Shoulder Balance
   b. Press
   c. All-Fours Support
6. Combatives
   a. Palm Push
   b. Bulldozer
   c. Breakdown
   d. Elbow Wrestle
   e.   Leg Wrestle

DPE pp. 526 – 542

Scatter as many tumbling mats as possible throughout the area in order to avoid waiting lines.

For most children, limiting the number of forward or backward roll repetitions to four or five will prevent fatigue and injury.

There is usually a wide range of ability among youngsters in this lesson. If necessary, start at a lower level than listed here to assure students find success.

After students learn the basic activities, emphasize three phases of correct performance:
1. Starting Position
2. Execution
3. Finishing Position

DPE pp. 543 – 547

Rotate partners to prevent one student from dominating another. For safety, use starting and stopping signals to ensure fair starts and fast stops.

Cog.—Momentum needs to be developed and applied when performing rolls. The student will be able to name three ways of developing momentum (i.e., tucking, starting from a higher point, preliminary raising of the arms).

PM.—The student will be able to perform at least two of the activities in each of the groups.

Aff.—Tumbling and stunts are activities in which there is a wide range of student ability which is evident to others. Discuss the sensitivity of the situation and the need to understand the shortcomings of others.

Cog.—The center of weight must be positioned over the center of support in balance stunts. The student will be able to describe and demonstrate this in his or her own fashion.

Cog.—Certain sports and activities offer a greater degree of aerobic conditioning. Contrast activities such as basketball, jogging, bicycling, rope jumping, and swimming with bowling, golf, softball, and football.

Aff.—Many people take drugs to help them handle stress. Unfortunately, they avoid dealing with the cause of stress. Drugs are short-term solutions and ultimately cause more problems than they solve. Discuss how drugs can cause physiological and psychological changes and addiction.

MOVEMENT EXPERIENCE— CONTENT	ORGANIZATION AND TEACHING HINTS	EXPECTED STUDENT OBJECTIVES AND OUTCOMES

Juggling with Scarves

Scarves are held by the fingertips near the center. To throw the scarf, it should be lifted and pulled into the air above eye level. Scarves are caught by clawing, a downward motion of the hand and grabbing the scarf from above as it is falling.

1. **Cascading**—Cascading is the easiest pattern for juggling three objects. The following sequence can be used to learn this basic technique.
   a. One scarf. Hold the scarf in the center. Quickly move the arm across the chest and toss the scarf with the palm out. Reach out with the other hand and catch the scarf in straight down motion (clawing). Toss the scarf with this hand using the motion and claw it with the opposite hand. Continue the tossing and clawing sequence over and over.
   b. Two scarves. Hold a scarf with the fingertips in each hand. Toss the first one across the body as described above.
   c. Three-scarf cascading. A scarf is held in each hand by the fingertips as described above. The third scarf is held with the ring and little finger against the palm of the hand. The first scarf to be thrown will be from the hand that is holding two scarves.
2. **Reverse Cascading**—Reverse cascading involves tossing the scarves from the waist level to the outside of the body and allowing the scarves to drop down the midline of the body.
   a. One scarf.
   b. Two scarves.
   c. Three scarves.
3. **Column Juggling**—Column juggling is so named because the scarves move straight up and down as through they were inside a large pipe or column and do not cross the body.
4. **Showering**—Start with two scarves in the right hand and one in the other. Begin by throwing the first two scarves from the right hand. Toss the scarves in a large circle away from the midline of the body and overhead as high as possible. As soon as the second scarf is released, toss the scarf across to the left hand and throw it in the same path with the right hand. All scarves are caught with the left hand and passed to the right hand.

DPE pp. 417 – 420

Scarf juggling should teach proper habits (e.g., tossing the scarves straight up in line with the body rather than forward or backward).

Many instructors remind children to imagine that they are in a phone booth or large refrigerator box—to emphasize tossing and catching without moving.

The fingers, not the palms, should be used in throwing and catching the objects.

Throwing the objects too high and away from the body is a problem students need to overcome.

Verbal cues such as "toss, claw, toss, claw" are helpful.

To perform three-scarf column juggling, begin with two scarves in one hand and one in the other hand.

Showering is more difficult than cascading because of the rapid movement of the hands. There is less time allowed for catching and tossing. The scarves move in a circle following each other. It should be practiced in both directions for maximum challenge.

Cog.—The student will be able to state the sequence of throwing the scarves in cascading with three objects.

PM.—The student will be able to consistently toss the objects up and directly in front of the body.

Aff.—Students must accept the fact that the more difficult the skill, the more practice it takes to learn.

Discuss the complexity of juggling and the need for applied and repetitive practice.

Aff.—Discuss the fact that accomplishing the skill once is not a goal. Performing the skill many times correctly is a goal of people who excel at skills.

MOVEMENT EXPERIENCE—CONTENT	ORGANIZATION AND TEACHING HINTS	EXPECTED STUDENT OBJECTIVES AND OUTCOMES

5. Juggling Challenges

  a. While cascading, toss as scarf under one leg.

  b. While cascading, toss a scarf from behind the back.

  c. Instead of catching one of the scarves, blow it upward with a strong breath of air.

  d. Begin cascading by tossing the first scarf into the air with a foot. Lay the scarf across the foot and kick it into the air.

  e. Try juggling three scarves with one hand. Do not worry about establishing a pattern, just catch the lowest scarf each time. Try both regular and reverse cascading, as well as column juggling.

  f. While doing column juggling, toss up one scarf, hold the other two and make a full turn. Resume juggling.

  g. Try juggling more than three scarves (up to six) while facing a partner.

  h. Juggle three scarves while standing beside a partner with inside arms around each other. This is easy to do since it is regular three-scarf cascading.

6. Juggling with Balls—Two balls can be juggled with one hand, and three balls can be juggled with two hands. Juggling can be done in a crisscross fashion, which is called cascading, or it can be done in a circular fashion, called showering. Cascading is considered the easier of the two styles and should be the first one attempted.

DPE pp. 420 – 421

Students easily become frustrated with this skill. It is a good idea to allow short bouts of practice. For example, 4–5 minutes of practice followed by a game would avoid long periods of failure. Further practice could be continued after the game for another 4–5 minutes.

After the basic skill of juggling is mastered, different types of objects can be used (i.e., pins, rings, and beanbags).

GAME (5 – 7 MINUTES)

Team Handball—*DPE*, p. 590

  Supplies: Team handball, foam rubber ball, or volleyball; cones; pinnies

  Skills: Running, dribbling, passing, throwing, catching

  The object of the game is to move a small soccer ball down the field by passing and dribbling and then to throw the ball into a goal area that is 3 m wide and 2 m high. In regulation play, each team has six court players and one goalie. The six court players cover the entire court. A player is allowed three steps before and after dribbling the ball. There is no limit on the number of dribbles. Dribbling is, however, discouraged because passing is more effective. A double dribble is a violation. A player can hold the ball for 3 seconds only before passing, dribbling, or shooting. Players cannot kick the ball in any way, except the goalie.

  One point is awarded for a goal. Violations and penalties are similar to basketball. A free throw is taken from the point of the violation, and defense must remain 3 m away while protecting the goal. A penalty throw is awarded from the 7-m line for a major violation. A major violation occurs when an offensive player who is inside the 9-m line in a good shooting position is fouled. During a penalty throw, all players must be behind the 9-m line.

  The offensive team starts the game with a throw-on from the center line. A throw-on also initiates play after each goal. All six offensive players line up at the centerline, and a teammate throws the ball to a teammate. The defense is in position, using either a zone or person-to-person defense. Offensive strategy is similar to basketball with picks, screens, rolls, and movement to open up shots on goal. With a zone defense, short, quick passes are made in an overloaded portion of the zone.

MOVEMENT EXPERIENCE—CONTENT	ORGANIZATION AND TEACHING HINTS	EXPECTED STUDENT OBJECTIVES AND OUTCOMES

The defensive strategy is similar to basketball, with person-to-person and zone defense being popular. Beginning players should start with the person-to-person defense and learn how to stay with an offensive player. The back players in the zone are back against the goal line, while the front players are just inside the 9-m line. The zone rotates with the ball as passes are made around the court.

Octopus—*DPE*, p. 584
    Supplies: None
    Skills: Maneuvering, problem solving
    Octopus is a game that gets its name from the many hands joined together in the activity. Children stand shoulder to shoulder in a tight circle. Everyone thrusts the hands forward and reaches through the group of hands to grasp the hands across the circle. Players must make sure that they do not hold both hands of the same player. Players also may not hold the hand of an adjacent player. The object is to untangle the mess created by the joined hands by going under, over, or through fellow players. No one is permitted to release a hand grip during the unraveling. What is the end result? Perhaps one large circle or two smaller connected circles.
    Teaching Suggestion: If, after a period of time, the knotted hands do not seem to unravel, call a halt and administer first aid. The teacher and group can decide where the difficulty is and allow a change in position of those hands until the know is dissolved. This should not be used as a competitive game because the difficulty of the knots cannot be equalized.

Bomb the Pins—*DPE*, p. 581
    Supplies: 8 to 12 bowling pins per team, 10 to 12 foam rubber balls
    Skill: Throwing
    A line is drawn across the center of the floor from wall to wall. This divides the floor into two courts, each of which is occupied by one team. Another line is drawn 25 ft from the centerline in each court. This is the line where each team spaces its bowling pins. Each team has at least five balls.
    The object of the game is to knock over the other team's pins—not to throw at opponents. Players throw the balls back and forth, but the players cannot cross the centerline. Whenever a pin is knocked over by a ball or player (accidentally or not), that pin is removed. The team with the most pins standing at the end of the game is declared the winner. Out-of-bounds balls can be recovered but must be thrown from inside the court.
    Variations: Pins can be reset instead of removed. Two scorers, one for each pin line, are needed. Rolling the balls is an excellent modification.

DYNAMIC PHYSICAL EDUCATION LESSON PLAN
Gymnastics and Bench Skills
Level III

Supplies and Equipment Needed:
1 8 1/2" playground ball per student
Tape player (aerobic dance)
Tumbling mats
6 benches
Parachute
Bowling pins

MOVEMENT EXPERIENCE—CONTENT	ORGANIZATION AND TEACHING HINTS	EXPECTED STUDENT OBJECTIVES AND OUTCOMES

INTRODUCTORY ACTIVITY (2 – 3 MINUTES)

Ball Activities

Each student has an 8-½" playground ball. The balls can be dribbled as in basketball or as in soccer. On signal, students stop, balance on one leg, pass the ball under the leg and around back and overhead, maintaining control and balance.

Variations:
1. Toss ball up in place of dribble.
2. Play catch with a friend while moving.
3. Have a leader challenge the class to try different stunts and manipulative actions.

DPE p. 256

Emphasis should be on movement rather than ball skill activities.

Spread the playground balls throughout the area so the time needed to secure and put away equipment is minimized.

Cog.—The student will explain the concept of making a toss that leads the catcher so he can move into the path of the ball.

PM.—The students will be able to toss the balls in front of themselves so movements are not interrupted.

FITNESS DEVELOPMENT ACTIVITY (7 – 8 MINUTES)

Parachute Fitness

Tape alternating segments of silence and music to signal duration of exercise. Music segments indicate aerobic activity with the parachute while intervals of silence announce using the chute to enhance flexibility and strength development.
1. Jog in circle with chute held in left hand. Reverse directions and hold with right hand.
2. Standing, raise the chute overhead, lower to waist, lower to toes, raise to waist, etc.
3. Slide to the right; return slide to the left.
4. Sit and perform curl-ups with twist—45 seconds.
5. Skip for 30 seconds.
6. Freeze, face the center, and stretch the chute tightly with bent arms. Hold for 8–12 seconds. Repeat five to six times.
7. Run in place, hold the chute at waist level, and hit the chute with lifted knees.

DPE, p. 285

Evenly space youngsters around the chute.

Use different grips to add variation to the activities.

Develop group morale by encouraging students to move together.

Use music to motivate youngsters.

To cool down, allow youngsters a minute to perform parachute stunts like the Dome or Mushroom.

Cog.—It is interesting to measure the breathing rate at rest and during and after exercise. Why does breathing rate vary?

Aff.—Many experts feel people are overweight due to lack of activity rather than eating too much. Discuss why this might be true.

Aff.—Goals should be set based on a person's capability. Discuss some types of goals students might set to maintain physical fitness. Some examples might be:
1. Jog 1–1 1/2 miles daily.
2. Do 10 push-ups daily.
3. Jump-rope for 10 minutes daily.
4. Play basketball every day for 30 minutes.
5. Run 30 miles in a month.

MOVEMENT EXPERIENCE—CONTENT	ORGANIZATION AND TEACHING HINTS	EXPECTED STUDENT OBJECTIVES AND OUTCOMES

8. Sit with legs under the chute. Do a seat walk toward the center. Return to the perimeter. Repeat four to six times.
9. Place the chute on the ground. Jog away from the chute and return on signal. Repeat for 45 seconds.
10. On sides with legs under the chute. Perform Side Flex and lift chute with legs.
11. Lie on back with legs under the chute. Shake the chute with the feet.
12. Hop to the center of the chute and return. Repeat for 30 seconds.
13. Assume the push-up position with the legs aligned away from the center of the chute. Shake the chute with one arm while the other arm supports the body.
14. Sit with feet under the chute. Stretch by touching the toes with the chute. Relax with other stretches while sitting.

LESSON FOCUS (15 – 20 MINUTES)

Gymnastics and Bench Skills

Gymnastics

Six groups of activities in this lesson ensure that youngsters receive a variety of experiences. Pick a few activities from each group and teach them alternately. For example, teach an individual stunt or two, then a tumbling skill or inverted balance, followed by a balance stunt, etc. Give equal time to each group of activities

1. Tumbling and Inverted Balances
   a. Straddle Press to Handstand
   b. Handstand Variations
   c. Headspring
   d. Walking on the Hands
   e. Walk-Over
2. Balance Stunts
   a. Handstand Stunts
   b. Front Seat Support
   c. Elbow Balance
3. Individual Stunts
   a. Pretzel
   b. Jackknife
   c. Heel and Toe Spring
   d. Single-Leg Circle
4. Partner and Group Stunts
   a. Quintuplet Roll
   b. Dead Person Lift
   c. Injured Person Carry
   d. Merry-Go-Round
5. Partner Support Stunts
   a. Angel
   b. Side Stand
   c. Partner Pyramids

DPE pp. 481 – 497

Scatter as many tumbling mats as possible throughout the area in order to avoid waiting lines.

For most children, limiting the number of forward or backward roll repetitions to four or five will prevent fatigue and injury.

Many of these activities are difficult. Do not hesitate to start at a level lower than listed here to assure students find success.

Avoid asking all students to perform in front of others. Allow students to work individually.

Teach youngsters to stand on the hips and shoulders when doing partner support stunts.

PM.—The student will be able to perform a forward and backward roll with at least two variations.

The student will be able to perform at least two activities from each of the categories.

Cog.—The student will be able to describe proper positioning of the hands and knees in partner support and pyramid activities.

Cog.—The student will be able to name at least three safety principles that are important tumbling and inverted balance activities.

Aff.—Tumbling is an excellent activity for overcoming personal fear of harm from the activities. Discuss how many athletes must conquer various fears and take risks in order to succeed.

MOVEMENT EXPERIENCE—CONTENT	ORGANIZATION AND TEACHING HINTS	EXPECTED STUDENT OBJECTIVES AND OUTCOMES

6. Combatives
  a. Catch-and-Pull Tug-of-War
  b. Stick Twist
  c. Toe Touch
  d. Crab Contest
  e. Shoulder Shove
  f. Power Pull
	DPE pp. 543 – 547
	
	Rotate partners to prevent one student from dominating another. For safety, use starting and stopping signals to ensure fair starts and fast stops.
		Cog.—When a forward roll is started, the center of gravity is moved outside the base of support. This causes momentum to be developed in the direction of the roll. What skills demand that the performer move into an unstable position?
		
		PM.—The student and his partner will be able to originate and demonstrate two partner support activities.

Benches
 	
1. Basic Tumbling Skills
  a. Forward Roll
  b. Backward Roll
  c. Forward Roll to a Walkout
  d. Cartwheel
2. Locomotor Movements
  a. Gallop
  b. Jump on and off the bench
  c. Hop on and off the bench
  d. Jump or hop over the bench
3. Movements alongside the benches — Proceed alongside the bench in the following positions.
  a. Prone position—hands on bench.
  b. Supine position—hands on bench.
  c. Turn over—proceed along bench, changing from prone to supine position with hands on bench.
  d. All of the above positions performed with the feet on the bench.
4. Scooter movements—sit on bench and proceed along bench without using hands.
  a. Regular scooter—feet leading.
  b. Reverse scooter—legs trailing.
  c. Seat walk—walk on the buttocks.
5. Crouch jumps
  a. Straddle jump
  b. Regular jump
  c. One hand—two feet
  d. One hand—one foot
6. Jump dismounts
  a. Single jump—forward or backward
  b. Jump with turns—1/2, 3/4 or full
  c. Jackknife
  d. Jackknife split
  e. Heel or knee slap
7. Jump followed by a stunt
  a. Jump—forward roll
  b. Back jump—back roll
  c. Side jump—side roll
  d. Shoulder roll
  e. Cartwheel
	DPE pp. 469 – 472
	
	Benches should be placed near the mats they will be used with so the transition is smooth and time efficient.
	
	Six benches, one group behind each bench.
	
	Place a mat at end of bench for dismounts.
	
	Use a dismount at the end of each activity. See numbers 6 and 7 for suggestions.
	
	Have the next person in line begin when the person in front of him is halfway across the bench.
	
	Have the youngsters perform a return activity on the way back to their line.
	
	Speed is not the goal. Move deliberately across the bench.
	
	Keep the limbs on the floor as far away as possible from the bench to achieve maximum developmental effect.
	
	Use the dismounts to add variety to each of the previous activities. Proper dismounting should be encouraged and can be associated with gymnastic routines.
		PM.—The student will be able to perform the forward roll on the bench.
		
		PM.—The student will be able to perform the locomotor movements across the bench.
		
		Cog.—The student will be able to identify which bench activities develop arm and shoulder girdle strength.
		
		Cog.—The student will be able to describe why quality of movement is necessary on the benches to ensure beneficial results.
		
		Cog.—Increased fat causes the heart to have to work harder. The resting pulse rate of an obese person is often 10 beats per minute faster than a normal weight individual. This amounts to approximately 14,000 extra beats per day due to excessive fat.
		
		Cog.—Flexing at the ankles, knees, and hips is important when landing after a dismount. This increases the time over which the force is absorbed. Students should understand the importance of absorbing force for a stable landing and minimizing the risk of injury.

MOVEMENT EXPERIENCE— CONTENT	ORGANIZATION AND TEACHING HINTS	EXPECTED STUDENT OBJECTIVES AND OUTCOMES

8. Allow students time to develop their own routines on the benches including dismounts and return activities.

GAME (5 – 7 MINUTES)

Pin Knockout—*DPE*, p. 586

Supplies: Many playground balls, 12 bowling pins

Skills: Rolling, dodging

Two teams of equal number play the game. Each team is given many playground balls and six bowling pins. A court 30 by 60 ft or larger with a centerline is needed. The size of the court depends on the number of children in the game. The object of the game is to knock down all of the opponents' bowling pins. The balls are used for rolling at the opposing team's pins. Each team stays in its half of the court.

A player is eliminated if any of the following occurs:

1. She is touched by any ball at any time, regardless of the situation (other than picking up a ball).

2. She steps over the centerline to roll or retrieve a ball. (Any opposing team member hit as a result of such a roll is not eliminated.)

3. She attempts to block a rolling ball with a ball in her hands and the ball touches her in any manner.

A foul is called when a player holds a ball longer than 10 seconds without rolling at the opposing team. Play stops and the ball is given to the opposing team.

The bowling pins are put anywhere in the team's area. Players may guard the pins, but must not touch them. When pin is down, even though it might have been knocked over unintentionally by a member of the defending team, it is removed immediately from the game. The game is over when all pins on one side have been knocked down.

Over the Wall—*DPE*, p. 585

Supplies: None

Skills: Running, dodging

Two parallel goal lines are drawn about 60 ft apart. Two additional parallel lines about 3 ft apart are laid out parallel to the goal lines in the middle of the game area. This is the wall. One player is it and stands on, or behind, the wall. All of the other players are behind one of the goal lines. The tagger calls "Over the wall." All of the players must then run across the wall to the other goal line. The child who is it tries to tag any player he can. Anyone caught helps catch the others. Players also are considered caught when they step on the wall. They must clear it with a leap or a jump and cannot step on it anywhere, including on the lines. After crossing over to the other side safely, players must wait for the next call. The game can be made more difficult by increasing the width of the wall. The taggers can step on or run through the wall at will.

DYNAMIC PHYSICAL EDUCATION LESSON PLAN
Gymnastics and Balance-Beam Skills
Level III

Supplies and Equipment Needed:
  Tape player for aerobic fitness
  Tumbling mats
  Six balance beams
  Manipulative equipment to be used on balance beams
  Cones
  Balls
  Pinnies

MOVEMENT EXPERIENCE—CONTENT	ORGANIZATION AND TEACHING HINTS	EXPECTED STUDENT OBJECTIVES AND OUTCOMES

INTRODUCTORY ACTIVITY (2 – 3 MINUTES)

Rubber Band

Students begin from a central point with the teacher. On signal, students move away from the teacher with a designated movement such as run, hop sideways, skip backward, double-lame dog, or Carioca. On signal, they sprint back to the central point.

DPE p. 258

Be sure plenty of room exists away from starting point.

Repeat this cycle several times.

Students can perform one or two stretching activities after returning to central point.

PM.—The student will be able to perform all of teacher-designated movements at an adequate level.

Cog.—The student will know the meaning of all movements called out by the teacher.

FITNESS DEVELOPMENT ACTIVITY (7 – 8 MINUTES)

Aerobic Fitness (suggested routine)

1. Rhythmic run with kick
2. Bounce forward and backward with clap
3. Rhythmic 2-count curl-ups
4. Crab Kick Combinations
     Repeat steps 1–4 four times.
5. Jump Jack variations
6. Knee lifts turning
7. Side bends
8. Leg extensions (seated)
     Repeat steps 5–8 four times.
9. Directional run (changing formations)
10. Bounce with body twist
11. Side leg raises (alternate legs)
12. Rhythmic Push-Ups
     Repeat steps 9–12 four times.

DPE pp. 305 – 307

May be done in scattered formation or in a circle.

A follow-the-leader approach is excellent.

Use music that stimulates students to exercise.

Alternate bouncing and running movements with flexibility and strength development movements.

While performing rhythmic running movements, students can move into different formations.

Place cue cards on the wall that list steps, number of repetitions, and "cue words."

Smile and have a good time—students will believe you enjoy fitness activity.

Variations may be made in the suggested routines.

PM.—The student will be able to perform all of the exercises in time to the music by the end of the week.

Cog.—The student will be able to recognize all of the exercises by name by the end of the week.

Cog.—The blood is transported back to the lungs in the veins. This system is called the circulatory system.

Cog.—The body adapts rapidly to hot, humid conditions. Within two weeks of practice and training in heat, the body will adapt and become more efficient. Primarily, the body sweats more rapidly and to a greater extent. The evaporation of sweat effectively cools the body. Discuss adaptation and the important role of sweating to maintain a constant body temperature.

MOVEMENT EXPERIENCE— CONTENT	ORGANIZATION AND TEACHING HINTS	EXPECTED STUDENT OBJECTIVES AND OUTCOMES

Gymnastics and Balance-Beam Skills

Gymnastics

Six groups of activities in this lesson ensure that youngsters receive a variety of experiences. Pick a few activities from each group and teach them alternately. For example, teach an individual stunt or two, then a tumbling skill or inverted balance, followed by a balance stunt, etc. Give equal time to each group of activities

1. Review activities taught in previous gymnastics lesson plans.
   a. Tumbling and Inverted Balances
   b. Balance Stunts
   c. Individual Stunts
   d. Partner and Group Stunts
   e. Partner Support Stunts

   f. Combatives

Balance Beams

1. Move across the beam in various directions, using the following movements:
   a. Slide
   b. Heel and toe
   c. Tiptoes
   d. High Kicks
   e. Grapevine
   f. Dip Step
   g. Student choice
2. Balance objects such as beanbags, erasers or wands while walking across beam. (Exploratory approach)
3. Use various equipment:
   a. Play catch with beanbags. Try different throws and movement.
   b. Bounce a playground ball and catch it, dribble it, play catch with a partner.
   c. Step over a wand, go under a wand, change direction.
   d. Go through a hoop.
   e. Jump-rope with an individual jump rope.
4. Half-and-Half Movements—Utilizing previously learned movements, the student goes halfway across the beam using a selected movement and then changes to another movement to travel to second half.
5. Movement Sequences
   a. Repeat the half-and-half movements, adding a particular challenge or stunt in the center. Examples include:
   — Balances—Front Balance, Backward Balance, Seat Balance.

DPE pp. 526 – 542

Scatter as many tumbling mats as possible throughout the area in order to avoid waiting lines.

There is usually a wide range of ability among youngsters in this lesson. If necessary, start at a lower level than listed here to assure students find success.

DPE pp. 543 – 547

DPE pp. 467 – 469

Balance beams should be placed near the mats they will be used with so the transition is smooth and time efficient.

Use at least six benches with equal numbers of students behind each bench.

Stress student choice and exploration.

Place a target on the wall in front of the beams. Ask students to visually focus on the targets while walking the beams.

Use a mat at the finishing end of the beam for students to perform their dismounts.

Assign a return activity for students so they are busy off as well as on the beam.

Stress quality of the movement across the bench as well as during the dismount.

If a child falls, have her step back on the beam and continue. This will ensure her of the same amount of practice as the gifted child.

Make sure each student performs a dismount. The dismount will discourage the student from running across the beam and will closely simulate the competitive balance-beam event.

A jumping box or other type of box placed near the front of each beam allows for efficient pick-up and put-away of manipulative equipment.

Aff.—Learning gymnastics skills helps a student's total body control. Discuss specific physical activities that require different amounts of body control.

PM.—The student will know proper spotting techniques when needed.

Cog.—The student will know that high-difficulty gymnastic stunts should only be attempted with teacher spotting when learning.

M.—The student will be able to balance themselves and an object while walking across the beam; a desirable goal would be for neither the object nor the child to fall off.

Cog.—For increased balance control, widen the base of support and lower the center of gravity. Discuss the impact of the narrow base of support found on balance beams.

Cog.—Balance is a learned activity. The student will be able to explain that practice and concentration are necessary for improvement.

Cog.—The student will be able to explain how changing arm and leg positions or direction of movement creates a new balance task for the body.

Aff.—Awareness of the status and prestige given to a skilled performer. Discuss the payoff when one is skilled, such as friends, money, prizes, etc.

Cog.—Balance activities are best performed when performers are relaxed. Increased leg strength also plays an important part in balance. Encourage practice at home where there is little fear of falling and embarrassment.

MOVEMENT EXPERIENCE— CONTENT	ORGANIZATION AND TEACHING HINTS	EXPECTED STUDENT OBJECTIVES AND OUTCOMES

— Stunts—Walk Through, Finger Touch.
— Challenges—Make a full turn, jump kicking up heels; do a push-up.
6. Allow student exploration.

GAME (5 – 7 MINUTES)

Octopus—*DPE*, p. 584
  Supplies: None
  Skills: Maneuvering, problem solving
  Octopus is a game that gets its name from the many hands joined together in the activity. Children stand shoulder to shoulder in a tight circle. Everyone thrusts the hands forward and reaches through the group of hands to grasp the hands across the circle. Players must make sure that they do not hold both hands of the same player. Players also may not hold the hand of an adjacent player. The object is to untangle the mess created by the joined hands by going under, over, or through fellow players. No one is permitted to release a hand grip during the unraveling. What is the end result? Perhaps one large circle or two smaller connected circles.
  Teaching Suggestion: If, after a period of time, the knotted hands do not seem to unravel, call a halt and administer first aid. The teacher and group can decide where the difficulty is and allow a change in position of those hands until the know is dissolved. This should not be used as a competitive game because the difficulty of the knots cannot be equalized.

Fast Pass—*DPE*, p. 583
  Supplies: One 8-in. foam rubber ball, pinnies
  Skills: Passing, catching, moving to an open area
  One team begins with the ball. The object is to complete five consecutive passes without the ball touching the floor. The team without the ball attempts to intercept the ball or recover an incomplete pass. Each time a pass is completed, the team shouts the number of consecutive passes completed it represents. Each time a ball touches the floor or is intercepted, the count starts over.
  Players may not contact each other. Emphasis should be placed on spreading out and using the entire court area. If players do not spread out, the area can be broken into quadrants and players restricted to one quadrant.

DYNAMIC PHYSICAL EDUCATION LESSON PLAN
Manipulative Skills Using Wands and Hula Hoops
Level III

Supplies and Equipment Needed:
  Taped music (for the introductory activity)
  Taped music (for the aerobic fitness routine)
  Wands
  Hula hoops
  Cassette recorder
  Cageball
  Tom-tom
  Deck tennis rings
  12 Yarnballs

MOVEMENT EXPERIENCE—CONTENT	ORGANIZATION AND TEACHING HINTS	EXPECTED STUDENT OBJECTIVES AND OUTCOMES

INTRODUCTORY ACTIVITY (2 – 3 MINUTES)

Moving to Music

Use different types of music to stimulate various locomotor and non-locomotor movements. Dance steps such as the polka, two-step, schottische and grapevine could be practiced.

DPE p. 256

If students have difficulty sensing the rhythm, a tom-tom may be used to aid them.

Emphasis should be placed on synchronizing the movement with the music.

Cog.—The student will be able to recognize the difference between 3/4 and 4/4 rhythm.

PM.—The student will be able to move, in time with the music, to six different rhythms.

Cog.—People need to warm up psychologically so they "feel" like moving. Discuss the importance of movement in setting the right frame of mind for fitness development activity.

FITNESS DEVELOPMENT ACTIVITY (7 – 8 MINUTES)

Aerobic Fitness

1. Bounce and do arm circles
2. Grapevine step with clap
3. Curl-Up variations
4. Treadmill combinations
    Repeat steps 1–4 four times.
5. Forward and side stride hops
6. Knee lift and kick combinations
7. Rhythmic windmills
8. Leg extensions (seated)
    Repeat steps 5–8 four times.
9. Rhythmic run with knee lift on every fourth beat
10. Rock side to side with double bounce on each side
11. Rhythmic Push-Ups (try them in the reverse position)
12. Bear hugs
    Repeat steps 9–12 four times.

DPE pp. 305 – 307

This is the final week of aerobic dance.

Students should be given the opportunity to lead.

Groups of four to six may be formed to create aerobic dance routines.

Use music that stimulates students to exercise.

Smile and have a good time; students will get a positive feeling about fitness activities.

Aff.—Leadership demands an increase in responsibility. Leaders must be concerned for the welfare of others as well as themselves. Discuss how the squad captain determines the work load for the rest of the group.

PM.—The student will be able to perform the exercises at an increased work load (longer duration) than the previous week.

Cog.—One measure often used to measure fitness is to count the pulse rate after exercise within 2 or 3 minutes. It might be interesting to measure pulse rate at various intervals after exercise. The more fit one is, the faster pulse rate returns to normal.

Aff.—A well-balanced diet provides fuel for physical activity. Discuss the basics of a good diet and the need for such.

MOVEMENT EXPERIENCE—CONTENT	ORGANIZATION AND TEACHING HINTS	EXPECTED STUDENT OBJECTIVES AND OUTCOMES
		PM.—The student will be able to work in small groups and create aerobic dance routines by the end of the week.

Cog.—Aerobic training increases maximal oxygen intake. A large part of the increase is due to increased stroke volume of the heart. More blood is pumped per heart beat due to increased capacity of the heart and stronger contractions. How is the heart strengthened? |

LESSON FOCUS (15 – 20 MINUTES)

Manipulative Skills Using Wands and Hula Hoops

Wands

Select some activities from each of the three groups: exercises, stunts and partner activities

Exercises Using Wands	*DPE pp. 427 – 431*	

1. Standing isometrics:
  a. Push hands together; chest high, overhead, behind seat.
  b. Pull hands apart; chest high, overhead, behind seat.
2. Wand overhead, with straight arms:
  a. Bend right, left, forward.
3. Wand twist:
  a. Twist right, left.
  b. Bend right, left.
4. Long sitting, wand overhead:
  a. Touch toes with wand.
	Watch posture. Stress good effort. Hold for 8 seconds.
	
	Stress full bends. Reach beyond toes.
		Aff.—Wand stunts demand a great deal of flexibility. Often, girls are more successful at flexibility than boys. This is an opportune time to discuss individual differences as well as ability differences between sexes.
		
		Cog.—The students will be able to explain in their own words that frequent stretching makes possible a wider range of motion and conserves energy.

Wand Stunts		

1. Wand catch:
  a. Practice different combinations.
  b. Do four-way routine.
2. Thread needle—V-Seat:
  a. Legs crossed.
  b. Legs together.
  c. Combination.
3. Thread needle—standing:
  a. Front-back, reverse side-to-side.
  b. Add Shoulder Stretcher.
4. Grapevine:
  a. First stage.
  b. Second stage—step out.
  c. Reverse.
5. Back Scratcher:
  a. First stage—down back.
  b. Second stage—down over seat.
6. Wand Whirl:
  a. Practice standing wand.
  b. Grab with hand, grab with one finger.
  c. Do right and left turns.
	Do one each way. Keep balance.
	
	Stress not touching the wand.
	
	Hold wand in fingertips.
	
	Allow kneeling, may be better for some. Use demonstration.
	
	Crossed-hands position, palms up. Use demonstration.
	
	Secure some skill in standing wand.
		Cog.—It appears to be impossible to improve reaction time. Reaction time is the time it takes to initiate a response to a signal. However, movement time can be improved through increasing strength, shortening the length of a lever, and decreasing the distance to be moved. Movement time is the time it takes to move a certain distance. Discuss a skill and what could be modified to improve movement time.
		
		Cog.—Knowledge of results is important when learning motor skills. Performers can evaluate their movements and make modifications for improvement. Discuss various aspects of a skill students should analyze to improve their performance.

MOVEMENT EXPERIENCE— CONTENT	ORGANIZATION AND TEACHING HINTS	EXPECTED STUDENT OBJECTIVES AND OUTCOMES

7. Twist under:
   a. Right hand, left hand.
   b. Twist right, left; reverse.
8. Jump stick
9. Wand balances
   a. Student choice—back of hand, shift back to front, change hands, sit, lie. Get up. Try balances on foot.
10. Crab leap
    a. Alternating feet.
11. Long reach—Perform with the wand in both the left and right hand in turn.

Partner Activities

1. Partner catch—one wand, two wands.
2. Partner change.
   a. Simple exchange
   b. Spin
3. Partner rowing
   a. Seated, legs spread, feet against feet.
   b. Overhand grip, row back and forth.
4. Stick twist—face, arms overhead, overhand grip.
5. Wand Wrestle—one hand outside.
6. Partner Pull-Up
   a. Sit, facing, knees straight, soles against soles.
   b. Bend forward, grasp wand
7. Wring the Dishrag
8. Ring toss with deck tennis rings—alternate back and forth

Hoops

1. Hula-hoop using various body parts such as waist, neck, knees, arms and fingers.
   a. While hula-hooping on the arms, try to change the hoop from one arm to the other.
   b. Change hoop from one partner to another while hula-hooping.
   c. Try leg-skippers—hula-hoop with one leg and jump the hoop with the other leg.
2. Jump rope with the hoop—forward, sideways, backward. Begin with a back-and-forth swing.
3. Roll hoop and run alongside it. Run in front of it.
4. Roll hoop with a reverse spin to make it return to the thrower.
5. Roll with a reverse spin and see how many times partner can go through it.
6. Roll with a reverse spin, jump the hoop and catch it as it returns.

Stick will slip. Must control.

Do *not* reverse jump. Get height. Practice without stick.

Keep distances short.

Distances short, use one step. Gradually increase distance. Add turns.

Hold wand instead of hands.

Try to get opponent to shift grip.

Try to wrestle stick away.

Stress equal start.

Both hands either inside or out.

Keep distances short at first.

DPE pp. 431 – 433

Scatter formation.

Hula-hooping demands that body parts are moved back and forth, *not* in a circle.

Have the class place their hoops on the floor when you desire their attention.

When jumping through hoops, encourage children to hold them loosely to prevent falls.

Use the hoop as a home area for children. This will keep them in a designated area.

The reverse spin must be taught and practiced. Many students find it to be a difficult skill.

Cog.—Teaching a skill in parts is effective when the skill is complex and contains many individual skills, and the learner has limited memory span. Explain and demonstrate to youngsters how skills can be taught in parts and then put together as a complete task.

Cog.—Practice sessions should be short when tasks are difficult and performers young. Also, when excessive repetition is demanded, sessions should be kept short. Students will understand the need for short practice sessions, distributed evenly over a long period of time.

PM.—The students will be able to hula-hoop on at least one part of their bodies.

PM.—The students will be able to place a reverse spin on the hoop, causing it to return to them.

Aff.—Many students will not immediately be able to hula-hoop or apply the reverse spin. Discuss the value of continued practice versus the alternative of quitting and never learning the skill.

Aff.—Discuss the value of learning a skill simply for one's own enjoyment and satisfaction.

MOVEMENT EXPERIENCE— CONTENT	ORGANIZATION AND TEACHING HINTS	EXPECTED STUDENT OBJECTIVES AND OUTCOMES

7. Roll with a reverse spin, kick it into the air and catch.
8. Balance the hoop on your head, try to walk through it ("thread the needle") forward, backward and sideways.
9. Use the hoop as a cowboy lasso, standing, sitting or lying down.
10. Try partner activities:
    a. Play catch with hoop.
    b. Hula-hoop on one arm, toss to partner, who catches it on one arm.
    c. Use two hoops for catching.
    d. Hoop with one hoop and play catch with other.

When throwing and catching two hoops, each partner should throw one and then progress to both hoops being thrown at the same time by one partner.

GAME (5 – 7 MINUTES)

Galactic Empire and Rebels—*DPE*, p. 583
  Supplies: None
  Skills: Chasing, fleeing, dodging
  This game can be played indoors or outdoors in a square that is approximately 100 ft on each side. Each team's spaceport is behind the end line, where the single space fighters are stationed, waiting to issue against the enemy. To begin, one or more space fighters from either team move from their spaceport to entice enemy fliers for possible capture. A flyer leaving the spaceport may capture only opposing flyers who previously have left their respective spaceport. This is the basic rule of the game. A flyer may go back to his spaceport and be eligible immediately to issue again to capture an opponent who was already in general space. The technique of the game is to entice enemy flyers close to the spaceport so that fellow flyers can issue and capture (tag) an opposing flyer.
  As an illustration of how the game proceeds: Rebel flyer 1 moves into general space to entice Empire flyer 1 so that he can be captured. Rebel flyer 1 turns back and heads for her spaceport, chased by Empire flyer 1. Rebel flyer 2 now leaves her spaceport and tags Empire flyer 1 before the Empire flyer can tag Rebel flyer 1. The Empire flyer is now a prisoner.
  A player captured by an opposing flyer is taken to the tagger's prison—both captor and captive are given free passage to the prison. In prison, the captives form a chain gang, holding hands and extending the prisoners' line toward their own spaceport. The last captive is always at the end of the prisoners' line with one foot in the prison. Captives can be released if a teammate can get to them without being tagged. The released prisoner (only the end one) is escorted back to her own spaceport and both players are given free passage.
  The game becomes one of capturing opposing flyers and securing the release of captured teammates. Flyers stepping over the sideline automatically become prisoners. One or two players in the spaceport should be assigned to guard the prison.
  Set a time limit of 10 minutes for the contest, and declare the team with the most prisoners the winner.

Jolly Ball—*DPE*, p. 584
  Supplies: A cageball 24 in. or larger (or a 36- to 48 inch pushball)
  Skill: Kicking
  Four teams are organized, each of which forms one side of a hollow square. Children sit down, facing in, with hands braced behind them (crab position). The members of each team are numbered consecutively. Each child waits until his number is called. Four active players (one from each team) move in crab position and try to kick the cageball over any one of the three opposing teams. The sideline players can also kick the ball. Ordinarily, the hands are not used, but this could be allowed in the learning stages of the game.
  A point is scored against a team that allows the ball to go over its line. A ball that goes out at the corner between teams is dead and must be replayed. When a point is scored, the active children retire to their teams and another number is called. The team with the fewest points wins the game. This game is quite strenuous for the active players, so they should be rotated after a reasonable length of time when there is no score.
  Variation: Two children from each team can be active at once.

MOVEMENT EXPERIENCE— CONTENT	ORGANIZATION AND TEACHING HINTS	EXPECTED STUDENT OBJECTIVES AND OUTCOMES

Circle Touch—*DPE*, p. 582

Supplies: Yarnballs

Skills: Dodging, body management

One child plays against three others, who form a small circle with joined hands. The object of the game is for the lone child to touch a designated child (on the shoulders) in the circle with a yarnball. The other two children in the circle, by dodging and maneuvering, attempt to keep the tagger away from the third member of the circle. The circle players may maneuver and circle in any direction but must not release hand grips. The tagger, in attempting to touch the protected circle player, must go around the outside of the circle. She is not permitted to go underneath or through the joined hands of the circle players.

Teaching suggestion: The teacher should watch for roughness by the two in the circle protecting the third. To avoid roughness, the game should be played in short 20 second bouts and then rotate in a new tagger.

Variations:

1. A piece of cloth, a handkerchief, or a flag is tucked into the belt in back of the protected child. The fourth child, the tagger, tries to pull the flag from the belt.

DYNAMIC PHYSICAL EDUCATION LESSON PLAN
Volleyball Skills (Lesson 1)
Level III

Supplies and Equipment Needed:
  One beanbag per student
  Apparatus for the Challenge Course
  Volleyball trainers or foam training balls, one for each student
  Cones
  Nets
  Hoops

MOVEMENT EXPERIENCE—CONTENT	ORGANIZATION AND TEACHING HINTS	EXPECTED STUDENT OBJECTIVES AND OUTCOMES

INTRODUCTORY ACTIVITY (2 – 3 MINUTES)

Vanishing Beanbags

Beanbags (one per student) are spread throughout the area. Students move throughout the area. On signal, they find a beanbag and sit on it. On the next signal or command, the students move again, with a few beanbags being removed during the interval. On signal, they once again sit on a beanbag. The object is to try not to be left without a beanbag move than five times.

DPE p. 256

Spread bags before class arrives, if possible.

Vary the locomotor movements and body parts to be placed on the bags.

Hoops may be substituted for beanbags.

PM.—The student will be able to move throughout the area without falling or bumping.

Aff.—Sportsmanship is necessary when students are put in self-officiating situations. Discuss the need for fair play in this and other activities.

FITNESS DEVELOPMENT (7 – 8 MINUTES)

Challenge Course Fitness

Design a course around the perimeter of the area using the following ideas:
  1. Step on jumping box, dismount to tumbling mat and do a forward roll.
  2. Run and weave through four wands held upright by cones.
  3. Handwalk across a horizontal ladder or do a flexed-arm hang from a climbing rope for 5 seconds.
  4. Step on and off three jumping boxes (small-large-small).
  5. Agility run through hoops.
  6. Perform jump turns.
  7. Leap over a magic rope held taut with two chairs or jumping boxes.
  8. Hop on one foot.
  9. Do a Log Roll across a tumbling mat.
  10. Alternate going over and under six obstacles (cones and wands or hoops).
  11. Crouch jump or scooter movements the length of a balance-beam bench.
  12. Slide through a parallel tumbling mat maze (mats stood on their sides).

DPE pp. 304 – 305

Design a Challenge Course that exercises all body parts.

Emphasize moving through the Challenge Courses with quality movements. The goal is fitness, not how fast youngsters can move through the course.

Distribute youngsters throughout the course rather than lining them up to start at one point. Faster moving youngsters can pass a station one time only.

Stop the class at regular intervals to perform flexibility and strength development activities for the shoulder girdle and abdominal region.

Change directions periodically. This will help prevent a build-up of students at slower moving stations.

Cog.—The student will be able to design a Challenge Course that exercises all parts of the body.

PM.—The student will be able to accomplish all the challenges successfully.

Aff.—Many different methods for developing and maintaining physical fitness are used in this curriculum. Discuss the importance of people's analyzing their likes and dislikes as they find an approach to fitness that best suits them.

PM.—The student will be able to negotiate all obstacles successfully while traveling around the Challenge Course at least three times within the allotted time.

MOVEMENT EXPERIENCE— CONTENT	ORGANIZATION AND TEACHING HINTS	EXPECTED STUDENT OBJECTIVES AND OUTCOMES

LESSON FOCUS (15 – 20 MINUTES)

Volleyball Skills

Skills

Underhand Serve

Face the net with the foot opposite the serving hand positioned slightly forward and the weight on the rear foot. Hold the ball waist high in the opposite hand. When serving, step forward with the opposite foot, swinging the serving hand forward with an underhand motion.

Overhand Pass

Position the feet in an easy, comfortable manner with the knees bent. Cup the forefingers and thumbs close together forehead high with elbows out. Ball contact is made at eye level by the force of spread fingers and arm and leg extension.

Forearm Pass (Bump)

Move rapidly to the spot where the ball is descending to ensure an accurate volley. Clasp the hands together so the forearms are parallel to the floor and the elbows are reasonably locked. While awaiting the ball, hold the forearms and hands between the knees. When contacting the ball, swing the forearms slightly upward with rapid leg extension. Contact is made with the forearms or fists.

Setup

Raise the ball with a soft, easy pass to position 1 or 2 feet above the net and about 1 foot away from it. Usually the overhand pass is used for the setup. The player who taps to the "setter" must make an accurate, easily handled pass.

Drills

Station (Small Group) Instruction

The teacher should instruct at a different station each day. Start at the station that demands the most instruction. Set up a system of rotation that assures all stations will be covered during the unit.

Station 1 - Partner work

Positioned about 20 feet apart, two players practice the underhand serve back and forth, catching the ball after each serve.

DPE pp. 719 – 721

Practice with a partner serving back and forth or against a wall.

Contact can be made with an open hand or with the fist. (Encourage student exploration.)

Foam balls (8 1/2") or beach balls increase success in early stages of learning.

It should appear as if the player is "looking through the window."

Do not contact the ball with the palm of the hands.

Again, foam balls (8 1/2") or beach balls are suggested in the beginning stages.

Do not swing the arms above waist high or the ball will travel backward.

Forearm contact is generally more accurate than fist contact.

Practice in groups of four to six.

The pass to the setter is usually a bump.

The setup is generally the second hit in a series of three.

DPE pp. 676 – 677

After the correct skill pattern is established, the receiver sets a target for the server by moving forward, backward, or to one side or the other.

Work in groups of two or three, depending on the number of balls and available wall space. If no wall space is available, one partner tosses the ball to the receiver. Following the volley by the receiver, the tosser catches the ball and the partners trade roles.

PM.—The student will be able to perform the following skills adequately:
1. Underhand serve
2. Overhand pass
3. Bump
4. Setup

Cog.—The student will be able to recite the basic rules of volleyball in the following areas:
1. Scoring
2. Rotation
3. Violations

Cog.—The student will know why forearm contact is preferred over fist contact when executing the bump.

Aff.—Teamwork is essential for group success. Discuss the need for cooperation among teammates before success in a competitive situation can be achieved.

Aff.—Cooperation is necessary when partner and group work are used to learn skills.

MOVEMENT EXPERIENCE— CONTENT	ORGANIZATION AND TEACHING HINTS	EXPECTED STUDENT OBJECTIVES AND OUTCOMES

Station 2 - Individual work

Stand 6 feet from a wall; throw the ball to the wall and volley it to the wall with an overhand pass. The player then catches the ball and gives it to his partner. Use the same drill to teach the forearm pass (bump). Allow two passes against the wall before a catch is made.

Station 3 - Individual work

Standing 6 feet from the wall, toss the ball against the wall and alternate an overhand pass with a bump.

Station 4 - Group work

Two groups of students scatter on opposite sides of the net. The children serve volleyballs from back of the baseline and recover balls coming from the other team.

Eight to ten balls are needed. The action is informal and continuous.

The game Shower Service Ball may be played.

GAME (5 – 7 MINUTES)

Volleyball Lead-Up Games

Keep It Up.—*DPE*, p. 726

Supplies: A trainer volleyball for each team
Skills: Overhand, forearm, and dig passes

Each team forms a small circle of not more than eight players. The object of the game is to see which team can make the greater number of volleys in a specified time or which team can keep the ball in the air for the greater number of consecutive volleys without error.

On the signal "Go," the game is started with a volley by one of the players. The following rules are in force.

1. Balls are volleyed back and forth with no specific order of turns, except that the ball cannot be returned to the player from whom it came.

2. A player may not volley a ball twice in succession.

3. Any ball touching the ground does not count and ends the count.

Teaching suggestions: Players should be responsible for calling illegal returns on themselves and thus interrupting the consecutive volley count. The balls used should be of equal quality, so that one team cannot claim a disadvantage. Groups should be taught to count the volleys out loud, so that their progress is known.

Mini-Volleyball.—*DPE*, p. 726

Supplies: A volleyball or trainer volleyball
Skills: Most volleyball skills

Mini-Volleyball is a modified activity designed to offer opportunities for successful volleyball experiences to children between the ages of 9 and 12. The playing area is 15 ft wide and 40 ft long. The spiking line is 10 ft from the centerline. Many gymnasiums are marked for badminton courts that are 20 by 44 ft with a spiking line 6.5 ft from the center. This is an acceptable substitute court.

The modified rules used in Mini-Volleyball are as follows.

1. A team consists of three players. Two substitutions may be made per game.

2. Players are positioned for the serve so that there are two front-line players and one back-line player. After the ball is served, the back-line player may not spike the ball from the attack area or hit the ball into the attack area unless the ball is below the height of the net.

3. The height of the net is 6 ft, 10 in.

4. Players rotate positions when they receive the ball for serving. The right front-line player becomes the back-line player, and the left front-line player becomes the right front-line player.

5. A team wins a game when it scores 15 points and has a 2-point advantage over the opponent. A team wins the match when it wins two out of three games.

The back-line player cannot spike and thus serves a useful function by allowing the front players to receive the serves while he moves to the net to set up for the spikers.

Teaching suggestion: This game can be modified to suit the needs of participants. Sponge training balls work well in the learning stages of Mini-Volleyball.

MOVEMENT EXPERIENCE— CONTENT	ORGANIZATION AND TEACHING HINTS	EXPECTED STUDENT OBJECTIVES AND OUTCOMES

Regulation Volleyball—*DPE*, p. 726

Supplies: A volleyball

Skills: All volleyball skills

Regulation volleyball should be played with one possible rule change: In early experiences, it is suggested that the server be allowed a second chance if she fails to get the first attempt over the net and into play. This should apply only to the initial serve. Some instructors like to shorten the serving distance during the introductory phases of the game. It is important for the serving to be done well enough to keep the game moving.

A referee should supervise the game. There are generally three calls.

1. "Side out." The serving team fails to serve the ball successfully to the other court, fails to make a good return of a volley, or makes a rule violation.

2. "Point." The receiving team fails to make a legal return or is guilty of a rule violation.

3. "Double foul." Fouls are made by both teams on the same play, in which case the point is replayed. No score or side out results.

Teaching suggestion: There should be some emphasis on team play. Backcourt players should be encouraged to pass to front court players rather than merely batting the ball back and forth across the net.

Variation: The receiver in the back court is allowed to catch the serve, toss it, and propel it to a teammate. The catch should be limited to the serve, and the pass must go to a teammate, not over the net. This counteracts the problem of children in the back court being unable to handle the serve to keep the ball in play if the served ball is spinning, curving, or approaching with such force that it is difficult to control.

DYNAMIC PHYSICAL EDUCATION LESSON PLAN
Volleyball Skills (Lesson 2)
Level III

Supplies and Equipment Needed:
  Challenge Course equipment
  Volleyball trainers and/or foam (8 1/2") training balls (one per student)
  Three or four volleyball standards
  Two or three volleyball nets

MOVEMENT EXPERIENCE— CONTENT	ORGANIZATION AND TEACHING HINTS	EXPECTED STUDENT OBJECTIVES AND OUTCOMES

INTRODUCTORY ACTIVITY (2 – 3 MINUTES)

Marking

"Mark" by touching partner; after touch, reverse and the other partner attempts to mark.

Variations:
 1. Use the eight basic locomotor movements.
 2. Use positions such as Crab Walk, Puppy dog Walk, etc.
 3. Allow a point to be scored only when they touch a specified body part (i.e., knee, elbow, left hand).
 4. Use signal to freeze, then student attempts to "mark" (or tag) partner. Reverse roles.
 5. Use a whistle signal to change partners' roles. (If chasing partner, reverse and attempt to move *away* from the other.)

DPE p. 257

Encourage students to "watch where they are going" so they won't run into each other.

Partners should be somewhat equal in ability.

Change partners once or twice.

PM.—The students will be able to move with enough agility and quickness to allow them to catch as well as evade their partners.

Cog.—The student will be able to verbalize a simple reason for warm-up prior to strenuous activity.

FITNESS DEVELOPMENT (7 – 8 MINUTES)

Challenge Course Fitness

Design a course around the perimeter of the area using the following ideas:
 1. Step on jumping box, dismount to tumbling mat and do a forward roll.
 2. Run and weave through four wands held upright by cones.
 3. Handwalk across a horizontal ladder or do a flexed-arm hang from a climbing rope for 5 seconds.
 4. Step on and off three jumping boxes (small-large-small).
 5. Agility run through hoops.
 6. Perform jump turns.
 7. Leap over a magic rope held taut with two chairs or jumping boxes.
 8. Hop on one foot.
 9. Do a Log Roll across a tumbling mat.
 10. Move through a tunnel made with jumping boxes covered by a tumbling mat.
 11. Crouch jump or scooter movements the length of a balance-beam bench.
 12. Slide through a parallel tumbling mat maze (mats stood on their sides).

DPE pp. 304 – 305

Design a Challenge Course that exercises all body parts. Allow students an opportunity to develop new challenge ideas.

Emphasize moving through the Challenge Courses with quality movements. The goal is fitness, not how fast youngsters can move through the course.

Distribute youngsters throughout the course rather than lining them up to start at one point. Faster moving youngsters can pass a station one time only.

Stop the class at regular intervals to perform flexibility and strength development activities for the shoulder girdle and abdominal region.

Change directions periodically. This will help prevent a build-up of students at slower moving stations.

Cog.—Challenge Courses were a common way of developing fitness in the armed services.

PM.—All students should be able to run the Challenge Course three times.

Aff.—There is no easy way to fitness. It demands self-discipline. Discuss the importance of possessing a positive attitude toward activity in later life.

P.M.—The student will be able to do all Challenge Course movements with adequate skill.

MOVEMENT EXPERIENCE—CONTENT	ORGANIZATION AND TEACHING HINTS	EXPECTED STUDENT OBJECTIVES AND OUTCOMES

LESSON FOCUS (15 – 20 MINUTES)

Volleyball Skills (2)

Skills

1. Review and use different drills to practice prior skills.
   a. Underhand serve
   b. Overhand pass
   c. Bumping (forearm pass)
   d. Setup
2. Introduce the overhand serve. Stand with the opposite foot in front and the opposite side of the body turned somewhat toward the net. Toss the ball straight up with the opposite hand so it comes down in front of the shoulder on the serving side. The striking hand comes forward, contacting the ball 1 foot or so above the shoulder. Weight transfer is an essential part of this skill. Contact is made with the fingertips (pads of fingers) or with the fist.
3. Introduce blocking
   A member of the defensive team forms a screen by extending hands and arms straight up while jumping straight up. The ball is not struck, but rebounds from the blocker's stiffened hands and arms.

Drills

Station (Small Group) Instruction

The teacher should instruct at a different station each day. Start at the station that demands the most instruction. Set up a system of rotation that assures all stations will be covered during the unit.

Station 1 - Individual Volleying
1. Volley the ball directly overhead and catch. Try to consecutive volleys before the catch. Next, alternate a bump with an overhand pass before the catch. Finally, try to keep the ball going five or six times in a row with one kind of volley; alternate kinds of volleys.
2. Volley the ball 15 feet overhead, make a full turn and pass the ball again. Vary with other stunts (i.e., touching the floor, a heel click, clapping the hands at two different spots).

Station 2 - Volleying with a Partner
Players are 10 feet apart. One player tosses the ball to the other, who volleys it back to the first player, who catches it. After several volleys by one player, exchange tossers. Players can try to keep the ball going back and forth with a designated number of volleys before one player catches the ball.

DPE pp. 791 – 721

"Opposite" refers to the hand or side opposite the serving hand or side.

The floater—a serve made with the fingertips that has no spin—is difficult for opponents to handle.

The blocker should leave as little space as possible between himself and the net.

DPE pp. 722 – 724

Many sequences of volleys are possible in this drill. Movement problems such as the following can be presented: "See if you and your partner can each execute a bump, then an overhand pass, then a bump before the catch."

Cog.—The "floater" is the most difficult variation of the overhand serve for the receiver to handle.

Cog.—The student will demonstrate understanding of when to use blocking.

PM.—The student will show increased proficiency in the following skills:
1. Underhand serve
2. Overhand pass
3. Jumping
4. Setup

MOVEMENT EXPERIENCE—CONTENT	ORGANIZATION AND TEACHING HINTS	EXPECTED STUDENT OBJECTIVES AND OUTCOMES

Station 3 - Serving to a Partner
   One partner serves to the other, who volleys the ball back. Exchange responsibilities after several serves and return volleys.

Station 4 - Setting and Blocking
   Setup should be reviewed from the previous lesson with a ball tosser, setter and ball retriever. A blocker can be added if sufficient skill exists.

Practice in groups of four to six depending on available balls and net space.

Rotate positions following each attempt.

GAME (5 – 7 MINUTES)

Volleyball Lead-up Games

Mini-Volleyball—*DPE*, p. 726
   See the Lesson Plan, Volleyball Skills (Lesson 1) for a complete game description.

Regulation Volleyball—*DPE*, p. 726
   See the Lesson Plan, Volleyball Skills (Lesson 1) for a complete game description.

Three and Over Volleyball—*DPE*, p. 727
   Supplies: A volleyball
   Skills: All volleyball skills
   The game Three and Over emphasizes the basic offensive strategy of volleyball. The game follows regular volleyball rules with the exception that the ball must be played three times before going over the net. The team loses the serve or the point if the ball is not played three times.

Rotation Mini-Volleyball—*DPE*, p. 727
   Supplies: A volleyball
   Skills: All volleyball skills
   If four teams are playing in two contests at the same time, a system of rotation can be set up during any one class period. Divide the available class time roughly into three parts, less the time allotted for logistics. Each team plays the other three teams on a timed basis. At the end of a predetermined time period, whichever team is ahead wins the game. A team may win, lose, or tie during any time period, with the score determined at the end of the respective time period. The best win-loss record wins the overall contest.

DYNAMIC PHYSICAL EDUCATION LESSON PLAN
Rhythmic Movement (Lesson 3)
Level III

Supplies and Equipment Needed:
  Tom-tom
  Apparatus for the Challenge Course
  Tape player and music
  Tinikling poles
  Pinnies
  Chalk or jump ropes
  6 Playground balls
  Jump the shot rope

Dances Taught:
  Jugglehead Mixer
  Ten Pretty Girls
  Klumpakojis
  Tinikling

MOVEMENT EXPERIENCE— CONTENT	ORGANIZATION AND TEACHING HINTS	EXPECTED STUDENT OBJECTIVES AND OUTCOMES

INTRODUCTORY ACTIVITY (2 – 3 MINUTES)

European Running with Variations

1. Run lightly counterclockwise.
2. Clap hands on every fourth beat.
3. Stamp foot on every second beat.
4. On signal, make a complete turn, using four running steps.
5. On signal, stop, pivot and move in the opposite direction.
6. Appoint a student to lead the class through various formations.

DPE pp. 252 – 253

Variations should be tried after the class has mastered the quality requirements of rhythm, spacing, and staying in line.

At times, stop the drumbeat and have the class continue running. The patter of their feet is a good measure of their success in the activity.

Cog.—Skilled runners do not need the beat of the tom-tom, but can keep time with the leader.

PM.—The student will be able to perform the variation and maintain the proper rhythm at the same time.

FITNESS DEVELOPMENT ACTIVITY (7 – 8 MINUTES)

Challenge Course Fitness

Design a course around the perimeter of the area using the following ideas:

1. Step on jumping box, dismount to tumbling mat and do a forward roll.
2. Run and weave through four wands held upright by cones.
3. Handwalk across a horizontal ladder or do a flexed-arm hang from a climbing rope for 5 seconds.
4. Step on and off three jumping boxes (small-large-small).
5. Agility run through hoops.
6. Perform jump turns.
7. Leap over a magic rope held taut with two chairs or jumping boxes.
8. Hop on one foot.
9. Do a Log Roll across a tumbling mat.
10. Alternate going over and under six obstacles (cones and wands or hoops).
11. Crouch jump or scooter movements the length of a balance-beam bench.
12. Slide through a parallel tumbling mat maze (mats stood on their sides).

DPE pp. 304 – 305

Change some of the challenges and add new ones designed by students.

Emphasize moving through the Challenge Courses with quality movements. The goal is fitness, not how fast youngsters can move through the course.

Distribute youngsters throughout the course rather than lining them up to start at one point. Faster moving youngsters can pass a station one time only.

Stop the class at regular intervals to perform flexibility and strength development activities for the shoulder girdle and abdominal region.

Change directions periodically. This will help prevent a build-up of students at slower moving stations.

Repeat the Challenge Course for the duration of the 7–8 minute fitness development section.

Some of the challenges may be changed if desired to increase motivation.

This is the final week of this fitness routine.

Cog.—Challenge Courses were a common way of developing fitness in the military services.

Cog.—Smoking increases the amount of carbon monoxide inhaled. Carbon monoxide limits the amount of oxygen that can be carried by the blood to the cells. Discuss how smoking could reduce physical performance.

Cog.—The student will be able to explain that in order to support stronger muscles, larger bones are developed. Muscles grow when exercised regularly, and bones become stronger in response to the increased stress.

Cog.—Young people who have completed college and want to teach, find it extremely difficult to secure a position if they are 25% overweight. Discuss how obesity affects the perceptions of people.

PM.—The student will be able to go through the Challenge Course at least four times.

MOVEMENT EXPERIENCE—CONTENT	ORGANIZATION AND TEACHING HINTS	EXPECTED STUDENT OBJECTIVES AND OUTCOMES

LESSON FOCUS (15 – 20 MINUTES)

Rhythmic Movement (3)

Begin each lesson with a dance or two students know and enjoy.

1. Listen to the music, clapping the rhythms and pointing out where changes occur.
2. Teach the basic skills used in the dance.
3. Practice the dance steps in sequence.
4. Practice with the music.

Make the rhythms unit an enjoyable one for students. Be enthusiastic when teaching rhythms.

1. Jugglehead Mixer (*DPE*, p. 399)

An American dance

Beginning with a mixer will help break the ice, and help pave the way for more difficult dances.

Basic dance steps:
1. Two-step
2. Elbow swing
Circle of couples facing CCW.

A variety of dances are listed. Time allowances will determine the number that will be taught.

PM.—The students will improve their techniques in the two-step to the point of utility in this dance.

Aff.—The students will enjoy this dance since it has a fun aspect.

PM.—The student will become more skilled in performing turns.

2. Ten Pretty Girls (*DPE*, p. 396)

An American dance

Basic dance steps:
1. Front, side, back step
2. Swing step
Arms or hands may be linked.

Begin with the music at slow tempo. As students become familiar with the dance, the tempo may be turned up to normal speed.

For each repetition of the dance, begin on alternate feet.

Groups of three in the circle; the center person moves forward on the three stamps.

PM.—The student will improve in the front, side, back step.

Aff.—The student will take pride in doing dances properly.

Aff.—The student will accept a new partner with proper courtesy.

3. Klumpakojis (*DPE*, p. 395)

A Lithuanian dance

Basic dance steps:
1. Walking
2. Stars
3. Polka step
Double circle, partners facing CCW.

At intervals during Part IV of the dance, shout "Hey, hey" or "Yahoo" spontaneously.

Cog.—The student will be able to recognize and react to the changes as indicated in the music.

MOVEMENT EXPERIENCE—CONTENT	ORGANIZATION AND TEACHING HINTS	EXPECTED STUDENT OBJECTIVES AND OUTCOMES
4. Tinikling (*DPE,* p. 389) **Teach the Dance Rhythm.** a. Teach the basic step rhythm using two parallel chalked lines or jump ropes. b. Practice a two-count weight transfer rocking sideways on the left and right feet. c. When students can shift the weight from side to side, introduce the uneven rhythm. This is a similar rocking motion where one hop is done on the left foot and two on the right. d. Practice the uneven rhythm moving in and out of the ropes, lines on the floor, or stationary poles. **Teach the Pole Rhythm.** a. Teach the pole rhythm by practicing a three-count clapping rhythm cued by the teacher with a tom-tom. The rhythm is clap (hands together); down (slap top of legs); down (same as previous). b. Clap the rhythm to the record. Slow the music down in the early learning stages. c. Allow everyone to practice the rhythm with the poles and no dancers. d. Add dancers doing the basic step. **Practice other steps and the circle movement.** a. Crossover step: begin with the right foot. b. Rocker step: face the poles. c. Circle the poles. d. Cross step. **Practice Formation dancing.** a. Line of poles individually; with a partner. b. Square formation. **Practice Variations with Equipment** a. Bouncing ball to self or to a partner. b. Individual rope jumping while performing the Tinikling dance.	A dance from the Philippines Small-group formations. Since 5th and 6th grade students have previously had a taste of the Tinikling dance, progress through the beginning steps should be made quickly. The initial step is used only to get the dance under way. Make sure the sticks go together on the *down*-beat, as this is an auditory cue for the dancer. This dance takes some time to learn. Don't be impatient, and allow them enough time to practice. Make sure that the people handling sticks are rotated often. The sticks should be kept low or the dancer's legs may be caught. Eyes should be up, not looking at feet or poles. Partners face, holding hands with the side to the poles. Begin with the foot nearest the poles. Students should be given some time to practice these skills as they are rather difficult to master.	Cog.—The student will know the origin of the dance. PM.—The student will be able to perform the basic Tinikling step as well as move the sticks to the proper rhythm. Aff.—Dancing is an activity that has been done for many years, in many cultures. Discuss the possibilities as to why this occurs. Aff.—One of the important facets to positive social adjustment is accepting individual differences. Discuss the importance of accepting others as they are and avoiding comparing, judging, and disapproving other's performances. Aff.—All sports activities contain rhythmic elements. Discuss the need for smooth, continuous rhythm in some of these activities: basketball, football, ice skating, track and field, etc. Cog.—The student will be able to master at least two of the other steps. Cog.—Motor skills are classified as open and closed. When the environment is constantly changing, the skill is open. If spatial factors and the environment do not change, the skill is closed. Identify examples of closed and open skills. PM.—The student will be able to bounce and pass the ball in a rhythmic manner. PM.—The student will be able to jump rope in a rhythmic manner while performing the dance.

GAME (5 – 7 MINUTES)

Whistle Ball—*DPE,* p. 588
   Supplies: A ball for each group of six to eight players
   Skills: Passing, catching
   Eight or fewer children stand in circle formation. A ball is passed rapidly back and forth among them in any order. The object is to be the player who stays in the game the longest. A child sits down in place if he makes any of the following errors:
   1. He has the ball when the whistle blows. (The teacher should set a predetermined time period, at the end of which a whistle is blown. The time period can be varied from 5 to 20 seconds.)
   2. He makes a bad throw or fails to catch a good throw.
   3. He returns the ball directly to the person from whom it was received.

MOVEMENT EXPERIENCE— CONTENT	ORGANIZATION AND TEACHING HINTS	EXPECTED STUDENT OBJECTIVES AND OUTCOMES

Teaching suggestion: One way to control the time periods is to appoint a child as timer and to give her a list of the time periods, a whistle, and a stopwatch. The timer should be cautioned not to give any advance indication of when the stop signal will be blown. An automatic timer enhances the game. When the game gets down to two or three players, declare them the winners and begin anew.

Jump the Shot Variations—*DPE*, p. 584
   Supplies: A jump-the-shot rope
   Skill: Rope jumping
   Before the following variations are tried, the jump-the-shot routines and variations taught previously should be reviewed.
   1. Two or more squads are in file formation facing the rope turner. Each player runs clockwise (against the turn of the rope), jumping the rope as often as necessary to return to the squad.
   2. Each player runs counterclockwise and tries to run around the circle before the rope can catch up with him. If this happens, he must jump to allow the rope to go under him. The best time for a player to start his run is just after the rope has passed.
   3. Players can try some of the stunts in which the hands and feet are on the ground, to see whether they can have the rope pass under them. The Rabbit Jump, push-up position, Lame Dog, and others are possibilities.

DYNAMIC PHYSICAL EDUCATION LESSON PLAN
Rhythmic Movement (Lesson 4)
Level III

Supplies and Equipment Needed:
 Individual jump ropes
 Tape player and music
 Beanbags
 Fleece balls or yarn balls
 Hula hoops
 Pinnies
 Scooters
 Cageball
 Small object (coin)

Dances Taught:
 Jiffy Mixer
 Horse and Buggy Schottische
 Oh Johnny
 Doudlebska Polka
 Korobushka
 Alunelul

MOVEMENT EXPERIENCE— CONTENT	ORGANIZATION AND TEACHING HINTS	EXPECTED STUDENT OBJECTIVES AND OUTCOMES

INTRODUCTORY ACTIVITY (2 – 3 MINUTES)

Popcorn

Student pair up with one person on the floor in push-up position and the other standing ready to move. On signal, the standing students move over and under the persons on the floor. The person on the floor changes from a raised to a lowered push-up position each time the partner goes over or under them. On signal, reverse positions.

DPE p. 258

Scatter formation.

Beanbags, fleece balls (yarn balls), hula hoops, or balls may be used.

Add many challenges while moving to both the locomotor movements and manipulative activities.

PM.—The student will be able to toss and catch an object while moving.

Cog.—The student will recite the fact that it is easier to toss and catch an object while standing stationary than while moving.

FITNESS DEVELOPMENT ACTIVITY (7 – 8 MINUTES)

Continuity Drills

Students alternate rope jumping with exercises done in two-count fashion. Exercises are done when the leader says "Ready." The class answers "One-two" and performs a repetition. Students can choose any push-up or abdominal challenge activity (*DPE, pp. 281–283*). Teachers or students can lead. Tape alternating segments of music (rope jumping) and silence (exercises) to signal duration of exercise.

Rope jumping—forward	25 seconds
Double Crab Kick	30 seconds
Rope jumping—backward	25 seconds
Knee Touch Curl-Up	30 seconds
Jump and turn body	25 seconds
Push-Ups	30 seconds
Rocker Step	25 seconds
Bend and Twist	30 seconds
Swing -Step forward	25 seconds
Side Flex	30 seconds
Free jumping	25 seconds

Relax and stretch for a short time.

DPE p. 303

Use scatter formation.

A number of enjoyable chants can be used (i.e., "Physical education" followed by a two-count response and repetition "is fun!").

Allow students to adjust the work load to their fitness level. This implies resting if the rope jumping is too strenuous.

PM.—The student will be able to perform the exercises with rhythm and in unison with the rest of the class.

Cog.—Exercise, if demanding enough, will cause the training effect to occur in a short period of time. Discuss the fact that 10 minutes of rope jumping is equal to 30 minutes of jogging.

Aff.—With the class moving together and "sounding like a team," it is a good time to discuss pride in group accomplishment.

343

MOVEMENT EXPERIENCE— CONTENT	ORGANIZATION AND TEACHING HINTS	EXPECTED STUDENT OBJECTIVES AND OUTCOMES

LESSON FOCUS (15 – 20 MINUTES)

Rhythmic Movement (4)

Begin each lesson with a dance or two students know and enjoy.

1. Listen to the music, clapping the rhythms and pointing out where changes occur.
2. Teach the basic skills used in the dance.
3. Practice the dance steps in sequence.
4. Practice with the music.

Make the rhythms unit an enjoyable one for students. Be enthusiastic when teaching rhythms.

A number of dances are listed. Time allowances will determine the number that will be taught.

Do not demand perfection when teaching dances. Children can be expected to make mistakes similar to learning any other physical skill.

1. Jiffy Mixer (*DPE*, p. 397)

An American dance

Basic dance steps:
   1. Heel-and-toe step
   2. Chug step
   3. Walking

This dance may be introduced in a single circle facing inward. As the dance steps are grasped, progress to a double circle of partners facing with the boy's (nonpinnie's) back to the center. Add moving on to a new partner.

Create a less formal atmosphere when performing mixers.

Mixers provide quick and easy accomplishment, thus reinforcing success through dance.

Cog.—The student will be able to recognize and react to the changes as indicated in the music.

PM.—The student will be able to put the parts of the dance together and make the partner change properly.

2. Horse and Buggy Schottische (*DPE*, p. 399)

An American dance

Basic dance skills:
   1. Schottische step
   2. Horse and buggy formation

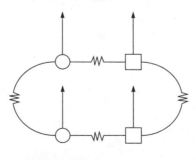

Couples should practice individually until they have mastered the dance. Then the groups of four can be put together into a circular formation.

This takes some practice.

PM.—The student will become more skilled in the schottische step.

PM.—The student will be able to apply the schottische to the horse and buggy formation.

MOVEMENT EXPERIENCE—CONTENT	ORGANIZATION AND TEACHING HINTS	EXPECTED STUDENT OBJECTIVES AND OUTCOMES

3. Alunelul (ah-loo-NAY-loo") (*DPE*, p. 401)	A Romanian dance
	
	The dance is called "Little Hazelnut." Stomping represents breaking hazelnuts.
	
	Basic dance steps:
	  1. Stomp
	  2. Step behind step
	
	Stomps should be made close to supporting foot.
	
	Dancers should be scattered, moving individually.
	
	After the dance steps have been learned, lines (side by side) may be formed with students holding the shoulder of the dancer(s) beside them.
	
	Do not demand perfection when teaching dances. Children can be expected to make mistakes similar to learning any other physical skill.
	
	As a change-of-pace activity, a tag game (or other simple game) may be taught between dances.
		Aff.—The student will begin to develop an appreciation for folk dancing.
		
		PM.—The student will be able to put the parts of the dance together and perform it successfully.

4. Korobushka (*DPE*, p. 402)	A Russian dance
	
	Basic dance steps:
	  1. Schottische step
	  2. Balance step
	  3. Walking step
	Double circle, partners facing, boy's (nonpinnie's) back to the center.
	
	Review dances students have learned previously. This is an enjoyable endeavor for youngsters and allows them to see progress they have made.
		Aff.—The student will develop some appreciation of the Russian culture.
		
		PM.—The student will be able to perform the schottische step well enough to employ it in this dance and in other dances.

5. Oh Johnny (*DPE*, p. 402)	An American dance
	
	Basic dance skills:
	  1. Circle the ring
	  2. Partner and corner swing
	  3. Allemande left with the corner gal
	  4. Do-si-do
	  5. Promenade
	This is a singing call that eliminates the need for a caller.
	
	Partners may be boy–girl or pinnie–nonpinnie.
	
	Corners become new partners for the next verse of the dance.
	
	Begin practice at slow tempo.
	
	This is a mixer.
	
	Partners change after each verse of the dance.
		Cog.—The student will recognize the proper figure on call.
		
		PM.—The students will be able to perform all of the basic square dance steps smoothly.

MOVEMENT EXPERIENCE— CONTENT	ORGANIZATION AND TEACHING HINTS	EXPECTED STUDENT OBJECTIVES AND OUTCOMES

6. Doudlebska Polka (*DPE,* p. 403)	A Czechoslovakian dance
	
	Basic dance skills:
	  1. Polka step
	  2. Clapping pattern
	  3. La, la, la step
	May be done in one large circle of part-ners, or in several smaller circles of partners scattered around the area.
	
	Any dancers without a partner go to the "lost and found" department in the center. They may reenter during the clapping portion of the dance.
		PM.—The student will be able to apply the polka step in this dance.
		
		Aff.—Students will be able to accept new partners with the proper courtesies.

GAME (5 – 7 MINUTES)

Scooter Kickball—*DPE,* p. 586
    Supplies: A cageball, gym scooters for active players
    Skill: Striking with various body parts
    Each team is divided into active players (on scooters) and goal defenders. The active players are seated on the scooters, and the goal defenders are seated on the goal line, with feet extended. The object of the game is to kick the cageball over the goal line defended by the opposite team. The players are positioned as shown above.
    The game starts with a face-off of two opposing players on scooters at the center of the court. The face-off is also used after a goal is scored. The active players on scooters propel the ball mainly with their feet. Touching the ball with the hands is a foul and results in a free kick by the opposition at the spot of the foul. A player also may use the head and body to stop and propel the ball.
    The players defending the goal are seated on the goal line. They may not use their hands either, but use of the feet, body, and head is permitted. (If scoring seems too easy, then the defenders can be allowed to use their hands.) Defenders should be restricted to the seated position at the goal line; they are not permitted to enter the field of play to propel or stop the ball.
    Teaching suggestions: If the sidelines are close to the walls of the gymnasium, out-of-bounds balls need not be called because the ball can rebound from the wall. The number of scooters determines the number of active players. The game works well if half of the players from each team are in the center on scooters and the other half are goal defenders. After a goal or after a stipulated time period, active players and goal defenders exchange places.
    Some consideration should be made for glasses; otherwise they might be broken. Any active player who falls off a scooter should be required to seat herself again on the scooter before becoming eligible to propel the ball.
    Variation: If there are enough scooters for everyone, the game can be played with rules similar to soccer. A more restricted goal (perhaps half of the end line) can be marked with standards. A goalie defends this area. All other players are active and can move to any spot on the floor. The floor space should be large enough to allow some freedom of play. Putting too many active players in a relatively small space causes jamming.

Touchdown—*DPE,* p. 588
    Supplies: A small object that can be concealed in the hand
    Skills: Running, dodging
    Two parallel lines about 60 ft apart are needed. Two teams face each other, each standing on one of the parallel lines. One team goes into a huddle, and the members decide which player is to carry an object to the opponents' goal line. The team moves out of the huddle and takes a position like a football team. On the charge signal "Hike," the players run toward the opponents' goal line, each player holding the hands closed as if carrying the object. On the charge signal, the opponents also run forward and tag the players. On being tagged, a player must stop immediately and open both hands to show whether or not he has the object.
    If the player carrying the object reaches the goal line without being tagged, she calls "Touchdown" and scores 6 points. The scoring team retains possession of the object and gets another try. If the player carrying the object is tagged in the center area, the object is given to the other team. They go into a huddle and try to run it across the field to score.

Chain Tag—*DPE,* p. 582
    Supplies: None
    Skills: Running, dodging
    Two parallel lines are established about 50 ft apart. The center is occupied by three players who form a chain with joined hands. The players with free hands on either end of the chain do the tagging. All other players line up on one of the parallel lines.
    The players in the center call "Come," and children cross from one line to the other. The chain tries to tag the runners. Anyone caught joins the chain. When the chain becomes too long, it should be divided into several smaller chains.
    Variation: Catch of Fish. The chain catches children by surrounding them like a fishing net. The runners cannot run under or through the links of the net.

DYNAMIC PHYSICAL EDUCATION LESSON PLAN
Juggling Skills and Pyramids
Level III

Supplies and Equipment Needed:
  Juggling scarves
  Fleece balls
  Foam tennis balls
  Individual jump ropes
  Tumbling mats
  Tape player
  Music

MOVEMENT EXPERIENCE— CONTENT	ORGANIZATION AND TEACHING HINTS	EXPECTED STUDENT OBJECTIVES AND OUTCOMES

INTRODUCTORY ACTIVITY (2 – 3 MINUTES)

Move, Exercise on Signal

Students do a locomotor movement, stop on signal and perform an exercise such as the following suggested activities:
1. Push-Ups
2. Curl-Ups
3. Crab Kick
Variations:
4. V-Ups
5. Treadmills

DPE p. 254

Many different exercises may be done. These should be selected to add challenge to this activity.

Vary the locomotor movements by adding quality (slow–fast, high–low) or direction.

PM.—The student will be able to perform the basic exercises on command.

PM.—The student will be able to perform the locomotor movement variations as well as the designated exercises.

Aff.—The body should be gradually warmed up, rather than moving into demanding activity immediately. Discuss this with the class with regard to need to self-pace and gradually work toward maximum output. Incorporate this principle into your teaching by demanding more as the introductory and fitness work progresses.

PM.—The student will be able to stop quickly with good balance.

FITNESS DEVELOPMENT ACTIVITY (7 – 8 MINUTES)

Continuity Drills

Students alternate rope jumping with exercises done in two-count fashion. Exercises are done when the leader says "Ready." The class answers "One-two" and performs a repetition. Students can choose any push-up or abdominal challenge activity (*DPE*, pp. 281–283). Teachers or students can lead. Tape alternating segments of music (rope jumping) and silence (exercises) to signal duration of exercise.

Rope jumping—forward	30 seconds
Double Crab Kick	30 seconds
Rope jumping—backward	30 seconds
Knee Touch Curl-Up	30 seconds
Jump and turn body	30 seconds
Push-Ups	30 seconds
Rocker Step	30 seconds
Bend and Twist	30 seconds
Swing -Step forward	30 seconds

DPE p. 303

Use scatter formation.

A number of enjoyable chants can be used (i.e., "Physical education" followed by a two-count response and repetition "is fun!").

Allow students to adjust the work load to their fitness level. This implies resting if the rope jumping is too strenuous.

Cog.—Two misconceptions prevail in regard to weight control. One is that exercise burns a small amount of calories and thus has no impact on weight, and the other is that exercise increases appetite. This ignores the fact that if a mile were run every day, the person would burn 12 lb of fat in a year. Activity does not appear to significantly increase appetite.

PM.—The student will be able to perform the exercises correctly and respond in unison with the rest of the class.

347

MOVEMENT EXPERIENCE—CONTENT	ORGANIZATION AND TEACHING HINTS	EXPECTED STUDENT OBJECTIVES AND OUTCOMES
Side Flex 30 seconds Free jumping 30 seconds Relax and stretch for a short time.		Cog.—When a person exercises regularly, additional capillaries form in the muscle tissue so that the muscle cells are better supplied with blood. The student will be able to describe this occurrence in her own words. Discuss the importance of regular exercise and acceptable types of exercise to cause the above effects.

LESSON FOCUS (15 – 20 MINUTES)

MOVEMENT EXPERIENCE—CONTENT	ORGANIZATION AND TEACHING HINTS	EXPECTED STUDENT OBJECTIVES AND OUTCOMES
Juggling Skills and Pyramids **Juggling with Scarves** Scarves are held by the fingertips near the center. To throw the scarf, it should be lifted and pulled into the air above eye level. Scarves are caught by clawing, a downward motion of the hand, and grabbing the scarf from above as it is falling.	*DPE* pp. 417 – 420 Scarf juggling should teach proper habits (e.g., tossing the scarves straight up in line with the body rather than forward or backward). Many instructors remind children to imagine that they are in a phone booth or large refrigerator box—to emphasize tossing and catching without moving.	Cog.—The student will be able to state sequence of throwing the scarves in cascading with three objects.
1. Cascading—Cascading is the easiest pattern for juggling three objects. The following sequence can be used to learn this basic technique.		
a. One scarf. Hold the scarf in the center. Quickly move the arm across the chest and toss the scarf with the palm out. Reach out with the other hand and catch the scarf in a straight-down motion (clawing). Toss the scarf with this hand using the motion and claw it with the opposite hand. Continue the tossing and clawing sequence over and over.	The fingers, not the palms, should be used in tossing and catching the objects.	PM.—The student will be able to consistently toss the objects up and directly in front of the body. Aff.—Students must accept the fact that the more difficult the skill, the more practice it takes to learn. Discuss the complexity of juggling and the need for applied and repetitive practice.
b. Two scarves and one hand. Hold the scarves with the fingertips in one hand. Toss the first scarf upward. As the first scarf reaches its zenith, toss the second scarf and catch the first one. Continue.		Aff.—Discuss the fact that accomplishing the skill once is not a goal. Performing the skill many times correctly is a goal of people who excel at skills.
c. Two scarves and two hands. Hold a scarf with the fingertips of each hand. Toss the first one across the body as described above. Toss the second scarf across the body in the opposite direction.		
d. Three-scarf cascading. A scarf is held in each hand by the fingertips as described above. The third scarf is held with the ring and little fingers against the palm of the hand. The first scarf to be thrown will be from the hand that is holding two scarves.		

MOVEMENT EXPERIENCE—CONTENT	ORGANIZATION AND TEACHING HINTS	EXPECTED STUDENT OBJECTIVES AND OUTCOMES

2. Reverse Cascading—Reverse cascading involves tossing the scarves from the waist level to the outside of the body and allowing the scarves to drop down the midline of the body.
   a. One scarf.
   b. Two scarves.
   c. Three scarves.
3. Column Juggling—Column juggling is so named because the scarves move straight up and down as though they were inside a large pipe or column and do not cross the body.

   To perform three-scarf column juggling, begin with two scarves in one hand and one in the other hand.

4. Showering—Start with two scarves in the right hand and one in the other. Begin by throwing the first two scarves from the right hand. Toss the scarves in a large circle away from the midline of the body and overhead as high as possible. As soon as the second scarf is released, toss the scarf from the left to the right hand and throw it in the same path with the right hand. All scarves are caught with the left hand and passed to the right hand.

   Showering is more difficult than cascading because of the rapid movement of the hands. There is less time allowed for catching and tossing. The scarves move in a circle following each other. It should be practiced in both directions for maximum challenge.

5. Juggling Challenges
   a. While cascading, toss a scarf under one leg.
   b. While cascading, toss a scarf from behind the back.
   c. Instead of catching one of the scarves, blow it upward with a strong breath of air.
   d. Begin cascading by tossing the first scarf into the air with a foot. Lay the scarf across the foot and kick it into the air.
   e. Try juggling three scarves with one hand. Do not worry about establishing a pattern, just catch the lowest scarf each time. Try both regular and reverse cascading, as well as column juggling.
   f. While doing column juggling, toss up one scarf, hold the other two and make a full turn. Resume juggling.
   g. Try juggling more than three scarves (up to six) while facing a partner.
   h. Juggle three scarves while standing beside a partner with inside arms around each other. This is easy to do since it is regular three-scarf cascading.

MOVEMENT EXPERIENCE—CONTENT	ORGANIZATION AND TEACHING HINTS	EXPECTED STUDENT OBJECTIVES AND OUTCOMES

Juggling with Balls

Two balls can be juggled with one hand, and three balls can be juggled with two hands. Juggling can be done in a crisscross fashion, which is called cascading, or it can be done in a circular fashion, called showering. Cascading is considered the easier of the two styles and should be the first one attempted.

DPE pp. 420 – 421

Students easily become frustrated with this skill. It is a good idea to allow short bouts of practice. For example, 4–5 minutes of practice followed by a game would avoid long periods of failure. Further practice could be continued after the game for another 4–5 minutes.

After the basic skill of juggling is mastered, different types of objects can be used (i.e., pins, rings, and beanbags).

Pyramids

Emphasis in this lesson is on smaller pyramid groups. Stunts using only two performers should be practiced as a preliminary to pyramid building with three students. Groups larger than three are not recommended since that increases the potential for accidents.

DPE pp. 541 – 542

The problem-solving approach can be used to encourage children to devise different pyramids.

Use about two thirds of the lesson focus time teaching juggling and one third forming pyramids.

Place a number of signs or pictures around the area to encourage different types of pyramids.

GAME (5 – 7 MINUTES)

Pyramid Building or Juggling

If desired, the game time can be used for additional work on pyramids or juggling. Otherwise play a favorite game or two.

DYNAMIC PHYSICAL EDUCATION LESSON PLAN
Relay Activities
Level III

Supplies and Equipment Needed:
  Long jump ropes (16 ft)
  Individual jump ropes
  Cones
  Tom-tom
  Equipment for relays
  Tape player
  Music

MOVEMENT EXPERIENCE—CONTENT	ORGANIZATION AND TEACHING HINTS	EXPECTED STUDENT OBJECTIVES AND OUTCOMES

INTRODUCTORY ACTIVITY (2 – 3 MINUTES)

Long-Rope Routine

Student begin in a loose column composed of four people holding the long jump rope in their right hand (held down to their right side).

First signal: Jog lightly in a column with one child leading.

Second signal: shift the rope overhead from the right side to the left side, transferring the rope to the left hand while still jogging.

Third signal: the two inside students release the rope and the two outside students begin turning the rope. The two inside students jump the rope until the next signal.

Fourth signal: The outside students move to the inside positions to jump while the inside students move out to turn the rope. The sequence is repeated.

DPE, p. 256

Use a tom-tom to signal changes.

Students should be in groups of four.

May want to have students carry two long ropes and work on Double Dutch on the third and fourth signals.

Students should move through the sequence with little hesitation.

Students may create their own activity for the second signal.

Students should change end holders without stopping the rope.

Challenge students to work on stunts and Double Dutch.

PM.—The student will be able to jump the long rope 10 times.

Cog.—The student will be able to develop one new idea to be used by his group on the second signal.

FITNESS DEVELOPMENT ACTIVITY (7 – 8 MINUTES)

Continuity Drills

Students alternate rope jumping with exercises done in two-count fashion. Exercises are done when the leader says "Ready." The class answers "One-two" and performs a repetition. Students can choose any push-up or abdominal challenge activity (*DPE*, pp. 281–283). Teachers or students can lead. Tape alternating segments of music (rope jumping) and silence (exercises) to signal duration of exercise.

Rope jumping—forward	30 seconds
Double Crab Kick	35 seconds
Rope jumping—backward	30 seconds
Knee Touch Curl-Up	35 seconds
Jump and turn body	30 seconds
Push-Ups	35 seconds
Rocker Step	30 seconds

DPE p. 303

Use scatter formation.

Other exercises can be substituted to add variation to the activity.

Allow students to adjust the work load to their fitness level. This implies resting if the rope jumping is too strenuous.

PM.—The student will be able to perform the exercises with rhythm.

PM.—The student will be able to jump-rope for 25 seconds without stopping.

Aff.—Lack of exercise is one of the key factors in heart disease. Symptoms of heart disease are often found in young people, and thus fitness activities may help retard this health problem. Discuss heart disease and the role of exercise.

MOVEMENT EXPERIENCE— CONTENT	ORGANIZATION AND TEACHING HINTS	EXPECTED STUDENT OBJECTIVES AND OUTCOMES

Bend and Twist	35 seconds
Swing -Step forward	30 seconds
Side Flex	35 seconds
Free jumping	30 seconds

Relax and stretch for a short time.

LESSON FOCUS (15 – 20 MINUTES)

Relay Activities

Introduce a variety of relays. The following are listed in sequence from easy to difficult. None of the relays require well-developed specialized skills (throwing, catching, etc.). This helps assure all students have the opportunity to contribute to their team's cooperative effort.
Partner Relays, (*DPE,* p. 595)
Carry and Fetch Relay, (*DPE,* p. 595)
Attention Relay, (*DPE,* p. 601)
Corner Fly Relay, (*DPE,* p. 599)
Pass and Squat Relay, (*DPE,* p. 599)
Rescue Relay, (*DPE,* p. 600)
Circular Attention Relay, (*DPE,* p. 601)
Potato Relays, (*DPE,* pp. 596–597)
Tadpole Relay, (*DPE,* p. 600)
Three Spot Relay, (*DPE,* p. 596)
Jack Rabbit Relay, (*DPE,* p. 598)

Teach relays with learning to understand the concept of cooperation, competition, playing under stress, and abiding by certain rules in mind, rather than teaching various skills.

Team should contain four to eight members. Change leaders often.

Rotate students into different squads so the makeup of each squad changes.

Have the children sit down when they are finished.

Put the least talented students in the middle of the squad so they do not stand out.

Emphasis should be on student enjoyment rather than winning at all costs.

PM.—The student will be able to participate in the relays at an adequate level.

Aff.—Relays involve performing under stress. Explain what happens to athletic performance when stress is too great. Mention the fear of looking stupid and being embarrassed.

Cog.—The importance of winning sometimes supersedes the reasons for participating in competitive activities. Discuss participating for enjoyment, skill development, and fitness maintenance.

GAME (5 – 7 MINUTES)

Relaxation Activity

Relays are spirited. It might be useful to spend a few minutes relaxing.
   1. In a supine position, practice some deep breathing with the eyes gently closed. Daydream while deep breathing about a favorite place.
   2. Tense a muscle group, take a deep breath and hold it for 6 counts. Slowly exhale and relax the muscle group. Do the same with other muscle groups.

DYNAMIC PHYSICAL EDUCATION LESSON PLAN
Track and Field Skills (Lesson 1)
Level III

Supplies and Equipment Needed:
Two stopwatches with neck lanyards (box for these for safety in the field)
Measuring tapes for the four jumps
Starter (p. 716)
Pits for the jumps with takeoff boards
8–12 hurdles
Stretch rope crossbar for high jump (p. 710)
High jump standards
Technique hints for each station (on poster boards)
Eight batons
Four sets of boxes and blocks for potato relay

MOVEMENT EXPERIENCE—CONTENT	ORGANIZATION AND TEACHING HINTS	EXPECTED STUDENT OBJECTIVES AND OUTCOMES

INTRODUCTORY AND FITNESS DEVELOPMENT ACTIVITIES (9 – 11 MINUTES)

Stretching and Jogging

Combine the introductory and fitness activities during the track and field unit. This will help students understand how to stretch and warm up for demanding activity such as track and field.

Jog for 1–2 minutes

Standing Hip Bend	30 seconds
Sitting Stretch	30 seconds
Partner Rowing	60 seconds
Bear Hug (do each leg)	40 seconds
Side Flex (do each leg)	40 seconds
Trunk Twister	30 seconds

Jog for 2–3 minutes.

DPE pp. 289 – 291

To prepare for strenuous activity, students should learn to warm up their body by walking or jogging, stretching, and finishing with jogging.

Avoid bouncing during the stretching activities. All stretching should be smooth and controlled movements.

Allow students to direct their warm-up activity. It is important that students be able to warm up without teacher direction.

Cog.—The student will be able to explain why stretching exercises and warm-ups are essential to track and field work.

PM.—The student will demonstrate the ability to put proper stress on muscles in stretching.

LESSON FOCUS (15 – 20 MINUTES)

Track and Field Skills

Orientation

1. Goal is self-improvement and developing proper techniques.
2. Each must accept responsibility for self-directed work. Try all activities.
3. Learn from the general sessions and from the technique hints that are given at each station.
4. You should rotate through two stations each day. The following period you will participate in two other stations activities. Please stay at your stations until time is signaled for rotation.
5. To measure the long jumps and the hop-step-and-jump, use the measuring tapes.

DPE pp. 704 – 710

Come to a central point. They should be ready to rest and listen.

Instructional charts listing two or three technique hints and, if possible, a diagram or picture should be posted for each event.

Emphasize care for the watches and show how they work.

Explain that height is a factor and that this is one reason the groups are formed. They are important particularly in the high jump.

Aff.—To succeed in track and field, one must work diligently and independently. Discuss the need for self-discipline in training.

Aff.—It is important to concentrate on good techniques, rather than performance at this point. Discuss the importance of learning proper technique before worrying about maximum effort.

PM.—The student will demonstrate the ability to use the measuring tapes accurately.

Cog.—The student will be able to explain how a stopwatch operates.

Aff.—Acceptance of responsibility for care of equipment.

MOVEMENT EXPERIENCE—CONTENT	ORGANIZATION AND TEACHING HINTS	EXPECTED STUDENT OBJECTIVES AND OUTCOMES
6. Use care with the stopwatches. They are expensive to purchase and also to repair. Put the lanyard around your neck when using stopwatches. 7. Announce the four groups. (Form groups according to formula in *DPE*, p. 710).		

Group Drills
 	
1. Explain starting:
  a. Standing start.
  b. Norwegian start.
  c. Sprint start.
2. Starting practice by groups.
3. Explain striding.
4. Stride practice.
	Use an entire group at one time.
	
	Stride about 70 yd and return to start. Repeat several times.
		Aff.—Acceptance by students of the group division is necessary if this approach is to work. Take time to discuss grouping, if deemed necessary.
		
		PM.—The student will demonstrate improvement in form, technique, and performance of:

Station (Small Group) Instruction
 	
The teacher should instruct at a different station each day. Start at the station that demands the most instruction. Set up a system of rotation that assures all stations will be covered during the unit.
		Starting
		  Sprinting
		  Striding
		  Hop-step-and-jump
		  High jump
		  Relay and baton passing
		  Standing Long Jump (optional)
		  Potato Shuttle Race
		  Running Long Jump
		  Hurdling

Station 1 - Starting and Sprinting 1. Front foot 4–12" behind line. 2. Thumb and first finger behind line, other fingers support. 3. Knee of other leg placed just opposite front foot. 4. On "get set," seat is raised, the down knee comes up a little, and the shoulders move forward over the hands. 5. On "go," push off sharply and take short, driving steps.	Sprint 25–30 yd or so. Have one child use the starter and count out the rhythm of the start. Should be a gradual rise of the shoulders. Foul rule applies. The runner can sprint forward and then take a jump as a return activity.	Cog.—The student will demonstrate knowledge about the points of technique of the above. Cog.—When sprinting, initial contact is made with the ball of the foot as compared with the heel or flat-footed contact made when running long distance. Discuss this and arm carry differences between sprinters and distance runners.
Hop-Step-and-Jump (Triple Jump) 1. Important to get the sequence and rhythm first, then later try for distance. 2. Sprinting.		
Station 2 - Running High Jump 1. Keep stretch rope low enough so all can practice. 2. Approach at 45°. 3. Good kick-up and arm action.	Can begin with the scissors style. Use only two heights in beginning practice. Avoid competition.	Cog.—Gravity and air resistance limit performances in the jumping events. Identify these factors and why altitude (Mexico City Olympics) has a positive impact on long jump performances.
Baton Passing 1. Decide on method of passing. 2. Incoming runner passes with left hand to right hand of receiver.	Space runners Change baton promptly. Avoid "blind" exchange.	

MOVEMENT EXPERIENCE—CONTENT	ORGANIZATION AND TEACHING HINTS	EXPECTED STUDENT OBJECTIVES AND OUTCOMES
3. After receiving, change to the left hand. 4. Estimate how fast to take off with respect to the incoming runner.		Cog.—The ratio of fast twitch versus slow twitch fibers is genetically determined. Fast twitch fibers contract rapidly and are useful in activities demanding speed and explosive power. Slow twitch fibers contract less quickly and are excellent for aerobic endurance activities. People are born with varying ratios and thus have a predisposition to succeed in activities in line with their given muscle fiber ratio.
Station 3 - Running Long Jump 1. Decide on jumping foot. 2. Establish check point. 3. Control last four steps. 4. Seek height.	Stress the foul rule. Hit with the jumping foot.	
Standing Long Jump or Shuttle Relays	Use either activity.	
Station 4 - Hurdling 1. At beginning, use one or two hurdles. 2. Leading foot is directly forward.	Practice striding along the hurdles before going over them. Keep in the infield, keeping track clear.	Cog.—Knowledge of what interval training is and can do for performance.
Striding for Distance 1. Work on pace. 2. Easy, relaxed strides.	Begin in straightaway and stride around curve. Best around the track.	

GAME ACTIVITY (5 – 7 MINUTES)

Track and Field Activities

Circular (Pursuit) Relays—*DPE*, p. 706

Circular relays make use of the regular circular track. The baton exchange technique is important, and practice is needed. On a 220-yd or 200-m track, relays can be organized in a number of ways, depending on how many runners are spaced for one lap. Four runners can do a lap, each running one quarter of the way; two can do a lap, each running one half of the distance; or each runner can complete a whole lap. In these races, each member of the relay team runs the same distance. Relays can also be organized so that members run different distances.

Shuttle Relays—*DPE*, p. 706

Since children are running toward each other, one great difficulty in running shuttle relays is control of the exchange. In the excitement, the next runner may leave too early, and the tag or exchange is then made ahead of the restraining line. A high-jump standard or cone can be used to prevent early exchanges. The next runner awaits the tag with an arm around the standard or a hand on a cone.

One on One Contests

Allow students to find a friend and have a number of personal contests in track and field events such as sprints, hurdling, high jump, and standing long jump.

DYNAMIC PHYSICAL EDUCATION LESSON PLAN
Track and Field Skills (Lesson 2)
Level III

Supplies and Equipment Needed:
  Four stopwatches with neck lanyards (box for these for safety in the field)
  Measuring tapes for the four jumps
  Starter (p. 716)
  Pits for the jumps with takeoff boards
  8–12 hurdles
  Stretch rope crossbar for high jump (pp. 710)
  High jump standards
  Technique hints for each station (on poster boards)
  Eight batons
  Four sets of boxes and blocks for potato relay
  Clipboards and pencils
  Recording sheets for each group

MOVEMENT EXPERIENCE— CONTENT	ORGANIZATION AND TEACHING HINTS	EXPECTED STUDENT OBJECTIVES AND OUTCOMES

INTRODUCTORY AND FITNESS DEVELOPMENT ACTIVITIES (9 – 11 MINUTES)

Stretching and Jogging

Combine the introductory and fitness activities during the track and field unit. This will help students understand how to stretch and warm up for demanding activity such as track and field.

Jog for 1–2 minutes

Standing Hip Bend	30 seconds
Sitting Stretch	30 seconds
Partner Rowing	60 seconds
Bear Hug (do each leg)	40 seconds
Side Flex (do each leg)	40 seconds
Trunk Twister	30 seconds

Jog for 2–3 minutes.

DPE pp. 289 – 291

To prepare for strenuous activity, students should learn to warm up their body by walking or jogging, stretching, and finishing with jogging.

Allow students to direct their warm-up activity. It is important that students be able to warm up without teacher direction.

Cog.—The student will be able to explain why stretching exercises and warm-ups are essential to track and field work.

PM.—The student will demonstrate the ability to put proper stress on muscles in stretching.

LESSON FOCUS (15 – 20 MINUTES)

Track and Field Skills

Station (Small Group) Instruction

The teacher should instruct at a different station each day. Start at the station that demands the most instruction. Set up a system of rotation that assures all stations will be covered during the unit.

Station 1 - Sprinting

1. 60 yard distance
2. 75 yard distance
3. Two trials

Hop-Step-and-Jump

1. Three trials
2. Record performances

DPE pp. 704 – 710

Stress legibility.

One watch.

Run individually.

PM.—The student will be able to perform creditably in the various events.

Cog.—Red blood cells pick up oxygen as they pass through the lungs. When exercising, a person breathes faster to bring more oxygen into the lungs. The heart beats faster to move more blood and transport oxygen to the muscles.

MOVEMENT EXPERIENCE—CONTENT	ORGANIZATION AND TEACHING HINTS	EXPECTED STUDENT OBJECTIVES AND OUTCOMES

Station 2 - High Jump

1. Begin at 3 foot, raise 6" at a time.
2. Two trials.
3. Record performances

Baton Passing

1. Practice while waiting for high jump turn.

Station 3 - Running Long Jump

1. Three trials.
2. Record all three, circle best.

Standing Long Jump

1. Three trials.
2. Record performances.

Shuttle Relays

Station 4 - Hurdling

1. Set up 60-yard hurdle course.
2. Give two trials.
3. Record best time.

Striding Practice

Striding practice can be done while waiting for turns on the hurdles.

Organization and Teaching Hints:

Use foul rule.

Watch for falling backward.

Practice striding beside the hurdles before going over them.

Expected Student Objectives and Outcomes:

Cog.—Smoking causes the heart rate to jump 10–20 beats per minute. The blood vessels constrict and the heart must pump harder to get blood through them. Discuss how this can be a detriment to good health.

GAME OR FUN ACTIVITY (5 – 7 MINUTES)

Track and Field Activities

Circular (Pursuit) Relays—*DPE*, p. 706

Circular relays make use of the regular circular track. The baton exchange technique is important, and practice is needed. On a 220-yd or 200-m track, relays can be organized in a number of ways, depending on how many runners are spaced for one lap. Four runners can do a lap, each running one quarter of the way; two can do a lap, each running one half of the distance; or each runner can complete a whole lap. In these races, each member of the relay team runs the same distance. Relays can also be organized so that members run different distances.

Shuttle Relays—*DPE*, p. 706

Since children are running toward each other, one great difficulty in running shuttle relays is control of the exchange. In the excitement, the next runner may leave too early, and the tag or exchange is then made ahead of the restraining line. A high-jump standard or cone can be used to prevent early exchanges. The next runner awaits the tag with an arm around the standard or a hand on a cone.

One on One Contests

Allow students to find a friend and have a number of personal contests in track and field events such as sprints, hurdling, high jump, and standing long jump.

DYNAMIC PHYSICAL EDUCATION LESSON PLAN
Track and Field Skills (Lesson 3)
Level III

Supplies and Equipment Needed:
  Four stopwatches with neck lanyards (box for these for safety in the field)
  Measuring tapes for the four jumps
  Starter (p. 716)
  Pits for the jumps with takeoff boards
  8–12 hurdles
  Rope crossbar for high jump (p. 710)
  High jump standards
  Technique hints for each station (on poster boards)
  Eight batons
  Four sets of boxes and blocks for potato relay
  Clipboards and pencils
  Recording sheets for each group

MOVEMENT EXPERIENCE— CONTENT	ORGANIZATION AND TEACHING HINTS	EXPECTED STUDENT OBJECTIVES AND OUTCOMES

INTRODUCTORY AND FITNESS DEVELOPMENT ACTIVITIES (9 – 11 MINUTES)

Stretching and Jogging

Combine the introductory and fitness activities during the track and field unit. This will help students understand how to stretch and warm up for demanding activity such as track and field.

Jog for 1–2 minutes

Standing Hip Bend	30 seconds
Sitting Stretch	30 seconds
Partner Rowing	60 seconds
Bear Hug (do each leg)	40 seconds
Side Flex (do each leg)	40 seconds
Trunk Twister	30 seconds

Jog for 2–3 minutes.

DPE pp. 289 – 291

To prepare for strenuous activity, students should learn to warm up their body by walking or jogging, stretching, and finishing with jogging.

Allow students to direct their warm-up activity. It is important that students be able to warm up without teacher direction.

Cog.—The student will be able to explain why static stretching is more effective than ballistic stretching for track and field warm-up.

PM.—The student will demonstrate flexibility during stretching.

LESSON FOCUS (15 – 20 MINUTES)

Track and Field Skills

  1. Utilize the last week of this unit to conduct a track and field meet. The same rotation plan and groups of students started the previous two weeks can be continued for the meet.
  2. Utilize the same stations, events, number of trials and scoring procedures outlined in last week's track and field lesson.

DPE pp. 704 – 710

Parents can be asked to help.

PM.—The student will demonstrate proper form and improving performance in track and field events.

Aff.—Students develop their skills at different rates, regardless of chronologic age. Discuss the need for sensitivity to individual growth patterns.

PM.—The students will work independently and diligently to keep the meet running on schedule.

MOVEMENT EXPERIENCE—CONTENT	ORGANIZATION AND TEACHING HINTS	EXPECTED STUDENT OBJECTIVES AND OUTCOMES

GAME OR FUN ACTIVITY (5 – 7 MINUTES)

Track and Field Activities

Circular (Pursuit) Relays—*DPE*, p. 706

Circular relays make use of the regular circular track. The baton exchange technique is important, and practice is needed. On a 220-yd or 200-m track, relays can be organized in a number of ways, depending on how many runners are spaced for one lap. Four runners can do a lap, each running one quarter of the way; two can do a lap, each running one half of the distance; or each runner can complete a whole lap. In these races, each member of the relay team runs the same distance. Relays can also be organized so that members run different distances.

Shuttle Relays—*DPE*, p. 706

Since children are running toward each other, one great difficulty in running shuttle relays is control of the exchange. In the excitement, the next runner may leave too early, and the tag or exchange is then made ahead of the restraining line. A high-jump standard or cone can be used to prevent early exchanges. The next runner awaits the tag with an arm around the standard or a hand on a cone.

One on One Contests

Allow students to find a friend and have a number of personal contests in track and field events such as sprints, hurdling, high jump, and standing long jump.

DYNAMIC PHYSICAL EDUCATION LESSON PLAN
Long-Rope Jumping Skills
Level III

Supplies and Equipment Needed:
  Squad leader exercise task cards
  Long jump ropes (16')
  Music for rope jumping
  Cageball
  Balls

MOVEMENT EXPERIENCE—CONTENT	ORGANIZATION AND TEACHING HINTS	EXPECTED STUDENT OBJECTIVES AND OUTCOMES

INTRODUCTORY ACTIVITY (2 – 3 MINUTES)

Personal Choice

Students select the type of Introductory Activity they wish to use in order to warm up. They may use one they have previously learned in class, or they may create one of their own. Emphasis should be on a balanced approach that works all major muscle groups.

Encourage students to keep moving.

It may be necessary to point out some activities to stimulate some of the youngsters.

PM.—The student will be able to create a warm-up routine that will physically warm her up for fitness activities.

Cog.—The student will be able to develop a balanced warm-up routine.

FITNESS DEVELOPMENT ACTIVITY (7 – 8 MINUTES)

Squad Leader Exercises with Task Cards

The class is divided into squads of five to seven students. Each group is given a task card that lists eight to ten exercises. One of the group members begins as the leader and leads an exercise. Each time an exercise is completed, the card is passed to a new leader. Use alternating intervals of music to signal exercising (25 seconds) with silence (5–8 seconds) to indicate passing the card. Suggested exercises:
Sitting Stretch
Push-Ups
Body Circles
Jumping Jack variations
Crab Kick combinations
Abdominal Crunchers
Treadmills
Toe Touchers
Leg Extensions

If there is a delay in starting an exercise, the squad should walk or jog.

DPE p. 300

Aerobic activities such as jogging or rope jumping may be used between strength exercises in order to develop the cardiovascular system.

A goal of squad leader exercises is to allow students the opportunity to lead other students. Teachers should give students freedom to modify the exercises.

Cog.—The student will be able to recognize the exercises by name.

Cog.—The student will be able to describe how overload is achieved (by increasing the number of repetitions of each exercise and by decreasing the amount of rest between each set of exercises).

PM.—The student will be able to do *quality* work on all exercises listed on the task cards.

MOVEMENT EXPERIENCE— CONTENT	ORGANIZATION AND TEACHING HINTS	EXPECTED STUDENT OBJECTIVES AND OUTCOMES

LESSON FOCUS (15 – 20 MINUTES)

Long-Rope Jumping Skills

Single Long-Rope Activities

1. Review previously learned jump-ing skills.
2. Have more than one youngster jump at a time. Students can enter in pairs or triplets.
3. Jump while holding a beanbag or playground ball between the knees.
4. While turning rope, rotate under the rope and jump. Continue jump-ing and rotate back to the turning position.
5. Play catch with a playground ball while jumping.
6. Do the Egg Beater: Two or more long ropes are turned simultane-ously. The ropes are aligned per-pendicular to each other; the jumper jumps the rope where they cross.
7. Try combinations of three or four ropes turning. The ropes are aligned parallel to each other and students jump and move through to the next rope.

Double Long-Rope Activities

1. Basic jump on both feet. Land on the balls of the feet, keeping ankles and knees together with hands across the stomach.
2. Jogging Step. Run in place with a jogging step. Increase the chal-lenge by circling while jogging.
3. Scissors Jump. Jump to a stride po-sition with the left foot forward and the right foot back about 8 inches apart. Each jump requires reversing the position of the feet.
4. Straddle Jump. Jump to the strad-dle position and return to closed position. Try a Straddle Cross Jump by crossing the legs on re-turn to the closed position. The straddle jumps should be per-formed facing away from the turn-ers.
5. Turnaround. Circle left or right us-ing the basic jump. Begin circling slowly at first and then increase speed. To increase the challenge, try the turnaround on one foot.
6. Hot Peppers. Use the Jogging Step and gradually increase the speed of the ropes.
7. Half Turn. Perform a half turn with each jump. Remember to lead the turn with the head and shoulders.

DPE pp. 446 – 451

Organize youngsters in two groups of four or five.

Design some type of rotation plan so all youngsters get a chance to jump and turn.

Make sure youngsters know the differ-ence between entering front and back door.

Youngsters who have problems jump-ing should face one of the turners and key their jumps to both the visual and audio cues (hand movement and sound of the rope hitting the floor).

When turning Double Dutch, rotate the hands inward toward the midline of the body (right forearm counterclockwise and left forearm clockwise). Students should concentrate on the sound of the ropes hitting the floor so that they make an even and rhythmic beat.

Double Dutch turning takes consider-able practice. Take time to teach it as a skill that is necessary for successful jumping experiences.

When entering, stand beside a turner and run into the ropes when the back rope (farther from the jumper) touches the floor. Turners should be taught to say "go" each time the back rope touches the floor.

Concentrate on jumping in the center of the ropes facing a turner. Use white shoe polish to mark a jumping target.

Exit the ropes by facing and jumping toward one turner and exiting immedi-ately after jumping. The exit should be made as close to the turner's shoulder as possible.

When students are having trouble with Double Dutch, allow them opportunity to return to single rope jumping.

Aff.—The student will appreciate the great deal of time and practice needed to become skilled at jumping rope.

Cog.—Physical activity appears to change the state of mind in a positive direction. People on regular exercise programs are more productive and bet-ter able to cope with stress. Discuss the benefits of aerobic activities such as rope jumping.

PM.—The student will be able to jump-rope with proper form in time to the music.

PM.—The student will master at least two of the more difficult maneuvers.

MOVEMENT EXPERIENCE— CONTENT	ORGANIZATION AND TEACHING HINTS	EXPECTED STUDENT OBJECTIVES AND OUTCOMES

8. Ball Tossing. Toss and catch a playground ball while jumping.
9. Individual Rope Jumping. Enter Double Dutch with an individual rope and jump. Face the turner and decrease the length of the individual jump rope.

The jumper must jump twice as fast as each rope is turning.

GAME (5 – 7 MINUTES)

Cageball Target Throw—*DPE*, p. 582

Supplies: A cageball (18- to 30-in.), 12 to 15 smaller balls of various sizes

Skill: Throwing

An area about 20 ft wide is marked across the center of the playing area, with a cageball in the center. The object of the game is to throw the smaller balls against the cageball, thus forcing it across the line in front of the other team. Players may come up to the line to throw, but they may not throw while inside the cageball area. A player may enter the area, however, to recover a ball. No one is to touch the cageball at any time, nor may the cageball be pushed by a ball in the hands of a player.

Teaching suggestion: If the cageball seems to roll too easily, it should be deflated slightly. The throwing balls can be of almost any size—soccer balls, volleyballs, playground balls, or whatever.

Variation: Two rovers, one from each team, can occupy the center area to retrieve balls. These players cannot block throws or prevent a ball from hitting the target. They are there for the sole purpose of retrieving balls for their team.

Sunday—*DPE*, p. 587

Supplies: None

Skills: Running, dodging

Two parallel lines are drawn about 50 ft apart. One player is it and stands in the center of the area between the two lines. All of the other children are on one of the two lines. The object is to cross to the other line without being tagged and without making a false start.

Each line player stands with her front foot on the line. The line players must run across the line immediately when the tagger calls "Sunday." Anyone who does not run immediately is considered caught. The tagger can call other days of the week to confuse the runners. No player may make a start if another day of the week is called. The tagger must be careful to pronounce "Monday" in such a way that it cannot be confused with "Sunday." If confusion does occur, "Monday" can be eliminated from the signals for the false start.

Teaching suggestion: "Making a start" must be defined clearly. To begin, it can be defined as a player moving either foot. Later, when children get better at the game, a forward movement of the body can constitute a start.

DYNAMIC PHYSICAL EDUCATION LESSON PLAN
Softball Skills (Lesson 1)
Level III

Supplies and Equipment Needed:
  Station 1: 2 batting tees, 4 balls, 2 bats
  Station 2: 2 balls
  Station 3: 4 bases (home plates), 4 balls
  Station 4: 2 balls, 2 bats
  Exercise task cards
  Station signs
  Tape player
  Music

MOVEMENT EXPERIENCE—CONTENT	ORGANIZATION AND TEACHING HINTS	EXPECTED STUDENT OBJECTIVES AND OUTCOMES

INTRODUCTORY ACTIVITY (2 – 3 MINUTES)

Personal Choice

Students select the type of Introductory Activity they wish to use in order to warm up. They may use one they have previously learned in class, or they may create one of their own. Emphasis should be on a balanced approach that works all major muscle groups.

Encourage students to keep moving.

It may be necessary to point out some activities to stimulate some of the youngsters.

PM.—The student will be able to create a warm-up routine that will physically warm him up for fitness activities.

FITNESS DEVELOPMENT (7 – 8 MINUTES)

Squad Leader Exercises with Task Cards

The class is divided into squads of five to seven students. Each group is given a task card that lists eight to ten exercises. One of the group members begins as the leader and leads an exercise. Each time an exercise is completed, the card is passed to a new leader. Use alternating intervals of music to signal exercising (30 seconds) with silence (5–8 seconds) to indicate passing the card. Suggested exercises:
Sitting Stretch
Push-Ups
Body Circles
Jumping Jack variations
Crab Kick combinations
Abdominal Crunchers
Treadmills
Toe Touchers
Leg Extensions

If there is a delay in starting an exercise, the squad should walk or jog.

DPE p. 300

Aerobic activities such as jogging or rope jumping may be used between strength exercises in order to develop the cardiovascular system.

A goal of squad leader exercises is to allow students the opportunity to lead other students. Teachers should give students freedom to modify the exercises.

Cog.—Know why it is necessary to increase the number of repetitions (overload principle).

PM.—The student will be able to perform all exercises at teacher-established levels.

Aff.—The students will demonstrate the self-discipline needed for independent group work.

MOVEMENT EXPERIENCE— CONTENT	ORGANIZATION AND TEACHING HINTS	EXPECTED STUDENT OBJECTIVES AND OUTCOMES

LESSON FOCUS (15 – 20 MINUTES)

Softball Skills

Station (Small Group) Instruction

The teacher should instruct at a different station each day. Start at the station that demands the most instruction. Set up a system of rotation that assures all stations will be covered during the unit.

Station 1 - Batting

1. Weight on both feet.
2. Bat pointed over right shoulder.
3. Trademark up on swing.
4. Elbows up and away from body.
5. Begin with hip roll and short step.
6. Swing level.
7. Follow through.
8. Eyes on ball.

Batting from Tee

1. Stand back (3 feet) from tee, so when stepping forward, ball is hit in front.
2. Show three types of grips.

Fungo Hitting

1. Students can be given this option instead of tee hitting.
2. Toss the ball up, regrasp the bat, and hit the ball.

Station 2 - Throwing and Catching

1. Show grips.
2. How to catch—Stress "give," eyes on ball.

Practice Activity

1. Throw around the bases clockwise and counterclockwise using the following throws:
   a. Overhand throw.
   b. Sidearm throw.
   c. Underhand toss.
2. If enough skill, roll the ball to the infielders and make the throw to first. After each play, the ball may be thrown around the infield.

Station 3 - Pitching Practice

1. Face the batter, both feet on the rubber, and the ball held in front with both hands. One step is allowed and the ball must be delivered on that step.
2. Ball must be pitched underhanded.
3. No motion or fake toward the plate can be made without delivering the ball.

DPE pp. 684 – 695

Squad formation.

Have signs at each of the stations giving both direction and skill hints.

Captain gathers equipment in designated spot before changing to next station.

Divide squad, with one batter, a catcher (next batter), and one or more fielders.

Points to avoid:
1. Lifting the front foot high off the ground.
2. Stepping back with the rear foot.
3. Dropping the rear shoulder.
4. Chopping down on the ball (golfing).
5. Dropping the elbows.

This is a higher level batting skill than tee hitting.

Rotate batters, catchers, fielders.

This will be review for most students.

Use "soft" softballs.

Rotate infield positions, including the "ball roller."

Set up regular infield staffed by a squad.

Divide squad into two groups. Each has a catcher, pitcher, and "batter," who just stands in position.

A home plate and pitching rubber are helpful.

Stressed legal preliminary position before taking one hand off the ball to pitch.

Aff.—Willingness to cooperate at each station is crucial to the success of the lesson. Discuss and emphasize the importance of cooperation among peers.

PM.—The student will be able to meet the ball squarely on the tee.

Cog.—The student will know the different points in good batting.

Cog.—Strenuous exercise causes blood pressure to go up. This occurs because the heart beats faster and more blood is trying to push its way through the vessels. Why do some people have high blood pressure even at rest?

PM.—The students will be able to increase their catching potentials and increase their accuracy in throwing (three styles).

Cog.—The student will be able to define and recognize good points of throwing and catching.

PM.—The student will be able to pitch in observance with the rules.

Cog.—The student will know the rules governing pitching.

PM.—The student will be able to pitch 50% of the balls into the strike zone.

Cog.—Softball is not a very effective sport for exercising the cardiovascular system. Most of the time is spent sitting or standing. Therefore, there is little, if any, aerobic activity.

MOVEMENT EXPERIENCE—CONTENT	ORGANIZATION AND TEACHING HINTS	EXPECTED STUDENT OBJECTIVES AND OUTCOMES
4. No quick return is permitted, nor can the ball be rolled or bounced toward the batter.		
5. Practice both regular pitch and windmill.	Rotate positions regularly.	
Station 4 - Throwing or Batting Fly Balls	Divide squad into two groups.	PM.—The student will begin to handle (catch) easy fly balls with confidence.
1. Begin with high throwing from the "batter,"	Leave a bat at the station.	PM.—The fielders will improve in estimating flight of the ball and getting under it in time.
2. Have the fielders return the ball with a one-bounce throw to the "batter."		
3. Show form for high and low catch. Show sure stop for outfielders.		
4. After initial stages, allow fungo hitting of fly balls if the "batter" is capable.		

LEAD-UP GAME (5 – 7 MINUTES)

Softball Lead-Up Games

Batter Ball—*DPE*, p. 697

Supplies: A softball, a bat, a mask

Skills: Slow pitching, hitting, fielding, catching flies

Batter Ball involves batting and fielding but no base running. It is much like batting practice but adds the element of competition. A line is drawn directly from first to third base. This is the balk line over which a batted ball must travel to be fielded. Another line is drawn from a point on the foul line 3 ft behind third base to a point 5 ft behind second base and in line with home plate. Another line connects this point with a point on the other baseline 3 ft behind first base.

Each batter is given three pitches by a member of his own team to hit the ball into fair territory across the balk line. The pitcher may stop any ground ball before it crosses the balk line. The batter then gets another turn at bat.

Scoring is as follows:

1. A successful grounder scores 1 point. A grounder is successful when an infielder fails to handle it cleanly within the infield area. Only one player may field the ball. If the ball is fielded properly, the batter is out.

2. A line drive in the infield area is worth 1 point if not caught. It can be handled for an out on any bounce. Any line drive caught on the fly is also an out.

3. A fly ball in the infield area scores 1 point if not caught. For an out, the ball must be caught legally by the first person touching it.

4. A two-bagger scores 2 points. Any fly ball, line drive or not, that lands fairly in the outfield area without being caught scores 2 points. If it is caught, the batter is out.

5. A home run scores 3 points. Any fly ball driven over the head of the farthest outfielder in that area scores a home run.

Three outs can constitute an inning, or all batters can be allowed one turn at bat and then the team changes to the field. A new set of infielders should be in place for each inning. The old set goes to the outfield. Pitchers should be limited to one inning. They also take a turn at bat.

Teaching suggestion: Many games of this type require special fields, either rectangular or narrowly angled. This game was selected because it uses the regular softball field with the added lines. The lines can be drawn with a stick or can be marked using regular marking methods.

The pitcher has to decide whether he should stop the ball. If the ball goes beyond the restraining line, it is in play even if he touched it.

Variations: Batter Ball can be modified for use as a station in rotational teaching, with the emphasis on individual batting and squad organization. One member of the squad would be at bat and would get a definite number of chances (e.g., five) to score. She keeps her own point total. The other squad members occupy the necessary game positions.

Tee Ball—*DPE*, p. 699

Supplies: A softball, a bat, a batting tee

Skills: Most softball skills (except pitching and stealing bases), hitting a ball from a tee

This game is an excellent variation of softball and is played under softball rules with the following exceptions.

1. Instead of hitting a pitched ball, the batter hits the ball from a tee. The catcher places the ball on the tee. After the batter hits the ball, the play is the same as in regular softball. With no pitching, there is no stealing. A runner stays on the base until the ball is hit by the batter.

MOVEMENT EXPERIENCE— CONTENT	ORGANIZATION AND TEACHING HINTS	EXPECTED STUDENT OBJECTIVES AND OUTCOMES

2. A fielder occupies the position normally held by the pitcher. The primary duty of this fielder is to field bunts and ground balls and to back up the infielders on throws.

Teams can play regular innings for three outs or change to the field after each player has had a turn at bat.

Teaching suggestions: A tee can be purchased or made from a radiator hose. If the tee is not adjustable, three different sizes should be available. The batter should take a position far enough behind the tee so that, in stepping forward to swing, she will hit the ball slightly in front of her.

Tee Ball has many advantages. There are no strikeouts, every child hits the ball, there is no dueling between pitcher and batter, and fielding opportunities abound.

Scrub (Work-Up)—*DPE*, p. 699

Supplies: A softball, a bat

Skills: Most softball skills

The predominant feature of Scrub is the rotation of the players. The game is played with regular softball rules, with each individual more or less playing for herself. There are at least two batters, generally three. A catcher, pitcher, and first-base player are essential. The remaining players assume the other positions. Whenever the batter is out, she goes to a position in right field. All other players move up one position, with the catcher becoming the batter. The first-base player becomes the pitcher, the pitcher moves to catcher, and all others move up one place.

Variation: If a fly ball is caught, the fielder and batter exchange positions.

DYNAMIC PHYSICAL EDUCATION LESSON PLAN
Softball Skills (Lesson 2)
Level III

Supplies and Equipment Needed:
  Station 1: 2 bats, 4 balls
  Station 2: 3 plates, 3 balls
  Station 3: 4 bases (regular diamond), ball, bat
  Station 4: 4 bats, 4 balls, home plates (optional)
  Exercise task cards
  Tape player
  Music

MOVEMENT EXPERIENCE—CONTENT	ORGANIZATION AND TEACHING HINTS	EXPECTED STUDENT OBJECTIVES AND OUTCOMES

INTRODUCTORY ACTIVITY (2 – 3 MINUTES)

Personal Choice

Students select the type of Introductory Activity they wish to use in order to warm up. They may use one they have previously learned in class, or they may create one of their own. Emphasis should be on a balanced approach that works all major muscle groups.

Encourage students to keep moving.

It may be necessary to point out some activities to stimulate some of the youngsters.

PM.—The student will be able to create a warm-up routine that will physically warm her up for fitness activities.

FITNESS DEVELOPMENT (7 – 8 MINUTES)

Squad Leader Exercises with Task Cards

The class is divided into squads of five to seven students. Each group is given a task card that lists eight to ten exercises. One of the group members begins as the leader and leads an exercise. Each time an exercise is completed, the card is passed to a new leader. Use alternating intervals of music to signal exercising (35 seconds) with silence (5–8 seconds) to indicate passing the card. Suggested exercises:
Sitting Stretch
Push-Ups
Body Circles
Jumping Jack variations
Crab Kick combinations
Abdominal Crunchers
Treadmills
Toe Touchers
Leg Extensions

If there is a delay in starting an exercise, the squad should walk or jog.

DPE p. 300

Aerobic activities such as jogging or rope jumping may be used between strength exercises in order to develop the cardiovascular system.

A goal of squad leader exercises is to allow students the opportunity to lead other students. Teachers should give students freedom to modify the exercises.

Cog.—The student will be able to verbalize why correct form is important when performing exercises.

PM—The student will perform all exercises at the teacher-established level.

MOVEMENT EXPERIENCE— CONTENT	ORGANIZATION AND TEACHING HINTS	EXPECTED STUDENT OBJECTIVES AND OUTCOMES

LESSON FOCUS (15 – 20 MINUTES)

Softball Skills

DPE pp. 684 – 694

Station (Small Group) Instruction

Aff.—Each player will work at the designated skill and attempt to improve his skill. Discuss the importance of practicing both strengths and weaknesses.

The teacher should instruct at a different station each day. Start at the station that demands the most instruction. Set up a system of rotation that assures all stations will be covered during the unit.

Station 1 - Game of Pepper

1. Practice bunting.
2. Practice fielding.

Divide squad into two groups. Change batters every six swings.

Stress easy underhand pitching.

PM.—The players will be able to play this game successfully in order to develop throwing, catching, and striking skills.

Station 2 - Pitching and Umpiring

1. Teach umpiring.
   a. Right hand—strike.
   b. Left hand—ball.

Need catcher, pitcher, batter, and umpire.

Pitch to three batters and then rotate.

The batter does not swing at the ball during umpiring practice.

PM.—The student will be able to "strike out" two out of three batters.

PM.—Umpires will gain increased skill.

PM.—The student will be able to demonstrate proper umpiring techniques in calling balls and strikes.

Station 3 - Infield Practice

1. Roll ball to infielders and make the play at first. After each play, throw around the infield.
2. If enough skill, bat the ball to the infielders in turn.

Set up regular infield, staffed by squad. Rotate where needed.

PM.—The infielders will gain in skill in infield play.

PM.—The infielders will learn to "play" the grounder at the most advantageous spot.

Station 4 - Batting Practice

Each batter takes six swings and then rotates to the field. Catcher becomes batter and pitcher moves up to catcher.

Use the squad. Have hitter, catcher, pitcher, and fielders.

Use two balls to keep things moving.

Pitcher must be able to serve up good pitches. Use a shorter distance for pitching.

LEAD-UP GAMES (5 – 7 MINUTES)

Softball Lead-Up Games

Scrub (Work-Up)—*DPE*, p. 699
  See the Lesson Plan, Softball Skills (Lesson 1) for a complete game description.
Slow-Pitch Softball—*DPE*, p. 700
  Supplies: A softball, a bat
  Skills: Most softball skills
  The major difference between regular softball and Slow-Pitch Softball is in the pitching, but there are other modifications to the game as well. With slower pitching, there is more hitting and thus more action on the bases and in the field. Outfielders are an important part of the game, because many long drives are hit. Rule changes from the game of official softball are as follows.
  1. The pitch must be a slow pitch. Any other pitch is illegal and is called a ball. The pitch must be slow, with an arc of 1 ft. It must not rise over 10 ft from the ground, however. Its legality depends on the umpire's call.
  2. There are ten players instead of nine. The extra one, called the roving fielder, plays in the outfield and handles line drives hit just over the infielders.
  3. The batter must take a full swing at the ball and is out if he chops at the ball or bunts.

MOVEMENT EXPERIENCE—CONTENT	ORGANIZATION AND TEACHING HINTS	EXPECTED STUDENT OBJECTIVES AND OUTCOMES

4. If the batter is hit by a pitched ball, she is not entitled to first base. The pitch is merely called a ball. Otherwise, balls and strikes are called as in softball.

5. The runner must hold base until the pitch has reached or passed home plate. No stealing is permitted.

Teaching suggestion: Shortening the pitching distance somewhat may be desirable. Much of the success of the game depends on the pitcher's ability to get the ball over the plate.

Babe Ruth Ball—*DPE*, p. 700

Supplies: A bat, a ball, four cones or other markers

Skills: Batting, pitching, fielding

The three outfield zones—left, center, and right field—are separated by four cones. It is helpful if foul lines have been drawn, but cones can define them The batter calls the field to which he intends to hit. The pitcher throws controlled pitches so that the batter can hit easily. The batter remains in position as long as he hits to the designated field. Field choices must be rotated. The batter gets only one swing to make a successful hit. He may allow a ball to go by, but if he swings, it counts as a try. There is no base running. Players rotate.

Teaching suggestions: Children play this game informally on sandlots with a variety of rules. Some possibilities to consider are these: What happens when a fly ball is caught? What limitations should be made on hitting easy grounders? Let the players decide about these points and others not covered by the stated rules.

Three-Team Softball—*DPE*, p. 701

Supplies: A mask, a ball, a bat

Skills: All softball skills

Three-Team Softball works well with 12 players, a number considered too few to divide into two effective fielding teams. The players are instead divided into three teams. The rules of softball apply, with the following exceptions.

1. One team is at bat, one team covers the infield (including the catcher), and the third team provides the outfielders and the pitcher.

2. The team at bat must bat in a definite order. This means that because of the small number of batters on each side, instances can occur when the person due to bat is on base. To take a turn at bat, the runner must be replaced by a player not on base.

3. After three outs, the teams rotate, with the outfield moving to the infield, the infield taking a turn at bat, and the batters going to the outfield.

4. An inning is over when all three teams have batted.

5. The pitcher should be limited to pitching one inning only. A player may repeat as pitcher only after all members of his team have had a chance to pitch.

DYNAMIC PHYSICAL EDUCATION LESSON PLAN— ALTERNATE
Rhythmic Movement (Lesson 5)
Level III

Supplies and Equipment Needed:
  Lummi sticks
  Tape player and music
  Scooters
  Cageball

Dances Taught:
  Lummi Sticks
  Klumpakojis
  Korobushka

MOVEMENT EXPERIENCE— CONTENT	ORGANIZATION AND TEACHING HINTS	EXPECTED STUDENT OBJECTIVES AND OUTCOMES

INTRODUCTORY AND FITNESS DEVELOPMENT ACTIVITIES (9 – 11 MINUTES)

This lesson may be substituted for any previous lessons. Use the introductory and fitness development activities given in the sequenced lesson plans.

LESSON FOCUS (15 – 20 MINUTES)

Rhythmic Movement (5)

Lummi Sticks

1. Without sticks, learn the chant.
2. Issue sticks. Show: vertical taps, tap together. Work on a three-count routine: (1) vertical tap, (2) tap together, (3) rest best.
3. Organize by partners. Children sit cross-legged, facing, at a distance of 18–20 inches. Work out the following routines:
   a. Vertical tap, tap together, partner tap right; vertical tap, tap together, partner tap left.
   b. Vertical tap, tap together, pass right stick; vertical tap, tap together, pass left stick.
   c. Vertical tap, tap together, toss right stick; vertical tap, tap together, toss left stick.
   d. Repeat a, b, c except substitute an end tap and flip for the vertical tap and tap together (i.e., end tap, flip, partner tap right, end tap, flip, partner tap left).
   e. Vertical tap, tap together, pass right and left quickly; repeat.
   f. End tap, flip, toss right and left quickly; repeat.
   g. Right flip side-left flip in front, vertical tap in place, partner tap right; left flip side- right flip in front, vertical tap in place, tap left.
   h. End tap in front, flip, vertical tap, tap together, toss right, toss left.
   i. Vertical tap, tap together, right stick to partner's left hand and left stick to own right hand. Repeat.

DPE p. 388

Various lummi stick rhythms records are available for teaching lummi stick activities.

Teach the various tap sequences to the students individually before organizing them in partners.

Hold stick with thumb and fingers (not the first) at the bottom third of the stick.

Stress relaxed and light tapping.

Partners provide their own chanting. Two or three sets of partners can work in unison.

This is called circling.

Cog.—The student will be able to sing the Lummi Stick Chant.

Cog.—Practicing skills incorrectly can make it difficult to learn them correctly later. Discuss the need for patience with one's self when learning new rhythmic activities. This prevents learning them incorrectly due to fear of failure and resultant peer pressure.

PM.—The student will get accustomed to the proper grip so it becomes automatic.

PM.—The student will be able to do the following—vertical tap, tap together, partner tap right (left), end tap, flip, toss right (left), end tap, flip, toss right and left quickly—and put these together in rhythm to the chant.

Cog.—The student will recognize and be able to do circling.

MOVEMENT EXPERIENCE— CONTENT	ORGANIZATION AND TEACHING HINTS	EXPECTED STUDENT OBJECTIVES AND OUTCOMES
j. Repeat previous routines, but reverse the circle. k. Devise own routines.		
Klumpakojis	*DPE* pp. 350 – 351	
Korobushka	*DPE* pp. 357 – 358	

GAME (5 – 7 MINUTES)

Scooter Kickball—*DPE*, p. 586
  Supplies: A cageball, gym scooters for active players
  Skill: Striking with various body parts
  Each team is divided into active players (on scooters) and goal defenders. The active players are seated on the scooters, and the goal defenders are seated on the goal line, with feet extended. The object of the game is to kick the cageball over the goal line defended by the opposite team. The players are positioned as shown above.
  The game starts with a face-off of two opposing players on scooters at the center of the court. The face-off is also used after a goal is scored. The active players on scooters propel the ball mainly with their feet. Touching the ball with the hands is a foul and results in a free kick by the opposition at the spot of the foul. A player also may use the head and body to stop and propel the ball.
  The players defending the goal are seated on the goal line. They may not use their hands either, but use of the feet, body, and head is permitted. (If scoring seems too easy, then the defenders can be allowed to use their hands.) Defenders should be restricted to the seated position at the goal line; they are not permitted to enter the field of play to propel or stop the ball.
  Teaching suggestions: If the sidelines are close to the walls of the gymnasium, out-of-bounds balls need not be called because the ball can rebound from the wall. The number of scooters determines the number of active players. The game works well if half of the players from each team are in the center on scooters and the other half are goal defenders. After a goal or after a stipulated time period, active players and goal defenders exchange places.
  Some consideration should be made for glasses; otherwise they might be broken. Any active player who falls off a scooter should be required to seat herself again on the scooter before becoming eligible to propel the ball.
  Variation: If there are enough scooters for everyone, the game can be played with rules similar to soccer. A more restricted goal (perhaps half of the end line) can be marked with standards. A goalie defends this area. All other players are active and can move to any spot on the floor. The floor space should be large enough to allow some freedom of play. Putting too many active players in a relatively small space causes jamming.

Sunday—*DPE*, p. 587
  Supplies: None
  Skills: Running, dodging
  Two parallel lines are drawn about 50 ft apart. One player is it and stands in the center of the area between the two lines. All of the other children are on one of the two lines. The object is to cross to the other line without being tagged and without making a false start.
  Each line player stands with her front foot on the line. The line players must run across the line immediately when the tagger calls "Sunday." Anyone who does not run immediately is considered caught. The tagger can call other days of the week to confuse the runners. No player may make a start if another day of the week is called. The tagger must be careful to pronounce "Monday" in such a way that it cannot be confused with "Sunday." If confusion does occur, "Monday" can be eliminated from the signals for the false start.
  Teaching suggestion: "Making a start" must be defined clearly. To begin, it can be defined as a player moving either foot. Later, when children get better at the game, a forward movement of the body can constitute a start.

DYNAMIC PHYSICAL EDUCATION LESSON PLAN— ALTERNATE
Rhythmic Gymnastics
Level III

Supplies and Equipment Needed:
  Record player (or cassette tape player) and records (or tapes)
  Jump ropes
  Hula hoops
  8 1/2" playground balls
  Ribbons
  Posters
  Cageball
  Assorted balls

MOVEMENT EXPERIENCE— CONTENT	ORGANIZATION AND TEACHING HINTS	EXPECTED STUDENT OBJECTIVES AND OUTCOMES

INTRODUCTORY AND FITNESS DEVELOPMENT ACTIVITIES (9 – 11 MINUTES)

This lesson may be substituted for any of the previous lessons. Use the introductory and fitness development activities given in the sequenced lesson.

LESSON FOCUS (15 – 20 MINUTES)

Rhythmic Gymnastics

Rhythmic gymnastics involves the combination of manipulating hand-held apparatus and graceful body movements to music. The apparatus used are jump ropes, hoops, 8-½" playground balls and ribbons. Individual routines utilize one piece of apparatus and are 1- 1-½ minutes long. Group routines utilize one or two different types of apparatus and are 2-½ - 3 minutes long.

Rope Movements

1. Single and double jumps forward and backward.
2. Circles on each side of the body holding both ends of the rope.
3. Figure-eight swings:
   a. Holding both ends of rope.
   b. Holding the center of the rope and swinging the ends.
4. Pendulum swing rope and jump.
5. Skip over rope turning forward or backward.
6. Run over turning rope.
7. Schottische over turning rope.
8. Cross rope over body and jump.
9. Holding the ends and center of the rope:
   a. Kneel and horizontally circle the rope close to the floor.
   b. Stand and circle the rope over-head.
10. Perform a body wrap with the rope. (Hold one end on the hip, wrap the rope around the body with the other hand.)

DPE pp. 436 – 440

Present a variety of ideas to students that may be useful in creating a routine.

Discuss differing degrees of difficulty of movements presented.

Avoid working in lines.

Emphasize covering the entire 40 ft x 40 ft area when choreographing a routine.

Be sure to provide students with ample time to practice skills individually. DO NOT ask student to perform dance and manipulative skills in front of others unless they have become comfortable with the activities.

To create a group routine, use a poster at each station and divide the children into each groups at each station:

Station 1
Combine five different jump rope movements together.

Station 2
Combine five movements together. One must go close to or on the floor.

Station 3
Combine four movements together and one tossing movement.

Station 4
Combine four movements together and one toss to a partner.

Aff.—The student will develop an appreciation for the amount of skill needed to perform a quality rhythmic gymnastic routine.

PM.—The student will be able to master a minimum of five jump rope skills that could be used in a rhythmic routine.

Cog.—The student will be able to correctly name at least five jump rope skills.

Aff.—The student will realize that more difficult skills require more time and practice to master. Discuss the need for repetitive practice.

PM.—The student will contribute to the creation of a 2 1/2–3 minute group rope routine.

PM.—The student will perform in the group routine created by the class.

372

MOVEMENT EXPERIENCE—CONTENT	ORGANIZATION AND TEACHING HINTS	EXPECTED STUDENT OBJECTIVES AND OUTCOMES

11. Upon completing a backward turning rope jump, toss the rope with both ends into the air and catch it.

Have each group teach its combination to another group until the entire class learns the routine. Put the routine to music.

12. Run while holding both ends in one hand and circling the rope backward on the side of the body. Toss and catch the rope while performing this.
13. While performing a dance step, toss and catch the rope.
14. Hold both ends of the rope and swing the rope around the body like a cape.
15. Perform leaps while circling the rope on one side.
16. Hook rope around foot and make shapes with the body and foot-rope connection.
17. Have students explore and create more movements.

Hoop Movements

1. Swings
   a. Across the body.
   b. With body lean.
   c. Around body and change hands.
   d. Across body and change hands.
   e. Overhead, change hands, swing down.
   f. Form a figure eight.
   g. Create poses using hoop and body.
2. Spins
   a. In front of the body.
   b. On the floor.
   c. Spin and kick one leg over and turn around.
3. Circling
   a. Extend arm straight in front of body. Circle on hand between thumb and first finger.
   b. While swaying from side to side.
   c. Horizontal circle overhead.
   d. Hold both sides of hoop and circle in front of body.
   e. Circle around waist (hula-hoop).
4. Tossing and catching
   a. One or two handed.
   b. Directional tosses.
   c. Toss overhead from hand to hand.
   d. Circle on side of body, toss into air and catch.
5. Rolling
   a. And run along wide of the hoop.
   b. And run through.
   c. And jump over.
   d. Roll over one arm, across the chest to the other arm.
   e. Roll up the front of the body.
   f. Roll down the back of the body.

The hoop movements should appear to be a graceful extension of the body.

To create a group routine, utilize student creativity in small groups to combine movements together. Then have each group teach its combination to another group, etc., until the students have created a group routine.

The movement of the hoop should be flowing.

Must always be in total control of the hoop.

All manipulative skills and movements should be coordinated with the music.

The hoop must always roll without bouncing.

PM.—The students will create a group routine combining movements learned in class and those invented individually. The routine will be set to music.

PM.—The students will be able to perform at least five activities with a hoop.

PM.—The students will be able to place a backspin (reverse spin) on the hoop, causing it to return to them.

PM.—The students will be able to coordinate body movements and hoop movements with the musical accompaniment to create a rhythmic hoop routine.

MOVEMENT EXPERIENCE—CONTENT	ORGANIZATION AND TEACHING HINTS	EXPECTED STUDENT OBJECTIVES AND OUTCOMES

6. Jumping
   a. As with jump rope.
   b. With a pendulum swing.
   c. Side to side.
   d. Leap through.
	Group and individual routines may be created in the same manner as the other apparatus described above.	PM.—The students will be able to create an individual or group routine by combining movements and setting them to music.

Ball Skills

MOVEMENT EXPERIENCE—CONTENT	ORGANIZATION AND TEACHING HINTS	EXPECTED STUDENT OBJECTIVES AND OUTCOMES

1. Rolling
   a. Under bent legs.
   b. Around the body.
   c. Down the legs.
   d. Down the arms.
   e. Down legs, lift legs to toss the ball off toes and into air and catch.
2. Bouncing
   a. Adapt basketball dribbling drills with graceful body movements.
   b. Execute locomotor dance type movements while bouncing.
3. Toss and catch ball in a variety of body positions.
4. Add locomotor movements to tosses and catches.
5. Perform body waves with the ball.
6. Throw the ball in a variety of ways (also bounce).
7. Allow for student exploration.
	When throwing, the movement should flow from the feet through the body to the fingertips.
	
	The ball should rest in the hand and not be grasped by the fingers. Fingers should be slightly bent.
	
	Bounces should be caught noiselessly.
		PM.—The students will be able to perform ball activities with the ball resting in their hands rather than grasping the ball.

Ribbon Movements

MOVEMENT EXPERIENCE—CONTENT	ORGANIZATION AND TEACHING HINTS	EXPECTED STUDENT OBJECTIVES AND OUTCOMES

1. Swings
   a. Across and in front of body.
   b. Overhead from side to side.
   c. Swing it up and catch the end.
   d. While holding both ends, the ribbon can be swung up, around and over the body.
2. Circling
   a. At different levels.
   b. Vertical or horizontal.
   c. In front of the body.
   d. Around the body.
   e. Run while circling overhead, leap as ribbon is circled down.
   f. Add dance steps and turns.
   g. Figure eights.
   h. Figure eight and hop through the loop when wand passes side of body.
3. Zigzag patterns
   a. Execute in air in front, around and behind body.
   b. Run backward while zigzagging in front of body.
   c. Run forward while zigzagging behind body low or high.
4. Spirals
   a. Execute around, in front or beside the body while performing locomotor dance steps.
   b. Execute while performing forward rolls, backward rolls.
	The ribbon wand may be held in one or both hands.
	
	Hold the wand lightly with the index finger pointing down the wand.
	
	The ribbon should be a graceful extension of the body movements.
	
	Try stations to develop creative routines:
	
	Station 1
	Combine three or four movements. One must travel forward. One must be a figure eight.
	
	Station 2
	Combine three or four different movements. One must go to the floor. One must travel backward.
	
	Station 3
	Combine four movements. One must travel forward. One must include a toss. One must turn in a circle.
	
	Station 4
	Combine four movements. One must include a leap. One must travel forward with the ribbon moving behind you. One must be a ribbon exchange. End in a pose.
	
	Create the feeling that the entire body is coordinated with the ribbon.
		Cog.—The students will understand the differences between the categories of ribbon movements.
		
		Aff.—Rhythmic gymnastics skills are activities in which there is a wide range of student ability. Discuss the sensitivity of the situation and the need to understand the shortcomings of others.
		
		Cog.—The students will be able to explain that when choreographing a rhythmic gymnastic routine, it must be at least 1 minute long and not more than 1 minute 30 seconds in length.

MOVEMENT EXPERIENCE— CONTENT	ORGANIZATION AND TEACHING HINTS	EXPECTED STUDENT OBJECTIVES AND OUTCOMES

5. Tosses
  a. The wand can be tossed and re-grasped while performing dance, locomotor or pre-acrobatic movements.
6. Exchanges
  a. During group routines, ribbon is handed or tossed to partner.
	After students learn the basic manipulative and dance skills, begin to stress proper form.
	
	Students may work in small groups and help each other. They can give constructive feedback to others.
		PM.—The students will be able to combine dance and manipulative skills successfully in order to create a rhythmic gymnastics routine.

Dance Steps

1. Dance steps may be added to any of the movements above. Suggested steps include:
   a. Chassé
   b. Runs, walks
   c. Schottische, polka, two-step, bleking, waltz
   d. Locomotor movements—skip, hop, gallop, slide, leap, jump, etc.
   e. Body waves
   f. Various turns—pirouette, tour-de-basque, tour jeté, fouetté

GAME (5 – 7 MINUTES)

Touchdown—*DPE*, p. 588
  Supplies: A small object that can be concealed in the hand
  Skills: Running, dodging
Two parallel lines about 60 ft apart are needed. Two teams face each other, each standing on one of the parallel lines. One team goes into a huddle, and the members decide which player is to carry an object to the opponents' goal line. The team moves out of the huddle and takes a position like a football team. On the charge signal "Hike," the players run toward the opponents' goal line, each player holding the hands closed as if carrying the object. On the charge signal, the opponents also run forward and tag the players. On being tagged, a player must stop immediately and open both hands to show whether or not he has the object.
  If the player carrying the object reaches the goal line without being tagged, she calls "Touchdown" and scores 6 points. The scoring team retains possession of the object and gets another try. If the player carrying the object is tagged in the center area, the object is given to the other team. They go into a huddle and try to run it across the field to score.

Circle Touch—*DPE*, p. 582
  Supplies: Yarnballs
  Skills: Dodging, body management
One child plays against three others, who form a small circle with joined hands. The object of the game is for the lone child to touch a designated child (on the shoulders) in the circle with a yarnball. The other two children in the circle, by dodging and maneuvering, attempt to keep the tagger away from the third member of the circle. The circle players may maneuver and circle in any direction but must not release hand grips. The tagger, in attempting to touch the protected circle player, must go around the outside of the circle. She is not permitted to go underneath or through the joined hands of the circle players.
  Teaching suggestion: The teacher should watch for roughness by the two in the circle protecting the third. To avoid roughness, the game should be played in short 20 second bouts and then rotate in a new tagger.
  Variations:
  1. A piece of cloth, a handkerchief, or a flag is tucked into the belt in back of the protected child. The fourth child, the tagger, tries to pull the flag from the belt.

Cageball Target Throw—*DPE*, p. 582
  Supplies: A cageball (18- to 30-in.), 12 to 15 smaller balls of various sizes
  Skill: Throwing
An area about 20 ft wide is marked across the center of the playing area, with a cageball in the center. The object of the game is to throw the smaller balls against the cageball, thus forcing it across the line in front of the other team. Players may come up to the line to throw, but they may not throw while inside the cageball area. A player may enter the area, however, to recover a ball. No one is to touch the cageball at any time, nor may the cageball be pushed by a ball in the hands of a player.
  Teaching suggestion: If the cageball seems to roll too easily, it should be deflated slightly. The throwing balls can be of almost any size—soccer balls, volleyballs, playground balls, or whatever.
  Variation: Two rovers, one from each team, can occupy the center area to retrieve balls. These players cannot block throws or prevent a ball from hitting the target. They are there for the sole purpose of retrieving balls for their team.

DYNAMIC PHYSICAL EDUCATION LESSON PLAN—ALTERNATE
Climbing Rope Skills
Level III

Supplies and Equipment Needed:
  Climbing ropes
  Tumbling mats (placed under the climbing ropes)
  Beanbags
  Hoops
  Wands
  Balls (optional)

MOVEMENT EXPERIENCE—CONTENT	ORGANIZATION AND TEACHING HINTS	EXPECTED STUDENT OBJECTIVES AND OUTCOMES

INTRODUCTORY AND FITNESS DEVELOPMENT ACTIVITIES (9 – 11 MINUTES)

This lesson may be substituted for any of the previous lessons. Use the introductory and fitness development activities given in the sequenced lesson.

LESSON FOCUS (15 – 20 MINUTES)

Climbing Rope Skills

DPE pp. 460 – 464

Supported Pull-Ups

1. Kneel and pull to feet. Return.
2. Site, pull to feet and back to seat.
3. Stand, keep body straight while lowering body to the floor.

Place tumbling mats under all the climbing apparatus.

The pull-up and hang activities are excellent lead-ups for students who are not strong enough to climb the rope.

Students should be cautioned to descend the rope *slowly* to prevent rope burns.

Cog.—The student will be able to describe the safety rules necessary when climbing ropes.

Hangs

1. Sit, pull body off floor except for feet and hold
2. Jump up, grasp the rope and hang.
3. Jump up, grasp the rope and hang and perform the following leg movements:
   a. One or both knees up
   b. Bicycling movement
   c. Half-lever
   d. Choice movement

Swinging and Jumping

Reach high and jump to a bent-arm position while swinging.
  1. Swing and jump. Add one-half and full turns.
  2. Swing and return.
  3. Swing and jump for distance or land on a target.

Swinging on the ropes should be done with bent arms and with knees tucked.

Caution the person waiting in line to wait out of the way until the person before her is completely finished.

Climbing the Rope

1. Scissors grip:
   Place the rope inside of the knee and outside the foot. Climb halfway up and practice descending using the reverse scissors grip before climbing to the top of the rope.
2. Leg around rest:
   Wrap the left leg around the rope and over the instep of the left foot from the outside. Stand on the rope and instep with right foot.

Students should be encouraged to learn the various techniques of climbing and descending.

Rope climbing is a very intense and demanding activity. A good idea is to break up the lesson focus with a game or relay. This will also offer leg development activity.

PM.—The student will be able to demonstrate proper techniques in the following activities:
  1. Climbing with the scissors grip
  2. Leg around rest
  3. Reverse scissors grip
  4. Instep squeeze

Aff.—Rope climbing demands a great deal of upper body strength. Discuss how muscular strength develops through overloading and increasing the demands placed on the body.

MOVEMENT EXPERIENCE— CONTENT	ORGANIZATION AND TEACHING HINTS	EXPECTED STUDENT OBJECTIVES AND OUTCOMES

Descending the Rope
 	
1. Reverse scissors grip
2. Leg around rest
3. Instep squeeze:
The rope is squeeze between the insteps by keeping the heels together.
 	
Stunts Using Two Ropes
 	
1. Straight arm hang: Jump up, grasp rope and hang.
2. Arms with different leg positions.
  a. Single and double knee lifts
  b. Half lever
  c. Full lever
  d. Bicycle—pedal feet like bicycle
3. Pull-Ups
  a. Same as Pull-Up on a single rope.
4. Inverted hands
  a. With feet wrapped around the ropes.
  b. With feet against the inside of the ropes.
  c. With the toes pointed and the feet not touching the ropes.
	If there are only a few climbing ropes, it would be a good teaching technique to have the nonclimbing students work on another unit. Some good units are beanbags, hoops, wands, and/or playground balls.
	
	Spotting should be done when students are performing inverted hangs on two ropes.
		Cog.—Exercise increases the diameter and density of bones. Why would this be important? Why do bones become stronger in response to exercise?
		
		Cog.—Rope climbing is excellent for developing upper body strength. Discuss the major muscle groups that are used and developed when climbing ropes.
		
		Cog.—The larger the diameter of the muscle, the greater the amount of force that can be generated. Identify various muscles of the body and their relative size.
		
		PM.—The student will be able to perform the following two-rope activities:
		1. Straight arm hang
		2. Hangs with different leg positions
		3. Pull-Ups
		4. Inverted hangs
		
		Aff.—Rope climbing favors those students who are small and carry little body fat. Discuss individual differences and how different sports favor certain types of body build.

GAME (5 – 7 MINUTES)

Whistle Ball—*DPE*, p. 588
    Supplies: A ball for each group of six to eight players
    Skills: Passing, catching
    Eight or fewer children stand in circle formation. A ball is passed rapidly back and forth among them in any order. The object is to be the player who stays in the game the longest. A child sits down in place if he makes any of the following errors:
    1. He has the ball when the whistle blows. (The teacher should set a predetermined time period, at the end of which a whistle is blown. The time period can be varied from 5 to 20 seconds.)
    2. He makes a bad throw or fails to catch a good throw.
    3. He returns the ball directly to the person from whom it was received.
    Teaching suggestion: One way to control the time periods is to appoint a child as timer and to give her a list of the time periods, a whistle, and a stopwatch. The timer should be cautioned not to give any advance indication of when the stop signal will be blown. An automatic timer enhances the game. When the game gets down to two or three players, declare them the winners and begin anew.

Touchdown—*DPE*, p. 588
    Supplies: A small object that can be concealed in the hand
    Skills: Running, dodging
    Two parallel lines about 60 ft apart are needed. Two teams face each other, each standing on one of the parallel lines. One team goes into a huddle, and the members decide which player is to carry an object to the opponents' goal line. The team moves out of the huddle and takes a position like a football team. On the charge signal "Hike," the players run toward the opponents' goal line, each player holding the hands closed as if carrying the object. On the charge signal, the opponents also run forward and tag the players. On being tagged, a player must stop immediately and open both hands to show whether or not he has the object.
    If the player carrying the object reaches the goal line without being tagged, she calls "Touchdown" and scores 6 points. The scoring team retains possession of the object and gets another try. If the player carrying the object is tagged in the center area, the object is given to the other team. They go into a huddle and try to run it across the field to score.

Chain Tag—*DPE*, p. 582
    Supplies: None
    Skills: Running, dodging
    Two parallel lines are established about 50 ft apart. The center is occupied by three players who form a chain with joined hands. The players with free hands on either end of the chain do the tagging. All other players line up on one of the parallel lines.
    The players in the center call "Come," and children cross from one line to the other. The chain tries to tag the runners. Anyone caught joins the chain. When the chain becomes too long, it should be divided into several smaller chains.
    Variation: <u>Catch of Fish</u>. The chain catches children by surrounding them like a fishing net. The runners cannot run under or through the links of the net.

Materials and Supplies for
Dynamic Physical Education for Elementary School Children

The following list is offered to help teachers identify an adequate equipment list for a balanced physical education program. The items are listed by priority in two categories—materials and supplies and capital outlay. Priority is based on cost, need, and versatility of the equipment. In other words, the first piece of equipment listed (playground balls) can be used to teach the most units making it the highest priority. The quantity of equipment is also listed to assure that the proper amount of equipment is ordered to facilitate a normal class size. Some of the equipment can be constructed (See Chapter 33 of *Dynamic Physical Education for Elementary School Children, Eleventh Edition*) for specifications and construction tips.

The majority of the equipment listed is available from **The Robert Widen Company, P.O. Box 2075, Prescott, AZ 86301.** The author has worked closely with this company in an attempt to assure only quality equipment which is durable and reliable is shipped. Equipment is shipped quickly and is guaranteed for one year from the date of shipment against defects in workmanship and materials. For a current price list or more information, call toll free at (800) 862-0761 or FAX to (602) 776-8742.

Priority	Material and Supplies	Quantity
1	8½" playground balls	36
1a	8" foam rubber balls (can be substituted for playground balls)	36
1b	8" vinyl covered foam rubber balls (an expensive substitute for playground balls, but they are much safer, more durable and give a true bounce. They can be used for all types of sport activities)	36
2	6" × 6" beanbags	72
3	Jump Ropes (plastic segments for beginners and speed ropes for experienced jumpers)	
	7 ft length	36
	8 ft length	36
	9 ft length	18
	16 ft length (long rope jumping)	12
4	Hoops (solid or segmented)	
	30" diameter	36
	36" diameter	36
5	Wands (36" length)	36
6	Traffic Cones (12" bright orange vinyl)	20
7	Tambourine	1
8	Plastic racquets (sized for elementary children)	36
9	Foam balls for racquet skills (2½")	36
10	Fleece Balls (3–4" diameter)	36
11	Floor Hockey Sticks and Pucks - 36 of each	36
12	Whiffle Balls (use for throwing, hockey, softball, etc.)	36
13	Individual Mats (20" × 40" × ½")	36
14	Individual Tug-of-war Ropes (made from garden hose and ⅜" nylon rope)	18
15	Juggling Scarves	108
16	Beachballs (18" to 20" diameter)	36
17	Soccer Balls (junior size or trainers)	18
18	Basketballs (junior size)	18
19	Footballs (Junior size or foam rubber)	18
20	Volleyballs (lightweight trainer balls)	18
21	Softballs (extra soft)	18
22	Softball Bats (wood or aluminum)	3
23	Frisbees	36
24	Magic Stretch Ropes	12
25	Cageball (24")	1
26	Pinnies (four colors - 12 each)	48
27	Ball Bags (nylon see-through mesh)	12
28	Team Tug-of-War Rope (50 ft length)	1
29	Stopwatches (digital)	6

Priority	Material and Supplies	Quantity
30	Batons (for track & field relays)	12
31	Scooterboards	18
32	Bowling Pins	24
33	Lummi Sticks	72

Priority	Capital Outlay Items	Quantity
1	Tumbling Mats (4 ft × 8 ft × 1¼" thick; 4 sides of Velcro fasteners)	8
2	Cassette Tape Player	1
3	Parachute and Storage Bag (28 ft diameter)	1
4	Electric Ball Pump	1
5	Heavy Duty Equipment (Ball) Carts	4
6	Balance-Beam Benches (12 ft length)	6
7	Jumping Boxes (8" height)	6
8	Jumping Boxes (16" height)	6
9	Audiovisual Cart with Electrical Outlet (for tape player, etc.)	
10	Sit and Reach Box (measure flexibility)	2
11	Utility Gym Standards (for volleyball nets etc.)	2
12	Field Marker (for chalking lines)	2
13	Climbing Ropes on Tracks (8 ropes)	